Kenneth Kaunda of Zambia

*To my mother
and
in memory of my father*

President Kenneth Kaunda

FERGUS MACPHERSON

Kenneth Kaunda
of
Zambia

The Times and the Man

LUSAKA
OXFORD UNIVERSITY PRESS
NAIROBI LONDON NEW YORK
1974

OXFORD UNIVERSITY PRESS

ELY HOUSE, DOVER STREET, LONDON W. I

Glasgow New York Toronto Melbourne Wellington
Ibadan Nairobi Dar es Salaam Lusaka Addis Ababa
Delhi Bombay Calcutta Madras Karachi Lahore Dacca
Kuala Lumpur Singapore Hong Kong Tokyo

OXFORD UNIVERSITY PRESS, P.O. BOX 2335, LUSAKA, ZAMBIA

Cover design by Chris Higson
Cover photograph
by Marion Kaplan

Made and printed in East Africa

Previous Publications

One Blood (Neczam, 1970)
One Finger (Neczam, 1974)

Contents

List of Illustrations   viii

Introduction by President Nyerere   xi

Chronological Table   xiii

1. Seeds of the Whirlwind   1

2. Family Background   23

3. Germination of a Vision   50

4. 'Welensky's Federation'—the Great Central African Plot   80

5. The Continental Crisis   99

6. First Fruits of the Vision   129

7. Extending Horizons   162

8. Times of Testing   194

9. Parting of the Ways   228

10. 'A Man Who Gathers Honey'   263

11. Non-violence on Trial—'A Flower in Seed'   307

12. Cha-Cha-Cha—Controlling a Fire   340

13. 'Man Must Come First'   384

14. Kwacha Ngwee—Into the Zambian Morning   426

List of Abbreviations   464

Select Bibliography   466

Acknowledgements   470

Index   473

Map (*inside back cover*)

List of Illustrations

1. The Kaunda family at Lubwa around 1923
2. Grave of Revd. David Kaunda at Lubwa
3. Kenneth Kaunda's house as Head Master, Lubwa, 1945
4. Kenneth Kaunda with Ellison Millambo, ANC Southern Provincial President, late 1953
5. Discussing the 'Moffat Resolutions', August 1954
6. Kenneth Kaunda soon after release from prison in March 1955
7. Roy Welensky addressing civil dignitaries at Kabwe, July 1957
8. Kenneth Kaunda in Lusaka Central Prison, June 1959
9. In London for the Northern Rhodesian Constitutional Conference, February 1961
10. A road block set up during 'Cha-cha-cha', 1961
11. Men of the Police Mobile Unit in action during 'Cha-cha-cha'
12. *Northern News* cartoon of Kenneth Kaunda, 30 October 1961
13. UNIP posters to greet the visit of Colonial Secretary Maudling, December 1961
14. Maudling with Governor Hone greets UNIP delegation
15. Betty Kaunda at work in House No. 394, Chilenje
16. UNIP rally at Kitwe, June 1962
17. At Africa Freedom Day Rally, New York, 10 July 1962
18. Kenneth Kaunda saying goodbye to his wife and their son Kaweche at the start of an election tour, September 1962
19. Kenneth Kaunda as Chairman with delegates to the PAFMECSA Conference in Zaïre, December 1962
20. Mass burning of identification certificates at Kitwe, December 1963
21. Kenneth Kaunda and Governor Hone garlanded by Asian well-wishers on return from London, 6 April 1963
22. Multi-racial ceremony for the burial of the Central African Federation, Chililabombwe, 31 December 1963

23. Kenneth Kaunda on an election tour in January 1964
24. The large house in Prospect Hill, Lusaka which Kenneth Kaunda occupied as Minister of Local Government and Prime Minister
25. A typical certificate of membership of the Lumpa 'church' of Alice Lenshina
26. A Provincial Officer calls on followers of Alice Lenshina to surrender, mid-1964
27. The Zambian Cabinet a month before independence
28. President Kaunda at the independence ceremony on 24 October 1964

The author is indebted to the following for the use of the photographs listed below: President Kaunda (1, 8), Zambia Information Services (2, 3, 7, 10, 11, 14, 18, 21, 27), Frank Ndhlovu (4), *Zambia Daily Mail* (5, 9, 19, 28), Bulaya Mpulumba (6), *Times of Zambia* Library, Ndola (12, 15, 16, 20, 24, 25, 26), National Archives of Zambia (13, 17), Wilson Chinengu (22) and *Times of Zambia* (23).

Introduction

by President Julius K. Nyerere

This book is about a man whose life is dedicated to Africa and its peoples, with special but not exclusive reference to his own country and its citizens. It does not need an introduction or recommendation, because the subject is its own justification. And there is certainly no basis on which I, as President of the United Republic of Tanzania, can presume to introduce my fellow-President, my colleague, and my friend, to the potential readers of this biography.

Yet I agreed to write this Introduction. I did so for two reasons. First, because it gives me an opportunity to pay tribute to an African leader to whom Tanzania owes a great deal. Second, because I believe that a study of this book will assist an understanding of modern Africa. And perhaps as a third consideration, I would like to think that greater understanding of President Kaunda's life and attitudes will encourage future generations of Africans—and others—to emulate the selfless service which he exemplifies.

Tanzania mainland became independent in December 1961. But until Zambia's independence in October 1964 our whole southern boundary marked the East African border of free and colonial Africa,—Zaïre was the front-line state to the West. And in that year the people of Mozambique, under the leadership of Frelimo, began their armed struggle against Portuguese oppression. Tanzania has felt the effects of that freedom war ever since.

But the policies of Zambia under the leadership of President Kaunda and UNIP, have meant that instead of our being a somewhat lonely front-line state, much of the real pressure has been taken from us. It is Zambia, with its much longer and more exposed borders with Mozambique, Rhodesia, Namibia, and Angola, which has borne the first brunt of the colonialist's anger, intrigue and attack. It is Zambia, and not Tanzania, which is now the real front-line state.

There was nothing inevitable about this development. The

Zambian economy which President Kaunda's government inherited was tied very closely with the economies of Rhodesia and South Africa. All Zambia's communications went South,—or through the Portuguese colony of Angola. Further, the Zambian economy was entirely dependent upon copper; and for the production of copper President Kaunda had to retain the only skilled workers then available—most of whom came from South Africa or Rhodesia because of the colonialist's racialist education and training policies.

It would have been very easy—and even understandable—if the UNIP Government had said very firmly to the rest of Africa, 'We are sorry, our hearts are with you, but we cannot join in the struggle for African liberation.' There were some voices of caution in the new state which wanted to do that. But President Kaunda stood by the principles he and his Party had proclaimed during their own struggle for independence. And despite enormous difficulties following the Smith Regime's Declaration of Rhodesian Independence, Zambia has accepted its destiny as the front-line of free Africa's confrontation with racialism and colonialism. Had she not done so, Tanzania's experience over the last nine years might well have been very different. We owe a great debt to President Kaunda and the colleagues who have supported and worked with him in these matters.

My reasons for believing that readers of this book will gain understanding, and encouragement for service will, I think, be clear when it is read! For the author accepts that you cannot write intelligently about President Kaunda except in the context of the independence struggle. Therefore the events of the period from the late 1940s are explained as the background and motivation for his work. It is impossible to read these things without understanding some of the problems which faced the first government of the independent state of Zambia—and by extension the governments of other newly independent African Nations.

History will be a more objective judge of President Kaunda than I can be. But history will not know from experience, as Tanzanians do, the importance to our freedom of the contribution he has already made to Africa. He has, and will be, chosen by the Zambians for the leadership of Zambia, and their leadership is their affair. But the cause of freedom and development in the whole of Africa has been served by their choice.

Chronological Table

1835 The Ngoni, under Zwangendaba, cross the Zambezi and move north.

1873 Death of David Livingstone.

1878 Birth of David Julizya Kaunda.

1881 Opening of Free Church of Scotland Mission at Bandawe on Lake Malawi.

1884 Admission of Christian agents to Ngoni kingdom of Mwambera, Malawi.
      Berlin Conference on 'Partition of Africa'.

1889 Royal Charter granted to British South Africa Company.

1890 B.S.A. Company secures the 'Lochner Concession' from Lozi King.
      Anglo-German concordat fixes boundaries.

1891 Katanga 'pedicle' seized for Belgian King.
      Nyasaland proclaimed as 'British Central Africa Protectorate' with Sir Harry Johnston as Commissioner.

1895 Opening of Mwenzo Mission by Free Church of Scotland.

1898 Defeat of Mpezeni's Ngoni and of Kazembe of the Luunda by British troops.

1899 B.S.A. Deputy Administrator moves from Blantyre to Fort Jameson (Chipata).

1903 King Victor Emmanuel of Italy fixes frontier between B.S.A. territory and Portuguese Angola.

1904 Evangelistic mission of Livingstonia students to region west of Luangwa River: David Kaunda visits Chinsali area of Bemba Chief Nkula.

1905 B.S.A. administrative headquarters for North-West Rhodesia moved to Livingstone from Kalomo.
      David Kaunda and wife, Helen, settle in Chinsali District.

1906 Railway from the south reaches Broken Hill (Kabwe).

1911 N.W. and N.E. Rhodesia combined as Northern Rhodesia by B.S.A. administration.

1912   Founding of Mwenzo Welfare Association by Donald Siwale, David Kaunda and others.

1913   Appointment of Scottish missionary to Chinsali District, (Lubwa).

1915   John Chilembwe rising in Nyasaland (Malawi).

1922   Start of major development of Northern Rhodesian Copperbelt.

1924   End of B.S.A. Company rule and establishment of N.R. Protectorate under Colonial Office.
Birth of Kenneth David Kaunda, 28 April.

1928   Birth of Betty Banda.

1931   World economic slump affects N. Rhodesia.

1932   Death of David Kaunda.

1933   Kafue meeting of African Associations.

1935   First African strike on the Copperbelt.

1936   Establishment of the United Missions in the Copperbelt.

1939   Establishment of Munali, in Lusaka, as secondary school for Africans.
Outbreak of Second World War.

1940   Second Copperbelt African strike.

1941   Kaunda goes to Munali.

1943   Kaunda returns to teach at Lubwa.

1945   End of Second World War.

1946   Kaunda marries Betty Banda.
Federation of African Welfare Societies established.

1947   Simon Kapwepwe, Malama Sokoni and Kaunda go to Tanganyika.

1948   Publication of Dalgleish Report on 'The Place of Africans in Industry'.
Appointment of first two African members of N.R. Legislative Council.
Kaunda teaching in Mufulira U.M.C.B. School.
N.R. African Congress formed out of Federation of Welfare Societies.
Victory of Afrikaaner Nationalist Party in S. Africa.

1949   The Banda/Nkumbula Memorandum against Federation.
Kaunda returns to Chinsali.

1950   Kaunda and Makasa elected office-bearers of Chinsali Branch of N.R. African Congress.

1951   Harry Nkumbula elected President of N.R. African Congress. Kaunda appointed Northern Provincial Organising Secretary of Congress.

1952   ANC's Supreme Action Council set up, with Kaunda as a member.

        Welensky's 'Red Indian' speech.

1953—Jan.   Nkumbula burns White Paper on C. African Federation.

    Apr.   ANC's 'Two-day National Prayer'.

    Aug.   Queen Elizabeth II signs Order-in-Council establishing Federation.

        Kaunda elected Secretary-General of ANC.

    Oct.   First issue of *Congress News*, edited by Kaunda.

    Dec.   ANC Report on Gwembe disturbances, sgd. by Kaunda and others.

1954—Jan.   ANC boycott of butcheries in Lusaka and other towns.

    July   Leg. Co. accepts the 'Moffat Resolutions'.

1955—Jan.   Kaunda and Nkumbula sentenced to three months' imprisonment.

    Apr.   Disturbances in the Northern Province.

    Aug.   'Nkumbula/Yamba Pact'.

1956—Aug.   Meeting of Congress leaders with European Unofficials.

    Sept.   N.R.G. Declares State of Emergency on Copperbelt.

    Oct.   Welensky succeeds Huggins, Lord Malvern, as Federal Prime Minister.

    Mar.   Ghanaian Independence.

1957—May   Nkumbula and Kaunda in England.

    July   Congress boycott of beer halls.

    Aug.   Fresh disturbances in northern provinces.

    Dec.   First joint conference of African Congresses of C. Africa, Lusaka.

        Kaunda returns from Britain.

1958—Mar.   Publication of the 'Benson Constitution'.

May	Kaunda leaves for Tanganyika and India.
July	Dr. Hastings Banda returns to Nyasaland (Malawi).
Oct.	Kaunda returns to Lusaka.
	ANC emergency conference: Kaunda and others 'split' from Nkumbula.
	ZANC formed.
Dec.	All Africa Peoples' Conference, Accra.
1959—Feb.	State of Emergency in S. Rhodesia.
Mar.	Nyasaland Emergency begins.
	ZANC banned. Chilubi riots.
	N.R. elections under 'Benson Constitution'.
Apr.	Evelyn Hone appointed N.R. Governor.
June	Kaunda sentenced to nine months' imprisonment, first in Lusaka, then in Salisbury.
July	African National Independence Party (ANIP) formed under leadership of Paul Kalichini.
Sept.	Mainza Chona leads United National Independence Party (UNIP).
Nov.	End of 'Mau Mau' Emergency in Kenya.
1960—Jan.	Kaunda released from prison.
	Visit of British Prime Minister MacMillan.
	Kaunda elected President of UNIP.
Mar.	Colonial Secretary Iain Macleod visits Lusaka.
Apr.	Monckton Commission in Central Africa.
	Publication of *Black Government* by Kaunda and Colin Morris.
	Sharpeville 'massacre' in S. Africa.
	Kaunda visits America and Britain.
May	Murder of Mrs. Lilian Burton near Ndola.
	UNIP declared an 'unlawful' society'.
July	Belgian Congo becomes independent.
Dec.	Federal Review Conference in London.
1961—Jan.	London Conference on N.R. Constitution.
Feb.	Kaunda's 'second Mau Mau' remark causes furore.
	Kaunda visits United Arab Republic and Ethiopia.
Mar.	More disturbances in Northern Province.
Apr.	Kaunda at 'Africa Freedom Day' in New York.

June	Macleod announces '15-15-15' constitutional proposals.
July	UNIP Conference at Mulungushi: Cha-cha-cha starts.
Aug.	Kaunda visits London for 'last appeal'.
Oct.	UNIP publishes *Grim Peep*.
Dec.	New Colonial Secretary, Maudling, visits N.R.
1962—Jan.	UNIP threatens 'country-wide strikes'.
Feb.	Maudling announces modified constitutional plan.
Mar.	Kaunda alleges plan by Welensky to arrest Governor.
Apr.	Kaunda in America to attend U.N. Committee on Colonialism.
May	Alice Lenshina tells Lumpa followers not to take part in politics.
June	The Kaundas hold a large inter-racial reception in Kitwe's Edinburgh Hotel.
Aug.	UNIP 'pre-election' conference at Magoye.
Sept.	Kaunda visits Tshombe in Katanga.
Oct.	General Election produces deadlock.
	Publication of Kaunda's *Zambia shall be Free.*
Nov.	'Caretaker' Government announced.
Dec.	UNIP and ANC form Coalition Government with Kaunda as Minister of Local Government and Social Welfare.
	Tanganyikan Independence.
	Kaunda chairs PAFMECA Conference in Leopoldville (Kinshasa).
1963—Jan.	Tension rises between Lumpa members and non-Lumpa in the north.
Feb.	Dr. H. K. Banda appointed Prime Minister of Nyasaland.
Mar.	ANC-UNIP clashes.
	UNIP National Council meets.
May	Kaunda awarded Honorary Degree of Doctor of Laws by Fordham University, U.S.A.
June	Victoria Falls Conference to dismantle Federation.
Aug.	Report published on 'Unrest on the Copperbelt'.

Sept.	New Constitution for N. Rhodesia announced.
Dec.	UNIP-Lumpa clashes in north.
	Big exodus of Europeans from N. Rhodesia.
	Kenyan Independence.
1964—Jan.	Army mutiny in Tanganyika.
	UNIP wins General Election: Kaunda appointed Prime Minister.
Apr.	Kaunda given control of N.R. Police.
May	London Conference on Zambian Independence.
June	S. Africa rejects Kaunda's offer to exchange envoys.
	Nelson Mandela and others sentenced to life imprisonment in S. Africa.
July	Malawi Independence. Lumpa 'War'.
Aug.	Kaunda rejects Life Presidency of UNIP.
	End of sixteen-day European Railwaymen's strike.
	Kaunda proclaimed President-elect of Zambia.
Sept.	UNIP Conference at Mulungushi.
	Banda dismisses Malawi Cabinet Ministers.
	Kaunda announces new Cabinet for Zambia.
Oct.	End of B.S.A. 'royalties'.
	Birth of the Republic of Zambia.

1

Seeds of the Whirlwind

'On the night of October 24th, 1958, Kenneth Kaunda and a substantial number of intelligent young men proclaimed the birth of the Zambia African National Congress.'[1] They did so after much secret discussion, because they believed that the attainment of national independence for the territory called Northern Rhodesia was a matter of growing urgency and that it could not be effected under the leadership of Harry Nkumbula, the President, since 1951, of the African National Congress. Their decision had two dramatic effects: it placed the burden of leading a new drive towards independence upon the shoulders of the thirty-four year old Kenneth Kaunda; and it put on the map of African and world politics the new word 'Zambia', which in six short years would become the name of the sovereign republic that was to replace the British Protectorate of Northern Rhodesia.

Though ZANC, as the new breakaway political party was called, was to be banned in less than five months, the whole subsequent story of the development of the thinly-populated region of 290,000 square miles north of the Zambezi was thenceforth dominated by ZANC's spirit, reincarnate in UNIP, the United National Independence Party. As our review proceeds, we shall be increasingly sharpening our focus on the character, thought, utterances and actions of the foremost of this group of radicals, and so note here how Kenneth Kaunda appeared to his fellows, as expressed by the man who shared 'restriction' with him at Kabompo in the North-Western Province after the proscription of ZANC. "He cares very little about his own personal troubles," said Frank Chitambala, "he is a man who is above them. He is my idea of a true national leader, faithful, honest and sincere. I believe he is a man of destiny . . . Kenneth is a very handsome and well-built African. His

complexion is very dark; his brown, deep, penetrating eyes look out
from a face of great determination. Grey is gradually taking colour
out of his black hair, which he combs upright making him look
like a Swahili warrior. He has a strong and pleasant voice which
seems to have had a narrow escape from stammer. During any
of his casual talks one might mistake him for a shy man who
would never address a crowd of people. He manages a shy and
dry-like smile, but from his heart. He listens more than he talks.
He is quick, merciful and full of humour."[2]

For Zambia, as for many other 'colonial dependencies' the
struggle for nationhood meant in effect seeking international
recognition of sovereign self-rule as a single nation for a region
which, before the colonial intrusion, had comprised a number of
smaller kingdoms and peoples. Here as elsewhere frontiers bore
little relation to the bounds of those old kingdoms. Instead they
represented the limits of expansion reached by one or another
colonial power in the great 'scramble for Africa' at the end of the
nineteenth century. The frontiers of modern Zambia reveal out-
standingly, as do those of Egypt, Libya and the Sudan, the geo-
metrical delineation determined as the 'scramblers' consolidated
their gains and accorded each other mutual recognition, however
reluctantly. Angola is separated from western Zambia by a straight
line drawn in 1903 by King Victor Emmanuel of Italy as chairman
of the commission charged with arbitrating the dispute of the
Portuguese and the British South Africa Company. Another such
straight line separates Zambia's South-Eastern Region from
Mozambique. The Zaïre pedicle that juts deep into Zambia in the
region of the Luapula River and reduces the country's 'waist' to just
over a hundred miles, was established in 1891 by the daring action
of an English officer and others in the service of King Leopold
of Belgium, who outstripped Cecil Rhodes's agents in determination
and brutality, killed King Msidi of Bunkeya and hoisted their
master's flag over the area that was soon to yield rich booty from
the copper mines of Katanga. Britain recognised this frontier in
1894. The rapier point of the Caprivi Strip, today under hostile
South African control and bringing that country's military presence
to a point just across the River Zambezi from Zambia's Sesheke
District, was determined by the Anglo-German concordat of 1890.
This agreement, which allowed Kaiser Wilhelm II's colonists

access to navigation on the Zambezi, also drew the line between the north end of Lake Malawi and the south end of Lake Tanganyika, which separated German Tanganyika from what was then called North-Eastern Rhodesia.[3]

Historians have given us various surveys of the thrusts of European imperialism in Africa that followed the Berlin Conference of 1884 and, more recently, attention has been given to the history of previous centuries in which the European adventurers had torn perhaps as many as fifty million Africans from their homes and put those who survived the horrors of the long sea passage into slavery in the plantations of America and the Caribbean. The colonial annexation of 'northern Zambesia' has had its interpreters, while the activities of bands of Christian missionaries of many denominations who converged on the area in the 'spiritual awakening' that followed the death of David Livingstone in central Zambia in 1873, have been recorded by individual missionaries largely as the chronicle of light entering darkness.[4] The reactions of colonial agents, traders and missionaries to Central African society have also been subjected recently to scholarly examination.[5] However, to understand Zambian nationalism, it is necessary to turn our focus in particular upon the reactions, revealed or suppressed, of the African peoples of the area to foreign conquest and to the social dislocation and turmoil that followed.

Central African historiography has been bedevilled by the word 'protection'. The traditional British historian tended to believe, like Rayner, that the British role was essentially that of 'trustee for the backward races of mankind', not allowing them 'to be exploited for the benefit of profit-seekers'. But even scholars more directly concerned with Central Africa have been ready, like Mulford, to believe that 'in the beginning Northern Rhodesia had been subjugated not by war but by treaties concluded between white men and the Territory's unsophisticated chiefs'; a view which, though it cannot survive a thorough scrutiny of those 'treaties' or of African testimony, yet so permeated the curricula of the territory's thin network of African schools in the middle of this century that the first officers of the Northern Rhodesia African Congress could state that 'African chiefs asked for and were graciously granted British Protection by Her Most Gracious Majesty, the late Queen Victoria.'[6] A decade later the much more

fiery Harry Nkumbula declared, in 1958, that 'the treaties...
stated that HMG had an obligation to train and prepare Africans
for self-government and independence.' More significantly, however,
Kenneth Kaunda's statement prepared for the Commission established to enquire into the circumstances of the banning of ZANC
in 1959 included these words: 'Northern Rhodesia is a Protectorate
whose status was reached through treaties freely entered into
between our forebears and representatives of Her Majesty the
Queen of Great Britain.'⁷

There is now well-nigh irrefutable evidence, however, that what
were being protected, when Rhodes' men moved swiftly north
of the Zambezi and Sir Harry Johnston held sway over what was
soon to be called Nyasaland, were the interests, actual and potential,
of the companies that claimed the untrammelled right to exploit
the lands they had subjugated. Some missionaries, like Francois
Coillard among the Lozi of King Lewanika and Alfred Swann of
the London Missionary Society's pioneering band at the southern
end of Lake Tanganyika, readily accepted the new colonial rulers
as agents of David Livingstone's dream of the three-pronged
advance, into regions ravaged by the Arab slave-trade, of Christianity, commerce and civilisation. Others, however, noted that
'when Europeans take the land they practically ENSLAVE THE
NATIVE POPULATION' and became aware that the devices of
'compulsory labour and oppressive taxation' and the 'rude triumphs
of the terror [that] big guns can inspire in the hearts of Africans'
were making mockery of the claims that this was a civilising mission.⁸
Indeed when Johnston openly avowed, in an article in *The Nineteenth Century* for November 1902, his plan to turn Central Africa
'into a labour recruiting ground for the Rhodesian and Transvaal
mines', the leader of the Scots mission at Blantyre pleaded that the
urgent need of the region was for 'the cultivation of its own soil
by the hands of its own children' and that 'it was for this that the
slave yoke was torn from his neck and not that he might be turned
into a serf of the colonist and capitalist.'⁹

It was conquest and not protective tutelage that was effected
by Rhodes and Johnston. Indeed, the latter would have liked an
alliance of British and Arab forces for, as he said, 'subduing and
taming irrational blood-thirsty wild beasts like the Angoni, Zulus,
the Wa-Wemba...and all the hundred and one races of Negro

robbers'.[10] Moreover a strategy of conquest can be detected which corresponds with the basic formulae of subjugation of which human history has so many examples. The stronger kingdoms must be tackled first, after which the lesser states and communities would succumb without struggle. The first master stroke, effected by the Lochner Concession, secured for Rhodes effective access to the land and the wealth of a region far larger than the Lozi kingdom of Lewanika, from whom the 'concession' was extracted. This was later to be used to justify the annual draining from the territory of the British South Africa Company 'royalties' all through the booming years of the Copperbelt's growth and up to the actual eve of Zambia's independence in 1964.[11] Further afield, King Mpezeni's Ngoni army was provoked to war early in 1898, and overwhelmed by the deadly fire of Maxim guns and Martini rifles. The King was called to witness the court-martial and execution of his son for 'raiding in British territory'. The Ngoni King 'never made his mark on a document [of treaty] yet [in this way] the North Charterland [Company] acquired its ten thousand square miles.' Moreover, as after the 'Matabele Rebellion' of 1896, a great number of Ngoni cattle were seized, though in the face of vocal criticism in Britain, most of them were later returned. Mpezeni's country, Johnston told the Foreign Office, was 'healthy and auriferous.'[12]

In the same year, small but well-armed British forces, supported by Sikhs, effected the humiliation of chiefs Ponde and Mporokoso in the north, while King Kazembe of the Luunda fled in the face of a British advance on his capital, a town of between 10,000 and 20,000 people. Those minor but decisive acts of conquest were carried out with vigour. As 'Bobo' Young of the British South Africa Company recorded: 'We set fire to what we left and Ponde's village was soon reduced to ashes.' It was Robert Codrington the Administrator, who, according to Young, sent 'the Nyasaland Army, Central African Rifles' to 'wipe out Kazembe'; though Young did not record the burning of the Luunda capital. Those exploits, however, were not expensive to the Company for 'our little scraps always paid for themselves from ivory we captured.' The African account of the rout of Kazembe claimed that 'the Europeans burnt the capital and many people died in it.'[13]

In the area of modern Zambia, the rest of the annexation was relatively bloodless, but no less effective. 'Chirupula' Stephenson, one of the most colourful of the early B.S.A. administrators, bluntly described the planting of the flag among the Lala people and the 'annexation' of the area that was to become the Copperbelt. 'We made no treaty, we referred to no treaty, we complied with no treaty. We walked in and,' after announcing the defeat of the Ngoni of Mpezeni not so far to the east, 'we forthwith began to "administer" the country.' But local memory speaks of the coming of the agents of Rhodes and Johnston as 'war', and recalls the seizure of cattle and fowls for the use of the conquerors as a regular feature of the conquest.[14]

The agents of Rhodes and Johnston, it is true, gathered collections of documents which they called 'treaties', 'concessions' and 'certificates of claim', many of which have been shown as spurious. No less spurious was such a 'treaty' as that which Alfred Sharpe claimed to have made with Nsama of the Tabwa whom he called 'King of the Bemba People' and by which Nsama was to receive £25 per year 'or the equivalent thereof in trade goods' in return for the 'concession' to Sharpe of the right 'to search, prospect, exploit, dig for and keep all minerals and metals'; for Nsama was not the Bemba King.[15] The colonial agents, however, had to produce 'treaties' to fulfil the requirements of the formula by which the major European powers, in the critical situation of a threatening cold war over the partition of Africa, had resolved, at the Berlin Conference, to legitimise the spoils of the scramble. Moreover, contemporary missionary comment affirmed the determination of the British agents to do no less than conquer, and if necessary to do so by war. The documents so drafted were thus not of any significance to the peoples they subordinated. To them, the conquest had to be accepted simply because of 'fear of guns'. Missionaries wanted to hope for the best and 'soon to be listening to sweet music in Central Africa . . . not the harsh grating of the Maxim gun, not the crackle of burning huts, not the groan of dying men, all hideous noises to our ears, but'—in echo of Livingstone's dream—'the gold waltz, and the rubber gavotte and the ivory fugue.'[16] But when, as a young nationalist, Kenneth Kaunda quoted in a political circular, lines describing the 'scramble' in stark terms, his readers knew that that was in fact how it had seemed in the experience of their fathers:

'Onward, Chartered Soldiers,
On to heathen lands,
Prayer books in your pockets, rifles in your hands.
Take your glorious tidings where trade can be done.
Spread your peaceful gospel—with a Maxim gun.
Tell the wretched natives, sinful are their hearts;
Turn their heathen temples into spirit marts.
And if, to your teaching, they will not succumb,
Give them another sermon with a Maxim gun.
Tell them they are pagans in black error sunk;
Make of them good Christians—that is, make them drunk.
And if on the Bible, still they dare to frown,
You must do your duty, take and shoot them down.
When the ten Commandments they quite understand
You, their Chief, must hocus, and annex their land;
And if they, misguided, call you to account,
Give them another sermon—with a Maxim from the Mount.'[17]

The imposition of 'civilised' rule in Central Africa was justified by the argument that it 'pacified' regions racked by 'tribal war' and the Arab slave-trade which David Livingstone had called 'the open sore' of Africa. One latter-day champion of white colonialism has spoken of the reports of early travellers of 'the sickening horror that possessed them when, again and again, they came upon the charred ashes where peaceful villages had stood . . .scenes of massacre and desolation . . . as the Makololo, the Angoni and the Shangaans ravaged the land, tearing through it in fiery rivers that . . . left behind a trail of waste and death . . . Colonists of a different colour were soon to come in and put an end to the Age of Blood.' Writing fifteen years after the end of the war in Europe and the Far East in which obliteration bombing had had its climax at Hiroshima and Nagasaki, he added that, 'as long as the Bantu were their own rulers neither the missionary nor the hunter could reform them.' 'The missionary himself was therefore wise to carry a gun as well as a Bible when he went forth.'[18] One of Northern Rhodesia's more petulant white politicians was to warn, soon after Zambia attained independence that 'the flames [were] sweeping closer to the borders of the Republic [of South Africa]' since 'in Central Africa which seemed quite stable a few years ago, the institutions of the West . . . are facing ruin. Only the Portuguese

flag is still fluttering in the breeze.'[19] Remote commentators might
see the conflict in Africa as stemming, in part at least, from the
invasion of 'communal societies' by bands of 'sturdy individualists'.
The tragedy, however, was that Europe and its sons and daughters
who emigrated to Africa were blind to the feelings and reactions
of the peoples so invaded, and took the apparent African submission
to indicate acquiescence under foreign domination.

The testimony of one senior Zambian in the Northern Province,
representative of evidence received in many parts of the country,
reveals the other side of the situation. 'The first Europeans arrived
in this country peacefully; first it was Mandala [the African Lakes
Company of John and Frederick Moir] and then the missionaries
. . .we welcomed them and lived together peacefully. . .and demanded
that they should learn the local language. . . . When you entered
the stores of Mandala the trader, even there you were well received.
Things began to change completely when other companies began
to arrive . . . . Things turned really very, very bad.' After describing
the long journeys which press-ganged carriers were obliged to
undertake between the two lakes and down to Kasama, Simon
Singoyi went on: 'We began to wonder whether we had really
been freed from our fetters. It did not take long before we experienced the introduction of the yoke . . . long chains which they used
to chain people's necks . . .several people together in a line. . . .They
would then force people to run about in the forest, tied together.
. . . People began to refuse to carry *katundu* [lit. loads: huge steel
boxes] and escaped into the bush, and it was terrible and dangerous
to sleep in the bush because of lions. . . .I myself saw these things
with my own two eyes . . .fetters, chains, cords and sjamboks. [whips]
. . .When you could no longer stand this [the weight of the load]
you would just dump the thing and flee into the forest, and they
would begin to hunt for you. This turned into a kind of war. . . .We
continued living under such conditions a nd treatment, being beaten,
imprisoned, chained together, until 1904 when an instruction
went to all our chiefs to assemble all their subjects in one place . . .
to get *katundu* from Karonga to Mbala . . . . After their arrival at
Mbala, people were lined up. . . and each one handed a piece of
printed and stamped paper . . . people begun to grumble . . . expecting to be paid some money. These pieces of paper turned out to be
tax receipts and people were instructed . . . to guard these papers

as they guard their two ears .... People complained to their chiefs and ... after this they agreed to offer them a few yards of cloth .... Things became harder and harder .... We hated these things very much .... The other terrible practice we disliked was carrying the bwanas in hammocks .... For example, Bwana Chimpindi [*sic*] ... had his *askaris* [African police], ... Tongas [from Nyasaland] and Chewas ... very harsh people. ... Sometimes, when these Europeans visited certain places ... and found grain stores filled with grain and the villages empty ... all people had fled into the forest, they set all grain stores on fire .... If they spotted a hen, they could never leave it alone ... they gave the hens to their carriers .... [For example] Bwana Macdonald ... when he was carried in a hammock, he would jump down with a bamboo stick in his hand .... After beating the hammock bearer, he would say "Because of your foolishness in allowing the branch to prick my skin, you will now pay for your stupidity." Then he would get hold of the poor man by the neck and grind his head against the rough surface of a tree until the skin began tearing off .... Everyone else was watching .... There was no peace at all. You could not cough nearby. "Who is bloody coughing here?" Mackinnon would shout. "Go and give him six strokes," and the messengers went and administered a beating to the one who had coughed.'[20]

From all corners of the country similar testimony can be heard from those who recall the coming of Europeans and the years that followed the imposition of their rule. 'There had been wars in the land, the wars of the Mashitu [Ngoni] and the Bemba, the wars of the Balungwana [Arabs] that had followed the early wars of the Bayeke and others. Then the Basungu [Europeans] came with their war [*nkondo*], and there was no peace in the villages.' For many this state of strife was especially symbolised by tax raids and by the public whipping of defaulters at Boma offices. 'They were taken to the Boma at Kapili,' said the old men at Nanzhila in Ila country, 'and there they were tied in sacks, whipped with a sjambok with thongs and then their wounds were sprinkled with salt. This was why the people fled from the villages.'[21]

The Royal Charter granted in 1889 by Britain to Cecil Rhodes' British South Africa Company served the interests of both parties. Britain had a stake in Central Africa secured for her, without charge on the tax-payer, by a company of determined men who, in turn, were able to operate with minimal interference from London. For the conquered peoples, the issues of European imperial rivalries, the quest for raw materials and for markets, the diplomatic niceties of the agreements reached at Berlin in 1884 did not, and could not, have significance.[22] What a District Officer in the north-western area of the country wrote to his parents can be accepted as more significant evidence of action which could not but be regarded as harsh and hostile by the victims of the conquest. That officer's letters were written in the decade following 1912. By then the recommendations of labour agents had been long put into effect, whereby 'a heavy hut tax' would force adult males to seek employment in the southern mines.[23]

It fell to 'collectors' and Native Commissioners to enforce this taxation. In one letter, written in 1913, the officer told how 'not a village has stayed in the northern part of the district—they have all fled in the night. There is no doubt that it is the 10/- tax that they revolt from [and] they are largely afraid of Pound [the Senior Commissioner] as having been the man who . . . threatens them with prison if they will not work and earn their tax . . . . 10/- seems the deuce of a tax to put on men who do not normally own more than a pot and a spear and a yard or two of calico.' Later he wrote: 'It raises my gorge to think of attempting to tax these poor savages . . . sacrificing every single item of improving administration and sticking to the dirty tax . . . . All that the tax has done is simply to frighten the people of us . . . . and depopulate the district . . . . If driving the people out was the object then the tax was barbaric, cruel, morally and materially a damned foolish thing for now we have no villages to bring us food . . . . The payment of tax is an outward expression oɪ obedience and subjugation.'[24]

'The first objective of the colonisers,' wrote the priest in charge of the White Fathers' mission at Kayambi in 1898, 'is to fill their own pockets; as for improving the lot of the poor natives that is the business of the poor missionary people who don't know the value of gold.' Frequently 'everyone was in the bush,' they recorded, as tax-raids were carried out and African *kapitaos* in B.S.A. employ 'had come beating, chaining and plundering the people on the pretext that they didn't want to pay tax.' If a hut did not have an acknowledged owner, it was to be burned. The priests on Chilubi Island in Lake Bangweulu noted the comment of a collector called

Francis that he had authority to burn all tax-defaulters' houses. Having found one village concealed in reeds on the lake, 'he had blown it up.' In 1905 the Unga people around the lake told the missionaries that they were 'ready for war with the Company because of the tax-raids'.[25]

One feature of Company rule that appeared not infrequently in missionary records was *la chaine*, as the White Fathers called it, the means by which such people as tax-defaulters were tied together in a 'chain-gang'. Though the White Fathers recorded, 'We have never preached revolt but full submission [to the British],' their journals, like those of the Scots missionaries in the area of modern Malawi and of the London Missionary Society in the region at the south end of Lake Tanganyika recorded many acts of overt brutality carried out by 'collectors' and administrators. The brutal methods of the Arab slave trade had had much to do with rousing British opinion and rallying support for action in Central Africa 'to heal the open sore': though men like Harry Johnston and A. J. Swann did not conceal their sympathy with the Arabs and defence of their 'colonising' efforts and various African testimonies have suggested that the Arabs were remembered primarily as traders and not generally as oppressors. Whatever their motives, however, they had undoubtedly used chains to fetter together the people whom they took as porters of the goods which they procured in Central Africa. Moreover, the numbers of people taken by Arabs whether for press-ganged porterage or for resale as slaves were, according to figures provided by contemporary observers, so high as to create grave social and economic deprivation in the villages from which they were removed. What is significant here is that the stronger instruders, whose sophisticated weapons drove the Arabs from the region, used guns, whips and chains to enforce their conquest and by taxation and press-ganged labour recruitment drove great numbers of able-bodied men from their homes. As one English missionary wrote in 1908, 'To obtain money for taxes and force the young men south to work, the Administrator told the people at a public indaba at which I was present that in future non-tax-payers would be put for three months on the chain. But that if young men cared, they could go south, get work and pay their taxes as well as those of their relatives. I hear that a labour agent has sent 900 down south . . . . It is iniquitous that this should be the case ....Many of these men return to their homes worse physically and morally as well as with a contempt for the white man that they did not show before .... Perhaps the Administration will find this out to their cost in the years to come.' If this was the view of a foreigner in the area, how much more did the local people resent the behaviour of their conquerors.[26]

The subsequent decades which can be called, in A. J. Wills's phrase, 'the African submission', were to witness traumatic and irrevocable upheaval. The pre-European trading systems of the region were shattered and vanished. Indeed, as has been recently claimed, whereas many accounts by visitors to East and Central Africa in the nineteenth century spoke of agricultural prosperity, a wide variety of foodstuffs and a vigorous body of entrepreneurs, the picture that emerges after three decades of white rule is one of stagnation and decay, extensive malnutrition, social dislocation and poverty, consequent upon the removal of so many adult males from the rural agricultural system and the psychological depression experienced by many of the women who remained. 'If the arrival of the Arabs had stifled local entrepreneurship, the entry of the Europeans dealt the death blow to local production.'[27] When, in 1922, there was a sharp increase in 'native tax', the General Missionary Conference protested in vain for a reduction of the tax; the Administration replying that this would be impossible, since 'the estimated native tax to be received is £90,000 while the estimated expenditure on district administration is £98,859.' The Conference, however, had heard that 'a very high percentage of the able-bodied male population (from 50 per cent to 75 per cent or more) is absent from the villages to work outside the Territory or far away from their homes, in some instances hardly one able-bodied man remaining.' This resulted in an 'increase in immorality among the girls and women left behind [and] very many separations and divorces,' while 'the old men, women and children can hardly do more than raise enough food for bare existence,' so that 'any improvement in methods of cultivation is out of the question.' Five years later and three years after the transference of government from the B.S.A. Company to the Colonial Office, the Conference declared 'that compulsory or forced labour for private enterprises is inadmissible in any circumstances', and went on to ask whether the 'natives of this country' should not now be given the franchise, albeit limited, and something 'like a Native Parliament be instituted.'[28]

The impact of colonial conquest on the use of land was thus far more disastrous than has been suggested by historians writing from the standpoint of the imperial power; and, as we are not concerned with Central Africa's long and chequered record of conflict and plunder but with what happened under the formula of 'protection', the evidence to hand reveals a situation fraught with bitterness. Today, well to the west of the railway line that runs north from Livingstone, they still recall the methods by which villages were removed to make way for large allocations of land to white farmers, such areas being proclaimed 'Crown Land'. Though Gann speaks of compensation, the local memory is of forcible eviction from good to poorer land, to the crackle of burning huts and with guns in evidence, but without compensation. Gann's mention of what was probably merely 'paper' compensation appears in a chapter entitled 'The Birth of a New Economy'. For the settlers this was certainly so. Land could be had at twopence or threepence an acre, though the *Livingstone Mail* called for free issues, as the reward of conquest. Indeed its fiery editor, Leopold Moore, asserted that since 'the native does not make the best use of his land . . . it should be confiscated by the stronger and more efficient race . . . and he be made to pay rent for it . . . [so that] economic pressure will bring him into the labour market voluntarily.' Labour was cheap and authority over it absolute. Immigrants from Britain or even from South Africa were finding what they affectionately called 'God's own country'. But for the African people, this was rather the death of their political and economic systems and the beginning of a new thraldom. In the Tonga and Ila areas, as elsewhere, tax-defaulters were constantly harried, sometimes being stripped naked and subjected to public flogging. But in May 1920, an assembly of 'settlers' in Livingstone resolved unanimously 'not to submit' to a B.S.A. proposal to introduce the direct taxation of European incomes.[29]

The 'African submission' was not, however, without signs of resistance. In 1909 there was 'an almost rebellious situation' in the Gwembe valley, not long after the officers in charge of the Serenje district had feared a mass exodus in protest against taxation. Moreover, though Wills believed that the reaction to taxation was

'nowhere unfavourable', as late as 1923 over half of the taxable
population was convicted of default and, eleven years later, the
Acting-Governor expressed amazement to find 'prisons in such an
unproductive region as Barotseland filled with tax-defaulters'
where there were '7,109 persons committed to prison in that year
for default'. It is impossible to conceive of people acquiescing in
such a system as, throughout the territory, the practice for years
was, in the cynical words of one Native Commissioner, 'to insist
on the natives of your district paying their tax in order to drive
them out . . . rather than exercise undue energy in finding employment for them.' Nowhere in the world would men accept such a
regime gladly. The smashing of the Ndebele and the Ngoni, the
signal 'chastisement' of Kazembe, and the arrogant presence of
guns wherever white men settled maintained the 'pacification'.
The John Chilembwe rising in Nyasaland in 1915 revealed a smouldering bitterness, and colonial policy was always to be alert to
any signs of trouble. The rise of 'separatist' churches and of the
Watchtower movement cannot be dissociated from the state of
widespread resentment. Moreover, in Northern Rhodesia there had
been sporadic signs of popular emotion. In 1907 the Sable Mine in
the Mumbwa area had been virtually shut down in face of the
threat of 'a native rising', and in 1909 the Lunda, described as
'most unequivocally defiant', boasted to local missionaries 'that
they had expelled the Government from their country.'[30]

Another phrase that greatly clouded the foreign historian's
perception of the realities of the colonial impact on Central Africa
was the formula 'indirect rule', which could easily be advanced in
validation of a paternalist regime. In fact, as local testimony
affirms, it made Chiefs into *kapitaos* or foremen of the foreign
rulers. As late as 1932, a Provincial Commissioner told an *Indaba*
at Mumbwa: 'If there is not tax money, there will be no money
to pay chiefs,' and then ordered the Chiefs to collect the taxes.
'If you cannot do this, you are not fit to be chiefs.' This was a
reaffirmation of established policy, and in consequence it was not
surprising that the institution of Native Authorities in 1930, in
development of the proposition of Lord Lugard's 'Dual Mandate',
had 'little to recommend it to the Native mind', as one official
said. As we shall see, the N.A.s and, later on, the variety of African
Councils created by the colonial Government were to prove uni-

formly incapable of giving genuine expression to popular feeling.
The parlous role of Chiefs was undoubtedly further vitiated by the
fact that so little attention was paid by the Administration to their
repeated pleas on behalf of their people. The depopulation of the
rural areas continued as the demand for labour for the southern
minefields increased, despite a mortality rate that was as high as
13 per cent in 1911, the appeals of the Chiefs having no effect.[31]

As late as 1934, one Chief described the situation thus: 'I ask that
taxes in the country be reduced because our people cannot earn
money to pay it. There are many taxes for people to pay. 10/- is
the tax for all men . . . . A man with a gun must pay 3/-. A man with
a bicycle must pay 3/6. Our people go to the mines to look for
work. They cannot find work and become weak and ill from hunger.
On their way home they die of hunger because they have no money
to find food on the journey. Sometimes they find work for very
little money, 5/- or 6/-. To earn money for tax a man must stay
away for many months. His wife is left with no one to cut her
garden. Then there is hunger in the village too . . . . The lives of the
people are spoiled and all our people are unhappy.' This picture
of widespread depression would, however, be incomplete if we
were to overlook the added sufferings of the years of the First
World War when in one district alone, 40,000 men were 'roped in'
as porters and when the mortality rate reached as high as 10 per
cent, with an official report for Lundazi describing the majority
of the 2,400 carriers enlisted in 1917-18 as returning 'in a pitiable
state of emaciation, due to starvation or dysentery'. To obtain
these vast numbers of porters from a territory already severely
drained, the Administration had applied further coercion upon
Chiefs and so further diminished their standing among their peoples.[32]

The original role of the B.S.A. Company's territory north of the
Zambezi was, as we have seen, to provide labour for the south.
But in 1902 a considerable ore-body of copper was discovered
near Chief Chiwala's court at a place that came to be called Bwana
Mkubwa, or 'big chief', in honour of the Native Commissioner,
Moffat Thomson, signalizing the beginning of mining in the territory.
Eight years later, as the railway line from the Victoria Falls bridge
was joined to the Congo system, digging began at Nkana, not far
from the rich Katanga copper field. By 1922, as the world demand

for copper rose and as the new flotation method of extraction was being developed, the Northern Rhodesian Copperbelt began in earnest. For Africans, this meant shorter journeys in search of wages but it also brought a rapid extension of the whole pattern of racial antagonisms summed up in the phrase 'the colour bar'. Gann has commented on it thus: 'Harsh treatment, danger and the many minor abuses inseparable from the control of vast numbers of semi-conscripts by a small harassed staff... made mining unpopular among Africans in the early days.' He has then sought to explain the situation by noting that 'under different climatic and geographical conditions, it has been the European trader, buying tropical products grown by Africans without foreign supervision who opened up the country economically, whereas the demands of mining enterprise, using techniques unknown to the local people, cast the African in the role of labourer rather than producer.' Elsewhere Gann gives prominence to the often nefarious role, in between the 'bwanas' and their 'native boys', of African *kapitaos*, and no doubt this special role was ripe for exploitation by unscrupulous men. But far more serious for the future of the territory was the entrenchment of social, economic, industrial and political discrimination against Africans in every aspect of the life of the country.[33]

In an African National Congress Circular of 1956, Kenneth Kaunda was to quote words written by Winston Churchill in 1921 when he was Colonial Secretary, thus: "It will be an ill day for the native races when their fortunes are removed from the Imperial and august administration of the Crown and abandoned to the fierce self-interest of a small population of white settlers."[34] Yet the whole story of the territory now called Zambia, from 1890 to 1964 was the record of the determined effort of such a minority to claim the right to rule by virtue of conquest and possession. The race relations of the territory gave baleful testimony to this determination. As townships appeared on the line of rail and elsewhere and settlers increased in number, they wanted 'boys' to do all the manual work required for their comfort, peel their vegetables, clean their shoes, carry their shopping baskets, look after their young children, take their fierce dogs for walks. But as 'kaffirs', 'natives' or 'munts', those so employed were forbidden to walk on the pavements of the white men's towns.[35] At one time in 1930, in Livingstone alone, there were forty-three people arrested in one month for that offence. In that same year Nelson Nalumango, who was to be one of the first two Africans appointed to the Legislative Council in 1948, was kicked and beaten by an African constable who found him standing on the sidewalk in Broken Hill. In that year, the European population of the Copperbelt had risen sharply to 11,000, many of whom came from South Africa. A bad situation was worsening.[36]

The protracted controversy between London and the leaders of European opinion in Central Africa over the latter's desire to effect the amalgamation of the two Rhodesias and Nyasaland led to various comparisons of the situation in the three territories, notably by the Bledisloe Commission of 1939. Such examinations inevitably underlined the differences between the declared 'native policies' of the two Protectorates, on the one hand, and the self-governing Colony of Southern Rhodesia on the other. No matter which party was in power in Britain, the Colonial Office was bound to respect informed opinion, both at home and abroad, in favour of a liberalizing of colonial policies, and so resist a move that would extend the 'avowed policy of segregation, under the name of "parallel Development" and the institution of the 'colour bar'. When the pressure mounted again in the post-war years for first Amalgamation and then Federation, the differences between official 'native policies' were again subjected to scrutiny. Moreover the memorandum prepared, in May 1949, by Dr. Hastings Banda and Mr. Harry Nkumbula in opposition to the proposed Central African Federation, contrasted the Southern Rhodesian 'cardinal principle [of] domination' with the 'cardinal principle [of] guidance and guardianship' in the northern territories.[37]

To the Africans of Northern Rhodesia and especially those who had worked in the south, those differences were not readily apparent. In the towns along the railway line and in the more remote rural townships, a universal colour bar operated. Trains carried 'native coaches'; access to cafes was forbidden to all Africans, for whom shopping in the towns meant queuing at 'hatches' or 'pigeon-holes' where they were liable to be addressed abusively; and there was total racial discrimination in employment by the big mining companies and other commercial and industrial undertakings. Post-offices and banks had separate entrances for 'natives'; medical and

educational services were completely segregated and those available
to Africans were minimally financed, equipped and staffed. Moreover, virtually without exception, the urban churches practised
total segregation, while social intercourse was severely condemned
by white opinion. As African opinion increasingly found its voice,
there was, as we shall see, a constant appeal to the enlightened
principles that had been publicised as fundamental British policy
during and after the war with Hitler's Germany. But this appeal
was made in the context of daily experience which belied those
principles and made all Africans conscious of that 'ostracism
symbolising inferiority' to which Kenneth Kaunda was to make
increasingly insistent reference.[38]

The balance sheet of Central African history, in the middle
decades between the beginning and the end of foreign rule, nonetheless contains some significant credit items. There was notably
the educational and medical work of Christian agencies. Government assistance for these undertakings was belated and niggardly,
especially in view of the wealth of the territory in comparison with
other British 'dependencies'. But missionary efforts in these fields
spread over the territory a thin but important network of village
schools and established a few rural hospitals, serving vast areas,
which especially symbolised the churches' ministry of compassion.
There were also the voices of a few individual missionaries and a
number of notable declarations by the General Missionary Conference which did not fail to attract the attention of the leaders of the
embryonic bodies of African protest and political action. And
there were some Government officials, both in the territory and in
London, who were convinced, in the words of one of them, that
'until such time as the native community are themselves in a position
to secure the expression of their views, by the participation of
elected representatives in the Legislature, it is essential that the
power of the Governor and his officers . . . to promote their interests
should not be impaired.'[39]

When white rule began, its officers were mainly tough adventurers, men with little academic training but with a love of hunting,
notable for their determination to work their wills on the vast,
ecalcitrant territories which they claimed for Rhodes' Company.[40]
The move to transfer authority in Northern Rhodesia, at the same
time as Southern Rhodesia became a Crown Colony, coincided

with the impact on Colonial Office thinking of Frederick Lugard's 'Dual Mandate in British Tropical Africa' and its exposition of the doctrine of 'indirect rule'. Thus the period after 1924 might be called the Lugard era. Then, imperceptibly at first, but markedly in the years following the Second World War, we find what we might call 'the Fabian men', officers whose university training had been associated with the serious reappraisal of Britain's overseas role which owed much of its inspiration to the Fabian Colonial Bureau. Thus in the years immediately preceding the drive by Godfrey Huggins and Roy Welensky for Federation, the Northern Rhodesian colonial service had a number of men in its service of whom Kenneth Kaunda was to record later that 'many of them are good men and I count some of them as my friends.'[41]

It is suggested, however, that it has been right to put first, in the record of the forces that prepared Northern Rhodesia for dramatic change, the factor of racial discrimination and inhumanity. This is not at all to overlook the beneficent factors which expressed themselves in the introduction of formal education, scientific medicine and other significant advances. It is rather to remind us that, here as elsewhere and at this time as always, there is an inevitable reaction against the oppression of man by man. Ironically, yet aptly, the first issue of the *Congress News* which Kenneth Kaunda produced in October 1953, carried this quotation from a speech by Roy Welensky in July of that year: "I believe that if any section aims at dominance this is what they have got to face. In the first instance they may be able to do it by legislation . . . but it will only be a passage of time when they will have to enforce it by force. I would suggest if that is their viewpoint that they must dominate by force, it is therefore inevitable that only bitterness and hatred will follow." We have seen something of the visible aspects of 'the African submission', how it was brought about and how it was maintained during the proud years of white supremacy. The men of the 'master race' were, however, characteristically deaf to the tremors of irresistible change, mistaking the silence for peace. In the third year of the Federation, as we shall see, Kaunda was simply echoing the hearts of his people when he wrote: 'Youth of Africa, on your shoulders lies the responsibility of attaining and thereafter maintaining for this country [within our lifetime] a policy in which there shall be the same law for all, a policy administered with regard to equal rights and entirely devoid of racial discrimination and all its components. You rest in peace only after that policy is attained.'[42]

---

[1]W. K. Sikalumbi, *Before UNIP* (forthcoming, NECZAM, Lusaka), Chap. VIII.
[2]T. Melady, *Kenneth Kaunda of Zambia: Selections from his Writings* (Praeger, 1964), 5, quoting Frank Chitambala.
[3]For the history of Northern Rhodesia and of European colonial expansion in Central Africa, see L. H. Gann, *A History of Northern Rhodesia* (Chatto and Windus, 1964); R. Hall, *Zambia* (Pall Mall Press, 1965); A. J. Hanna, *The Beginnings of Nyasaland and North-eastern Rhodesia* (O.U.P., 1956); R. I. Rotberg, *The Rise of Nationalism in Central Africa* (Harvard, 1965).
[4]Early missionary accounts of work in Central Africa include L. Decle, *Three Years in Savage Africa* (Methuen, 1898); W. A. Elmslie, *Among the Wild Ngoni* (Oliphant, 1899); F. Coillard, *On the Threshold of Central Africa* (Hodder and Stoughton, 1902); H. Johnson *Night and Morning in Dark Africa* (London Missionary Society, 1902); J. Stewart, *Dawn in the Dark Continent* (Oliphant, Anderson and Ferrier, 1903). See also Bibliography in R. I. Rotberg, *Christian Missions and the Creation of Northern Rhodesia* (Princeton, 1965) 208-224.
[5]See H. A. C. Cairns, *Prelude to Imperialism* (Routledge and Kegan Paul, 1965).
[6]See H. S. Meebelo, *Reaction to Colonialism* (Manchester, 1971), which refers especially to northern Zambia; R. M. Rayner, *Nineteenth Century England* (Longmans, 1938), 332. D.C. Mulford, *Zambia—the Politics of Independence* (O.U.P., 1967), 4.
[7]NAZ: SEC/NAT/353, Kaluwa to S.N.A., 15/7/48; ANC: speech by Harry Nkumbula at All Africa Peoples' Conference, Accra, 8-12/12/58; RH, Oxford: 103/2, 'Sworn Memorandum drawn by Kenneth David Kaunda . . . for the Commission to probe into the banning of the said Zambia African National Congress' (undated).
[8]*Life and Work* (Blantyre Mission of the Church of Scotland), December 1894, March 1892, and April 1893.
[9]*Scotsman*, Edinburgh 29/12/02, letter by Revd. Dr. Alexandar Hetherwick of Blantyre Mission, headed 'Exploiting the African'.
[10]RH, Oxford: MSS.Afr.s.84(1,2)—Report by H. H. Johnston on the Nyasaland-Tanganyika Expedition, 1889-90, 36 ff.
[11]The cessation of the payment of B.S.A. 'royalties' was announced by Zambia's Finance Minister, Arthur Wina, on 23/10/64.
[12]See J. A. Barnes, *Politics in a Changing Society* (Manchester, 1954) 85-93; and FO: 2/127, Johnston to Foreign Office 6/2/97.
[13]See *NR Journal*, Vol. II, No. 2,1953, 'Bobo Young relates his exploits', 65-71; M. Gelfand, *Northern Rhodesia in the Days of the Charter* (O.U.P., 1961) 87; Central Bantu Historical Texts II, 110-111, for an African account of Kazembe's subjugation; and White Fathers, Rome: Luapula Diary, August 1900.
[14]J. E. Stephenson, *Chirupula's Tale* (Geoffrey Bles, 1937), 63; and e.g. testimonies of participants in Lundazi Seminar in Oral Records of Local History, and of Singoyi and Nansala, *et. al. vide infra*, footnotes 16, 22 and 21.
[15]See Hall, *op. cit.*, pp. 54-86, and esp. 77 ff, citing, on p. 82, T. W. Baxter, 'Occasional Papers of the National Archives of Rhodesia and Nyasaland', No. 1, Salisbury, 1963, p. 27, giving texts of some 'treaties'.
[16]See Nat. Lib. Scot.: 7879, Folio 76, letter, W. A'. Elmslie to Free Church Mission Secretary, Edinburgh, 9/4/1896; White Fathers, Rome: Kayambi Diary, 26/12/1896; testimony received at Oral History Seminars, Kasama and Lundazi, June 1972; and TI-FM/William Kawandami of Mbereshi, 9/5/73.
[17]*Life and Work*, January 1897.

[18]C. E. Lucas-Phillips, *The Vision Splendid: the Future of the Central African Federation* (Heinemann, 1960), 59, 64. See also H. M. Bates, *Report on the Rhodesia.* (Melrose, 1953), 106.

[19]G. van Eeden, *The Crime of Being White*, (Nasionale Boekhandel Beperk 1965), 165.

[20]TI-FM/Simon Singoyi of Chilanga village, Isoka, a retired evangelist of the United Church of Zambia, interviewed with others, 26/4/71.

[21]Macpherson Collection: e.g. TI-FM/ Benjamin Shankwaya; Chose Ngana, Shadreck Samalumo, Nanzhila, 19/4/73; Nansala Manyeta, Zebron Sambwa, Yakobe Lusuma, Noah Kapika, Serenje, 15-19/10/73; Samson Maphara, Edward Gondwe, Lundazi, 21/6/72; and papers of Oral History Seminars, Kasama, 3-5 June 1972, and Lundazi 23-25 June, 1972.

[22]See RH, Oxford: MSS, Afr. 71, Chartered Incorporation of the B.S.A. Company, and 'General Acts of the Brussels Conference', 2/11/1890.

[23]*Ibid.:* MSS. Afr. s. 228, report to B.S.A. by Lawley on potential labour resources of Northern Rhodesia, 7/12/1898.

[24]MSS. Afr. s. 779, letters of Theodore Williams, 8/5/13, 23/9/13, 7/10/13.

[25]White Fathers, Rome: Diaries, Kayambi, 8/10/1898, and 19/7/04; Chilubula, 6-8/12/02; Chilubi, 12/2/05, 16/3/05, 11/6/05.

[26]*Ibid.*: Kayambi, 9/2/02; Chilubi, 2/2/04, 9/5/11; Kayambi, 20/3/13; Chilubula, 4/11/04, 6/1/05; C.C.W.M., London: Letters, C. Africa, P. W. Jones to L.M.S. Directors, 28/5/1899; Wright (Niamkolo) to Directors, 8/12/08; TI-FM/Nansala Manyeta *et. al.*, and for one estimate of number of slaves taken by Arabs see Nat. Lib. Scot.: 7904 Folio 11, letter of Edward Young, engineer with Livingstonia.

[27]A. J. Wills, *Introduction to the History of Central Africa* (O.U.P., 1963). esp. 225 ff; R. Gray and D. Birmingham (ed.), *Pre-Colonial African Trade* (O.U.P., 1970), 227. See also T. O. Ranger, *The Agricultural History of Zambia* (Historical Association of Zambia, Neczam, 1971) and W. Rodney, *How Europe Underdeveloped Africa* (Bogle-L'Ouverture, 1972).

[28]General Missionary Conference (a) Kafue, July 1922 and (b) Livingstone, July 1927; and note esp. paper delivered by the Anglican Bishop, Alston May, pp. 181 ff. of 1922 Report. In 1918, the tax yield in Solwezi District was £1,300 against administrative costs of £1,200 (RH, Oxford: MSS. Afr. s. 780—T. R. Williams, letter, 5/8/18).

[29]Gann, *op. cit.*, p. 135; TI-FM/Benjamin Shankwaya *et. al.*; *Livingstone Mail*, 18/11/11, 16/12/11 and 13/5/20.

[30]Wills, *op. cit.*, p. 226; NAZ: NW/A. 2/1/3-A Administrator to High Commissioner, Johannesburg, 10/11/09; P 3/3/3/, Minute on 'Native Taxation' by Acting Governor Charles Dundas, 26/4/34; KSK 1/1/1, Coxhead, N.C., Fort Jameson, to Hughes, N. C. Serenje, 24/8/04; KJJ 2/5, Ag. Collector to D.C., Kafue, 2/8/07, on Sable Mine crisis; KSE 6/1/1, Annual Report, Balunda District, 1908-1909, p. 4. Note also G. Shepperson and T. Price, *Independent African* (Edinburgh University Press, 1958) for an excellent study of the Chilembwe Rising in particular and the African reaction to conquest in general.

[31]Macpherson Collection: as in footnote 21; and NAZ: KJJ 3/1, Mumbwa District Notebook, Vol. I, pp. 143, 145; and see KSZ 7/1/1, Annual Report, Luwingu Sub-district, 1912-13, for figures of migrant labour mortality.

[32]NAZ: KSD 4/1, Mpika District Notebook, p. 484, report of Indaba, 26/10/34; and data on the effects of the First World War, extracted from records in NAZ by Dr. W. A. Hunton in his Quarterly Progress Report No. 2 of May 1968, to the Kenneth Kaunda Foundation, a report on historical research.

[33]*The Birth of a Plural Society* (Manchester, 1958), 122-126; and Gann, *A History*, p. 124.

[34]*ANC Circular*, Vol. II, No. 3, 31/3/56, quoting from Churchill's *My African Journey*, (Holland Press, London, 1908), 25.

[35]'Munt' was an insulting term of address used over an extensive part of southern and central Africa by white men to black. It is a corruption of *muntu* (singular

of *bantu*) meaning 'person' in a very large number of sub-Saharan languages.
[36]See Hall, *op. cit.*, pp. 114, 117.
[37]See Royal Commission Report on Rhodesia and Nyasaland (Cmd. 5949 of 1939), the Bledisloe Report, esp. p. 252; and Sokoni Papers: 'Federation in Central Africa', sgd. H. K. Banda and H. Nkumbula, 8, Ayleston Avenue, Brondesbury Park, London, 1/5/49.
[38]K. D. Kaunda, and C. Morris, *Black Government* (United Society for Christian Literature, Lusaka, 1960) esp. p. 47. Note: The writer's personal experience and observation, from 1946 onwards, confirmed this description of Northern Rhodesia society. The main N.R. newspaper, the *Northern News*, provides interesting insights into the prevalent attitudes of white society and the universal application of segregation in the twenty years before Zambia's attainment of independence.
[39]NAZ: SEC/Misc/10, Ormsby-Gore to Governor Hubert Young, 15/9/37; and for a study of the role of missionary societies and churches, see J. V. Taylor, and D. A. Lehmann, *Christians of the Copperbelt* (S.C.M. Press, 1961) and Rotberg's controversial *Christian Missions*.
[40]For glimpses of some B.S.A. men, see Brelsford, *A Generation of Men* (Stuart Manning, 1965); and *NR Journal*, esp. Vol. II, No. 3, 1954, article, H. T. Harrington 'The Taming of North-Eastern Rhodesia', pp. 3-20; and sundry notes on 'Abandoned Bomas'.
[41]K. D. Kaunda, *Zambia Shall be Free* (Heinemann, 1962), 59.
[42]ANC: *Congress News*, Vol. I, No. 1, (October 1953); and Vol. III, No. 2, (December, 1956).

2

Family Background

The arbitrary delineation of the borders of what is now called Zambia paid little or no attention, as we have seen, to the boundaries of the kingdoms subjugated at the end of the nineteenth century. It is, however, important to study the main peoples and kingdoms of pre-colonial days, not only so that their political interaction and trading can be sketched, but also in order to attempt to understand the social systems and customs on which the impact of European intrusion fell. Moreover, this type of attempt to reconstruct African history from an African standpoint must be seen as a recent departure from the earlier assumption that Central Africa was without significant history before 'the scramble'. It is now amusing to recall how, when Kenneth Kaunda was teaching a senior class in Mufulira's larger primary school in 1948, one of the few books available told of how, when David Livingstone went to Africa, he found some friendly native chiefs; the reader having to transport himself in imagination to Britain so that he might watch the missionary-explorer going to 'the dark continent'. Instead it is now clear that the period of 'the African submission' was a relatively brief era during which Arabs from the east coast and explorers, traders and conquerors from Europe worked their will, by virtue of superior arms, upon Africa.

In recent years, the peopling of Zambia by various groups of Bantu and the establishment of the more notable centralised governments in pre-colonial centuries have been usefully summarised for the general reader.[1] Though we are far from having a detailed picture of pre-colonial centuries, local traditions, widely corroborated, trace the rise of the major kingdoms to the arrival, over at least some decades, of 'hero-kings' from Luba or Kola, to the north-west of Zambia in the southern region of modern Zaïre.

Whether these incursions were made by small but well-armed bands who subdued the local peoples and demanded tribute and obedience, much as William of Normandy did in England, or whether the region witnessed the large-scale immigration of foreigners, is not yet clear. But it can be assumed that, just as the Anglo-Saxon invaders at the close of the fifth century A.D. drove the native Celts into the inhospitable Welsh mountains—as far as they could be pushed—so the vigorous invaders from Kola and Luba pushed the native pre-Bantu Twa and other groups of hunter-gatherers into the malarial swamps of Bangweulu, Lukanga and Kafue.[2]

It can also now be assumed that the Tonga of Zambia's Southern Province were among the earliest Bantu intruders to settle in the area, arriving perhaps around A.D. 1200. Like their close neighbours, the Ila, the Tonga may have derived from the region to the east of Lake Tanganyika and it is worth noting that old men of the other group called Tonga, on the west shore of Lake Malawi, the group to which the Kaunda family belonged, have claimed to share a common origin with the Zambian Tonga. The great majority of Zambia's Bantu peoples were consolidated thereafter by successive waves of immigrants from the Luba and Lunda Empires of the large region around the watershed of the great rivers, Congo and Zambezi. Though again it is far from clear whether those immigrants left their homelands in organised expeditions or as fugitives, they clearly succeeded in shaping a network of greater and lesser states in the area of Zambia; a number of those of Lunda origin continuing for some time to pay tribute to the Lunda emperor, Mwata ya Mvwa, 'Lord of Death'. From Luba and Lunda there thus originated at least the consolidation of authority in the Aushi, Lamba and Lala, Lenje, Bemba and Bisa, Kaonde and Lozi, and the eastern and southern Lunda states as well as other lesser communities. Probably however, those incursions were preceded by others of Luban origin which constituted the migrations known as Maravi and contributed to early state-formation in parts of the region now known as Malawi. The peoples along the Tanganyika-Malawi corridor, though claiming Luban hero-kings, seem to have derived, at least in part, from homelands to the north, possibly around the great lakes of East Africa.[3]

Sociologists and anthropologists can undoubtedly establish

the existence of a wide variety of customs and beliefs among peoples living in different parts of an area as large as Zambia. Family structures that are matrilineal, for instance, are markedly different from patrilineal systems. But it is still possible to make certain valid general statements of the African way of life in the region at which we are looking, statements which can assist us in appreciating some of the human properties which were to be severely assaulted by the arrival of 'modern' people from western Europe. The peoples upon whom fell the impact of invasion by sturdy individualists from Europe, were essentially communalists, for whom the primary purpose of life was the continuation and strengthening of the community. The teaching of their children was the responsibility of the elders of the village and was designed to train boys and girls, by precept and rigorous physical discipline, to fill their mature roles as husbands and fathers and wives and mothers. In the poetic language of Professor Mbiti, for such communities 'children are the buds of society and every birth is the arrival of "spring." ' There could thus be no place for casual marriages based merely on the individual's choice of a partner. The part played by senior kinsfolk in choosing or ratifying a partner was not interference but the rightful operation of corporate responsibility. So too childlessness could not be lightly regarded. Fertility was of prime importance, and the barren woman became 'the dead end of human life, not only for the genealogical line but also for herself,' whose infertility was 'an irreparable humiliation for which there is no comfort in traditional life'. By the same logic, man's use of the earth was symbolically related to the fertility of the earth, which could not be used without prayer. Nor could a new village be built without a sacrifice of purification. Man was vitally involved in the processes of causation. He could not blame fickle chance. All evil had a human cause and malice was a major crime against society.[4]

The social cohesion of pre-colonial Zambia was undoubtedly derived from a cosmology in which man, set below the Supreme Being and the 'ancestral spirits' in the spiritual hierarchy, belonged together with other creatures in the community of life. It was not irrational, therefore, to ask the 'flour of peace and testimony', placed reverently where it seemed sensible to build a new village, to testify whether or not the spirits approved what was technically a good site. The blowing of a breeze and the scattering of the flour would be a clear indication of the response of the ancestors, as would be the discovery of the flour undisturbed.[5] Man was not in arrogant isolation from nature, free to work his will on the 'things' that made his environment. Rather there was a comprehensible dialogue going on, under the auspices of the spirits, which dare not be despised. It was perhaps of this sense of rapport with the universe that Kenneth Kaunda wrote when he described the emotion aroused as, during his political rustication in 1959, he sat by the bank of the Kabompo river. 'On both sides of the river are huge trees, deep green in the rainy season. They seem to be jealous of one another and appear to be pointing fingers of strange accusation at each other as the wind blows them backwards and forwards. Just as this one great sheet of water makes a sharp bend at the grassy feet of this princely high ground ... the silent waters burst into noisy protest as they clash with the enduring rocks ... Here I seemed to be getting nearer and nearer to understanding the language of nature.'[6]

It would be wrong, however, to deduce from such a sketch of certain aspects of social life in past centuries that Central African society had been stable. Perhaps the close knitting together of members of what were relatively small communities was a safeguard against the divisive forces of decades, if not centuries, of turbulence. This state of turmoil was certainly widespread at the time of the European conquest, which was also the period of the childhood of Kenneth Kaunda's father. It is important, therefore, now to turn our attention to the antecedents of the Kaunda family and the environment in which its latter story was set, and to note the special significance of the powerful new intrusion into the eastern areas of the region by the Ngoni.

Under the leadership of one Zwangendaba, a group of Nguni-speaking Jere had fled from the rising power of their overlord, the Zulu king Shaka, after a battle on the Mhlatuze River in Natal in 1818. The Ngoni flight, however, became a great pilgrimage, outsripping in length Israel's famous exodus from Pharoah's Egypt. Perhaps the most celebrated event of the great northward thrust was the crossing of the Zambezi in 1835 at Zumbo when, after much beer-drinking, the Ngoni were terror-stricken while in the river by an eclipse of the sun, in consequence of which people and cattle perished. Ngoni tradition tells also of the parting of the

waters as Zwangendaba struck them with his staff and of the pre-
mature birth of the hero-captain's son, Mbelwa. This event took
place not long before the Kololo of Sebituane, another breakaway
group from Shaka's kingdom, invaded what is now Zambia's
Western Province from across the Zambezi, and established so
effective a conquest that, even though they were routed by their
victims less than thirty years later, they left behind a lasting influence
upon the language and social customs of the Lozi.

The great northward trek of the Ngoni was to last for the best
part of twenty-five years and to take them as far north as Lake
Victoria. Thence there began the backward journey of strong
companies of Ngoni into the area of modern Malawi and Zambia,
where the three kingdoms of Mwambera, Mpezeni and Gomani
were to be established. Zwangendaba himself, who had led his
warriors and their dependants across the Zambezi in late 1835,
had died in Tanzanian Ufipa in 1848. For our purpose the kingdom
of Mwambera is of special significance. After Zwangendaba's
death, factions had fought bitterly over the issue of a successor and
in consequence the nation had split. Mwambera's goup moved
south-east into northern Malawi and in 1855 began their conquests
there by killing Chikuramayembe VII, ruler of the Kamanga
kingdom at the foot of the Nyika mountains. Eventually
Mwambera established his capital near Ekwendeni, in the area
between modern Mzimba and the Lake. There followed a period
in which by constant raids and captures, the Ngoni sought to
incorporate members of the local tribes into their army and for a
generation a group, whom van Velsen calls the Ngoni-Tonga,
lived in this vassalage. The Ngoni wars and the heroism of their own
warriors are still vivid in Malawi Tonga memories, but 'the Tonga,
soft and untrained, were no match for the virile hillfolk in their
disciplined strength and . . . warfare was now going on perpetually
. . . raids, attacks and massacres.' Mwambera became more determined to kill off the older Tonga and conscript the young men as
a subservient militia for future conquests. '*Mututomera iphere,
kusal' injumbura,*' the Tonga heard the Ngoni say, 'Let's kill the
old men and let only the youngsters remain.'[7]

The lakeshore Tonga kingdom had probably been formed
towards the end of the eighteenth century by the integration of a
number of separated groups around the time when ivory traders

were coming across the lake from the east. Lacking strong leadership, the Tonga at first fell easy prey to the attacks of the Ngoni who raided, not so much for booty as for young men to train as warriors. Under this harsh military regimen some of the Tonga became captains in Mwambera's army, and so, using their new skills, a group of Ngoni-Tonga staged a sudden rebellion and broke away from their masters, to re-establish themselves on the lakeshore. When the Ngoni pursued them, the rebels, under Mankhambira, won a notable victory in a fierce battle at the Chinteche river in 1875. It was just as this rebellion took place that the first missionaries from Scotland were landing at Cape Maclear.

Three years later, in the cool season of 1878, while the war was still raging savagely, Julizya Kaunda was born at Lisali in the Mwambazi district of Tongaland, about sixteen miles from Nkhata Bay. His father, Mtepa, had taken part in the fighting and was killed when his son was a little child. It is believed by Kenneth Kaunda's cousin Herbert, who still lives at Lisali, that Julizya's maternal grandfather, Chapukwa Muchirwa, was actually a founder of the Tonga state, and by van Velsen's estimate of the date of the consolidation of Utonga, the Tonga state, this is credible. The name 'Julizya' meant 'cause to open', a fitting name for the man who was to open the Bemba chiefdom of Nkula in Zambia to evangelism and education twenty-six years later. The name 'Kaunda' is of obscure origin. It could mean 'the coverer'. Locally the Kaundas were jokingly referred to as the men who would not eat monkeynuts, in memory of the abstemious habits of a forebear.[8]

While Julizya was still a toddler, word came to the Tonga of a terrible massacre on Mount Hora, up whose treeless rocky sides the Ngoni had driven a band of rebellious Tumbuka, slaying them as they came down in desperation to seek for water. This was in 1880, and increasingly thereafter Tonga and other families preferred to move into Mwambera's kingdom rather than face the terror of his soldiers. Among the Kaunda family at Lisali it is recorded that, soon after her husband's death, NyaChirwa, around 1885, took her children, three girls and a boy, up through the hills to Emfeni, near to the large Ngoni village of Elangeni established by the most important regiment or 'segment' derived from the great wife of Hlatshwaya, Zwangendaba's father. It was there that Julizya grew up, probably spending the earlier years herding cattle, and learning the hard discipline of a regimented society so different from the weaker matrilineal communities of the lakeshore.[9] Writers on the Ngoni agree that, despite their long trek north under Zwangendata or indeed perhaps as a result of it, they developed a strong regimented social system which they planted wherever they settled. Barnes, an expert on Ngoni sociology, who described them in the period 1821-1898 as 'an armed nation on the march', portrays a typical Ngoni village in the period preceding the European intrusion as 'containing hundreds of huts built round a central cattle byre . . . Clusters [of huts] were grouped into divisions, each usually under the control of a village lieutenant . . . . Several divisions made up a village under a headman or regional governor . . . . New people came into the system in two ways: by birth and by capture. Captives were placed in the system by decree of the Paramount Chief and his regional governors.'[10]

Obviously a young alien among the Ngoni, like Julizya Kaunda, would know the rigours of such a system perhaps more harshly even than a Ngoni boy would, and would often have to think matters out for himself, in the face of taunts. Most Ngoni villages were large and Elangeni, with its royal associations, was one of the notably concentrated communities, with upwards of a thousand houses as well as large cattle herds.[11] Julizya was six years old when, though murderous raids on the Tonga were still going on, Mwambera in 1884 agreed to admit Christian agents from Bandawe on the lakeshore. This was the place to which the Livingstonia Mission from Scotland had moved in 1881 from Cape Maclear. Robert Laws, the leader of the Livingstonia team, had sent an appeal, soon after starting work on the lakeshore, to Dr. James Stewart, founder Principal of Lovedale, for a team of African evangelists from South Africa to assist in the effort to gain admission to Ngoniland. The outstanding member of the group of volunteers was William Koyi, and it was directly as a result of his courage and determination that Mwambera agreed to the opening of a few schools and then to the establishment of a mission settlement at Njuyu in the heart of his kingdom. It was in consequence of the evangelistic outreach of Njuyu that young Julizya Kaunda was received into church membership and received the name David.

The rooting of the church in Ngoniland merits special study in the field of Christian sociology. The initial bitter resistance was superseded by a strong response to the gospel, which was to produce outstanding leaders and a unique treasury of indigenous praise. Thus David Julizya Kaunda's experience as a young Christian was within an exceptionally fresh and vibrant church whose hymns combine a great sense of glory with a highly perceptive understanding of the stresses and struggles of man's life. In this connection, Tonga commentators have drawn attention to the fact that four outstanding church leaders of Tonga origin grew up in Ngoniland and went to serve in widely-separated places. They were Jonathan Chirwa, who in 1902 wrote a hymn, '*Ine umoyo wane ndi Yesu*'-'For me, Christ is my life', which is sung throughout and beyond Central Africa; Hezekiah Tweya, also a hymn-writer; Andrew Mkochi; and David Kaunda, who was to go farthest afield.[12]

There is strong reason to assume a direct relationship between these men and William Koyi, who at the time of his death, aged forty, in 1886, had earned the name Mtusane, 'the bridge-builder, the go-between', by virtue of his work in bringing peace between the Ngoni and their neighbours. Biographers must often be tempted to force connections between events and people to add colour to the life-story of their subject. However, when we are recalling the formative events and forces that built up the experience and character of Kenneth Kaunda's father, and when it is noted how closely Elangeni lay to Njuyu, it is not at all fanciful to presume that, even as an eight-year-old, Julizya had seen Koyi and felt the influence of his personality. As Koyi moved around Mwambera's land it was common for over 1,500 people to gather to listen to him, and many children would be sure to be in those crowds. By any standard, Koyi was a man whose personal courage confirmed his teaching. This is borne out by the recorded testimony of missionaries who worked with him. Moreover in the first encounters with agents of colonialism, Koyi had not only acted as an interpreter but had sharply rebuked the insults delivered by some of them to the Ngoni 'Prime Minister and his councillors' and their 'filthy and degrading language'. Even after his death, there is no doubt about the fundamental effect upon bright boys of Julizya's generation which was exerted by the whole movement of social and cultural upheaval, of which Koyi had been a pioneer.[13]

The memories of the old people in Malawi who recall the young

David Kaunda cannot now fill in many details of his early years at Elangeni, but they confirm that he moved from elementary school in the village to Ekwendeni Mission for Standards II and III. Ekwendeni had been established as a mission centre in 1889. From there, David went for his upper primary schooling and for the 'normal course' in teacher training to the Overtoun Institution on the high plateau of Khondowe in the country of the Phoka people. Most of the students of the Institution had to live in dormitories, and all members of the community were required to share in the manual labour needed to carry through the ambitious building programme. One of the oldest residents of the Khondowe Plateau, Mgonera Mkandawire, father of the present Principal, vividly remembers the start of building operations in which he took part and recalls young Julizya as a student of serious disposition, strong in body, very courteous and given to stammer slightly when annoyed. Similarly the widow of the late Revd. Peter Z. Thole, another of the hymn-composers, recalls David in the years before he went to the Institution as a very upright young man, '*munyamata wa kunyoroka nkanira*'. Hanock Ngoma, a classmate, now living near Chinteche on the lakeshore road from Bandawe to Nkhata Bay, has recalled how David found his studies hard, and this memory is confirmed by a minute of the Mission Council of 1913 which recorded a decision that David Kaunda who had twice unsuccessfully submitted a thesis be asked to do one 'in the vernacular' and if successful be given back-pay. In addition to confirming the young man's scholastic difficulties, this minute shows that Overtoun Institution expected its former students to go on studying while in the field and that Kaunda, though engaged in the tough work of pioneering far from home, was still required to keep up with the Institution's programme of assignments.[14]

While young David was growing up in Mwambera's kingdom, his future wife, Helen NyamuNyirenda, born around 1885, was also in Ngoniland, at Chisanya village near Ekwendeni. Her father, Mugagana Nyirenda, was a Phoka from the mountains westwards of Khondowe. NyaNkonjera, her mother, was from the Henga valley between Khondowe and Ekwendeni, but the couple had somehow come to make their home among the Ngoni. In 1893, however, they moved north to Karonga in Kyungu's kingdom of Ungonde (Konde), sending their daughter thence to Overtoun

Institution in 1900. The girl was known to friends by the name
Tukaya. At Overtoun, she became one of the first tiny band of
female students. Her brother, Robert Gwebe Nyirenda, who died
late in 1967, was to become a prominent personality in the Karonga
District whose outspoken views on matters of public concern bore
fruit in his grandson's bitter opposition to the Central African
Federation, as a result of which he was held in detention during
the Nyasaland Emergency of 1959.[15]

In the first years of the century, it was decided by the Livingstonia
Mission that a reconnaisance party should be sent westwards
across the Luangwa River to Lubemba, the country of the Bemba
tribe. A station of the Livingstonia Mission had been established in
January 1895, midway between the northern tip of Lake Malawi
and the southern tip of Lake Tanganyika, at a place called Mwenzo
just a few miles from the present Zambia-Tanzania border at
Tunduma. In June of that year the Livingstonia Mission Council
approved the plan of the Revd. Alexander Dewar to move south
from this new station in Mwanga country to 'seek an opening among
the Awemba'. Now, in 1904, the student team reached as far west
as the Chambeshi, some thirty miles from Chinsali, and after a few
weeks in Bembaland began trekking eastwards again back to
Khondowe. In a written report, one of the team, who might well
have been David Kaunda, wrote thus: 'In the months of August,
September and October, the Livingstonia Church sent away some
men to the Bemba land to teach and to preach the good words of
Jesus-Christ our Lord. The Bemba are very ready to receive Christ
as their King. I witness this because I was one of them who went
there. I and Samson were teaching and preaching in Chibeza village:
the chief of the Biza people and many people came around our
preaching of Jesus crucified. They were also happy to hear that
God loves them as well as ourselves.' But it was not possible to
overcome the opposition of the Edinburgh Committee, despite
the fact that Dewar's successor, James Chisholm, was very aware
of 'an open door' in the area of Chief Mubanga, and it was not until
June 1906 that Laws, in a letter to Edinburgh, made his first mention
of Chinsali as the next place to be opened after Chitambo.[16] The
beginning of evangelistic and educational work among the Bemba
of Nkula in late 1904 or early 1905 was thus 'unofficial'. David
Kaunda was one of the Overtoun team who explored Chief Nkula's

eastern region of the Bemba kingdom. When the team returned to Khondowe, he went with them but, though there appear to be no written records of discussions concerning his future work, it is known that he soon returned to Chinsali in response to the urgent invitation of Chief Nkula. The Kaunda family recall that his imagination had been fired by the prospect of opening new work in Bembaland and so, hastening his inter-tribal marriage to the young Helen NyamuNyirenda, he went west again across the Luangwa. Kenneth himself has said that, on receiving the Chief's call, transmitted through 'Bobo' Young to Dr. Laws, his father was at first reluctant but soon realised that he must go.[17] A memorial stone, set in the wall of the church building at Lubwa, states simply: 'Kaunda brought the Gospel, 1905.'

In the Chinsali District to this day it is David Kaunda who is remembered as the missionary pioneer of the area, yet there is no reference to him in the writings of the Livingstonia missionaries and their biographers. Robert Laws himself in his *Reminiscences* wrote thus: 'South of Tanganyika are the Bemba tribe, a fierce, turbulent, fighting race, meting out cruel punishment such as destroying eyes and cutting off noses, lips and ears. I saw one woman with thumbnails allowed to grow particularly long, her appointed task being to gouge out the eyes of condemned criminals. The Revd. Mr. McMinn at Lubwa began work among these people . . .' In his chapter on 'Other Stations' under the heading 'Lubwa-Chinsali', Laws recalled that 'after a season of spiritual revival, the people were roused to think of the needs of their fellow-countrymen who had not received the Gospel.' 'This led to simultaneous expeditions from our Mission stations for the purpose of evangelisation. The missionaries from Livingstonia struck westwards till they came to the Chambezi River . . . and some of our native teachers remained for a time in the country to the south [of Mwenzo], returning a number of weeks later to the Institution . . . This eventually led to the opening of a station at Lubwa . . . Mr. McMinn was appointed.'[18] Laws was in very many ways a far-sighted strategist, yet these passages indicate that, in keeping with the thinking of many in the missionary enterprise of the time, he was not aware that what David Kaunda was doing during the eight years between his arrival in Chinsali and the appointment of McMinn as Missionary-in-Charge was courageous work of great

significance, fully worthy to be listed among the pioneering undertakings of the church in Central Africa.

The journey of Kaunda and his young wife, across the River
Luangwa and into Nkula's country, at the Chief's invitation,
armed only with their Bible and their youthful hope, appears
the more romantic when we recall the comment of other visitors
to Bembaland at that period. James Henderson, who was to direct
the Overtoun reconnaisance team, had paid a visit to Mwenzo in
1896 and wrote thus to his fiancée: 'The Awemba ([*sic*]—Bemba)
are to the uplands what the Angoni were to Nyasaland only perhaps
more so. They are a great tribe occupying a vast extent of country
and held under most despotic rule. ... About two days' march
from Fife lives Cheitmkuru ([*sic*] Chitimukulu) the head Chief
of the northern section of the tribe and a veritable master of cruelty.
I should not like to say how many people we saw up there who had
been maimed by him. I spoke to one man whose ears and nose had
been cut off and his eyes put out by this cruel brute . . . . Up to last
year he avoid conflict with the whites but then . . . on Mlozi's
instigation, he changed his tactics. Mlozi's scheme seems to have
been to make an alliance with the Awemba and the Angoni to sweep
the white man out of the land . . . . The Awemba occupy a position
not at all unlike that of the Mahdi's people in the Sudan.'[19]

On his first visit to Chief Nkula's area, David Kaunda stayed
at a village called Fonkofonko on the river Lubu, about eight miles
from Chinsali and from the Chief's *umusumba* or capital. When he
returned from Khondowe with his young wife, they went to live
at Chinsali, where he was on terms of mutual respect with the
British South Africa Company Commissioner Robert Young,
nicknamed 'Bobo'. Young built a school and a teacher's house
there. While still holding the rank of Assistant Collector of the
Company, Young had been sent by Charles McKinnon, Collector
at Ikawa, to open an outpost as near as possible to Chief Chiwale.
A site was found at Mirongo on the Lualizi and Young took up
residence there in 1897. Despite grave threats of extermination by
the Bemba whose villages were as near as eighteen miles, Mirongo
survived. On 16 August 1904, however, Young opened a new post
at Chinsali, not long before the Kaundas arrived. Except for two
periods of extended furlough in 1907 and 1911, 'Bobo' was at
Chinsali until his retirement in 1916.[20]

Chinsali was the Kaunda's home until the arrival of McMinn in 1913, when they moved to Nkula and spent two years there. Their first child, Katie, was born in 1907 and their son Robert in 1912. During those first eight years, Kaunda earned two striking names among the local people, Chendaluta,—'the tireless traveller', and Nkandabantu,—'he who disciplines the people'. But his integrity impressed itself strongly on those who came under his influence; and one former pupil wrote, 'I liked his soft, strong voice.' He became a champion of the local community both when relations were bad with the local British South Africa Commissioner at Chinsali, during Young's furlough, and when there was famine in the area.

In Bembaland, as in Malawi, Kaunda is still remembered as a patient and compassionate man, given only now and then to exhibitions of anger. Old friends of his at Lubwa, like Eneah Mumba and Tom Isabi, still remember with laughter a sharp clash between Kaunda and one of the men who was in charge of the Boma when Young was overseas. The Commissioner took exception to the practice of beating a drum at Chinsali on Sunday mornings to call people to prayer. Probably his wife objected to being awakened early. He therefore called Kaunda and ordered him to stop the drum-beating. Kaunda refused. This was the established call to prayer and it would continue. In fury, the Commissioner decided to punish Kaunda severely and bring him into public contempt. A carpenter was told to make a set of harsh wooden stocks and the evangelist was placed in them outside the Boma. Quietly Kaunda took his 'punishment', his only request being for his Bible. As the day wore on, an endless line of people stopped to greet their teacher, bringing him food and chatting with him. At last the Commissioner had to admit defeat. It was not Kaunda who had become a laughing stock. 'Bobo' Young would not have made this mistake, for he knew how highly the people regarded the Kaundas. When famine struck, there was no better and more reliable centre for the distribution of emergency food supplies than their house.[21]

Initially Nkula's people must have regarded the Kaundas as 'foreigners'. Moreover, Kaunda was a subject of the Ngoni and the Ngoni-Bemba wars had been bitter and lingered vividly in local memory, even though, when they ended, a 'joking relationship' began to develop between the two peoples. However, David

Kaunda's plan of campaign in the Chinsali District was based on
initial thorough touring of the area, carried out fearlessly, and the
careful selection of men to attend intensive courses in literacy,
scripture reading and arithmetic, after which they were sent out to
conduct 'schools' in the villages for limited periods, returning for
further instruction from Kaunda himself. In his report for 1907,
he wrote of the rapid expansion of Chinsali. 'Many are coming
searching school. They do not wish me to go away but to make
Chinsali as my home. They are very much willing to hear the
words of God preached among them. Many are crossing the
Chambesi River in search of school.'[22] The band of student-
teachers grew and the level of their education rose, until a number
of them began to establish permanent centres of education and
evangelism throughout the district. Included among the early
team of teachers were Daniel Besa, father-in-law of Simon
Kapwepwe, and Robert Sokoni, whose son John Malama Sokoni
was from the start one of President Kaunda's companions and
confidantes.

The evangelist's pioneering task in the chiefdom of Nkula was
not an easy one. Simon Kapwepwe, whose father was a 'Boma
Messenger' at Isoka, records that the Chinsali District was initially
'colonised' by soldiers of the Bemba chief, Mwamba, in the early
wave of expansionist adventures eastwards of the river Chambeshi,
probably in the latter part of the eighteenth century. For this task
he selected warriors from Mupika, Mpolokoso, Makasa, Luwingu,
Kankomba and Kasama, and this army became known as *'umulilo
ushibwelela numa'*—'the fire that does not retreat'. The eastern
reaches of the Chinsali District were then called 'Ichinga', the
fortification against Bamuchime, the Bemba name for the Ngoni.
As the years passed, there were thus found in Chinsali men who had
seen battle with Mpezeni's Ngoni. To their sons the arrival of
David Kaunda in their district, unarmed and accompanied only by
his girl-bride, coming dauntlessly to make his home among them,
symbolised the bravery of the Ngoni. Yet, understandably there
were some who, after some years, saw Kaunda as a rival to the
power and influence of their chief, and they whispered to Nkula:
'Kaunda wants to take over your kingdom.' At first the Chief
believed them, and Kaunda came to hear of this suspicion. In
anger he called his band of young teachers and said, 'Let's go to

Mwenzo and shut the school.' His older son recalls how Helen said: 'No, let the Chief's people first come and beat and injure the teachers and tear their clothes, so that Chisholm [at Mwenzo] can be sure of this opposition. Don't just go.' Kaunda heeded her and next day beat the drum as usual to call the pupils to school. This so impressed the Chief that he sent his hunter to kill a fine buck and gave the meat to the Kaundas as a sign of trust and respect. Thus Kaunda resumed his work of tireless travelling through the vast district where, for fear of wild animals and enemies, the people were still living in stockaded villages. When they asked him how he could move without fear, he would point up and say, '*Ni Lesa.*'— 'It is because of God.'[23]

In the young church which David Kaunda founded there was, however, also a certain amount of jealousy towards this powerful foreigner. 'He works just for money,' some of them murmured and this ill-feeling probably delayed McMinn's plan to send Kaunda to Khondowe to finish his theological training. Like all the first teachers appointed by missions, Kaunda was paid in money in the midst of a community in which money was new. According to the first statistical returns of the Livingstonia Mission for Lubwa-Chinsali, presented in 1913 just after Robert McMinn had been stationed there, David Kaunda was then earning fifteen pounds per year. The returns list a total of forty-five centres of evangelism and education, including schools strategically sited at the head-quarters of the Bemba Chief Nkula and the neighbouring Biza Chief, Chibesakunda, whose chiefdom lies to the south-east of Lubwa. These schools had a total of 2,517 pupils, of whom 996 were girls, and were served by around 100 village teachers. The roll of communicant church members stood at 286.[24] This, in a district of around 15,000 square miles, was no mean achievement after eight years and compares interestingly with Dr. Chisholm's statistical returns for the Mwenzo district, dated 8 March, 1904. The first eight years of work there had resulted in the establishment of 32 schools, with a total of over 1,000 pupils, taught by 59 teachers and monitors. In Chinsali, McMinn found Kaunda's system of school fees which cost a pupil one penny per month. Families of pupils were responsible for feeding the teachers and monitors.

Much of the trekking on foot was through tsetse fly belts and lion-infested country, yet in eight years Kaunda managed to establish

schools as far to the south-east as Lundu and Chibale, in the scorch-
ing Luangwa valley, as well as westwards to the banks of the river
Chambeshi and at Shimwalule in the north, the village that stands
by the sacred grove in which the Paramount Chiefs of the Bemba
are buried. Schools had been planted not only in the Bemba areas
but also at the courts of the Biza Sub-Chiefs, Chibesakunda,
Mwenge and Kabanda. Nineteen-thirteen was the centenary of
David Livingstone's birth and it is noteworthy that it was an
increase of missionary offerings in Scotland for the occasion that
made possible the posting of a Scots missionary to Lubwa.[25]

'Bobo' Young, as we have seen, is still remembered as a relatively
good man, but the presence of British administrators in the country
inevitably provoked thoughtful men to critical comment, as it was
all too common for some of those officials to treat the local people
with brutality. Thus it was that, on the occasion of the annual
refresher courses for teachers and evangelists held at Mwenzo and
attended by the staff of both the Mwenzo and Lubwa districts,
there were regular discussions in the evenings about the problems
that arose from British rule. Donald Siwale recalls how a group of
senior teachers, including David Kaunda, Peter Sinkala, Hezekiah
Kawosa and himself, came to the conclusion that something must
be done to give expression to the opinions of the people about
matters of government. They had been particularly incensed at
the reference by a European to Headman Kasichila of Mwenzo,
priest of the grave of the WinaMwanga legendary hero-chief
Musyani, as 'that boy'. At one stage they discussed the matter with
Dr. James Chisholm of Mwenzo who warned, perhaps half-seriously,
that any organised action on their part could bring British guns,
and that they were 'seeking trouble for themselves by entering into
politics'. Richard Hall in his *Zambia* records that Siwale wrote to
Levi Mumba, an Ngoni living at Ekwendeni and an old fellow-
student at Overtoun Institution, for advice about the best way in
which to organise a body similar to the North Nyasa Native Association. There were very close contacts at that time between Mwenzo
and the Livingstonia and Karonga fields of the Scots mission,
where 'native associations' had been formed at Chinteche, Karonga
and Mzimba in 1912. The Mwenzo Welfare Association thus took
birth and, though its formal constitution is dated 1923, which
was the year in which its Secretary sent a copy of its rules to the

Secretary of Native Affairs in Livingstone, Donald Siwale's testimony indicates that it was in fact in being before the First World War. It seems highly likely to have been formed before the arrival of Robert McMinn effected savings on the mission budget by convening the Chinsali District teachers' refresher courses at Lubwa, instead of Mwenzo. Nineteen-twelve is thus a more probable date for the formal establishment of the Association, which can be regarded as the first organised body of African political expression in Northern Rhodesia in the context of colonial rule. Siwale recalls David Kaunda's enthusiastic participation in the meetings and activities of the Association and how when Kaunda poured out his troubles to him, they would talk into the night and the Chinsali pioneer would go back home with renewed enthusiasm.[26]

As Hall points out, the purposes of the Mwenzo Welfare Association, as set out in the rules as submitted to the colonial administration, were 'guarded'. 'The members thereof are to be persons of good knowledge and character. It is an open question for educated chiefs and Europeans to attend and join it as full members if they choose to do so. The aim of the Association is neither directly nor indirectly to subvert the authority of the government or of any lawful establishment, nor to induce the community to do so. It is rather one of the helpful means of developing the country in the hands of the two necessary connecting links—the government and the governed. It aims at making the people understand the necessity and value of order and the importance of being law-abiding citizens —also the necessity and value of industrious labour and in short the value of civilisation as against ignorance, laziness, disloyalty and anarchy.' As old students of Overtoun Institution, some of the authors of this declaration may well have been aware of the conviction of Robert Laws that, as he told Sir Alfred Sharpe, the first Governor of Nyasaland in 1907, the people of the country, who at that time were already paying tax to the amount of £31,000 per annum, 'should have some means of expressing an opinion on public matters and legislative changes which concerned themselves'. Moreover, the Presbyterian system of church polity under which Kaunda, Siwale, Sinkala and others were reared, was based on the doctrine of human equality and of conciliar government.[27]

When Robert McMinn was appointed to Lubwa in 1913, David Kaunda became Head Master of the school there. He had written, in 1907, that 'a European missionary should quickly take place at Chinsali', for 'there are many people and many villages—over 100 villages, east, west, south and north, just in deep sleep.' Nevertheless, it must have been a strange experience to have a Missionary-in-Charge taking over the control of the evangelistic and educational work which he had started and built up in the far-flung district. McMinn referred to Kaunda as 'assistant at Lubwa'. However, there was to develop a bond of cooperation between them. The local people tell how, when Kaunda died in 1932, McMinn lay over his dead body, crying sorely. Yet there had clearly been an element of supplanting, albeit unwitting, in McMinn's approach to Kaunda's work. Moreover, McMinn frowned upon social intercourse and, as was the unhappy wont in many mission stations, there were in the church building a group of comfortable pews in the transept reserved for white people only.

It is true that many of the first white people in Central Africa came from lands in which social stratification was accepted by many benevolent people without question and where indeed the gap between rich and poor was often regarded as part of 'God's order'. But it is most important to realise how the manners of foreigners appeared to the local people. Missionary diaries confirm that, whereas there was virtually no social 'coming and going' between white and black people on their stations, any visitor who was white could expect to receive the hospitality of missionary houses. The White Fathers' diaries contain repeated references to their receiving as guests men who, as agents of Rhodes' Company, were in the area to collect taxes, burning the houses of tax defaulters and often removing them for extended periods of forced labour in chain gangs. There can be no doubt that this caused amazement to the local people who at once contrasted this ready association with their oppressors with the words of the Christian gospel. Naturally they would generalise about white people as Europeans have so often generalised about 'natives'. The spectacle, for example, of a white trader known widely for his hard drinking and for his constant abuses of Africans as 'baboons', sitting in the special pews of a church building on a mission station, was naturally a cause of deep offence to the people of the area.[28]

Kenneth Kaunda tells in his *Zambia Shall be Free* how as a little child he felt the influence of his father. The following passages endorse the reputation of the pioneer as expressed in his nickname Nkandabantu: 'He was a strict man, always expecting to be obeyed without question. He ruled his family with a firm hand, but only once did he beat me. Until the day I die I do not think that I shall forget that beating my father gave me. I was sore for days afterwards and he had to treat me with soothing medicines.' Kenneth was only eight when his father died, having been born twenty years after his parents' marriage, in 1924, and to mark the fact, called Buchizya which in the Tumbuka language of his mother's family, means 'surprise' or 'the unexpected one'. It was during Kenneth's early boyhood that his father, who had been a teacher since 1904, took his theological studies at Overtoun from 1927 to 1929, and was ordained, just a few years before his death. Something of the atmosphere of life in Kenneth's early years is best conveyed by quoting him again: 'My father was for many years headmaster of the school but, in later life, he was ordained as a minister of the Church. This responsibility meant that he frequently went off on tours round the villages, visiting his people. My dearest memories of him concern the family how before he departed on these tours he would call my mother and my brother and sisters and we would sing hymns and he would pray with us. How I loved to sing with him. Indeed, my mother has often told me that as a very young child I would stand up on the occasions to imitate him as he beat time to the music. The sweet music of those hymns in the soft language of Bemba, my mother tongue, gave me my first love of singing which has never left me. My father was a fine preacher, though I remember none of his sermons since, as a child, we always came out of the church before the preaching began.'[29]

David Kaunda's death at the age of fifty-four was a sudden blow to his family and to the thousands who had come to know him in his twenty-eight years in the Chinsali District. He had gone, with a band of church elders, to conduct communion services in the Mwalule area, and was on his way back to Lubwa when he suddenly fell ill. A rough stretcher was improvised as he was too ill to walk. As the party passed the Boma at Chinsali, the District Commissioner came out to see what had happened and on hearing that it was Kaunda they were carrying, he sent for the Government stretcher and insisted that it be used to take him home. When the group reached the Kaundas' house they found that young Kenneth was gravely ill, the family fearing that he would die. Mrs. Helen Kaunda recalled vividly that her husband, rallying from his coma and hearing that his child was ill, prayed a short emphatic prayer in four languages, Tonga, Tumbuka, English and Bemba. In it he begged that Kenneth might live and he himself might 'depart in peace'. Then he told his wife to open the food box he had used on his journey to Shimwalule so that his companions might be fed. Having seen to this duty, he prayed for peace in the country and said: 'Father God, let your Kingdom come in this land.' In a short while he was dead. Little Kenneth cried bitterly for days, for, as he writes, 'all my memories of him are sweet ones.'[30]

We have been given some more homely glimpses of Kenneth Kaunda's childhood in the booklet prepared in 1964 by John Sokoni and Merfyn Temple. Here we see a little boy preserving his memory of a visit to his father's birthplace far in the east by modelling the lake steamer in clay. '*Nine Kaunda wa pa nyanja*'—'I am Kaunda of the Lake,' he would say as he pushed his clay model of the Lake Nyasa steamship *Ilala* over the sand by his mother's door. Sokoni and Temple give, in direct speech, a prayer said by the youngest of the Kaunda family at evening prayers, thus:"O God great Spirit, maker of all things and father of us all, bless our family and all the boys and girls in our school and all the visitors who come to this house. Look after us while our father is away. Give us plenty of food to eat and look after the dogs who guard us at night. Care for the chickens and the pigeons in the yard and preserve them from the hawks in the sky. Please take care of our father on his journey. Don't let any lions come on the road. Make him like the Good Samaritan to all sick people. Keep his boots from wearing out on the stones and find some boys to clean them in the evening."[31]

All through Kenneth's childhood and youth, education was the great hunger of his country. It is necessary to appreciate both the scale of the achievement of his father and other teachers in the establishment of a network of village schools throughout the area and, no less, the adversities under which education was started and developed. As late as 1954 the writer can recall glimpsing from his office window at Lubwa a band of youngsters coming on to the mission estate. The average age of the group would be around eleven but the leader might be as much as fifteen years of age. They came to the office and, having knelt in courteous greeting, they handed over a bunch of letters from their Head Master and his colleagues. They had been on the way a full five days and after a short rest, while they collected boxes of chalk, hoe blades, exercise books, slates, pencils, a football, their teachers' salaries and some items like salt, cloth, and paraffin which they purchased for their teachers' personal needs, they would set off for the long trek home. Once back, and while following the prescribed time-table for Standard III or IV or V, they would have to help with brick-making for a classroom block and take turns at work in the school garden. Everything had to be done by local effort and so the Head Master had to seek to enlist the help of headmen and villagers so that the longed-for brick building might at last replace the pole-and-mud structure that had served so long. The Government had given £180 for the building of the two-classroom and office block. 'It's up to the people themselves, if they want education,' was the regular comment. There was no money for more than one teacher's house or for dormitories. Yet thousands of pounds had been voted for a hostel for a relatively small number of white primary pupils in Lusaka.

In this context Kenneth Kaunda's description of his own experiences of education is worth quoting verbatim: 'My father had planned for me the best education possible, which at that time, could only be obtained in South Africa. He planned to send me as soon as I had received my basic education to live with Z. K. Matthews, but of course that was not to be. The method of teaching young children in the nineteen-twenties was to gather them under a tree on which was hung a cloth painted with the letters of the alphabet. I well remember sitting for hours under a shady tree chanting "a-e-i-o-u", then forming the letters with my finger in the sand. We would smooth out a little area near where we were sitting and the teacher would wander round among the children correcting our letters. Each cloth was called *Nsalu* and when we had *Nsalu* one, two and three, we were promoted to the first class when we were allowed to use slates. There was no free universal education at that time and every parent had to find half-a-crown a year. Just before my father died, I had been ill with influenza and so unable to attend the opening of the school. When I did at last present myself at school the teacher asked for my two-and-sixpence, and when I told him that I had no money, he sent me back to my mother to get the half-crown. I ran sobbing to her, but she had no money in the house and she wept with me. Fortunately, a kind neighbour came to our aid and lent us the money which was in due course repaid. For so small a thing in those days could a child for ever forfeit the privilege of his life's education.'

The reader will find more intimate memories of Kenneth's early life in his autobiography from which these words are quoted. It is possible, however, to add further tints to the portrait from the record of his boyhood friends. Robert Makasa, whose elder brother had been one of David Kaunda's helpers, has known Kenneth from early childhood. John Malama Sokoni has been mentioned above as the son of one of David Kaunda's first students and as a lifelong friend of Kenneth. The Sokoni's home was at Kamangu in Chief Chibesakunda's area of the Chinsali District, south of Lubwa, but when Robert Sokoni went to see his teacher, he often took this children with him and little Kenneth Buchizya Mtepa and Malama became playmates while very young.[32]

In their little book, Sokoni and Temple record an incident which evidently imprinted itself on Sokoni's memory. Kenneth was thirteen at the time and he and Sokoni spent a lot of time together. One day, as they sat on a tree trunk near the football field at Lubwa Mission, Kenneth told his friend of a dream he had recently had. "I was in the millet gardens walking alone looking at the trees and watching birds. In the distance I saw a crowd of people. They were men and women, old and young, and when they came up to me they clapped their hands and greeted me. I was frightened and wanted to run away. But I stood there and smiled and then I thanked them and they went away." Young John could offer no clue to the dream but warned his friend that it was dangerous to mention dreams, especially to grown-up people. Kenneth replied that he remembered how his father used to say that he wanted him to grow up to be a minister of the gospel. The little boy had been told of his father's dying prayer and may well have wondered if the dream had to do with his father's hopes for him. However young Kenneth was more than a dreamer, though very shy. Sokoni tells how one day 'a crowd of boys came running down the path.' They had come from nearby Maluba, the village of flowers, to play football against the boys from Galilee, as the school area of the mission station was called. A series of rough games followed as they kicked their skinless tennis ball around the field. The Maluba boys were bigger than the others and took a defeat by one goal badly. The slanging match that followed ended in a challenge to the Galilee group to pick a boy to fight a big fellow from Maluba. Though Kenneth David was one of the youngest of his group, Galilee chose him and a fierce fight began. Kenneth at first was worsted but, as he lay panting, saw his big opponent rushing on him again and kicked out violently. The Maluba champion fell in a heap and Kenneth leapt up and sat on him triumphantly. The shout "We've won! Galilee for ever!" incensed the big boy so badly that he drew a knife and slashed out at Kenneth's head. At the sight of blood, all the other boys fled and the bully took fright and followed them. It was a David and Goliath story that would naturally gain significance as the young Kenneth's gift for leadership came to light later.[33]

The death of Sokoni's father in 1930 resulted in the lessening of contact between the families, and it was not until John Malama went to school at Lubwa in 1940 to do Standard V, that their friendship really blossomed again in the year preceding Kenneth's admission to secondary school in Lusaka. Kenneth, having completed Standard VI though only sixteen, was then doing the second-year course that led to the award of an Elementary Teacher's Certificate. Though the youngest in his year, Kenneth had already participated in a minor local strike by way of what he looks back on as the youthful questioning of authority. In the face of the urgent need for teachers, the mission authorities had decided to allow the group who followed Kaunda to complete their course in one year. In hot protest, the seniors demanded that they should therefore be regarded as having completed their course. Thus in late 1939, in the company of Phiri N. Kapika, who was to be another close political associate, Kaunda went on strike. 'In fear of family displeasure,' he has recalled, 'I did not know what to do then and where to go.' Despite a fair share of the troubles and crises of childhood and youth, however, Kenneth has recorded that 'Lubwa, set among the lovely hills of Chinsali . . . was a good place to live. Old Mr. McMinn . . . my own father and the other missionaries had created out of nothing a busy community of order and peace, which I look back upon with a deep thankfulness, realizing how much I owe to my early training in that place.' And he has added

that 'there were always numerous guests and visitors in our home.'
'During the term time there were always boys with us, some of my
father's friends who could not find school fees and whom my
parents out of kindness had taken in.'[34]

As he passed from young childhood into boyhood, stronger
friendships naturally formed and the close friendship between
Simon Kapwepwe and Kenneth began in 1934 when Kapwepwe
was twelve years old. Very soon, as he recalls 'they were calling us
twins and the two families were thus brought into close association.'
'We had grown up together,' Kapwepwe has recorded, 'from two
complementary backgrounds. Kenneth was brought up with a
missionary background: I was brought up with a Government
station background. He is thus sometimes very patient and what
I consider to be too slow. I sometimes go too fast. The balance
has been very good. It has not only been in politics but even in the
things we were trying to plan as boys.' In spite of this quality,
Kenneth as a boy was, according to his friends, sometimes very
short-tempered and Kapwepwe attributed this to the stammer
that he inherited from his father. 'As you know, when someone
annoys you, you talk very fast, but with a stammering person it
chokes him up and he expresses himself only with his fists—or by
walking away.' This, he recalls, troubled Kenneth quite a lot as a
young teacher. If a boy in his class gave him trouble he sometimes
had to stop teaching and leave the class until he had regained
mastery of himself. 'I was very shy in my early days and Kenneth
was very shy,' he adds, 'and this attached us together.' It is interesting to note that Kapwepwe's aunt, Ba Nandalama, loved to recall
Kenneth's father as not only a 'tireless traveller' but as a 'political
leader', because of his effective action on many occasions as a
representative of the people to the Government officers at Chinsali.
For instance, one year at harvest time in April or May, there was
drumming and dancing going on at Masandiko's village, about a
mile from Chinsali, and the Commissioner ordered a messenger to
remove the drums and stop the noise. The evangelist, however,
went to him and pointed out that the people were enjoying innocent
pleasure. He argued his case so effectively that the drums were
sent back and the dancing resumed. 'In those days for a Commissioner to listen to a black man was something the people could not
believe.' But Ba Nandalama and the senior Kapwepwe spoke

often also of David Kaunda's patience. 'Even if you were talking rubbish, he would not tell you to go away,' and this quality was yet another that his young son was to inherit.[35]

Thus the boy who was in 1941 picked from among his peers to go to secondary school was a shy, sensitive lad, bothered by a stammer, who had outstripped many of his age-group in his studies and so had had to face the task of teaching boys older than himself. As the son of their revered teacher, his growth had been watched by many people, and the staff of Lubwa Mission in particular hoped for great things from him when he would be ready to return from the south. At the small farm at Shambalakale where his mother had gone to live after her husband's death, there was a sad parting as Kenneth set off. There had developed a special attachment between mother and son which had perhaps been strengthened by various incidents involving roughness on the part of the older son, Robert, to his little brother. There were twelve years between the boys, and so Kenneth would tend to be specially sensitive to Robert's harsh words and actions. His intense shyness was in conflict with his desire to imitate his heroes, and it is recalled how, in an effort to fulfil the plea of the Revd. David Maxwell-Robertson for kindness to suffering people, Kenneth used to carry old women's loads and help his mother with the collecting of firewood and with drawing water from the nearby stream. He was finding delight in guitar music and his instrument was slung over his shoulder as he set off for Lusaka in August 1941.[36]

---

[1]See B. Fagan, (ed.) *A Short History of Zambia* (O.U.P., 1972). esp., Chap. VII, by A. Roberts, 'Migrations from the Congo', pp. 101-120; Hall, *op. cit.*, pp. 1-34; and for a notable historical reconstruction from oral records, J. Vansina, *Kingdoms of the Savanna* (Wisconsin, 1966), esp. Chaps III and VI.
[2]B. Fagan, *Southern Africa* (Thames and Hudson, 1965) 32 and 143-152.
[3]See useful maps in Roberts (in Fagan, *A Short History*) p. 102, and Hall, *op. cit.*, p. 13; and note testimony of some senior Malawi Tonga on their common origin with the Zambian Tonga given to the writer at Chinteche, Malawi, in September 1968. See also R. G. Wills, *The Fipa and Related Peoples* (International African Institute, 1966), Part XV of the Institute's *Ethnographic Survey of Africa*.
[4]For valuable material on the traditional African way of life, see J. Mbiti, *African Religion and Philosophy* (Heinemann, 1969) esp. p. 110; P. Tempels *Bantu Philosophy* (Presence Africaine, 1952); and E. W. Smith, *The Secret of the African* (U.S.C.L., 1938).
[5]See T. C. Young, *Customs and Folklore of the Tumbuka-Kamanga Peoples* (Livingstonia, 1931), 12 ff.
[6]Kaunda, *op. cit.*, 110-111.

[7]See J. Omer-Cooper, *The Zulu Aftermath* (Longmans, 1966), esp. p. 68; J. K. Rennie, 'The Ngoni and European Intrusion,' *Zambesian Past*, ed. E. Stokes and R. Brown (Manchester, 1966), 302 ff; J. van Velsen, *Politics of Kinship* (Manchester, 1964), 16; and W. P. Livingstone, *Laws of Livingstonia* (Hodder and Stoughton, 1921), 185.

[8]Based on testimony of Herbert Kaunda and others, given to the writer, Sept. 1968

[9]*Ibid.* and testimony of NyaShaba, widow of the late Revd. Peter Z. Thole.

[10]Barnes, p. 7; Omer-Cooper, p. 70; and J. Barnes 'Marriage in a Changing Society' (Rhodes-Livingstone Papers, No. 22, O.U.P. 1951), 1-2.

[11]See Barnes, *Politics*, pp. 102-104.

[12]For the record of the spread of Christianity in northern Malawi, see W. P. Livingstone, *op. cit.* and J.W. Jack, *Daybreak in Livingstonia*, (Oliphant, Anderson and Ferrier, 1901); and note, for examples of indigenous Christian hymns, *Sumu za Ukristu* (Church of Central Africa Presbyterian, Hetherwick Press, 1961) and *Izingoma* (Ngoni Hymns, Livingstonia, 1956).

[13]For reference to Koyi, see W. P. Livingstone, *op. cit.* and Jack, *op. cit.* and Nat. Lib. Scot.: 7876 Elmslie to Edinburgh 20/8/85.

[14]Testimonies of Mgonera Mkandawire, Hanock Ngoma, Wesley Manda and NyaShaba to the writer, Sept. 1968; and Minutes of Livingstonia Mission Council, 1913, by courtesy of the Principal, Overtoun Institution.

[15]Testimonies of NyaShaba (see Footnote 14) and TI-FM/Helen Kaunda and her family, Shambalakale, Chinsali, 2/1/69.

[16]Nat. Lib. Scot.: 7878, Folio 281, Laws to Mission Secretary, Edinburgh, 4/10/1895; 7879, Folio 16, Dewar to Edinburgh, 9/1/1896; Livingstonia Letters 1905, report of Revd. A. G. MacAlpine on Bemba pupils at Bandawe and Livingstonia Mission Council's readiness (Oct. 1904) 'to take the initial steps for opening a European station in the Mirongo district [i.e. Chinsali] probably somewhre on the Luvu [sic]'. (that is, the Lubu River) and see W. V. Stone, 'The Livingstonia Mission and the Bemba,' *The Bulletin of the Society for African Church History*, Vol. II, No. 4 (1968), 311-322.

[17]TI-FM/Helen Kaunda, 2/1/69; and TI-FM/KK, 5/2/69.

[18]*Reminiscences of Livingstonia* (Oliver and Boyd, 1934), 189 and 201.

[19]See M.M.S. Ballantyne and R.H.W. Shepherd (eds.) *Forerunners of Modern Malawi* (Lovedale, 1968), quoting James Henderson's letter to his fiancee, 14/5/1896.

[20]See NAZ: KTQ/1 Chinsali District Notebook Vol. I.

[21]Testimonies of Eneah Mumba, Tom Isabi, Abraham Mwanamwenge, to the writer, 1969; and letter of Revd. Alfred Mvula to Macpherson 25/9/68. The Commissioner who acted during Young's furlough in 1907 was J. C. de Jong.

[22]Stone, *op. cit.*, citing Livingstonia Report, 1907, 55.

[23]TI-FM/S.M. Kapwepwe, 8/11/69 and FM/Helen Kaunda and family, 2/1/69.

[24]Statistical Returns for Lubwa Mission, 1913, seen by writer when working at Lubwa, 1951-54.

[25]NAZ: KTQ 2/1, Chinsali District Notebook Vol. I.

[26]TI-FM/D. Siwale, 1969; and Hall *op. cit.*, p. 113.

[27]Hall, *op. cit.*, pp. 113 and 121; W. P. Livingstone *op. cit.*, p. 328; and see also Shepperson and Price, *op. cit.*, pp. 118-121 for note on early protests against colonial rule.

[28]Stone, *op. cit.*, pp. 313-314, citing *Other Lands* (Church of Scotland Missionary Magazine), July, 1913, article on David Kaunda by McMinn; White Fathers, Rome: e.g. Nyasa Diaries, 1895-1906, II p. 21, (April 1898), 125 (April 1903), 540 (March 1905) and Mambwe, 21/11/1892, Chilubula, 8/12/02, 25/5/03 and Chilubi, 9/5/01.

[29]Pp. 5-7.

[30]TI-FM/Helen Kaunda, 2/1/69; Kaunda, *op. cit.*, p. 5.

[31]*Kaunda of Zambia* (Nelson, 1964), 9.

32*Op. cit.*, pp. 9-10; TI-FM/M. Sokoni, 6/10/69.
33Temple and Sokoni, *op. cit.*, Chap 3.
34TI-FM/KK, 5/2/69; and Kaunda, *op. cit.*, p. 7.
35TI-FM/S. M. Kapwepwe, 8/11/69.
36TI-FM/KK, 5/2/69.

3

Germination of a Vision

The 'bus' in which young Kenneth Kaunda was carried from Chinsali to the line of rail was a rattling old open five-ton lorry. In its front compartment the two seats were reserved for 'Europeans only'. If there were no white travellers, the seats must remain empty. The journey was divided so that the bus would arrive in the evening at places like Mpika, Mkushi and Kapiri Mposhi where there were hotels. But these hotels again were strictly for white travellers, and African travellers had to sleep either beside log fires in the open or, as at Kapiri Mposhi, in a corrugated iron shed with a beaten earth floor, entirely unfurnished. Yet there was a constant stream of travellers from the rural areas of the country towards the railway line. The great invisible realm of the tsetse fly in the Northern Province had denied cattle to the Bemba and some of their neighbours. Unlike the Mambwe and Mwanga further north and the Lozi and Tonga groups in the south, the Bemba were not thus tied to their rural economy since their wealth was not in livestock; though interestingly cattle figured in their language and lore. Not surprisingly, therefore, when the copper mines began calling for labour, and the pressure of taxes was intensified, they were the first to go just as some of them had gone earlier to the mines of Katanga. Thus it happened that their language, ChiBemba, became the *lingua franca* of the Copperbelt. It has travelled with the ceaseless movement of people up and down the country ever since.

The Chinsali District sent a very large number of men to the towns. By 1958, the Northern Province was given as the home area of 29.3 per cent of the total labour force of the Copperbelt, which was 13 per cent more than the next largest source area, the Luapula.[1] 'Buses' were infrequent and often subject to breakdown, sometimes stranded for days on the roadside. Consequently they were full to capacity as they hammered along the corrugated gravel tracks. Many passengers had to stand, their legs jammed among heaps of suitcases, bundles, big tin basins, bicycles, baskets of live hens, sacks of meal or salt and tins of paraffin, with often one or two forty-four gallon drums of petrol as well. A few agile youths would probably manage to perch on the drums. The rest, including women with babies on their backs and sick folk trailing to a distant hospital, might well have to stand all the way. Then, as the lorry squealed to a halt at some roadside store, children from the nearest village, set well back from the road, would run forward with little bowls of groundnuts, roasted or boiled, or bananas or mangoes in season. Big clay pots would appear with water and the driver and his 'lorry-boy' and other men would often slip round the back of the village for a long drink of *bwalwa*, the home-brewed beer of the region. As night fell, the people crowded on the truck would often suffer from the sharp drop in temperature. Once a pile of logs to make fires for night stops had been added to the lorry's load, the songs and laughter of the day would drop to weary whispers.

Kaunda has written of the hazards of that journey in 1941, aggravated by a drunken driver, and has described his particular horror at the night shelters for African travellers, especially at Kapiri Mposhi. The rough shed of corrugated iron stood there on the right side of the road, going south, and not far from the railway station. The hotel for Europeans was further on. In common with others for whom this was their first experience of long-distance travel, young Kenneth was oppressed by the move from home life where no one was a stranger to the rough anonymity of the night stopping places. 'I had been travelling for days with no opportunity to wash properly and I was longing for a bath. ... Now I was shown a communal wash-place which was indescribably filthy. I hung around for hours trying to pluck up courage to go in and hoping against hope that some moment would come when I could have the place to myself. The lavatory was disgusting, I could hardly bring myself to use it .... I still shudder when I think of it.'[2] Had he been 'the right colour', he would have had a bath run in for him, at the hotel across the road, by a shoeless servant in a white tunic with a red fez. Instead he had to face a grim night on a concrete floor, clutching his cash and any other valuables for fear of the silent visitation of *bakabwalala*, pickpockets and thieves, found around such night-sheds at all the main bus stops. The writer, making the same journey six years later, realised how far beyond the Copperbelt the power of inflexible discrimination had penetrated the Protectorate.

From Kapiri, the last one hundred and twenty miles of the journey were made by train, and again the race barrier was undisguised. First- and second-class coaches, furnished in strong washable cushion fabrics, were at the disposal of white travellers, for whom bedding was provided. The train might well be carrying only a handful of them and so the rest of this reserved accommodation moved along unoccupied. There was a restaurant car for white passengers. Third-class compartments were provided with wooden benches. Indians and 'better class' Africans might travel in them. But the vast majority of local travellers had to be squashed into the barely furnished 'native' or fourth-class carriages, known as *dobo-dobo*. Toilet facilities were minimal and the air was soon heavy with the odours of congestion, babies unrefreshed on their mothers' backs and fruit skins rotting on the floor.

There were twenty-nine boys in the class that Kenneth was joining in Lusaka, drawn from many parts of the territory. There was therefore a lot of shy excitement as they became aware of each other on the station when they dropped off the train, clutching their bundles. For all of them, the name Munali was magic. Not more than thirty of the primary schools in the country had reached Standard VI[3] by that time, and of the approximately 450 pupils in them only thirty could find places in Munali. When those few met, they were not, as Form I pupils would be now, just into their teens; they were moving to manhood. Kaunda, for instance, at seventeen, already held an Elementary Teacher's Certificate, yet he was younger than many of the others. They were therefore to tackle their new adventures in education with mature seriousness. They had all, like young Kenneth, made their first letters and figures in the sand in the shade of some great tree that served as classroom. As they had seen so many of their fellow pupils in primary school 'weeded out' by the Standard II and Standard IV examinations, they had dreamed their dreams of unknown experiences ahead. Kaunda had certainly been among the dreamers. At the age of thirteen he had a dream which was perhaps inspired by the Genesis tale of

Jacob's young son, Joseph. In it he saw some of the 'big men' of the district, John Mpuku, Daniel Besa, Abraham Mwanamwenge and old Stefano, coming along the road between the church building and 'old Galilee', the school village at Lubwa, carrying bundles of grass. As he approached, also carrying a small bundle, the *bakalamba* fell down and began clapping their hands. When he told his mother and sisters about it, Kaunda has recalled, 'they were very angry.'[4]

Munali had been founded in 1939 as part of a scheme for 'native training' sponsored by the Governor, Hubert Young, and actively developed by Julian Tyndale-Biscoe, Director of Native Education. There was all along considerable white opposition in the territory to any development of African education and so the Northern Rhodesia Government reacted with timidity. One Unofficial Member of the Legislative Council had denounced the possible emergence of what he called a 'class of Babu natives—all book learning and no desire to work—dissatisfied with their positions and a nuisance to everybody.' This was the settlers' 'unrelenting hostility to the idea that well-educated Africans should replace whites in employment at lower rates of pay'. With his ear to the ground, yet missing the deeper tremors, the Secretary of Native Affairs, Sandford, reiterated as late as 1940 that Government must not assist Africans to enter such trades and professions as were then in European hands 'and must therefore refrain from providing training *en masse* which would inevitably increase competition'. Despite the 'Africanisation' policy that had been urged in the early thirties, notably by the Labour Colonial Secretary, Sidney Webb, Lord Passfield, the Government was definitely applying brakes upon development, and especially in African education.[5] In the mounting controversy between the European 'self-government' group, the B.S.A. Company and Colonial Office, Roy Welensky claimed in the Legislative Council that the territory was far from poor, but that in 1939 while the mines were contributing about £492,000 to the Protectorate exchequer, which was 70 per cent of the total annual revenue, around £500,000 per annum was going to the Chartered Company.[6]

The Governor supported Tyndale-Biscoe's insistent suggestion that the school should be called Munali, which had been one of the names given to David Livingstone, and was translated as 'the leader'. It has been also said to mean 'the red one', presumably in reference to the colour of the explorer's skin, while others regard it as a corruption of the Dutch *mijnheer*. Though it began as a junior secondary school, Munali aimed to provide a sound education that could be developed until its pupils were fit to be presented for the English General Certificate of Education. The school was originally sited on the high ground to the south-east of Lusaka, not far from the Governor's residence. Its first head was Frederick Hodgson, an expert in technical training, none of whose first eleven pupils were over twenty years of age. Hodgson impressed his pupils by his vigour and thoroughness, seemingly embodying the familiar words he often used at morning assembly: 'Lord, make us good, hard-working and kind.'

Kaunda spent only two years at secondary school, but looking back he was to find that ten men who have been Zambian cabinet ministers were Munali 'old boys' of subsequent years. By its very nature, a school like this provided an ideal seed-bed for a conscious movement towards national solidarity. As a boy at Lubwa, Kenneth had thought of himself as a *mwina-Chinsali*—a Chinsali man, but it was at Munali, he has said, 'that Northern Rhodesia began to make sense to me.' As geographical and historical horizons were extended in the classroom, the student who sat with his head slightly tilted, listening intently, was on the way to becoming a citizen of the world. But as the awareness of the extent of man's multifarious life on earth grew, so also did the realisation of the stark fact of 'man's inhumanity to man'.

From his own testimony and that of early associates, Kaunda was very sensitive to injustice even as a small boy. When his brother Robert, twelve years his senior, was blamed by their mother for whacking little Kenneth with a Boy Scout scarf, he retorted: 'He is just too soft, this fellow.' The little boy's reaction was that of hurt at the injustice of so unequal an encounter, rather than that of a young Spartan. Similarly, when, at a time when Mrs. Kaunda was away from home, he was scoffed at as he rode with short legs on his late father's bicycle, what pricked him was that the account of the event was distorted. 'Even the one who taught you to ride was stupid,' his brother had said, and that sounded like a terrible slight on their father. The little boy's sad letter to his mother was dismissed by the older boy as 'lies'. 'Why,' young Kenneth thought, 'should anyone want to say that the true story is false?' At Munali he found it senseless that older boys should mar the newcomers' first weeks at school by so much bullying. This was not his idea of fun, and so he used to shelter the tearful victims beneath his bed at night, especially when he was made a house captain. 'One of these little boys,' Kaunda recalls, 'is now a Permanent Secretary.'[7]

The most profound influence during his Munali days was, however, that of a quiet, gentle, African teacher from South Africa, Daniel Sonquishe. With one or two others, Kenneth began to spend time after school hours in Sonquishe's bachelor house. He then took to doing small chores for his teacher as he had done for the Maxwell-Robertsons at Lubwa. The schoolmaster's way of life deeply impressed him. Out of a monthly salary of around £13 he regularly sent £10 or more to his crippled father in 'the Union', as South Africa was then called. Yet he managed both to live simply and to take care of some of the poorer boys in the school. He had a quiet gaiety and loved music, so that as he discovered this common interest in some of his pupils, they formed a guitar and vocal group called The Evening Birds which was somehow able to find enough money to visit the Copperbelt. In these concerts Kaunda was lead guitarist. He thus had his first glimpse of what has been called 'the crucible' of Central Africa, and of the total social separation of the people in the beautiful, ornamented 'European townships' from dwellers in the uniform rows of little one or two-roomed houses of sundried or burnt brick in the 'native locations' and 'compounds'. The concerts of Sonquishe's group therefore had to be given in the open air, as, apart from a few school classrooms and church buildings, there were no halls in the African areas of the Copperbelt. The audiences were large, however, and included many cheering, clapping children. Organised entertainments were few and The Evening Birds received lusty reactions from their listeners such as greeted the few showings of Western and Charlie Chaplin films in the open air cinemas now being erected in the 'Government locations'. The Copperbelt was obviously a place of excitement and there was much laughter as Sonquishe commented on the panorama of life on the mines.[8]

Sonquishe's pupils knew, however, that their gay, soft-spoken master had a tough core. Often he would go into town for shopping and systematically defy the unpublished law by which 'non-whites'

were forbidden to enter the main doors of shops. Hatches or
pigeon-holes were provided for Africans at the side or back of the
buildings. What surprised him, Sonquishe told his pupils, was that
some shopkeepers would change their manners when they realised
that he was not a 'local boy', and that people from countries like
South Africa and Somalia were better treated than those from
Kenya, Tanganyika, the Congo or Nyasaland. They, like the local
people, were often greeted with angry shouts in Chikabanga and
ordered to '*hamba lapa weendo*'. At the 'window' they could wait
for hours for service, which was often accompanied by more abuse.
Certain white shop assistants took sharp exception to being addressed by African customers in English. Sonquishe did not go to seek
better treatment than his fellow *nie blankes*, to use the shocking
title of non-entity by which South Africa still labels all who are
'not the right colour'. He however firmly rejected the humiliating
practice whereby the majority of the shop's customers were herded
round the back like cattle. 'You boys have still a chance here,'
he told Kaunda and his friends. 'Don't lose it as we have lost it in
South Africa.'[9]

There was laughter in plenty at Munali, but, though Kaunda
broke through his shyness to become a keen sportsman, as he was
also a keen Scout, he came to look back on the Munali years as a
period of vital enlightenment that came to him through Sonquishe
and through the healthy atmosphere of argument and debate.
He recalls how when he was chosen to move a motion that 'rats
are found only in dirty houses,' the debate ended in debacle when
a huge rat shot across the floor of the dining-hall. But despite
peals of jeering laughter, such debates had the effect of sharpening
the pupil's logic and powers of expression. At Munali, moreover,
pupils were required to use only English, thus widening their
vocabularies and perpetuating their common mistakes simultaneously.
English quotations, proverbs and maxims were thus firmly fixed in
their memories, as we shall see from Kenneth's later writings.
As the son of a pioneer of Christian education and evangelism
who had been socially and politically aware, he had been nurtured
in what has been called the Golden Rule: Do to others as you would
have them do to you. In secondary school, the influence of the
Christian understanding of life was felt not merely in the prayers
at morning assembly. The whole enterprise of formal education

in the Protectorate had been begun by Christian agencies and was still to a very large extent managed by them. It is obviously therefore important to look at the missionary impact on the territory as we try to trace the embryonic growth, in Kaunda's mind, of a powerful urge towards a radical creative change in the organic life of Northern Rhodesia.

If we are to attempt to see the situation as it appeared to the local people, the effect of brutal conquest and rapacious exploitation must not be minimised. Yet it is essential to note the influence of other factors which undoubtedly affected the way in which the swift and thorough change was made. High in any list of such factors must be put the positive, ameliorative results of missionary work in the territory as well as the impact of 'the Christian way' on Kaunda personally. Though the names of Rhodes and Livingstone were often to be bracketed together, it is important to remember that Livingstone was far from being an uncritical supporter of colonialism. Despite his firm belief that Christian evangelism and Christian commerce were the key to Africa's future, Livingstone was associated with vocal opposition to the colonists' action in seizing land that provoked the so-called 'Kaffir War' of the eighteen-forties and to their brutal methods of smashing the 'rebellion'. Thus, as one biographer has said, 'he was well known as a champion of native rights and ... as a spreader of disaffection.' Nothing however dimmed his conviction that 'the spirit of missions is the spirit of our Master, the very genius of His religion .... It requires perpetual propagation to attest its genuineness.'[10]

The missionary movement that followed Livingstone's death has been the subject of much praise and some sharp blame. What matters most here, however, is to realise the reactions of the local people and where possible their expressed attitudes to various foreign impacts. In relation to the expansion of Christianity, it is necessary to include the phenomena of independent churches, separatist churches and the 'Ethiopian Movement' in our study of continental African history in this century. Moreover, in any given area, the dispassionate observations of sociologists can help us to see how Christianity, for instance, related to those whom its agents deemed the recipients of their mission. One such commentator has described the Northern Rhodesian situation thus: 'The missionaries' crusade against slavery, their establishment of schools, their medical and welfare work, and the vistas they opened to the elite were all profoundly significant. The Africans accepted many of the secular values of the missionaries, and these provided the base and the shape for a benevolent image with which these Africans could identify. The African's Christianity contrasted sharply to the deeply religious conversions of American negroes in the Deep South . . . In Northern Rhodesia there was no equivalent of these revivals and of the "getting religion" experiences of the American "Bible Belt" . . . The secular work of the missionaries, their devotion to African welfare, their sincere belief in the brotherhood of man, and their promise that those who accepted their training "would enjoy the fruits of civilisation which were displayed in everyday European life", these were the values which sparked the revolutionary changes in Africa . . . The missionaries became the protagonists in the struggle for African rights and were the first representatives of African interests in the Northern Rhodesia legislature.'[11]

If then a balance sheet were to be drawn up of the missionary movement in Zambia including actions in the sum of the whole, with the liabilities listed first, the debit column would include such items as:

aiding the actions of exploiters;

assuming the essential evil of everything African;

seeming to equate Christianity with western civilisation;

assuming the role of masters;

assuming the social behaviour of 'Europeans' without question;

operating social *apartheid;*

leaving a clamant gap between missionary manners and 'the teaching of the King';

not reading the signs of the times.

Because of the first, Coillard among the Lozi and Swann of the London Missionary Society in the north, for example, seemed to be willing parties to the actions which subsequent researches have proved to have been predatory. For, as we have seen, the scramble brought a kind of cold war from Europe into the heart of Africa and the race to plant flags was ruthlessly pursued at the expense of the native peoples, to whom the scramblers appeared as 'brigands; to use the word used by Basil Davidson. Charles Domingo, leader of an independent church drawn from the membership of congregations of the Livingstonia mission, wrote in 1911 that "the three combined bodies, Missionaries, Government and Companies, or gainers of money—do form the same rule to look up the native with mockery eyes."[12] Branding everything African as evil, some missionaries undoubtedly helped to dislocate society and create serious moral vacuums by outlawing various customs which had served to strengthen it. In particular, customs and ceremonies that emphasised the relations of the sexes were often condemned and a 'waste howling wilderness' of moral confusion resulted.

Similarly, by the seeming identification of Christianity with western civilisation, it was all too easy to assume that the way to equality was by the ladder of 'Europeanisation'. 'We will give the African equality,' ran the formula of Welenskyism, 'when he shows himself fit for it.' Moreover, the problem of authority brought innumerable crises as missionaries attempted to grapple with social evils, using the only yardstick they knew, as is especially illustrated in the records of the Paris Evangelical Mission among the Lozi, the London Missionary Society at the southern end of Lake Tanganyika, the White Fathers in Bemba country, and the Scots missionaries in southern Malawi. Historians whose personal inclinations have been to gloss over the element of brutality in the establishment of British 'protection' have been able, with documented evidence, to elaborate upon the blunders of missionaries when faced with crises of 'temporal authority', and to stress the gravity of their errors. Indeed, whether the judge is a modern agnostic, an apologist of exploitation, or one of the exploited peoples of the 'non-white' world, Christians cannot escape the condemnation of words and actions on their part which contradict the gospel.

In Zambia, until recently, it was generally assumed that where a missionary worked, he was in charge. The title 'bwana' which was used for all other white men, with the same connotation as 'baas' in South Africa, was given to missionaries; and this indicated a one-way traffic of at least nominal respect. Undoubtedly, many missionaries were thus denied many needed opportunities of learning from the local people; for no man can fail to be deprived if he is regarded as automatically 'having the last word'. 'Goodness' in the people round about him will inevitably be a synonym for docility, which has a universal genetic relation to sycophancy. Attitudes such as these, so often unconsciously developed, meant that the social behaviour of some missionaries looked little different from that of the administrator, that mission stations demonstrated *apartheid* and that people, who kept quiet lest they be accused of disrespect, noted the gap between 'what the Bible said' and how its messengers behaved. The fact that the tea party after the football match on the mission's field was so often for 'whites only'—be they District Officers, store-keepers, tourists, believers or unbelievers —made many of the local residents of the station wonder what 'the body of Christ' meant and how such behaviour related to 'the building of the Christian community'. For *apartheid* was utterly offensive, however easily it was defended and practised by Europeans. It meant only: 'We will keep you at a distance, down there.' To be posted to a mission station was the last assignment that many an African minister, priest or teacher would want. Relationships were thus often unfruitful, a particularly severe commentary on an enterprise whose Founder had said so unequivocally, 'By their fruits you shall know them.'

The credit side of the balance sheet, however, is impressive and helps to explain why the Christian cause has 'cash in hand', as it were, in the country today. Among these 'assets' should be listed:

the message of universal human brotherhood in God's family;

the challenge of justice and social righteousness;

the establishment of schools upon the premiss of a moral universe;

the expression of compassion through healing;

the strengthening of the nuclear family through Christian marriage.

Though the simultaneous arrival of the evangelist and the alien ruler made it seem to some that the former called people to close their eyes in prayer while the latter grabbed the land, it is clear that the situation would have been far worse if the missionaries had not come. It was not possible for Europeans, in whatever role they came to Africa, to dissociate themselves from the acceleration of technological progress in Europe. They therefore appeared as pace setters, holding the key to power and progress. Because this was so, it was a matter of the greatest importance that formal education should be started by agencies whose fundamental motivating principle was that man was the 'child of God'. The vision of the Hebrew prophet Isaiah of the leopard lying down with the

kid[13] was translated by Scots missionaries and read to the people
of the lakeshore of Malawi where wild animals often brought
terror and death. Undoubtedly to many the notion of concord in the
forests and fields was ludicrous. But after some years, there was an
occasion when, at a celebration of the sacrament of communion,
the minister had a Ngoni church elder on one hand and on the
other a Tonga, one of David Kaunda's people who had been victims
of Ngoni raids. 'Now I have seen it,' someone exclaimed after the
service. 'The leopard has lain down with the kid.' For this was no
sentimental notion, but the imagery of a real experience of the end
of terror.[14]

Moreover the Christian agencies released forces which produced
a creative tension in the minds of African people, which in turn
sharpened their awareness both of injustice from white to black
and of their territorial and consequently continental, oneness.
Jesus Christ, arraigned before Pontius Pilate, had been charged
with 'stirring up the people'. The cry at a meeting in Lusaka of
the Zimbabwe African National Union (ZANU) that 'Jesus
Christ is our leader' can be understood in the light of the impact
for justice and humanity which 'the way of Christ' has had in so
many parts of the world. South Africa has counted many Christians
among the martyrs for humanity. In the ten years of the Central
African Federation, the churches were to make increasingly urgent
pleas for a non-racial society in the face of the reactionary trends
of the Welensky regime; the churches 'in the field' being supported
in many cases by the 'home' churches in Britain and elsewhere.
More significantly the voice of certain churches had been raised
early against the more brutal manifestations of colonial rule;
to wit, the Blantyre missionaries' warning in 1896 that 'few in this
country know the significance [of the Native Question] ... upon
which, as upon a stone of stumbling they will come to grief.'[15]
Indeed, because of the genealogical relationship of Kaunda's
Lubwa to Livingstonia and to Lovedale, it is worth noting the
pronouncements on public issues of the pioneers of the Scots
missions.

The first decades of this century saw a widespread process whereby
villages split up into smaller family settlements, which has remained
the pattern since. Chiefs found increasing difficulty in exercising
authority, and it was to increase the problem of providing schools.

But it happened undoubtedly because the stockades that used to surround villages could now come down. In part, this could be attributed to the 'pax Britannica'. The Roman Empire had affected mobility in its far-flung provinces in the same way. It was also, however, because of the positive declaration of Christian agents that, under God, all men must live like brothers. The dismantling of stockades has often been described by Zambian witnesses as a direct result of the peace-making work of the church. While the Boma still stood for a harsh foreign presence in the land, people were beginning to move from church school to church school. The example of men like David Kaunda, as we have seen, was of great importance in this respect. All manner of old fears thus began to recede. As Choirmaster of the Mufulira congregation of what is now called the United Church of Zambia, Kenneth Kaunda in 1948 taught a song, with African words and tune, which thanked God, the great Rock, for causing people to spread and multiply and for giving Christ as 'the conquerer of all evil things'.[16] Because the Christian message in effect extended horizons and transcended the frontiers of old kingdoms with the proclamation of the 'Kingdom of God' as relevant to all mankind, the schools which the missionaries started premissed their teaching on the doctrine of a moral universe. Their educational philosophy was thus heavily biased in favour of moral values. The founding of hospitals and itinerant medical services was seen by many as evidence of the sincerity of these beliefs, love not just in word but in deed.

Monogamy has been held, by all the missionary churches, to be a requirement for communicant membership. Insistence upon 'one man—one wife' may often have been made without any realisation of the social function of polygamy. It always, however, brought the nuclear family, the spiritual and physical union of man and wife, into new significance. At a time when great numbers of men were moving from the closely interwoven life of rural villages to the welter of the copper mining towns, it undoubtedly was of importance that the pattern of Christian marriage should be available for their use.

Though Lubwa was far from the line of rail, young Kenneth Kaunda had grown up in a situation in which all aspects of the missionary situation mentioned above, were part and parcel of his daily life. His boyhood memories of Lubwa were generally happy, yet there were there a number of factors which mitigated strongly against the planting of a truly responsible and indigenous church, such as the sparse population of the area, the constant drift of young men to the south, over-taxed missionary resources and the lack of foresight in fostering the church's independent growth. He had known of animosity of some local men against 'outsiders', and especially the moves to delay his father's theological training, as we saw above. What had impressed him most, however, was the 'very Christian' comment of old John Mpuku that "it is not always the boy from your own village who kills the lion." As he came back home, he was to look more critically than before on the life of the mission station and to be in turn blamed by some of the missionary staff for being aggressive. Undoubtedly he was displeased at the insistence of the missionaries that he should return, for he had been selected with seven others, towards the end of his year in Form II at Munali, for admission to Form III. He was only nineteen years of age and therefore, by the standards of that time, younger than most of his school-fellows. But Lubwa Mission required him to return because of the acute shortage of teachers for the senior primary classes. Almost immediately he was appointed Boarding-Master and would certainly have among his pupils in the dormitories some young men senior to himself. Though it was disappointing to him to be recalled from Munali, the prospect of new responsibilities was challenging. Both the disappointment and the challenge sharpened his observation of mission life and he found that there was already 'this feeling of unfairness'. He returned in 1943 when the war in Europe was at its height and when the missionary staff was under unavoidable strain. His family had moved some time before to a small farm behind the hill on which Lubwa was built and there was increasing uneasiness in their relations with the mission and with the local church. His brother, Robert, states that he called the farm Shambalakale because 'certain sorrows had started for them long ago.' It seemed to Kenneth that somehow the church was not fair to its senior workers. 'There were very old people who had worked very hard for the church and,' he has said, 'I felt that the principle of looking after these people was not there at all.' 'Some who worked with Father, it was as though they had never existed. This was a very sad thing indeed to me.'[17]

Though he had many friends among the young people of the community at and around Lubwa and was, as he has said in his autobiography, well-liked by his pupils, he was aware of the disfavour not only of some of the missionaries but of certain senior leaders of the local church. It is easy to see how a young man who, as he has written himself, took 'a very great interest in clothes,' would come under adverse comment,[18] especially as his Lubwa pupils began to copy his special styles of tailoring suits and shorts. The analysis of popularity is never easy. In the case of young Kaunda it could well be that his zest, his high standards, his humour, his love of music would be enough to make people like him. One close associate of the period has suggested, romantically, that the tough Bemba people of Chinsali, offspring of the warriors who had won the area for Chitimukulu, responded naturally to a young man of Tonga-Tumbuka stock. 'Once you fail in Tumbuka society you are not accorded any respect,' and likewise among the Bemba 'to be defeated is a shame, they must go forward all the time.' Therefore 'the leadership of Kenneth is not an accident,' just as earlier 'the people of Chinsali got attached to David Kaunda because of his courage.' 'His coming to that land was not something to be taken lightly. So with Kenneth, because he matured quickly to fit into a position where his temperaments were just as good as that of an old man, he was accepted much faster than just a mere brilliant young man ... brilliancy would not have helped him, but ... in this society his mastery of himself has been helpful.' This self-mastery in him may have started early. 'The beating by his father ... gave him a big silencer on his fighting instinct ... He must behave if he was going to be a great man as his father had wished.'[19]

Kenneth had developed considerable facility in playing the guitar while at Munali, and Malama Sokoni has recorded that, as soon as he was home, he began to spend a lot of time with Simon Kapwepwe, Julius Chatepa Mfula and Sokoni, teaching them to play. Kapwepwe had come to know Kaunda well in 1934 and the friendship with Sokoni went back even earlier, as we have seen above. As these friendships revived in 1944, they would spend time, often with others as well, chatting into the night. As Kenneth and his friends talked, Kapwepwe would recall what he had heard from his father who as a B.S.A. Company policeman, had taken part in

numerous 'punitive actions' against villagers. In 1912, the senior
Kapwepwe had been promoted, after four years as bugler, to the
rank of Head Warder, and the District Commissioner had recorded
that he was now the best candidate for the post of Head Messenger.
At that time, there had been an intensive campaign of tax collection,
involving widespread beatings in villages. Then, as arrangements
were being made for the transfer of the territory from Company
rule to Protectorate status, there was another period of harsh
behaviour by administrative officials. The first period may well
have provoked the beginnings of the Mwenzo Welfare Association,
and the second wave of brutality may have led to a revival of the
Association's activities. Indeed Kapwepwe heard from his father
that this whole period 1909 to 1923 was 'very rough'. It is worth
noting that Kapwepwe developed his political consciousness early
and, as he has said, he 'got the rubbing of politics' much more than
his friends, especially from his brother-in-law, Nashon Chiabwe.
This man had been employed for some years in Ndola and Abercorn
by Messrs. Thom and Co., who traded in many parts of the territory.
He was sent to Isoka thereafter and took an interest in Kapwepwe
when he was learning at the local school. 'He started talking about
experiences on the Copperbelt and how Europeans were mistreating
Africans; and how he was trying to refuse to be suppressed.' From
his father, Kapwepwe heard of many occasions on which he had
objected to the orders which, as a Government employee, he had to
carry out. So 'in 1940-41 we started formulating our minds that
something was wrong.'[20]

Kaunda's return and his renewed association with these boyhood
friends did not pass unnoticed. 'Dr. Brown was not happy with
him and wanted him to go and teach at Chibesakunda. The reasons
were not advanced except that Kenneth was very cheeky and would
spoil other teachers ... But Mr. Cato would not accept this.'
Kapwepwe, who qualified as an elementary school teacher in 1945,
was also recommended for a posting well away from Lubwa and
the main road. They therefore began to wonder why they should be
'so much disliked'. 'These people are missionaries,' they murmured.
'What is this, that anyone who is a little bit enlightened must not be
near them?'

George Cato was from South Africa, but the people at Lubwa
saw that his relations with young Kaunda were good. 'If Cato

knew he had no money in his treasury he would say so,' but obviously in a helpful way that enabled his African colleagues to understand the difficulties. However because of the attitudes of some of his missionary colleagues, the older mission employees as well as the lower-trained teachers began to wonder why 'the Kaunda group, the middle group' were viewed with suspicion. Kenneth was courteous in his dealings with these senior people in the community and indeed they generally understood why, for instance, as the most highly educated local teacher, he resisted the proposed posting away from Lubwa. But it was realised that by expressing disappointment and criticism openly he was being regarded as a potential troublemaker. Special note was taken of words that he spoke, with considerable feeling, in the course of preaching at a Wednesday afternoon service, about what he considered the church's failure to care for its old servants.[21]

Meanwhile, almost simultaneously, there were two apparently contradictory developments in the district. The group at Lubwa who resented 'outsiders' had intensified pressure for the removal of the Nyasalander, Kaleya, who was Head Master of the Upper Primary School. The District Commissioner, Reeves, was believed to have advised the missionaries to heed this demand in order to reduce tension. But, in the forward-looking, outgoing Chinsali Welfare Association, thinking was developing along lines that transcended parochialism and the same Commissioner informally remarked to the Association that it was high time that 'native interests' in the territorial Legislature were represented, not by a white man, but by an African. Sir Stewart Gore-Browne of Shiwa Ng'andu visited Chinsali from time to time as M.L.C. for 'native interests' and generally met the Association on such occasions. But there was a growing conviction in favour of what the District Commissioner had put into words, even though for another five years there would be no African member of Leg. Co. Another District Commissioner, Maddocks, who was aware of the stirring among young men in the territory 'reported that he had seen many educated men in other stations but that Kenneth Kaunda was different and must be watched'.[22]

Lubwa was a place of contrasts. Old Mr. McMinn maintained to the end a severe and aloof approach to African people. His local nickname, Ngungu, bespoke his aloofness. But his restless, dynamic and quick-tempered colleague, David Brown, is still remembered as a man of ready and sincere compassion. The sight of handcuffed men being led past the Annandale Hospital by Boma Messengers raised his indignation, and once or twice he demanded that they be unfettered. He was a man of emphatic utterance and action and was a bitter opponent of Roman Catholicism. For years he distributed widely a Bemba translation of a booklet entitled *50 Reasons why I am not a Roman Catholic*. This passionate attitude led the Director of African Education to oppose his nomination as Manager of Schools in the Chinsali District in view of 'his fanatical anti-Catholic disposition and his irresponsibility in opening schools without permission'.[23] But Brown's medical work in the hospital and on extended district tours was marked by this quality of ready compassion. Because Lubwa provided a microcosm of the contradictory postures of Christian missions in Africa, it is necessary to take note of the impact of such experiences on Kaunda and his fellows.

It is thus alarming to realise that, in an apparently small matter affecting the fitting of collars to pupils' school shirts, the fact that Principal Cato showed appreciation of the boys' request, as voiced by Kaunda, caused delight to the African staff. 'It was a small thing,' Kapwepwe said, 'Nevertheless it meant a lot in those days for a European agreeing with your suggestion, and we felt satisfied that we were also considered as human beings.' There was therefore plenty to discuss, especially informally, at meetings of the Chinsali Welfare Association, of which Kaunda became a member soon after his return, and whose Secretary was Samson Mukeya Mununga. Indeed serious consideration was given at one time to the establishment of a Lubwa African Institute, on the model of the Kasama Institute, to provide a forum for free discussion without Government surveillance. The name 'African Institute' connoted to participants an organisation more radical in character than a welfare association. It is interesting to note that though the Kasama Africans' Institute, which, according to the Provincial Commissioner, had 'been long moribund,' was described by its Secretary in his minutes of November 1950 as 'non-political', it however was to devote a full meeting in 1952 to the discussion and rejection of the plan for Federation, as a threat of 'Malanite infiltration' and eventual Amalgamation.[24]

Kaunda was appointed to the upper primary school at Lubwa, as we have seen, in 1943. The Head Master then was Henry Chibuta, who had been seconded by the Government from Munali to the Church of Scotland mission station for a period of two years. This had been arranged because Hubert Siwale, a matriculant and son of Kaunda's father's friend, Donald, had declined appointment to Lubwa. In August 1945, Chibuta left for Kasama and Kenneth became Head Master. He however, continued his various outside activities, including increasingly active membership of the Welfare Association. He was also playing a lot of football, while he kept up his music and was leader of the organisation for younger boys called 'Trekkers'. This was in fact a Wolf Cub pack, the junior section of the Boy Scout movement. The organisations for African boys were not, however, allowed to use the names 'Scouts' and 'Cubs', as these were reserved for Europeans only! They were therefore called 'Pathfinders' and 'Trekkers' respectively. Ironically, the founder of this boys' movement for international brotherhood was Robert Baden-Powell who had gained prominence from his exploits against the Ndebele in the so-called 'Matabele Rebellion' of 1896; and the discriminatory term found to denote African Cubs was derived from the Dutch word that had been used to describe the great northward pilgrimage of the Afrikaaners from Cape Province to the Transvaal in 1836. In the British Protectorate of Northern Rhodesia a boy had to be white to be a Scout or Cub. Despite this, Kaunda and many of his generation were to continue in Scouting and to help to recover the movement's original non-racial character.[25]

The range of Kenneth's extra-curricular activities led to an affectionate relationship between him and his pupils. One of them recorded how at the time of the long holiday at the end of 1945, the rains had been so heavy that the pupils who came from the Church of Scotland's mission at Chasefu, in the Lundazi District of the Eastern Province, could not cross the numerous rivers of the Luangwa Valley. They came to Lubwa because there were no upper primary classes at Chasefu. The group numbered thirty-four, and there was a food shortage in Chinsali District. But Kaunda and his mother looked after them all at Shambalakale for six weeks.[26] However, Kenneth's bachelor life was not to last long.

In 1946, on a journey to Mufulira in the Copperbelt for a

Pathfinder Training Camp, Kenneth was introduced by a cousin at Mpika to Betty, daughter of John and Milika Banda. John Kaweche Banda had met his wife accidentally when carrying bags of flour to Fort Jameson during the First World War. As Milika Sakala had a husband who had become one of the 'lost ones' in Johannesburg, John's marriage with her was by elopement. Seven years later, in 1923, they had their first child, Grace. Betty, the second child, was born on 17 November, 1928, and called Mutinkhe after her paternal grandmother. During her childhood her father was an employee of the African Lakes Corporation, which had been founded in Nyasaland in 1879 by two Scots brothers, one of whom, John Moir, had worn spectacles which were called '*mandala*', in consequence of which the A.L.C.'s chain of shops through Central Africa were known as Mandala Stores. After some years at Serenje, John Banda was transferred to Chinsali, where he became acquainted with David and Helen Kaunda. 'There were no medical facilities at Chinsali,' Betty Kaunda has recalled, 'so whenever I became ill, I was taken to Lubwa mission . . . On these occasions my parents always entrusted me to the care of the Kaunda family at Lubwa.' She was still a small child when her father was transferred to Mpika. She was seventeen when she was introduced to the young man of twenty-two who had been only seven when she had left Chinsali.[27]

Kaunda has written of his engagement and marriage to Betty Banda that as soon as he saw her, he knew his mother had chosen well for him. Betty had returned in May 1946 from the Mbereshi station of the London Missionary Society on the Luapula River in the chiefdom of Kazembe, where she had obtained an Elementary Teacher's Certificate. 'Auntie' Helen Kaunda from Lubwa visited her parents soon after and plans were laid for the betrothal of Kenneth and Betty. Though, according to 'tribal' origin he was Tonga-Tumbuka of Malawi and she was Kunda, the customs of Bembaland were followed as arrangements were swiftly made for their wedding. It was solemnised a few weeks later at Mpika by the Lubwa evangelist, John Mpuku, on 24 August, 1946. The Mpika Head Master in whose school Betty was teaching was highly displeased by the hastiness of the marriage, but to no avail. A second reception was held at Lubwa three days later. Beer was conspicuously absent from the celebrations. The restiveness of which his friends

have spoken did not, however, leave Kenneth as he established his
bride in their home at Lubwa. As he has recorded, he was happily
married but the irksomeness of his mother's 'apronstrings' made
him long to 'break away'. There was no diminution in his zest for
teaching, and Sokoni has recalled how at that time he was trying to
impress upon his pupils the value of self-sacrifice and self-reliance
and the importance of farming.

Kaunda's autobiography does not offer a real clue to the serious
decision to leave home before the birth of their first child. Kapwepwe,
however, has stated that he and Kenneth and John Malama Sokoni
were 'completely fed up' with the strained relations that had developed with 'the mission management'. Obviously the malaise at
Lubwa was serious enough to be noticed by visitors. Gore-Browne
told the Provincial Commissioner that the atmosphere was 'rather
depressing', worsened by the effect of a severe food shortage.
In reply, Howe, the Commissioner, wrote that Lubwa had been
'going downhill rapidly since Maxwell-Robertson left'. He did not,
however, comment on Gore-Browne's observation that 'Northern
Rhodesia politicians would be surprised at the strength of the feeling
expressed [on Amalgamation] in all the rural areas.' The political
disquiet was inevitably a disturbing factor at Lubwa as elsewhere.
Nevertheless Kenneth's own words about Lubwa must be noted:
'I think that I can say in all honesty that the one thing that has
influenced me more than anything else in my first years was the
deep belief of my parents and the fact that I was living on a mission
station in a community based on love, friendship and kindness.'[28]

The writer, who had arrived in the Protectorate in November
1946 to work as a member of the United Missions in the Copperbelt,
was sent to Lubwa in April 1947 for a period of Bemba language
study. He met Kenneth Kaunda there and they had long talks
together. What was so significant to him was that Kaunda was
clearly exceptionally concerned about the future of continental
Africa. During one long chat in the shade of a wild-fig tree at the
mission, Kenneth spoke of racial oppression as a 'great burden of
evil' and said that he believed a way must be found to remove it
without bloodshed. The 'non-violent positive action' of Mahatma
Gandhi, he said, was perhaps the answer, giving as it had done in
India a practical political application to the way of Jesus Christ.
It seemed as though his visible restiveness stemmed as much from

this continental concern as from the local stresses of which he was so keenly conscious. Not long before, a new student had come to Lubwa Training School from Chitambo, the Church of Scotland station two hundred and forty miles south. He had been late for morning worship one Sunday soon after his arrival and had entered the building by the door nearest to the road from the dormitories. At the front of the seats occupied by the missionaries, there was one pew vacant and the student sat there and closed his eyes in a silent prayer as was the habit in Christian congregations. He was tapped sharply on the shoulder by a woman missionary and ordered to 'go to his own place'. As he told his fellow students what had happened, there was a wave of deep resentment. When Kaunda and the writer were talking under the fig tree, he recounted the event with deep feeling, Kapwepwe's telegram five months later found him ready to go, even if he was not then fully conscious of the nexus of pressures that were prompting so serious a move.

Kapwepwe and Sokoni had been investigating the possibility of employment in Tanganyika and had gone north to start work in a high school at Malangali. In Mbeya, the two men, being short of cash, had 'stolen a rest-house'. Hopeful of early appointment, Kapwepwe and Sokoni decided to call Kenneth to join them. Leaving Betty with his sister at Chinsali Boma, he therefore set off in September 1947. With very little money in his pocket, Kenneth went north by bus. The Principal of Malangali had said he was sure his friends would be empoyed, but asked them to wait until he received official authority from the Director of Education in Dar es Salaam. The Director consulted the Director of Education in Northern Rhodesia, and the school Principal had to tell them sadly that they were not to be appointed. Kapwepwe's account of this experience has stressed that they were sure that this rejection was not accidental. There on the mountain at Mbeya they realised something of the magnitude of the obstacles in their way. 'We agreed that we must now fight for independence until we got it. We should not work for Europeans. If we had to, it must be on condition that we earned sufficient for our wives and children and to enable us to go on fighting. We should not accept any permanent or pension-able jobs, and we must try to teach our people very seriously about this.' Kapwepwe formed the opinion that, had their applications to Malangali been accepted, they might have 'fallen politically asleep'.

Life had been pleasant there and they had enjoyed playing and singing with the local people. For him, the realisation they shared on the mountain at Mbeya was the beginning of a clear, political commitment from which there would be no turning back, and which strengthened the bond between them. For Kaunda, the Mbeya experience brought a fresh understanding of the need for intensive agricultural and forestry work in Northern Rhodesia. Because capital was essential for such enterprises, whatever work he would find must enable him to start accumulating money for this purpose. Their pocket money, however, was too little to get them back to Chinsali and so the three stopped at Isoka and stayed with the store-keeper, Nashon Chiabwe. The thirty shillings that Kapwepwe had left with Chiabwe was enough for their fares to Chinsali, where they spent two weeks. There they had to give an evasive answer to the plea of Revd. William Bonomy, a new member of the Lubwa staff, to return to teaching, for they were set on seeking work in Lusaka. On the way south, Kenneth stopped at Mpika to play his guitar for his wife's people at Christmas.[29]

While Sokoni went to Kitwe and found work with the Standard Trading Company, Kaunda joined Kapwepwe in Lusaka and they were signed on as instructors in the army, with the rank of Sergeant. This work, they believed, would give them uniforms and free food and so they would be able to send money home. There was no danger that they would be involved in fighting. However at four o'clock on the same day, the Commanding Officer called them to say that they were not to be employed. Giving them each half-a-crown for a day's work, he asked them not to ask him for a reason for their discharge. Naturally it seemed as though the same confidential files must have been consulted, and this impression was strengthened when Kapwepwe was called for an interview at the office of the Senior Education Officer for the Southern Province. There a junior officer put a number of questions to him about his previous employment and having confirmed that he was Simon Kapwepwe from Lubwa, Chinsali, told him that there was no work for him at present.

Kenneth Kaunda meanwhile had gone south with the idea that he might try to find some temporary work there. He had been accepted for a teaching post under the Salvation Army near Salisbury, but was late and found it filled. However, he was sent to another of the mission's schools at Bindura Mine, eighty-five miles away. 'I had been travelling for five days with never an opportunity to take a bath; I was tired and dirty and in a strange country without friends. All my thoughts were of home and the parable of the Prodigal Son was never far from my mind. . . . I must have presented a strange sight to the eyes of the headmaster of that school when I stood on the doorstep of his house. I had a bulky rucksack on my back, a large box of books, a bundle of blankets on my head and my guitar on my shoulder. My hair was full of dust and my clothes were dirty and crumpled. The first thing I did was to ask where I could wash. I was told that the river was three miles away but there was a place down the road where water could be obtained. I set off and after some time I passed a filthy pond where cattle up to their knees in mud were drinking. I went on, keeping my eyes open for the place where I could wash, feeling more tired, more hungry, more dirty with every step. After what must have been a mile and a half walk, I asked some people passing by where was the place to wash. They directed me back to the cattle pond. . . . When I finally got back to the school, I was given a meal so badly prepared that I could hardly choke it down.'

Kenneth therefore decided that somehow he must go back home. He managed to sell some of his clothes as he had no money for a return fare so soon. Taken aback by the ticket clerk's demand for a 'pass' before he could be allowed to board a train for the north, he fumbled in his pocket and pulled out his church transference certificate from Lubwa. The clerk glanced at it and issued the ticket. 'I had exactly three-and-sixpence left for food,' he has recorded, and so he carefully divided the loaf of brown bread that he bought so that it would serve him for the four days of the journey. In Bulawayo a violent fight between a white man and an African cripple left a sharp impression on his mind as he made the long, sticky journey to Livingstone in a 'native class' railway coach. At the Victoria Falls he found some of his old Lubwa pupils at the railway station and they took him for a bath and a meal before he went north again to the Copperbelt.[30]

In Kitwe Kenneth had a fortunate meeting with John Sokoni, but found him far from cheerful. The Standard Trading Company had just paid him off, after a month's work, with one pound. Kapwepwe meanwhile had found a teaching appointment under

the United Missions in the Copperbelt, at Wusakile, the huge
Compound growing up near Kitwe on the road going south.[31]
Wusakile, like other such housing schemes for African mine
employees, consisted of rows of box-like houses with corrugated
iron roofs. 'When the sun shines on such dwellings,' Kaunda said
in his plea for a 'colour-blind society', 'the hut becomes an oven;
when the rain falls it becomes a well in the middle of a swamp,'
for the tarring of roads was confined to the 'European townships'.
'When it is cold,' Kenneth added, 'the hut is like a refrigerator.'
Lack of ceilings made this exposure worse.[32] The United Missions
was responsible for the administration of all the African schools
in the Copperbelt. The U.M.C.B., as it was generally called, had
been formed in 1936 as a cooperative agency of the London Missionary Society, the Church of Scotland Mission, and the Methodist
Missionary Society, with the Anglican Church's Universities
Mission to Central Africa participating as 'team members' in the
fields of education and welfare. By early 1948, Kaunda, Kapwepwe
and Sokoni were all employed by the U.M.C.B. as teachers. His
own appointment surprised Kapwepwe because Betty Kaunda's
brother, who was employed by the U.M.C.B., had shown him a
confidential file with a comment from Lubwa to the effect that his
politics were 'still in the bad, and could ripen any time.'[33]

Kenneth had previously applied for a post as Organising Secretary
of a new venture initiated by the European Mineworkers' Union's
President, Brian Goodwin, aimed at incorporating African miners
into the Union. He did not know, at the time when his application
failed, that the scheme of incorporation was strongly rejected by
African miners who felt it would leave all power in the Union's
affairs in European hands.[34] Kenneth had therefore to look elsewhere
for work and was appointed at £4 per month, as an Assistant at
the African Welfare Centre run by the Municipality in the Chingola
Location. Welfare work among Africans on the Copperbelt was
meagre and there was considerable antipathy towards it on the
part of influential Europeans. In his job at Nchanga, Kaunda was
'terribly bored'. For a man with experience as a Head Master and
formal education up to Form II, this was a miserable assignment.
His wife, Betty, and Panji, their infant son, had come from Chinsali
to join him now and so he went to visit the School Manager at
Mufulira and was appointed to the Mine School there, under the

headmastership of Patrick Mkandawire. As at Lubwa, he found himself in charge of the school's boarding department. The salaries of teachers were fixed by the African Education Department, the Manager of Schools acting merely as paymaster. Kaunda received £5.13.6 per month as a teacher with the equivalent of the Higher Teacher's Certificate, while Betty's salary was £3.3.6.[34]

In his *Birth of a Dilemma*, Philip Mason wrote in 1958 that Central Africa was 'the meeting place not only of black people and white people but of different ideas as to how they should behave toward each other. It is thus the key to Africa.' The same insight had earlier inspired commentators like Basil Davidson whose book had been quickly banned by the South African government. 'Northern Rhodesia', he said, 'forms a reservoir of cheap migrant labour for mining operations, and this, today as yesterday, is Northern Rhodesia's most important function within the pattern of white supremacy in southern and central Africa.' He went on to show how 'in their attitude to Africans the white settlers cannot be said to differ in any essential way from their fellows in Southern Rhodesia or South Africa.'[35] Kaunda and his friends were now seeing at close quarters how true it was that the British Protectorate was allowing the development of a replica of the worst of South African *herrenvolkism*, in terms of the daily experiences in the towns of the voteless masses of African people. Twelve years later, Kaunda was to declare: 'I am a "nationalist" living in a society that you white men call multi-racial but it rejects me and my claims. I am regarded in my own country as a second-class citizen. I ask you to look at this society and I ask all Europeans to look at it for once through the eyes of an African.'[36]

It was this situation that he was observing closely in Mufulira. His autobiography speaks of what he learned as he found himself 'suffering the indignities of the colour bar'. Yet, though he worked for only one year in Mufulira, his reaction was far from negative. He was Conductor of the choir of the huge congregation of the Church of Central Africa in Rhodesia and among the items which he taught the choir was the song referred to above, in praise of God the Great Rock, and the spiritual 'Yonder come the children—Lord, I lay down my life.' He also joined the local Pathfinder Scout troop as a leader. Moreover since the combined earnings of Betty and himself were so small that they could not hope to find capital

for the farming enterprise of which he still dreamed, they began
the 'Mokambo' project, whereby from the Zaïre border post of
that name they bought second-hand clothing which could be sold
at a small profit in Mufulira. On the first Saturday after he received
his salary, he would gather a goup of pupils and they would stride
along the thirteen miles to the border and 'come back wearing the
strangest assortment of clothes.' In addition the plight of some of
the pupils worried him. They had great difficulty in finding their
boarding fees and so, with the Head Master's approval, he started
what would now be called a 'young farmers' club'. By buying seeds
instead of vegetables from the Government boarding grant, the
boarders were able to open up an extensive vegetable garden and
considerably augment their diet.[37]

Kaunda had not, however, forgotten active politics. As Vice-
Secretary of the local branch of the Northern Rhodesia African
Congress, he took part in recruiting new members and, as he has
recorded, helped some of his pupils to save their pennies until
they had found enough for subscriptions to it. He also attended a
meeting of an informal body called the 'Afro-European Friendship
Group', which met in the house of the missionary Manager of
Schools and was denounced by certain sections of the European
community. It was a time when, though virtually unheeded in the
local press, the Congress, which had been formally established in
September 1948, was formulating a radical opposition to the
situation in the Territory. In a confidential report on a Congress
Committee meeting called to deliberate the issue of Federation,
the Secretary, Nabulyato, wrote thus: 'NR ... is ruled on the basis
of trusteeship, i.e. until the wards of Trusteeship are matured to
rule themselves. ... Mr. Welensky says (African Weekly, 3/11/48)
that "like Sir Godfrey Huggins, I also believe in amalgamation
but ... straight amalgamation would meet with considerable
opposition from the African people". So we see Federation is
the same as amalgamation. Mr. Welensky is likely to bring the
miseries of civil war to NR. All Africans must be cool and non-
violent else we lose our land. ... Sir Stewart advises us to demand
a sort of Treaty ... but as most Treaties have proved to be "scraps
of paper", ... we are not prepared to do so.... The secret of
Federation is to subordinate the African's interests. ... NR is
rich and other countries like SR look upon her enviously ... to

make her a white man's home .... If we want peace, Christianity and UNO are there to mould our future. This does not mean that we [are] blind pacifists, we know our needs .... I further see imprisonment for some of you.' One senior civil servant on seeing this document, jotted his comment thus: 'Very well written ... gives impression of European influence,' but Nabulyato's words found an echo in Kaunda's heart.[38]

Despite the variety of his activities in Mufulira, Kaunda was still sure that he would not stay in teaching. The African Provincial Council for the Western Province received two nominations in 1948 for membership of the territorial African Representative Council, of which his name was one. He told Sokoni that, if he were elected, he would know that he should stay in the province. 'If I don't go in though, it means that God is telling me to go back home.' His good prospects of election were reversed as a result of heavy lobbying involving Kasokolo and Nelson Nalumango, who were appointed in 1948 as the first two African Members of the Legislative Council. This was the signal for him and Sokoni to resign from their posts in the Mine School. They made their definite decision near the end of 1948, and Kapwepwe also resigned. In April 1949, they were on the way home.[39]

If political awakening was going to be truly effective, the rural areas must be involved. It was inevitable that scattered villages, out of touch with newspapers and radio, would lack the chances for discussion and organisation that existed in the towns. Kaunda and Sokoni therefore laid plans for this work of political organisation before they left the Copperbelt. What they had in mind was to relate their campaigning closely to cooperative enterprises that might help to awaken the villages. For, as we saw earlier, their province was heavily denuded of manpower. To this end they bought bicycles, sewing machines and cloth patches and, with a solemn resolve to be punctual at any meetings which they might organise, they bought stout watches. The journey north with their families has been described by Kaunda in his autobiography. Because money for their fares was short, he and Sokoni had to cycle from the Lukulu River, north of Chitambo Mission, to Mpika. For years that was a lion-infested region. His account of the preparations for the journey testifies to the strong sense he has always had of 'how providential the Creator is'.[40] This uncom-

plicated belief in the love of God offers an important clue to the
understanding of his thought and action.

It was very clear to Sokoni that his friend was thinking long
thoughts. The man cycling beside him was not an iconoclast but
a prophet in the making; preparing not just to denounce but to
testify to a vital, universal truth. The encounters of the last eight
years had radically changed the direction of his life and sharpened
his thinking. 'Kenneth,' Sokoni once commented, 'is at times like
an elephant who was seen by seven blind men.' 'It is sometimes
difficult to pinpoint his characteristics but you can always say that
he is seeing a number of years ahead.'[41] Sonquishe of Munali
had joined with various apparently adverse forces in hoeing over
the fertile character of the young Kaunda. The seeds of a strong
vision were now germinating fast.

[1]*NR Annual Report*, 1958.
[2]*Op. cit.*, p. 14.
[3]Now called Grade VII.
[4]TI-FM/KK, 5/10/71.
[5]For a scholarly study of educational developments see T. Coombe, *Origins of
Secondary Education in Zambia* (Harvard, 1968), esp. p. 237 ff.; also Gann,
op. cit., p. 266.
[6]*NR Hansard*, 25/11/43, pp. 152-163.
[7]TI-FM/KK, 5/2/69, with ref. to former Munali pupils, R. C. Kamanga, K.
Konoso, P. Matoka, E. Mudenda, J. Mwanakatwe, M. Sipalo, A. Wina, S. Wina,
G. Zulu, who were to become Ministers in the Zambian government.
[8]Kaunda, *op. cit.*, pp. 16-17.
[9]TI-FM/KK, 5/2/69; and note that other names for the S. African town 'lingo',
Chikabanga, were 'Kitchen Kaffir', 'Chilapalapa' and 'Fanikalo'.
[10]J. Macnair, *Livingstone the Liberator* (Collins, 1940), 132-133; and W. G.
Blaikie, *Personal Life of David Livingstone*, (Murray, 1913), 69.
[11]H. Powdermaker, *Copper Town* (Harper and Row, 1962), 54-55.
[12]B. Davidson, *African Awakening* (Jonathan Cape, 1955), 60; and Shepperson
and Price, *op. cit.*, p. 163.
[13]Isaiah 11: 6.
[14]W. P. Livingstone, *op. cit.*, p. 294.
[15]Shepperson and Price, *op. cit.*, p. 75, citing *Life and Work in British Central
Africa*, No. 106, p. 11.
[16]The first verse of this song, in Bemba, ran thus:
   Tuletota, mwe Lesa, mwe Chilibwe libwe,
   Mwe balenga bantu kusanda,
   Mwatupelyo Mwana, ni Yesu Kristu,
   Kachimfya wa fibi fyonse.
[17]TI-FM/KK, 5/2/69, and FM/R. M. Kaunda, 1969.
[18]Kaunda, *op. cit.*, p. 19.
[19]TI-FM/SMK, 8/11/69.
[20]TI-FM/JMS, 6/10/69 and FM/SMK, 8/11/69; NAZ: KTQ(2/1) *Chinsali
Dist. Notebook*, Vol. I, and note that, after independence, Abercorn was renamed
Mbala.
[21]TI-FM/SMK, 8/11/69.

[22]Testimony of Henry Chibuta, Kaunda's predecessor as Head Master at Lubwa, given to the writer, 1971; and TI-FM/SMK, 8/11/69; note that Gore-Browne's estate should be spelled *Ishiba Ng'andu*, Bemba for 'lake of the royal crocodile'.
[23]NAZ: SEC/E/67, Tyndale-Biscoe, confidential letter to Chief Secretary, 16/3/42.
[24]*Ibid.*: N/2195, minutes of Kasama African Institute, 4/11/50 and 23/7/52.
[25]Lord Robert Baden-Powell (1857-1941) was Founder and World Chief of the Boy Scout Movement, which developed from interest in his handbook on scouting written after military service in Africa; see T. O. Ranger, *Revolt in Southern Rhodesia 1896-7* (Heinemann, 1967) for refs. to Baden-Powell.
[26]M. M. Temple, 'Profile of Kenneth Kaunda', *Black Government* by Kaunda and Morris (U.S.C.L., 1960), 9; and note that one of the Chasefu boys taught by Kaunda is Professor Lameck K. H. Goma, B.Sc., M.A., Ph.D., Vice-Chancellor of the University of Zambia. See also S. A. Mpashi, *Betty Kaunda* (Longmans, 1969) 18-23; TI-FM/SMK, 8/11/69 and FM/JMS 6/10/69; and Kaunda *op. cit.*, p. 23.
[27]Mpashi, *op. cit.*, p. 10.
[28]*Zambia* 22-23; TI-FM/JMS, 6/10/69; NAZ: SEC/NAT/117, Gore-Browne to Prov. Commissioner, 20/1/47 and 27/1/47; and Hall, *Kaunda—Founder of Zambia* (Longmans, 1964), 15.
[29]TI-FM/SMK, 8/11/69; Kaunda *op. cit.*, p. 24.
[30]Kaunda, *op. cit.*, pp. 23-27.
[31]TI-FM/JMS, 6/10/69.
[32]Kaunda and Morris, *op. cit.*, pp. 41 ff.
[33]TI-FM/SMK, 8/11/69; and note that, at this period the Head Master of Ndola Main School, managed directly by the Govt. was Nelson Manda, former husband of Kaunda's eldest sister, Katie. The leader of the U.M.C.B. was the late Revd. A. J. Cross, a Baptist missionary and father-in-law of the writer.
[34]See A. L. Epstein, *Politics in an Urban African Community* (Manchester, 1958), 91-92; and Kaunda, *op. cit.*, pp. 28-29. The writer was Manager of Schools, Mufulira, from 1946-1950.
[35](O.U.P., 1958) pp. v and 1; and Davidson, *Report on Southern Africa* (Jonathan Cape, 1952) esp. pp. 240-255.
[36]Kaunda and Morris, *op. cit.*, p. 41.
[37]Kaunda, *op. cit.*, pp. 31-36.
[38]NAZ: Sec/Nat/353, Nabulyato's confidential memorandamu, 28/12/48.
[39]TI-FM/JMS, 6/10/69.
[40]Kaunda, *op. cit.*, pp. 36-37.
[41]TI-FM/JMS, 6/10/69.

4

'Welensky's Federation'— the Great Central African Plot

The plan that Kaunda and his two friends had made on the mountain at Mbeya was not easily fulfilled. The money which they had dreamed of accumulating as capital for cooperative agricultural projects had been consumed instead by the cost of daily living and of travel. They therefore had to start by tackling their farming on their own, and Kenneth set to work as soon as they arrived at Shambalakale. 'He worked very hard', said his wife. 'I had never seen a man of such determination. He used to work from morning to sunset. His mother and I went to help him water the vegetable garden at four o'clock in the afternoon. We soon had plenty of vegetables and sold them at Lubwa Mission.'[1] He was in good health and his temperate living, which totally excluded alcohol, was an important asset. More hands were required in the fields, however, and so he decided to renew his contacts with the Zaïre second-hand clothes trade, in order to increase his income. This meant cycling over three hundred miles each way. When he reached Zaïre, he would purchase bundles of old clothes and consign them to himself by Messrs. Thatcher Hobson's bus. Then, cycling back to Chinsali as hard as he could, he would be there to receive the bundles. The bus of course went south from Mufulira via Ndola and then turned north at Kapiri Mposhi, the total distance to Chinsali being around 540 miles. The route he followed by bicycle was east-north-east from the Zaïre Pedicle across the Luapula and Chambeshi to Chinsali. Such earnings were, however, haphazard and so he agreed to an urgent plea from Lubwa to start teaching again, on a part-time basis. His plan was to keep the afternoons for farming. He had also to fit in regular visits to Sokoni's 'cooperative farm' at Kamangu on weekends. They were developing their projects under the auspices of what they called the Chinsali Youngmen's Farming Association. In addition to staple crops, the scheme included poultry and a promising little orchard of guava, pawpaw, mango, banana and citrus.[2]

The magnetism of the Welfare Association gripped him again, however, as soon as he was home in the Chinsali District. More and more its activities began to eat into his afternoon and evening programme. Here was a natural base for the introduction of the African Congress with which he had associated himself in Mufulira as soon as word had reached the Copperbelt that the Federation of Welfare Societies had taken this new name. Late in 1949 Kaunda wrote to the new Congress General Secretary Robinson Nabulyato, for advice about the opening of a branch in Chinsali. As Nabulyato's reply was encouraging, he discussed the idea with Sokoni and another boyhood friend, Robert Speedwell Makasa, who had been away from the district for some years and had returned while the others were on the line of rail. Together they brought the matter before the Welfare Association, where, as Kaunda has recorded, it was given 'a cautious welcome'. Older men like Daniel Besa, disciple of David Kaunda and father-in-law of Simon Kapwepwe, had favoured the younger men's activities in the Welfare Association. But the Congress was obviously a different type of organisation. 'Let them start this thing and Government will deal with them' was the attitude of some of the *bakalamba*. Early in March 1950, however, the Chinsali Branch of Congress was formed. Five weeks later, Kaunda reported to Nabulyato that there were now twenty members, and he stated also that the Branch appreciated 'the idea of British Citizenship' and wanted full information from Congress Headquarters about any developments in the quest for a new status for Africans in the Protectorate. He also wanted details of a report that a member of the Governor's Executive Council had been dismissed 'because of supporting the African on the Federal Proposals....' 'We understand,' he added, 'that it was on the disrecommendation of Mr. Welensky that that was done. If it be true, was and is His Excellency showing us that he is in favour of the Federal Proposals as they stand?'[3]

The African Congress had in fact been born in 1948 from the recently established Federation of Welfare Societies, bodies which had pioneered the articulation of protest. In the first decades of the

century, with their Chiefs now little more than low-paid civil
servants, the people, coerced, taxed and voteless, seemed dumb.[4]
Their services were demanded for the comfort of the conquerors
who, however, did not want to find them 'in their way'. All the power
in the land was in alien hands. The Welfare Societies, timorous and
stammering though they may have appeared, uttered the first
coherent 'voice of the people'. Tragically, the colonial Government
kept on asserting, or at least pretending, that such utterances were
unrepresentative and irrelevant; while this African 'voice' reiterated
the affirmation of respect for the British Government and loyalty
to the Governor. In April 1950, the Chinsali Branch of Congress,
over Kaunda's signature, presented a letter of welcome to the new
Secretary for Native Affairs, which praised his predecessor and said:
'We are glad because it is you, sir, the man we regard as our Senior
Teacher, the man who will not deny us the slightest chance of
learning . . . [and who will] cope up with [*sic*] such a huge mass
of men, women and children, especially in time of thick and thin
when the passing clouds are trying to cover the horizon of our
hopes, faith and freedom which lies within the bounds of the Great
British Empire.' The Government's response was negligible, probably, in part at least, because of the elaboration offered, as in
Kaunda's message, of the nature of the 'passing clouds'. For he and
Makasa referred explicitly to 'the enslaving aims of most settlers'
as 'derogatory, ostentatious and very trying to the health of our
country as a whole'.[5]

A few Europeans were unhappy about this voicelessness of the
people. Thirty-six years after the 'pacification' of the territory by
British forces, Sir Stewart Gore-Browne, soon after his election to
the Legislative Council, asked whether there was any chance of
finding some way of consulting Africans on matters affecting their
lives. He was prompted to ask this because he had recently addressed
a gathering of Africans on the subject of the amalgamation of the
two Rhodesias and discovered that the great majority of those
present had no confidence in the ability of their Chiefs to be their
spokesmen. Yet in 1948 he expressed a strange complacency.
'I do not think I am flattering ourselves unduly when I say that in
Northern Rhodesia we are ahead of other territories in the way we
consult our Africans.' Here was the use of 'we', which was to be
heard constantly from Welensky; the 'we' that meant Europeans,

the 'proprietors' of 'our Africans'. In the same fateful year, Gore-Browne was to put before an African gathering in Mufulira his proposal for partition of the country into a white state, covering the line of rail and related to Southern Rhodesia, and a number of African states in the rural reas. Kenneth Kaunda was among those who protested hotly, demanded African self-government instead, and walked out. That was the year of the birth of the African Congress.[6]

To understand official blindness on the issue of African opinion, we have to note not only the fierceness of settler opposition to any 'concessions' but also the fact that the colonial regime was committed to a policy of indirect rule. The schizophrenia of the Northern Rhodesia Government from 1924 to 1953 can be traced to the impossibility of evolving this policy to its logical end while accommodating the mounting pressures of the settler doctrine whose fulfilment was in something like Afrikaaner *baaskap*. The fact that the explicit declaration of a policy based on 'the paramountcy of native interests' in Northern Rhodesia was the work of a British Labour Colonial Secretary only aggravated the tensions. It is not easy to believe that Passfield, as a Labour politician, was unaware that paramountcy as formulated in 1922 by the Conservative Duke of Devonshire in respect of Kenya had not been intended for a moment to apply to African interests *vis-à-vis* European interests. Devonshire had been attempting to tackle the problem of Asian versus 'native' interests. When Passfield extended the formula to the 'plural' situation of Northern Rhodesia, he could not look for anything but fierce hostility from white people in Rhodes' Northern Territory.[7]

The *Livingstone Mail* from 1906 onwards is an important text of settler sentiment. The reaction of its editor, Leopold Moore, to Passfield's pronouncement had strong support from white Northern Rhodesians. 'The natural trustees of barbarous and less developed races are their more civilized neighbours. The assumption of trusteeship by the Imperial Government is uncalled for and inadvisable.' In the alluring sunny climate of the Northern Rhodesia savanna, however, with cheap domestic labour, spacious houses and the pleasures of social relaxation at sundown, one of the toughest problems of the modern world was going to demand a solution. In the 'dis-ease' of their dilemma, many colonial admini-

strators, perhaps understandably, took the timorous line of trying
to stifle the real reactions of the African people, as is so clearly
seen from the record of official dealings with Welfare Societies
and then the Congress.[8] What was written in 1959 by Guy Clutton-
Brock about colonial civil servants aptly describes many of their
counterparts in Northern Rhodesia: 'men of high integrity, ability
and fine character, conscientious and with a keen sense of duty', but
'well paid in a poor country, with extensive leave, good conditions
of service and a pension to come . . . temporary sojourners who do
not have to live with their mistakes'. There were some, however,
whose commitment was outstanding. Kaunda speaks especially of a
D.C. at Chinsali, Roy Stokes, who 'was one day tackled very
seriously about his sympathies with us . . .' 'This took place at
Senior Chief Nkula's village. I don't remember what the trouble
was exactly but this man found courage to speak and he spoke.
I can well remember the expression of utter disgust on the Government officials' faces.'[9]

Welfare Associations began to appear rapidly in the early 1930s
and it is interesting to note that one of the prime movers in the
formation of the Ndola Association was Ernest A. Muwamba, a
Tonga from Malawi, born near the birthplace of David Kaunda.
At its meeting in November 1930, this body was advised to 'prohibit
foolish words so that the government will not stop us'. It was
committed to 'creating peace and prosperity', an echo of the
objectives of the Mwenzo Association, which now experienced a
brief revival. Similar associations were formed soon after in Broken
Hill, Mazabuka and Lusaka. The minutes of a Lusaka meeting in
1931 protested hotly against the behaviour of butchers towards
African customers 'as though the native was a dog'—a type of
behaviour which the writer witnessed on a number of occasions
in Mufulira in the years 1946–50. The record of the emergence
of such associations in Choma, Luanshya, Abercorn, Kasama and
Fort Jameson provides a sad commentary on the official reaction
as expressed in particular through the S.N.A., Moffat Thomson.
As Rotberg mentions, the cry of one Choma Native Welfare
Association member, "Do you think the government will ever agree
for a black man to have a piece of land near the township?"
prompted Thomson to warn the Chief Secretary against the mingling
of Europeans and Africans. While the Acting-Governor was telling

the Lusaka Association that there was no colour bar in the Protectorate, the S.N.A. was working for the extension of the pass system and for the removal of protesting Africans from 'urban compounds'. In 1933 he stated categorically that the Associations must not discuss the issue of the amalgamation of the two Rhodesias and remarked in passing that men from Nyasaland were 'professional agitators'. In response to this, the Associations began to plan a united territorial association and arranged for a public meeting at Kafue, thirty miles south of Lusaka, in 1933.[10]

The Kafue meeting is worthy of special note here. Firstly, as was the practice in most of such meetings at that time, and later, it was opened with prayer. Secondly, despite all the increasing irritations and insults experienced especially by people in the towns, it began with these words: 'We are here to make a recognition that should cement the existing friendship between the government, the settlers and the Africans.' The Government, however, chose to detect subversion in these stirrings of the Welfare Associations. On the ground that the members of the associations, being 'detribalised' or 'alien', could not speak for 'natives living in the tribal areas'—a formula redolent of the whole dogmatism of South Africa—Moffat Thomson urged the Chief Secretary to forbid the associations to pursue any matters that were not strictly 'non-political'. Thus began a decade of decline for the Associations. Rotberg cites one last abortive effort, made in 1937 at 'illegal' meetings at Chief Chongo's court in the Mazabuka area, to form a Northern Rhodesia African Congress on the model recently offered by Southern Rhodesia.[11] The succession of timorous men went on using the semblance of indirect rule in an attempt to silence that very self-expression which was to be proclaimed so soon among the primary war aims of the Western powers.

In May 1946, however, the seemingly dormant Welfare Societies established their Federation at last, but found no real change in the official reaction. Two months later, in a memorandum on the Federation submitted to the Governor's Executive Council, the Federation was said to be aiming at 'developing independently of the African Provincial Councils', but nonetheless the S.N.A. invited the Chairman, Dauti Yamba, and the Secretary of the new organisation to meet him.[12] But, he stated officially, the Federation 'is representative of no one but itself'. Kaluwa, however, continued

his protracted and meticulously courteous overtures. When the
Federation fixed its general meeting for 10 July, 1948, he wrote to
ask the S.N.A. to 'send an official to take notes for the SNA's information'. The Federation also wanted to discuss the selection of
delegates to a London conference on the proposals and the submission of a memorandum from the Federation to the Colonial
Secretary; the issue of Amalgamation or Federation; Gore-Browne's
relation to the London delegation; and official recognition of the
Federation of African Societies. Hudson, the S.N.A., agreed to this
meeting, at which he rejected the idea that the African Representative Council was not 'representative of all the people'.[13]

A Federation of the Rhodesias and Nyasaland, Hudson assured
Lipalile and his colleagues, would not be established 'until Africans
had been fully consulted'. The Colonial Secretary had given this
guarantee. Yet the S.N.A. stated his view that, 'as they were not
aware of the meaning of federation', there should be no Africans
present at any preliminary discussions of proposals for closer
association of the three territories. He then reiterated in writing his
refusal to approve a delegation to London from the Federation.
Safeli Chileshe and Moses Mubitana were, however, to be Govern-
ment-sponsored delegates.[14] This letter to Kaluwa was written at
the moment of the birth of the African Congress, for it was this
General Council of the F.A.S. that unanimously constituted the
Northern Rhodesia African Congress, and affirmed its opposition
to the Governor's renomination of Gore-Browne as representative
of African interests. It called for the replacement of the 'misleading
name', Northern Rhodesia, by the designation, 'Queen Victoria's
Protectorate', and reaffirmed African opposition to white 'responsible government', Amalgamation and Federation. It went on to
appeal for funds for the new Congress 'from the African public
and Europeans interested in African welfare and development'.
It then elected Godwin Mbikusita as its President, Robinson
Nabulyato as Secretary and Mateyo Kakumbi, carpentry instructor
of the Chitambo Mission of the Church of Scotland, as Treasurer.[15]

The first formal Congress memorandum to the Government
contained these words: 'As the policy of the Colonial Office Rule
is to educate and civilise Africans and then let them rule themselves,
it is earnestly hoped that this said promise will be fulfilled. As no
English blood was shed by Africans when the English first entered

in Northern Rhodesia, it is hoped that the Colonial Office will, as before, protect the interests of Africans from the oppression of European settlers. ... It is hoped that their say on anything in Northern Rhodesia will not be outweighed by any demand from the European settlers, such as responsible Government, Amalgamation or Federation. ... Northern Rhodesia African chiefs asked for and were graciously granted British Protection by Her Most Gracious Majesty, the late Queen Victoria, therefore they think it would be ingratitude and disloyal to break away from the government of her great grandson's direct representative .... It is only this year when Africans will sit in the Legislative Council and nobody has seen what they can do, therefore it would be unfair to hurry up the Africans to Responsible Government.'[16]

The Northern Rhodesia African Congress now published its objectives. It saw its task as a commitment 'to promote the educational, political, economic and social advancement of the Africans in full cooperation with the Government, Native Authorities, Missionary Societies, the African Representative Council and other such organisations which have the welfare of the Africans at heart.'[17] It planned also 'to break the tribal bars ... to foster the spirit of unity among Africans'. In view of the vast disparity of educational expenditure on African and European children, the total non-enfranchisement of Africans, the industrial colour bar and humiliating social discrimination, this expressed desire to cooperate with every possible agency was the more remarkable. Undoubtedly it was prompted by prudence, but it certainly should have elicited a positive response. However little sign of response there was, it seems to have sharpened the argument within the upper echelons of Government as to how this new body should be treated.[18]

Robinson Nabulyato, as Secretary, began immediate planning for the first General Meeting of the Congress and therefore asked the S.N.A. whether African civil servants might be office-bearers of Congress. He also sent an invitation to the Governor to open the meeting, fixed for 24 December. The Chief Secretary told the S.N.A. that he believed that the Congress was trying 'to invest itself with a good deal more importance than it in fact possesses' in order to win financial backing from Government. The conflict was sharpening.[19]

A confidential memorandum of the Congress Executive set down the African conviction on the existing gulf between African and European interests. 'When we think of native policy the Colonial Office ... has failed to wield its influence in Southern Rhodesia ... How much more of the failure of the Colonial Office shall be experienced under the Central African dominion of the Federated States? The secret of Federation is to subordinate African interests. ... Under Federation it is said that rights now enjoyed will be safeguarded, this shows no African progress. ... We are ... not prepared to alter our present colonial rule to that of the Federal government ... we now claim that Colonial Office rule is better for us at present. ... We must keep to a bird in the hand which is worth two in the bush ... persuasion from other people shall be regarded as snakes .... Partnership ... is a ladder for Europeans in Northern Rhodesia to climb on us.' The idea that the African people did not grasp the meaning of Federation was wrong, said the memorandum. 'We see its meaning ... to enslave the African'—and, Nabulyato warned his members, 'I further see imprisonment for some of you.' Here was a tremor that Government could not fail to record. The Acting S.N.A. therefore sought to quieten African fears. The Governor and the Colonial Secretary, he told a meeting of Congress in July 1949, had guaranteed that 'full account would have to be taken of African opinion before any alteration affecting African interests could be considered.'[20]

As Kenneth Kaunda threw himself into the task of letting the people of the north hear the news of the birth and activities of the African Congress, he realised that at last an authentic voice was making itself heard. He knew too, however, that the forces ranged against the young Congress were determined and powerful. He therefore began at once a programme of publicity designed to inspire the people of his district with the aim of Congress and the need for as many sub-branches as possible. Therefore, since 'after heated discussion' the Congress General Meeting in Lusaka in July 1950 had 'reached the conclusion that, since UNITY IS POWER, we shall need the cooperation of every African,' it was clear that informed people must start to establish Congress everywhere by means of sub-branches, and from the outset 'keep clean records' of their activities. But, he said, 'Some people are busy planting "DISUNITY" among Africans. "Beware of wolves in sheep's clothing"... The Congress is not an enemy to the Government ... it is in fact a recognised mouth-piece of the African people ... The Congress is not financed by any outside Bodies, so for its existence it relies on what you as an individual can do ... you are allowed by the Constitution to start a branch from 6 to 50 people.' Then he added: 'The Congress is open to all people whether Christian or pagans, magicians or witch-doctors ... every person who has welfare of N. Rhodesia at heart. These are times of thick and thin, so please if you would like to start up a Branch write back to the Secretary, Sub-head Office, Lubwa.' A few months later, welcoming the Revd. Henry Kasokolo, he called on the Member of the Legislative Council to strive for unity though it was a difficult job 'to try and cope up with [*sic*] such a mass of men, women and children whose position is never certain'. The Chinsali Branch, he said, wanted Kasokolo 'to convey to His Excellency the Governor and all the Officials concerned that we the Africans of this Territory have deep confidence in His Majesty the King's Government and like to say plainly that we have no desire to branch from the present system of direct rule from the King's own Government.'[21]

The story of his subsequent labours and his elevation to national leadership demands that we sketch now the growth of the movement for European 'responsible government' in which already Roy Welensky was seen as the dominant figure. Kaunda was to say of him that he had 'never uttered a single word that would have encouraged Africans'. As Prime Minister of the Federation, Welensky was to speak of 'we' when referring obviously to Europeans only. Ten years after its inception he was to see that Federation dismantled to make way for the sovereign nations of Malawi and Zambia. Had he behaved otherwise, the pace of Central African history might have been different. If he had not resorted so frequently to blatantly racist utterances, echoing the accents of Godfrey Huggins, he might have participated in a process whereby pressure could have been brought to bear on Southern Rhodesia and South Africa to stop putting the clock back. Instead, his legacy was a situation of exacerbated racial antagonism. Kaunda and his friends, from the outset, saw the Federation plan as essentially of the same nature as both Amalgamation and Partition, a conspiracy to consolidate minority rule and white supremacy. 'If you took some sour beer,' Kenneth often said as he cycled from village to village, 'and put it in another calabash, do you think it will change just because you have changed the calabash?' The emergency of Welensky thus signalled a dangerous sharpening of conflict.[22]

In Britain the official view was increasingly influenced by the need to prevent Central Africa from passing into the orbit of South Africa, as this would bring a number of serious threats not only to the continent of Africa but also to British control of important raw materials. Whitehall hoped that, though Amalgamation could not be accepted, the territories would endeavour to make the new Inter-Territorial Council a success. The post-war years saw a wave of anti-imperialist feeling sweeping over Europe, bringing sharp criticism against the British Government for oppressive colonial practices and associating the cause of the working classes of Europe with that of the voteless peoples throughout Britain's overseas possessions. To Welensky, this meant that Britain was now in effect blaming the settlers for the exploitation and the blunders which she herself had made. The British Labour Government's plan for colonial development evoked a proposal from him that instead Britain should stop taxing companies in the Protectorate and divert the vast B.S.A. royalties back to Northern Rhodesia. Welensky's character oddly compounded 'an instinctive sympathy with the underdog' and a determination to protect 'white working class standards' from 'undercutting by poorly paid Africans'. Gann has neatly summarised the opposing viewpoints of the post-war period thus: 'Whilst many of the more radical Labour supporters overseas now saw in Rhodesian settlers nothing more than an overpaid and under-brained pigmentocracy ... many settlers envisaged their opponents as a motley crew of headline hunters, society ladies with bored BBC accents, ... parsons with bees in their bonnets and Research Fellows in barbarology with grants to count the cats in Kuala Lumpur... the sooner Downing Street control was ended the better things could turn out for the country!'[23]

While the *Northern News*, which Welensky owned, continued to see the struggle as between the settlers and Whitehall, the men who would at last procure the dismantling of Welensky's Federation sixteen years later were taking the measure of the odds against them. But before the final battle, there must be a period of escalation, in which some notable figures were to rise and fall, while others would change sides and yet others would drop by the wayside.

One of the most important pioneering figures of the period was Harry Mwaanga Nkumbula, with whom Kenneth Kaunda was to be in close association during the crucial years of the imposition and initial impact of the Federation, and whose career thus merits attention here. Born in 1916 at Maala in the Namwala District and educated first at two Methodist Mission schools, Nkumbula was early influenced by George Padmore's *How Britain Rules Africa.* 'This is certainly an age of white supremacy,' Padmore wrote, '. . . because it is the age of the mighty gunpowder.' 'I started from there,' Nkumbula has said. After a few years' service as a teacher in Methodist schools, he was transferred to the United Missions in the Copperbelt and posted to Mufulira in 1942. He became Secretary of the local Welfare Association, and when the issue of Amalgamation was brought to the forefront by Welensky, tried to organise a meeting about it which, however, the District Commissioner forbade. Government's reaction was to require Nkumbula's transfer from Mufulira. In Kitwe, he plunged again into Welfare Association work and was a founding member of the Kitwe African Society. Godwin Mbikusita was President and Nkumbula Secretary of this body which he has described as 'the first political institution'. One of his close associates at this period was Dauti Yamba, also a U.M.C.B. teacher, who according to the personal recollection of Kenneth Kaunda's friend, John Malama Sokoni, had visited South Africa and come back, in 1942, with the idea of forming an African Congress. Soon after, Nkumbula heard from S. K. Mwase, Senior Boma Clerk in Kitwe, that the Government was alarmed by his activities. 'You are being deported from the Copperbelt,' Mwase told him. This Mwase had been a founder of the Livingstone Native Welfare Association in 1930 and had corresponded with Marcus Garvey, the Jamaican Pan-Africanist. In 1945, he was to write to Nkumbula again, asking for the return of papers on Levi Mumba and the Nyasaland Association and giving news of the Kitwe African Society. 'What about forming NR Congress?' he wrote. 'This is the only country which has now no Congress.'[24]

It may well be that Gore-Browne, aware of official hostility to Nkumbula, was trying to give him an opening for further study. Thus it was decided to send Nkumbula to Makerere in Uganda. However, through the procuring of a British Council scholarship, he was removed from Makerere and sent to the London School of

Economics in 1946. In England he was to meet George Padmore
and his entourage which included Kwame Nkrumah of Ghana,
Jomo Kenyatta of Kenya, Hastings Banda the Nyasaland doctor,
and the South African author, Peter Abrahams. 'We juniors,'
he has recalled, 'just sat and listened, but the whole discussion
hinged on how Africa shall be free.' This intense involvement in
pan-African affairs, however, interfered with his studies and he was
referred in certain subjects. On his return to Northern Rhodesia,
he was to learn that the scholarship had been cancelled and also
that the Federation of Welfare Societies had become the Northern
Rhodesia African Congress.[25]

Angered by the offer of a low-grade Government appointment
which he flatly refused, Nkumbula tried to secure himself an
independent income in a very unusual way. The Ila people, perhaps
from some immemorial association with the coast of Africa or
perhaps through Arab contacts, had a belief that a sea-shell—*mpande*
—must be placed on the graves of their notables to ensure the welcome of God. Such shells abounded at Beira on the coast of Portuguese Mozambique, and so Harry began a series of trips to the coast
which resulted in a revival of the market for shells among the Ila
and kept him in funds. He was just about to set off on one of these
journeys in July 1951, when Robinson Nabulyato visited him at
Namwala and invited him to address the African Congress on the
closer association of the Central African territories. Though not a
member, he agreed because he had been joint author with Hastings
Banda of a pamphlet, issued in London in May 1949, entitled
Federation in Central Africa.[26] At the meeting, both Mbikusita
and Nkumbula addressed the Congress. Mbikusita's mild expression
of willingness to consider Federation if certain conditions were
met was followed by Nkumbula's rejection of any closer association
with Southern Rhodesia. He was supported by, among others,
Simon Zukas of Ndola. Immediately strong pressure arose, first
in whispers and then openly, for a fresh election for the presidency.
In the crowded Kabwata Hall, the Chinsali Branch of the Congress
was represented by Kenneth Kaunda and Robert Makasa. The
pro-Mbikusita campaign was led by Gordon Chindele. 'You need
a moderate,' was the plea. 'Let Nkumbula be secretary.' This led
Kaunda, Makasa and Dixon Konkola to begin lobbying for
Nkumbula. 'Harry for the job now,' they said. As Nkumbula had

been speaking, Kaunda had shouted out, 'Long live Harry. Death to the traitor,' like, as he has said himself, 'a small agitator'. At the end of the meeting, members of the executive, like Nabulyato, Kakumbi, Yamba, Chileshe and Kaluwa, pressed Nkumbula to stand for the presidency against Mbikusita. Nkumbula gained twenty-four votes, Safeli Chileshe three and Mbikusita one. A new era of action had begun.[27]

The Brondesbury Park memorandum, prepared by Hastings Banda and Nkumbula, is notable because it was circulated widely and, as Kaunda has said, 'we read that and began to go into libraries and read of the extinction of the Aborigines in Australia.' 'We began to read *Venture* from the Fabian Society and it meant a great deal to us.' The case against Federation, Banda and Nkumbula said, was that it would sever the 'direct' political and cultural ties of Northern Rhodesia and Nyasaland with Britain and end 'the policy of deliberate tutelage'. On his return from England, Nkumbula was to find that his people were suffering from 'a terrible inferiority complex' that made them lie down under daily humiliation. Very few were challenging the gross insults that accompanied 'pigeon-hole shopping' or the conditions imposed upon African travellers by rail or road. 'It was unimaginable then,' he has stated 'that white and black should ever sit together.' 'Afrikaaners were joined by people of British origin and even by religious bodies, to keep Africans down. We were convinced that this treatment must end . . . When I took over Congress, I found it impossible to go straight into politics. Our first job was to remove the inferiority complex.'[28]

As Kenneth Kaunda mounted his bicycle and went into the villages of the Chinsali District, he met saddening evidence of the spirit of 'submission' and sometimes he would feel that he was 'the only person mad enough to go on with this thing'. Yet, more and more he found a response as he asked his listeners to recall their own experiences in southern Africa and also in the two European wars. 'Those who had gone to Rhodesia affirmed the sense of oppression. Heads would nod in meetings to point out that the land was no longer the people's.' Chiefs were muzzled. Any extension of the Southern Rhodesian system would mean more individual suffering, frustration and fear. In the villages, as in the urban compounds, what counted was not printed statements of Whitehall policy but how Government officials behaved towards the local people in the face of the mounting pressures upon them to let the country go the way of Godfrey Huggins. The action Kaunda and others were taking was readily labelled as 'agitation' by those in authority. His thinking then and his subsequent actions were not, however, directed towards rabble rousing. Instead, there was an urgency in the situation because the dark cloud of inhumanity seemed to be moving up swiftly from southern Africa. The Bemba proverb, '*Mangilile mulamba talatulula*'—'Let me make haste before the storm breaks', describes the mood of those days. It was not going to be easy to counter the threat of the amalgamationists, overt or disguised. It was going to be a race against time.[29]

In March 1950, Kaunda was elected Secretary of the new Chinsali Branch of the N.R. African Congress, to which we have referred, with Makasa as Chairman and Simon Sula, the clerk at Lubwa Mission, as Treasurer. Makasa was at that time Head Master of the Lower Middle School at the court of Chief Nkula.[30] Kaunda has described the months that followed as one of the 'most amazing' periods of his life. On the weekends, Makasa and he would cycle long distances, 'singing hymns which the Rev. R. D. McMinn and Revd. P. B. Mushindo had translated from the Church of Scotland hymn-book.' Those were dangerous journeys for there were lions and leopards in the district and the men had a sense of placing themselves 'more than ever before, entirely in the hands of our Creator'.

Kaunda's own summary of what they discussed with the people on those exhilirating trips merits quotation here. 'What was the message that the Chinsali people were receiving at this time? We had to make our people conscious that they were human beings just as good or as bad as any other . . . . this message was not difficult to put across to our people. I was aware that most of our people who had gone to fight in defence of the British Empire had suffered for nothing; we were only employed as hewers of wood and drawers of water, and we could not eat from the same tables nor share the same beds in hotels. I would ask which was more important: to prepare someone else's meals and beds or to share them? Was it not common sense that a person who prepared your meals and made your bed and looked after you was controlling your life? How stupid it was for anyone to say you may control my life but

I will not sit at the same table with you because you are stinking or because you are black. Then there was my most popular story. This was the story of an African soldier who was not even called a soldier, but an *askari*, and yet sent to fight against Hitler, who was a horrible racialist. In fact, we went to defend the so-called Western or Christian values. I would point out the differences that existed in pay, uniform, food and in all other conditions of service. I would then portray this *askari* demobilized with none of the promises made to him fulfilled. This *askari* would suffer so much, he would end up a road labourer. Then he would ask for a lift from his road foreman who would put him at the back of a Government van while his dog shared the front seat with him. At an hotel, the Big Bwana would leave him to look after his luggage while he himself went in to take a meal. The dog would be given some food while this ex-*askari* would have nothing. Then they would arrive in town and this man, who risked his life just like his English counter-part, would go to a shop to see inscribed above the door, NO DOGS ALLOWED INSIDE. To his surprise when window-shopping he would see an actual dog right inside through the window. On his attempting to get inside he would be met at the door with a glib "Get out of here, you nigger, *bobojana*" (meaning monkey). "No Kaffirs allowed in here". Then would his own fellow black man come to order him out. "*Tata, kabiyeni kunse uko ku ntolokoso ekushitila abafita muno mwa babwana epela*". Then this ex-*askari* would look back to the days before the Second World War. He would remember how campaigns were conducted to recruit him, and others like him, the differences between a black and white service-man, the promises he had been given of what could be done for him on being demobilized. Then he would come nearer to where he was: how his road foreman exposed him to the heat, the cold or the rain, while he shared the warmth and all with his dog. He would end up by asking, "Where is the partnership in this country that Welensky talks about?" From there on he would decide to join the Northern Rhodesia African Congress.'[31]

In the Western Provincial Council in March 1950, Mufana Lipalile had spoken of the distrust of the doctrine of 'partnership' which was being presented as the guarantee of the international credibility of the scheme for Federation. It 'has a good sound ... and gives us the feel that there are two oxen, one black and one white, pulling the wagon... But ... one bull says, "I must go ahead and you must come behind me all the time". In that way, I do not see how the plough can go.' A member of the Northern Provincial Council spoke more forcefully. 'If a man is given food and he vomits, can he eat again what he has already vomited? And when a man vomits food, it means that it is not good for him. Most of us know that our friends in Southern Rhodesia are slaves.'[32]

In Chinsali, the little 'sauce-pan' radios were 'open' as never before as people listened apprehensively. Creech Jones, the Labour Colonial Secretary who had cheered them somewhat by his visit in 1949, had lost his seat in the February 1950 elections in Britain. James Griffiths, his successor, had agreed to Huggins' demand for a conference of officials to draft a Federal Constitution, and the subsequent discussions brought the word 'partnership' into further disrepute but in no way checked the arrogant utterances of Huggins. Nabulyato's invitation to Nkumbula to postpone a sea-shell collecting trip to Beira and address the Congress instead was an index of mounting anxiety and the sense that a voice was needed that would be free of the ambivalence of Mbikusita. Meanwhile, Congress had added to its ranks Reuben Kamanga, Justin Chimba, Mungoni Liso and Simon Zukas, Ndola editors of *The Freedom Newsletter* and founders of the Anti-Federation Action Committee, which declared bluntly that 'the years of courting between Government officials and the settlers have resulted in the birth of an illegitimate child.'[33]

When Kaunda and Makasa met them at Kabwata in Lusaka—though only twenty-seven people were there—the air was already charged with tension and anticipation. The Welensky plot was thickening. The years which Gann describes under the chapter heading 'Progress and Closer Union' were threatening to force back the hands of the clock of history and aggravate beyond repair the profound disharmony of Central Africa. When the marked man from Namwala stood to address the Congress, the effect was electric. Kaunda had had a glimpse of him once seven years before when they had been on the same bus going north from Kapiri Mposhi. Presumably Nkumbula had been on his way to visit Gore-Browne. His emphatic action in insisting that the bus driver give proper care to a sick passenger impressed Kenneth greatly.[34]

In the Kabwata Hall he saw him as the man for the hour, and as Makasa and he travelled back to Chinsali, his heart was on fire.

---

[1]Mpashi, *op. cit.*, p. 29.

[2]Kaunda, *op. cit.*, pp. 38-39.

[3]Makasa Papers: Kaunda and Makasa to Nabulyato, 10/4/50; and TI-FM/KK, 5/2/69.

[4]Note that in 1938 the Provincial Commissioners' Conference proposed increased payments to Chiefs, some of whom were then receiving only £6 p.a.

[5]Makasa Papers: NR African Congress, Chinsali Branch, sgd. Kaunda and Makasa, 'Welcome Address to Secretary for Native Affairs', 21/4/50.

[6]*NR Hansard*, No. 26 (May 1936), and No. 50 (Nov. 1948); and TI-FM/KK, 5/2/69; and note, (NAZ: Sec/E/67) recommendation of Ag. Director, Native Education, C. Opper, for 'native membership of Education Advisory Boards'.

[7]UK Command Paper 3573 (Passfield) of 1930, based on Duke of Devonshire's Memorandum, 'Indians in Kenya,' 1922.

[8]For *Livingstone Mail*, see British Museum Newspaper Library, Colindale, London; and see Hall, *Zambia*, pp. 103-111.

[9]*Dawn in Nyasaland* (Hodder, 1959), 133; and Kaunda, *op. cit.*, p. 43.

[10]NAZ: Sec/Nat/332, report of meeting, 3/6/31, and S.N.A. to C.S., 19/6/33; and see Rotberg, *Rise*, pp. 115-134.

[11]NAZ: Sec/Nat/447, letter of 24/2/25, ref. 8/NAT/A/7/2, and Sec/Nat/348.

[12]*Ibid.*: see Sec/Ea/14, Governor to Colonial Secy., 13/7/39, Sec/Nat/358, S. Prov. Commissioner to C.S., 14/8/46 and record of meeting at Secretariat, 2/12/46.

[13]*Ibid.*: Sec/Nat/353, letter of Kaluwa, 15/5/48; and S.N.A. to Kaluwa, 31/5/48; and record of meeting, Hudson (S.N.A.) and Price (Ag. C.S.) with Lipalile and Adamson of F.A.S., 29/6/48.

[14]*Ibid.*: Sec/Nat/353, S.N.A. to F.A.S., 10/7/48.

[15]*Ibid.*: Report of Federation of N.R. African Societies, 9-13/7/48.

[16]*Ibid.*: Kaluwa to S.N.A., 15/7/48.

[17]*Ibid.*: N. R. African Congress Constitution.

[18]Note: statistics for education of African and European children, 1930-39 (cited by Coombe, *op. cit.*, Table at end):

	African	1939	European	1939
1930 enrolment,	79,131	123,993	1930-879	1,480
1930 expenditure	£32,095	£ 47,694	£33,110	£44,300

i.e., In 1939, expenditure on African Education, approx. 12/- per head to cover buildings, salaries and equipment; on European, approx. £23.4/- per head p.a.

[19]NAZ: Sec/Nat/353, C.S. to S.N.A., 21/9/48; S.N.A. to Secy., N.R.A.C. 29/9/48.

[20]*Ibid.*: N.R.A.C. memo (strictly confidential) sgd. Nabulyato, 28/12/48; and note on S.N.A.'s address to N.R.A.C., July 1949.

[21]Makasa Papers: Kaunda's first circular to Chinsali District, 1950; Kaunda and Makasa to Kasokolo, 4/1/51.

[22]TI-FM/KK, 5/2/69 and 13/2/69. Welensky, born in 1907, was the son of a Lithuanian Jewish father and an Afrikaans mother.

[23]*A History*, pp. 263 and 390; and see also RH: Fabian Papers, Gore-Browne to Rita Hinden, 30/7/43.

[24]Padmore (Wishart, 1936); TI-FM/HMN, 15/6/71; and ANC 1/6, Mwase to Nkumbula, 1/3/45.

[25]TI-FM/HMN, 15/6/71.

[26]Sokoni Papers: see Chap. I, footnote 37.

[27]TI-FM/HMN, 15/6/71, and FM/KK, 13/2/69. Note: Rotberg, *Rise*, p. 234 mentions that Mbikusita was believed to have reported Zukas to the police.

[28]TI-FM/HMN, 15/6/71.
[29]TI-FM/KK, 13/2/69.
[30]The Chief Nkula of that period is now Paramount Chief of the Bemba.
[31]Kaunda, *op. cit.*, pp. 40-42.
[32]NAZ: Minutes of Western (Copperbelt) Provincial Council, 28-30/3/50, and of Northern Province Council, 15/4/50.
[33]TI-FM/HMN, 15/6/71; ANC: pamphlet of the Ndola Anti-Federation Committee, *The Case against the Federal Proposals*, 20/8/51.
[34]*A History*; TI-FM/KK, 13/2/69.

5

The Continental Crisis

The events in Central Africa which we have reviewed so far cannot be understood in isolation. Belatedly, though now insistently in the United Nations and elsewhere, it is recognised that the fortunes of the south or the west, the east or the north or the central regions of the African continent impinge inexorably upon each other. The huge land mass which was glibly described only sixty years ago as dark and empty of significance is now one of the more important factors for the future of mankind. The striking fact for us here is that Kenneth has been, from the outset of his adult years, a continental thinker. To ignore the historical drama beyond the borders of Northern Rhodesia or the Central African Federation would therefore be to lose sight of elements in his development which are essential to a fair picture of him. Now that we have sketched some of the main trends in the political crisis of Central Africa up to the time when it was clear that Federation was coming, we ought to look at the surrounding scene in order to place Kaunda, and no less Welensky, in context; without, however, losing sight of either the drama within Northern Rhodesia or the exploits of Kaunda himself.

As we have seen, British criticism of the Huggins/Welensky position was greatly muted by the switch from Labour to Tory in Britain, which replaced Griffiths by Oliver Lyttelton at the Colonial Office. The ascendancy of John Foster Dulles in the Eisenhower administration in the U.S.A. after 1952 was to extend an international climate in basic sympathy with Welensky. Increasingly the Southern Rhodesian statute book was imitating the South African. It was not just a policy of admitting fewer Africans to the voters' roll, but of removing them all from it. By 1938, African voters there had been reduced to 39 while white voters numbered

24,587. Ten years later, encouraged by Dr. Daniel Malan's sweeping victory in the South African elections, Huggins promised to exclude Africans altogether. While Attlee sat in Downing Street and Harry Truman in the White House, he had held his hand. But in 1951, the way seemed clear again. The financial qualification for the franchise was trebled and so was the educational criterion. 'The minimum income figure jumped to £240 (which a dozen years later is still three times the average for all African wage earners) and the property figure to £500.' Here were factors that could be manipulated at will. It was thus not just that 'African advancement' was being delayed in Southern Rhodesia; an *apartheid* state was being positively consolidated at the moment when 'Federation' was adroitly invoked as an expedient substitute for 'Amalgamation'.[1]

There can be no doubt that Huggins was emboldened by the trend of affairs south of the Limpopo. Daniel Sonquishe had told Kenneth Kaunda and his Munali school-mates something of the triumph of inhumanity in South Africa. As the oppression hardened after 1948 through the rule of Malan, the South African statute book filled up with a mass of 'laws' whereby the 'non-white' population would be confirmed in their homelessness, forbidden to enjoy the basic securities of family life, and constantly subject to harrying by the police. By an Act of Smuts' government an urban African who had his wife or children staying with him for more than seventy-two hours without an official permit had been guilty of a crime, as were his family. Scores of such 'laws' reveal the blatancy of *baaskap*. Moreover, as ex-Senator Brookes, one time Principal of Adams College in Natal, has written: 'It is impossible to exaggerate the effect of the colour question on the limiting of civil liberty. . . restrictions on the freedom of the non-whites have inevitably brought in their train great and increasing restrictions on the freedom of the whites.'[2]

Inevitably the unflagging drive of the white supremacists in South Africa has brought forth a succession of brave men and women determined to wage 'the struggle for a birthright'. The 1955 'Freedom Charter' gave expression to a pent-up cry for justice which could in no circumstances be called seditious by reasonable men. 'We, the people of South Africa, declare for all our country and the world to know: that South Africa belongs to all who live in it, black and white, and that no government can justly claim authority unless it is based on the will of all the people; that our people have been robbed of their birthright to land, liberty and peace by a form of government founded on injustice and inequality; that our country will never be prosperous or free until all our people live in brotherhood, enjoying equal rights and opportunities; that only a democratic state, based on the will of all the people, can secure to all their birthright without distinction of colour, race, sex or belief.'[3]

By 1941, the land listed as for African use was only 9.6 per cent of the total land of the country. 'A cautious authority' stated that the 'native reserves' of the Northern Transvaal were 'situated mostly in dry bushveld country, which affords little support for agriculture and stock-raising ... for the most part the natives are concentrated along the non-perennial streams, leading a precarious existence and obtaining water from pools in the river-beds.' 'Before the coming of the Europeans,' he went on, 'there was a large concentration of natives on the fertile, high-rainfall area of the Levubu River.' Now on the dry scrub-lands, there were, on the average, eighty-two persons per square mile. The result is that 25 per cent of the white population 'have prescriptive rights to 87% of the land.'[4]

The men of the Northern Rhodesian African Congress, in the years following its birth, were thus increasingly aware of the urgency of underlining the long-felt dread of 'white supremacy' and galvanising their people's determination that it would not be allowed to transfer the shaping of their destiny from the good intentions of the Colonial Office to what Winston Churchill once had called 'the fierce self-interest of a small population of white settlers'. However, as Rotberg had aptly said of the Churchill Government that came to power in 1951: 'Lyttelton and his fellow conservatives not surprisingly persuaded themselves that the federal form of amalgamation would benefit the British balance of payments, its world-wide strategic posture, the financial interests of the City of London, the British-backed copper companies of Northern Rhodesia, and the tobacco firms of Southern Rhodesia.' The Churchillian cast of mind missed the incongruity of calling the perpetuation of white superiority and black inferiority by the name of 'partnership'. For them, Welenskyism, as a compromise between the extremes of white supremacist *apartheid* and black nationalism, seemed to be the expedient formula. For the Africans, this was a time when their overseas friends seemed perilously few.[5]

When Kaunda and his associates looked north, there was little cheer to be found there. The history of what was called the Congo had been no less chequered, over the past half century, than that of Northern Rhodesia. In 1885, a secret act had transferred the Congo from the paper control of the 'International Association of the Congo' to King Leopold, in person, as his *domaine privé*. Immediately his 'forest guards', under the authority of tough soldiers of fortune, set about the massive recruitment of forced labour, especially to extract the wealth in rubber from a territory as large as western Europe. When the King finally yielded authority to his Government at the end of 1908, the way had been prepared for vast capital undertakings especially in the Katanga, which had been secured for the King by Captain Stairs in 1891. The railway line from South Africa and the Rhodesias reached Elizabethville in 1910 and the administration of the colony became more vigorous and, in many ways, effective. But responsible reports of beating, plundering, rape and the destruction of villages by state officers continued to reach the outside world. Nevertheless despite a 60 per cent drop in copper production during the world economic 'slump' of 1930-1932, the Congo's economy grew fast. The 'happy colony' saw a rapid expansion of its various industries between 1914 and 1945. Its post-war prosperity has been described as 'unequalled in any African colony'. The Belgian Congo Government proclaimed a policy of universal elementary schooling, and apologists of its policy claimed that 'under the regime of paternalism', though all higher civil service posts were reserved for Europeans, 'the racial question did not arise'. But, as the world was to know in a few year's time, there was a mounting ferment going on under the seeming placidity[6].

In Tanganyika, which shared a frontier with Northern Rhodesia between the lakes, there was a less depressing situation. It has been suggested that 1937 could be given as the year of the start of a conscious nationalism there. From 1922 there had been an organisation called the Tanganyika Territory African Civil Servant's Association. In 1929, the Tanganyika African Association was formed out of T.T.A.C.S.A., and twenty-five years later the Tanganyika African National Union was to be born from T.A.A. One significant flash-point came in 1951 when the Government announced a plan to move 3,000 African peasants from land in the Meru area which was to be given to European farmers. Kirilo Japhet, spokesman of the Meru people, supported strongly by Julius Nyerere and S. A. Kandoro, set out on a country-wide pilgrimage 'to wake up all Tanganyika'. This was how things stood in the year when Britain opened the door to a Central African Federation and Harry Nkumbula took over the Presidency of the Northern Rhodesia African Congress.[7]

Kenya was much further away, but the situation there was more akin to Southern Africa, and grim news from Kenya would soon figure prominently on the front pages of Welensky's *Northern News*. In legislation, Kenya followed a pattern not unlike that of South Africa; the size and self-assertion of the white settler population making it difficult for the Government to do otherwise, especially since the South African model was superficially successful. After the Second World War, the Governor, Sir Phillip Mitchell, introduced portfolios for European Unofficial Members of the Legislative Council. By 1951 'with thousands of acres lying idle in the "White Highlands", the so-called squatters were being evicted from the settlement areas and sent to the already overpopulated and greatly eroded Reserves.' As the resentment and the repression mounted, the horrific explosion drew near. 'Mau Mau was a desperate attempt by desperate people to change a system of economic and social injustice,'[8] and its 'hymns' thrummed with the longing for the restoration of the country to its owners. 'Tell the elders to shut up, they let our lands be taken. Tell the young men to rise up in arms so that our land may be returned to us'[9]. The long trampling upon people as inferior could not go on. The maelstrom was advancing upon Kenya rapidly as Kenneth Kaunda cycled through the Chinsali District and beyond, telling the news of Congress and singing the songs of the Christian gospel.

West and south-east of Northern Rhodesia lay the two large Portuguese 'provinces' of Angola and Mozambique. Here the 'civilising mission' of the European masters was five centuries old. But what had gone on for decades in 'the silent kingdom' had been steadily building up a corporate sense of insufferable injustice in the hearts of the defenceless African people. Here, perhaps more than anywhere else in white-ruled Africa, the authorities particularly resented the role of missionaries, especially those of the

Protestant Churches. In Angola there was a number of abortive risings against Portuguese rule, notably in 1902, 1904, 1910 and 1914, while similar unsuccessful resistance was attempted in Mozambique between 1895 and 1912. Thereafter, the rulers settled down to decades of relentless repression. Forced labour was the rule and, according to J. Duffy in his *Portuguese Africa*, Africans 'took the role of humble animals'.[10]

It is true that Northern Rhodesia could proclaim an official policy which acknowledged no colour bar and yet the whole social and economic life of the Protectorate operated on the basis of total and pervasive racial discrimination. But there was a difference. The 'white supremacists' were not left to work their own will unhindered on the 'indigenous peoples', because the 'metropolitan' authority was increasingly under pressure to apply more liberal policies. The situation that confronted the new African leaders, and especially Kenneth Kaunda and his closer associates, was one in which it was urgent to make and maintain contact with the Colonial Office in London. Daniel Sonquishe, Kaunda saw, had been right. It now seemed too late for a change in South Africa, and in Portugal's colonies, short of bloodshed. In Northern Rhodesia, however, despite the proximity of those regions of despotic oppression, there was still a chance. His activities in the 1950s were to be marked by a determination, unblighted by despair, to demonstrate the justice of his people's cause and open the way to a radically different new situation.

In the years that followed his return to Chinsali, therefore, we can trace the development of what we may call vital 'positive negatives' in his political philosophy. The only way to break the entail of racism was a dynamic non-racial approach. Its strength would lie in the basic commonsense of man whereby people know right from wrong. Similarly the only clue to the removal of violence from the crisis areas of the continent, as indeed of the world, would be positive non-violence. Violence, by its very nature, escalates. The future of Northern Rhodesia lay in checking the spiral of repression, revenge and more repression. We shall see later how the two other vital 'positive negatives' of non-alignment in foreign relations and of non-partisanship in the quest for a national political philosophy have played a vital part in Kaunda's thinking. Meanwhile it is important to note one early influence on him in particular, that of Mahatma Gandhi, the greatest apostle of non-violence.

When, as we noted above, Kenneth Kaunda and the present writer talked at length, at Lubwa in early 1947, about the future of Africa, Gandhi figured very much in their discussion. Two years later, after the Mahatma's assassination, the writer lent Kenneth a book on Gandhi which he read thoroughly, as evidenced by his thumb-marks on its pages! For Kenneth, Gandhi was not only one of the world's greatest men, besides whom, in terms of their human impact, imperialistic sabre-rattlers and arrogant racists were political pygmies. Gandhi had been personally involved in the early struggle for a better Africa. When he had gone to South Africa as a young lawyer, the plight of indentured labourers, often victims of brutal assault, had deeply concerned him as a lawyer, especially when he realised that the law laid down that, if such labourers left work, they were deemed guilty of a criminal offence. At the same time, taxation of Indians was extended. As he battled in the law courts for the victims of this system, he began thinking deeply about the great issues of humanity. 'Thus God laid the foundations of my life in South Africa,' Gandhi himself said, 'and sowed the seed of the fight for national self-respect.' His teaching, that violence was not the answer to violence, was not likely to be readily accepted however, for it involved a rare evaluation of man as the centre of all endeavour, so important that it was right to be ready to suffer in order that justice might return. As one newspaper reported of Gandhi's teaching: 'They had two ways of self-defence —to kill and be killed or to die without killing. He would teach them the latter.' This was emphatically pacifism and definitely not passivism. The right answer to aggression, Gandhi believed 'was a form of non-violent resistance which would render the fruits of aggression unobtainable by the aggressor'.[11]

Kaunda was on his travels in Southern Rhodesia when Gandhi was slain by an assassin's bullet while going to prayer on 30 January 1948. Cynics would be quick to dismiss the Mahatma as a failure in the end. But Gandhi and Jesus had a special magnetism for the twenty-four year old Kaunda. He saw them as realists with a vision and rejected the popular notion that this was a contradiction in terms. 'Gandhi,' he has said, 'tried to organise things in such a way that the state must eventually wither away—for the whole state machinery has in it the seeds of violence—when man would do to others what he would like them to do to him. If this were not possible, Jesus Christ would not have said it all. He realised that it is possible and . . . I am encouraged by this . . . . In spite of so much violence, man will come to realise that non-violence is the only way . . . . Because we have not yet attained perfection we are bound to get lost as we do from time to time.'[12]

It had been most important for Kenneth Kaunda's thinking that he had completely rejected the proposal either to amalgamate or to federate the three Central African territories; he was thus spared the pettifogging exercise of splitting hairs in an effort to marry African aspirations with white supremacy. That memorable meeting in Mufulira in 1948 when Gore-Browne had outlined his Partition plan and Kaunda and others had shouted their rejection of it and stormed out of the hall, had been for him a kind of catharsis. He had seen Simon Kapwepwe tear up a copy of the Partition proposals, shouting "The country is one and is going to remain one." He had heard Gore-Browne say that he must "get away before bricks start flying". But beyond the immediate commotion of that meeting, he had seen a vista of another kind of future altogether for his country. Henceforth the future would mean much more than the past; plans for a new nation must increasingly absorb his mind and infect the thinking of his colleagues, thus setting them free from the sterile reiteration of the wrongs done to their people. On his return to the north, as we have seen, Kaunda found many people apparently acclimatised to that 'inferiority complex' that so much troubled Harry Nkumbula. Many seemed to react as his wife, Betty, did. 'The word "Congress" . . . was spreading around the district but most of us did not understand what it was all about. . . . One day I gathered up the courage to ask him to explain what these Congress activities were and their ultimate aim. He told me that he and his friends wanted ultimately to take over the government from the hands of the European colonialists . . . . White men are very clever and powerful, I thought, how on earth could Kenneth and Makasa and Sokoni, even if helped by the villagers, take control of the country? . . . . His mother and I began to get anxious about him.' Yet, for him, that was a period of great exhilaration. The two years back at home had given him a splendid experience of the grass roots of political action. 'Now people realised, by the thousand, not only that what was happening is wrong but also that, if they come together, they can remedy the wrong.' 'In this way,' he said, 'I warmed up Chinsali to a comparatively high level of political consciousness.'[13]

The Kabwata meeting of the Congress that had replaced Mbikusita by Nkumbula as President had also appointed Kenneth Kaunda as Northern Province Organiser. This meant a vast extension of his work and was also the start of a period of sharper encounters. Soon after his return, the Governor visited the province and came to Chinsali. Kaunda and Makasa joined the official reception for the Governor at the Boma, wearing bark-cloth skirts, and this action caused immediate offence. In the confrontation that followed with the head of the Lubwa Training School, the two men argued that the Lozi ruler, Mwanawina, had worn traditional costume when receiving the British Royal visitors in 1947. Undoubtedly, their tongues were in their cheeks as they pointed out this parallel, for obviously they had decided that it was necessary to draw attention to the fact that the Governor was not on an amiable visit to his docile subjects.

Kaunda had up till then been continuing his part-time teaching, but the relationship of himself and Makasa to the mission was severed forthwith. Moreover, the use of the mission hall for Congress meetings was forbidden. The Lubwa Station Management Committee—a body established in execution of the Church of Scotland mission's policy of 'integration of Church and Mission'—had unfortunately gone into abeyance, and so the ban on Congress meetings was made by the missionary responsible for the school buildings, without consultation of the local community. In various ways, Lubwa Mission and its work in the 15,000 square miles of the Chinsali District were under a strain. The rainy season of 1951-52 found Kaunda out in the villages as much as possible, while at Lubwa and in the surrounding area resentment smouldered against his dismissal at the very time when the 'hated Federation' seemed inescapable. The continued use of special seats in the church building at Lubwa by some white people served to strengthen the feeling of ill-will. The *chilundu* incident at the Chinsali reception had not only released Kaunda for even fuller commitment to Congress work; it had released in Chinsali, even more than in neighbouring districts, a wave of united anti-Federation sentiment. In the words of one former colonial officer, 'This was a bad period. Governor

Rennie was building up the Security Forces for the coming clash on Federation. All PWD [Public Works Department] energies were concentrated on police quarters. The education officers were having to supervise their own building programmes and the standard of education naturally suffered.'[14]

At its now active headquarters in Lusaka, the Congress was intensifying its efforts to delay the coming of Federation. The case against the scheme was presented repeatedly, stressing that Federation must mean a marked reduction in the influence of Whitehall on the territory's affairs. Referring to 'treaties and agreements between Her Majesty's Government, Queen Victoria and the African chiefs', the Congress stated that 'the African Chiefs sought British Protection', rather than Portuguese, German or Belgian, 'because they had a certain amount of trust and confidence in the representatives of the British Government.' This, they said, had 'remained unshaken until the intentions of the officials who produced the Closer Association Report were made known'. Here was interesting evidence of the fact that fifty years after the conquests which we recounted in Chapter I, there had developed a widespread acceptance of the 'official' history of the acquisition of the territory which presented it as 'protection' granted in response to the requests of chiefs. More important, however, the statement testified to the good relations which had been built up between a notable number of colonial civil servants and the local people in the preceding two decades.[15]

In February 1952, there was what Kaunda called 'a very explosive conference' of the Congress at which the complete rejection of the Federation plan was voiced by a number of delegates, including Simon Zukas. Also present was Commander Thomas Fox-Pitt, who had been in provincial administration for a number of years but had been 'retired' because 'his part in politics embarrassed the government.' The cynical attitude of the new regime in London was quickly felt. One of its influential members had said, after a visit to Northern Rhodesia, that the way to deal with a man like Nkumbula was to 'give him £40 a month and he would eat out of your hand'.[16] Huggins was openly appreciative of Lyttelton's attitude and had succeeded in persuading Governor Rennie to espouse Federation whole-heartedly. But though the 'moderate' view had been expressed by Safeli Chileshe that, since the territory could not remain static, 'responsible Africans' would give earnest consideration to the Closer Association Report, huge African gatherings on the Copperbelt totally rejected it. At Kitwe it was declared that 'Africans have at heart the strong feeling of becoming a nation within the Commonwealth.'[17]

There was now, Nkumbula declared, 'a rising tide of nationalism'.[18] While the political ferment mounted, the industrial scene was far from peaceful and the Government must have been troubled by the fact that the unsettled Copperbelt was giving such full support to the new Congress line. The past year had seen a marked growth in the authority of the African Mine Workers' Union which even the *Northern News* had praised as having 'gained greatly in prestige.'[19] A strong African Railway Workers' Union had recently been formed, and the British National Union of Mineworkers had endorsed the significance of the growth of trade unionism by inviting Lawrence Katilungu, the pioneer trade unionist, and other union leaders to visit Britain. In response to the swift escalation of the whole situation in the territory, the February Conference of Congress established a Supreme Action Council which Sikalumbi describes as consisting of nine members 'including five seats to be filled by the Trade Union Congress . . . to be empowered to issue orders for action in the name of Congress up to and including the serious step of calling for a national stoppage of work . . . [and] call for mass action at any moment during the time of the Federation crisis that they think tactically wise.'

A statement from the Action Council added that, if Federation were imposed, 'there would be a total stoppage of work in the territory, chiefs would be asked to stop people going to the towns, and women and children in in the Copper Belt would be sent to their villages.'[20] Kenneth Kaunda, who was a member of this new body, recorded that 'the Executive Council was left to deal with ordinary matters but the Supreme Action Council was to direct the fight against Federation.' The sharpness of the Attorney-General's reaction to the news of this action was such that the Congress replied by publicly declaring that its action had been forced upon it 'by the refusal of the Government of the UK and of NR to pay attention to the unanimous opposition' to Federation. As feeling ran high, members went out to buy red ties to show that they were ready to shed blood for their country. Undoubtedly the ties were seen by their opponents as proof of Communist leanings.[21]

When Kenneth Kaunda reached home, news awaited him of a local crisis. The new Missionary-in-Charge, he was told, had made reference, from the pulpit, to Congress which had displeased some of the local committee. In fact, the sermon in question had been based on words in John's Gospel about the 'voice of the Son of God'. The missionary had referred to the various voices that kept on calling for men's allegiance and spoken of the disturbing voice of Welensky in Central Africa. He then said that, since Christians must 'test every spirit', the answer of 'hate for hate' must also be rejected by them. At the same time, charges of seditious action had been laid against Simon Zukas and, despite a vigorous Congress campaign to raise funds for his defence, evidence against him had been given by Godwin Mbikusita. News of his deportation to Britain was made public on the first of March. Soon afterwards Kaunda was on his way to a meeting in Broken Hill of the Supreme Action Council which was far from happy. The absence of a number of members was cause for alarm and it looked as though fear of harsh Government action might be going to frustrate the Council's programme. It was at that time that, as he has recorded, he posted a 'terribly angry letter to the missionaries at Lubwa'.[22]

The letter was two and one half pages in length, closely typed. It interpreted the missionary's sermon as 'preaching . . . the preservation' of the white race and quoted a passage from George Bernard Shaw's *Man of Destiny*, which said that "when he [the Englishman] wants a new market for his adulterated Manchester goods, he sends a missionary to teach the Natives the Gospel of Peace. The natives kill the missionary; he flies in arms to the defence of Christianity; fights for it, conquers for it; and takes the market as a reward from heaven." The letter then said that the African people 'killed no European in this protectorate and we are going to make sure we kill no European, missionary or otherwise for political reasons. . . . We are not struggling against the British Government but against the Federal case.' Some months elapsed before the misunderstanding about the message of that sermon was resolved. It had revealed the tenseness of the atmosphere and the need for much closer cooperation in a situation in which the missionary concerned was being increasingly marked by Government for the anti-Federation convictions which he shared with a number of his colleagues. As Kenneth was travelling through the province now and living at his farm, a few miles from Lubwa, he and the missionary did not meet again for some months.[23]

The Kaunda family was finding life far from easy in those days for lack of money. Kenneth's salary as a teacher had stopped abruptly after the *chilundu* incident and his monthly allowance as a Congress Provincial Organiser amounted to £10 at most and came in very infrequently. The patches of cloth which Betty had brought home in a bundle from Mufulira were now required to extend the life of well-worn clothes. As the Congress allowance had to be used for food and transport costs when Kenneth was touring the province, very little of it could be spared for house-keeping. As his father had been on behalf of the church and the schools, he was now *chendaluta*, the tireless traveller for Congress, very seldom seen at home. As he sat by crackling fires under the stars in village after village, his guitar on his knee, he would sing hymns with the people and teach them new songs of national aspiration, unaware of any clash between their themes. 'Fierce raged the tempest o'er the deep,' rendered in Bemba, was among his favourite hymns. Easily he would move from it to a composition of his own, knowing that his hearers knew well what he was singing about:

'Others cry out for smart berets;
We cry for our country.
Others cry out for suits;
We cry for the iron in our soil.
Our wealth has been taken from us,
Alas, our iron.
Mothers, cease your weeping;
Fathers, do not cry.
I ask, "What are you going to do about it?" '[24]

At the end of the rainy season of 1952, Harry Nkumbula made a tour of the Northern Province and paid a brief visit to Shamba-lakale. 'He was a VIP,' Betty Kaunda has recorded, 'and treated so majestically that we women wondered what sort of food would be suitable for him.'[25] There was of course a meeting of the Chinsali Branch of Congress at which the National President spoke of their determination to oppose Federation. Lubwa was very near, and

Nkumbula came by car and met some of the residents, but did not visit the missionary staff. Keen interest was shown by Chinsali people in the forthcoming delegation to London which the Congress was sponsoring and for which funds were urgently required. In three weeks, £3,000 were raised throughout the territory. When in fact the delegation reached London, it was unable to do much more than pour the sorrows of the African people into the sympathetic ears of some Labour Party friends. Yet Nkumbula's statement was clear and incisive: entrenched protective clauses for the majority in a minority-ruled state were of little or no value. 'The only safeguard is the African himself when he is able to stand on his own feet and defend his rights . . . until then we shall not consider it [Federation].'[26]

At this period, in Kaunda's own words, 'old Harry was tops.' In a typed statement to a public meeting in Lusaka in June, Nkumbula emphasised his view that Welensky, 'a Pole of humble education,' was strenuously inveigling 'feeble-minded British people in Northern Rhodesia' into a scheme whereby the territory would be opened to continental European immigrants. So, he said, 'I must say one thing that I have always avoided . . . the best government for the Black people is government fully manned and run by the Black people of Africa. This is also true of any race . . . I do not accept Welensky's or Huggins' Governments. They are to me foreign and foreign they shall remain.' Shortly after issuing this circular, Nkumbula reported on 'the first delegation to Britain to campaign against Federation' and gave a new slogan: 'Change of power from the white minorities to the legitimate black majorities'. The imposition of Federation against the wishes of six million Africans would 'make life intolerable for the Whites in Central Africa'.[27] Such a remark could not pass unheeded. 'Here is the true basis of African opposition to Federation,' said the London Committee of the United Central Africa Association. 'It is the crudest and most dangerous kind of racialism.'[28]

Events were accelerating now, and official reaction to the situation revealed mounting disquiet. Worried that a meeting of Chiefs called by Congress might well 'pass an anti-Federation resolution', the Eastern Provincial Commissioner urged that 'we ought to do all we can . . . e.g. by warning chiefs . . . that they are being bamboozled by Congress.'[29] When Clement Attlee, leader of the British Labour

Party, visited the Protectorate in August 1952, he met with thirteen Chiefs, the two African M.L.C.s and four politically-minded men who were listed in the sederunt as interpreters. The Chiefs, however, were unanimous in their opposition to Federation and the record of the meeting, produced by the Congress, reveals Attlee's impatience with this consensus. 'I see you don't want to federate with Southern Rhodesia and that all safeguards are useless: is that so?' 'Yes', replied all thirteen Chiefs, 'it is so.'[30]

The Government reacted swiftly, and Kaunda's autobiography gives an extract from a meeting of the S.N.A. with the Chiefs four days later. As it was the ANC that had called the Chiefs to meet Attlee in Lusaka, 'the Secretary for Native Affairs, through the District Commissioner, Lusaka, sent two District Messengers to ask the African National Congress to allow the Chiefs to see him on 23rd August, 1952.' Despite this odd tangle of protocol, the S.N.A. warned the Chiefs not to surrender their power to Congress and not to support it financially. Kaunda's comment stressed that this was a grave turning-point. 'The DIVIDE AND RULE policy had never been more openly displayed. From this time, the campaign of persecution and prosecution of Congress men and women was fully launched and some terrible things were done in the name of maintaining law and order.'[31]

Welensky's confidence, however, was growing and the Government's hands were increasingly tied. As, day after day, he figured in the *Northern News*, someone suggested that its name should be changed to 'The Welensky News'. The British Government's Harry Hopkinson declared blandly that African 'pro-Federationists were intimidated and so could not speak.' The press meanwhile publicised an attack on the Federal scheme as an attempt to impose outdated ideas on the Rhodesias. Power must be transferred directly to White Rhodesians, it said.[32] Into this ferment, the Congress made a proposal for phased progress towards 'a self-governing state of Northern Rhodesia', and the ANC position was strengthened by the acceptance of the proposed constitution by the Chiefs and Delegates Conference which had been held in Lusaka at the time of Attlee's visit. Nkumbula's Presidential Address hailed the conference as 'the first time in the history of this country that Chiefs and Commoners . . . have been able to come together to discuss matters that affect them and their country'. He referred with concern to the arrival of twenty-seven armoured cars from Kenya and an air detachment from the Middle East 'to intimidate our struggle against Federation'. In conclusion, he said that he was aware that his recent statement about the necessity of 'government fully manned and run by the black people' had caused uneasiness among Europeans. In view of this disquiet, the Congress now proposed phased progress towards self-government, whereby racial minorities would be well represented. The forty members of an Upper House or Senate, with power to veto legislation passed by the Lower House, would comprise four equal groups, representing the following sections of the population: African Commoners; Europeans; Asians and Euro-Africans; and African Chiefs. The Governor would be Head of State under the Queen.[33]

This Congress proposal was a serious attempt to reassure Europeans and Asians that, under a system whereby the vote would be extended to Africans as British Protected Persons, their interests would not be submerged. But Britain had, as Hopkinson publicly stated, decided to stand 'one hundred per cent behind the Federal Plan', and only a division of European opinion in Southern Rhodesia could now prevent its execution. The Chiefs pleaded in vain for an end of the punitive deposition of Chiefs by Government for their support of the people's cause, whereby 'the prestige and honour of chieftainships' was suffering.[34] Governor Rennie, however, offered no formulae of reassurance for the Africans of the Protectorate, as though unaware that Welensky, a few weeks earlier, had made his famous 'Red Indian' speech, and used words which had reverberated to the far corners of the land. "I say this to the Africans: ... if they do not come with us, they will meet the same fate which came to the Red Indians in the United States of America: they disappeared."[35]

Despite all the blood and thunder of 'cowboy and Indian' films, the details of the extermination of countless Red Indians in the westward surge of the American colonists were not likely to be known to either white or black in Northern Rhodesia when Welensky made that threat that he claimed was not one. Even today, few realise the dimensions of the strategy of extinction that opened their 'Canaan' to the land-hungry invaders from Europe. What everyone did know was that the Red Indian peoples had virtually vanished from their ancestral lands. Nearer home, as we have seen, white conquest in Africa had been characterised by ruthless exploitation, dispossession and oppression. Now, as Nkumbula was voicing his people's serious questioning of the 'treaties' by which their rulers had taken the country from its owners, Welensky's careless utterance was bound to be heard as a brutal threat, especially since, as the Revd. Paul Mushindo told the S.N.A., many Africans regarded him as an 'honest man who . . . reveals many white men's feelings in Central Africa against Africans . . . what many Europeans think and plan against Africans'.[36] The times were certainly 'out of joint', and rumour—always a powerful factor in history—rooted everywhere like rank weeds. Welensky's 'Red Indian' speech was like a deliberate broadcast of the seeds of such a noxious growth.

This was the period when the Capricorn Africa Society was beginning its activities. Under the leadership of Colonel David Stirling, this 'multi-racial' organisation proclaimed as its aims the abolition of all forms of racial discrimination, the preservation of the best elements of all cultures, the establishment of a common patriotism for all races and the attainment of a territorial Constitution which would guarantee equal freedom of speech, religion, association, access to public services and to the qualifications required for the practise of any trade, profession or calling. 'All men of whatever race,' it declared, 'are born equal in dignity before God.' 'The outstanding responsibility placed on the individual is the exercise of the vote' and so 'Caprafrica' believed that 'this right must be EARNED by the individual.'[37] For a number of years it carried on extensive publicity, but made little impact, though Ndabaningi Sithole of Rhodesia described it, seven years later, as 'one of the few beacons of hope in multi-racial Africa'.[38] In the eyes of Kaunda and his associates, 'Capricorn was dirty because of the people using it.'[39] Rotberg has stated bluntly that 'Welensky . . . paid Frank Kaluwa, an agent of the Capricorn African Society, to "sell" Federation to rural Rhodesians.' Pages of a diary, believed to have been that of one Abel Nyirenda, reported his visits in 1952, to various Chiefs and leading citizens, including Congress members, in a persistent attempt to persuade them of the benefits of Federation. Congress files for the period include a number of letters from members to Nkumbula hotly disclaiming any associations with Capricorn. Chiefs were told by Nyirenda that they would 'go up in Federation'. Most significantly, he also reported meeting Welensky and receiving from him an advance of £20 plus £10 for travelling expenses. Nine days later he sent a telegram to Welensky 'for more travelling expenses'.[40]

Despite the high-sounding aims of Capricorn Africa, it fell into immediate disrepute with the men who looked for a resolution of the Central Africa dilemma which would remove from the Welenskyites the power to call the tune. In a situation of perilous non-communication, Fox-Pitt pinpointed the threat of the interplay of dark fears. To this 'that great statesman Welensky', added the 'scare of a Communist master-plan behind all African disturbances', so that, trading on the current Foster Dulles phobia in world affairs, he 'need make no further effort to produce a sane and civilised solution to the problems that produce unrest'.[41] Thus the words 'Capricornist' and 'informer' had become terms of abuse and, as Sikalumbi has said, 'by the use of these two names, many responsible, well-to-do or reasonable Africans were temporarily forced into oblivion . . . to the disadvatage of Congress and the country . . . . This type of propaganda created hatred and mistrust both among Africans and between Africans and Europeans'.[42]

Nineteen fifty-three thus began gloomily. As Gann graphically wrote, 'suspicion stalked the land; and Federation to many became a magical word of evil.'[43] But the new year found Kaunda already an experienced field organiser. For weeks he was on tour without communication with either his home or the Congress headquarters. In order to establish branches of the Congress as well as answer the many queries of both supporters and doubters, he tried to spend adequate time in the villages. Because of the difficulty of keeping in touch with what was going on elsewhere, he felt when he reached a Boma that, in his own words, 'it was as if it was daylight'. His longest trip lasted three months and was made in the latter part of the wet season of 1953. It took him from Chinsali north through the Isoka District, where he spent time helping to find suitable men to serve as Chairmen and Secretaries for the newly formed ANC branches. With not a penny in his pocket, he had to depend on local hospitality. Between the mission station at Mwenzo and Mbala he witnessed the birth of two branches, one of them at Chief Nsokolo's court. It was there that he had lengthy conversations with a research scholar who was studying the economy of the Mambwe

people, and who inspired Kenneth with a number of lively suggestions.[44] Nsokolo supported the Congress openly and organised
the collection of funds to be sent to its Lusaka headquarters.
Moreover, he had attended the Chiefs and Delegates Conference
mentioned above. Kaunda was sure that his eventual deposition
was on account of this support. Boma and police plainclothes
agents were never far away as he travelled, and so the reactions of
Chiefs and Headmen to the Congress were bound to be noted.[45] In
Chinsali, a rumour spread that Boma Messengers were announcing
'an order from the Boma that people should not pay extra money
to the chief, money which was mostly to counteract Federation'.
Kenneth therefore wrote to the D.C. 'with all the respect . . . that
I hold for a European officer', that if this were true, he could 'see
nothing but the fall in grade of the long respected BRITISH
JUSTICE and FAIR PLAY and the beginning of serious misunderstanding in the already sickening and suffocating atmosphere of
RACIAL DISCRIMINATION . . . . To my knowledge, people
are told what they are donating for and do so on the basis of loving
their precious land and their posterity and I wonder if messengers
have a right to interfere.'[46]

In Kasama, using the local African Institute as a base of operations, Kaunda was able to exploit the exceptional enthusiasm of
Joel Nkhata, the District Organising Secretary, and to be sure that
there would be no friction between ANC and the Institute.
Nkhata accompanied him on some of his journeys in the area
around Kasama on which they had to wait sometimes for hours
for swollen streams to subside. As people were eating food made
from millet, *bwali bwa male*, which Kaunda found indigestible,
he had to be content on various occasions with a tiny dish of beans.
All the time he was looking for men who would be ready to bear
the strain of the coming struggle. A number appeared who 'would
hold posts at the level of branch and constituency officials but were
not bold enough to face what they knew would be coming'.

Looking back, he has commented that his provincial tours did
not succeed in discovering many who would stay on until the
end of the struggle. 'I had many friends at home,' he said, 'but
Simon and Makasa and Sokoni stood out clearly.'[47]

On these journeys he carried what he later called 'a friend who
never leaves my bookshelf', Ralph Waldo Trine's *In Tune with*

the Infinite. At the end of this book there is a section entitled 'A Resolve for Today' which may be seen as shedding light on the mystical pragmatism of Kaunda's character: 'I believe that my Master intended that I take His teachings in the simple, frank, and open manner in which He gave them, out on the hill-side, by the calm blue waters of the Galilean sea, and out under the stars of heaven. I believe that He knew what He meant, and that He meant what He said, when He gave the substance of all religion and the duty of man as love to God, and love and service for His fellowmen . . . . I am resolved in all human contact to meet petulance with patience, questionings with kindness, hatred with love, eager always to do the kindly deed that brings the joy of service—and that alone makes human life truly human. I shall seek no advantage for myself to the detriment or the harm of my neighbour, knowing that it is only through the law of mutuality that I can fully enjoy what I gain—or can even be a man.'[48] Kenneth's long absences from home, however, made his family wonder if he was just trying to dodge his responsibilities.

Looking back, Kenneth Kaunda has said that the tremendous potential support on the Copperbelt and among the Chiefs for the anti-Federation cause was not exploited as it should have been. 'I think we were really afraid for our skins . . . we just managed to get to the verge of getting to prison and then withdrew.' If the organising machinery had been developed and the real feelings of the great majority of the people articulated, 'no British Government would have dared impose Federation on us.'[49] Welensky and his friends overseas were aware of this. In particular, the British Secretary for Commonwealth Relations, Lord Salisbury, expressed the urgency of accomplishing Federation, before African opposition increased 'and you might have trouble'. The most understandable 'fear for their skins' on the part of the Africans—in a situation in which the overwhelming physical power in the hands of the authorities was being rapidly expanded—would lessen, Salisbury knew, if Britain temporised. After the imposition of Federation, the repository of power would be the Huggins/Welensky regime and Britain would have successfully washed her hands of the dilemma. As the Kenya crisis escalated and more and more British ground and air strength was committed to the Mau Mau conflict, it would be a welcome relief to leave Central African security in Federal hands.

In this mood, Lyttelton approved the Huggins/Welensky demand that, if there must be an 'African Affairs Board', it should be incorporated into the Federal parliamentary structure. Yet there was, in fact, no lack of sane and serious counsels in Britain to point out the gravity of the situation. 'The fundamental error we are making in Africa,' the *London Observer* had warned, 'is to place people in a position which offers them no peaceful and constitutional way of expressing their grievances and getting these redressed. We are driving them into enmity and towards violence.'[50]

At this point, it is important to summarise some of the main events of the first months of 1953. The Congress held a conference in January in London with Chief Mpezeni of the Ngoni, an English lawyer named Bryden and Commander Fox-Pitt on the crucial land-ownership issue. The proceedings of the Conference revealed the almost unlimited powers which had been claimed for the British Crown by the Foreign Jurisdiction Act of 1894. By the formula of jurisdiction by cession or conquest, it had provided the basis for a long series of Orders-in-Council dealing with the disposition of land. As one jurist had said, 'It matters not how the acquisition has been brought about.' The Crown had absolute power, and no inhabitant of such 'acquired' territories could look for redress, for 'such rights as he had under the rule of predecessors avail him nothing'.[51]

Harry Hopkinson, Minister of State at the Colonial Office, had exclaimed, on his burlesque African tour, that 'African opinion on the subject [of Federation] hardly exists.' The postponement of the scheme would 'invite contempt for Britain's ability to rule and . . . mean victory to an African political minority', which would give them 'authority to be nationalistic'.[52] But Harry Nkumbula, in a special statement on the Federal White Paper of January 1953 depicted a situation in which, in the face of known African aversion, extensive repression was being mounted. He said this to an audience of over eight hundred and in the presence of a number of Chiefs, with Kaunda translating his speech into Bemba. He referred to secret official missives on the security situation and to Welensky's 'threats of the extermination of the Black Race'. He saw the European domination of both the territorial legislatures and the proposed Federal Assembly as proof that the next step after Federation would be Amalgamation with Dominion status. He found no reassurance

in the proposed status and composition of the African Affairs
Board. Because of the gravity of the situation, he announced that,
on that evening, a copy of the White Paper would be burned.
'Should Federation be imposed,' he warned, 'measures would be
taken to paralyse the industries of this country' with the full support
of African trade union leaders. Finally, he proclaimed a 'two-day
national prayer' against Federation to be held on first and second
April. The 'White Paper' was then solemnly burned.[53] Within a
few days after issuing this statement, Nkumbula and the ANC
Treasurer, Safeli Chileshe, circulated an 'appeal to all Africans,
Europeans, Indians and Euro-Africans who believe in building
a sound social pattern', for £10,000 to erect an inter-racial social
centre in Lusaka, under the auspices of the Congress.[54]

An interesting account of the rally at Chilenje in Lusaka has
been provided by a European broadcaster who was present. Recalling
Nkumbula's speech, he wrote: 'I had expected a spell-binder, a
fiery demagogue, but he spoke with all the detachment and manner-
isms of touring district commissioners, and like them he spoke
through interpreters.' What aroused the crowd was the burning
of the White Paper. 'Women ululated shrilly. Fists were clenched.
"Kill them! Kill them!" shouted a hoarse voice near me.' There
were banners bearing the words: 'Self-government our only ultimate
goal'. The broadcaster had noted at once that Nkumbula was
greeted by the Ngoni royal salutation, '*Bayete*'. 'We [the Europeans]
were creating new loyalties: Bemba and Ngoni, chiefs and radical
politicians, were all getting together to oppose Federation.' After
the burning, the crowd broke into singing again, 'another song of
Kenneth Kaunda's, full of allegory about Northern Rhodesia's
coat of arms, the fish eagle holding a fish in its talons:
"Vultures are flying high and low.
Brothers, watch the vultures!
What will they pick up next?
What will they pick up next?
A fish—or something bigger?
Brothers, allow them no more,
Allow them no more!
They are coming armed with sharp beaks,
To frighten the live
And to feast on the dead.

Where are you brothers?
Where are you brothers?
Are you watching?"
'Here was the essential allegorism of old Africa, which projected
its anthropopathism upon the birds and the beasts. What *were*
Africans thinking?' that broadcaster kept asking himself and was
given this answer one day, on the eve of Federation by a petrol
pump attendant, 'Without land, we shall be as wild pigs driven
from place to place.'[55] The crowd at Chilenje represented a concentration of emotions that Huggins and Welensky did not know
existed, evidenced in the solemn personal promise which was
required of those attending the conference of Congress delegates,
trade unionists and representatives of other African organisations,
at Kitwe in March 1953: 'I promise to the Almighty God that
because the proposed federal plan is a wicked plan I shall continue
to fight against it. I shall be ready to perform any services that this
national movement shall require of me until the liberation of my
people from white domination.'[56] The Protectorate was smouldering
ominously.
    The two days of National Prayer were not as successful as
Nkumbula had hoped, though certainly not, as Gann describes
them, 'a resounding failure'.[57] The effect on Lusaka's Chilanga
Cement Works was noted by a *Northern News* cartoonist. Lawrence
Katilungu, President of the African Mine-Workers' Union, was
not ready to lend his union's services to the occasion, though he
claimed to be in personal support of the idea. It may be, as Kaunda
has said, that the trade unions had been built up by Katilungu
'on such a luxurious basis' that not many trade unionists were
prepared to go to prison. But a considerable number of clerks in
Government employ observed the two days, were promptly dismissed, and at once became full members of Congress. Nkumbula
himself claimed that the 'national prayer' was a good cover for
the real political purpose of the occasion. Though the number who
responded was small, the two days have a rightful place in history.
The event drew public attention and indeed sparked a rumour of
Nkumbula's imminent deportation. Coming soon after Nkumbula's
open challenge to the churches on the Federation issue, it undoubtedly quickened both anger and serious thought among white
churchmen in particular.[58]

More significantly, the two days brought before Nkumbula's listeners the need to consider the use of strikes and boycotts as political weapons. It also gave him an occasion, a few days later, to address another gathering and offer an assessment of the value of the two days. He now claimed that, by instructing employers to dismiss participants, and by evicting them from their houses, the Government was using intimidation. Charges and counter-charges of intimidation were thereafter to be a constant feature of the political struggle. 'We have warned the Government they cannot hope to have that economic progress with a labour force so wounded in their own hearts by the imposition of a plan which is so subtly designed as to rob them of their elementary human rights . . . The Central African Federation would . . . bleed to death.' Nkumbula went on to speak of reports of a huge gathering in the Eastern Province and of Government threats against Chiefs there. He declared that 'the Congress policy involves among other things, nonco-operation and passive resistance but without violence.' Those who were not prepared to suffer should say so at once.[59]

The news of the recent formation of a cinema club 'for approved members of the African community' could only add a tiny touch of comedy to the situation. What mattered was that the final plans for Federation had been initialled in London, and the signed plea of 120 Chiefs to the Queen for 'your protection until there is a government in this country in which we shall feel safe' brought no response. Increasingly the Congress headquarters were now receiving letters urging them, for instance, to declare the country independent of Britain in the event of Federation being established. Meanwhile Dr. Alexander Scott, of the *Central African Post*, addressed the Congress and urged them to oppose Federation peacefully. The United Federal Party was established in May, and on first June it was announced that Welensky was to be knighted. There was talk of a multi-racial university for Central Africa, and the House of Commons in London began a debate of the Federal Bill, which concerned itself mainly with questions of how African interests might be safeguarded.[60]

June was to witness a new wave of *apartheid* legislation in South Africa under Verwoerd; and intensification of bombing raids against the Mau Mau, especially in Kenya's Aberdare region; the announcement of the resignation of eight Nyasa Chiefs as an anti-

Federation protest; an instruction by Governor Rennie to African teachers to 'keep out of politics', and a number of brave attempts to make a success of special celebrations on second June for the coronation of Queen Elizabeth II. In Broken Hill, ANC was able to block an inter-racial march and persuaded Africans to boycott the ceremony.[61] In Kaunda's home area, the coronation was marked by partly concealed tremors. Children from village schools, some over a hundred miles away, streamed into Chinsali Boma, many of them wearing the little coronation badges which had been distributed by the Provincial Education Officer through mission school managers. Chief Nkula was late for the ceremony, and so the youngsters formed themselves into a long column, little ones at the front and older pupils at the back. Walking, rather than marching, as if to pass the time, they sang their way through a repertory of songs often sung at school firelight concerts. 'The Paper Football', 'Rabbit told you', and 'Let us praise our teachers' were sung, as the concourse of adults waited wearily. The repertory included another song which was often heard in the schools at that time: '*Cha bulanda, cha bulanda, Basungu bapoke chalo chesu*'— 'It is sad, it is sad. The white people have taken our country.' Some more songs were sung and then at last the Chief appeared, and a brief formal ceremony took place, which included the planting of a tree. No member of the local community was willing to do the planting, however. As the company dispersed, and the children went to eat and prepare for the long walk home, at least superficially it seemed as though Chinsali had celebrated 'successfully'. However, under the heading 'Youth Misleaders' the magazine *East Africa and Rhodesia* reported that the House of Lords in London had heard of the coronation occasion at Chinsali. Lord Noel-Buxton had said schoolchildren threw away and stamped on their coronation medals and 'sang a near-seditious song as they marched past the DC'. 'What', asked the lord, 'has the Department of African Education . . . to say to this incident?' The explanation of the incident, said the magazine, must be sought 'outside juvenile circles'.[62]

But Nkumbula took the opportunity, far away in Lusaka, to mark the day by another declaration which questioned Britain's legal right to impose Federation on the Protectorate, and warned that H.M.G.'s 'desired strategy to combat infiltration of the

Malanite philosophy and that of the Soviet Union' was being based
on 'a sandy foundation'. Marxism would not provide an answer
to Central African problems, he affirmed, but nonetheless it might
'find a fertile ground on an angered people'. Congress was pledged
to non-violence but there could be no guarantee that violence
could be avoided. People must not go on selling their labour to
white men for wages. 'Get back to the land,' he called, 'before the
landgrubbing [sic] settlers have taken the last inch of your soil.'⁶³
Almost immediately, a wave of anti-colour bar demonstrations
began, at first mainly in Ndola and Broken Hill, and a few people,
including Dixon Konkola, were arrested. The *Northern News*
reported that 'passers-by generally ignored the demonstrators.' The
Lusaka boycott of butcheries was led by Safeli Chileshe, a man of
gracious manner and tact, and was effected without serious incident.
But the *Northern News* carried bitter letters against the publication
of a photograph of the daughter of Sir Stafford Cripps and her
African fiancé. The Christian Council, however, reiterated its
'deep concern' over the imposition of Federation. In Luanshya,
the Chamber of Commerce called for 'courtesy to *bona fide* African
customers', while the local African Urban Advisory Council
condemned recent incidents 'provoked elsewhere by groups of
hot-headed Africans'. On first August, the Queen signed an Order-
in-Council by which the Federation of Rhodesia and Nyasaland was
formally established.⁶⁴

As a member of the Supreme Action Group, Kenneth Kaunda
was now more closely in touch with Congress headquarters activities.
But he was devoting as much time as possible to his work as Provincial Organiser in the north, and his thoughts were long and serious.
He has recalled how, on the evening of a day of hard cycling with
Robert Makasa, they had had to stop to mend a puncture. It was
after midnight when they finished the repair, and suddenly Kaunda
said 'What would happen if all the big leaders of Africa—Nkrumah,
Kenyatta, the Nigerians—all met to discuss?' They had not then
heard of Julius Nyerere, Milton Obote or General Nasser, but they
talked at some length of the common problems the African leaders
could share if they met. But as they gathered the people in the
villages, they were aware of increasing depression. People had
thought of the struggle as only against the threat of Federation.
When the news came that Her Majesty in London had signed the

fatal instrument, many thought, 'It's now finished.' Kenneth has said that this is what made the issue of a nonviolent struggle against Federation most important. For him the matter was not settled. Rather what had happened was that the battle had been joined. But by any statistical reckoning, the African ranks were pathetically weak in the face of the high confidence of Welensky's followers. Naturally the glowing picture of swift economic advance led many anxious hearts to hope that after all the future might be better than they feared. It was clear that a number of 'moderate men' would grope for some form of compromise. It was alarming to Kaunda that even Nkumbula should have momentarily come out in support of Partition as an alternative to Federation. 'This was a trend in the old fellow, that when he came against a blank wall, he always wanted an escape route.' Instead he himself was searching for a deeper philosophy and, as his autobiography mentions, he was reading the life of Abraham Lincoln and a variety of writings on the Indian independence struggle. Interestingly, Arthur Mee's *Talks to Boys* also gave him food for thought at that time. His memories of provincial touring include an alarming encounter with a lion.[65]

In July, the Congress Secretary sent out calls to provincial delegates to come to Lusaka for a conference. The notice addressed to the Chinsali Branch found Kenneth and his baby son, Panji, both ill. Because of their great confidence in Dr. John Todd, who had gone from Lubwa to rebuild the hospital at Chitambo, he and Betty decided to have the little boy treated by him. Betty has described the vicissitudes of that journey and how, when she eventually reached the bus stop, four miles from Chitambo, she heard that Kenneth had just passed on his way south to Lusaka.[66] For the 400 delegates gathered in the Chilenje Welfare Hall, the mood of the conference was inevitably gloomy. Sikalumbi has recalled that Nkumbula, 'with a fallen heart', expressed the view that there was nothing to be gained by boycotting the two seats assigned to Northern Rhodesian Africans in the Federal Assembly. New ways of resisting Federation must be devised, he said, and obviously this was the view of most delegates. The conference, realising the dangers of any one Congress standing alone, resolved to organise a regional 'Pan-African Conference'. It then proceeded to elect its executive committee and the list of the new 'Cabinet' called forth a comment from the *Central African Post* to the effect that Nkumbula was now the only moderate.[67]

The atmosphere was very tense as nominations were made and elections, by secret ballot, took place; for it was clear that, despite the despair, there was a new militancy in the air. The committee included Konkola, now on the honours list as a 'prison graduate', Paskale Sokota, M.L.C., Robinson Puta and Job Mayanda. The election of a Secretary brought the tension to its height and Nkumbula knew he must find a completely independent person to count the votes. A journalist who was covering the conference, Frank Barton, was asked to check the ballot and it was soon clear that the winner had a very large majority. The new Secretary-General was the man whose outstanding field work in his home province was now well-known, Kenneth Kaunda. As he stood up, dressed in an old shirt and well-worn shorts, the delegates cheered uproariously. The shy, determined, tireless young rural organiser had captured their confidence. His appointment resulted in the first appearance of his name in what claimed to be the national newspaper, the *Northern News*. Solemnly the Congress resolved to examine its attitude to the African members of the Federal Parliament. It also agreed, after discussions with both the A.R.C. and the African T.U.C., to set up a national council to continue the struggle against Federation, in consultation with the sister bodies in Southern Rhodesia and Nyasaland.[68]

---

[1]P. Keatley, *The Politics of Partnership* (Penguin, 1963), 299-300.
[2]See L. and N. Rubin, *This is Apartheid* (Christian Action, 1965) for a summary of S. African racist legislation; and E. H. Brookes and J. B. Macaulay, *Civil Liberty in South Africa* (Oxford, 1958), 5.
[3]See M. Benson, *The Struggle for a Birthright* (Penguin, 1963); and A. Luthuli, *Let my People Go* (Fontana, 1962), 175 and 210 (Appendix B) for text of Freedom Charter.
[4]See SA House of Assembly Debates, 17/5/49; Davidson, *Report* p. 62, quoting S. H. Fraenkel, *Capital Investment in S. Africa* (Macmillan, 1938), 127; and 28, quoting Dr. Eiselen, Head of Native Affairs Department. Population returns of SA Bureau of Statistics, 2/10/67, were:

Africans	..	..	..	12,750,000
Whites	..	..	..	3,563,000
Coloureds	..	..	..	1,859,000
Indians	..	..	..	561,000
				18,733,000

[5]Rotberg, *Rise*, p. 237.
[6]See G. Martelli, *Leopold to Lumumba* (Chapman and Hall, 1962); C. Legum, *Congo*

Disaster (Harmandsworth, 1961); and B. Davidson, *Africa Awakening*, 62-82.

[7]See J. Iliffe, 'Tanzania under German and British Rule,' in *Zamani*, ed. B. A. Ogot and J. A. Kieran (E.A.P.H. and Longmans, 1968), 290 ff; and note that Nyerere was studying at Edinburgh University from 1949-52. See his *Freedom and Unity* (Oxford, 1967), for extracts from an unpublished paper of that period on 'The Race Problem in East Africa' (pp. 23-29), which confirms the similarity between his early thinking and that of Kaunda, though they did not meet until 1958.

[8]See B. A. Ogot, 'Kenya under the British, 1895 to 1963,' in Ogot, *op. cit.*, 255 ff.

[9]L. S. B. Leakey, *Defeating Mau Mau* (Methuen, 1954), 53 ff.

[10](Cambridge, Mass. 1959), 154.

[11]See H. S. Polak *et. al.*, *Mahatma Gandhi* (Odhams, 1948), and esp. pp. 308-310.

[12]TI-FM/KK, 4/9/72.

[13]TI-FM/KK, 13/2/69; Mpashi, *op. cit.*, pp. 29-30; and NAZ: Sec/Nat/660, Chinsali District Reports 1950 and 1951, which noted increasing Congress activity led by Kaunda and Makasa.

[14]SOAS: Fox-Pitt Papers, Pkt. 34, p. 34 (August 1950).

[15]ANC/2/7, memo. of 4/8/51, and ANC/2/4, memo. of 11/9/51.

[16]*Zambia*, p. 46; SOAS: Fox-Pitt Papers, Pkt. 34, pp. 24-26

[17]*NN* for period, especially 6/2/51, 20/2/55, 13/3/51, 27/3/51, 3/4/51, 3/8/51 and 25/9/51.

[18]ANC: President's Address to Working Committee, 25/12/51.

[19]19/1/51.

[20]*Op. cit.*, p. 9, citing Congress resolution of February, 1952; and RH: Supreme Action Council statement, 27/2/52.

[21]Kaunda, *op. cit.*, pp. 47-48.

[22]*Ibid.*, p. 49.

[23]The new 'Missionary-in-Charge' to whom Kaunda sent this letter, dated 25/3/52, was the present writer. See Kaunda and Morris, *op. cit.*, p. 11; and note that the quotation from Shaw is from *Plays Pleasant and Unpleasant* (Constable, 1908), 201.

[24]Cited in P. Fraenkel, *Wayaleshi* (Weidenfeld and Nicholson, 1959), 132.

[25]Mpashi, *op. cit.*, p. 31.

[26]RH: Memo by Nkumbula 3/5/52. The Congress delegation to London consisted of Chiefs Chitimukulu of the Bemba and Musokotwane of the Tonga, Nkumbula and Lawrence Katilungu.

[27]TI-FM/KK, 13/2/69; and ANC: Nkumbula's Statement to Public Meeting, Mapoloto African Township, 26/6/52.

[28]ANC: UCAA Leaflet, *Central African Federation—a Test of African Opinion*, quoting *EAR*, 14/8/52 on Nkumbula's statement.

[29]NAZ: N/0001/2/5, P.C., Fort Jameson to C.S., 11/8/52.

[30]ANC: Report of NR Chiefs' interview with Attlee, 19/8/52; and *NN*, 2/9/52.

[31]Kaunda, *op. cit.*, pp. 50-52.

[32]*NN*, 22/7/52, 23/8/62.

[33]ANC: Presidential Address, Kabwata Welfare Hall, Lusaka, and Proposed Constitution for a Self-governing State of N. Rhodesia, as adopted by the Chiefs in conference, 19-25 August, 1952.

[34]ANC: letters of chiefs to S.N.A., 21/8/52.

[35]*Ibid.*: Resolution passed at Chinika, Lusaka, 14/12/52, which cited Welensky's speech of 3/7/52.

[36]Mushindo Papers (by permission of his son): letter of the late Revd. P. B. Mushindo, Member of African Representative Council, to S.N.A., 11/3/52.

[37]ANC: *Capricorn Africa Society—Statement of Aims and Precepts* (undated leaflet).

[38]*African Nationalism* (Oxford, 1959), 168. Sithole is the leader of the banned Zimbabwe African National Union in Rhodesia.

[39]TI-FM/KK, 13/7/71 and 5/2/69.

[40]Rotberg, *Rise*, p. 244; and ANC: Pages of Diary of Capricorn agent, Nyirenda, May-September 1952.

[41]ANC/5/14, Fox-Pitt to Nabulyato, 19/11/52.
[42]*Op. cit.*, p. 12.
[43]*A History*, p. 427.
[44]TI-FM/KK, 13/2/69. The research scholar was W. Watson, author of *Tribal Cohesion in a Money Economy* (Manchester, 1958), a study of the Mambwe people.
[45]TI-FM/KK, 13/2/69 and Kaunda, *op. cit.*, p. 53.
[46]Makasa Papers: Kaunda to D.C., Chinsali, 4/2/53.
[47]TI-FM/KK, 13/2/69, and note that Joel Nkhata's brother was Alick, one-time clerk at Lubwa and then broadcaster and composer of songs, many of them political.
[48](Bell, 1970, but first published 1897), 207-208.
[49]TI-FM/KK, 26/2/69.
[50]*Observer*, 15/3/53; and see H. Franklin, *Unholy Wedlock* (Allen and Unwin, 1963) esp. p. 65.
[51]*EAR*, 4/9/52.
[52]*Ibid.*
[53]ANC: President's Statement on the White Paper of January 1953 (Cmd. 8754), delivered 22/3/53.
[54]ANC/2/7, letter of appeal, 8/2/53, and see NAZ: Sec/Nat/119, Revd. E. G Nightingale's proposal for an inter-racial rendezvous. A.R.C. had proposed an inter-racial social club in September 1948 (Sec/Nat/119).
[55]Fraenkel, *op. cit.*, pp. 161 and 171 ff.
[56]Sikalumbi, *op. cit.*, p. 17.
[57]*A History*, p. 431.
[58]TI-FM/KK, 13/2/69 and FM/HMN, 15/6/71.
[59]ANC: President's Statement on the effects of the National Days of Prayer, 11/4/53.
[60]*NN*, 19/1/53 and 29/1/53; ANC: Press Communique, 14/4/53, and CEO/0A/7, letter to U.N. Secretary-General, ref. U.N. Charter, Article 73 on political, economic and social advancement to self-government, 20/4/53.
[61]*NN*, June 1953.
[62]*EAR*, 16/7/53. The writer attended the Chinsali ceremony.
[63]ANC: President's Statement on the Imposition of Federation, 2/6/53.
[64]*NN* for the period.
[65]TI-FM/KK, 13/2/69 and 12/3/69; and Kaunda, *op. cit.*, pp. 52-54.
[66]Mpashi, *op. cit.* 32-33.
[67]Sikalumbi, *op. cit.*, p. 25, which cites the *CAP*.
[68]*Ibid.*, and Hall, *Zambia*, 159, *NN*, 21/8/53 and TI-FM/JM Sokoni, 6/10/69. Kaunda was opposed by Mukuka Nkoloso, the only other candidate being George Kaluwa who was at the time Vice-General Secretary and, according to Kaunda, 'for all practical purposes General Secretary, because Mr. Nabulyato could not apparently work with Mr. Nkumbula'.

6

First Fruits of the Vision

August 1953, said Roy Welensky, meant the fulfilment of his dreams. For the Congress, it seemed on the surface to spell the final collapse of confidence in the distant royal Protector and to bring a sense of deep frustration. For Kenneth Kaunda it marked a point of no return. He might still hanker after the fields and the little orchard of Shambalakale, but that was not the road he would now take. His friend Sokoni had advised him against accepting appointment as Secretary-General for family reasons. 'But it was a call so strong that he could not disobey it.' The seeds sown in his soul during the past decade were now going to yield their harvest and, though only twenty-nine years of age, he was soon to become his people's 'guide, philosopher and friend'. Till then, the Congress had been led in effect by one man, Nkumbula, supported by colleagues for whom his words rang true but who would have hesitated to utter them themselves. But these cautious men no longer held office. Now, while humbly and loyally serving his President, Kenneth was increasingly going to share with his people something much more than a protest against injustice, more than a demand for decent treatment— the conviction that here at the crucial core of the troubled continent must be created a society in which a man's humanity should be honoured as his birthright to freedom.[1]

Our task now is to follow the events of the first fateful years of Federation and to examine Kaunda's contribution to the shaping of the future. It is of special importance to trace his own thinking and so the brief chapter of his autobiography headed 'Secretary-General of Congress' calls for our attention. In particular perhaps it is note-worthy that he wrote without bitterness about the corps of colonial servants who, as he saw it, were increasingly required 'to carry out a system that sets them into opposition to the very people they are supposed to guide with a fatherly hand'. For example, he said, 'at the time of the imposition of Federation, the DCs and DOs had to travel round their districts to persuade the people to accept it. Some DCs have told me they did this very unwillingly.' He expressed a concern which the writer often heard expressed by African people, that the Government's 'terrible record' of shifting provincial officers from one language area to another often denied these men the chance to 'become a friend of the people and know their language'. Though he spoke for many when he complained that 'the well-meaning, imperialist DCs' had not realised that Africans were people, 'not cattle to be herded together and driven here and there', it is clear from the records of the colonial period that Northern Rhodesia had experienced briefly what has been called, in the context of Tanzania's history, an 'age of improvement'.[2] Despite the meagre Government expenditure on matters related to the welfare of the African people, there was a universal desire for schooling and the pioneer medical work of Christian agencies, however scanty, was widely appreciated. There was, moreover, a quick awareness among the people of the efforts of certain officials, in Kaunda's phrase, 'to lead them to better things'.[3]

Yet, in the same chapter, he exclaimed that he wished that he could write a book with the old ANC's files beside him, 'to tell the wretched story of how the Provincial Administration tried to use the Chiefs to crush Congress in the rural areas'. Part of the tragedy certainly stemmed from the fact that, as Britain moved towards Huggins and Welensky, it fell to her officers in the distant colonial field to try to implement harsh and benighted policies and, for those who had eyes to see, to witness the wanton demolition of a structure of confidence that had been slowly built up in the preceding years. The S.N.A.'s confidential Quarterly Newsletters to Provincial Commissioners had shown an early awareness that Congress had 'many good men in it' and that the fact that 'many of the more intelligent and well-meaning Africans' were bitter and resentful was not at all surprising in view of the 'provocative remarks made by candidates for Legislative Council and the insulting articles in the local press'. Officials had long been no less aware of the Unofficials' increasing 'ruderies to Government, distortions and odd antics' and the 'pathetically Gilbertian' aspects of a tricky situation. The more perceptive officers knew enough of the local situation to be very anxious about Welensky's mounting pressure, which was frequently turned angrily upon senior civil servants. They knew well that, for instance, the people were 'very nervous about the security of their land which is understandable' and that the abasing of the 'most unprovocative and helpful' Dalgleish Report had done great harm too.[4] The Federal scheme, described by the British Liberal Party as 'conceived in fraud', was eventually implemented by the persistent bullying of the representatives of the protecting power. Because they were not strong enough to resist the bullying, they had to face inevitable opposition as they struggled against the rising tide of popular anger at the seeming victory of the masters of the plot. The British newspaper, *The New Statesman*, saw the move to Federation as following 'the well-worn track towards white-settler Government'. In detail, Kenneth Kaunda had spelled out in Chinsali his people's deep misgivings a year earlier in what the District Report described as 'a valuable soap-box attack on Federation and Partnership'. 'Despite all the talk of British ideals,' said Kaunda, 'there is no democracy in Northern Rhodesia.'[5]

There was another factor in the whole ferment that Kaunda was well aware of, namely, a vocal rejection of Christianity in protest against those missionaries who seemed to have come to pave the way for the seizure of the land and against the continued existence of the scandal of 'colour bar churches'. A public meeting convened by Dauti Yamba in April 1953, had condemned the 'political chicanery' of the imminent Federation, warned of 'high indignation' among Africans in the three territories, called on Chiefs to end cooperation with colonial officials and pledged itself to passive resistance and the burning of Identification Certificates. Eight years were to pass before *ifitupa*, as the certificates were called, would actually be burned. It had then declared that 'instead of worshipping the Almight [*sic*] God through Christian religion all Africans should worship our ancestors' spirits . . . .' 'When all these have failed we shall, last but not least, offer our blood to the Government.'[6] The student of Central African history must also be aware of the political significance of religious protest movements. In various dramatic ways, including some pathetic extravaganza, the religious protest movements all sought to articulate the longing for the end of the subjugation of their peoples, the coming of a new order, the establishment in eschatological terms of 'the new Jerusa-

lem'. Persistently they inveighed against missionaries for failing to
live according to their messages. The existence of openly racist
'European congregations' sharpened the sense of anger against
this contradiction. They did not, however, in general, want to
turn from Jesus Christ. Kenneth had reason to be able to understand
this stirring. 'I shall never stop believing in the God of Jesus,'
he told the writer in a moment of depression at Lubwa in 1953,
'but I am beginning to doubt the God of the Church.'[7]

   Kenneth and his family moved from Chinsali to Lusaka on 11
November 1953. After his appointment as Congress Secretary-
General he had spent some time in Lusaka, making himself familiar
with the paper work of ANC and also looking for accommodation
for his family. When he went north to collect Betty and their two
small boys, Panji and Wazamazama Ngombo, he knew he was going
to take them to a difficult situation. With Nkumbula's approval,
he was going to use the Congress office in Chilenje as a house to
begin with. 'The office had two small rooms', Betty Kaunda has
recalled, 'and a kitchen two yards by three yards.' 'Life was not easy,
living in a busy office where clerks tapped their typewriters and
banged on the table at every typing error they made.' For the wife
of an ex-Head Master and small farmer, these conditions must
have been extremely trying. She had to rise very early, put away
the blankets, clean the room and leave it for the clerks. 'I used to
sit in the tiny kitchen all day,' she said. She and the children ate in
the kitchen, as the office was used as a staff dining-room. A big
tree near the house gave her shelter when she was 'bored in the
kitchen'. To make matters worse, 'secret meetings were very often
held in this office after dark.' 'The meetings at night were my worst
times for I was not allowed into the house till the end of the meeting
and these meetings often dragged on and on till midnight; then
my husband would come out and tell me to go in and sleep.' Months
passed in this way before an old house with three small rooms
was found for the family in the Mapoloto section of the Chilenje
suburb of Lusaka. The kitchen was built apart from the house as
was often the practice in 'compounds' and 'locations'. Its grass
roof leaked badly. When heavy rain fell at night, they had to wake
up, pile the blankets on the children in an attempt to keep them
dry and then stand in a dry corner till dawn. Ants swarmed into
the house constantly and in addition the red soil of the area stained

clothes badly. Betty spent much time, therefore, battling against adverse elements and seeing less and less of her busy husband.[8]

What kept him busy was a wide variety of activities related to the building up of a political organization at a time when pessimism was in danger of begetting apathy in the hearts of some of his fellow countrymen. Nkumbula had a number of worries to share with him. He had recently sternly warned propagandists of a faction calling itself 'Power in the Eastern Province' to cease their sectional activities.[9] Moreover, the press reports of the Congress conference in August had provoked some sharp racist comments. One of these, from Salisbury, sneered that the delegates 'were little better than the baboons on the kopjes until the arrival of the white man'. 'Start at the BOTTOM', the letter said, 'and climb up slowly, then maybe in *many years to come* you may be qualified to fit into decent WHITE "society". We know you don't want the Confederates in NR but you will probably get them. They know how to handle you.'[10]

Nkumbula then passed to Kenneth a letter from another European who used the obscure language of religious fanaticism and chided the Congress for lack of 'thankfulness to the Government and settlers' for such things as 'towns, roads, farming and bridges, etc.' Kaunda replied thus: 'You must have studied the life of that holy figure, Jesus Christ, in a terrible way.' Africa's old empires which had existed 'long before any white man stepped in a shoe', had risen and waned but now there was a fresh 'upthrust from our long suffering under the jack boots of you, imperialists . . . not even your Hydrogen or Atomic bombs will destroy the *LOVE* that we have for a truly multi-racial democracy; a government in which those who form the majority of the population must form the majority of the government. I know you fear this DAY—but as sure as the sun rises from the east and sets in the west, and never rises from the south to set in the north, that DAY is COMING.' Asserting that 'when the whites were going to crucify Him [Jesus], an African bore the Cross,' Kaunda went on: '. . . We, the Africans . . . move about with religion. To me a white man only remembers God when he is actually in the Church or in trouble. In the football field, at work, etc., he is without a feeling of the Holy Presence. Alas! now after mixing up with [*sic*] people who pride themselves in saying that they brought the Gospel here, my people are fast

losing their being intensely religious. As sincere [*sic*] as I believe
in Christ, I must tell you that most of your people have introduced
Christianity in this and other continents, etc., with a self-seeking
motive. With the introduction of Christianity, have we not only got
half-way sort of personal security and peace at the highest price,
price of losing liberty. One Zulu priest has said, "When Europeans
came, they had the Bible and we had the land, but now we have
the Bible and they have the land". I share this with him, but like
him, Christ has an undoubted place in my heart.' Then he ended
with a flourish of contempt: 'Keep your religious sermons to the
uncountable sirs so and so who have an empire for . . . eh! Give
them more spiritual food, feller, and come to us after your sirs are
constipated—for this is your practice in everything else. You
usually give the African the devil-may-care for residue . . . Meet
you in heaven, feller. Bye-bye!'[11]

More seriously and positively, the plan for a 'regional conference
of the Pan-African Conference' at once began to demand Kenneth's
energies. He wrote to 'African National organisations' in many
countries, announcing a two-day assembly to be held in Lusaka
in mid-October. 'Our *uniform suffering* under the jack boots of
our capitalist and imperialist oppressors *should*,' he wrote, 'bring us
together . . . from there we should work our way out to suit a
true multi-racial democratic African Continent.' In a second circular
he declared enthusiastically that 'the wind of freedom' was blowing
from east to west and north to south, and that 'the Africans who
from the coming of intruders have been nothing but criminals
of want' were now awaking. 'Help make this great idea a success,'
he pleaded. 'Long live this great continent—sons and daughters of
Africa—shoulder to shoulder.' A memorandum from the Revd.
Michael Scott was to provide the basis for the Conference's agenda.
It called for inter-territorial action for the progressive elimination
of the colour bar in the East and Central African protectorates
and therefore proposed a detailed study of how discrimination was
working in economic, industrial, social, political and religious
relations. Attention was therefore to be given to issues like migratory
labour, land tenure, community development, and fundamental
education. The Conference would then tackle the crucial matters
of economic, social and constitutional reform. In Scott's words,
it would aim to 'help the African resistance movements to clarify

a positive programme for their people as well as the negative programme of non-cooperation they are pledged to.'[12]

Kaunda issued a third circular letter aimed at building up enthusiasm for the Conference. Referring to the Central African Federation, he told his counterparts in other countries that his people had fallen prey to a 'haunting beast with sharp claws, a bird of prey with hoofs on . . . .' 'If at any time some of us believed that the British Imperialists have meant well with us, they have seen for themselves what is what . . . . Oh, well, true white christians and liberals in this country are few and more so in Britain—so our salvation lies in our own hands . . . .' 'Non-cooperation without violence,' he added '. . . is capable of achieving greater success than most of us have the power to foresee.' He was highly excited at the prospect of a large inter-territorial assembly in Lusaka, but it became apparent that it was going to run into serious obstacles. He wrote sadly to the 'shadow cabinet' of ANC about the lack of response from the 'sister-organisations' of Nyasaland and Southern Rhodesia. 'Things nowadays don't seem to be very normal, do they?' he said, in the conversational style that often appeared in his official correspondence. September had indeed been an anxious month. The disturbances in Nyasaland, notably at Luchenza, had been attributed by the Governor to the Nyasaland African Congress. Strong arm measures had been taken to suppress them and soon afterwards the Nyasa chiefs had formally abandoned their 'non-cooperation' policy. At home, while Godwin Mbikusita and Lawrence Katilungu joined the Moral Rearmament movement, alarming disturbances took place in the Gwembe Valley and among the Samfya fishermen on Lake Bangweulu. In both cases Congress was blamed for fomenting trouble and therefore Nkumbula and Kaunda set out to show that the people in these two widely separated areas had simply reacted against harrassing Government regulations.[13]

Meanwhile a sharp attack on 'Kaunda and his gang' was made by the Secretary of the Northern Rhodesian African Educational Organisation, John Musamba, bemoaning the resignation of 'outstanding men like Mr. Chileshe, Mr. Yamba, Mr. Kaluwa and Mr. Nabulyato' from the Congress Executive. Musamba called Kaunda a 'political pariah' and suggested that if they did not believe in democracy, it was high time that he and his henchmen 'packed their bags and baggages and went to Kremlin [*sic*].' 'If they still

believe that a spear and an axe will achieve their purpose and that
their black God from the Congress will turn bullets into water,'
he said, 'they are doomed to failure.'[14] The new ANC initiative in
galvanising public opinion would have to reckon with this kind of
opposition. But, more ominously, Welensky suddenly showed his
hand, as it were, by an angry rejection of the Colonial Secretary's
proposals for very limited change in the composition of the Northern
Rhodesian Legislature. Official members were to be reduced from
nine to eight. European Unofficials were to be increased from ten
to twelve and two more African members were to be added. In a
fierce speech, Welensky took the 'greatest exception' to proposals
which involved only a '20 per cent increase in the number of
European elected members against a 100 per cent increase in the
number of African members.' The increasing vigour of the Confederate Party, and especially of John Gaunt, posed a threat, however,
not only to the aims of the Congress but to Welensky's role
as spokesman of European 'settlers'.[15]

Nkumbula in a press communique declared that the Colonial
Secretary could not be relied on to have 'the courage to disappoint
Welensky' for he had 'met the settlers' demands a hundred per cent
in both the Constitutions'. In London the Labour leader, Attlee,
had just expressed the view that although 'the Central African
Federation did not appear to accord with the desires of the African
people . . . it was not the job of a great movement like the Labour
Party to encourage resistance to Acts of Parliament passed at
Westminster.' Some Labour M.P.s had shouted 'Shame', but for
the Congress the omens were bleak: Britain was 'climbing down'
in the face of Welensky's bluster.[16]

It was therefore most important for Congress to enunciate an
acceptable alternative to the Federal and Confederate programmes.
A few days after reading of the planned removal of 20,000
Africans from the Nairobi area 'to counter Mau Mau activity'
and of Malan's new bill in the South African Parliament to remove
'coloureds' from the common voters' roll, Kaunda issued a circular
entitled *Nationalism and Parliamentary Democracy* which began by
declaring that the imposition of Federation had been made possible
because 'the imperialists [could] count on the strength of the British
troops which they are ruthlessly using in crushing down the national
aspirations of the colonial peoples.' In execution of the Congress

policy of 'non-cooperation without violence', Congress had decided, he stated, that European farming and the scheme for European housing were, in particular, 'detrimental to African interests'. It would therefore press for the withdrawal of African labour in these two spheres, while intensifying an anti-colour bar campaign in hotels, restaurants, public lavatories, churches, post-offices and shops. It would launch a vigorous membership drive, and also strive to integrate the activities of all African organisations in the country, providing a Council to link the Congresses of the three territories, and urge the development of Pan-African cooperation.

All these moves would aim towards 'the introduction of a straight democratic franchise,' for 'if we Africans are decided to continue fighting against human injustice, we will be well advised to link up our national movements with the established foreign parliamentary system. We must see to it that more and more of our men find their way to the Parliamentary institution whilst . . . we intensify our national aspirations.' Congress therefore had decided not to boycott the Federal elections. The issue was so important that all African councils, trade unions and societies would be asked to support 'a method of electing the two African members to the Federal Parliament . . . .' 'A Federal Parliament in which there were no strong African members could the more easily alter the constitution so as to enable Governors of each Territory to nominate two of their African stooges.'[17] Keen observers in the Protectorate, like the more profound commentators in the British press, saw troubled times coming, but the Governor of Southern Rhodesia, Sir John Kennedy, predicted 'progress, prosperity and tranquility' in Central Africa. His counterpart in the north, Gilbert Rennie, at the same time described Kaunda as an 'agitator'. He was undoubtedly angered by reports of remarks that Kaunda had made a few days earlier in Livingstone when he had declared: 'We want the franchise now . . . we are not afraid of guns or atomic bombs . . . . As long as power remains with the whites it is a police state and no peace can prevail . . . unless and until foreign power is removed.' Such tranquility as there was was, as we now know, a long lull before the storm. Battle positions were being taken up; the 'Federation for ever' men against those who would now say explicitly that 'Federation must go'. Between them, in no-man's land as it were, there moved a number of African figures, men whose subsequent careers were to take them in widely divergent directions.

The elections to the African Representative Council brought a number of these 'moderates' into the forefront; people like Safeli Chileshe, Robinson Nabulyato, Lawrence Katilungu, Francis Chembe, George Kaluwa and Mateyo Kakumbi. In Southern Rhodesia, in an apparent access of moderation, delegates to the Supreme Council of African Organisations unanimously rescinded its policy of non-cooperation and nominated three candidates for the Federation election of African M.P.s, including Joshua Nkomo. Meanwhile the civil disobedience among the Bangweulu fishermen had led to eighty-two convictions, some of which involved caning. Various Chiefs were deposed and deported to other areas. Opponents of the African Congress saw this as a notable defeat for it. Despite the apparent gap between the 'moderates' and the 'extremists', however, and despite the officials' hope that they could exploit it by favouring the former group, there was no breach between them and they generally held each other in high regard. Kaunda has recalled a long discussion with Dauti Yamba and the late Mateyo Kakumbi, on a visit home from Salisbury, and with Chileshe and Sokota. 'We youngsters,' he said, 'were trying to reconcile these old men.' At last Kenneth said, 'Look, old men, if you are tired of leading us, leave this thing in our hands and we will finish the job.' 'If you have failed the nation, we will not fail it.' Some time later Sokota was to say to him 'Ken, remember these words you spoke. It has come true.'[18] Meanwhile, in reaction to Lyttelton's timid proposal for two more African M.L.C.s, Welensky announced the withdrawal of all co-operation by elected members with the Government. These were 'dictated terms' he said, which had been rejected by both Europeans and Africans. This petulant piece of double-talk came two days after his forecast of 500,000 European residents within a decade.[19]

From the time of the ANC elections in August 1953, there was a great increase in the volume of circulars and correspondence flowing from its Chilenje headquarters. Though there was no hand-over from the previous secretary, Kaunda, with the help of Wittington Sikalumbi, started the organization of files, etc., and Congress pronouncements began at once to make a sharper impact than before. In addition to writing the letters cited above, Kenneth formed an editorial board consisting of himself, Sikalumbi and

Titus Mukupo to launch a periodical newssheet which they called the *Congress News*. The first two issues appeared in October and November. As police surveillance of ANC activities was growing fast, Kaunda and Nkumbula were charged with illegal publication. They were arrested but not imprisoned. It soon was verified that in fact the newssheet had been duly registered by the Postmaster General and the Central African Archives. However, it was at this time that Kaunda's name began to be well-known in the Protectorate. The brief encounter with the police over the *News* led to the suspension of further publication until January 1955, but the first two issues had drawn attention not only to the major matters which it discussed but to the personality of its chief editor. As Sokoni has said, 'We see an immediate change in Congress organisation when he took over.' 'The monthly circular became a very inspiring instrument.'[20]

Volume I, number 1 of October 1953 was a circular of twelve quarto pages. Its contents were as follows: Editorial; 'Africa Awakening'; 'News of Africa' from Northern Rhodesia, Nyasaland, Kenya and South Africa; 'The Message' from Kaunda himself; 'H.Q. Notes'; 'What some people have said'; and 'A smile'. In a brief editorial note, there was an apology for having to write in English. Lack of money precluded publication in local languages. This was followed by an apt quotation, cited above, from one of Welensky's speeches which warned against "any section" trying to "dominate by force".[21] 'Africa Awakening' (by the President-General) was a lengthy extract from the circular issued by Kaunda in October under the title *Nationalism and Parliamentary Democracy*. There followed a quotation from a statement by the Africa Bureau in London on the consequences of the imposition of Federation in the face of genuine and widespread African opposition. A brief analysis of political parties described Dendy Young's Confederates as 'advocating an *apartheid* policy,' while the 'half-and-half' United Federal Party had 'chosen to be vague in their pronouncements on . . . race relations . . . with an obvious hope of pleasing everybody'. The Northern Rhodesia news section also included a brief report on the Samfya disturbances in the form of an extract from the *Northern News* without comment.[22] The paper went on to report on recent charges of sedition against Nyasaland Congress men and the return of official robes to Chiefs by the Government there as a sign of the end of the Chiefs' non-cooperation policy. The item on Kenya quoted, from the paper *Africa and the Colonial World*, allegations of police brutality, including the burning of houses and shooting of women. From South Africa there was a brief note on the introduction of colour-bar buses in Cape Province with separate doors and compartments for Europeans and Africans. The last section of quotations included Kwame Nkrumah and Jawaharlal Nehru on the evil of imperialism and a brief word from Gandhi on 'non-violence'. It meant "conscious suffering", the Mahatma had explained. "It does not mean meek submission to the evil-doer but . . . putting of one's whole soul against the will of the tyrant," whereby "it is possible for a single individual to defy the whole might of an unjust empire."

'The Message' from Kaunda himself as Secretary-General, thanked the 'dear honourable Chiefs and people' for the first battle which they had fought and lost like men against 'a beast with talons or a bird with hoofs' which he called 'Amalgafeder-partnership'. But 'more fighting lies ahead,' he said. Paraphrasing words of Jesus Christ, he urged everyone to be 'patient as a dove but as cunning as a snake' in dealing with 'dangerous elements who will try and make you forget your place'. The situation in South Africa gave a grave warning against believing in 'safeguards' provided by oppressors. 'Divide and rule' was still the policy used by those in power and so he made an urgent plea for unity 'to save the nation as a whole, for it only is Power.' 'The fight is long,' he concluded, 'the road bad and dangerous, but one thing we are sure of is, FREEDOM for us in the end.' Here was a declaration of an objective no less than national independence. The Banda-Nkumbula plea of 1949 for the *status quo ante* was a thing of the past. Kaunda was saying openly what he had said to his wife: the African people must prepare to rule their own country. There was no explanation of the meaning of the 'nation'. He knew that his readers would know exactly what he meant.[23]

Number 2 of Volume I, which was published in the following month, continued the focusing of vital issues. From Southern Rhodesia came the news of the abandonment of its non-cooperation policy by the All-African Convention. There was a short article, meant to be the first of a series, entitled 'Back to our land'. Readers were invited to study 'what we all, as the trustees of this land,

should do to save it from land-hungry people, destruction by
our own poor use of it and . . . exploiting its wealth of which it
has plenty'. In contrast to this call was a report that the South
African Government was bringing in legislation whereby 'under the
new Native Labour Bill, no native, man or woman, would be allowed
to belong to any registered trade union.' The quotations for November were from Thomas Payne and Wendell Phillips. "Tyranny,"
said Payne, "like hell, is not easily conquered; yet we have these
consolations within us, that the harder the conflict, the more
glorious the triumph. What we obtained too cheap, we esteem too
lightly . . . . It would be strange indeed if as celestial an article as
freedom should not be highly rated." The brief passage that followed
from Phillips was headed 'Violence Condemned'. "When you have
convinced thinking men that it is right and humane men that it is
just, you will gain your cause. Men always lose half of what is
gained by violence. What is gained by argument is gained for
ever." Here was a paper, radically different from official publications
for Africans, which widened horizons, deepened awareness of major
issues at stake and offered clear moral principles for political
action, by using the technique of brief reporting without deceit.
The master mind behind its visionary realism was Kaunda's.

The second issue included as well, a longer section entitled
'What do you know about the Dalgleish Report?'. Here again
it was clear that Kaunda was doing his homework. He reminded his
readers that the Report had been the work of a Commission
appointed in 1947 by Governor Waddington. He quoted its terms of
reference and its major recommendations, including the provision
that the promotion of Africans in the mining industry must not
result in the discharge of any European currently employed. There
followed a summary of the views of politicians on the Report,
comments made in reaction to the announced intention of the
African Mine Workers' Union to press for its immediate implem-
etation. Welensky regarded it as 'dead'. The Confederates were no
less hostile to it. 'About the only liberal voice heard in the Federation', that of Dr. Alexander Scott,[24] condemned vigorously
Welensky's assertion that 'the African must wait another two
generations before he can hope for a better job.'

The history of the Northern Rhodesia Copper Mines offers a
sombre demonstration of the effects of a *laissez faire* policy in

colonial affairs. It had been recognised as late as 1941 that African wages which had been reduced in the time of the depression had not been increased after the depression had ceased. Yet between the depression and that date, the dangerous riots of 1935 and 1940 had taken place. It was generally agreed by officials that the major cause of the 1935 riots was the sudden increase in 'native tax' but 'over-crowding in locations, ill-treatment by Europeans, the mis-understood system of pay and bonus, the prosecution of "loafers" and the influence of the Watch Tower' were listed as contributory causes. The notice fixed on the door of the Nkana beer-hall in April, over the nom-de-plume 'I am glad', had merited more attention than it received from either Government or the mine management: 'See how we suffer with the work and how we are continually reviled and beaten underground. Many brothers of ours die for 22/6,' it said. But the strike had been quelled by a show of superior force, and a smouldering quiescence had followed.[25]

In April 1940, there had been a second major disturbance. In defiance of an agreement between the mining companies and their union, European miners struck for higher wages in March 1940. After a ten-day halt to all mining, they were awarded a five per cent increase and increased overtime rates. According to the D.C. at Chingola, this 'European unrest and the consequent visit of the Acting Chief Secretary and Mr. Roy Welensky kept District Commissioners out of touch with the African public.' The sudden outbreak of the strike in Nchanga caught them unawares. It began when while drawing rations, 'an African woman was assaulted by a Compound Assistant on the orders of the European Compound Manager.'[26] The award to the white strikers further underlined the injustice of the situation. As the strike of African mine labourers spread, once again troops moved in. The climactic third of April ended with thirteen Africans dead and sixty-nine wounded. Another Commission of Enquiry followed, against the wishes of Governor Maybin, and inevitably it recommended that, along with a rise of an extra 2/6 per month in African wages, there must be a serious move to hasten African advancement. The P.C., Ndola, referring to the mine ration system which had provided the *casus belli* at Nchanga, expressed his disquiet: 'The contention that it is either necessary or desirable for married women to turn out at 3 o'clock a.m. to draw rations, or that they appreciate this arrangement will

1 The Kaunda family at Lubwa around 1923
Revd. David Kaunda (d. 1932) and Mrs. Helen Kaunda (d. 1972) with,
standing right, Katie; kneeling left, Bertha (d. 1937) and Robert; and
centre, Joan.

2 Grave of Revd. David Kaunda at Lubwa

3 Kenneth Kaunda's house as Head Master, Lubwa, 1945

4 Kenneth Kaunda, sitting, with Ellison Millambo, ANC Southern Provincial
President, late 1953
Millambo wrote at the bottom of the photograph: 'Seest thou a man diligent
in his business; he shall stand before kings.' (Proverbs 22:29)

5 Discussing the 'Moffat Resolutions', August 1954
Front, left to right: S. H. Chileshe, M. L. C.; M. Kakumbi, M.P.;
L. Ng'andu, M.L.C.; R. Nabulyato, M.L.C.; D. Yambo, M.P. Behind.
left to right: P. Sokota, M.L.C.; K. D. Kaunda; H. M. Nkumbula; E. M,
Liso and A. Hiwa, representing ANC

6 Kenneth Kaunda in his Chilenje house soon after release from prison in March 1955, wearing a black toga as a sign of political protest

7 Roy Welensky addressing civil dignitaries of Kabwe Municipal Council at the opening of the new offices, July 1957

8 Kenneth Kaunda in Lusaka Central Prison, June 1959, the photograph being taken hurriedly and without official permission

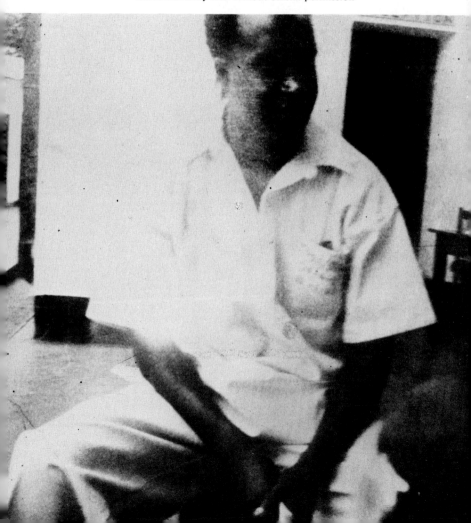

9 In London for the Northern Rhodesia Constitutional Conference, February
1961: Paramount Chief Undi, Chief Mapanza, Chief Chikwanda,
L. Ng'andu, M.L.C., K. D. Kaunda and N. Sipalo, UNIP

10 A road block set up during 'Cha-cha-cha', 1961

11 Men of the Police Mobile Unit in action during 'Cha-cha-cha', 1961

12 *Northern News* cartoon: 'Men in the North, no. 10—Impressive Politico', 30 October 1961

13 UNIP posters to greet the visit of Colonial Secretary Maudling, December 1961

14 Colonial Secretary Maudling with Governor Hone greets UNIP delegation at Governor's House, December 1961
Left to right: Mainza Chona, Arthur Wina, Sir Stewart Gore-Browne, Solomon Kalulu, Aaron Milner and Kenneth Kaunda

15 Betty Kaunda at work in House No. 394, Chilenje, where the Kaundas lived from January 1960 to December 1962

16 UNIP rally at Kitwe, June 1962

18 Kenneth Kaunda saying goodbye to his wife Betty and their son Kaweche at the start of an election tour in the Landrover known as 'Mama UNIP', September 1962

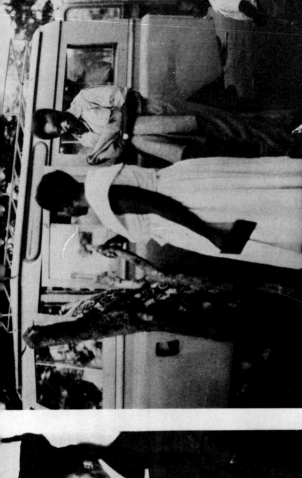

17 At Africa Freedom Day Rally, New York, 10 July 1962: Oliver Tambo of South African ANC, Kenneth Kaunda, Raouf Boudjako of Algeria and Eduardo Mondlane of Mozambique liberation movement, FRELIMO

19 Kenneth Kaunda as Chairman with delegates to the PAFMECSA Conference at Leopoldville (Kinshasa) in Zaïre, December 1962. The group includes Jomo Kenyatta on Kaunda's left

20 Mass burning of identification certificates at Kitwe, December 1963

22 Multi-racial ceremony for the burial of the Central African Federation, Chililabombwe, 31 December 1963

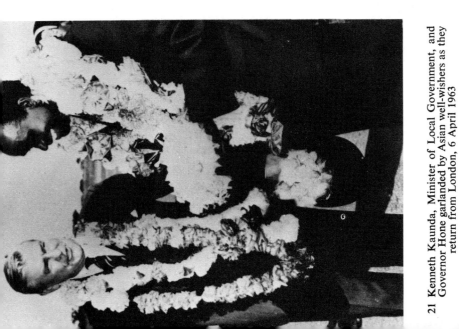

21 Kenneth Kaunda, Minister of Local Government, and Governor Hone garlanded by Asian well-wishers as they return from London, 6 April 1963

24 The large house in Prospect Hill, Lusaka (formerly owned by the R.S.A. Co). which Kenneth Kaunda occupied as Minister of Local Government and then as Prime Minister, from December 1962 to October 1964

23 Kenneth Kaunda on an election tour in January 1964, with Chief Moono of Mombwa

Alexander Grey Zulu is standing behind his left shoulder

25 A typical certificate of membership of the Lumpa 'church' which some followers of Alice Lenshina regarded as a 'passport to heaven' during the violent conflict of mid-1964

26 A Provincial Officer calls on followers of Alice Lenshina to surrender during the Lumpa 'war'

27 The Zambian Cabinet, announced a month before independence. Seated, left to right: A. G. Zulu (Transport and Works), S. Kalulu (National Resources), H. D. Banda (Housing and Social Development), R. C. Kamanga (Vice-President Designate), M. M. Chona (Home Affairs), N. Mundia (Commerce and Industry), S. Wina (Local Government). Standing, left to right: A. W. Gaminara (Secretary to the Cabinet), P. Matoka (Information, Post Office and Telegraphs), S. N. Kapwepwe (Foreign Affairs), J. Skinner (Justice), A. N. Wina (Finance), M. Sipalo (Health), M. J. Chimba (Labour and Mines), E. K. Mudenda (Agriculture), J. Mwanakatwe (Education), E. S. Kapotwe (Senior Principal, Cabinet Office), D. Joy (Principal, Cabinet Office)

28 President Kaunda receiving the 'Instrument of Government' from the Princess Royal at the independence ceremony on 24 October 1964

be exceedingly hard to justify and it is obvious that a better scheme must be drawn up.' He also suggested 'that the European personnel is too large and that some of it could be replaced by African boss-boys and capitaos with increased efficiency and economy.' 'Everything is set,' wrote another senior Government official later, 'for a struggle between the races which is certain to come eventually unless an unexpected change in the European attitude takes place or the managements are in a position to resist pressure from the European union.'[26]

During the years following the second strike, there were a few outward signs of change, though official ambivalence was seen at once in the correspondence about a proposal of the General Missionary Conference, sharply rejected by the Mines, that African advancement and the use of money to provide improved welfare services were urgent.[27] Government feared that action on African advancement would incite the 'amalgamationists' to push for union with Southern Rhodesia and the adoption of its 'native policy'.[28] Recognition was, however, accorded at the instigation of the Labour Commissioner, R. S. Hudson, to associations of 'boss-boys' or gang foremen. The first African trade association, the African Shop Assistants' and Tailors' Committee, was formed in 1943. Then the post-war Labour Government in Britain began to press for the extension, in number and authority, of African bodies of local government, Creech Jones at the Colonial Office urging the use of the elective principle in local government. The African Representative Council, established in 1946, was designed, as Gann points out, to serve the Government's desire to 'channel the intelligentsia's political ambitions away from the Welfare Societies and to create a common link between the "new men" and the chiefs'.[29] It was chaired by the Secretary for Native Affairs. Everything about its establishment and its operation was paternalistic. Nonetheless acknowledged leaders of African opinion began to be heard at its meetings.

In part at least because of Government's negative attitude to freely elected bodies, the smouldering situation on the Copperbelt remained potentially explosive, constantly exacerbated by the resolute resistance of the European mineworkers to African advancement. It is therefore not surprising that Kaunda should have given such prominent place to the Copperbelt situation in the second

issue of *Congress News*. As 1953 drew to a close, wise men became
a little more articulate in the pleas for appreciation of the malaise
of Central Africa, but those who were bent on dragging back the
minute hand of the clock of history were redoubling their efforts.
Ronald Prain of the Rhodesian Selection Trust declared that the
future of the mines depended on finding a solution to the colour
barrier. 'A policy of blindness can lead only to a rude awakening,'
he said. 'The present situation is intolerable.'[30]

At this time, decisive action was taken by the Federal authorities
to wreck the Pan-African Regional Conference in Lusaka. Only
one delegate, Hla Aung from Burma, was allowed to enter Federal
territory. The rest were debarred, but it was not until the Northern
Rhodesian delegates had gathered that it was known that their
foreign guests would be absent. Kenneth Kaunda had, by circulars
sent out in November, continued to generate enthusiasm for the
Conference. 'That times of great calamity and confusion have
ever been productive of the greatest minds cannot be disputed,'
he wrote in a letter appealing for funds for the delegates' meals and
accommodation. 'Effort and not ease, difficulty and not facility,
contribute to the making of men.' Then, after describing graphically
the 'flare of confusion' that was rising from the greed of the western
world for the wealth of Africa, he offered his challenge: 'I appeal
to you ... to start changing history now.' The conference would
include representatives of ten African countries, 'coming together
for the first time to deal with our common problems ....' 'They are
expensive men and they must be attracted to our country by our
nice treatment. We are big and so must play big .... Help now by
subscribing and thereby start changing history.' Then in a long
letter, written a few days later to Miss Mary Benson of the Africa
Bureau, he reaffirmed Congress policy: 'We shall never be agents
of any system which would mean taking to violence. Perhaps
Government is unaware of the fact that we understand our people
better than they do .... Wherever true Congress leaders have gone,
even where Government has worked tricks on chiefs, etc., our
people have looked up to them with a degree of love and trust which
only a handful of Europeans in this country can have, and they
would mostly be missionaries .... The respect Government officers
get is not real. It comes from fear and hate. This they enjoy, not
knowing how it comes.'[31]

When the Conference, Pan-African in name alone, at last met, twenty-five men from Northern Rhodesia sat with Hla Aung, facing a sad collapse of their dream. Pastor Meembe of the African Methodist Episcopal Church had opened the gathering with words which, in Kaunda's view, gave the lie to the frequent charge that the African politicians were 'anti-Christian racialists'. 'We are all brothers, for we are all children of God,' Meembe had said. .... 'If people do not belong to our race, colour or nation, we must not hate them....God's children must work together to banish sin .... I believe this is the aim of this Conference .... White and black should live and work together.' The sederunt list, however, had some notable inclusions. In addition to five Chiefs and eleven full delegates of ANC, there had been representatives of the Shop Assistants' and Railway Workers' Unions, the ex-Service Men's Association and a new body called the National Youth League. In another circular to 'all secretaries of African Organisations' and sympathisers in Africa, Asia, Europe and America, Kaunda recounted the story of the debarring of delegates and blamed it on the British Government. 'One could have thought,' he said, 'that people coming together in the open was not dangerous in the least.' The programme prepared by 'the saint-like Revd. Michael Scott' was for a constructive conference. 'There is an in-let of grievances flowing into Africa but there is no out-let. ... What shall we do? In any case ... we shall not stop at this. ... It has never been possible ... to crush an idea [which] is thinner than air. .... An idea can never be successfully fought by banning those who entertain it.' The circular carried an appendix setting out 'proposals for the structure of the Pan-African Council,' with headquarters at Kano in Nigeria.[32]

In the meantime, Kaunda had produced a closely typed five-page report on the Gwembe disturbances at the end of which were the words: 'Read over and adhered to before us this 17th day of December, 1953. (sgd). K. D. Kaunda, W. K. Sikalumbi and E. L. Mungoni'. The report told how, in May 1953, the Congress District Organising Secretary, Simon Mambo, had come to ask the Chiefs and Headmen to call a meeting and how the Chiefs had sent out their messengers to call people together. Harry Nkumbula had then been present at a second meeting at which donations were handed over to Congress. People had begun to

refuse to participate in forced labour or the compulsory communal
storage of kaffir-corn and cassava planting. The District Commissioner was reported to have gone, with Boma Messengers, to
various villages where he had threatened to 'fix these people'.
A week later, he returned with 'four lorries full of African Constables
with three Europeans,' and announced a ban on Congress in the
district. 'We have come,' said the signatories of the report to
Kaunda and his colleagues, 'to let you know of the torture in our
land . . . also to ask if it is possible for us to interview some big
Government officials who just hear that people in Gwembe are
bad, that . . . they may be persuaded to think otherwise and try to
rectify the conditions at home.' Kaunda decided to let the Secretary
of Native Affairs know what he had heard from those witnesses.
As the S.N.A. refused to meet a Congress delegate with the eight
witnesses, the report was submitted to him in writing. 'These men
desired to see you,' he wrote. 'It is out of the question to ask them
to see their District Commissioner. They simply wouldn't go near
him. They fear him because of the things he has done to them.'
The last paragraph of his covering letter reaffirmed the Congress
policy of 'non-cooperation in matters detrimental for African
interests, without violence'.[33]

Federation had begun badly. The industrial situation was simmer-
ing threateningly. 'The struggle for African advancement in industry
is coming to a head,' declared Lawrence Katilungu. 'The talking
stage is now over.' But the United Federal Party won the Northern
Rhodesia elections in mid-December with a working majority
of twenty-three. Meanwhile omens from the south were grim.
Malan was acting with renewed determination to 'end non-segrega-
tion' in South Africa's universities, and the fanatical 'Union Defence
Force' was urging him to annex Swaziland which it called 'a dagger
directed at South Africa'. From Salisbury came the news that,
despite the protestations of non-racialism, the new University
College was not to have 'mixed' hostels. While Lyttelton said he
was confident of a solution to Northern Rhodesia's problems, the
New York Times had second thoughts on the Federation. 'Either
the Central African Federation will become a white-dominated
dominion,' it prophesied, 'or Southern Rhodesia will join South
Africa,' a comment which endorsed the stark statement of the Ndola
Anti-Federation Committee, made over two years earlier, that

'to call domination by the name of partnership is to call a lion a fish'.[34]

For the Congress, the new year opened with plans for the extended boycott of shops which practised racial discrimination. 'One of the things we have got to put right in this great but young country,' Kaunda declared in a widely distributed circular, 'is the evil of colour bar.' A newspaper note on the opening of the two new white secondary schools at Kabulonga in Lusaka revealed, however, that the assumptions of the colour bar were still, for many white people, unshaken. 'The plan to provide fully for students seeking secondary education' would become apparent, said the paper, quite ignoring African aspirants for secondary schooling. But whereas the educational colour bar, like the racial barrier in industry, simply kept doors closed, the daily scramble of Africans at the hatches of the country's shops, while white people used the main doors and shopped at leisure and in comfort, provided a visible scandal and had long provoked bitter resentment. After the first round of the new campaign in Lusaka, Kaunda expressed appreciation of the 'well-disciplined fight' that had been put up by Congress officials, the picketing group and its leaders and 'the general African public' against discrimination in the butcheries. This had been done despite 'severe beating of some of the picket group members by capitalistic forces'. One shop which had not enforced 'pigeon-hole shopping' previously, had now removed internal barriers. 'This was a most welcome reaction' and Kaunda said of the shop's proprietors, 'All we have for them is respect and we wish them the best luck.' The boycott of the other three butcheries went on, however. 'Now then, keep the heat,' he added. 'Now is the time for a country-wide drive for our elementary human rights.' The ANC Action Group, for which recruiting and training had started in October, now numbered one hundred and twenty. Their training emphasised discipline and non-violence.[35]

A distinctive style and theme were emerging in Kenneth's writings now. The style, racy and vivid, kept before his readers the evil of what he called 'Malan *apartheid* and Herrenvolkism'. But the dominant theme was clearly the coming liberation of the 'nation', for which it was necessary that 'HQ instructions' should be carried out in all parts of the land. This in turn meant that the National Executive Council of the Congress had to work vigorously at the formulating and expounding of policy in order to keep ahead of popular action. Moreover, just as he did not forget to praise the butcher who removed the barriers in his shop, he consistently appealed to basic decency and common sense. In telling his readers of yet another clash with Government officials over Oliver Lyttelton's forthcoming visit, he rejected outright the officials' claim that Congress's policy of 'non-cooperation' precluded it from the right to an interview with the Colonial Secretary. 'Non-cooperation' related to matters 'detrimental to the African interest'. Lyttelton's visit was in no sense regarded as detrimental. But he added: 'Let us hope that the good old British spirit will prevail over groundless hatred next time we have an important Government guest.' 'I deliberately used the word "hatred",' he said, 'because it was used by this official in his official capacity.' The injection of an incisive brightness, almost gaiety, into his circulars was of considerable value at a time when sullen resentment was smouldering everywhere. In the same spirit of innate generosity, he stressed repeatedly the full realisation that the Protectorate could be 'nothing else but a place for a multi-racial society'. To replace the settlers' 'policies based on their pseudo-psychology of racial superiority, we must take to constructive measures'.[36]

The delicate work of boycotting butcheries owed much of its success to the good sense of the local leaders. In Lusaka, the Congress Branch Chairman, Lewis Changufu, developed Safeli Chileshe's technique of constructive discusssion successfully and so hastened the end of discrimination in the first of the butcheries to accept the boycotters' demands. Similarly, in Ndola, under Justin Chimba's leadership, the boycott quickly produced what the *Northern News* had to acknowledge as 'a clear victory for the African Congress'. Congress members there offered their labour free to close two pigeon-holes and knock out an extra door to avoid congestion at the Standard Butchery. Though arrested on the second day of the boycott, Chimba had come out of prison committed to positive measures. But the situation was always electric and the news that Matthew Nkoloma was in court for assaulting a European in Kitwe Post-Office was alarming. A one-day stoppage by the General Workers' Union confirmed the tenseness of the atmosphere.[37]

In Mufulira, however, where Andrew Mutemba was in the forefront of the local boycotts, the D.C. had intervened helpfully with the result that the manager of the butchery had ordered the end of discriminatory practices and indeed advised European employees who objected to his instructions to resign. On receiving a copy of the D.C.'s letter to Mutemba, Kenneth immediately wrote to express his gratitude to the D.C. and the butchery manager. 'We have been accused of being anti-white and anti-government,' he wrote. 'The truth is that we are not, not in the slightest sense of the terms: all we are is ANTI-WRONG. ... Let us hope that many other people will now brave the field and follow your example.'[38] By contrast, it was somewhat pathetic that the Chief Secretary should issue a press statement condemning 'the great trouble' caused to the butcheries, 'and to the African people who want to buy meat', by the boycotts. The police, he said, had 'done very good work' in protecting shoppers. 'People who had complaints' should go to the District Commissioner as they had always done.[39] The whole statement implied that the smooth relations of Government, the Chamber of Commerce and the Urban Advisory Council, the butcheries and their customers, had been upset by the boycotts.

As Congress branches exchanged congratulations on the progress of the anti-colour bar campaign, Kenneth was promoting another exercise in corporate action in the form of a special fund to send a promising student to the United States to study medicine. The student, Julius Chabala, was sent to various Congress branches with a letter of introduction from Kaunda, despite the unhappy state of Congress finances.[40] For Dr. Hastings Banda, in a recent letter congratulating Kenneth as a man of 'honesty and integrity' on his election as National Secretary, had urgently requested the repayment of at least £200 of the £600 which he had advanced a year earlier to George Kaluwa, Chief Mpezeni III and their fellow delegates when they were in London over 'the land case'. 'It would have been terrible,' Banda wrote, 'if these two men had been allowed to starve in London ... unable to return home, all simply because Congress officials had mismanaged funds.'[41] However, Kaunda now also informed branches of a plan of 'floating a fifteen thousand pound capital to open an All-African Butchery in Lusaka'. In a circular about this, Kaunda also spoke of 'a wide plan on AGRARIAN development, for ... we must treat it [the land] as our sacred trust.' There was a proposal also to launch a new secondary school, to be managed by Chiefs. Those three schemes, however, were not to be realised for lack of adequate support. Congress had still to organise and control its financial system.[42]

The campaign against discrimination in Livingstone had meanwhile run into serious difficulties through lack of organisational skill, and the official reaction had been sharp. Kaunda's advice to the Branch Secretary there was to 'send two or three strong members . . . to get trained here in how to deal with such business for one week.' 'This', he said, 'must be very private indeed. We don't want to expose ourselves to the enemy, we must be smarter.' To comfort the Livingstone group, he told them how twenty-seven men and women had been jailed for their part in the Lusaka campaign. Signing off 'Yours in earnestness of freedom'[43] or 'in earnestness for self-determination and independence,' he was trying to instil confidence into small groups which were ill-prepared for the fierce reactions of the police. It was time, he realised, for a detailed message to all ANC provincial and district officials to restore confidence and extend understanding of the policies to be carried out.

As news spread that African national organisations elsewhere were discontinuing the 'non-cooperation' policy, letters came to ANC headquarters asking if it was to be discarded in Northern Rhodesia also. Kaunda's new circular therefore reiterated the maxim, non-cooperation without violence, and spelled out again the reasons for it. It would continue until there was a 'government of the people for the people based on the noble principles of democracy'. He then recounted the events of the boycott campaign, and claimed that it was not until Congress announced the end of the boycott that the campaign ended, 'thus showing the government that the final word . . . had to be given by the . . . Congress'. But the Congress was being depicted as an organ of racial extremism. Kenneth therefore made a fresh and emphatic declaration on this issue. If Congress were to 'preach racial hatred,' he said, 'it would be making the same fatal mistake the whiteman has made in Africa . . . which honest men of all shades of colour are jointly trying to be put right.' But he went on to show how grievous the colour bar was to African people who had 'joined the forces which had fought and crushed NAZISM'. From war experiences in which, 'under the same gunfire, pay, etc. were based on colour,' Africans had come back home to hear the cry of 'partnership' but feel the full rigour of humiliating discrimination. Congress was therefore

pledged to change that state of affairs by 'that democratic weapon—
THE VOTE'. Again, as was increasingly his wont, he used an
apt quotation from James Russell Lowell, "They are cowards
who fear to speak for the fallen and weak." Therefore Africans
'had to find a way of sweeping the dirty surrounding rather than
shrinking in silence'. It was shameful that the 'foremost and obvious'
evil of the commercial colour bar had to be fought for seven weeks
before fair treatment could be secured. 'Congratulations—less
talk and more work—well done, Lusaka .... Keep the national
heat up ... your nation first and your good selves next as its
servants.' It was important, therefore, to express explicit appreciation to 'all those white friends who agreed by negotiation ... to
remove all colour-bar practices in their places ... for those days
when colour was a certificate to warrant honour or dishonour are
gone.'[44]

The organisation of the Congress offices and of the National
Executive Council were matters of urgency in early 1954. Correspondence with district officials revealed that, while the success of
the Lusaka boycotts had influenced the butcheries in various smaller
urban centres up and down the line of rail, important decisions
were being delayed by poor attendance at Council meetings.
Kenneth's desk meanwhile was increasingly piled with letters
from the provinces, some of which revealed the inexperience of the
Congress officials who wrote them. In particular, he had to rebuke
the Branch Chairman in Fort Jameson for allowing his juniors to
act irregularly. 'I knew you,' he wrote, 'long before I came to this
office and I expect better things from you than just nasty letters
and telegrams ....' 'It is up to you to be the guiding star.'[45]

The role of teacher, or, to use Julius Nyerere's Swahili title,
Mwalimu, was increasingly being thrust upon Kaunda. Because of
this, it is necessary to study his circulars in detail as evidence of
the development of a cogent and viable philosophy for political
change, and to note how his regular references in circulars to events
elsewhere in Africa and beyond and to memorable words of great
leaders served to break down the sense of isolation which tended
to grip his people after the fateful imposition of Federation. People
had to be made to feel their solidarity nationally and continentally.
In a further circular, headed 'How far have we gone?' Kenneth
began by characteristically emphasising what might 'go without

saying'. 'Needless here to remind,' he wrote, 'that the great wheel
of change is still on the move . . . .' 'Our spoke in this wheel is bound
to come to the top if only we can influence the present events.
. . . What you are doing in your big or small town or in a small
lonely village, another of your faith is doing elsewhere.' This to
him was 'simply wonderful'. 'As that great West African leader
said: "The fight is hard, the pace is fast, the obstacles well nigh insurmountable, our enemies are legion. But the benefits of freedom,
unity and peace are beyond compare." ' This same circular illustrating the cost of the struggle, gave numbers of those imprisoned in
different places, including Livingstone where 'twelve men and
three ladies [were] serving sentences from one to twelve months
in Her Majesty's Hostels—Our Protector!' In face of the fact that
there were many who still had a 'slavish mentality', members were
given a new instruction with a catchy new verb in it: 'ENROL AND
ENROL until you ANCOLISE the whole country.'[46]

The concept of partnership was naturally a difficult one for
African people to accept. Nothing in their personal experience
gave grounds for believing that the word was used genuinely.
Huggins had uttered a definition which gave the lie to the pretension
of 'Welenskyism' in terms such as these: 'Don't worry about
partnership. What we mean by it is the partnership of a man and
his horse. They don't eat or sleep together, but there is a working
understanding between them.' Good liberal people among the
white population seriously and, sometimes desperately, wanted to
promote real partnership. But the new rulers had other ideas.
Kaunda therefore sounded a loud alarm when, under the title
'Southern Rhodesia comes to Lusaka', he drew attention to the
grave news that night passes for Africans were to be introduced
in the capital.

For long the European mine townships in the north had been
insulated by a *de facto* curfew on Africans in them. But the proposal
at this time to establish the pass system by municipal legislation
in Lusaka was a blatant betrayal of the promises which had been
successfully used to sell Federation abroad. For too long the
Africans had 'bowed like dumb animals' to oppressive legislation
until it had appeared that 'silence means consent'. Now, he pleaded,
'Let us all join hands to stump [*sic*] out all that is unworthy of man.'
'We have no weapons that are physical but we have that which no

power can crash [*sic*]—Love for Freedom! I can give you one assurance ... all progressive people of any racial group are with us. .... So, awake, awake, and be the decent man you are.... There is nothing for nothing.'[47]

Kaunda's first Annual Review summed up the past year as a 'trying period of great mental and physical strain' which had nonetheless revealed 'the bare truth that lies in the making of our difficulties into stepping-stones to success'. One of the difficulties was that, despite repeated calls from around the country, the 'national leaders' were unable to visit the provinces as they should due to lack of funds. Moreover 'many young men who joined the ranks of the movement and whose sincerity one could not honestly doubt have come and gone, leaving the most needy places leaderless.' This had prevented the right interpretation of Congress policy and allowed others to 'use that chance to make their selfish ends meet'. The debarring of the Nyasaland Congress President from entering Northern Rhodesia and the consequent delay in the formation of a Central African Council of Congresses; the merciless wrecking 'by the powers that may be' of the Pan-African Regional Conference; and the piecemeal banning of the ANC in six districts, were blows that had to be faced. So was the lack of an answer to the request for a Congress delegation to meet the Colonial Secretary. So too was the failure of a number of cooperative projects, through financial bungling and, in the case of poultry and groundnuts, the inroads of wild cats and jackals. But Aggrey was right, he concluded: "You have been made to believe you are chickens. You are not, you are eagles. Stretch out your wings and fly."[48]

This first Annual Review was presented to the Sixth Annual Conference of ANC. Significantly, it was a minister of the African Methodist Episcopal Church, Revd. Dr. S. J. Tladi, who conducted the prayers at the opening of the Conference on 17 August. The agenda was lively. Nkumbula chose, as the theme of his presidential address, a review of the pattern of political parties in Central Africa. But there was little in it that was forward-looking. The hypocrisy of 'partnership' provided the main body of the speech, sharply illustrated by the overwhelming defeat in the Federal Parliament of Dauti Yamba's motion calling for equality of treatment for all races in public places. This was the motion that had called forth Huggins' sneer: 'You cannot expect a European to

form up in a queue with dirty people, possibly an old *mfazi* with an
infant on her back, mewling and puking and making a mess.'[49]
In Nkumbula's view the Federal Prime Minister's attitude and the
support it commanded fully offset the principles of what had come
to be called the Moffat Resolutions. John Moffat, having first
visited the Congress headquarters to discuss what he proposed to
say, won the backing of the majority of Leg. Co. members in Lusaka
for a motion that sought to free Africans and Europeans alike of
the fear that the other race might dominate them 'for its own racial
benefit'. But this humane plea did not have the force behind it that
Huggins knew he could rely on, and as Hall has observed, 'In
later years, Moffat's inability to win African support for his middle-
of-the-road Liberal Party could in part be traced to the refusal
of the Northern Rhodesia Government to implement his resolutions.'[50]

The 1954 ANC conference took place in an atmosphere so charged
that Rotberg, in his tenth chapter, refers to it as 'the bitterness'.[51]
Yet the resolutions before it sounded a note of constructive planning.
'In preparation for a democratic method of electing members to
the Federal and Legislative assemblies, municipal councils, etc.',
it was proposed to form a Congress political party. A closer association with Nyasaland was to be sought, going as far as 'the integration' of the two Protectorates. Congress was exhorted to launch
a national mass-literacy campaign, and to approach Government
with a view to establishing a grant-aided inter-racial college to
provide 'a good foundation for future race-relationships'. Similarly,
the Northern Rhodesia Government was to be asked to build a
technical college for Africans. Meanwhile, to widen popular awareness of the issues at stake in the land, the Conference approved the
principle of starting 'an all-African paper for Central Africa'.
It was also announced that the Congress intended to build an
inter-racial hall to which its offices and guest accommodation would
be attached. The report of the Conference concluded by recording
that, at the close, delegates sang *Lesa shipaleni Africa* and *Mwe
bombeni, bombeni, bombeni,—chulileni Africa*, meaning 'God,
please bless Africa' and 'You [people], work, work, work and suffer
for Africa'.[52]

After the delegates had dispersed, Kaunda wrote to the S.N.A.
advising him of six resolutions of the Conference, and stressing

that, by 'intimidating and dismissing Chiefs and Civil Servants who associated themselves with Congress, the Government would 'achieve nothing but stimulation of the interests of Africans in the national organisation'. The declaration of the Nyasaland Congress President as a prohibited immigrant was then deplored. Finally, the Government was warned that there would be organised resistance to 'pass laws and other humiliating class legislation.' A few days later, Kenneth wrote again to the S.N.A., asking for the Government's support for the establishment of an inter-racial college and a technical college for Africans.[53] Copies of both these letters went to the Colonial Secretary in London, as well as to African members of the Federal Parliament and the Legislative Council and to various friends. To the British Labour M.P., Mr. Fenner Brockway, he said, 'I fully realise that while we have sympathisers the world over, the battle for freedom must be fought and won by us here.' However, ANC accepted 'very very warmly indeed' the offer of affiliation to the rapidly growing 'Congress of Peoples against Imperialism'.[54]

For many years it had been customary for African boys and girls to have 'Christian' names derived from Europe, many being of biblical origin and adopted while attending mission schools. Probably the Lozi had been less given to this practice than others. Now, when strong stirrings of national self-consciousness were abroad in the land, a conscious desire appeared to revert to pre-colonial names. In answer to a letter from a pupil of Munali school, Kaunda sent congratulations on such a change of name. The boy had written: 'My names are now family ones as I am an African.' 'Let us give all honour to Africa by Africanising ourselves,' Kaunda replied. 'Let people civilise us if they can but let us not make them westernise us.' But he at no time wished to change his own two names, Kenneth David. His first name was dear to him because his father had chosen it for him, while the second was, of course, his father's own name. This was so even though his mother and close friends often referred to him as Buchizya Mtepa; Buchizya being the name given at birth meaning 'the unexpected one', and Mtepa being the name of his paternal grandfather.[55]

During his first year as Secretary-General, Kenneth's vision of his people's awakening bore fruit fast. But, though ANC might accelerate its output of informative circulars, it did not have access to the press or radio. The picture presented by the newspapers of the territory and likewise by official pronouncements on Central Africa in Britain was a very different one. Early in the year the Colonial Secretary had told the House of Commons that the Federal Prime Minister and the Nyasaland Governor had given him 'encouraging news on the way Africans were cooperating'. The *Northern News*, in a series on the 'issues' in the Protectorate, saw the elections as a contest between the Federal Party and the Colonial Office, a view apparently endorsed by the U.F.P.'s victory in ten out of twelve electoral seats in Leg. Co. It was a question of 'whether the modicum of power which has been won by European elected members will be retained and extended or whether all power will return to the Colonial Office from which it was wrested in fifteen years of united struggle'. The paper went on to aver that 'any reckless experiment in African advancement . . . would involve immediate action by the electorate in Southern Rhodesia . . . [and] force Huggins and Welensky to commit political suicide.'[56] There could hardly have been a fuller exposure of the fundamental fraud at the core of the Federation. But, moreover, the press comment revealed that, despite the openness of Congress comment and action, African political action was being pushed into the role of a sort of underground movement to be increasingly harassed by official repression.

There were still very few references to Kaunda in the public press, but it was noteworthy that on the day after he was reported as having stated that ANC members who had been convicted for violence during the Lusaka boycott campaign would be 'disciplined' on their release, the *Northern News* carried a centre-page article on the Congress which attempted an analysis of Nkumbula's leadership. His achievement had been in 'the concentration of resources to reject Federation', but now that it had been established, the movement needed 'someone with greater qualities of organisation and steadiness'.[57] From the start it was clear that Nkumbula would not figure prominently in the actual leadership of the various campaigns which the Congress was now organising and that Kaunda was much closer to the campaigners. It was he whom the press had quoted as saying that it was Congress pressure that had effected the end of the colour bar in the Lusaka butcheries. His commitment to this struggle was endorsed by his wife's participation in the boycotts as a member of the recently formed Congress Women's League. Their home life was soon deeply affected by their continual involvement in the campaign. Kenneth had gone to watch how African customers were treated and it had been then that he vowed never to eat meat again. Indeed when supporters in the Eastern Province sent the Kaundas a big parcel of fresh pig meat, Kenneth persuaded Betty that they should not eat it while thousands were doing without meat. Betty has told how, when the campaign was won after ten hard weeks, Kenneth continued to refuse meat and so she decided that the whole family must abstain with him. His vow had been not to eat meat till his people were free, but he did not want to deprive the family and so began a system whereby the office messenger brought meat to Betty. Kenneth has continued his 'no meat' rule ever since.[58]

About the time of his vow, another tricky issue had arisen, this time relating to beer. The Government ban on the brewing of 'native beer' was so patently discriminatory that the Congress leaders protested against it. Women then began to brew beer plentifully in defiance of the law and as a source of income. Though as 'teetotal' as her husband, Betty began to join the other illicit brewers without telling him until she had some money to show for her labour. 'He did not encourage me,' she recalled, 'but thanked me all the same.' He knew she had taken part in the protest of the women at the D.C.'s office shortly before and had been choked by tear gas fired by the police. The sharp action of the D.C. was followed by illegal brewing and more arrests and thus the campaign became part of the whole movement of 'non-cooperation without violence'. In consequence, secret drinking in *mikotokoto* in the forests kept the police increasingly busy. 'In some ways the whole thing was funny,' Betty said, 'and both the police and the raided women enjoyed the exercise.'[59]

Official anxiety about people of the different races meeting seemed to increase with the advent of Federation. The case of Simon Zukas was interpreted as being a matter, not just of a subversive person, but of a dangerous European influencing Africans. When the ANC hired the Chilenje Hall, under the clause in the permit forbidding 'tribal dancing and Tsaba-tsaba dancing' there was a postscript in ink specifying that any 'Europeans, Indians or Euro-Africans attending the conference must obtain individual entry permits, by order of the Director of African Affairs'.[60] For the same reason, Nkumbula had been listed as a prohibited immigrant in Southern Rhodesia at the same time. Hastings Banda's plan, after the Federation was established, to start a non-racial practice in Lusaka was blocked by a similar 'P.I.' order. Now, in August 1954, when Nkumbula and Kaunda went to Salisbury to meet the African M.P.s, they were stopped at the airport by immigration officials, presented with banning orders and turned back. The wording of the orders, as Kaunda remarked, was further testimony to the distorted thinking of an unjust regime. As 'alien natives', they were to be expelled from the Colony of Southern Rhodesia. 'How can you be an alien if you are also a native?' he asked.[61]

It was the Colonial Secretary's view that 'Africans would revert to darkness if they were given the vote.' On such a premiss, Whitehall was not to be expected to appreciate in which way the wind was blowing in Africa. Therefore, though Verwoerd was reportedly planning the compulsory shifting of over one million 'non-whites' from their homes in South Africa and Operation Anvil in Kenya was carrying through the 'intensive screening' of around twenty-five thousand Africans with a notable increase in the number of executions, the white supremacists in Central Africa could rely on Lyttelton's essential good will towards them. Thus towards the end of Federation's first year, Huggins warned, without fear of a rebuke from London, that 'the European' would resist with all his ability and resources any further political advancement if the African Federal M.P.s formed what he called 'a colour party'. This meant in effect that, while European privilege was securely entrenched on a rigid colour basis, any corporate advocacy by those M.P.s of the cause of the African people would be deemed provocation of racial conflict. In such an atmosphere, while the Revd. Percy Ibbotson, now an M.P., bade Africans be patient, the Boy Scouts' Travelling Commissioner declared that the joint training of white and black Scouts was now out of the question.[62] It was as though no one heeded the insight of Nabulyato, who had warned that 'bottled opinion' would inevitably lead to 'blood politics' and added wistfully: 'I wish we could exchange skin pigments for just an hour and probably we would be just a little wiser in legislating.'[63]

Towards the end of Federation's first year Kenneth Kaunda

issued two more major circulars. The struggle, he said in the first, was against those who wanted Africans 'to remain picks and shovels for ages to come,' those who were 'keeping pus—bad pus—in the lung'. He was therefore worried by subtle attempts to blind people so that they would not see what was really happening. 'Wolves, wolves, wolves, ho! be careful,' he cried, for there were those who were 'nicely clad in sheep's skins' and who were trying to persuade people to form a party to oppose the Congress. So Congress called upon its 'STREET BOYS to preach the truth and nothing but the truth and shame the devil.' "This generation," he quoted, "is sentenced to hard labour." Should we then drop the struggle? Nay, not after we have done so much. . . . Courage, old fellers, courage. . . . But let us remember that our Canaan, the Promised Land whose shrines have been destroyed, is yet far. To rebuild these destroyed shrines, we offer you nothing but toil, sweat, tears and the like.'[64] The second circular announced the decision of the Congress National Executive Council to prepare a five-year development plan and called upon people of every 'creed, colour and religion' to send in suggestions for the formulation of such a programme, for political, economic and social progress 'with special attention paid to Agrarian Planning, Health, Mass Literacy'. Proposals for the financing of this programme were also sought. 'Let it be remembered by the man and woman who was born to serve this nation sincerely that "Difficulties melt like snow in the sun when a brave heart faces them." Kenneth concluded with a formula for success, more inspirational than mathematical, which he presented thus:

$$\frac{\text{Love} + \text{Faith} + \text{Patience} + \text{Sacrifice}}{\text{Truth}^{65}} =$$

---

[1]*NN*, 7/7/53; and TI-FM/JMS, 6/10/69.
[2]*Op.cit.*, pp. 55-59; and Ogot, *op. cit.*, pp. 298 ff., Iliffe's article on Tanzania.
[3]Kaunda *op. cit.*, p. 59; TI-FM/D. Siwale (in Mwanga), 20/4/71; and for valuable studies by Zambian educationists, see J. Mwanakatwe, *The Growth of Education in Zambia since Independence*, (O.U.P., 1968) and H. F. Makulu, *Educational Development and Nation Building in Independent Africa* (S.C.M. Press, 1971).
[4]NAZ: Sec/Nat/109 S.N.A.'s Confidential Quarterly Newsletters, 2/4/48, 17/7/48, 4/10/48. Note also *Report of the Commission Appointed to Enquire into the Advancement of Africans in Industry*, chaired by Andrew Dalgleish (Govt. Printer, Lusaka, 1948).
[5]NAZ: N/0001/2/8, sundry notes from District Reports, letters of officials, press comments, (including undated quotation from *The New Statesman*) and report of Chinsali Welfare Society and Kaunda's address to it, 5/7/52.

[6]*Ibid.*: N/0001/2/8, resolution proposed by Amonson Mugala at a meeting convened by Yamba, 14/4/53.

[7]For religious protest movements, see Rotberg, *Rise*, pp. 133-135, and Shepperson and Price, *op. cit.*

[8]Mpashi, *op. cit.*, p. 34.

[9]ANC: circular by Nkumbula, 23/6/53.

[10]*Ibid.*: letter to Nkumbula from 'Commonsense', 19/8/53.

[11]*Ibid.*: letter from H. Johnston, Kalinda Mine, P.O. Dett, S. Rhodesia, 25/8/53 and Kaunda's reply, E43-36 of 10/9/53.

[12]*Ibid.*: Kaunda's circulars, D/6-21 of 26/8/53 to Secretaries of 'African National Organisations in South Africa, British South-West Africa, Basutoland, Bechuanaland, Swaziland, etc., Kenya, Uganda, Zanzibar, Tanganyika, Southern Rhodesia, Nyasaland'; and D/6-53, attaching Revd. Michael Scott's Memorandum.

[13]*Ibid.*: Kaunda's circular C/6-59 of 17/9/53; letter to 'shadow cabinet', B/1-92 of 5/10/53; Kaunda, *op. cit.*, pp. 186 ff. (Appendix IV); and ANC: Kaunda to S.N.A. D/27-197 of 18/12/53; ANC/5/22, letter of Colonial Secretary to Revd. Michael Scott, claiming that Nkumbula had been 'intent on stirring up trouble' in the Gwembe Valley, 14/10/53; and NAZ: KTE-2/1, Gwembe District Notebook, p. 385, recording 'loyal cooperation' of local Native Authority.

[14]ANC/2/7, letter of J. Musamba.

[15]*NN*, 25/9/53.

[16]ANC: Press Communique, 13/10/53; and *NN*, 2/10/63.

[17]ANC: Kaunda's circular, 13/10/53.

[18]Sikalumbi, *op. cit.*, pp. 29-30, naming three deposed chiefs as Milambo, Kasoma and Mulakwa; and TI-FM/KK, 5/2/69.

[19]*NN*, 25/9/53, 6/11/53, 9/11/53 for speeches by Welensky.

[20]TI-FM/JMS, 6/10/69.

[21]*NR Hansard*, July 1952.

[22]*NN*, 30/9/53.

[23]ANC, *Congress News*, Vol. I, No. 1, (October 1953).

[24]Owner of the *Central African Post*. His Progressive Party had recently withdrawn from the political scene.

[25]NAZ: Sec/Lab/139—record of discussion between Revd. J. G. Soulsby (Methodist) of NR Missionary Conference and C.S., 13/6/41; Sec/Lab/67—report by D.C., Luanshya, on 1935 'strike'; and *Report of the Commission Appointed to Enquire into Disturbances on the Copperbelt* (Govt. Printer, Lusaka, 1935) and 'Evidence taken by the Commission' (Lusaka, 1935) pp. 416-417.

[26]*Ibid.*: Sec/Lab/132—report of D.C., Chingola, 21/3/40; 769-2/MW/C/3 of 19/4/40 and 219/8 of 8/4/40; and Sec/Lab/71, letter of H. F. Cartmell-Robinson, 2/2/44.

[27]*Ibid.*: Sec/Lab/139—letter of Revd. A. J. Cross, Secy., General Missionary Conference, to C.S., 4/6/41; and of Secy., Chamber of Mines, to C.S., 24/6/41.

[28]*Ibid.* : Sec/Lab/139—P.C. Ndola, to C.S., 21/8/41.

[29]*A History*, p. 385.

[30]*NN*, 23/11/53.

[31]ANC: Kaunda's Circular B/1-153(2) of 17/11/53; and Kaunda to Mary Benson, A/42-156 of 19/11/53.

[32]*Ibid.*, A/70-180 of 30/11/53; Minutes of Regional Pan-African Council, 10-11/12/53; Kaunda, *op. cit.*, pp. 148-149; ANC Circ. D/6-202 of 28/12/53; and note that the Pan-African meeting was attended by Albert Kalyati, later Mayor of Kitwe, representing Shop Assistants; Timothy Kankasa, later Minister of State, Foreign Affairs, representing Ex-Servicemen; Wilson Chakulya, onetime General Secretary of the T.U.C. and later Minister of Labour, representing the National Youth League. Kaunda described Chakulya as 'brave enough to face anything'. (TI-FM/KK, 13/2/69).

[33]Kaunda *op. cit.*, pp. 186-196; and see NAZ: KTE/2/1, Gwembe District Notebook, esp. pp. 240-242 and 385.

³⁴See *NN* for the period; *NN*, 19/1/54 for quotation of *New York Times* comment; and see Chap. IV, footnote 33.
³⁵ANC: Kaunda's Circular B.1/54 of 24/1/54; and Sikalumbi, *op. cit.*, p. 32.
³⁶ANC: Circular B.1/54.
³⁷*NN*, 9/2/54; and ANC/2/7, Dixon Konkola to Kaunda and Sikalumbi, 5/2/54.
³⁸ANC: Kaunda to D.C., Mufulira, 19/2/54.
³⁹ANC: press statement of C.S., A. T. Williams, 20/2/54.
⁴⁰Chabala had moved in 1947 from Lubwa, Chinsali, to Mufulira, where he had lived with the writer and completed his primary education. His secondary education was at Adams College, Natal, where his fees were paid by Dr. Hastings Banda, now President of Malawi. The refusal of NRG to give him a university scholarship was followed by the opening of the Congress fund. He studied in the U.S.A. for nine years, having been initially assisted by Bishop Frederick Jordan of the African Methodist Episcopal Church. See ANC/2/7, A. Mutemba to Kaunda f./6-72 of 26/2/54.
⁴¹ANC/2/7—Dr. H. K. Banda to Kaunda, 7/2/54.
⁴²ANC/2/7—Kaunda's Circular of 3/3/54 re various schemes; and Sikalumbi, *op. cit.*, p. 37.
⁴³ANC A/21-95, Kaunda to Livingstone Branch Secretary, 4/3/54.
⁴⁴ANC: Kaunda's Circular 1/b.3/54 to all ANC Provincial and District Officials, 5/3/54.
⁴⁵ANC: Kaunda to Branch Chairman, Fort Jameson, A/73-119 of 7/4/54.
⁴⁶ANC: Kaunda's Circular 1/B.4/54, 12/4/54.
⁴⁷*Ibid.*: p. 2, para 3. Note also Sikalumbi, *op. cit.*, p. 38, ref. Ndola Municipal Council's ruling that African women had to carry their marriage certificates, which provoked a riot at the Boma by '600 women and 200 men'. For reference to Huggins' definition of partnership, see Keatley, *op. cit.*, p. 224.
⁴⁸ANC: Kaunda's Circular, A/23-258 of 15/8/54.
⁴⁹Federal Assembly Debates, 1, 28/7/54.
⁵⁰*NR Hansard*, No. 82 (July, 1954); and Hall, p. 169.
⁵¹pp. 258 ff.
⁵²ANC/DHR/2/7, circular by Kaunda.
⁵³*Ibid*: Kaunda to S.N.A., B/5-291 of 4/9/54 and B/5-197 of 8/9/54.
⁵⁴ANC/3/UK, Kaunda to Brockway, 31/3/54 and 5/8/54.
⁵⁵ANC/2/7, letter of Mwewa Lubansa, 27/8/54, and Kaunda's reply, A/21-301 of 9/9/54; and TI-FM/KK, 5/10/71.
⁵⁶*NN*, 12/2/54—19/2/54.
⁵⁷*NN*, 27/2/54.
⁵⁸Mpashi, *op. cit.*, pp. 37-40.
⁵⁹*Ibid.*: pp. 40-41.
⁶⁰NAZ: Sec/Nat/353; ANC-CEO/0A/2, *proforma* dated 19/2/53.
⁶¹Kaunda *op. cit.*, pp. 60-61.
⁶²*NN*, 26/5/54 and 16/6/54; and *London Times*, 6/5/54.
⁶³*NR Hansard*, 28/4/54 for speeches of Nabulyato and of Chileshe, Sokota and Lakement Ng'andu opposing the 'Picketing Bill'.
⁶⁴ANC: Kaunda's Circular B/1(6)-54 of 13/9/54.
⁶⁵*Ibid.*: 1/81-365 of 26/9/54.

7

Extending Horizons

What so radically aggravated the Central African situation in the period after 1945 was the threat of the further extension of attitudes which dressed up exploitation as *apartheid* and used the persuasive arguments of 'separate development' to perpetuate inhuman domination. A Rhodesian M.P. had once remarked that 'the conqueror considered . . . that one of the fruits of victory was the women of the conquered race.' Thus in Rhodesia as in South Africa, legislation initially laid down drastic sentences for African men who had illicit relations with white women while condoning the behaviour of European men who took black concubines. One impartial observer, in the period preceding the First World War, reported that he found 'a great many of the white men living with Kaffir women in Northern Rhodesia' while the number of men in Matabeleland who had African concubines was 'positively appalling'.[1] The huge 'coloured' population of southern Africa and the parlous plight of Northern Rhodesia's Euro-Africans in their social no-man's-land in the pre-independence period, testify to a factor in the racial tangle of the continent which charged the whole situation with explosive and irrational emotions, dangerously akin to those of America's southern states.

The importance of this factor must not be overlooked when we review the period in which the long-dominant and confident slogans of 'white superiority' began to be articulately countered by plans to build a 'multi-racial democracy'. A glance at the population statistics confirms something of the magnitude of the threatened clash. In 1953 the ratio of Africans to Europeans in Northern Rhodesia was 40:1. It had dropped to 31:1 by 1963. In Southern Rhodesia, however, the high-powered immigration campaign mounted by Huggins increased the colony's white population from

82,836 in 1946 to approximately 168,000 on the eve of Federation. The cost of this increase, from public and private funds combined, was over £2,000 million.[2] These figures give point to Welensky's plan to have around half-a-million Europeans in Northern Rhodesia by the early nineteen-sixties. On the face of it, it would have therefore been logical to regard the situation as a simple confrontation of one race with another. As we have seen, various white politicians spoke constantly in terms of stark racism; their 'we' was essential an exclusive one. Every now and then there were evidences of an indiscriminate reaction on the part of Africans, especially when in crowds, against all Europeans.[3] Yet what Kenneth Kaunda was expounding, from the outset, was a philosophy for a 'multi-racial' society: it does not matter what colour you are: you are a human being, a 'child of God', which is the only viable formula for man's life in the world. The leadership Kenneth offered, therefore, was much more akin to that of Martin Luther King than to that of the disciples of Malcolm X. It is thus not surprising that he should enjoy and return the friendship of people in Britain and elsewhere who saw the justice of his cause. Increasingly he was to establish spontaneous and lasting relations of this kind. What is of special interest now is that he began to do so early in his career.

Though contacts with African organisations in the neighbouring territories could not be extensive, the nationalist movements were quick to hear of Europeans who were sympathetic. Thus the name of Guy Clutton-Brock, pioneer of an inter-racial farm in Southern Rhodesia, came early to the notice of the Congress office in Chilenje. Just before Christmas, Kaunda wrote to him, acknowledging two letters and thanking him for a donation of £17 sent in response to the Congress appeal for '£3,000 needed to campaign against Interterritorial Control Act, Deportation Orders, Immigration Policy, etc.' He wanted Clutton-Brock to know the situation in the north. The letter, which had included a kindly reference to Mrs. Clutton-Brock, ended thus: 'We wish you a Happy Xmas Day when men of all colours shall together and sincerely sing, "All glory be to God on High, Goodwill and peace to men." '[4]

This relationship with the Clutton-Brocks was reciprocally warm from the start, even though they were to have little opportunity to meet in subsequent years. Clutton-Brock has said of Kaunda that he appeared 'uncommitted to anything other than the service of his fellow men. ... He was certainly not committed to anything to do with himself nor to any ideology ... perhaps he is one of the few free men in the world.' As for so many people, Kenneth impressed Clutton-Brock by a number of small but spontaneous kindnesses on their few meetings. But, most of all, he appeared as one of 'the three men of top quality in Africa', the others being, in Clutton-Brock's view, Julius Nyerere and the late Dunduzu Chisiza of Malawi. 'His freedom has bound him to the service of his fellow men as head of a modern state.' To a man of the deep insights of Clutton-Brock, this bondage must sometimes mean for Kaunda in the future being 'bound hand and foot, compelled to do things which are really against his nature,' for 'anyone with integrity going into politics and being chosen by the people to lead must, in many detailed situations, be called upon to act against his deepest belief.' In terms of the quality of Christian inspiration which the two men shared, Kenneth's role might demand of him that particular sacrifice of which Deitrich Bonhoeffer had spoken as he faced the ultimate suffering as Hitler's prisoner, namely, the sacrifice of 'one's most treasured principles'. But what especially impressed Clutton-Brock was the 'very wonderful thing, not a "miracle" but an indication of the basic purity of Man, that men such as Kenneth Kaunda and Julius Nyerere have been thrown up through all the ferment to lead in this crucial part of the world at this moment'.[5]

Some time previously, an Indian businessman in Lusaka, Rambai Patel, had obtained a considerable amount of literature on the Indian struggle for self-determination, which was available to Congress leaders, some of it being translated into local languages. Kaunda read those books and pamphlets avidly and began to hope for a chance some day to visit India. It was true, as he has said, that Asian immigrants in Central Africa gave relatively weak support to the Congress cause but this, he believed, was because most of them were in commerce and feared the consequences of official displeasure upon their incomes, if they were to ally themselves with African aspirations. In South Africa, where there were a number of Asian professional men, the picture was different. In Northern Rhodesia, Kaunda said, 'those who supported us were always hunted.' The few who risked this 'hunting', including the late T.L. Desai, a lawyer in Lusaka, helped to enliven further Kenneth's early interest in India. The cause of his people was not, he was now sure, a lonely one. There were friends, actual and potential 'the world over'. Letters from Simon Kapwepwe, then in India, painted a vivid picture of Gandhi's country in the first years of her independence.[6]

Kaunda was, however, very suspicious of some of the advocates of 'inter-racialism' at home. Early in December, he wrote a long letter to Harry Franklin, who had succeeded Nightingale as Specially Nominated M.L.C. for African Interests. It was in fact a detailed questionnaire on Government policy regarding such matters as: land; development of African agriculture; the responsibilities of Native Authorities and the vexed question of the deposition of chiefs; African education, including plans for developing secondary schools and a university as well as industrial and technical institutions; public service posts of responsibility for Africans; town planning and racial zoning in urban areas; and the promotion of social intercourse between the races. Franklin's answer was somewhat evasive. His description of inter-racial social intercourse was distinctly rosy and he surprisingly included the Boy Scouts and the Girl Guides as agencies of such meeting. Three weeks earlier, a Ndola European Guide Captain had resigned over the rejection of her plan to let the Guide Hall be used by African Guides for a Christmas party and the threat of the parents of seven white girls to withdraw them if the hall were so used. The churches were conspicuously absent from Franklin's list. Swiftly the correspondence became fiery, until in May 1955, Franklin closed it with a brief note: 'There is no point in our continuing to write long letters to each other, since it is clear to me that the bitterness in your heart and the ignorance in your mind is unlikely ever to be dispelled.' He then urged Kaunda to visit the Kabulonga Club, of which he himself was Chairman.[7]

The Kabulonga Club in Lusaka was a social centre run by the United Northern Rhodesia Association. Kaunda hesitated for a long time before he registered himself as a member of it and even then he did so out of loyalty to Harry Nkumbula. 'I just didn't see the use of it,' he said. 'You form an association for a definite purpose. We couldn't improve things through such an association. It had to be done through political action.' He added that as time went on, his misgivings increased as the 'doubtful role of Harry Franklin, in relation to his fellow Harry, increased' in the mid-fifties.[8] The club was to remain sufficiently in the public eye to provoke a senior schoolboy at Munali to ask Kaunda, in 1957, to warn people 'more militantly ... to think twice before joining such things'.[9] Back in 1955 and 1956, Kaunda 'attended it seldom'. He once heard a Negro professor give a lecture there and 'went four or five times to play games, draughts, table tennis, etc'. It was there, however, that he formed an intimate acquaintance with Father Patrick Walsh, who also met Nkumbula and the Wina brothers, Sikota and Arthur, at the club. 'Kaunda struck me as the outstanding personality among them all,' Walsh has recalled, 'and I formed the opinion then that he was the man who would emerge as the future leader of the country.' 'His sense of dedication, his self-discipline and absolute sincerity were characteristics that anyone who had close contact with him could not fail to notice. He was the very antithesis of what Welensky and others described as power-hungry agitators.' For Walsh, the club was the only place where Africans and Europeans could meet together.[10]

This meeting place of the United Northern Rhodesia Association has provided another vignette of Kaunda as he appeared to Peter Fraenkel the European broadcaster, who, as we saw above, had attended the Congress rally in March 1953. 'It was not easy to make conversation with him,' said Fraenkel. 'He was a taciturn, embittered young man, one of those who "see nothing save their own unlovely woes." When at last, the conversation turned to his early years at Lubwa, he answered somewhat truculently, "I was a very troublesome youth.... I would insist on asking awkward questions ... like why the European missionaries had padded seats in church but my father, who had been working for the mission longer than most of them, had to sit on a wooden bench like the rest of the African congregation. I demanded to know whether it would be the same in their heaven."' The sharpness of this reply set the broadcaster thinking: 'Generations of kindly missionaries have retired from Lubwa ... to Scotland,' he mused, 'convinced that they have sacrificed a lifetime's labour and lived in poverty to convert and raise up the heathen.' 'They have forgotten about the padded seats. Partial acceptance is not enough.'[11] Now, in the new situation of turbulence, news came of an ANC group breaking the church colour bar in Broken Hill and a clear assertion by Andrew

Mutemba that the copper of the country belonged to its people who 'must look forward to controlling it', served to demonstrate that every form of discrimination and exploitation was now coming under fire.[12]

Not long after Mutemba uttered this claim, Guy van Eeden revived Gore-Browne's old scheme of partition of the territory and called for a white-ruled dominion excluding Nyasaland, Barotseland and Northern Rhodesia's Northern Province. A month later, on Christmas Day, Kaunda issued a press communique totally rejecting the plan. The proposal, he claimed, 'would destroy the spirit of the Federal Constitution and the Moffat Resolutions which are a serious attempt to solve racial problems' and 'mean a complete defeat of the possible integration of men and women of different colours'. It would lead to the 'wholesale eviction of a possible one and a quarter million Africans' and the fierce repression of African political aspirations. Moreover the African states would stagnate economically since 'the White State' would include all the industrialised areas. 'It can be argued,' he said, 'that the White State might be generous to the African States.' But history did not support such a hope for 'the tendency of the white people in Africa has always been to hold the African back.' The last reason for rejection was that 'the African' regarded 'the industries and the areas where these industries lie as part of his property just as much as they are the property of the investor of capital.' People were therefore urged to oppose the van Eeden scheme 'tooth and nail'.[13]

Congress was in effect a political party now and had to be organised on a country-wide basis so that its activities could be developed throughout the year. An annual conference was no longer sufficient, nor was the work of an active headquarters office any longer adequate. When Kaunda called on people to 'ANCOLISE all our beautiful mountains and valleys', something more was required than a general interest in what Congress was doing. There was a hierarchy of national provincial, district and branch officers on paper, but Kaunda, as Secretary-General, was aware that in many places this organisation was still far from effective. In his second last circular of 1954, entitled 'HQ Instructions' he had combined detailed regulations for local officials, to make 'integrity and efficiency better' with exhortations to confidence and courage. Those regulations referred to such matters as the use of receipts, keeping of district and provincial registers, inspectoral powers of senior officials, careful filing, financial reports and disciplinary action. Moreover, Kenneth was clearly developing his policy of acknowledging and listing adverse elements in the situation and then adding specific words of inspiration. 'It is not for us to lament over these things—ours is a more noble duty to fight all these off.' Congress men and women in jail must, he said, be prayed for. 'You will also ask God to give you wisdom and courage ... in your struggle for self-determination and independence.' But this meant action, for 'someone has said, "Our oppressors understand only the language of organised strength." A friend of Revd. Michael Scott had written to say that similar movements elsewhere in Africa were watching events in Northern Rhodesia. 'Go out,' he said, 'and organise our people honestly and efficiently so that we reach that goal—HOME RULE, before those other people who are following our example.'[14]

As the year ended he published another ringing exhortation. 'The old days when we used to depend on what we called British Protection are no more. Exploitation and all the evils that go with it were there but we had some hope that we would one day protect ourselves after the right kind of tuition.' Instead however, 'the Tory government has sold us to a handful of reactionary settlers ... let no other man once more deceive you that he will protect you. .... Now stand up, be bold, be strong, be the man you were born to be. .... In you God has put all the power—so stand up and serve your nation. Stop that old habit of speaking and not doing things ... for ... this beast FEDERATION ... has started by passing Act after Act that will end in Central Africa becoming a second South Africa.' Local officers were then asked to advise people not to participate in the celebration of such public holidays as 'Rhodes and Founders Day; Empire Day, Federation Day', for those were in fact celebrations of the enslavement of the people, 'easily gained wealth, the extravagant and luxurious lives' of the ruling race. 'Remember to non-cooperate—but without violence.'[15]

It was, however, industrial unrest that was filling the headlines in those days. More than ten thousand African employees of the building industry had been on strike, including bricklayers in Government undertakings, for two weeks in October. The Master Builders' Association declared that the African demand for increased wages would force them to employ more Europeans and so delay African advancement further. The Government warned its building employees of dismissal if they were not back at work by the eighteenth and promised in any case to deduct pay for the period of the strike. The threat by the Mine Workers' Union to join eight other unions on strike increased the tension at a time when, as Mason observes, 'the European Union, as usual, was in favour in principle of African advancement, in practice against any step that might have led to it.' In all the negotiations of the period, the Rhodesia Selection Trust was notably more favourable to African advancement than was the Anglo-American Corporation, and this further complicated matters. Though Lawrence Katilungu called off the miners' strike at the beginning of November, the situation was deteriorating, and there was angry resentment on the part of the A.M.W.U. against the mining companies' plan to admit Africans, promoted to supervisory posts, to the Mines African Staff Association. The African Union saw this as another 'divide and rule' move.[16]

As a new strike began at the turn of the year, the Government was now showing marked nervousness over the relationship of the growing African trade union organisations to the Congress. On 4 January there was a call-up of all European men, between seventeen and twenty-nine years of age, for military training, patently related to what van Eeden described as an 'explosive racial situation' in the mining towns. Two days later Harry Nkumbula, Wittington Sikalumbi and Kenneth Kaunda were charged with being in possession of prohibited literature, arrested and released on £25 bail until their trial four days later. In Fort Jameson, two ANC officials, Frank Chitambala and Dominic Mwansa, were sentenced to six months imprisonment on a similar charge. On 12 January Sikalumbi was acquitted by the Lusaka magistrate's court, but Nkumbula and Kaunda were sent to prison for two months with hard labour. In a speech applauded by over a thousand people, Dixon Konkola, ANC's Acting Secretary-General, told a rally at Chilenje on the day of the trial that the Congress was preparing the country for self-government. 'In any country,' he said, 'when the leaders of any national movement are sent to gaol, it is the beginning of freedom.' At the same time, the General Manager of the Rhokana Corporation told visiting British educationists:

'We will never have a Mau Mau here because we have started on far better lines than anywhere else in Africa.'[17]

Kenneth Kaunda has described the occasion of his arrest in his autobiography. The Congress headquarters naturally kept a number of publications which the Federal authorities would not like, but one in particular, the magazine sent by Fenner Brockway, *Africa and the Colonial World*, was regarded as especially offensive by the police prosecutor. The raid on the Kaunda home in Chilenje began in classical style, in the early hours of the morning, when Kaunda was still asleep. The blue warrant of search was produced and the police officer, not unkindly, said 'Kenneth, we are asking you to go to your office.' *Africa and the Colonial World* had recently been banned, as Kaunda records, when Frank Barton, editor of the *Central African Post*, raised a hue and cry about it. The Congress report on the disturbances in the Gwembe valley had been published in the magazine and this had undoubtedly hastened the ban. The *Northern News* quoted a police statement that 'red pamphlets' had been found at the ANC office. The pile of banned papers had not yet been posted to Southern Rhodesia as Fenner Brockway had suggested on hearing of the ban in Northern Rhodesia. The various items of literature had, however, been tied together for disposal, according to Sikalumbi. When the police had arrived at the Chilenje house, Betty Kaunda heard them mention prohibited literature and assumed at once that they were looking for the translations into Bemba of the pamphlets about Gandhi and Nehru and the Indian independence story. As soon as they went off with her husband to the Congress office, she 'removed all the books from the house and hid them in a large pot in the kitchen and covered it with an empty sack'. But, she has recorded, 'I had not observed the CID men who were posted at a distance around the house.' The result was that when the police officers returned, they went straight to the kitchen, pulled the books from the large pot and checked the titles on a list of prohibited publications which they carried. 'They had quite a big catch,' Betty said.[18]

The trial, before the Resident Magistrate, lasted three days. When the conviction of the two men was announced, a crowd of over one thousand gathered in Chilenje to protest. The *Northern News* report printed Kenneth's surname as 'Kaonde'. Though 'there were no incidents', the crowd sang lusty political songs.

'This is our land. It is not the Europeans'. It is ours. We will have it. We will fight for it.' In his summing up, the magistrate described some of the literature found in the possession of Kaunda and Nkumbula as 'cheap, disreputable and scandalous'. 'The identity of the political organisation to which they belong is quite immaterial,' he said. 'What is important is that both the men and the books are political.' Betty Kaunda's view was that it was the books on the Indian struggle that were 'red hot' in raising the political morale of the people. As Kenneth went off under arrest, he was reassured to know that Simon Kapwepwe, who had returned on 6 January from his four-year 'sojourn in India', would help to look after his family. Immediately gifts began to flow in from Congress members in many parts of the country, for the care of the two leaders' wives and children. In Sikalumbi's words, 'the tomtoms beat out the news, "Support the just cause." ' Kapwepwe had arrived wearing a 'kind of jumper' made of cheap cloth which was sometimes called 'the Kapwepwe shirt'. According to Hall, this shirt, made of black cloth, 'was adopted as a uniform by some Congress enthusiasts'. Kapwepwe also introduced black armbands as a sign of mourning for the imprisoned leaders, and, Hall says, immediately 'took over the presidential chair'.[19]

In prison, however, Kenneth was aware that he and his President had different attitudes to their new situation. Because the food in jail was of poor quality, Kenneth proposed that they should go on hunger strike on behalf of themselves and their fellow prisoners. It seemed to him that Nkumbula was not at all in sympathy with this idea. He appeared badly shocked by the experience of being arrested. Kaunda told him not to worry. He had been reading about the Indian and the Irish struggles and was himself 'prepared for anything'. Looking back, Kaunda could trace the small beginning of a parting of the ways at that time. He was aware that the struggle ahead might well demand further privation and so decided to follow a way of life devoid of compulsive habits. He would eat even more simply than hitherto and continue his total abstinence in the matter of alcohol. He had never used tobacco. Harry Nkumbula, however, seemed to be wanting more of 'the soft life'.[20] He appeared to be less and less committed to the labour required to bring a new nation to birth; though he had said recently that his people were determined to 'get' their country.[21] Indeed the message he delivered at Chibolya, Lusaka on his release from prison had much of the earlier fire as he spoke of the suffering needed so that the pioneers of the movement might 'be the rocky foundation of our people's freedom and national independence'.[22]

Simon Kapwepwe's return to the Protectorate had been dramatic and, as Hall says, he 'became almost overnight a rallying force in the nationalist movement'. Four years in India had given him a close view of the activities and techniques of a popular movement that had faced severe repression triumphantly, and his temperament was such that he was bound to want swift action in his homeland, related both to 'breaking the yoke of white domination' and galvanising the human resources of the nation. Already Harry Nkumbula was becoming concerned by the activities of the Action Group and the tension between the young radicals and himself. Kapwepwe's impact was so sharp that Nkumbula sent him a letter from prison, in which he pleaded, 'Please don't destroy my Congress.' The young man who was in jail with him was, Nkumbula knew, a boyhood friend of Kapwepwe. It might be true as the returned radical often claimed that his 'pushing' and Kaunda's 'caution' were complementary to one another, and that when Simon was 'very rushing' Kenneth would 'take the brakes'. But for Nkumbula, Kapwepwe embodied a challenge to which historians would later trace 'the origin of the dissension within the leadership which was to split Congress in 1958'. For Kenneth however, during those weeks behind bars, there was added another anxiety to his apprehensions about his leader, namely the serious illness of his youngest son, Tilyenji. On compassionate grounds he was allowed to visit his family, under guard and in the uniform of a convict, rough sailcloth shorts and shirt marked with black arrows.[23]

Shortly before he was arrested, Kenneth had produced the first number of a revived and condensed *Congress News* under the title of the *Official Gazette*. Unlike the pioneer *News*, this paper used a stilted form of 'bureaucratic English'. 'It is hereby notified that under and by virtue of the powers conferred upon this National Executive Council . . . the said Council has expelled the Hon. Sokota, P., Esq., MLC, from the post of a Treasurer General.' Similarly, under the heading: 'Auditors, appointment of', it announced that 'Mutemba, A. B., Esq., and Chimba, J. H., Esq.,' had been given responsibility for auditing Congress accounts on a territorial basis. The final paragraphs of Volume I, Number 1, however, were in Kaunda's now well-known conversational style. 'My friends old and new,' he wrote, 'Northern Rhodesia wants the sacrifice of a thousand men and women. . . .' 'No great work can be done without sacrifice, so lay down your comforts, your pleasures, your names, your fame and position now that your nation has called you to things higher than your own life. Cultivate the virtue of obedience and others will obey you . . . remember that the darkest hour comes shortly before dawn . . . and dawn is drawing nearer and nearer as we struggle.'[24] The second issue of the *Gazette* was presumably the work of Dixon Konkola as Acting Scretary-General. It announced two decisions of the N.E.C. which were to be observed everywhere: the wearing by ANC officials of 'national dress' in the form of 'a black simple shirt and collarless . . . of a cheap material not exceeding 2/6d a yard', and the annual observance of 6 January as a 'day of sorrow' to commemorate the arrest of Nkumbula and Kaunda.[25]

The official date for the release of the two 'top leaders' was 3 March and a massive procession was planned to welcome them. They were, however, released on the second and so the Government avoided a possible confrontation with an agitated crowd. However, four days later 'a crowd of more than eight thousand' assembled in the 'compound' called Chibolya, on the outskirts of Lusaka. The meeting place was fenced and so, according to Sikalumbi who was one of the organisers, it was possible to know how many attended by the amount of money collected at the gates. The printed programme for 'Good Sunday, 6th March 1955—Reception of our Leaders' was given to each admitted at the rate of '3d all round'. Singing and dancing, which were to become regular features of political rallies, were interspersed throughout the programme, while police spotter planes droned overhead. The meeting was opened and closed with prayers and the two leaders were greeted by the Ngoni royal salute, '*Bayete*'. After the speeches of Kaunda and Nkumbula, Bemba *mishikakulo* or jesters' orations, were performed. Nkumbula's lengthy speech was perhaps something of an anticlimax for a crowd primed to receive marching orders. It consisted largely of a reiteration of his outline of the evils of the colonial system, and he spoke fiercely about Huggins' recent remark about 'pests' that must be removed to let Federation work.

He linked this comment to Welensky's 'Red Indian' remarks of July 1952. His address ended with an outline of constitutional proposals drafted in prison. In a brief speech delivered before Nkumbula's, Kenneth Kaunda warned that 'by rejecting an evolutionary solution' to the racial tensions of the territory, the Government was 'fast heading for worse than South Africa'.[26]

Immediately on his release, Kaunda wrote to the Colonial Secretary on the need for a new Constitution for Northern Rhodesia. The Congress plan which he now submitted would, he claimed, give Europeans 'safeguards in the cabinet'. It was in fact, the second of the three alternative schemes which Nkumbula had outlined at Chibolya the day before. Whereas the first scheme had prescribed 'a cabinet of ten ministers', the one submitted to Lennox-Boyd added the words 'parity in the Cabinet'. By way of a *quid pro quo* it removed from Nkumbula's first scheme the explicit 'safeguards for minorities, e.g. special or reserved seats for them in the House of Representatives'. The primary principle of the first two schemes was the enfranchisement of 'British Protected Persons' and 'a single common roll for Black and White'. On behalf of 'the Africans of Northern Rhodesia', Kaunda 'demanded' that the constitutional scheme be considered.[27] At the same time, he cabled the Federal Governor-General protesting against Huggins' remark about 'pests' and demanding the right of secession.[28]

In another letter written on the same day to the Chief Secretary in Lusaka, Kaunda set out a list of nine matters on which the Chibolya meeting had passed 'protest resolutions'. These included complaints against the deportation of Tanganyikan Africans 'on the pretext that they were Mau Mau suspects' and of Sangala, President of the Nyasaland Congress. Congress, Kaunda said, had noted that when Europeans went on strike on the Copperbelt, dismissal did not follow. ANC therefore protested against the recent dismissal of Africans who had participated in the extended strike, which the Labour Commissioner had recently described as legal, in the face of the Mines' refusal to discuss wages, bonuses and savings. The Government Labour Department was biased in favour of European employees and so people had 'no confidence' in it. Once again, Kaunda recorded popular anger at the recent enactment of the Inter-Territorial Movement of Persons Bill and the Picketing Bill, and called the continued deposition of Chiefs 'intimidation', which, like the barring of Congress from certain districts and the extension of police powers of arrest, was changing their 'peaceful country' into a 'police state'.

The final protest was against the continued representation of African interests by Europeans specially nominated to sit as members of Leg. Co. A copy of this letter went to African members of the legislature but not to the Governor's special nominees.[29] However, Kaunda wrote to the European members for African interests in both Leg. Co. and the Federal Parliament to assure them that this protest was not in any sense 'something born out of personal hatred, but . . . a challenge to the system which is very wrong. . . .' 'We ask you to consider this as a timely and sincere warning,' he said. 'But should you fail to resign forthwith, we shall consider you as people who have personal interests and shall thereafter have no alternative but to make your position very unpleasant in future.'[30] When Harry Franklin reported this threat in the Legislative Council, Kaunda replied, though the press, that the 'unpleasant' experience predicted would be rejection 'by the majority of Africans when he sought their views'.[31]

The record of events of this period, given by Wittington Sikalumbi, confirms that there was considerable bitterness and suspicion in the land which produced tensions within Congress ranks. Nkumbula was not long out of prison when he spoke emphatically against the wearing of black shirts. The more radical men regarded this as an 'indication of a new spirit of moderation'. Safeli Chileshe, who was one of the old Congress Executive which had been replaced by 'militant' younger men in 1953, came under attack for employing Southern Rhodesians in his shops in Matero and Chinika. For some time a boycott of his shops was organised by ANC. This was a strange episode in view of the recent kindly reference to Chileshe made by Kaunda at a public meeting on a Congress 'day of national prayers'. The general uneasiness, which manifested itself in a new rumour about poison in the cheap popular brand of cigarettes called O.K., was rising in direct proportion to the intensified organisation of Congress activities throughout the country.[32] Kenneth Kaunda's statement on 'national prayers' in April was, however, designed to encourage people. They were not doing a new thing, he said. The ancient Israelites, in times of bondage, had gathered together in prayer. Soon people would be remembering,

during Holy Week, 'the suffering that our Lord and Saviour under-
went'. It was the wont of imperial regimes to hold their own holy
days to celebrate and rejoice over 'what they draw from these
empires' and 'cunningly make the ruled join . . . and . . . sing
"Hosanna, hosanna" for their empires.' But, he declared, 'we find
consolation in the fact that history has proved . . . that such ignorant
rejoicing by the oppressed has always had a limit.' Congress meanwhile was being criticised by some for 'running without an official
opposition'. Kaunda's thinking on the role of an opposition party
was to change considerably in the light of political developments
consequent upon the attainment of independence nine years later.
Now, however, he asserted that the time for an opposition would
come when there would be open elections on an unrestricted franchise. 'If we don't then [have an opposition party], we would be
running as dull a government as the Federal Party is running today.'
His brief speech went on to refer to the bitter rejection of motions
in the Federal and territorial legislatures, whereby African members
had sought legislation to outlaw racial discrimination in public
places. 'My fear is,' said Kaunda, 'that our children will not have
the same slavish patience that we have of allowing people to push
us here and there as if we were footballs.' He concluded by announcing the steady growth of the Congress Women's League. 'Among
the first people to go to jail for a national cause were some mothers.
. . . We cannot afford to leave them behind.'[33]

The first quarter of 1955 ended with some discernible recognition
of the weight of African attitudes. Huggins was asked by Yamba,
in Parliament, why he had not responded to an invitation to attend
the Bandung Conference of the Afro-Asian nations, an assembly
which, in the view of Father Trevor Huddleston, was 'the first
indication of a shift in the balance of power . . . a warning to
those . . . so anxious to maintain white civilisation . . . that they
have neighbours'.[34] 'The date and time chosen,' Huggins replied,
'. . . made it impossible for me, because of my duties here, to
attend'; thus avoiding open disparagement of the Afro-Asian
nations. North of the Zambezi the Attorney-General affirmed that
under common law, African travellers had a right to hotel accommodation unless the proprietor had reasonable grounds for refusing
them. Moreover Leg. Co. approved a Government inquiry into
racial discrimination, by way of amendment to a motion by Sokota

calling for the outlawing of the colour bar in shops, hotels and cafes.[35] At the same time there was a rapid increase in the number of registered branches of ANC. The rate of growth was such that Kaunda had to warn against impostors who went where branches had not yet been formed, pretending to be official recruiting agents. There was also an increasing flow of mail to Kaunda's desk as evidenced by his final note in the May *Gazette* thanking all who had written 'suggesting that the Leader have a short rest at a quiet place for a couple of weeks.' 'We shall see if we can induce him to do so,' he wrote. As membership contributions increased, Nkumbula the 'nation-builder and liberator' was on tour much more intensively than before, very often accompanied by Kaunda.[36] The African Representative Council was also demonstrating an increasingly critical attitude to affairs in the Federation. A motion, for instance, which called for a review of the deposition of Chiefs was passed unanimously by the Council'[37] Meanwhile the reaction of village peasants to their colonial rulers was becoming yearly what Hall has called a 'perpetual cold war in the bush'.[38]

It was in the north and the east that disturbances broke out sharply at this time. Kaunda kept Congress members informed of the course of those events through what was briefly called the *ANC Official Gazette*. The key figure in the troubles at Fort Jameson was Dominic Chitulushi Mwansa, the Provincial President of ANC. As noted above, he had been sentenced to six months imprisonment along with Chitambala for possessing prohibited literature. On 6 June, 'seven thousand men, women and children from all over the province' gathered to welcome the men from prison and a riotous situation developed. Kaunda received a telegram which reported 'arrest of youth . . . police force government officials rioted and fired teargases on Youth League . . . and wounded . . . public declared strike . . . restriction of movement to Africans . . . national flag withdrawn . . . strike suspended pending your advice . . . position critical cable to London immediately'. He replied that stoppage of work and demonstrations 'of any kind which lead into violence' must stop at once. Three senior ANC leaders in the Eastern Province were summoned to Lusaka. The organisation of the party was being put to severe testing, but the authority of the National Executive was shown to command respect. The three Fort Jameson Congress officials were imprisoned soon after until the end of the year, on the charge of 'unlawful possession'.[39]

In the north, at Chisanza, on the shore of Lake Tanganyika and at Chinsali, a number of arrests were made for defiance of 'native authority orders', the persons involved being Congress members. The lakeshore incident was attributed by the Provincial Commissioner to incitement by Robert Makasa who, he said, 'like Kenneth Kaunda, his predecessor in office in Kasama . . . is a shrewd and determined troublemaker'.[40] Kaunda attributed the lake-shore arrests to 'trouble that took place between Government officials and the African populace', and said that in Chinsali the District Organising Secretary had been jailed for 'stopping his fellow Africans from giving free fowls, eggs, flour and other food-stuffs to European Government Officers'. The accused had protested that officers on tour should buy what they required. More signi-ficantly, there was an organised boycott of the chain of shops called Thom's Stores which were managed by a man called Orr-Gliemann, well-known for his extreme racist attitude. This man had spoken angrily of Africans as 'munts' in an altercation with Kollenberg Lesa, Kasama District Secretary of ANC. 'Blacks,' he was reported to have said, 'were baboons . . . who had been washed, cleaned and could also wear suits because of the white man's coming to Africa.' At a public meeting at the end of March, a full-scale boycott had been declared, which Robert Makasa, the Congress Provincial President, called upon the Chiefs in the province to support. At Chinsali, where the Lumpa cult of Alice Lenshina was drawing crowds from far and wide, the pilgrims to her village did not join in the boycott. Soon after the shop there was destroyed by arson. The arsonist was caught and imprisoned for five years. Then in July, charges were brought against Makasa and other Congress members for conspiring to injure the trade of Thom and Company. The heaviest sentence of eighteen months' hard labour was imposed on Makasa.[41]

It seemed noteworthy to Sikalumbi that when the Chinsali shop was burned, Thom's Store at Lubwa, only five miles away, was not. There can, of course, be no proof that the arsonist or his colleagues, if he had any, had reasons which led them to burn one shop and not another. It was the case, however, that Lubwa had a special relationship to the local Congress leadership. From the point of view of the District Commissioner, Lubwa Mission was 'the *alma mater* of a fair proportion of leading malcontents'. Though the D.C. claimed that Congress efforts to incite people to refuse to offer foodstuffs to touring officers had been 'effectively dealt with', he recorded an increase in Congress activities, naming John Malama Sokoni as ringleader. He was specially concerned over the way in which ANC men were taking part in the large gathering at Kasomo, the village of Alice Lenshina Mulenga, which attracted more people than ordinary political meetings would attract. The Acting Provincial Commissioner commented thus on the situation in Chinsali District: 'The Church of Scotland at Lubwa has long confused free thinking with no discipline ... In Chinsali district, alone in this province, the organisers [of ANC] have been sufficiently acute to preserve a nuisance value and yet avoid making themselves liable to prosecution ... Lenshina has been at hand to cast a mystic spell into this noxious pot.'[42]

The 'Lenshina Movement' or 'Lumpa Church', as it has been called, was, as we shall see, to play an increasingly notable and latterly sinister part in the affairs of the country between 1955 and the coming of independence. It originated from a small village seven miles from Lubwa and about the same distance from the Boma at Chinsali; and it was on 18 September, 1953, that Alice Lenshina Mulenga was introduced to the Missionary-in-Charge at Lubwa and some of the local church leaders, and told how she had 'died, not once but four times, each time "rising again" when mourning had begun'. At her last rising, two days earlier she had gone, in response to a call from Jesus Christ, she said, to the river nearby, alone. There she had seen Jesus, who had shown her 'a sign' and told her to go to the '*abena kubuta*' or 'people of the whiteness'. She was then encouraged by the missionary and the elders to renew her faith and help revive the church in her home area. In its origins the 'Lenshina Movement' seemed to be neither heretical and schismatic nor primarily political. Tragically it was to clash with both the local churches and the Boma from 1955 onwards. By that year the movement had spread to the Kasama, Isoka, Chinsali and Mpika Districts and eastwards to Lundazi. By 1956, according to Rotberg, 2,600 members of the United Church in the Chinsali District had been lost to Lenshina. We shall have occasion to refer again to Lenshina's 'Lumpa Church'. By 1955, it was already of political significance insofar as it was providing added impetus to the swelling movement of protest. But an official report on the Northern Province saw the movement as attracting people away from political agitation. 'The charnel-house of surrendered bones and horns and other witchcraft paraphenalia at Lenshina's village represents a far greater reality to the average African than the windy talk of politicians who seem sometimes to forget the real problems of the people.'[43]

While reporting on the arrest of Congress members in the east and north and noting also the release of some who had been imprisoned for their part in the Lusaka boycotts in 1954, Kaunda commented sadly on further deposition of Chiefs. Nkomesha of the Soli had been dethroned for refusing to have land on which there were villages demarcated as a forest reserve. His case illustrated the ambivalent role laid upon Chiefs: having formally agreed to what was then called a 'native authority regulation', he now rejected it when his people resisted the application of it. 'It is a pity,' Kenneth wrote, 'that Government is taking this line towards chiefs who have the interests of their people at heart.' It was reported that Nkomesha's people wanted to take his case to court. 'We wish them the best of luck!' said Kaunda, using a form of lightsome felicitation by which he was expressing 'very best wishes'. Nkomesha now joined the roll of honour of deposed chiefs along with 'Chiefs Milambo (fish trouble), Nsokolo (bad laws), Mulakwa (fish trouble), Kasoma Bangweulu (fish trouble), Mphamba (coming to attend Regional Pan-African Conference, Lusaka in December 1953), and Kambwali'. 'These names,' he said, 'will be preserved by all who love our nation until the day when Africans will themselves write the history of this country. Let Africa rest in peace!'[44]

Harry Nkumbula was increasingly concerned at this time over the legality of the appropriation of mineral rights in the territory by the B.S.A. Company. An undated five-page 'general survey of the situation in Central Africa' had spoken of 'cunning treaties' and stated that, under the British 'Foreign Jurisdiction Act of 1890', there was not a single African who owned land in his own right. In June 1955 Nkumbula addressed a circular letter to 'all Honourable Chiefs of Northern Rhodesia (except Barotseland)', on the land issue. It was clear, he asserted, that the B.S.A. claim to mineral rights on the territory was an invalid extension of the concession extracted from Lewanika of the Lozi by Lochner. 'There were more than 600 chiefs in this country who were not under Lewanika's jurisdiction and who did not sign any treaty with the Company.' Congress was therefore seeking advice from lawyers in England. But this would cost about £200,000. Therefore he was appealing urgently for an initial £10,000, within the next six weeks, to enable the lawyers to start their work. Kaunda reported that, by 25 July, £260 had come in from three Chiefs. The objective was nowhere in sight. At a time when ANC was also launching a funeral fund and a building fund for new offices, the heavy lawyers' fees demanded an unprecedented drive for funds from all over the country and abroad. Tragically, by the end of the year, their local lawyer was convicted for misappropriation of just over £1,000 and sentenced to eighteen months' imprisonment. The subsequent history of the land case was far from happy, and it was soon overtaken by other issues.[45]

In the difficult months of 1955, the Congress Executive was worried by the activities of people 'of all colours' who were trying to woo Africans away from the political objectives which ANC considered vital and urgent. Kenneth issued a series of warnings against these agents 'of those who delight in your slavery'. The issue really was the crucial clash between gradual liberalisation and radical change. It was highlighted by two remarks of Anglican clergymen which were given prominence in the local press. The Archbishop of Canterbury, on an extended African tour, believed that Federation was the answer to Central Africa's problems and warned against the quest for a 'quick solution' of racial tensions. England, he said, had already taken over one thousand years and was still not perfect! Two years earlier, he had told the House of Lords that federating the Central African territories would allow the Africans of Northern Rhodesia and Nyasaland to come 'to the aid of their brethren in Southern Rhodesia'.[46] This was the authentic voice of naive paternalism. The voice of Trevor Huddleston, in his farewell message on being obliged to leave South Africa, was fundamentally different and it was this voice that echoed in Kenneth's heart. The other voice, which he described was 'diabolic', wanted to keep the African people, Kaunda said, 'in your right place—a ditch from which you must look up to them for everything and they look down upon you as underdogs.'[47]

Denunciation of the subtle influence of a soporific 'liberalism' as a will-of-the-wisp was not, however, enough, in Kaunda's view. Characteristically he saw that people needed a positive programme of cooperative action and so he gave prominence in the *Congress Circular* to a statement on what joining the Congress meant. This statement merits quotation in full:

'— Your membership in African National Congress—entered *now*—will help make possible:

— the fight for the franchise which should make it possible for us to participate fully in the running of our Protectorate's affairs according to our ability and not according to our colour!

— the fight against colour discrimination in public places, like post offices, hotels, rest rooms, eating places, theatres, parks, play grounds and many others.

— the fight to get Africans safeguarded against the prevailing police brutality and unlawful arrests.

— the fight for higher posts for Africans in the Protectorate's and Federal Civil Services, military and police forces according to merit and not according to colour.

— the fight for better treatment of our chiefs in the way of salaries etc., as we first declared at the conference of August, 1952, and also to stop all sorts of intimidation and illtreatment of chiefs and their Native Authority employees by Government officials.

— the fight against the system of Government officials compelling African villagers to give them free fowls, eggs, flour, etc.

— the fight against the prevailing night pass system.

— the fight for more and better educational and health facilities and for free economic progress of Africans in both urban and rural areas.

— the fight for African advancement in commerce and Industry.

— the fight against the establishment of a common native policy for the Federation.

— the fight against any move towards the establishment of a unitarian Government for the tripartite states that make the Federation.

— IN SHORT, WE WANT TO SAFEGUARD OURSELVES for we can trust nobody else to protect us!'[48]

The crux of this programme of action lay in the first objective listed: the fight for the franchise, 'SELF-GUARDS and not SAFE-GUARDS', as he said. All the people of the country must be allowed the unfettered right of participation. This was implicit in the statement of one of the letters by an African reader to the local press: 'Africans ask for no more than to be accepted as people and respected as human beings.'[49] To those who believed in the inalienable right to participate, this was a *sine qua non* of elementary social justice. But the incipient crisis within the leadership of Congress was to centre, as we shall see, upon the clash of a 'radical' and a 'moderate' view, upon the issue of whether Africans were seeing themselves as subordinates seeking promotion or as people demanding human rights as embodied in the United Nations Charter. For generous Europeans there was a special conflict to be faced. To speak out for justice was to risk immediate unpopularity. It was therefore 'a big thing' for a white man to take positive steps towards seeking better treatment for Africans. Yet to do no more was to appear to belong to that section of the community against which Kaunda had uttered his 'public warning'. To understand the character and beliefs of this man who readily made lasting friendships irrespective of race, yet branded as 'diabolic' and 'anti-African' the activities of those who would 'appear to be very sympathetic ... but were in fact "enemies"', one has to see that for him, 'freedom and national independence' were pre-requisites to creative inter-racial relations. Kaunda, as a thirty-one-year-old visionary, was more radical than many of the 'extremists' who would readily have joined an 'anti-white campaign'.

As the Federation moved into its third year, race relations were certainly not improving. Consequently it was going to be increasingly difficult for either Europeans or Africans to act with mobility and sensitivity. 'Partnership' as Gore-Browne had said early in 1955, was seen increasingly as 'utter humbug'.[50] Welensky was instead busy promoting the recruitment of Greeks and Italians to work on the Rhodesia Railways, heedless of the bitter frustration this caused to Africans. Dr. Scott wrote angrily against this action. 'He is,' he said, 'a dyed in the wool Conservative who, after his trade union career just cannot help himself and will do his best to keep the Africans on the railway in their humble hopeless place.' But Scott's appeals fell 'on deaf ears', as Kenneth wrote, 'and

instead the privileged class and legislators had raised more and
more oppressive legislation ... to stop the indigenous people
demanding their legitimate rights'. In the *Circular*, he was more
specific: 'The Italians and Greeks brought by Sir Roy and his
company—obviously to increase white population—have protested
vigorously [against Dr. Scott] some using dirty language. We feel
these people and those who brought them here must be told the
hard facts of what a situation they are creating here. ... Firstly ...
[they] are creating a new class ... a poor class. Now as is the
Government policy all these must be treated better than Africans
in all walks of life—result added on frustration of Africans. Secondly,
these people, having little or no education, will naturally want to
protect themselves from competition with Africans and so will
adopt an attitude that will leave the Africans more frustrated—and
a frustrated people can do anything.'[51] 'Before we are crushed,'
said Yamba in a letter to all members of the A.R.C., 'we must
struggle to see that our grounds are truly well maintained' for
'things are changing very fast and mostly against our advancement
both in politics and industry.' Therefore 'before the end of the present
life of the Legislative Council and the Federal Parliament' Africans
must be admitted to the Common Voters' Roll. As an interim step,
the joint proposals of what has been called the 'Nkumbula-Yamba
Pact' demanded racial parity in Leg. Co. The British Government
had been silent for over five months on the Congress request for
urgent constitutional talks. In submitting the new compromise
proposals which, for instance, allowed for an income qualification
as high as £200 p.a., Kaunda called upon national, provincial
and district officials of Congress to comment on the memorandum.
'Let us do it now or else we will be late again,' he wrote. But the
omens were poor, for, as Yamba and Nkumbula said, the Moffat
Resolutions had been 'disgracefully turned by the Federal Parliament'. The Resolutions, which had appeared like a tree ceremonially
planted to adorn the land, were already withering fast for lack of
attention.[52]

The 'Five-Year Development Plan' was now very much on the
minds of the National Executive Committee and a special committee
of five, including Nkumbula, Kaunda and Sikalumbi, was established to consider how best such a plan could be implemented.
The Plan was 'to plant the spirit of self-help in the minds of our

people as we develop in political, economic and social circles'. Though the Plan itself was not to see the light of day, as the Congress moved into the various crises of 1956, a series of significant memoranda appeared exposing the failure of the Federation to remove African fears on such matters as land, education, justice and parliamentary representation. Implicit in those documents was the sense that Federation was entrenching itself effectively and that therefore demands for the removal of grave wrongs must be presented as cogently as possible. Kaunda was personally involved in the research required in the preparation of the memoranda. African fears about land were based, Congress argued, on 'escape clauses' in the territorial ordinances in respect of 'native trust land' and 'crown land', and on the fact that, in the absence of 'a democratic legislature under full adult franchise', these 'escape clauses' could nullify 'safeguards'. Congress therefore called for the establishment of a 'Board of Africans' which must be consulted by the Governor in all matters affecting 'native reserves' and 'native trust land' and which could have its views transmitted to Whitehall should the Governor act against its wishes. The A.R.C. was not 'a truly democratic body' and could not be relied on therefore to defend African interests adequately. The proposed 'Board of Africans' must be empowered to safeguard African rights in matters concerning reservation of land as Forest Reserves, Protected Forest Areas, Game Reserves and Fishing Areas. Moreover, it was wrong that Africans were 'being kept back from the full development of their land by insufficient title' which precluded them from receiving Government loans. There must be freehold and leasehold tenure for Africans and safeguards, vested in Native Authorities, to avoid the reversion of land to mortgagers in the event of borrowers not repaying loans.[53]

On secondary and higher education for Africans, the ANC memorandum on this issue pointed out that while two hundred Ugandans were studying at British universities, only ten Africans had been sent overseas by the Northern Rhodesia Government. 'This,' said Congress, 'is particularly surprising when the revenues of the two countries are compared.' Indeed a comparison of relevant statistics for East Africa in general, as well as for West Africa, and those for Northern Rhodesia, forces us to conclude that there was a powerful factor operating in the Protectorate against African

education.⁵⁴ Congress also noted that the 'multi-racial' character
of the University College in Salisbury had been explicitly belied
'in planning to house European and African students in separate
hostels'. There were white South African lecturers at the college,
but no African had been appointed to the staff. A more fundamental
failure lay in the fact that the Government's educational programme
could not provide more than a trickle of candidates for university
studies. There was only one junior secondary school for girls,
at the Methodists' Chipembi Mission; but 'it is so badly equipped
that the students are handicapped in their studies. They work by
candle and lantern light. They have no library and no science or
domestic science equipment.' In the field of technical education,
not only was there minimum opportunity for Africans 'to take
advantage of the agreed plan for African advancement in the mines
or of advancement in industry'; there was actually on the statute
book the explicit exclusion of Africans 'from the terms of the
Apprenticeship Ordinance'.⁵⁵

The rising chorus of protests from Africans in the Federation
was, Congress insisted, being answered not by negotiation but by
repressive legislation specifically aimed against 'nationalists'.
It was therefore most serious that prison administration had been
centralised under the Federal Government. The fear was that a
penal system similar in its harshness to that of South Africa was
being rapidly developed under Huggins' rule. 'The majority of
prisoners ... are committed by the Territorial Courts,' the ANC
Memorandum said, and 'it is wrong that the Courts should be
part of an administration different from that which administers
the prisons.' The prisons, like all other governmental institutions,
operated a rigid colour bar. 'The African prisons,' Congress
claimed, 'are schools for thieves, breeding ground of homosexuality,
overcrowded disease centres, factories for recidivists rendered
unfit for a life of freedom, the core of the growing interacial hatred
that every prisoner fosters inside his mind as a compensation for
his miseries.' It was a system 'administered by settler politicians
answerable only to their fellow Europeans who have not heard of
modern penal reform and would not tolerate any system that tried
to make re-education and not retribution the motive of the prison
system'. Because the territorial laws were such that 'every young
person on his or her first visit to settled [i.e. where 'settlers' lived]

areas', was liable to arrest 'through ignorance', many who could not pay fines were imprisoned on trumpery charges and 'forced to consort with the people the system has corrupted'. Meanwhile the prisons, being Federal, were exempt from scrutiny by the Colonial Office Committee on the Treatment of Offenders. Her Majesty's Government was therefore 'earnestly requested' to include the prisons issue on the agenda of the 'Conference to be called under Article 99 of the Federal Constitution', which was of course the Review Conference, proposed for 1960. The reference to so remote a date was a measure of deepening gloom.[56]

The Congress memorandum on parliamentary representation began therefore by stating that Africans would 'accept nothing short of full adult franchise with no reserved seats or other special safeguards for minority groups, as the ultimate means of electing Legislative Assemblies and Councils with sovereign authority in the Federation and in Northern Rhodesia'. But they agreed 'to advance to this by steps that remain within the bounds of practice and constituted politics'. The six-page memorandum set out proposals for the attainment of a first step in 1958 with parity as the primary principle. It ended with a warning of 'unpleasant happenings if Britain should heed demands for a United Government, Dominion Status and Apartheid by European Settlers'. But it bespoke a new mood. Federation seemed to be accepted as the framework within which a programme of liberalisation would be pursued. In retrospect, this document can be seen as highly significant. For it adumbrates the coming split in the Congress which was to overshadow the next three years and play into the hands of Welensky. This period was also inevitably going to put a heavy strain upon Kenneth Kaunda's loyalty to his leader and to sharpen his own political thinking in consequence.[57]

The inner tensions of ANC were felt not only at the headquarters in Lusaka. The wave of criticism of the Action Group swept out to the Copperbelt as well as to the Eastern and Central Provinces. 'Some elements in it had been unruly and insubordinate to the locally elected Congress branch leaders,' Sikalumbi has recorded. The activists were providing the bulk of the voluntary labour that was building the new offices in Chilenje as well as in gathering funds. Nkumbula was evincing growing suspicion of the Action Group as an embryonic opposition to his leadership. The National

Executive Council resolved to tighten its control of the group by absorbing into the Congress central treasury the funds it raised from the extra levy of one shilling per month from its members and from other special efforts. Significantly, a decision had been taken at the same time to send Nkumbula to Britain in October as a one-man delegation. The huge gathering at Kabwata to speed the President on his way and the procession to welcome him back two months later suggested that his leadership was not in doubt. But the trip was, in Sikalumbi's opinion, 'abortive'. Lennox-Boyd, the Colonial Secretary, declined his request for an interview, even though, in contrast with ANC's demand for a £50 income and £100 property qualification for the franchise, the 'man of destiny' was ready to agree to £150 and £250 respectively. Nkumbula reported that Lennox-Boyd's rebuff had evoked sympathetic action by a number of leading Labour Party people on behalf of Congress. Understand-ably afraid of the further worsening of race relations in Central Africa, these allies would, however, naturally welcome what appeared as a flexible approach by Nkumbula. But the sixty-day trip had not appreciably accelerated action on the land case nor had it in any way cracked the solidarity of the concordat operating between Whitehall and Salisbury. Moreover, the Kariba project was clearly going ahead without regard to the Gwembe petition or indeed the protests of white Northern Rhodesians.[58]

In July 1955, the Legislative Council had agreed to the establish-ment of a special committee to examine the extent of racial discrimi-nation in the territory and to the appointment of African members of it. Undoubtedly the steadily increasing volume of protest against the totalitarian operation of the colour bar had accelerated this move. As the liberal *Manchester Guardian* said: 'A colour bar is a colour bar whether the line is drawn by a government or by a social convention, by employers or trade union.' Here lay the crux of the fierce resistance of the European Mine Workers' Union to proposals for African advancement, and the different reactions of the two mining companies revealed a significant difference in interpretation of the future. The Anglo-American Corporation secured a measure of agreement with the E.M.W.U. by accepting the Union's claim to a right of veto. Because the Rhodesian Selec-tion Trust would not allow the veto, the E.M.W.U. threatened strike action, and did not make its agreement with R.S.T. until

September. The demand for the veto had been based on the white
union's determination 'to protect our way of life and to ensure
that our children and their children will be able to enjoy the standards
we have set'. R.S.T., however, was apparently not ready to submit
to the claim that the ultimate power to prevent the logical development of advancement in the industry on a criterion of capability
only should be vested in a union established on the premiss of race.
Right-wing European politicians, like Rex L'Ange, were shocked by
R.S.T.'s attitude; and conversely it earned modest praise from the
A.M.W.U. But, said the Secretary of the African Union, Matthew
Deluxe Nkoloma, it was 'about time the Africans were consulted
on advancement', and the 'combined African front' of the A.M.W.U,
the African Salaried Staff Association and the A.T.U.C. protested
in December that, for jobs in which white miners had received
on the average £139 a month, Africans were to earn between
£24 and £36. There was concern too that the agreements committed
the mines 'to use every endeavour' to persuade the Government
to provide adequate technical training facilities for Europeans.[59]
Meanwhile, the African Congress, as we have seen, had explicitly
committed itself 'to fight for African advancement in commerce
and industry'. ANC's relations with the African trade union movement were to face various vicissitudes in the coming years, but there
was a broad basis of unanimity between them.

In the more overtly political field the last months of 1955 witnessed
the continuance of rancour. Government pressure on Chiefs to
restrict or forbid Congress activities in the Northern Province in
particular was worrying officials, as we have seen. The area had been
described by the S.N.A., Stubbs, as 'no longer notable for the
good manners and cheerfulness of the African people and as an
area in which chiefs governed well and were respected'. The Bemba
supreme council, known as Ilamfya, refused to ban ANC despite
the alleged threat of the District Commissioner to recommend the
deposition of Paramount Chief Chitimukulu. The Chief who
initially agreed to move that the ban be imposed 'ended up by voting
against it'. Kaunda thanked 'the Ilamfya Council and all other
Native Authorities who . . . refused to yield to Government pressure
to ban Congress' and warned of the danger of 'driving African
Nationalism underground'. For, he said, 'underground movements
are not pleasant movements for anyone anywhere.' As pressure

mounted to set recognised African 'authorities' against the Congress, people must be ready. 'Stand for the right as you have always done,' he pleaded.[60]

The flickering flame of optimism was hard put to it to counter the action of people in power which revealed their determination to block all African aspirations. One such move was the inter-govern-mental scheme to promote cheap charter air flights to bring in more European immigrants. As Dr. Scott had said, this meant the increase of anti-African discrimination. 'What makes me more eager than ever to champion the cause of Africans is a contemptuous Italian voice over the phone speaking to me of Africans as "Kaffirs." ' Meanwhile into the situation had come the sad voice of a spokesman of the Euro-African community, protesting that they must not be 'classed with Africans'. It was thus not insignificant that the Government's military call-up 'for defence training', had involved 800 Europeans along with 150 'Asiatics and Coloureds', while totally excluding Africans. It was those who controlled the money and the fire-power who, as 1956 dawned, were orienting southern and central Africa towards a racial confrontation.[61]

Welensky and Lord Malvern, as Sir Godfrey Huggins was now called, had chosen a path of political ambivalence, and thus van Eeden spoke for both of the white 'opposition' parties when he declared that, since Malvern's and Welensky's 'obscure platitudes about partnership' were being countered by 'the idea of black domination', the white population must 'put a Government in power before very long' that could cope with the African political resurgence. Kaunda's response to such pronouncements was simple and, for those willing to hear it, cogent. 'People who want to rule by force are sowing the wrong seed,' he said, 'and it does not require a philosopher to see that one reaps the fruits of what one sows. On the other hand Dr. Scott and his group, as few as they are, we think are men who will, should their number grow, save our races from the fate that may come about if things go at the pace they are going now. The reason is not far to seek; these few Euro-peans are, should they succeed, going to bring about some satisfaction in the minds of the have-nots by treating them as they would have others treat them. After this satisfaction...goodwill between races will then follow and everybody will be happy.... Europeans would be well-advised to follow Dr. Scott's policy for they have everything to gain by it.'[62]

---

[1]See Keatley, *op. cit.*, pp. 244-271, citing, on p. 244, Max Buchan, a Rhodesian M.P., and Sir Aubrey Woolls-Sampson, pp. 245-246
[2]*Ibid*, p. 238.
[3]P. Mason, *Year of Decision—Rhodesia and Nyasaland, 1960* (O.U.P., 1960), 113, citing shout of an African mob against a white football referee. In Malawi, in February 1959, the writer heard a song, sung by youths, '*Batuba, chokani*'— 'White people, get out'.
[4]ANC/5/2—Kaunda to Guy Clutton-Brock, A/24-476 of 23/12/54. Clutton-Brock's inter-racial farm was at St. Faith's Mission, Rusape, S. Rhodesia. He was a member of the African Congress there.
[5]Clutton-Brock to Macpherson, 25/1/70; and note that (a) Dunduzu Chisiza, from northern Malawi, was deported from S. Rhodesia in 1956 for political activities. Thereafter he was among those who urged Dr. Banda to return home and a leading organiser of the Nyasaland Congress. After detention by the Governor in 1959-60, he prepared a five-year plan for national development and organised a notable Economic Symposium. He died in a road accident on 3/9/62; and (b) Dietrich Bonhoeffer, a German theologian, was arrested in 1943 as an opponent of Hitler's Nazi regime and executed in 1945, aged 39.
[6]TI-FM/KK, 13/2/69 and 26/2/69. Note that Simon Kapwepwe had gone to India in 1951 on a scholarship, procured by Mbikusita, and was studying leatherwork and journalism.
[7]ANC/3/34, Kaunda to Franklin, A/49-444 of 2/12/54 and Franklin to Kaunda, 30/12/54; ANC/2/7, Franklin to Kaunda, 19/5/55.
[8]TI-FM/KK, 13/7/71.
[9]ANC: Rupiah Banda to Kaunda, 13/10/57.
[10]TI-FM/Walsh, March 1970.
[11]Fraenkel, *op. cit.*, pp. 130 ff.
[12]*NN*, 16/6/54, 3/7/54 ff, 19/8/54.
[13]ANC: Kaunda's press statement on 'partition', 25/12/54.
[14]ANC: Circular 1/B-(9)54 of 28/12/54.
[15]ANC: Circular 1/B-(10)54 of 29/12/54.
[16]Mason, *Year*, p. 107.
[17]*NN*, 3/1/55, 5/1/55, 12/1/55; and see *London Daily Telegraph* comment on Copperbelt strike that the average African miner's wage was about one-tenth that of a European, 4/1/55.
[18]Kaunda *op. cit.*, pp. 63-64; Sokoni Papers, note by Kaunda on arrest, which mentions also *African Newsletter* and *Spotlight on Africa* sent by 'someone called Rauch'; Sikalumbi, *op. cit.*, pp. 47-48, stating that ANC also received literature from the British Communist Party, the Women's International Democratic Federation in Berlin, and the Council for African Affairs in New York; and Mpashi, *op. cit.*, p. 43.
[19]*NN* for the period; Mpashi, *op. cit.*, p. 43-44; and Hall, *Zambia*, p. 174. Note that, according to the ANC *Official Gazette*, Vol. II, 1/2/55, the Acting President-General was Robinson Puta.
[20]TI-FM/KK, 13/2/69.
[21]See Mason, *Year*, p. 114.
[22]ANC, *News Supplement*, 6/3/55, containing Nkumbula's 'Statement and Message'.
[23]See ANC, Agenda for 'Emergency Session' of N.E.C., 19-21/1/55; Sikalumbi, *op. cit.*, p. 44; Rotberg, *op. cit.*, p. 291; Hall, *Zambia* pp. 176-177; and TI-FM/SMK, 8/11/69. Hall uses the actual phrase (p. 177).
[24]ANC *Official Gazette*, No. 1, Vol. I, 1/1/55.
[25]ANC *Official Gazette*, No. 1, Vol. II, 1/2/55.
[26]Sikalumbi, *op. cit.*, p. 51; ANC: Official Programme for 'Good Sunday',

6/3/55, and note that *mishikakulo* are the 'mirthful harangues' traditionally presented to a Bemba king by his jester.
[27]ANC: Kaunda to Colonial Secretary, A/70-107 of 7/3/55.
[28]ANC: 'List of Telegrams', 7/3/55.
[29]ANC: Kaunda to C.S., A/27-110 of 7/3/55.
[30]ANC: Kaunda to all European Nominated Members for African Interests, NR Leg. Co. and Federal Parliament, A/70-111 of 8/3/55.
[31]*NN*, 7/8/55.
[32]Sikalumbi, *op. cit.*, p. 53; and ANC: Statement by Kaunda on 'National Prayers', 2/4/55.
[33]*Ibid.*
[34]T. Huddleston, *Naught for your Comfort* (Collins, 1956), 251.
[35]*NN*, 19/3/55, 25/3/55.
[36]ANC: *Official Gazette*, No. 1, Vols. IV and V, 7/5/55 and 18/6/55, respectively, for reports of registration of 35 Congress branches between 1/3/55 and 6/5/55 and 37 in the following six weeks. Note that, in 1955, 96 branches were registered in approximately equal numbers in the Southern, Eastern and Central Provinces, 21 on the Copperbelt, smaller numbers in the Northern and North-Western provinces, 7 in S. Rhodesia, and none in Barotseland.
[37]A.R.C. Report No. 13, 8/6/55.
[38]*Zambia*, p. 175.
[39]ANC: *Official Gazette*, No. 1, Vol. V, 18/6/55.
[40]NAZ: N/0001/2/15/2, P.C. to S.N.A. (Conf. 208), 8/4/55; Sikalumbi, *op. cit.*, p. 54. At Chinsali, Abinaar Kakungu and at Chisanza, Windi Zimba and others were the ringleaders. Note that lake-shore race relations had been strained in the early 1950s by the arrogant and abusive conduct of a fish-trader called Finlay-Bisset, who later, in September 1961, assaulted the U.S. Assistant Secretary of State, Mennen Williams.
[41]ANC: *Official Gazette*, No. 1, Vol. V, 18/6/55; Sikalumbi, *op. cit.*, p. 55; and note that Thom's Stores had branches at Kasama, Fort Roseberry (now Mansa), Kawambwa, Abercorn (now Mbala), Mprokoso, Mpika, Isoka and Chinsali.
[42]NAZ: KTQ.2/1—Chinsali Tour Report, No. 4 of 1955, Annexure 1; and N/00003/2/15/2 Minute of Ag. P.C., Heathcote, to S.N.A. (Conf. 212).
[43]The quotation is from the *NR Annual Report on African Affairs, Northern Province, 1955*. See also F. Macpherson, *Occasional Papers* No. 1 (International Missionary Council, London, 1958), 2-5; Taylor and Lehmann, *op. cit.*, 248-68; Rotberg, 'The Lenshina Movement', *Rhodes-Livingstone Institute Journal*, No. XXIX (June 1961); *Report of the Commission of Inquiry into the former Lumpa Church* (Gov't. Printer, Lusaka, 1965), 4. For a further scholarly study, consult A. D. Roberts, *The Lumpa Church of Alice Lenshina* (O.U.P., Lusaka, 1972). The Missionary-In-Charge, Lubwa, at the time was the present writer..
[44]ANC: *Official Gazette*, No. 1, Vol. VI, 25/7/55; and note that Kaunda frequently wished people 'the best of luck'. The Bemba word *ishuko*, often translated 'luck' means in fact something more akin to 'blessing', belonging as it does to traditional belief in personal causation of all that happens and so excluding the notion of 'pure accident' or casual, random and inexplicable 'luck'.
[45]ANC Circular, 'General Survey of the Situation in Central Africa', undated; Circular A/1-55 of 15/6/55 (sgd. H. M. Nkumbula); *Central African Post*, 9/12/55 and 28/12/55. The lawyer was Robert Maltman, then aged 26.
[46]*CAP*, 15/4/55; and UK, *Hansard of the House of Lords*, 2/4/53.
[47]ANC: *Official Gazette*, No. 1, Vol. V, 18/6/55 and *Congress News Circular*, No. 1, Vol. VI, 25/7/55 and Vol. VII, 8/9/55.
[48]ANC *Congress Circular*, Vol. 1, No. IX, 15/11/55 and subsequent issues.
[49]*CAP*, letter of Hosea Soko, 6/4/55.
[50]See Rotberg, *Rise*, p. 272.
[51]ANC: *Congress Circular*, No. 1, Vol. X, 31/12/55.
[52]ANC: 'Joint Statement on Constitutional Changes', sgd., Yamba and Nkumbula (undated); unreferenced Circular, by Kaunda, on 'Constitutional Changes', 28/8/55; and letter of Yamba to all A.R.C. members, 28/8/55.

[53]ANC: *Congress Circular*, No. 1, Vol. VI, 25/7/55; undated Memoranda, attached to Presidential Circular, 12/2/56; Kaunda, *op. cit.*, p. 69; and see *NR Orders in Council:* (a) *Native Trust Land, 1947, Section 5* and (b) *Crown Lands and Native Reserves, 1948, Section 6.*

[54]W.M.C. (Lord) Hailey, *African Survey* (O.U.P., revised 1956) 1258, 143-7, gives the following figures of:

(i) *Enrolment at Secondary Schools:*

	N. Rhodesia	Nyasaland	Tanganyika	Uganda
1947	248	—	3,286	4,746
1952	1,210	362	26,802	9,438

(ii) *Expenditure on Post-Secondary Education in Pounds* (scholarships, teacher training and other) for 1952:

	N. Rhodesia	Nyasaland	Tanganyika	Uganda	Kenya
European	13,900				
African	6,600	2,700	157,400	345,600	137,400
Including for scholarships only	3,500	2,700	11,300	4,100	15,700

Note: Uganda was spending £229,000 on its University College in 1952.

(iii) Populations, (totals being 1953 Estimates).

	N. Rhodesia	Nyasaland	Tanganyika	Uganda	Kenya
Total	1,960,000	2,501,010	7,965,000	5,300,000	5,405,966
Including Europeans	50,000	4,387	20,300	7,000	42,200

(iv) *Growth rates of Primary School Enrolments of Africans* (p. 1258).

	N. Rhodesia	Tanganyika	Uganda
1947	169,834	131,987..	143,592
1952	156,164	227,468	272,766

(v) *Secondary School Enrolment by Races:*
In 1959-60 while 21,671 European children (including small numbers of Asian and coloured children) were in secondary schools in the Federation, the figures for African enrolment in Secondary schools were:

S. Rhodesia	N. Rhodesia	Nyasaland	
3,300	2,108	1,300	TOTAL—6,708.

[55]ANC: *Memorandum on Education;* and ref. apprenticeships, see *Laws of Northern Rhodesia, Cap. 187, Sect. 3, 2(a).*

[56]ANC: *Memorandum on Prisons*, citing Concurrent Legislative List (Part II, Item 60).

[57]ANC: *Memorandum on the Representation of Africans and other Races in the Federation of Rhodesia and Nyasaland and in Northern Rhodesia.* This undated Memo and the two cited in footnotes 55 and 56 above were attached to a Presidential Circular, dated 12/2/56.

[58]*Op. cit.*, pp. 59 and 63; and note that four Labour Party members who specially supported the African cause were: A. Creech-Jones, James Griffiths, Eirene White and Fenner Brockway.

[59]*NN*, 25/8/55, quoting *Manchester Guardian* on this; and *NN*, 12/9/55 ff.

[60]*NN*, 3/5/55, quoting Stubbs; and ANC: *Congress Circular*, Vol. 1, No. X, 31/12/55.

[61]*NN*, 12/9/55, 1/12/55; ANC: *Congress Circular*, Vol. I, No. X, 31/12/55; and note that (a) 72 cheap charter flights for white immigrants were planned for 1956, and (b) the Euro-African spokesman quoted in interview with *NN*, 12/9/55, was Tom Sayer.

[62]ANC: *Congress Circular*, No. 1, Vol. VIII, 18/10/55, quoting *NN*, 12/10/55, report of van Eeden's speech; and Vol. I, No. X, 31/12/55.

8

Times of Testing

Nineteen fifty-four and 1955 had heard the articulation of the African voice in the Federation. Hesitancy had been replaced by clarity and cogency. In Kenneth Kaunda's personal life those years had witnessed a symbolic parallel in his conquest of the stammer which had harassed him from infancy. As we saw earlier, his father had stammered in moments of emotion and strangely it was the youngest child, the 'unexpected one', who had inherited this affliction. But when Simon Kapwepwe returned from India, he was 'absolutely amazed' to hear Kenneth speak at a public meeting for an hour 'with no stumbling at all'. As soon as the meeting was finished, Kapwepwe asked him what had happened to him. It was by holding a walking stick and tapping it on the floor each time a stammer threatened that Kenneth had worked the cure. Thereafter when speaking in public he liked to have a plentiful supply of drinking water to prevent his throat from drying. Speaking in quick short phrases which further checked the stammer, he quickly discontinued the use of the stick. The coming years were, however, to put him under considerable strain when speaking of 'man's inhumanity to man'[1] and on various occasions he would have to pause to dry his tears and regain his composure. But by 1955 he was marked as an articulate and gripping speaker who would freely blend passionate conviction with laughter. As people near his home at Shambalakale said, 'He is the one most like his father,' especially in respect of his judgements, his humour and the clarity of his convictions.[2]

These years had also widened the circle of his friends and demonstrated his ability to strengthen bonds of trust with people of very different temperaments. The inevitable tension in the political arena between what are sometimes called 'freedom fighters' and those called 'intellectuals' was felt even in the early years of the movement. Kaunda's thoughts on this tension and how to use it creatively were set down later in his correspondence with the Revd. Colin Morris. As the team was being gathered, Kaunda 'did not project himself very much but did everything possible to project the leader'. It was he, however, who had the 'great power of bringing people together'. The band of 'activists' included men who had been teachers, clerks, artisans and professional trade unionists. While Kaunda spoke and wrote of Nkumbula as the 'man of destiny', he also managed to strengthen relations with 'radicals' such as Justin Chimba, Hyden Dingiswayo Banda, Munukuyumbwa Sipalo, Reuben Kamanga and indeed Simon Kapwepwe. Moreover, he was anxious to win the support of the country's few university graduates. When Congress was beginning to plan an invitation to James Johnson, a Labour Party sympathiser from Britain, Kenneth paid a surprise visit to Munali Secondary School to ask for the support of John Mwanakatwe and Joseph Mwemba who were teaching there. They were both graduates, Mwanakatwe having studied for his B.A. by correspondence and being the first Northern Rhodesian African to hold a degree. For him, the meeting with Kaunda was 'fascinating' and served to bring him a new understanding of the Congress cause.[3]

For Kaunda, the 'intellectual' must be 'essentially an engaged man applying modern knowledge and training to political purposes ... temperamentally ... attracted to nationalism because neither colonialism nor tribalism would allow him scope for the exercise of that critical faculty which is the most precious fruit of his training'. He was aware that colonial rulers would try to apply a 'divide and rule' policy to emergent intellectuals, 'patronising and advancing them within narrow limits, so cutting them off from their own people in the hope of rendering the nationalist movement impotent'. South Africa provided many baleful examples of African intellectuals 'tainted with this touch of white patronage'. This must not happen in Northern Rhodesia. The few who had secured 'higher education' must be inspanned to the popular movement towards radical change which must therefore appeal to critical reasoning as well as to the emotions of a nascent patriotism. The intellectual would be inevitably exposed to the processes of cultural alienation inherent in the university world as well as to the seductive allurements of 'some ideology which was not in the country's best interests'.

The strongest deterrents to such pressures upon him would be the historical validity and reasonableness of the coming 'revolution', whereby his training, critical insights and enthusiasm would be harnessed to the tasks of nation-building. The intellectual and the freedom fighter should then be able to find their community of interest. But, as Kenneth realised from the outset, it was going to be necessary to work consciously and constantly to 'achieve a harmonious relationship between these two key elements'.[4]

Just as the tension between such groups adumbrated the crises of later years, so for a number of individual freedom fighters their dedication in the fifties was costly and might well mean a harvest of frustration and disappointment. In popular politics, this can readily sow the seeds of future factions. 'Why are we forgotten now?', a cry which the writer heard on the Bangweulu islands in 1970, can easily become the lament of patriots whom the pace of events passes by when their main battle is won; and it is not possible to guarantee that all loyalty will be rewarded. But Kenneth wanted to find ways to 'reinforce their strengths and neutralise their weaknesses' no less than those of the intellectuals, for the future would certainly require their patriotism. He therefore realised that the national leadership of the Party must merit more than distant respect. 'The simple manner and the politeness . . . his forthrightness, modesty and humility',[5] which Mwanakatwe noted in Kaunda, served to make the Congress headquarters appear friendly and considerate to all who called there. In Kaunda they found a man who would, as Kapwepwe recorded, 'listen to every person regardless of his status in life'. The description of his late father as one who 'loved people so much' that even if they were talking rubbish he would not tell them to go away was increasingly applicable to Kenneth.[6]

The role of ready listener and counsellor was, however, made far from easy by the fact that his family were living under cramped conditions and very short of money. Despite the salary scales theoretically approved for Congress officials—whereby the Secretary-General should have received £360 p.a.—the actual amount paid to him at the start of 1955 was £5 per month.[7] His wife therefore had to join other women in the back-breaking task of charcoal burning, which meant spending hours in the forest. She and Sikalumbi's wife purchased licences for tree-cutting and then walked twelve miles daily to and from the allotted cutting area. There they had to fell their trees, cutting them into logs of four to five feet in length. Lastly the logs had to be carefully piled and covered with earth to ensure that the fire kindled in them would slowly trans-form the logs into charcoal. Betty Kaunda was expecting another child then, and so the husbands of the two women had to find the money to hire a vanette to transport the charcoal in sacks to Chilenje. The house was far too small for the family and the endless visitors who came to see Kenneth. When his mother came to stay in the middle of the rainy season, she had to sleep in Betty's kitchen. Even the two-roomed house to which they moved early in 1956 was cramped and inconvenient and the charcoal burning had to go on to reduce the cost of living. The family still saw little of Kenneth, except when he was weary at the end of his hectic days. But Betty knew that his work was exacting and sometimes dangerous.[8] After a meeting in Lusaka in the end of January 1956, a gang of Africans and Indians chased Nkumbula and Kenneth, shouting abuse and threatening violence. For the family this was alarming proof of the cost of leading the Congress.[9]

'The beginnings of "Moderation versus Activism"' is how Wittington Sikalumbi has described the end of 1955 and the first months of 1956. In the industrial field, the leadership of Lawrence Katilungu was subjected to repeated challenge by a growing number of A.M.W.U. men who wanted to use strike action to force the pace of change and who rejected the separation of industrial and political action. Katilungu's use of the finesse of finely balanced negotiation taxed their patience. The outbreak of widespread strikes was to culminate in the Government's declaration of a State of Emergency in the Copperbelt in September. As this rift widened, there followed the inevitable growth of sympathy for 'moderation' from supporters at home and abroad. By corollary, the 'activists' became more agitated and strident and the official reaction to them grew in severity.[10]

In the affairs of the Congress, a similar pattern of tension was emerging. Sensing it early, Sikalumbi had suggested to Kaunda that they should plan to find funds for Nkumbula to take a course in law for about three years, since some Congress men were becom-ing uncertain of his leadership. For the 'activists' the United Northern Rhodesia Association was increasingly suspect. The co-existence it seemed to represent was almost 'Capricornist'. Sikalumbi, though he joined it along with Nkumbula and Kaunda, was 'not happy and instead wanted secret action groups'.[11] The 'moderates' were men who were increasingly fatalistic about Federation and who therefore believed that the African political organisations must avoid direct confrontations and instead intensify negotiation for the reduction of racial discrimination. They had been watched as politically dangerous men a few years earlier when, for instance, they had proposed in Chingola, that 'African salaries in common should be one third [that] of the average male European' and called for 'a money allotment per head per school child regardless of colour'.[12] The young militants who were now pushing into the forefront of the territory's affairs wanted an end to foreign domination. They had found spokesmen in the men who had launched the *Freedom Newsletter*, which had proclaimed 'votes for all' as the objective of a programme based on 'the preservation of peace'. They had declared from the outset that 'war is cruel; war is wasteful . . . it hits hardest these poor people . . . who are hardest hit already.'[13] The task therefore was 'to unite our people for peace'. Kenneth Kaunda was at one with this objective. The deportation of Simon Zukas had flashed a danger signal. 'Moderation' in negotiating for less racial discrimination was not enough. The forces of oppression were strong and growing more confident. The organisation of the nationalist movement was a prerequisite for the triumph of non-racialism and the principles of the United National Charter of universal human rights.[14]

But Kaunda's leader, the 'man of destiny', was losing his fire, and the signs of the times were alarming. Thus as Kenneth sought to strengthen unity in the Congress and to revive Nkumbula's spirit by the knowledge of a strong, coherent popular movement behind him, he was aware that the shadows were lengthening over Africa. The tragic war in Kenya had worked its devastation, and greatly counterbalanced the progress which the United States, Belgium and the People's Republic of China had noted in Tanganyika's march to self-government.[15] Oliver Lyttelton's proposed Constitution for Kenya of 1954 might look for progress towards multi-racialism but many Africans, no less than Afrikaaners in the south, had seen what happened when 'white' bombers rained their fury on 'black' villages. For men like Tom Mboya and Oginga Odinga, 'multi-racialism' was a snare and a delusion; they did not see the change of heart in the white supremacists without which the formulae emanating from Whitehall would avail nothing.

Far more serious for Northern Rhodesia, however, was the trend of events in southern Africa, for it was with the Pretoria Government that the Federal rulers proclaimed cordial relations. Kenneth saw 'sheer madness' at work in South Africa where the *Africa Digest* had recently been added to the list of one hundred and forty-eight publications banned by the Strijdom Government. The banned list, he noted, had increased by forty-four in the first week of 1956, widely seen as reprisal for the Bureau's relief fund for victims of the Bantu Education Act of 1953.[16] Verwoerd had then spoken of the Government's plan to give 'the Bantu' a system that would 'stand with both feet in the Reserves and have its roots in the spirit and being of a Bantu society'. But to check the influence of those who believed in 'a policy of equality' which would 'create expectations in the minds of the Bantu which clash with the possibilities of the country', it was necessary to put 'Bantu Education' directly under the control of the Minister of Native Affairs. For 'equality' would mean abolishing the differential between the £43.88 p.a. spent on each white child and the £2.66 for each African pupil. 'The Voice of Vichy', as Father Trevor Huddleston called the 'moderates', hoped that, since Verwoerd could not personally supervise what happened in classrooms, African teachers could be relied on not to 'teach inferiority'. The S.A. African National Congress, however, had urged parents to boycott the operation of the Act by keeping their children away from school. Verwoerd's reaction was swift: the children who had joined the boycott would never be readmitted to school anywhere in the Union of South Africa, and their teachers would be dismissed at once.[17] In the Central Africa Federation in 1955 expenditure on what was called simply 'education' but which excluded African education, was £3,992,958 for a total of 52,246 pupils. The education of 199,020 African pupils, students and artisan trainees cost, according to the African Education Report for 1955, a total of £2,304,036, of which £1,010,036 came from the funds of local authorities.[18] The parallels with the south were grim. The 'humbug' of partnership could not obscure the direction of racial policies in Central Africa.

Nor was it only in the field of education that the oppressive

regime was operating in the south. The evacuation of thousands
of people from Sophiatown to Meadowlands, in pursuance of the
1954 Natives Resettlement Act, and the proposed Gwembe resettlement scheme shared a 'highest common factor' that spelled bitterness
for poor Africans. The interests of the rich masters were paramount.
Of course Sophiatown was a slum, but what prompted the eviction
of its people, at gun-point, was the determination to remove what
were crudely called 'black spots' from the neighbourhood of white
Johannesburg. In Southern Rhodesia, the Land Apportionment
Act continued to operate for the benefit of Europeans. Godfrey
Huggins had called it 'the first step in the social segregation of the
native, getting him into separate areas'. Between 1949 and 1957
'over 80,000 natives have been removed' from Crown Lands,
claimed the Secretary for Native Affairs. The effect of the processes
of 'land apportionment' was not only to describe as 'a squatter'
any African whose ancestral home was in an area designated
European; by 1961, forty-one million of the colony's ninety-seven
million acres would be reserved exclusively for the use of Europeans.
Moreover, whereas in the mid-twenties, more than half of Rhodesia's
urban Africans had been living more than fifty per cent below the
'poverty datum line', in 1958 an appendix to the Plewman Commission Report was to reveal that 57.1 per cent of urban Africans were
existing below what was called the 'extremely impoverished' line, an
index 35 per cent below the 'poverty datum line'.[19] In Northern
Rhodesia, average earnings of African town dwellers were £6 below
the 'poverty datum' of £14.11s per month. Such well-concealed
figures demonstrate why 'closer Association' with the south was
horrific to Northern Rhodesian Africans. 'This kind of thing must
not go on' was the conviction of Kaunda and his friends, and
therefore they were heartened by the personal popularity of
Nkumbula among the Gwembe people and the hope they received
from him of a new recognition of human dignity. For, as the valley
dwellers said, 'he started the fight to change things.' 'Now messengers do not dare to terrorise us any more. There is no more carrying
loads for European officials or those of the Local Authority.'[20]

At this time, Labour M.P.s were pressing questions in West-
minister on such matters as the Public Order Ordinance, the Riot
Damages Bill and the colour bar in shops, hotels and offices.[21]
The Congress cause had also won the sympathetic interest of the

novelist Doris Lessing. Moreover, Governor Benson's 'astonishingly forthright' statement about getting rid as soon as possible of Colonial Office Rule had caused anger and embarrassment in Britain. Thus, when Kaunda blamed the Governor for 'taking sides', he was joining a chorus of protest. Benson's revelation that 'one chap' who was very keen to give self-government to Northern Rhodesia was the Colonial Secretary himself sounded an 'alarm bell' for Africans, said Kaunda. For His Excellency had associated not only himself but his master in Whitehall with what could only mean 'European self-government' as demanded by 'reactionary white leaders'. A few days after the Governor's speech, Welensky warned against 'self-government preaching' by Africans. The voteless majority must therefore 'start preparing for a long political battle'. The recent reaffirmation in the House of Commons that the status of the Protectorate would 'not be altered without the consent of the majority of the inhabitants' gave little confidence when 'the top representative of the Crown to which we owe allegiance' had spoken 'as if he were a settler'.[22]

As the Congress launched a new campaign against shops practising discrimination, Harry Nkumbula spoke bitterly of the country as 'the darkest spot in the whole British Colonial empire'.[23] Yet the campaign was to reveal to his followers clear signs of his growing hesitancy. Indeed, men like Sikalumbi believed that it had been a speech by Kaunda, who had 'stormed the platform' at Matero, that had really triggered the new campaign.[24] Congress leaders did not show drafts of their speeches to each other as they all 'knew the policy'. Kaunda had had to speak at Matero at short notice as Nkumbula had suddenly gone 'to see friends at Monze, including the late Daisy'. He chose to speak on 'non-violence' and described it as a force that no power could crush. The press gave big headlines the following morning to his words. He has recalled that Nkumbula was 'furious' because of the impact of the speech and attributed his reaction to 'plain jealousy'.[25]

On 2 April the boycotts began in Lusaka and spread swiftly to other towns. The first press comment was that there was little public reaction to the boycott, which was aimed against the continual rise in prices of commodities specially required by Africans and also to 'teach the African more controlled spending'. Immediately, however, there were charges of coercion by Congress members, and

a magistrate imposed sentences of three and four months' imprisonment on two women so charged. Sentences were suddenly stiffened
as picketing became more vigorous. Kaunda was blamed by a letter
to the press for having 'no regrets' about the hunger being suffered
by 'hundreds of Africans' whose purchases had been damaged
or seized by ANC men and who must 'now pay exorbitant prices
to the few protected Congress shopkeepers'. The editor, however,
replied by quoting what Kaunda had actually said, thus: 'Apart
from the hooliganism, we have nothing whatever to regret about
this boycott . . . . There is too much hooliganism going on . . . we
are not at all pleased with irresponsible actions by some Africans'.
A few days later, Nkumbula said that the campaign was to
stop.[26]

Commentators differ on the decision to end the boycotts. The
Congress Circular said that 'non-Congress people (some employed
by anti-Congress elements) . . . turned the non-violent struggle into
one of violence.'[27] Mason quotes the demand of a meeting of European Associations for 'immediate steps to amend the laws of the
territory to ensure that no African political organisation can achieve
such domination'. Rotberg concludes his review of the wave of
boycotts by asserting that it 'served its economic purpose impres-
sively; hatches disappeared permanently, and the local bus company
began to provide services to the main locations'.[28] What concerned
Sikalumbi and others at the time, however, was the belief that
Nkumbula's decision to end the campaign had been taken at
Harry Franklin's instigation. The relationship between 'the two
Harrys', as Kaunda called them, had somehow changed from its
early bitterness. Franklin was wielding a strange influence upon
'the leader', they felt, though there is no mention of his part in the
boycott issue in Franklin's own record of the politics of the Federation. Increasingly, prominent Congress men were to be offended
by Franklin's influence over Nkumbula. As early as April 1956,
it became known that Franklin wanted to 'hoodwink' Nkumbula
into believing that Congress would be recognised by the Northern
Rhodesia Government if only it were a responsible and well-
behaved party, and that this could be effected 'if it purged itself
of its extremist secondary leaders'. Members of the National
Executive Committee were even more astonished when Nkumbula
brought Franklin to their meeting on 20 April.[29]

Franklin's view of the future of Central Africa fell far short, however, of what Kenneth Kaunda regarded as essential, His leadership of the United Northern Rhodesia Association was inspired by the 'liberal' view that the first objective must be to persuade people of all races to understand each other, whereby the 'evolution of the African would be accelerated'. Hence his growing influence on Harry Nkumbula seemed to Kaunda and his colleagues to be highly insidious. The association of 'the two Harrys' could only mean a dulling of Nkumbula's vision, and the ineptitude of both Franklin and Nkumbula in forcing Franklin's presence upon the ANC National Executive Council provoked sharp resentment which was to culminate in 1957 in a walk-out by some members in anger at Franklin's use of the term 'barbarians'. 'We simply could not treat Congress at this time of our development,' Kaunda said, 'as if we were an African Welfare Association with ex-DC "Bwana" Franklin coming to call us all sorts of names.' Unwittingly, Franklin contributed to the coming alienation of Nkumbula from the bulk of his followers.[30]

The answer, as Kaunda saw it, did not lie in hoping for a change of heart. "Woe to the nation," a Hungarian landowner had once said, "which raises no protest when its rights are outraged! It contributes to its own slavery by its silence. The nation which submits to injustice and oppression without protest is doomed." Kenneth chose these words for the front page caption of the April 1956 issue of the *Congress Circular*. The boycotts were right. They were a direct protest against injustice. It was therefore a matter of great rejoicing that the extended boycott in Mufulira— 'second in length only to the wonderful Lusaka boycott of butcher shops of January and February 1954'—ended with the acquittal of four leading Congress men, Andrew Mutemba, Mungoni Liso, Emmanuel Chalabesa and Matthew Mugara. On the advice of Dr. Scott, ANC had secured the services of Leslie Blackwell, a Q.C. from Salisbury.[31] Kaunda has given an account of the trial and the issues at stake. The men had been charged with conspiracy to damage trade. The magistrate, in acquitting them, said that 'he had no hesitation in saying that the boycotters had sufficient justification for their action'. Nkumbula went to Mufulira for the trial and stood with the acquitted men to receive the cheers of a crowd of about three hundred, thus signalising, as a British journalist said, 'an enormous boost to Congress throughout the entire African population'.[32]

The legal victory did not pass unnoticed and Kenneth joyfully quoted the *London Observer* comment that "a growing body of opinion in Rhodesia takes the view that the only practicable solution is to accept the fact that the African National Congress is representative of African opinion and to recognise the organisation." The issue of the *Circular* in which he made this quotation had, as caption, words of Canon John Collins: "Love evokes love and hate evokes hate." The behaviour of the police in making arrests during the boycott campaign had provoked a bitter reaction and, as was his wont, Kaunda saw fit to report it. For the call to 'non-violence' would fail if it obscured the harsh realities of the situation. The treatment of Robert Makasa on his arrest after the boycott. of Thom's Stores in Kasama and of Edward Mungoni Liso, ANC's Western Provincial Senior President, who was apprehended in Lusaka in connection with the Mufulira affair, had been blatantly brutal. Liso 'was handcuffed to an African constable, marched through the streets to the railway station, with some Special Branch boys shouting and jeering at him, taken to Ndola by train and there, similarly handcuffed, was marched through the streets on several occasions.' It was similar treatment to that meted out to Makasa who had been handcuffed from Kasama to Livingstone, 'a distance of 1000 miles and a journey by bus and train for six days'. The land was going to be increasingly threatened by the indiscriminate reaction of 'law and order' to widespread expressions of popular emotion. It was going to be very hard to keep before the people the necessity of positive action by non-violent means.[33]

The *Circular* continued to reflect the major issues that pressed upon the country and especially on the Congress; and the headline captions bore the imprimatur of the thinking of the Secretary-General. The January issue declared that 'minority rule in any multi-racial society breeds rule by force in favour of the minority: result—unpleasant happenings. . . .' 'If people have to live together they must avoid anything which might hurt their companions or neighbours, or else no social life is possible.' Because the European communities had been sealed off from Africans, such words were bound to be misunderstood. When Welensky had said of Harry Nkumbula that it was "the voice of Moscow speaking through this African gentleman", he had brought to Central Africa more than a hint of the sinister propaganda of Strijdom and Verwoerd. If the electorate could be persuaded that the African cry for justice was inspired by agents from behind the 'Iron Curtain', it would then be possible to regard 'agitators' as traitors to the strategic interests of 'the free world'. Insistently, certain 'white supremacists' hammered at the theme that Africans wanted to drive all Europeans away, and this emotional weapon served to promote the polarisation of the races.[34]

At the start of 1956, the *Circular* introduced a new character to the political stage in the person of 'Keen Observer'. This imaginary enquirer voiced key questions which Kaunda then answered. The first two questions that Keen Observer raised were concerned with 'European fears that if we [Congress] took the reins of Government we would drive them into the sea' and also with 'the President-General's comment on Communism at Margate, London, when addressing an international gathering, attended by men and women from all over the world'. There were, Kenneth noted, 'popular European leaders of the two opposite camps in the Federation' who were saying that Africans were implacably anti-European, but, he said, 'We are as the sun rises from the east and sets in the west, confident that it won't be long before the Whiteman and the Blackman are on the same footing in all walks of life.' 'Now when this stage is reached (and we mean it to take place non-violently) and according to the British way of life, the majority will have to rule. But this does not in the least mean that any of the races which are in the minority will be driven out of the country, does it?' Again, on Communism in Africa, Harry Nkumbula had made a clear and simple reply. 'He had not known any African leader or group of leaders in his country who had interested themselves in any ideologies, communistic or otherwise.' His people's demands were simple: 'bread and butter and a decent place where to lay our heads and the opportunity to release our energies in the administration of our country'. If to make such demands for 'better this and that for our people is to be communists, then we are hundred per cent so.' 'But is it true?' Kaunda asked. 'No, it isn't. Ours is a simple nationalism. . . . we are also people like you, . . . we are now all sons and daughters of this country in which you have found us and in which we have allowed you to found homes.'[35]

Keen Observer had picked up these statements of plea and protest
and put them alongside Welensky's warning against "self-government preaching by African leaders" and John Gaunt's "forcing
motions" in Leg. Co. on the territory's constitutional development. Here again was the distortion of Rhodes' maxim of 'equal
rights for all civilised men', and Kaunda asked, 'Can any sincere
person in the Federation either wholesale condemn Africans as
uncivilised or accept all Europeans as civilised?' These provocative
statements might well form 'the beginning of real political racial
struggle if handled unimaginatively,' for, as Kenneth quoted in
the March Circular, "Some of the things that come not back
are the spoken word and the neglected opportunity."

History's ultimate judgment on the colonial period in African
history may well show, as has been suggested, that 'white rule will
be seen as a brief interlude, lasting less than one hundred years
from first to last.' 'But it will surely be regarded as a crucial period
too; one in which the immemorial ways of African customary life
were broken and discarded and the new industrial system was
imposed—with all that that must come to mean in terms of the
prosperity of the entire population of the country . . . . The settlers
did not act from philanthropy. . . . They were . . . the bringers
of a new world; often harsh exploiters and yet ultimately benefactors
to mankind in this part of Africa.'[37] Kenneth Kaunda was responding, as he was, to his taxing vocation not because he despised the
benefits of 'modern civilisation' but because there were forces
at work which would recklessly seek to oppose the tide of history
and intrench exploitation in the African continent. He therefore
had to be a 'radical'.

As the tension between 'moderatism' and 'activism' grew, he
received a racy letter from young Henry Chipembere, a Bachelor of
Arts and Member of the Nyasaland Legislature. The Congress
there had just won 'a sweeping victory' in the Leg. Co. elections.
Chipembere was a graduate in politics and history of Force Hare
and, he wrote, 'politics is almost a disease in me.' He was yearning
to hear of the fortunes of the N.R.A.N.C. 'How is that mighty
national movement faring?'[38] The early dream of one movement to
speak for the African peoples of the three territories was proving
elusive, and the ascendancy of 'young militants' in Nyasaland
served to extend the tension between 'activists' and 'moderates'.

Kaunda had been sent by Nkumbula to visit Sangala, the Nyasaland Congress President, to explain in person ANC's request to Wellington Manoah Chirwa to join a delegation to London to campaign against Malvern's rumoured plan to press for sovereignty for the Federation before 1960. Kaunda travelled with Anderson Hiwa, one of the Congress trustees. To avoid publicity, he wore old overalls and cap and went ostensibly as Hiwa's 'lorry-boy'. Kaunda's impression of Sangala was of a man who was 'not able but brave'.[39]

At this period Kaunda put a lot of work into organising a 'constitutional changes conference of selected African leaders'. London's continued failure to respond to the Congress proposals became more disturbing as cordiality between Salisbury and Whitehall grew. The selected leaders were to comprise two trade unionists, the four Leg. Co. members and the two African Federal M.P.s along with four Congress men.[40] Friends in Britain were perturbed, Fox-Pitt told Kaunda, because ANC's constitutional proposals 'for step-by-step advance to full democracy' though detailed and never revolutionary, received no publicity, and so it seemed as though the only reasonable approach was that of the Capricorn Africa Society.[41] Fenner Brockway had earlier sent a long questionnaire to Nkumbula about the size of ANC and the distribution of its branches in the territory, 'spontaneous discontent' among the Gwembe Valley people and proposals for their compensation on eviction; for Congress had received and reproduced the Government's reply on the petition to the Queen to the effect that the Colonial Secretary had advised her that 'the petition did not represent the views of those for whom it claimed to speak or reflect any genuine grievance, and that it should not be granted'. The Labour M.P. also wanted information about the extent of bans on Congress, conditions at the 'inter-racial' university college in Salisbury, educational developments required for Africans, and ANC's specific proposals for constitutional change. M.P.s wanted to press the British Government 'to raise the level of African life . . . so that the African people can play a democratic part in the development of the colony'. James Johnson reported that H.M.G. had reaffirmed that the territory's status would not be altered 'without the consent of the majority of the inhabitants'.[42]

ANC sent, through Kaunda, a donation of fifty pounds to the

Congress of Peoples against Imperialism, of which Fenner Brockway was an active member. There was no lack of goodwill among such people and organisations in Britain towards the Congress cause. Any sign of a narrowing of the gap between the races was welcome to them, and Kenneth reported to Fox-Pitt in August that there had been 'for the first time in history' a meeting of Congress leaders with European Unofficial Members of Leg. Co. 'Their attitude was quite good' and the formal meeting ended by both parties seeing the need of more such meetings. It seemed as if 'the top men in the elected circles' might be ready to offer Congress 'quite a big place' in planning for the future of the Protectorate. 'But,' he added, 'we are watching very carefully for this could turn out to be a big hoax.' The 'New Look' policy of Harry Nkumbula was, however, distinctly disturbing to some of his colleagues. Sikalumbi went with Nkumbula, Kaunda and Chimba to the meeting with the Unofficials which took place in the lobby room of the Legislative Council building. The four African M.L.C.s were also present. He has described what happened thus: 'Nkumbula handed the leader of the Unofficials, John Roberts, a statement of the Congress "New Look Policy". Among other things the statement said:

'There are many things that the Congress must do which would take a little time. We must control our members and our branches better. We must control and educate on better lines our extremists. On both sides, both Africans and Europeans, there is room for better understanding.

'By this statement, by bringing the Congress onto constitutional practice, and by assuring Africans of this country that the Government of Northern Rhodesia is impartial and genuinely interested in improving the conditions under which Africans live, I am quite confident that race relations will improve to the satisfaction of every decent person in this country.

'We will do our best to work for the development of Northern Rodesia and all its people, but for this we need the help and sympathy of all liberal-minded Europeans.'

The discussion reached an important stage when Malcolmson said, "Now Mr. Nkumbula! We know that you have the following and the command of the African people of Northern Rhodesia. Whenever you call for a boycott people obey you, we recognise your authority and we can make you sit next to Mr. Roberts today. Now what do you want next?" Nkumbula replied, "We want respect from the other section of the community, the Europeans". The three of us, Kenneth Kaunda, Justin Chimba and myself, looked into each others' faces and did not believe what we had heard.'[43]

Kaunda's account of the meeting supports this view. 'This was not the type of thing we were working for. Respect every man wants but it doesn't come fast. Once power is acquired, respect and self-respect follow. Yes, Sikalumbi and Chimba were very upset and so was I. I had to contain their tempers at the time and try to keep the party together. Thereafter I was busy carrying on a patching exercise.' Chimba expressed his shock vehemently: 'Is it true that we have been toiling and going to imperialist prisons because we want respect from the white nincompoops?' The suspicion was growing that Nkumbula had somehow been 'bought'. It was their belief that Franklin 'was really the man who frightened Harry out of his wits and . . . tampered with him so badly' probably 'just in order to lead information on behalf of the Colonial Government'. Sikalumbi has recalled that Nkumbula had recently quoted a proverb of the Ila people that 'the coward hyaena grows older.' What it meant was that a person who feared powerful people would not be hurt, that in this situation 'if Congress feared the whites they would not go to prison.' The new situation was highly ambiguous. What, for instance, did 'bringing the Congress onto constitutional practice' mean when the rights and liberties of the African people were threatened further by the plans of Unofficials? Consequently the disquiet of some members about Nkumbula's decision to end the boycotts became more vocal. Kaunda was determined, if at all possible, to keep the unity of Congress. While standing by his loyalty to Nkumbula and 'minimising his own popularity', he was trying hard to convince Nkumbula 'that people wanted more than access to toilets, cafes, shops, etc.' His inner disquiet was growing, however, and thus we find only a brief mention of the meeting in one of his *Circular* letters.[44]

In July, papers lay on Kenneth's desk relating to a conference to be held in Cairo under the auspices of the 'African Liberation Committee', a special committee of all the liberation movements in Africa 'for united action to overthrow European imperialism in Africa'. The ANC was listed as a participant along with sister organisations in Nyasaland, Southern Rhodesia, and South Africa, the Basuto African Congress, similar bodies from Tanganyika, Uganda, Zanzibar and Madagascar, along with nineteen associations and parties from West Africa, Mozambique, Angola and North Africa. The main items on the agenda were announced as: 'Coordination of our activities; future plans; Pan-African Youth Conference'. The political committee of the Conference had as its task 'to survey the overall picture of colonialism and racialism in Africa and to suggest ways and means of effective coordination of all African movements in order to establish forces able to mobilize our people and fight in a systematic manner to eradicate all evil systems obtaining in Africa today: Colonialism and Racialism'. The Secretary-General of the Cairo conference was Munukuyumbwa Sipalo, a young Lozi who had studied economics at Delhi in India.[45]

The Northern Rhodesian Government's *Annual Report* of 1955 on African affairs claimed that the year had seen a diminishing of 'post-Federation fears and uncertainties'. This assessment may have been made in view of the sense of fatality about Federation that undoubtedly had fallen on many people and also of the effects of increased police activity. In his chapter entitled 'A time of frustration', Kaunda has said that '1955 was an unsatisfactory year from the point of view of Congress activity.' This may well have contributed to the emergence of what Hall called a 'new dynamism' in 1956, with which Sipalo and Kapwepwe were connected. 'In 1956,' Kapwepwe recorded, 'I was elected Treasurer of the party and came closer again with Kenneth.' 'But I differed very greatly with Harry—a playboy, drinking and dancing. We two, Kenneth and I, were dedicated through our up-bringing at the mission . . . . This frightened Nkumbula who started being very nasty to me—coming to snatch the keys of the treasury, because he didn't get money from me for drinking. Harry said: "This chap is not from a Christian place, he is from a Boma, so why is he so particularly against drinking?" Kenneth said this was how we had been brought up. Nkumbula now started to throw me out of the party. When Sipalo came he was very close to me, eating from my house. Nkumbula had no time for Sipalo, not interested in intelligent and dedicated people.' Obviously, however hesitant he was himself becoming, Nkumbula must have sensed the self-confidence of Kapwepwe, who claimed that in India he had become 'the leader of all African students from all of Africa' and, as their spokesman, had 'had to meet governors and the Prime Minister himself'.[46]

In August, ANC held its seventh annual conference at which some new names appeared on the National Executive Committee. It had been expected that Sikalumbi would become Treasurer, but instead Kapwepwe replaced Sokota, and Titus Mukupo replaced Konkola as Deputy Secretary. Mayanda, who had protested with Mukupo against the 'New Look' was replaced by one of the earliest 'Action Group' men, Reuben Kamanga. Edward Mungoni Liso, who had been one of the victors of the recent legal contest with Government in the Mufulira boycott case, took over from Robinson Puta as Deputy President. It was not a 'New Look' Cabinet.[47] In commenting on the elections, in Keen Observer's column of the *Circular*, Kaunda warned that the masses now behind the ANC would not be content with resolutions passed at conferences and then forgotten. He had previously issued in advance of the conference, a lengthy Annual Review along with a briefer summary of the history of Congress. He prefaced this summary by underlining that the National Committee must be answerable to the conference which should be the decision-making body. The conference must in turn act most responsibly in electing its Executive. 'As an elected member,' he said, 'I am by all democratic practices entitled to swaying your minds if you can listen to me; but because the national cause I consider above politics, I have deliberately decided not to make any attempt at using this document or any other for personal interests.' 'But I should here be failing in my duty if I didn't point out to you that we have ahead of us higher ascents and deeper chasms than we have already gone through.' Unity was therefore essential. Inspiration could be drawn from the struggles of other peoples. The local struggle was now a serious one and called for the best leadership. Therefore, he wrote, 'I find interest in exposing some mean characters at this Conference... small men [whom] nature disfavoured by planting in them equally small minds... [who] find pleasure in deserting the battle scene leaving greater men to face the dark clouds and reappearing on the scene when conditions are more stable. ... Such people... are simply sell-outs.'[48]

Clearly the potential for explosion, both within the Congress and in the country at large, was increasing. Over the past year there

had been a number of violent incidents in which the drivers of cars
involved in accidents had been stoned by angry mobs. On the mines
and on the football fields the same type of mood was noticeable.
The Riot Damages Ordinance of 1955 was not only an index of
the unrest in the land. Its provision for fining people living in an
area where unrest took place was provocative of more resentment.
Inevitably Congress meetings 'provided a focus and a forum for
a deeper unrest', providing as they did the only platform for protest.
Inevitably too, such tremors affected the copper mines.⁴⁹ Police
action meanwhile was visibly harsher. The phenomenon of young
white officers wielding power indiscriminately was to characterise
the Central African scene as it had done in Kenya and elsewhere.
Apprehension rose when the Congress H.Q. received word smuggled
from Salisbury's Central Prison of the treatment of Northern
Rhodesian prisoners there, which served to confirm African anger
at the inclusion of prisons on the list of Federal departments.
The secret message reported: 'We are kicked as if we were oxen
without an owner. ... To crown it all when we complain to the
Prison Superintendent he ... orders those who beat us to go and
shut us up on half the prison prescribed diet for seven days. ... We
are given European prisoners as warders. ... These beat us just
at any time. If one raises a hand to shelter one's head, the Superintendent steps in and recommends six strokes. ... We are told this
is not a protectorate but a white man's land.' In a letter of protest
to the Director of Prisons in Salisbury, Kaunda wrote: 'Such
torture really belongs to the world of fascism, complete despotism
and savagery.'⁵⁰

From 26 to 28 June, 1956, there was a brief strike on the Copperbelt triggered by African miners' resentment against what they saw
as a discriminatory regulation requiring the wearing of leg guards.
The official answer was that jobs done by Europeans did not call
for such protective wear. But this only served to underline the
continuing colour bar in industry, and, as Mason pointed out,
those 'rolling strikes' were really directed at 'the whole situation,
the pay rates ... at European political supremacy, at all that is
included in the "colour bar".' Tension rose fast and the press spoke
of a widespread sense of 'panic', with European passions running
high. There was a bitter protest against the trade testing of Africans
which Cousins, the Labour Commissioner, had recently instituted,

whereby Africans could hope to move into certain categories of skilled employment. 'Who the hell is Mr. Cousins?' one European demanded. 'With the abortion of government that we have...we shall see our livelihood and that of our children undermined by fumbling, misguided, idealistic, so-called Liberals who...think of the African...in sickly sentimental terms.' The Government's reaction to this tide of events was the declaration of a State of Emergency on the Copperbelt on 12 September, and the immediate arrest of over three dozen union leaders. Mungoni Liso was among those arrested as well as Matthew Nkoloma who was then in jail for three years, despite a ruling by the Chief Justice in his favour. The arrests made in the absence of Katilungu, who had expressed support for Nkumbula's 'New Look', were seen by many Africans as an attempt by Government to widen the gap between 'moderates' and 'activists'.[51]

Thus it was that in the tense areas of political and industrial life there began the decline of the forerunning father-figures. Kenneth Kaunda continued his strenuous efforts to avoid an open breach in Congress, in the face of the Government's increasing insistence that 'unrest and opposition to authority' in the rural areas as well as on the line of rail were fomented by the Congress. Messages from imprisoned ANC men certainly stirred people's emotions. Frank Chitambala, for instance, wrote from his cell a circular headed 'Her Majesty's Hostel, Fort Jameson', in which he said that Europeans had 'changed their Bible for our land.' 'Now we have their Bible and they have the land. Now there is a new awareness among the African people.... The wind has blown and the tide is changing.' His letter then cited how Hawkins, the famous sailor of Elizabethan England, had 'sailed his slave raiding boat JESUS with 400 Africans at £25 per head'. Shortly before, Chitambala had issued another message, also from prison, to the 'Black Youth of NR'. It was a four-page document, poorly developed and very emotional, but it set out seven purposes for a proposed Youth Conference, which would be called 'to infuriate the youth of this territory with the present situation'. Its tasks would then be 'to declare to Britain and the world that NR is an African state; to urge NR and UK to speed constitutional reforms; to advise NRG that all Bills should be published before discussion in Leg. Co.; to insist that franchise is a birthright; to press for complete secession; and to draw up a

National Policy and political programme for self-government Now and Independence'.[52]

As the Federal economy prospered, European immigration increased and the World Bank voted a £28,000,000 loan for the Kariba project, effective communication between Government and African organisations was shrinking fast, and official answers to increasingly blunt questions in the African Representative Council were becoming patently evasive. A question on the burning issue of colour-bar practices in shops asking why, under Section 8 of the Public Order Ordinance, No. 38 of 1955, Government had not taken legal action against offending traders, was answered by Stubbs thus: 'It is presumed that by "action" a prosecution is meant. Such a prosecution, to be successful requires proof of the intention stated in the section, namely "to excite enmity". Such an intention in the case of the imposition of a colour bar would be extremely difficult to establish as it is very doubtful whether it exists.' The M.L.C. Malcolmson, unaffected by his meeting with Congress leaders, scoffed at African nationalism as 'a silly cock crowing on its own dunghill' and his colleague Rendall blamed the 'paramountcy' policy of the Government for the rise of Congress. The Associated Chamber of Commerce called for action against the Congress as 'subversive'. But Nkumbula had declared opposition to any defiance campaign and pledged to work for better race relations; and soon after he was congratulated for this in Leg. Co.[53]

The Copperbelt State of Emergency had led to a determined effort by the Government to secure assurances from influential Africans that order would be restored. The Bemba chief, Chitimukulu, issued a call to his people on the mines to return to work, only two days after the A.M.W.U. President, Katilungu, who had said he was returning to 'save his union from destruction', had instructed all A.M.W.U. men to end the strike. His call was printed on thousands of leaflets which were dropped by plane over the African townships of the Copperbelt, and miners began to stream back at once. There were, however, stoning incidents and one disturbance at Luanshya involving members of the Lenshina sect from Chinsali. From London, Dixon Konkola attacked the copper companies and the government of both Rhodesias for the state of unrest, but Governor Benson blamed the Copperbelt situation on the 'duping of unsophisticated Africans' by 'rogues, crooks and self-seekers'. When the official enquiry into the unrest began, the Congress was accused of using the A.M.W.U. 'as a tool for the attainment of their political, nationalistic and racialistic objects'.[54] When ANC went into conference, Nkumbula voiced his bitter disappointment with the reaction to his gestures of goodwill. 'I've extended the hand of friendship,' he said, 'but nothing happened.' But, though the 'New Look' policy was out of favour, Nkumbula defeated Yamba for the presidency by 151 votes to 7.[55]

On 3 October, 1956, Godfrey Huggins, Lord Malvern, retired from the premiership of the Federation. He had been Prime Minister for twenty-three years. Welensky suceeded him as was expected, at a time when the British Labour Party's 'meddlesome ideas' were provoking the anger of him and his colleagues. William Wroth, angered by Mrs. Barbara Castle, went as far as to warn of a 'Boston Tea Party'. In the Gold Coast, people awaited the publication of a White Paper on an 'Independence Constitution' for 1957. Malvern marked the occasion of his retirement by declaring that white people had not come to Africa to help the local people but to earn a living and in consequence develop the country. However, the Government took the positive step of announcing that it was considering legislation which would be a first step to outlawing the colour bar in shops, offices, and other business premises. At the same time the Chief Justice ordered the immediate release of the fifty-four detainees for whom Leslie Blackwell had acted as counsel, and two days later a new Chief Secretary was appointed to the Protectorate in the person of Evelyn Hone. Kaunda was to say of him later: 'We could not have had a better friend.'

Yet in the confusion of the northern Protectorate, it was hard to 'see the wood for the trees', and Congress's 'man of destiny' was under assault from many quarters. The Nyasaland Congress leaders were 'thoroughly and persistently' snubbing him over his alleged remark that some Nyasalanders would opt for 'self-government within the Federation'. The political committee of the N.R.T.U.C. was talking of 'major differences' with Congress, and the restriction orders served on most of the Mumbwa detainees freed by the High Court confirmed official suspicion of ANC's influence within the Mineworkers' Union. Into the midst of this turmoil came Alan Lennox-Boyd on his long-promised visit, protesting that he wanted

his 'informal talks' to be restricted to constitutional proposals
only. ANC, still sore over his refusal to meet Nkumbula in London
a year previously, resolved to prepare a new petition.[56]

On New Year's Day, 1957, the Governor announced the end of
the State of Emergency on the Copperbelt and spoke of his 'high
hopes' for the days ahead. But the Colonial Secretary was using
cliches about 'government in the hands of civilized and responsible
people', which gave no cause for African hopes of a new British
awareness of the power of the forces of repression in this part of
Africa. On the contrary, his assurance that Britain had no intention
of imposing 'the dead hand of Whitehall' indefinitely seemed to
give approval to the remark of Governor Benson that had so
outraged African opinion. The visit included, at the end, and after
public protests and sharp British press comment, a reluctant meeting
with Nkumbula on 22 January, 1957. Commenting on it in the
Circular, Kaunda said that it was common knowledge that the
Governor had advised against the meeting. The African reaction
took the form of a 'monster meeting of some fifteen thousand men,
women and children ... at Kabwata ... demanding the recall
of the Governor'. Before leaving Lusaka, Lennox-Boyd issued a
statement which said that he had assured Nkumbula that 'the
part played through him [as Colonial Secretary]' by the British
Government would not be removed until Africans 'had the same
trust in the Federal Government as they had in the Colonial Office'.
On his way back to London, however, he held a press conference
in Johannesburg and spoke bluntly of his views on Africa. 'I met
many settlers,' he said, 'who, if anything, have more right to live
in the Rhodesias and Nyasaland than many of the Africans.'[57]

The first months of 1957 saw a continuation of hot statements
reported in the press. Welensky reiterated that Federation was
'here to stay'. Jonathan Chivunga, ANC's Ndola District Secretary,
echoed Konkola's description of Federation as a 'police state'
and called on people to 'kill this octopus'. John Gaunt's Dominion
Party issued a manifesto which cited corruption charges against
leading politicians in West Africa and in Northern Rhodesia,
revelations in the Barotseland courts of witchcraft and murder,
the return of slavery in the Sudan, and Mau Mau in Kenya as
proof that 'advance forward from sheer barbarism and savagery to
any civilised state must take at the very least three or four genera-

tions'. Extreme European views were not appeased by the news that Nkrumah, first Prime Minister of the state soon to be called Ghana, had invited Nkumbula to independence ceremonies there. Nkumbula went to Ghana therefore as a 'Prime Minister's Guest' and was accorded magnificent hospitality.[58] The A.T.U.C. meanwhile came out in opposition to Dixon Konkola's plan for a Socialist Party, which was one of a number of political ventures that failed to rival ANC effectively. But 'while Congress was still ... harping on parity of representation as the only possible way for a multiracial society,' Konkola's call for 'one man one vote' found a ready echo in the hearts of many activists.[59]

Not long after the Colonial Secretary's visit, Roy Welensky went to Britain. His cordial relations with Lennox-Boyd had led him to decide to press for significant advances for the Federation, and he returned with a concordat commiting H.M.G. to agreement in principle to the enlargement of the Federal Parliament which was to open the way to a number of amendments to the Federal Constitution. In retrospect, the concordat could be said to have sounded the death knell of Federation, as we shall see below. It certainly had the immediate effect of sharpening the voice of African protest. As earnest of this, Munukuyumbwa Sipalo was beginning to appear more in the public eye with his plea for the sweeping away of 'tribal cobwebs' in the nationalist movement.[60]

For Kaunda and Nkumbula, however, 1 April brought a nasty experience in Kitwe's Astra Cafe which confirmed that little progress had been made in 'changing men's hearts' in Northern Rhodesia. Kaunda has described the incident along with his earlier rough experiences in Mufulira in 1949. Kapwepwe's memory of the stir that it caused among Congress people and other friends was that Kenneth demonstrated great self-control even under severe provocation. He believed that the scene of the trouble was Kitwe's Astra Cinema Cafe. Nkumbula and Kaunda wanted a light meal as they passed through the town and had been told that the Astra might provide something. Since it was a 'white area there were no African eating houses nearby'. On entering the cafe, Kenneth went to the counter to ask for sandwiches but was told by 'a young girl of about seventeen that "boys" were not served at the counter'. His account goes on:

'When I told her that I was not a 'boy' and all I wanted was a dozen sandwiches, she spoke to an elderly white woman who was apparently in charge. On asking me what I wanted, she repeated that "boys" were not served at that counter. I repeated in my turn that I was not a "boy". At this point I was dragged out of the cafe by my clothes by a European man who had already dragged Harry Nkumbula outside the cafe. This white man hit Harry and called him a cheap, spoiled nigger. Five other white men joined him in attacking us and we defended ourselves. White men and black men passing joined in the fight, and an *apartheid* type of brawl took place. This was my third and last fight.

'We were ordered to leave the premises but we refused on the grounds that the white men who had started the fight could get away if we did so. In the end we were given an escort of an African policeman despite the fact that we were the complainants. The white men went to the Charge Office unescorted.

'At the Charge Office we were asked to make a statement. Harry Nkumbula began by saying that the girl at the counter refused to serve us. Before he could end his sentence the white superintendent of police who had come to stop the fight said, "You cannot call a white lady a 'girl' or a 'woman'." Harry ignored this and went on to say that "after that an elderly woman came . . ." but again, before he could finish his sentence, the superintendent said, "I say, you cheeky nigger, you cannot call a European lady a woman".

'Then this police officer called Harry to a room and closed the door and beat him up. Harry told this officer that he was lucky he was wearing Her Majesty the Queen's uniform, or one or other [*sic*] of them would have been killed.

'When the case came to court, our demand that we should be medically examined by a doctor chosen by us was refused and we therefore chose not to continue the case.

'The following morning after the incident a group of mineworkers went to the cafe and said to the proprietor, "We have heard that our leaders were beaten up here. We have come to have revenge". There was a police guard on the cafe and the leader of the group was arrested and fined.'[61]

The cafe incident took place at a time when the general unrest in the land was revealing a dangerous tendency among what Sikalumbi called 'rogue followers of Congress' to take the law into their own hands. This was seen in the rough handling of people who wanted to form other parties, but who were denounced by Congress leaders. There was a constant apprehension about rival parties among some Congress leaders, who believed that unity was of paramount importance. Kaunda himself said some months later, in a letter to Titus Mukupo, that it was not yet time for opposition parties to the cause of ANC. 'Once we have the vote,' he wrote, 'then one does not care how many blinking parties are formed.' 'Some of us will have done our duty and hope to settle down to peaceful farming. But until then, we must guard jealously what has been achieved in the way of national unity.' Here was something vital to uphold and to 'fight for', yet so easily undisciplined fists could take over the 'fight' and wreck the dream of a unity in dedication and service that Kaunda cherished. He was therefore trying to impress upon his people that disciplined unity was a powerful factor of change.[62]

Kaunda's first circular letter of 1957 to all Congress organisers and officials in the country sounded a rallying call to fight the 'many evil things which in the past we accepted with slavish timidity'. The boycott campaigns had demonstrated the effectiveness of concerted action and he said 'as a result of this UNITY they are scared stiff.' The decision to launch the anti-colour-bar boycotts which had brought 'imprisonment, most brutal attacks by the police, unlawful detentions and confinements', had, however, given the African people 'some little place in the Central African sunshine'. The new focus on injustice had led to some improvement in 'chiefs' wage-structure' as well as in the treatment of African civil servants by white. Such concessions were, however, 'but crumbs of bread'.[63]

It was primarily awakening, and not agitation, that was Kaunda's conscious role at this period and, though increasingly aware of his leader's weaknesses, he still saw him, as Mainza Chona has confirmed, as 'the only one strong enough to be able to whip up the spirit of the independence struggle in the minds of the population'.[64] Like many political activists who have believed in the authority of 'the voice of the people', he held that the thoughts of the people must be enlivened so that they could become vocal. This, he was convinced, had urgency. It was a race against time, and the opposing forces were confident of their superiority. The study of his writings

at this testing period reveals his overwhelming sense of the irration-
ality of human divisions. 'Ninety-nine out of a hundred Europeans
will not have an African sit side by side with them in a hotel, cafe,
restaurant, cinema hall . . . [or] stand in the same queue at the post
office . . . [nor] tolerate his presence even when he brings them
money in their shops. . . . But have a closer look around . . . and . . .
you will see an African doing practically all the cooking for them,
spreading their beds, looking after their children and a thousand
and one other tender household jobs. Which of the two requires
more careful handling, preparing meals . . . [or] sitting together
dining? Don't tell us the latter for we shall have reason to cry,
"Oh, judgment thou art fled to brutish beasts and men have lost
their reason" '. Therefore, 'THOU SHALT NOT BUY FROM
ANY SHOP WHERE THOU ARE DISCRIMINATED AGAINST
ON GROUNDS OF COLOUR.' Kaunda wanted his readers to
realise that they in fact held the potential power for change within
themselves though 'for years now the African people have with a
slavish timidity accepted everything that was said by a white man.'
The present situation demanded white acceptance of a simple
formula, 'Do unto the African what you would have him do to
you.' Yet instead there was talk of the use of force. 'They can do
what they please with Mr. Nkumbula and any of his colleagues
. . . they can even start shooting and maybe they would meet
with some temporal [*sic*] success' but 'the African people are
more than ever before determined to go on with their non-violent
struggle of putting the wrong right.' Man was man and different
from the beasts. 'You might succeed in pushing him around for a
while but you can't do so all the time.'[65]

Some European elected members had visited Southern Rhodesia.
'It is quite true,' Kenneth said, 'to say Africans of Northern Rhodesia
are not happy at all with the present way of handling their affairs—
but it is very misleading to suggest that the Native Policy of Southern
Rhodesia . . . would make them happier.' The visit, he claimed,
was 'a Hand on the Wall' for the African people. Many white
people were still being persuaded that European solidarity would
guarantee African docility. The voice of Congress, as Kaunda
sought to interpret it, was a call to the whole population to 'give up
racial prejudice, jealousy and conceit and learn to work unitedly
for the good of the country.' Therefore the *Circular* quoted another

anonymous saying: "Success . . . does not attend those who are timid and balance everything." 'The great wheels of change' were turning fast and 'unless Africans can move along just as fast in understanding this complex world [and] its funny inhabitants, . . . we will be lost in the mists of man-planned selfishness. . . . We must make ourselves some of the planners and drivers of this great machine of change.' This message was not a call to recover the 'African past' and its centre was impervious to the propaganda that sought to justify 'Bantu-hood'. Man is man, in his needs and aspirations, the world over. 'The bear [*sic*] truth is,' Kenneth said, 'man, it doesn't matter of what colour, is all round a creature of hopes, ideals and aspirations.' Stages of social attainment might vary, but the fact that some people were 'awaiting development' was 'no certificate to warrant the developed one to exploit the undeveloped one selfishly'.[66]

There was a touch of wit in the *Circular* that let its readers laugh while they were grasping its serious messages. For instance, in Northern Rhodesia, 'the surest way of not getting lost when you want a native friend who lives in a native compound is to look for a dusty and corrugation-ridden road.' 'It is sure to lead you to a native location where you may locate your native friend.' So also 'an African may move about even after 10 p.m. without the police worrying for passes or any other documents . . . as long as he is driving a car or lorry.' 'Does this suggest to you that if there was a car at every native hut in a native compound the pass system would end?' In another issue, an eye-catching paragraph appeared: "I am running so that I should be at Kabwata in time to listen to what our national leader and liberator Harry Mwanga Nkumbula and his lieutenants will be telling us about the new cunning ways that the settler government is trying to employ in attaining a higher status for the Federation in Salisbury", replied Ndaupyata to a question put to him by a pressman . . . . "I see, you are now going to learn more about hating the white" . . . . "Ha, ha, ha, but man that isn't true. All we are told by our leader is the bear [*sic*] truth that this is simply our country in which other people have founded homes and that they together with us must find a good way of living . . . not as at present whereby we are wholesale treated as hewers of wood and drawers of water." Memorable phrases were also needed to underline the dynamic thinking that the *Circular* sought to generate. Canon Collins's aphorism, "Love evokes love and hate evokes hate" was one such as was the quotation from 'a friend'; "The soil of my country is my heaven, the good of my country is my good—Oh, my country, thou mother of my strength, take away my weakness, take away my unmanliness and make me a man." Kenneth believed that he must insistently reiterate this sense of conscious common purpose. "You and I are passionately eager to advance ourselves peacefully," Kenneth quoted from 'a friend of the exploited'. "We have been backward; we are backward. We have been left behind . . . in the world race. . . . It is time for us to bring happiness and prosperity to our people and to discard all the age-old shackles." The charge to man, as given in Genesis, was "to be fruitful and multiply and replenish the earth and subdue it". There was no mention of grades of man or of dominion by one man over another. So again came the challenge: 'Let every good citizen regardless of his colour work for this great day—a day of equal opportunity for every one.'[67]

This voice of reason and justice was coming much more insistently in Northern Rhodesia from 'the have nots' than from 'the haves'. 'Settler' society still made it difficult for the voices of white men of humanitarian views to be heard. Among the voiceless masses, Kaunda claimed, 'the truth that the African National Congress tells all people who care to listen is what has made it so popular, NOT intimidation as is so often alleged.' As George Padmore had said, "Pan-Africanism stands for racial coexistence on the basis of absolute equality and respect for human personality. . . . Politically Pan-Africanism seeks the attainment of government of Africans, by Africans, for Africans with respect for racial and religious minorities who desire to live in Africa on the basis of equality with the black majority." Because Kaunda and all those who shared this aim spoke of Africa, Welensky warned of African 'racialism'; yet, as the *Circular* quoted, it was he who had spoken of his dream of 100,000 Europeans in Northern Rhodesia from all over the western world, saying, "just let them have a white skin and be willing." The flow of immigrants at the rate of 24,000 a year, in response to this programme, was, in Kaunda's view, cause for alarm insofar as the objective was overtly racist.[68]

In December the *Circular* appeared twice, with renewed calls for active participation in the processes of change. "The old order changeth, yielding place to new", it quoted, but warned that change did not come on its own. People must then take 'the ANCO way'. So 'let every true citizen of Northern Rhodesia work for the day when our present *apartheid*-type political, economic and social set-ups will be buried with due ceremony.' Christmas was near and soon 'the Holy Bells' would be ringing. 'If Christ came here on earth today,' asked Kaunda, 'what would He think of the Christian world?' Though 'in theory the Christian world does exist, in practice it does not,' for 'the Holy men of the day are busy blessing such brutal actions of murder, rape and arson of the weak by the strong because of money.' But peace never dropped 'like manna from heaven'; it had to be purchased. There were two states that were sometimes called peace, '(a) the peace that is imposed upon a people by an alien ruler and (b) the peace that is established by the people themselves.' But the choice was clear. As 'a socialist friend' had said: "The means of life . . . should be owned and controlled by the whole community. . . . A person who is dependent upon the will or consent of another for the privilege of earning a livelihood by labour is verily a slave . . . a nation whose workers are dependent upon a small fraction of non-producers for access to the instruments of wealth production is a nation of slaves and tyrants." Now 'Africans in Northern Rhodesia on realising that they have been chloroformed into slavery are coming up at a speed that is leaving the oppressor gasping for air.' The picture was vivid and would set men talking, and so he added that the way forward was by joining ANC, 'the only political organisation which has detected the oppressor's cunningness and is bold enough to challenge his action without either hating him or seeking his favour'.[69]

The chapter in Kaunda's autobiography entitled 'African Opinion' quotes from the last circular of 1956. There was in the country what he called 'pandemonium'. The Governor had just stated that there was "bitterness and bitter rivalry at this Christmas time when 99 per cent of us want to have peace and goodwill." As so often in times of deep unrest through patent injustice, the official formula was to attribute the confusion to a tiny minority of dissident men against whom the forces of law and order must be invoked. Hence the State of Emergency on the Copperbelt. But the current European strike at Bancroft was, Kaunda suggested, 'over a similar issue to the one that led African miners to decide on strikes', yet

Government's reaction seemed 'partial'. The last quotation of the year affirmed that there must be revolution in the social and political life of the territory, but "a revolution by peaceful means . . . using brains instead of bombs", which would allow each child to develop its manhood and "rob the privileged classes of their liberty to exploit labour." ' He then quoted words of a white missionary 'friend' that described accurately what the European intrusion had done in southern and central Africa. "Our unregulated and unrestrained profit-making urge . . . has led us to scour country-sides for labour, leaving the human remains to fend for themselves in desolate villages without the manpower to produce enough food; it has caused us recklessly to divide families and destroy the moral basis of the family." Now the great upheaval had begun or, in the image of Nnamdi Azikiwe of Nigeria, the African giant was stirring from sleep. 'From Cape to Cairo,' Kenneth wrote, 'and from Cape Guardafin to Cape Verde there is turmoil and restlessness.'[70]

'Northern Rhodesia has come to the crossroads,' and the time had come for decision and action. This was the conviction that Kaunda was sharing with all who heard him speak and read what he wrote. The pressure of events caused a delay in producing the next issue of the *Circular*. When at last it was published, marked 'Feb./April 1957', it appeared over the signature of Titus Mukupo, Acting Secretary-General. Mukupo was chosen for this post because, in response to an invitation to attend the Labour Party's Conference on Commonwealth Affairs, Kaunda was to accompany Nkumbula to Britain. It had been hoped to raise sufficient funds to allow three delegates to go, but fund-raising processes were still arduous. The conference was to take place at the Beatrice Webb House in the town of Dorking in Surrey, with delegates drawn from twenty-six countries, including the 'old dominions' of the British Commonwealth along with 'emergent' nations and still 'dependent' territories. Kenneth had had an earlier hope of visiting Denmark but, as he has recalled, 'my leader found it difficult to find a replacement who would not be claiming a monthly salary.' Again, there had been a plan to send him to an international socialist conference in Rangoon in 1956, but the Government declined to issue a passport as he might be "mixing with communists". Now he was on his way to London, proud to accompany the National President and determined to find every opportunity of presenting their people's case.[71] He departed at a time when the main burdens of his mind had lesser irritants added to them. Two weeks before departing for Britain he had pleaded guilty to driving a car without adequate insurance cover, and in a letter recording the plea, he had asked for 'His Worship's judgment' as soon as possible.[72] For nearly four years he had been at the hub of the 'national awakening'. His early vision had not dimmed. Rather his focus had sharpened. His conviction of the urgency of 'non-violent positive action' was more mature now after the first tense confrontation between Congress and 'the authorities'. But, though there was a boyish delight in his heart in the anticipation of new experiences, he was convinced that his country stood at a crucial crossroads and that the urgent issues of the hour concerned not only Northern Rhodesia but the rest of the continent as well.

---

[1]Phrase from line one of 'Man was made to mourn', by Robert Burns.
[2]TI-FM/SMK, 8/11/69.
[3]TI-FM/A.G. Zulu, 22/2/69 and FM/J.M. Mwanakatwe, 22/5/70.
[4]K. D. Kaunda, *A Humanist in Africa: Letters to Colin Morris* (Longmans, 1966), esp. pp. 81-111.
[5]TI-FM/JM, 22/5/70.
[6]TI-FM/SMK, 8/11/69.
[7]ANC: Nat. Exec. Council Organisation—Memo giving estimates of salaries, etc., 19/3/54.
[8]Mpashi, *op. cit.*, pp. 45-47.
[9]*NN*, 28/1/56, ref. Askari (ex-soldiers) Memorial Hall meeting.
[10]Sikalumbi, *op. cit*, pp. 64 ff.
[11]TI-FM/W. K. Sikalumbi, 8/6/71.
[12]Emmanuel Papers: report of Chingola African Urban Advisory Council, meeting with S.N.A. and John Moffat, sgd. M. Lipalile, 12/10/51.
[13]Vol. I, No. 1, ed. Nephas Tembo, Justin Chimba, Simon Zukas, 30/1/52.
[14]Art. 73 of the U.N. Charter pledges member states 'which have or assume responsibilities for the administration of territories whose peoples have not yet attained a full measure of self-government . . . to ensure . . . their political, economic, social and educational advancement, their just treatment and protection from abuses'.
[15]*NN*, 9/3/56.
[16]ANC: *Congress Circular*, Vol. II, No. 2, 29/2/56; and note (a) that the *Africa Digest* was published by the Africa Bureau, founded by Revd. Michael Scott, and (b) that the S.A. ban on 'objectionable publications' was based on Customs Act No. 55 of 1955.
[17]See M. Horrell (ed.), *Bantu Education to 1968* (S.A. Institute of Race Relations, 1968); *SA Hansard*, 17/9/53, col. 3576; and Huddleston, *op. cit.*, pp. 159-178.
[18]Federal Annual Report on Education, 1956; and note that, while African Education Reports (e.g. 1955) gave totals of expenditure, N.R. European Education Reports, for the three years prior to Federation, stated that 'without dnduly delaying the publication of this report, it is not possible to provide uetailed financial statistics.'

226

Kenneth Kaunda of Zambia

[19]See Benson, *op. cit*, pp. 179-188; Keatley, *op. cit.*, pp. 294-296; Clutton-Brock, *op. cit.*, pp. 65 ff; and Sithole, *op. cit.*, pp. 39 ff.

[20]E. Colson, *Social Consequences of Resettlement*, Kariba Studies, IV (Manchester, 1971) 208.

[21]ANC: Fabian Colonial Bureau to Nkumbula, 27/2/56 and 6/3/56, citing such M.P.s as George Craddock, James Hynd, James Griffiths.

[22]ANC: *Congress Circular*, Vol. II, No. 2, 29/2/56, with reference to Governor's statement to all-white Business and Professional Women's Club; and ANC/5/23, Fox-Pitt to Kaunda, 9/3/56, citing debate in House of Commons.

[23]ANC: *Presidential Circular*, 12/2/56, and ANC/2/7, Nkumbula on the boycott campaign, 8/4/56.

[24]*Op. cit.*, p. 67.

[25]TI-FM/KK, 7/9/71. Matero is a large suburb, northwest of Lusaka.

[26]*NN* for the period.

[27]ANC: *Congress Circular*, Vol. II, Nos. 6-7, 31/7/56.

[28]Mason, *Year*, p. 115; and Rotberg, *Rise*, p. 277.

[29]Sikalumbi, *op. cit.*, p. 68.

[30]Kaunda, *Zambia*, pp. 94-95; and see Franklin *op. cit.*, esp. pp. 20, 24, 31, 93, 173-176, 196 ff.

[31]ANC: *Congress Circular*, Vol. II, No. 4, 30/4/56.

[32]Kaunda, *Zambia*, pp. 74 ff; and see Sikalumbi, *op. cit.*, p. 73; *NN*, 12/7/56; and ANC extract, unreferenced and undated, from article by a British correspondent 'Boycotts in N. Rhodesia—the African Side of the Case'.

[33]ANC: *Congress Circular*, Vol. II, No. 6-7, 31/7/56.

[34]ANC: *Congress Circular*, Vol. II, No. 2, 29/2/56 and Vol. II, No. 1, 31/1/56, quoting Welensky on Nkumbula.

[35]ANC: *Congress Circular*, Vol. II No. 2, 29/2/56, pp. 3-4; see also RH: 102/1 for long speech by Nabulyato, 1951, who said: 'It is always on the alert on behalf of African interests. Congress does not know anything about communism'; and Sithole, *op. cit.*, pp. 131-145.

[36]ANC: *Congress Circular*, Vol. II, Nos. 1 and 2.

[37]W. Rayner, *The Tribe and its Successor* (Faber and Faber, 1972), 204 and 226.

[38]ANC/5/12, Chipembere to Kaunda, 6/4/56.

[39]ANC/5/12, Nkumbula to Sangala, 4/9/56; and TI-FM/KK, 7/9/71.

[40]ANC-DHR/2/7, confidential letter by Kaunda, 6/5/56.

[41]ANC/5/23, Fox-Pitt to Kaunda, 20/6/56 and 9/7/56.

[42]ANC/3/UK, letters from Fenner Brockway, 22/12/55, 25/1/56 and 2/8/56; and from Johnson, 3/6/56.

[43]ANC/5/23, Kaunda to Fox-Pitt, 9/8/56; and Sikalumbi, *op. cit.*, pp. 70-71.

[44]TI-FM/KK, 26/2/69 and 13/7/71; *CAP*, 3/8/56; and Rotberg, *Rise*, pp. 278-9. Among the Unofficials present were Malcolmson, Tucker, Beckett and Roberts. See RH, 103/1 for Kaunda's undated pre-Conference circular, which gave the date of the meeting with the Unofficials as 'July 1956'.

[45]ANC/5/24, programme of the Cairo Conference.

[46]*NR Annual Report, 1955:* Kaunda, *Zambia*, p. 65; Hall, *Zambia*, p. 172; and TI-FM/SMK, 8/11/69.

[47]TI-FM/KK, 5/10/71.

[48]ANC: *Congress Circular*, Vol. III, No. 1, 31/10/56; and RH 101/3, Secy-General's 'Summary' report, undated, to 7th Annual Conference, August, 1956.

[49]See Mason, *Year*, p. 113.

[50]RH 103/1—Note by Fox-Pitt of prisoners' letter, translated from Bemba, 8/5/56; and Kaunda to Director of Prisons, Salisbury.

[51]*Year*, p. 116; *CAP*, 20/8/56; Mason, *op. cit.*, p. 113, quoting *Union News*, February, 1956; and note figures for African and European miners' earnings quoted by Mason (pp. 104-105) respectively, thus: 1955, £134 : £1943; 1956, £160 : £2295; 1957, £189 : £1910; 1958, £200 : £1699. Note also RH 103/1, note on sharp rise in early 1955, of B.S.A. 'unappropriated profits' from £5,196,000

to £7,285,000; and letter of Dixon Konkola, President, A.T.U.C., to Ag Governor, calling for end of State of Emergency, 21/9/56; and Hall, *Zambia,*. p. 177.

[52]See *NR African Affairs Report*, 1957; RH 103/1 and 103/2, circular letters by Chitambala, 29/9/56 and 6/8/56.

[53]*NN*, 26/6/56; and Hall, *Zambia*, p. 166, noting that the Federation's output had risen from £265,000,000 in 1953 to £369,000,000 in 1956, and that net figures of European immigration were: 1954, 5,000; 1955, 11,000; 1956, 18,000. The total white population was 37,000 in 1951, 64,000 in 1955, and 80,000 in 1963. Also A.R.C. Minutes 15/6/56, Col. 101 and note also Cols 102 and 227 illustrating continuing protest in A.R.C. Minutes, 7/6/57, Col. 150 and 210 ff. *NN*, 6/7/56, 19/7/56, 8-9/8/56, 17/8/56, 18/8/56, 23/8/56, 1/9/56; and *CAP* 30/3/56.

[54]*NN* for period, and TI-FM/Sikalumbi, 8/6/71.

[55]ANC: President's Speech to 7th Annual Conference, 7/10/56.

[56]*NN*, 1/11/56; TI-FM/KK, 9/4/71; and *NN*, 31/12/56.

[57]ANC: *Congress Circular*, Vol. III, No. 3, January 1957; and *NN*, 25/1/57.

[58]*NN*, 2/2/57 ff.

[59]Sikalumbi, *op. cit.*, p. 88.

[60]ANC: *Congress Circular*, Vol. III, No. 4, Feb/April, 1957, sgd. Titus Mukupo, Ag. Secy.-General, for notes on Welensky's 'concordat'; and *NN*, 15/2/57.

[61]Kaunda, *Zambia*, pp. 33-35; TI-FM/SMK, 8/11/69; *NN*, 2/4/57. Kaunda's account adds this comment: 'This very month, March [1962] the Vice President of the Christian Council of NR, the Revd. M. S. Lucheya, entered a cafe with his European colleague, the President of the Council, and was refused a cup of tea. Can anyone wonder that we sometimes feel bitter about the European settler who treats us like some kind of subhuman species in the land of our birth.'

[62]Sikalumbi, *op. cit.*, p. 89; Kaunda, *Zambia*, p. 84.

[63]ANC/DMR/2/7—Kaunda's Circular, 1/57 of 2/1/57.

[64]TI-FM/MM Chona, 26/4/69.

[65]ANC: *Congress Circular*, Vol. II, No. 3, 31/3/56 and No. 4, 30/4/56.

[66]ANC: *Congress Circular*, Vol. II, No. 5, 31/5/56.

[67]ANC: *Congress Circular*, Vol. II, No. 5, 31/5/56, Nos. 6-7, 31/7/56 and Nos. 8-9, August, 1956.

[68]ANC: *Congress Circular*, Vol. III, No. 1, 31/10/56.

[69]ANC: *Congress Circular*, Vol. III, two issues, both numbered 2, 5/12/56 and 31/12/56. "The old order changeth . . ." was quoted from Tennyson's 'Idylls of the King—the Passing of Arthur', line 407.

[70]*Zambia*, 78 ff; and ANC: *Congress Circular*, Vol. III, No. 3, January 1957.

[71]TI-FM/KK, 13/2/69, and note that Beatrice Webb was the wife of Sidney Webb, Lord Passfield.

[72]Sokoni Papers: Kaunda to Clerk of Court, Livingstone, 14/5/57.

9

Parting of the Ways

Man's road of life is seldom a long straight line. For many, it is the corners that count, the occasions when a man is faced with a change of direction. Whether we call such moments corners or watersheds or flash-points, we see a number of them in the life of Kenneth Kaunda. Munali and the meeting with Daniel Sonquishe; the experience with Kapwepwe and Sokoni at Mbeya; the impact of Bindura and the Copperbelt; his appointment as ANC's Northern Province Organising Secretary; his election in 1953 as Secretary-General of the Congress; and now his trip to Britain. Nineteen fifty-seven was a year of turmoil in Northern Rhodesia but, though he was away from home for seven months of it, from early in the year, 'Kaunda became much more important as a national leader.' Four years earlier he had been marked for the post of Secretary of Congress because news had passed around the country that his organisational work in the north was outstanding. Now in 1957 the murmurings against Nkumbula were increasing and it was natural that more and more Congress members should mention Kaunda as the man who must lead them forward. Sikalumbi has described him as an intellectual who was a 'non-smoking, non-drinking character with a good deal of reserve, and deeply religious'. But, he added, 'I have since observed that Kaunda has realised that religious activity, the arts, social development, industry, leisure and all other such forces are linked in varying degree with the political network'; thus equipping him for the work of 'the creation of sympathy on the part of the masses for the cause of freeing Northern Rhodesia from imperialism and colonialism—the great and filthy octopus that needed to be struck, not only at the end of its tentacles but squarely in the centre of its slimy organism'. To 'cut these tentacles' Kaunda had to 'create faith among his followers. . . .' 'When he noticed that his followers failed to grasp his sincere expression he would retire in tears.'[1]

For years, Kenneth had been following events in other parts of the world closely. Ghana's independence showed that Britain was willing to be persuaded by a people's proven determination. South Africa continued to strive to decimate any such determination in the hearts of the oppressed. Portugal's African 'provinces' endured a similar system virtually incommunicado. The Congo remained an enigma of paradoxical contrasts, with fierce repression of political stirrings, as Kaunda had noted.[2] Meanwhile, in East Africa, despite the scale of the Mau Mau 'bloodbath', it seemed as though the dawn of African self-rule was breaking. In Nyasaland, the 'inspiring news' was being broadcast that 'within a few years', Dr. Hastings Banda would return. But Welensky, who had recently said that 'the African with his close ties with the Colonial Office and his facile propaganda has many ways of making himself heard in the United Kingdom,'[3] was himself reaping the reward of his support of the British adventure at Suez. As we saw in the last chapter, he had secured a 'concordat' with Whitehall that was to increase his confidence greatly.

Harry Nkumbula and Kenneth Kaunda went straight to Dorking in Surrey on reaching London Airport as the Commonwealth Conference of Labour Parties started there on 27 May. Tom Mboya of Kenya was also there, as well as delegates from other African countries. A communiqué issued at the close of the Conference warned against the 'grave risks involved in unduly delaying the liberation of the subject peoples of the world. . . . Self-government should be granted in an atmosphere of goodwill.' On the specific issue of the crisis in Central Africa, the Conference condemned 'the creation of the Federation of Central Africa . . . against the wishes of the African peoples . . . [and demanded] that they be given the right of self-determination and that all three territories be granted a democratic constitution based upon adult franchise of one man one vote'. Deep resentment was felt against the South African Government's refusal to renew the passport of a delegate from the Labour Party there. 'We of the democratic socialist parties,' the Conference declared, 'pledge ourselves to continue with renewed vigour the fight against those evil forces in the world that keep your bodies, but not your spirits and beliefs, in captivity.'[4] But

it was at once clear to Kaunda that many people who felt driven
to criticise and condemn the racial attitudes of some Europeans
pinned their faith on the triumph of good sense and fair play at the
1960 Federal Review Conference. As one English churchman wrote
near to the date of the Review: 'I believe it is still possible for the
ideals underlying the federal scheme to be fulfilled.'[5] To Kaunda
and his close colleagues these 'ideals' had been mere words from
the outset because the architects of Federation were fundamentally
opposed to partnership in the accepted meaning of the term.
Thus it was that Kaunda was convinced soon after his arrival in
England that the 'kind and polite and sympathetic' people whom
he met there were, as he said, 'like my European liberal friends
in Rhodesia, ... political babes in the wood.' 'They would never
really believe what I said about the oppression of my people in
the rural areas. While they were dismissing me as a gentle extremist,
I was getting letters from our organisers in the Northern and
Eastern Provinces which deeply wounded me.'[6]

In Britain, Nkumbula and Kaunda found that Rhodesia House
in London was 'engaged in very intensive propaganda to hoodwink
the British public....' 'They painted us,' Kaunda said, 'as extremists
who had no regard for human values and whose sole interest was
to gain power so that we could drive white people into the sea ...
[and] they succeeded in causing a great deal of fear in certain
influential quarters.'[7] Nkumbula, in a memorandum sent to the
Colonial Secretary, pointed out that when Welensky and other
leaders threatened 'subversive' action by reference to the Boston
Tea Party, they were not 'in any way checked'. The two Congress
leaders wanted to lay before Lennox–Boyd a number of problems
which seemed to their people 'so urgent and desperate',[8] but there
was delay in granting an interview.

Harry Nkumbula stayed in Britain from the end of May to
8 July. In June, he took part along with Kaunda in confidential
talks about Central Africa with the Revd. Michael Scott, Colin
Legum, Thomas Fox-Pitt and the Africa Bureau's Secretary,
Jane Symonds. Fox-Pitt believed that more and more Europeans
in the three territories were becoming disenchanted with Federation,
though for reasons very different from the grounds of African
opposition; but Nkumbula and Kaunda were told that 'from
the London end it seemed unlikely that the Federation could come

to an end'. It was suggested that Welensky's pressure for dominion status might be foiled by an approach to the Commonwealth Prime Ministers.[9]

During June, Creech Jones wrote to Nkumbula to assure him that his Party was 'very alive to the African view' on Federation, on which, he said, his own attitude was known to Congress. James Johnson asked the two leaders to advise him whether the Federal franchise qualifications as outlined by Julian Greenfield, would 'be welcomed by the African community'.[10] Fox-Pitt, as usual more aware of the roots of the African resistance to Federation, sent Kenneth a note on Cecil Rhodes' utterance about 'equal rights for all civilized men', with the comment that his definition of a civilized man was rarely quoted. 'Rhodes,' he said 'went far beyond the Tredgold plan or any modern plan.' 'You could accept his ruling and have more voters straight away than the Europeans.' 'But,' he added, 'it is interesting to think in this Christian country that neither Rhodes, Tredgold, Garfield Todd or Welensky would have thought Jesus and the Twelve Apostles fit to have a vote.' 'The only rule is universal suffrage.' To Africans, as interpreted by Sikalumbi, it appeared that Tredgold's Report on the Franchise rejected adult suffrage because by allowing an African majority in the legislature, 'it would lead to a worse type of racial representation.'[11]

Two students from Northern Rhodesia, Mainza Chona and Fitzpatrick Chuula, were studying law in London at that time. When they heard of the visit of the Congress leaders, they invited them to Chona's lodgings in Hampstead. ANC's demand for parity in the legislature seemed to the students to fall far short of what was necessary. Nkumbula said he would demand 'only what he would get' and that Labour Party supporters thought parity might be granted. 'Meanwhile,' Chona recalled, 'K.K. was quiet.' When he did speak he pleaded that those who were outside 'should not think that people in Northern Rhodesia were already organised for independence'. Congress was at work awaking a 'conscious need of independence', but found some opposition among a number of educated people who 'thought that Africans could not rule themselves . . . ' 'When political education had taken ground, they could demand higher things'. This was why Congress was at present 'pressing for parity'. Chona and Chuula were not satisfied, however, and so they arranged to meet Kenneth alone. 'This time,' said Chona, 'we tried to persuade him to take over the leadership of ANC and pointed out Nkumbula's well-known defects. . . .' 'We told him that Nkumbula was a disgrace to Northern Rhodesia because, when he came to London, his behaviour did not bring the political movement a good name.' But Kaunda 'was not ambitious' and argued that Congress needed the leadership of a senior man. The students then invited him to go with them to Windsor, where they hired a rowing boat on the lake near the royal castle. Again they tried to convince him that 'Harry Nkumbula was not strong enough', but he was not ready to yield to their pressure. This time, 'K.K. said that many people were conscious of the problem but that talking to Harry Nkumbula might see some improvement.'[12]

Chona and Chuula were, nonetheless, 'very impressed by K.K.'s honesty . . .' 'He did not indulge in any activities that would embarrass the movement.' Moreover, 'he lived in very humble digs, somewhere near Swiss Cottage, paying £2 per week.' 'His leader was in a hotel at £2 per day for bed and breakfast. Kaunda was not drinking or smoking. When compared with Nkumbula he was an extremely good, modest, dedicated man . . . with the characteristics we would like to see in a nationalist leader. He made a very good impression on all who met him in London. . . . Though he was critical, he spoke in such a way that he showed he was sincere . . . and had no hatred.'[13] But Nkumbula's capriciousness during his few weeks in Britain was a great embarrassment to Kaunda. Two days before we were due to meet the Colonial Secretary, Mr. Nkumbula decided to fly back home. I tried to argue with him about the necessity of his meeting Mr Lennox-Boyd but he replied by asking me whether I was afraid of meeting him alone. I told him it was not a matter of being afraid but that I was only the humble Secretary-General. . . . It was important for him to hold on only for two more days and then he could leave. But he decided to go back home, and he did. The result was that we did not see the Colonial Secretary and I was told to see Lord Perth, Minister of State for the Colonies.' Kaunda is quoted elsewhere as having said that the six weeks with Nkumbula in London were 'one of the worst times' of his life. 'I felt desperately miserable. We seemed to be getting nowhere at all. Harry seemed to have lost his sense of direction. I thought of giving up politics entirely.'[14]

Kaunda has recorded that, during all his time in Britain, Titus Mukupo kept him well informed of what was happening in the Protectorate.[15] A boycott on beer halls operated by Municipal Councils was being threatened and the *Northern News* had said that official 'indolence' was aiding the Congress. ANC was looking forward to the visit in July of another Labour sympathiser, George Thomson. Mukupo also reported that Betty Kaunda had left for Chinsali.[16] This was another period of privation for the Kaunda family. 'I was glad for the sake of the movement,' Betty has recalled, 'but for the six months he was away, I suffered a lot with the children.' 'I became noticably thin, as the ration allowance was very little and was paid out irregularly.'[17]

In June, Kaunda also received copies of correspondence by Robert Makasa, ANC Provincial President for the Northern Province. Local Congress officials had been angered by news that 'two young men were arrested at Nseluka's village' for refusing to sell eggs at a price fixed by the District Commissioner. Makasa's letter to the Provincial Commissioner protested hotly against the behaviour of a certain D.C. 'Bless God,' he wrote, 'Abercorn has now got a strange kind of District Commissioner with a full dictatorial character just as a Nazi Statesman . . . to come and fight against the African National Congress which he said to me on the 8th of this month [was] to be done away with forthwith within three months' time.' A few days later, however, Congress in Kasama told the District Commissioner of arrangements for a provincial rally and invited 'lectures from each Departmental officer on how the African public should help in the development of the province'.[18]

Just after Nkumbula left London, a letter arrived for him from Dixon Konkola, accusing him of making statements against Konkola in Northern Rhodesia and of 'activities' against him in London. Konkola was therefore resigning from the N.R.T.U.C. and the Railway African Workers' Union. 'I have also applied,' he wrote, 'to the Secretary-General of the United Nations Organisation for voluntary exile from this country because of political persecutions.'[19] This news coincided with the arrival of a long letter from Reuben Kamanga, Deputy Treasurer of ANC, who was glad that Kenneth had secured a 'one-week scholarship from the Labour Party' to study party organisation, in preparation for the time when the

Congress Political Party would become 'really active for the purpose of elections'. Leg. Co., he reported, had, like the Nyasaland legislature, passed a bill to enable the Federal Parliament to enlarge itself, despite the solid opposition of African M.L.C.s. Congress had meanwhile cabled the Chairman of the Commonwealth Prime Ministers' Conference 'saying that Sir Roy had no right to represent Northern Rhodesian Africans'. The total of registered Congress branches was now 355. Arrests were on and a telegram from Kasama had reported 'mass arrests of people, particularly women in Kasama'. The letter ended by saying that people were very happy at the news of Kenneth's movements. 'They are following newspaper reports daily especially with the announcement of the old man of "one man one vote" and also "our goal—independence of Northern Rhodesia". . . . We expect meetings throughout the country when you come.'[20]

Kaunda was still in his lodging near Swiss Cottage when a copy reached him of an article published by *Reynolds News* on Northern Rhodesia, the heading of which 'was misleading in that it might convey to some other people that we are planning MAU MAU'. In a letter to the Labour M.P., Johnson, Kenneth made an important statement, quoted later in his autobiography, on non-violence. 'I have been on the field now for just over six years. The rate at which my people are becoming politically awake is frightening, and already we are seeing a situation arising whereby our present Congress Executive could be replaced by a more radical one, which might think our present methods of non-violence as a not fast enough method of redressing our grievances. . . . I have never in the past thought of any African calling the present Executive of the African National Congress a compromising and dangerously moderate council, but this is already happening and all I am asking the British Government is to help us to settle these matters peacefully by telling them the danger of growing African opposition to these undemocratic set-ups. I would be the last person to advocate violence because apart from the fact that it does not pay, we have only our people to get killed. What is the point in having the people one struggles for killed? Who is going to profit by those rights once they are achieved with half the population gone? In spite of the truth in my statement, I would be doing a disservice if I did not tell the British public what dangers lie ahead. I repeat what I have said for the sake of emphasis. We have no intention of running MAU MAU in our country but there are those dangers.' He then mentioned a cable 'received from home that speaks of mass arrests, maximum sentences imposed without trial and no bails and appeals allowed. . . .' 'All I can say is whatever crime one commits at most there should be a trial and chance to appeal. . . . It worries me to think of what the reactions to these injustices will be in future.'[21]

Kenneth made an elaboration of this point in a letter to *Reynolds News*. The 'settler press' in the Protectorate was reacting in a 'rather deplorable' way to his activities in Britain and asserting that he was demanding adult franchise and using 'threats of force'. He certainly was making the first demand but 'the settlers should know better than anyone else that the RANC has never advocated violence. . . .' 'There is no doubt', he went on, 'that the Settlers bitterly resent any African being allowed free speech in this country [Britain] to present the African point of view. I will not be surprised if on my return to Rhodesia I find that I will be refused permission to travel again. . . . But what happens to me is unimportant. What is important is that the British people realise . . . the chaos which may ensue if the Settlers insist on overriding popular African feeling.'[22] Meanwhile Gore-Browne was in London and invited Kenneth 'to meet Colonel David Stirling and to hear from him what his plans for the future in Africa are . . . but it's essential to keep Capricorn as such out of it'. The meeting with Stirling took place but, as Kenneth recalled, 'he did not try to impose his ideas on me.' 'I was beyond recovery! He spent time in asking me how I saw the future and I told him that I saw it as tough, but that we'd win and establish a non-racial society.'[23]

Another vivid description of affairs at home came in a letter from Simon Kapwepwe, which began with the words: 'Dear Mtepa'. Mtepa was Kenneth's grandfather's name, by which his closest relatives and friends sometimes addressed him. Because of moving continuously from province to province, Kapwepwe had not been able to write sooner. Kenneth's wife had been at home, 'busy in the field helping the old folks'. The boycott of municipal beer halls was '100% effective' although, in Kapwepwe's words, 'we were weakened by . . . the soldiers being outsiders of Northern Rhodesia.' There were many arrests and special courts were sitting at night to deal with the sudden increase in cases. 'The general feeling of the African people,' he went on, 'is feverish and we as leaders have received threatening letters that we are very weak because we are compromising with the government. They feel that we must now work straight for a full African government, with interests reserved for the minorities.' After commenting on bad conditions in African hospitals, Kapwepwe said: 'The awakening of Africa is wonderful . . . . I think to be very precise the time for building multi-racial society [*sic*] is gone. I have lost hope and practically all Africans are anti-multi-racial society.'[24]

It was a matter of concern to Kaunda that the early unity of the Congress movement had suffered from recent stresses due to the consequences of the 'New Look', which increased after a significant event which has been recorded by Sikalumbi. 'At a large public meeting at Kabwata on 2 July, 1956, Dominic Mwansa called upon all Congress members to bring their identity certificates, or *situpas*, on 9 July to set them on fire. This type of speech received good publicity in contrast to Nkumbula's "New Look" policy, but it was a headache to both the Congress leaders and the Government officials. The Secretary for Native Affairs, F. N. Stubbs, telephoned to invite various Congress leaders who were available to meet with him in his office. Stubbs asked if what Mwansa said was correct and if identity certificates would be burned then or in the future. He was assured by the Congress leaders that such a fiendish act as burning *situpas* had not been done by Mwansa on the ninth and would not happen. After the meeting the Congress leaders waited in the corridor while Nkumbula stayed to talk privately with the Secretary for Native Affairs'.[25]

As this disquieting situation developed, the news from the Northern Province testified to the growth of protest and conflict. The D.C., Kasama, was 'rumoured to have said that he would extinguish the Congress in Kasama District in two months' time'. Meanwhile, one of the highest members of the Bemba royal court, the Mwanangwa, was touring with District Officers jailing and fining people 'for minor offences like refusing to shout welcome for the D.C., failing to give free gifts to the D.C.s such as chickens, eggs, meals, etc.' Chalabesa declared that African hospitality to white men 'since Livingstone' was 'proverbial' but, he asked, 'What has come of civilisation . . . that hospitality has got to be demanded at pistol point?' Seventy people had been jailed or fined, the number

including 'pregnant women, deformed people and juveniles'.
Congress members had demanded an interview with the Paramount
Chief, Chitimukulu, and found him 'a confused and frightened
old man, . . . between the horns of a dilemma', whether to support
the administration in the 'terrorising of the people' or to 'protect
the people from naked tyranny and the rape of their rights'. Then
'at midday on the very Sunday,' Chalabesa wrote, 'we rushed to
Kasama for a meeting scheduled for 1 p.m. . . . at the location there
was pandemonium. The D.C. Davies and D.O. Andrew in khaki
shorts and shirts and Kapasos [special departmental messengers]
and messengers in full uniforms with guns and tear gas bombs . . .
were at the meeting place beating up people and arresting 16 men
and women. . . . At the time of writing the trials are on. And
can you guess who the Magistrate is? Why, the very arresting
officer, District Commissioner, J. H. R. Davies.' It was the conviction
of local ANC men that the plan of the Government officials was
'to keep the tension high by beating up . . . and terrorising the
people thereby provoking them to act' and then 'declare a state
of emergency. . . .' 'We do not know,' said Chalabesa, whether
this is a protectorate of the old democratic country or that of a
Nazi totalitarian police state.' 'What we are afraid of is the legacy
of hatred, suffering and mistrust that this high-handed tyranny will
leave behind.' The letter ended with a style of salutation borrowed
from Kwame Nkrumah and now popular among Northern Province
Congress men, 'FORWARD EVER AND BACKWARD NEVER,
even if stars fall. ALL COMRADES SEND THEIR BEST
WISHES.'[26]
Chalabesa's report was corroborated by Malama Sokoni, acting
Provincial President, who added: '*Ifintu nafinyongana sana kuno*,
boy'—'Things have become all tangled here, boy.' ANC, he said,
had been 'formally banned on 12 August. Meanwhile four school-
girls had written to 'the secretary for laws' in Lusaka protesting
against their imprisonment 'for two weeks without any case record
written'. They were 'very anxious to sue Mwanangwa's court'
and wanted to know if it was true that the Federal Government
now disallowed appeals and whether there was 'a new law passed to
arrest and imprison schoolboys and girls if their parents are guilty'.
As the crisis grew, ANC officials had been busy recording the testimony, signed and thumbprinted, of people who claimed to have

been ill-treated by Government officers and their African Messengers. The breakdown in relations between District Officers and the local people had been worsening fast, despite a plea by ANC that the Central Government, by a statement of the acting Chief Secretary in Leg. Co. in July 1956, had declared that every senior Government official should 'keep in touch with the African National Congress as representing not all Africans but . . . a body of African opinion'.[27]

From the other side, the Northern Province disturbances were blamed almost entirely on intimidation by 'agitators' inciting 'hooligans', 'toughs' and 'thugs'. The 1955 *Annual Report of the Province* had said that it was 'easy to allow too much weight to the activities of a minority of soured, frustrated but very vocal individuals and to overlook the things that matter most to the majority of rural Africans'. The District Commissioner, Chinsali, reported that 'in face of [*sic*] popular pressure, the politically inclined soon abandoned the idea of using Lenshina's gatherings as a forum of political agitation,' yet something was discernible 'in the demeanour, utterances and in the songs of Africans, particularly women'. The 1957 Report for Kasama stated that 'the struggle in the political arena between the Native Authority and the African National Congress . . . was brought into the open during the year.'[28]

In London, while invitations were coming to him to attend more Labour Party conferences, Kaunda received a long letter from Justin Chimba, reporting on his own arrest as well as on the growth of Congress in the Eastern Province. Chimba was bitter about the educational statistics for the Protectorate which he saw as proof of 'a deliberate move to hamper the African progress'. John Mwanakatwe had meanwhile been appointed Principal of Lukashya Secondary School in the Kasama District, but housed in 'a condemned house' while the white head of the nearby Trade School was living in what should have been the Principal's house. 'With all the bitterness said above and the rest untold mistrust, I just do not see any future of harmonious Government in this Country of discontentment,' Chimba wrote . '. . . but who is that African who will sit down and let these mischiefs pass unchallenged?' 'Stick to your courses, we have here a hope that you will come out to this country with [a] more determined mind than ever.'[29] In a letter to

Lennox-Boyd, Kaunda had asked for a personal interview so that he could explain the reason for the grave 'position at home'.[30] On the same day he wrote to Mukupo pleading for more information for the benefit of sympathisers in Britain. 'You will be surprised at the amount of sympathy we have here,' he said, in addition to the known support of men like John Hatch and James Johnson. He was seeking a meeting with John Profumo of the Colonial Office.[31] Profumo's reaction to the questions of Labour M.P.s was to cite the Governor's account of the Kasama disturbances, which claimed that, at a Congress meeting on 28 July, attended by about 150 people as well as Boma Messengers and Kapasos, 'Congress leaders villified and abused the messengers in provocative and insulting language.'[32]

It was at this time that Kenneth was introduced to one John Papworth, by a man called Douglas Edmonds who was on a brief visit to England from Northern Rhodesia. Edmonds, who owned a mineral bottling factory, had incurred the enmity of a number of Europeans by his open espousal of the Congress cause. The meeting with Papworth came at a time when Kaunda was finding that his meagre financial resources could barely cope with the cost of his rent and food as well as correspondence and bus and rail fares. Papworth, who was at the time working as a journalist, invited him to his home and an interesting friendship developed swiftly between them. To Papworth as they met, Kenneth was 'an African chap who was being kicked out of his lodgings and was very unwell'. At that period of his life, Papworth was an atheist. He at once became aware of Kenneth's 'profound sense of religion'. He saw him as 'a very ordinary man with very ordinary qualities who at a closer look appeared remarkably unusual'. With an atheist's scepticism Papworth found that Kenneth's religiousness aroused 'a certain derisiveness' in him, largely because he regarded Ralph Waldo Trine's book, *In Tune with the Infinite*, as 'trite and mediocre'. This was the book of spiritual meditations which Kaunda has mentioned in his autobiography. Soon after they met, they spent a weekend at Papworth's cottage in the Cotswolds and went on long walks together. From the quick association of their personalities, Papworth came to see Kaunda as 'not a profound intellectual' but as a man of 'quite tremendous insight'. Their subsequent weeks together deepened the impression of gentleness and sensitivity. 'I have never seen him react to other persons in terms other than a most tremendous respect for them as individual human beings.'[33]

Though, as he has said, Kaunda formed generally favourable impressions of Britain, 'which had not yet been invaded by Powellism', he was troubled by certain manifestations of class discrimination. When James Johnson took him to a steel works in Rugby and told the manager that 'this young man from Northern Rhodesia is looking for places for some of his followers to come and learn to be engineers,' the manager's reply gave him his 'first experience of a real Tory'. 'Where can we get the money from?' he said. 'Everybody here today is demanding a hot bath and a decent place to sleep.' Kenneth felt that this reply revealed that the man 'genuinely believed that the bath which he himself enjoyed daily was not a thing for the workers at all.' At the same time, a Scottish nurse who had worked for some years at Lubwa and Mwenzo and who invited him to visit her in Edinburgh wrote protesting against the current strike of bus drivers. Kenneth wrote at once to say that he was in sympathy with the strikers.[34]

The news from home during August was of spreading unrest and Kaunda was angered by further evidence that, as Nkoloso stated, 'the Provincial Administration which is supposed to be the representative of the Queen and our protecting power does its best to set our own Chiefs against us.' Mukuka Nkoloso was reporting a grave situation in the Luwingu district where Chief Shimumbi was taking drastic action against Congress people. 'In the name of our most gratious [sic] Queen Elizabeth II ruling over us,' he wrote to the P.C., Kasama, 'I am directed by the convention of all the people in Chief Shimumbi's country to complain to you that we all the people in this part of the country are treated inhumanly by Chief Shimumbi alone.' Fields were being burned and people were being imprisoned for belonging to ANC, 'contingents of messengers and other mobilised troops' were 'in armed chase against all [the] Congress community'. Since, as he claimed '99.75% of the whole Luwingu population' was on 'the Congress side . . . it is likely that Luwingu soon will be the next to what has taken place in Kenya.'[35]

Titus Mukupo wrote again, at length, to Kaunda in London with news of the continuance of the boycott of Copperbelt beer halls, the unrest in the north, the forthcoming Congress case in court against the 'illegal detention' of the men who had been held at Mumbwa, tensions between the Trade Unions, led by Katilungu, and the Congress, and rumours of a new African political party being formed to oppose ANC. Meanwhile Congress was growing fast, with a total of 375 registered branches, and the country was 'resounding with the rhythm of one man, one vote'. The reaction of Europeans was varied. Some were 'benumbed like lizards on a cold morning' while others were confused or resentful. 'But they have all got the message.' There was an epidemic of 'Asian flu' in Central Africa which was gravely affecting schools attendance, but Kenneth's family were all well in Lusaka.[36]

Kaunda replied at length, beginning thus: 'My dear Tito, Well, on seeing bits of red in my typing, I thought I should tell you that it is my ribbon that is at fault and not that I have gone RED. I'm still as pink as pink I ever was.' He was wanting to know whether Congress had formulated any new franchise policy, 'or should I still stick to ONE MAN, ONE VOTE?' Meanwhile he was finding 'the study of British politics extremely interesting', especially because he was meeting Conservatives and 'balancing up their theories against those of the Labour Group'. He then gave more details of his introduction by 'Jimmy Johnson' to the manager of the Rugby street Works. To Kaunda, this man's attitude was 'the shock of his life', and he added: 'After this I knew what it meant to deal with a conservative mind. You just can't deal with them by reasoning. Their minds are fixed.'[37]

The era of the dissolution of colonial empires saw the extension across the globe of political systems based, to a greater or less degree, on socialist principles. Kaunda's remarks, quoted above, certainly confirm that a 'nationalist' like himself was both unable to fathom 'Tory' mentality and, on the other hand, spiritually at home among socialists. But he had been careful not to commit ANC to more than fraternal relations with, for instance, Papworth's short-lived International Society for Socialist Studies. Congress leaders were keenly aware how readily Welensky would dub them 'Communists' on the slightest pretext. From the international political 'left', however, there was a natural desire to know the posture of the new African movements against colonial rule, and a few days after the I.S.S.S. Conference, Kenneth received a letter from Brussels asking for an explicit statement on 'the socialist content of the African nationalism of Rhodesia'. The writer wanted an article from him for publication in the Belgian socialist weekly, *La Gauche*, with specific answers to two other questions: (1) In the Belgian Congo, the European and African workers are still members of the same unions. Why is it not the same in Northern Rhodesia which is near the Katanga Province? (2) What were the importance and the result of the Copperbelt strike, which happened a few years ago? What about the eventual other strikes? In consequence of this correspondence, the Belgian socialist procured the publication of an article by Kaunda entitled 'Les Africains de la Federation d'Afrique Centrale disent "Non" a l'Apartheid'. In translation into French, the style he used in the *Circular* was not lost, as thus: '*Ne croyez pas nos ennemis. Nous serions tellement heureux de vivre aux cotes de L'Européen. Mais jamais plus nous accepterons de vivoter sous leur talon.*'[38]

'I was not able to enjoy my stay in Britain as much as I should have done,' Kaunda wrote in his autobiography, 'because I always carried with me the burden of the struggle going on at home.' October now brought him further evidence of the discord in the leadership of Congress. In response to a letter, presumably from Kapwepwe, he wrote to say that he was not surprised to learn of attempts to undermine the National Executive by using Kapwepwe's name. But 'to know a person thoroughly is one of those rare gifts that nature helps one to enjoy.' His letter was an obviously strenuous effort to calm Kapwepwe's resentment against Nkumbula, who had apparently given credence to whisperings against the Treasurer. 'Knowing you as I do,' he wrote, 'I did not doubt my past analysis of the situation—if I may repeat—that someone was trying to work for a division between you and the Old Man.' 'I dismissed as utterly impossible that you would work against the NEC. Our elected six are one of the strongest teams and [I] am proud to be its secretary. . . . It is a sign of political maturity that you show no resentment that the PC did not approach you immediately he heard those rumours about you. You will yourself remember how many times we have withheld information from some of our own friends— personal friends I mean—when we have in the HQ heard they were trying to undermine the national work. . . . As you rightly point out differences of opinion in a lively party like ours must be there

but as you say again we shall not wash our dirty linen in public.'
He concluded by thanking Kapwepwe for encouraging him in his
work in Britain. 'I am leaving no stone unturned to learn what I
can in the short space of time at my disposal.' But for a month
he had been unwell. 'I am no longer the healthy chap you knew.
I am hopelessly weak. At times it is stomach trouble, at others as
today a sharp headache, cold and cough. . . . Don't tell anyone
or else Betty with her already reduced figure will break down
completely. I am sure I will recover.'[39]

Meanwhile Kenneth's plans for an eight-month visit to India
were well-advanced. He would be studying elementary economics
and political science at the University of New Delhi, going there
from London because of the difficulty he would have to face if
he applied for a passport from Lusaka. Instead he had managed
with 'no small struggle', to have his passport extended from the
original three-months period to eighteen months. 'I intend to travel
as widely as I can—regardless of what consequences will be when
I get back home. . . . It is a pity our means of spreading the painful
things that go on in Central Africa are so limited while opponents
have got all sorts of ways of propagating whatever suits them.'
In telling Mukupo of the offer of an Indian Government scholarship,
he bade him 'get on holding the Fort.' 'Eight months in a world of
"Russian moons" isn't terribly long.' But he wanted news of the
suspension of Munukuyumbwa Sipalo by Nkumbula and pleaded
that Mukupo and 'the Old Man' would keep John Hatch and the
Fabian Colonial Bureau, Africa Bureau and Anti-Slavery Society
as fully informed as possible.[40]

October ended with more disquieting news from Mukupo,
this time relating to the Congress financial records. The arrest of
Kamanga, over the case of the boycotting of Gush's store in Fort
Jameson, had meant that the books had to be collected from him
by Kapwepwe. The Chief Secretary, Evelyn Hone, had formally
demanded the books for inspection. But Kapwepwe instead stayed
on in the east to await the judgment on Kamanga and his fellow-
accused. 'The feeling one gets,' Mukupo wrote, 'is that one cannot
entirely dismiss accusations against Mr Kapwepwe in the NEC.'
'He seems to be doing this quite deliberately. We've only got a day
to go. Government are really bent on finishing us up and on 25th
[*sic*] they published the new Societies Bill which is a severe piece

of legislation.' Nkumbula was holding Kapwepwe responsible for
any action taken against ANC.[41] Mukupo himself was meanwhile
struggling to get the Premier Press going, with inadequate assistance.
Mistrust was mounting, for Nkumbula was still stalling on the
land case issue while the London Solicitor was pleading with Kaunda
to expedite matters.[42]

In London, invitations were still flowing in, asking Kenneth to
speak to various groups, large and small. He was, however, distressed
by the manner of Nkumbula's speedy return to Northern Rhodesia
and by his failure to respond to numerous messages which it then
fell to himself to attempt to answer. George Padmore, the outstanding Pan-Africanist, then editor of the Pan-African News
Agency, had been very anxious to arrange for Nkumbula to visit
Ghana and had procured a visa for him, 'but he did not report to
the Ghana office to get it'.[43] More serious was the 'Old Man's'
departure without meeting the Colonial Secretary, although an
appointment had been fixed. When eventually Kaunda was allowed
to meet Lord Perth, the Minister of State for the Colonies, some
weeks after Nkumbula's departure, it seemed to him that the meeting
'achieved nothing'. He said of Lord Perth: 'I found him quite
unsympathetic. He began to lecture me about the need for patience
and I am afraid we parted company not on the best of terms.'[44]
Perth shared the view of Lennox-Boyd that Federation must be
accepted and consolidated. Criticism of this attitude was certainly
growing in Britain with the realisation, as Papworth said in a
letter to *The London Times*, that there was 'not one body of *African*
opinion on record as approving the "Federal" scheme, whilst
hostility to it has been intense, insistent, ubiquitous and quite
unremitting . . . growing so tremendously that the strong and
frequently violent attempts by the white administration to stifle
it are rapidly turning the Federation into a police state'. Yet Lord
Home was still insisting that he found 'no real opposition to Federation'.[45]

In November, Kaunda, still staying at Papworth's home, sent
a carefully reasoned statement to the Commonwealth Secretary
criticising the Constitution Amendment Bill and in particular
rejecting Lennox-Boyd's claim that the Bill gave 'representation
in the Common Roll to Africans'. 'The qualifications for the
ordinary roll are so high,' he declared, 'that only 3,000 Africans

out of a population of 7,000,000 can register. . . . I am quoting
the figures given by the Federal Minister of Law.' This Bill, he
said, 'coupled with the Franchise Bill that is following it, leads
our countries a long way down the path to subordination and servi-
tude along which our brothers in the Union of South Africa have
been forced.' 'Surely it must be clear to you how desperately we
in Central Africa will struggle against such a fate. . . . Our only
hope lies in the secession of the two northern Protectorates and
the fulfilment of the pledges to help us towards independence that
were made by Her Majesty's Government in the past.'[46]

On the same day, Kenneth wrote to Titus Mukupo, thanking
him for 'quite a bit of news, good and bad'. He was worried by
the 'unbearable' pressure of work on his deputy. He wanted more
news of 'the boys and girls on the CB [Copperbelt] . . . labelled
as rebels of Congress' and of 'the grumbling members' of the
so-called 'Chileshe-Scott-Stirling Party'. In particular, he asked
whether Kapwepwe had arrived back from Fort Jameson 'in time
to save the situation' regarding the Congress accounts. His report
on his 'short studies . . . especially on party organisation' was
well advanced. He was 'negotiating for scholarships', mainly in
Ghana, for students from Northern Rhodesia. Meanwhile, he
had not yet received confirmation of his own scholarship to New
Delhi. In London, he said, 'I am still staying with this wonderful
and kind friend where am not paying anything for meals and
accommodation.' 'Otherwise sobs would have come already.' He
asked for the second time, that Mukupo should write on behalf
of Congress, to thank Papworth.[47]

The Sokoni Papers, from which much of the material in this
chapter has been derived, appear to be the largest single collection
of 'nationalist papers' extant, though the Sikalumbi Papers also
contain valuable material, especially for the period after 1958.
Many of Zambia's political leaders testify that, in the subsequent
struggle, constant raiding of their houses by the 'security forces'
resulted in the loss or destruction of the bulk of documents and
letters relating to those crucial years. Many of Kaunda's own papers,
left in Sokoni's care, were lost in a fire. It is worth remarking,
at this stage, that the papers which we have been citing confirm
that the Congress leaders, both at home and in their activities
abroad, constantly appealed to principles of humanity and

democracy as they pleaded their cause with the metropolitan and territorial Governments. Despite the 'intensive propaganda' of the Federal Government 'to hookwink the British public' by portraying African leaders 'as extremists who had no regard for human values and whose sole interest was to . . . drive white people into the sea', Kaunda and his colleagues continued to appeal to the best elements in 'the British way of life'.[48]

The inhumanity of exploitation in Africa was, however, brought into sharp focus at this time by the receipt of a letter to ANC from an Angolan leader in exile in the Congo, Haldane Roberto, who had come across the testimony of a British Baptist missionary about the way in which the Portuguese had pretended that a letter from Dom Pedro V, King of Kongo, to the King of Portugal, thanking him for the gift of a carved chair, constituted a deed of submission to Portugal. Dom Pedro's letter was exhibited by the Portuguese to the 1885 Conference of Berlin. The Baptist missionary, describing that event of 1884, told how he had asked why he had not been asked to witness the King of Kongo's letter 'for all the other white men in Sao Salvador signed it'. 'Because we felt sure,' he was told 'that you would not do it until the King thoroughly understood the real purport of the letter.' Roberto wanted ANC to bring this matter to the attention of the governments of Ghana and the Sudan.[49]

Another interesting letter, which Mukupo had to deal with, came from Chikako Kamalondo in New Delhi. It was meant for Kaunda but addressed to him by the pseudonym, Miss Panji Tushuke. Panji, meaning 'perhaps', was the name of the Kaundas' first child, whose second name, Tushuke, in Bemba, meant: 'May we have good fortune'.[50] In a situation in which the Protectorate Government harassed the only organ of popular African political opinion yet did not proscribe it, secrecy had to be combined with openness by members of Congress. There was reason to believe that correspondence might be intercepted, as illustrated by a letter received at the Congress office from a schoolboy who wanted the African people's bitter opposition to Federation to be expressed more visibly through demonstrations—'of course non-violent'— when visitors from abroad arrived; by boycotting 'these new inter-racial clubs'; and by the production of an independent African newspaper. The writer concluded thus: 'I am at present not a member of Congress as such but I heartily believe in it. . . . When one is sharpening a spear to kill an enemy, he shouldn't tell him that it is for him he is sharpening. So I think that I shouldn't be open with my feelings against Whitemen and their devilish imperialism when I am still getting their education which I term—spear for my future fight. I ask you to keep this my poor letter as private as I have kept myself behind the curtain.'[51]

The exacerbation went on. Nkumbula was claiming that his life was threatened by extremists opposed to the ending of the boycotts. Inevitably the issue of non-violence arose on several occasions, following reports of Congress supporters using sticks and stones during the beer hall boycott campaign in Lusaka, and the arrest of women who clashed with police in Chingola when attempting to stop a lorry loaded with beer from reaching a beer hall. An African schoolboy was said to have written, against an examination question, 'What is the function of African Congress?' the answer 'To teach us to hate whites'. Nkumbula had told the novelist, Doris Lessing, that 'the example of Kenya must surely make it plain to responsible people what might happen if African bitterness is ignored.' Anti-Congress feeling, in such an atmosphere, was heightened by the report of Kaunda's article to *Reynolds News* in Britain, mentioned above. The *Northern News* gave it the headline: 'An uprising in Rhodesia could make Mau Mau "seem just a picnic", Kenneth Kaunda'. Nkumbula and Mukupo were at pains to deny Congress support for violence, but Safeli Chileshe accused ANC of intimidation and said that the Constitution Party aimed 'at dealing a death blow to the doctrine of racial hatred and malice'. Nkumbula retorted that Chileshe and Katilungu had abandoned the anti-Federation struggle by joining the new party. John Gaunt was, however, demanding the total proscription of Congress, and Nkumbula then played into the hands of white opponents by suggesting the deletion of the 'non-violence' clause in ANC's constitution. The fiery Dominic Mwansa's prophecy that white immigrants would soon 'fall away as do the waters of Mosi-oa-Tunya', the Victoria Falls, merely added fuel to the fire.[52]

When Evelyn Hone, the Chief Secretary, denied any knowledge of 'hate schools' or a secret army being organised by Congress and rebuked the exaggerated statements of the press, Gaunt was

incensed by his reassurance and a United Federal Party member
asked whether 'the apprehension felt on the Copperbelt by the
general public'—meaning Europeans—was not accepted by the
Government. From a different standpoint, Revd. Merfyn Temple,
the Constitution Party's Chairman, warned of the real danger of
'war, strife and revolution' if Africans were denied a responsible
role in the Territory's government. 'We believe that democracy
is a possibility here—not a universal franchise, that would be
disastrous—but a qualified franchise.' Neither white domination
nor African nationalism offered practical solutions. Immediately,
Dingiswayo Banda, Ndola District Chairman of ANC, attacking
the *Northern News* for fomenting 'terrific trouble' in the Protectorate,
declared that the Congress aim was 'a black government'. Then,
in early December, the first joint conference of the African
Congresses of Central Africa, meeting in Lusaka, resolved that
'the only course open to Nyasaland and Northern Rhodesia' was
'their dismemberment from the Federation'. The impasse appeared
all but complete.[53]

It was in this tense atmosphere that four hundred and sixty
ANC delegates assembled in the Kabwata Welfare Hall, Lusaka,
on 9 December, 1957, for their Eighth Annual Conference. 'The
official opening was delayed' until the next day, 'to coincide with
the Declaration of Conscience being made all over the world . . . in
protest against detained leaders who were undergoing trial for
treason in the Union of South Africa.' Solemnly thereafter Mukupo
read goodwill messages from the British Labour Party, the Afro-
Asian Conference, Messrs. Mutemba and Chalabesa on behalf
of the sixty-five restricted Congressmen of the Northern Province,
and 'the Secretary-General, Mr. K. D. Kaunda, who was in Britain'.
After a review of a revised draft Constitution, Nkumbula addressed
the Conference on his visit to Ghana for her independence celebrations and 'the exciting experience of living for 21 days in an
independent African state for the first time'. But at home the
troubles in the north where 'villagers were continually fleeing . . . for
fear of the Mobile Unit', and the deteriorating race relations
everywhere had brought Central Africa to 'the brink of an abyss
and a single false step might send it headlong into the bottomless
pit of misery'. As Nkumbula was elaborating this point, his speech
'was interrupted by the unexpected arrival of Mr K. D. Kaunda'.

The Conference at once broke into loud cheering with shouts of 'Africa, Africa', and Kaunda 'was asked to say a few words by the National President'.[54]

It was a telegram from Harry Nkumbula that had brought Kenneth's return home, but there had also been a letter from Kapwepwe saying, 'Come home or you'll find the party split.' 'I arrived,' he has recorded, 'with 10/- in my pocket, after paying £1 to a taxi driver.' 'I found my wife very thin for lack of food.'[55] The experience of a sudden return was a deeply emotional one, and characteristically he was overcome for some minutes when Nkumbula called him up to the front of the hall to 'say a few words'. He knew that, despite the inner dissensions of ANC, men like Mukupo had worked strenuously to preserve the unity and purpose of Congress, as was testified by the quality of the three issues of the *Congress Circular* produced in his absence. They had maintained the note of challenge and sober teaching admirably. Lincoln's famous Gettysburg definition of democracy had appeared as a caption and 'Arise, arise, Young Africa, allow not your dear Africa to be moved away from under your feet.' 'God has stopped making other worlds. If your Africa goes, you will have no other' could well have come from Kaunda's pen. And the June *Circular* which had provided a digest of material sent by Nkumbula from Britain, had another memorable caption: 'Everywhere round the world the clock of freedom is ticking. You hear the tick-tock, yes, but at what tick shall freedom be yours?'[56]

The dissensions within Congress were therefore of the gravest concern to Kaunda, realising as he did how they were affecting the public image of the party and playing into the hands of its powerful opponents. As soon as he had greeted Betty on 10 December, he went straight to Kabwata Hall and he records that at once he had to try 'to patch things up'. Matters were not made easier by the appearance of an article in the *African Times*, by Frank Barton, entitled 'Kaunda, the Man to Watch', who 'goes to church every Sunday and plans twenty years hence'. 'This aroused suspicions,' he said, 'which I had greatest difficulty in allaying.' 'I was determined that Congress must present a united front to the world in its fight against oppression.' Thus, strengthened by Kaunda's support, Nkumbula managed against significant opposition to retain the 'non-violence' clause in the Constitution but his own earlier vacillation on this cardinal issue, followed by his reaffirmation of it as soon as Kenneth was back, certainly lent credence to the second assertion of the *Africa Times* that Kaunda was 'the second most important African in the country' and 'even if he remains No. 2 man he will become the power behind the throne.' Nkumbula's nervous efforts to restore his position by demanding that Congress accord him as President extra powers, provoked the inevitable reaction that his demands 'looked like dictatorship'. Kenneth therefore decided to issue a statement which the *African Times* published, thus: 'I feel that I cannot step into Nkumbula's shoes. I am very happy to serve my people as Secretary of Congress as long as they want me but the lack of the qualities I know to be necessary for a national president makes my blood run cold at the suggestion that I am "heir apparent" and "on the point of taking over". My short study of British political institutions while in Britain strengthened my loyalty to Mr Nkumbula as a national leader and president because after the little I was able to see I am convinced, more than ever, that he is pursuing the right course.'[57]

Kaunda had, moreover, taken this line explicitly from the moment of his return to Lusaka. The minutes of the Annual Conference, reported that, 'giving a vote of thanks to Mr Nkumbula . . . and assuring him of the undivided loyalty of the rank and file, Mr Kaunda said that Mr Nkumbula's initials H.M.N. stood for "Here is the Man for the Nation."'[58] Because Kenneth had not allowed himself to be involved in Nkumbula's clashes with a growing number of hostile critics while himself maintaining a widening circle of cordial relationships in the movement, he was able, at least temporarily, to help to patch up the internal differences. His conviction that the political impasse in the country must be resolved revealed itself in the press report on the day after the Congress Conference ended headed 'Congress seeking talks'. The Conference unanimously urged 'the National Conference to open constitutional talks with the Northern Rhodesia Government and that an all-Party Conference be summoned to discuss the future constitutional changes immediately'. Negotiations were opened in response to this initiative and there followed, on 7 February, a historic first meeting between a Governor and national officers of the Congress, lasting three hours. The two men took with them a memorandum which merits quotation here:

'Congress has, for a period of seven years now, put forward proposals for Government consideration and such proposals have found their way to the waste paper baskets. Indeed, as a result of this, an attitude of resentment and frustration among African leaders and their followers has been created. . . . We have made ourselves abundantly clear . . . that there shall be no need for a qualitative franchise, apart from age and sanity, since reserved seats for the minority groups shall be created which will remove the danger of the minority groups being swamped by Africans. This is Congress' proposal, and Congress's proposal is the proposal of the Africans of the Protectorate of Northern Rhodesia. . . . Furthermore, we wish to give this warning to the authorities that if it is the desire of the British Government in the United Kingdom and the European settlers in Central Africa to build a healthy plural society in this part of the world, this is the time to do it . . . . A qualified franchise now being proposed will leave hundreds of thousands of Africans without a vote. Naturally, these will organise propaganda campaigns against the privileged few which will create an atmosphere of unrest in the Protectorate— which is bound to embarrass the Government . . . and plant fear in the minds of the minorities. In such a situation, it is idle and absolutely mischievous to talk about building a healthy and sound multi-racial society'.[59]

Though they were couched in unequivocal terms, Kaunda recorded his belief that the Congress proposals 'were so moderate that the Government would find it difficult to dismiss them'. But, he said, 'it did not take me long to discover how wrong I was.' 'The British lion, aged and toothless as it now is, was not a beast to be approached moderately unless you meant to sell your people to it.' He added words which summarised the dilemma of men urgently seeking a halt to white domination while avoiding a stark confrontation: 'I remember Governor Benson asking me "Mr Kaunda, don't you think Europeans would paralyse the Government if we accepted your proposals?" In reply I said, "Are you implying, Your Excellency, that for our demands to be met we have got to be in a position to paralyse Government?" My question was never answered.'[60]

It was customary, during the years of the struggle, for liberal

Europeans to take African reports of brutality perpetrated by police, especially members of the Mobile Unit, and Boma Messengers, sometimes led by white officers, 'with a pinch of salt'. The Congress Conference, however, gave a summary in its Minutes of the report, district by district, which the Northern Provincial Secretary, Ng'andu, had submitted; and Congress headquarters were receiving a growing volume of testimony in which those accused of assault and those allegedly their victims were named. Tragically such testimonies could be paralleled from other parts of Africa where well-armed forces under white direction had undertaken 'pacification'. During subsequent years, there would be a grave increase in the amount of such evidence brought to light by African nationalists or their supporters. Just before Christmas, 1957, yet another such testimony came in, this time from a man who claimed that he was the victim of officers on both sides of the Zambezi around the Gwembe area of the valley Tonga. 'When I went to Gogwe Boma [Southern Rhodesia],' he said, 'I was beaten badly by a white policeman by the name of Wood . . . because I refused to move from my old village to another place where the Government of SR is taking all people who stay near the Zambezi valley' on account of the raising of the water level by the Kariba dam.[61] In a letter to Revd. Michael Scott, Kaunda told how, on his return he found 'the Police Mobile Unit still hovering over the Northern Province'. 'Fines imposed on Congress card-holders are,' he wrote, 'extraordinarily heavy.' 'Both imprisonments and fines are many times done or imposed without any trial. Tear gas bombs, beatings and handcuffings are being used as scare methods.'[62] The sjambok had long been a symbol of white supremacy. The intensified use of it as an instrument of political coercion was to strengthen African determination not to submit any longer.

Immediately on his return to Lusaka, Kenneth resumed the editorship of the *Congress Circular*,[63] which in the December issue reproduced with approbation a comment from the *African Times* that "the conscience of the Christian Church has at last been aroused . . . in the Federation", as shown by the protest of churchmen against the new franchise proposals. "Gone are the days," exclaimed the *Times*, "when the Church confined itself to proclaiming the Kingdom to come."[64] The *Circular* then added the words of Wellington Chirwa, the Nyasaland Federal M.P.,

that 'the British government . . . was incapable of refusing anything given to them by the Federal Government [because] they
feared Europeans might cause a Boston Tea Party. But the Africans
would cause something even greater.'[65] It further announced that
in passing prison sentences of eighteen months on Reuben Kamanga,
Justin Chimba and J. J. Mwanza for their part in the boycott
of Gush's business in the Eastern Province, the magistrate was
reported to have said that he was giving longer sentences 'because
they are leaders of Congress'.[66]

As with hostility, so with sympathy, the first months of 1958
felt the breath of a number of capricious breezes. Extremism
expressed itself in an unsigned letter to Kaunda from 'The Union of
Eastern Kingdom', warning him to 'do something' or else he would
'disappear'. The *Northern News* gave publicity to this threat in
early February. The new Constitution Party seemed to be serving
as a nursery for new relationships. Though one member 'sharply
criticised Congress as a racialistic body',[67] the Party invited ANC
to attend its convention and unanimously approved a motion,
introduced by Safeli Chileshe, calling for legislation to 'abolish
the monster of social and economic discrimination'. Colin Cunningham, who later became a bitter enemy of Zambia, was at
this period a trusted friend and Kaunda asked ANC's Eastern
Province officials to arrange a 'small tea party' for him as 'guest
of honour' when he went, with Kenneth, to represent the Congress
leaders there in their appeal against conviction.[68]

Perhaps more significant, however, was a message of condolence
from the Governor to Kenneth on his being struck by lightning,
less than a week after the Congress leaders' visit to Government
House. The shock had not seriously injured him, though he had
to stay in bed for a few days. It had happened during a violent
downpour of rain. The impact of the lightning lifted him from
his chair and his back was injured as he dropped on it again. Still
shocked, he left the office and cycled home, where for some time
he was unconscious. Governor Benson must have written as soon
as the incident was known, and Kaunda replied quickly thus:

'May it please Your Excellency to allow me to say I am
most grateful for the message of condolence and your wishing
me a quick recovery.

Except for lack of strength I am now alright, Sir.

Further, I am very sorry that Mr Nkumbula did not come back to meet Miss Margery Perham as arranged. I can only guess something has gone wrong somewhere because I know he was just as anxious as I am to meet her. . . .

Once again I beg Your Excellency to accept my thanks for your kindness in my hour of trouble.'[69]

At the same time, the Revd. Colin Morris, minister of a white congregation on the Copperbelt, was praising a Moral Rearmament film for being far ahead of the insights of the Church, 'still languishing in the era of parish magazines and Sunday School nativity plays', but he felt that the showing of 'freedom' films to Africans might be dangerous. While Morris groped for an answer to the problem raised by M.R.A.'s overestimation of man's ability to deal with his problems by goodwill, the Chingola Branch of Congress reacted sharply to the official ban on the showing of 'the African produced and African-acted film' to Africans in the Protectorate. The incident of the ban and the comments on it offered a microcosm of the sharpening conflict between paternalism and the rights of man. Not insignificantly the formation of the African Congress Youth League was announced a few days later, on the eve of the publication of the Government's *Proposals for Constitutional Change*.[70] Kaunda's reaction to the proposals was clear. 'The division of normal human beings into "ordinary", "special" and "ungraded" (voteless) is unethical, unchristian and contrary to Western democratic values. What is the difference between the universal enfranchised African in Basutoland [and] Nigeria . . . and ourselves in Northern Rhodesia? . . . Why do we demand one man one vote? The history of the struggle of British women for the vote shows that when voteless classes are enfranchised Parliamentarians pay more attention to them. Soon after 1918 . . . Government became concerned with things of interest to women such as housing, maternity, education, food prices, etc. . . . Through the vote people get rid of anger and frustration. The vote is a safety valve.'[71]

The *Circular* now bade the youth of Africa be uncompromising in the struggle to gain full control of their God-given land by demanding and working for 'ONE MAN ONE VOTE now and at all costs'. But it also chided those who were 'not worrying who elects who to the municipal council to demand an end to "colour bar", ever rising hut rents—with no lights in them, bad unlit roads, bad sanitation, no water taps brought to your half-finished huts, heaps of rubbish unremoved for months where millions of flies raid your "native" hut in a "native" location'.[72] In April, Kaunda was himself elected to serve on the newly constituted Municipal African Affairs Committee in Lusaka.[73] Meanwhile, he renewed the call to 'ANCOLISE the entire Protectorate' and also praised 'the fighting parson', Colin Morris, quoting with approval the words of the *African Times* "Let the churches act now lest tomorrow it be too late."[74] It was noteworthy that Morris and also Henry Makulu were in the Constitution Party, both calling for an end to the colour bar and urging people to ignore past evils and work for the 'cooperation of all races'. Indeed Makulu believed that there was now 'such a feeling of unanimity in the country as had never existed before' and that since Northern Rhodesia was in fact a multi-racial state, 'equality had to be brought to its logical conclusion'. Early in April, it was reported that, as a result of a meeting in Kansuswa, near Mufulira, 'at night', the two parties, Congress and Constitution, had begun 'finding common ground', while recognising basic differences.[75]

Soon afterwards and just as the Bemba Chief, Chitimukulu, declined to meet Welensky, the ceremonial burning of the White Paper on the 'Benson Constitution' by Nkumbula was enacted at Kansuswa, on 25 May. Thereafter the ashes were buried under a 'little cross made of twigs'. Congress then published its 'Black Paper', signed by Nkumbula and Kaunda, which revealed that in February they had found the Governor 'already irrevocably committed' to 'almost all of the proposals of the white settlers'.[76] Though Nkumbula had issued a circular earlier rejecting the proposals, which was duplicated for large-scale distribution in May, Kaunda received a hot letter attacking Nkumbula for doing 'A BIG NOTHING'. The writer wondered if Congress was now a 'mop for the Constitution Party or a proof of the extravagant and illiterate who fight for the destruction of their own name—Congress'. Any further association with the Constitution Party would 'mean a split which is already threatening'.[77] Soon afterwards but from a different standpoint, Sikalumbi, who had resigned from ANC and associated himself with the Constitution Party, described the Congress as 'one man's organisation' and as 'an ageing woman who is fast losing her personal charm'.[78]

During this period of worsening relations, Kenneth was active in the provinces. With Frank Chitambala and Reuben Kamanga, he toured the area of Fort Jameson in a campaign to revitalise Congress in the province. It was the wet season and Kamanga has recalled tough journeys through black sticky mud and Kaunda's comment about their bicycles being 'very clever'. 'We've been riding on them, now they want to ride on us.'[79] A similar extended tour was made in the Luapula and Northern Provinces by Kaunda along with local ANC men, and he came back from these journeys very unwell with severe irritation of his chest caused by dust. As he began to journey in the Southern Province the illness worsened and he had to consult the Salvation Army doctor at Chikankata, near Mazabuka. Kapwepwe has said that Kenneth was 'found to be just exhausted' for he was 'the most travelled politician, wont to climb escarpments by bicycle'.[80] The doctor was disposed at first to be critical of men committed to politics and challenged Kaunda by saying, 'You people don't believe in God.' Thereafter, Kaunda has recorded, 'he would stop at my bedside for long and interesting discussions' and a lasting friendship developed between the two men, despite the presence of police surrounding the ward. Kenneth was in the hospital for nearly a month, and Nkumbula thought he had contracted tuberculosis.[81] From his hospital bed, however, he went back to Lusaka to prepare for a trip to Dar es Salaam for a conference of the World Assembly of Youth.

The hope of a visit to India now revived with the active help of a Lusaka trader, called Patel, affectionately nicknamed Kanjombe, who asked a friend in Dar es Salaam to help to arrange a trip to India from there. Kaunda, who flew to Tanzania on 29 May, had his first meeting there with Julius Nyerere, leader of the Tanganyika African National Union. Kaunda's visit to India, at the invitation of the Indian Council for Cultural Relations, gave him a chance to meet Jawaharlal Nehru and other leaders who were attempting to put the spirit of Mahatma Gandi into political planning and action, people who 'had taken part in those non-violent demonstrations which had helped to win India her independence'. Knowing his time was short, he resisted offers of 'VIP treatment' so that whenever possible he could move at will and see something of the conditions of life there. As he toured some of the districts where

Gandhi had worked, it struck him that 'people there seemed very lost . . .' 'The problem of India was so colossal that I didn't think they were even beginning to tackle it.' Yet non-violence had been used there with notable effect and this was a source of inspiration. 'It was a wonderful experience,' he has written, '. . . but it was only an interlude in our long struggle.'[82] In January, he had commented in the *Circular* on Gandhi as 'the Father of India . . . the man who put the powerful weapon of "non-violence" into practice.' 'With it he defied one of the then most powerful imperial and world powers—the British Empire.' There was now a fresh insistence in Kaunda's utterance on 'non-violence', but it called for selflessness. 'For years,' he wrote, 'Gandhi brought suffering upon his own body and ended up a victim of a dirty tool of imperialism . . .' 'it was perhaps fitting that he should end like that . . . a more noble end could not be found.' He then concluded with a reference to Northern Rhodesia. 'For the last seven years, our national leader has stressed the need for being non-violent in our struggle. This has worked wonderfully well. . . . But . . . there is a limit to everything. Last year's Annual Conference saw leaders hard put to defending this principle. Most delegates were in favour of removing the clause. . . . We are aware that violence would invite South African troops, British troops, American troops too. . . . Congress leaders realise, therefore, that they have a moral duty to keep their people away from imperial bullets.'[83]

At that time, however, what was uppermost in the minds of Congress leaders was the imminent split in their organisation. By August, 'the foundations of a breakaway movement were well laid'.[84] Though Nkumbula had personally burned the White Paper, as we have noted, Sikalumbi has said that the 'Black Paper' that refuted it was the work of Kaunda, Kapwepwe, Kamanga, Mukupo, Solomon Kalulu and Chimba, and that Nkumbula merely 'seemed to accept it'.[85] While Colin Morris warned that Europeans were 'priming a time-bomb for their children', Nkumbula spoke fiercely of the prospect of independence for white-ruled Central Africa as a 'bottomless pit'. Moreover, Congress was beginning to call for an end to the B.S.A. Company's 'milking' of the wealth of the Protectorate. But behind this clarity of utterance the dissensions within were becoming intolerable, and Nkumbula accused men in 'high Congress places' of intriguing against him. Then, on 27

August he named Kapwepwe, Chitambala, Jonathan Chivunga
and a former ANC Copperbelt President, Jeremiah Mulenga, as
the arch-plotters, and announced plans for a Congress general
election. 'If Nkumbula is unwilling to go to jail in the interests of
national aspirations,' retorted Chitambala, 'he should stand down.'
This was followed by an attack by the Ndola Branch on Nkumbula's
trips to Britain and Ghana 'with neither material nor political
benefits to show. . . .' 'His actions,' the statement declared, 'are
politically inexpedient, morally undesirable and economically
selfish.' Nkumbula had his champions, however, and so the conflict
developed fast. The Provincial Secretary in the north then joined
the fray by declaring that people should 'look for another leader
before it is too late'. Justin Chimba incurred Nkumbula's anger
by blaming him for the disturbances in the Gwembe Valley. The
expulsion by Nkumbula of the men he accused of intrigue and of
a big number of provincial officials was then resisted by the Central
Provincial Executive Committee.[86] Immediately thereafter, on
2 October, an emergency conference of ANC to 'deal with the new
Constitutional proposals of the Colonial Secretary and the deep
rift between senior officials' of the Congress was announced.[87]

Chimba was now in the forefront of the attack on Nkumbula's
leadership. He had written to Kenneth urging his return. 'Either
you come to lead a different party or you come now, to try to heal
the deep wounds in Congress ranks.'[88] Kapwepwe also wrote
telling him of 'the young people's opposition' to Nkumbula, and
added that he himself had 'made up his mind'.[89] All along Kaunda
had 'remained aloof from the various quarrels', as Sikalumbi had
said, and in the words of Hyden Banda, it sometimes seemed that
'under the supervision of Harry he did not go far,' though they knew
he was 'progressive'. As anger rose, however, Nkumbula began
to say that Kenneth had been 'sabotaging Congress letters' and
that he was a Nyasalander who looked to Dr. Hastings Kamuzu
Banda for political affiliation, and who 'suffered from the Bemba
mentality and ineptitude which he learned from the people among
whom he grew up'.[90] The news of Nkumbula's trip to London
increased Kaunda's alarm, for the President-General had posted
a memorandum to the Colonial Secretary which he was to have
handed over in person and then 'slept through an appointment with
Lennox-Boyd'. Despite the trenchant declarations he had made

at the Annual Conference in July against the 'Benson Constitution' and the Colonial Secretary's refusal to meet a Congress delegation, Nkumbula then began 'flirting with the Constitution Party' and let it be known that he thought the official proposals should be given 'a fair trial'. This, Kaunda has said, 'was the final straw'.[91]

On 12 October, he was back from India. The National Executive met on the twenty-first and on the twenty-second he was working in the office till late. Kapwepwe and he then had a long chat in Nkumbula's tea-room at Chilenje till 3 a.m., which they resumed the next day. On the twenty-third Kaunda 'agreed that they should break with Nkumbula'.[92] When delegates gathered for the Emergency Conference on the twenty-fourth, it was clear that Nkumbula was determined to maintain his new attitude to the 'Benson Constitution', 'in alliance with Franklin's Constitution Party which was a protegé of the Capricorn African Society', as Hall has asserted.[93] Various young Congress men attacked Nkumbula for his accusations against Kaunda, and then Kapwepwe announced his resignation. 'I've discovered you cannot lead up to independence,' he told Nkumbula. 'I must step out. I have closed the books. The balance in the bank is 15/3d.' Between fifteen and twenty 'fellows from Chipata, the north, the Central Province and the Copperbelt' rose and followed Kapwepwe. 'One hour after, K.K. walked out with one or two more.'[94]

'We left the African National Congress without anything,' said Kaunda. 'All we had was a tide of anger against us. On October 24th, the Zambia African Congress was born at a meeting held at Broken Hill to which sixty delegates had been called with only a week's notice.'[95] The decision to break away from ANC had thus been taken before Kaunda himself had agreed to join the 'rebels'. Nkumbula had described the situation 'during the past three weeks' as 'going from bad to worse.' 'I have had to have my house guarded by Congress men', he said.[96] Certainly the 'split' had been coming for some time. There had been a number of informal meetings at which restive men had been 'examining the structure of ANC'.

As soon as the walk-out had been made, keen discussion began about what to call the new party. 'Muchinga,' the name of the country's largest mountain range, and 'Zambesia' were rejected. Then, whether it was first proposed by Kapwepwe, Sikalumbi or Kaunda himself—or indeed taken from a poem written by Arthur

Wina in 1953—'Zambia' was chosen, because it 'would be easier, particularly for children, to say and would prevent tongue-biting', as Sikalumbi has written.[97] The die was cast. The structural unity of the African resistance movement was broken, and this would lead to dangerous crises and conflicts. But the birth of ZANC released at once into the political arena a new dynamic force.

---

[1]Sikalumbi, *op. cit.*, p. 90.
[2]ANC: *Congress Circular*, Vol. III, No. 2, 5/12/56, p. 4.
[3]*London Times*, 4/1/57.
[4]Sikalumbi Papers: resolutions of the Commonwealth Conference of Labour Parties, 28/5/57. The S.A. delegate denied her passport was Mrs. Jessie McPherson, one-time Mayor of Johannesburg.
[5]G. Broomfield, *1960—Last Chance in the Federation* (U.M.C.A., 1960), 2.
[6]Kaunda, *Zambia*, p. 83.
[7]*Ibid.*, p. 82.
[8]Sikalumbi Papers: Nkumbula, from Bentinck House Hotel, London, to Colonial Secretary, 13/6/57.
[9]ANC/5/22, 'Confidential' notes, by Jane Symonds, on the talks, 19/6/57.
[10]ANC/Britain: Correspondence with M.P.s.
[11]ANC/5/23 Fox-Pitt to Kaunda, 21/6/57; and Sikalumbi, *op. cit.*, p. 86. Tredgold's Franchise Report was criticised by Colin Leys, *European Politics in Southern Rhodesia*, (O.U.P., 1959), p. 215ff; and esp. p. 224 for treating the vote as 'a skill' and not 'an inalienable right'.
[12]TI-FM/MMC, 26/11/69.
[13]*Ibid.*
[14]Kaunda, *Zambia*, 93-94; and Hall, *Kaunda*, 24.
[15]Kaunda, *Zambia*, 83.
[16]Sokoni Papers: Mukupo to Kaunda, 18/6/57.
[17]Mpashi, *op. cit.*, p. 47.
[18]Sokoni Papers: ANC District Chairman to District Commissioner, 8/NRG/D/KA of 14/5/57, 15/5/57, 23/5/57 and 30/5/57, attached to 22/ANC/NRG-107, Makasa to Provincial Commissioner, 14/6/57; and unreferenced letter, ANC Provincial Secretary to D.C., Kasama, 22/6/57.
[19]Sokoni Papers: Konkola to Nkumbula, 8/7/57 headed 'Defamation of D. Konkola'.
[20]Sokoni Papers: ANC letter, Kamanga to Kaunda, 4/7/57.
[21]Sokoni Papers: Kaunda to James Johnson, 25/7/57.
[22]*Reynolds News*, undated; RH 103/1, Kaunda to Ken Wanstall.
[23]Sokoni Papers: Gore-Browne to Kaunda, 24/7/57; TI-FM/KK, 5/10/71.
[24]Sokoni Papers: Kapwepwe to Kaunda, 12/7/57.
[25]Sikalumbi, *op. cit.*, pp. 77-78 and 84; and TI-FM/KK, 13/7/71.
[26]Sokoni Papers: Chalabesa to Kaunda, c/o Transport House, London, 30/7/57.
[27]*Ibid.*: Sokoni to Kaunda, 8/8/57; letter of Stephania Nseluka, Delefinas Lwipa, Mbilister Chipimo and Senephe Mwango of Nseluka School, 25/7/57; testimony of Mutale Kasepa, taken by the Acting District Organising Secretary, M. C. Mutale, headed 'Forced Labour and Beatings', 3/7/57; and letters of protest by M.C. Kashitu, 19/7/57 and Captain Banard, 31/7/57, of which copies were sent to Kaunda; letter of ANC Provincial Secretary, Kasama, to the S.N.A., 5/6/57 which cited the statement made by the acting Chief Secretary, Unsworth, in Leg. Co. on 24/7/56.
[28]NAZ: *Annual Reports, N. Province*, 1955 and *1957*.
[29]Sokoni Papers: Chimba to Kaunda, 10/8/57.

[30]*Ibid.*: Kaunda to Colonial Secretary, 10/8/57.
[31]*Ibid.*: Kaunda to Mukupo, 10/8/57.
[32]*Ibid.*: Profumo to J. Johnson, M.P., 15/8/57.
[33]TI-FM/J. Papworth, 27/2/72. Papworth's house was at 22 Nevern Road, London, SW 5.
[34]Sokoni Papers: Kaunda to Mukupo ('Dear Tito'), 10/8/57, and TI-FM/KK, 13/2/69. The nursing sister was Miss Margaret Turnbull.
[35]Sokoni Papers: Mukuka Nkoloso to P.C., Kasama, (undated), and to ANC Provincial President, 31/8/57.
[36]Sokoni Papers: Mukupo to Kaunda, undated (probably mid-September), ref. ANC/3/4.
[37]*Ibid.*: Kaunda to Mukupo, 21/9/57.
[38]*Ibid.*: Ernest Glinne to Kaunda, 27/9/57; and quotation from Kaunda's article in *La Gauche*, 7/12/57.
[39]*Ibid.*: Kaunda to 'Dear Lad', undated, acknowledging letter of 26/9/57. The 'elected six' were: Nkumbula, Mungoni Liso, Mukupo, Kapwepwe, Kamanga and himself.
[40]*Ibid.*: Kaunda to Mukupo, 21/10/57.
[41]*Ibid.*:Mukupo to Kaunda, 21/10/57 and 28/10/57.
[42]*Ibid.*: Kaunda to Lake, 8/11/57, and Lake to Kaunda, 11/11/57.
[43]*Ibid.*: Padmore to Kaunda, 25/10/57.
[44]Kaunda, *Zambia*, 83 and 93-94.
[45]Sokoni Papers: Papworth to *London Times*, 22/10/57, quoting Home.
[46]*Ibid.*: Kaunda to Secretary of State for Commonwealth Relations, 8/11/57.
[47]*Ibid.*: Kaunda to Mukupo, 8/11/57.
[48]Kaunda, *Zambia*, 82.
[49]ANC, unreferenced: Roberto to Nkumbula, in French, from Leopoldville, 15/9/57. The missionary was Revd. J. Weeks.
[50]ANC/5/24: Kamalondo to Kaunda, 18/9/57.
[51]ANC, unreferenced: Rupiah Banda, Munali Secondary School, to ANC, 30/10/57.
[52]See *NN*, July to October, 1957. Specific references, in order of appearance in the text, are 3/7/57, 3/8/57, 2/8/57, 15/7/57, 9/8/57, 28/8/57, 5/9/57, 28/9/57, 24/10/57, 26/10/57, and 31/10/57.
[53]*NN*, 20/11/57, 23/11/57, 5/12/57.
[54]ANC: Minutes of 8th Annual Conference, sgd. T. Mukupo, 9-12/12/57.
[55]TI-FM/KK, 26/2/69.
[56]ANC *Congress Circular*, Vol. III, Nos. 4, 5, 6, for Feb./April, May and June.
[57]TI-FM/KK, 13/2/69; Kaunda, *Zambia*, 84; *African Times*, 13/12/57 and 17/1/58; *NN*, 22/1/58; and Sikalumbi, *op. cit.*, p. 94.
[58]ANC: Minutes of 8th Annual Conference, 9-12/12/57.
[59]ANC/2/4, letter of 24/1/58, giving full text of Memorandum to Governor.
[60]*Zambia*, 85-87. The description of British policy as 'toothless' was used again in *The Voice of UNIP*, August 1961; in a UNIP Memorandum to the Belgrade Conference, September 1961; and in 1967 by the Zambian High Commissioner to London, Alinani Simbule, who, in reference to her handling of the Rhodesian 'rebellion', described Britain as 'a humbled, toothless bulldog, wagging its tail in front of Rhodesian Premier Ian Smith and fearing him like hell'. See R. Hall, *The High Price of Principles* (Hodder and Stoughton, 1969), 156-7.
[61]ANC: unreferenced 'Statement by Saul Siabeza of Siamwembo Village, Chief Siamupa—Gogwe District, SR' dated 20/12/57 and marked by Siabeza's thumbprint.
[62]ANC/5/22, Kaunda to Scott, 27/12/57.
[63]The December Vol. V, No. 7 issue was entitled simply *Official News*, but the January 1958 issue resumed the title *Congress Circular*. The numbering of this publication showed some confusion, e.g. May 1957, Vol. III, No. 5; June 1957, Vol. IV, No. 6; December 1957, Vol. V, No. 7.

⁶⁴Quoted from *African Times*, 13/12/57.
⁶⁵*NN*, 17/12/57.
⁶⁶See also ANC/5/23: Fox-Pitt to Kaunda, 10/1/58.
⁶⁷Dr. A. C. Fisher; and see *NN*, 17/2/58.
⁶⁸ANC/2/3, Kaunda to Ag. Prov. Secretary, Fort Jameson, 28/1/58.
⁶⁹ANC: CEO/OA/2—Kaunda to Governor, 14/2/58.
⁷⁰*NN*, 12/3/58, 14/3/58, 19/3/58, 22/3/58.
⁷¹Kaunda and Morris, *op. cit.*, pp. 68-69.
⁷²ANC: *Congress Circular*, Vol. V, No. 1, 31/1/58.
⁷³*NN*, 10/4/58.
⁷⁴ANC: *Congress Circular*, Vol. V, No. 1, 31/1/58; and see also Vol. V, No. 7, Dec. 1957 (called *Official News*).
⁷⁵*NN*, 26/3/58, 4/4/58, 18/4/58.
⁷⁶*NN*, 28/4/58, 23-26/5/58. Note that 'the Black Paper' offered constitutional proposals for 'the transition period from now to 1964'.
⁷⁷ANC/2/4: A. J. Soko to Kaunda, 25/4/58.
⁷⁸*NN*, 31/5/58.
⁷⁹TI-FM/R.C. Kamanga, 1969.
⁸⁰TI-FM/SMK, 8/11/69.
⁸¹TI-FM/KK, 13/2/69; and Kaunda *Zambia*, 89-90. The doctor was Dr. S. G. Gauntlett.
⁸²TI-FM/KK, 13/2/69; Kaunda, *Zambia*, 91-92.
⁸³Vol. V, No. 1, 31/1/58. Note Kamanga's view that the theme of non-violence appeared 'particularly after his [Kaunda's] visit to India.'
⁸⁴Hall, *Zambia*, 182.
⁸⁵Sikalumbi, *op. cit.*, p. 95; TI-FM/RCK, 1969.
⁸⁶*NN*, 31/5/58, 14/6/58, 2/8/58, 23/8/58, 28/8/58, 5/9/58, 6/9/58, 23/9/58, 27/9/58.
⁸⁷ANC: Circular calling Emergency Conference, 11/9/58.
⁸⁸TI-FM/KK, 13/2/69.
⁸⁹TI-FM/SMK, 8/11/69.
⁹⁰Sikalumbi, *op. cit.*, p. 97, and TI-FM/H.D. Banda, 9/5/72.
⁹¹Kaunda, *Zambia*, 92.
⁹²TI-FM/SMK, 8/11/69. Hall states, (*Zambia*, p. 182), that Kaunda returned in August, but Betty Kaunda (Mpashi, *op. cit.*, p. 51) speaks of his five months' absence and return in October.
⁹³Hall, *Zambia*, p. 183.
⁹⁴TI-FM/SMK, 8/11/69.
⁹⁵Kaunda, *Zambia*, 98.
⁹⁶*NN*, 25/10/58.
⁹⁷Makasa told the writer about the suggestion to call the new party Muchinga; note that Hall (*Zambia*, p. 182) attributes 'Zambia' to Kapwepwe, Kamanga attributes it to Sikalumbi and H. D. Banda attributes it to Kaunda; and see Rotberg, *Rise*, 291, footnote, for reference to A. Wina's poem.

10

'A Man Who Gathers Honey'

As a little schoolboy, Kenneth Kaunda's future had once depended on his mother's urgently finding half-a-crown. Later on, as he moved in and out of school teaching, money was always scarce and his monthly earnings had to be augmented by strenuous work in leisure hours. If he had not sold a jacket and a sweater at Bindura in Rhodesia in 1948 he would not have had the money to return to the Northern Protectorate. At the time of his dismissal in 1951 over the bark-cloth incident at Chinsali, teachers' salaries were still small. Shortly afterwards, the Government increased teachers' pay and awarded arrears of payment in what was widely regarded as an effort to placate the increasingly vehement opposition of schoolmasters to the coming Federation. But there was nothing available to the man then cycling through the Northern Province as Congress's Organising Secretary. Though ANC, as we saw above, had set out pay scales for its full-time officers, the Secretary-General never received what was supposed to be his salary. Thus the privation of daily life went on for his family. When after months of thrifty living in Britain, he returned to Lusaka in December 1957, he had no more than ten shillings in his pocket. Six months later, when he was on his visit to India, 'Asian flu' struck his family and Betty found herself as 'tight as ever'. 'The ration allowance paid by the Congress office was at irregular intervals. Sometimes I was given £2 to last a month. . . . Budgeting was my greatest problem,' she said. 'But I was able to face these difficulties in the knowledge that they were part of our struggle for our country's freedom.'[1]

Kenneth's return from India brought new worries, for Betty soon realised that the conflicts within the Party's leadership were coming to a head. Once again, as he had done in 1953, he came

one evening to ask her to leave the house for a while as there had
to be a meeting held there at once. For her, the birth of ZANC
meant a costly sorrow. 'After a while Kenneth came and asked
me to lend him half-a-crown. "But, my husband, the two and six
is all I have. If I lend it to you, what will the children eat tomorrow?"
"Give it to me", he said gently. I unwrapped the two shillings
and sixpence from my handkerchief and gave it to him. He went
back to the meeting in my house. When the meeting broke up and
everybody had left the house, Kenneth and I went to Simon Kapwepwe's house for a soft drink, *umunkoyo*. At Simon Kapwepwe's
house, glasses were laid on the table and the drink poured. Then
Simon stood up and said, "Ladies, let us drink to the health of
ZANC. Please repeat the words." At first I did not want to say
the words after him for I did not know what the word ZANC
meant. He insisted that I say the word "ZANC". I gave in and said
"ZANC."[2]

The birth of ZANC had come from within the African political
movement. It had not been engineered from outside. As Lewis
Changufu has said, Kaunda himself had not joined in the increasingly vocal opposition to Nkumbula. When others blamed the
'Old Man', 'it was very difficult to know whether he [Kaunda]
had accepted your word or not.' 'He was seeing the faults very
clearly but would not comment. That is why it took us a long time
to break away.'[3] But the breaking of Congress into two sections
opposed to one another on grounds of personality rather than
policy undoubtedly increased the possibility of Africans being
'played off' against one another by the enemies of their aspirations.
Almost at once, as Betty Kaunda has recorded, bitter feelings
developed between the supporters of the two Congresses which
was to put Kaunda's philosophy of non-violence to a severe testing
and encourage the propaganda of those who claimed that, left
to themselves, the African people would 'revert to barbarism'.
'The policy of the new party . . . was to be passive and tolerant.
He [my husband] insisted we should not retaliate when members
of the other Party trespassed and used abusive language against
us. We women are curious creatures. The hatred between the men
of the two Parties who relaxed compared with the hatred between
us, the wives, who were so hostile and so ridiculous that we often
did not even talk or greet each other. . . . The men of our Party

sometimes complained against the different view enforced by my husband, saying, "This leader, Kaunda, takes everthing in a too Christian way. If he would one day allow us to have a showdown with these Congress ruffians, we could easily beat the daylight out of them all." '⁴

Understandably the fear of faction fighting brought a new degree of disquiet in various parts of the Protectorate and people were urged to ostracise ZANC because its Constitution was unknown and it would 'want a policy of violence'. Meanwhile Government tightened its check on the movements of African politicians, especially the 'rebels' who now formed ZANC, while Nkumbula, on the eve of a trip to London with the Chewa Paramount Chief Undi to seek talks at the Colonial Office, declared of ANC that 'there aren't any senior officials. They all walked out.'⁵

At its first meeting, ZANC appointed Kaunda as President, with Sipalo as Secretary and Kapwepwe as Treasurer. Paul Kalichini, Sikalumbi and Kamanga were their deputies respectively. According to Simon Kapwepwe, Kenneth was not anxious to accept the presidency and urged that Kapwepwe should hold the top post. This, he said, 'showed K.K.'s modesty.' 'He has to be pushed to be in front. This is his greatness. He has never been selfish, always wanted to be a servant.' Kapwepwe was therefore annoyed that, as it seemed, Dixon Konkola should want the presidency of ZANC for himself. 'This wasn't a play. We were designing the future of the country and wanted someone acceptable to Africans and Europeans, not someone fiery. . . . If one of those suspected of communism [e.g. Sipalo or Kapwepwe] were appointed, N.R.G. would treat us with great contempt. K.K. was cool-minded.' It was easy to have the agreement of Chimba, Chitambala, Sinyangwe, Masaiti, Makasa, Banda, etc. to Kaunda's nomination and so, according to Kapwepwe, 'the election was unanimous', though Grey Zulu recalls that 58 voted for Kaunda and 4 for Konkola.⁶ Moreover on the day of the first ZANC public meeting, Nkumbula, to test the strength of the new body 'asked for a meeting in Kabwe just a few yards from our meeting'. Reuben Kamanga recalls that 'our meeting was well-attended and his meeting was a flop.'⁷

ZANC's headquarters, Kaunda has recorded, 'was hut number 280 at the New Chilenje township'. 'We had to live there as well as use it for our office. We drew up a scheme of work for each day

and also we kept a careful record of all work done. This scheme
of work was a sheet of paper headed, "Where is it?" Each one of
us had to go out every night of the week to a location, compound
or section of a township as had been assigned to us on the list.
We had just three points to deal with. The first was to tell people
why we had broken with the African National Congress; the second
was to explain in detail why we had rejected the Benson constitution
for the territory. The third was an appeal for membership and
subscriptions. . . . Our slogans became very popular. We invented
and introduced easy slogans so that all our followers could repeat
them, for the more people you had shouting them the better for
the popularity and membership campaign of the party. Within a
few weeks, we grew to something very considerable.' Sipalo claimed
that the first round of public meetings on the Copperbelt drew
crowds of up to five thousand and that in the Northern Province,
one hundred and seventy branches of ANC had switched allegiance
to ZANC, along with well over a hundred branches elsewhere.[8]

The breach between Kaunda and the 'Old Man' was personally
painful to both. On the day when Kenneth 'walked out', Nkumbula
was very dispirited and wept. Titus Mukupo—'perhaps because
he thought we were being ambitious'[9]—reacted to the birth of
ZANC by accepting Kaunda's post in ANC from Nkumbula,
then going on a 'pepping-up' tour of Congress branches on the
Copperbelt, and vigorously refuting ZANC's claim to have won
over many ANC branches. As Nkumbula was in Accra in
December it fell to Mukupo to implement the *volte face* over
Benson's Constitutional Plan, and, according to Sikalumbi, 'he
immediately began the registration of Africans' which resulted
in a total of 7,617 African voters out of an electorate of 30,234.
Since the new Constitution made about 25,000 Africans
eligible for registration, there was little reassurance here for
ANC.[10]

In his chapter, 'Federation—Genesis and Exodus', Hall has a
section entitled 'Accra and After', in which he states that 'Welensky
blamed the African resurgence on the Afro-Asian bloc and the
communists, tracing the growth of a conspiracy against "civilised
standards" to the Bandung Conference of 1955 and the Cairo
gathering of December 1957; [then] came the climax in the All-
African Peoples' Conference at Accra.' Hastings Banda's return

to Nyasaland in July 1958, after over forty years' exile, had certainly marked a watershed, and undoubtedly the Ghana Conference heightened the fervour of those participating in it. Thus, because Welensky regarded it as 'a meeting of extremists', the Federal Government's tight security net around Dr. Hastings Banda in Southern Rhodesia, was to be expected.[11] For it was there, in the schizophrenic situation of the University College, that the Northern Rhodesia athlete Yotam Muleya ran against an international champion, 'winning the three miles by a hundred yards against Gordon Pirie and all comers'. This happened at the same time as the announcement by the College Principal that because an African scholar was to marry a French-Canadian bride, he could not be appointed to the staff. The College had not failed to hear the comment of the Chairman of Southern Rhodesia's Amateur Athletics Association on Muleya: 'We shouldn't compete with natives at any time. Mr—whatever his bloody name is—this Kaffir has never even sent a formal application to run . . . we don't count natives' performance as records.'[12] Not surprisingly when Dr. Banda shouted before a crowd in Salisbury's New Highfield location: 'To Hell with Federation. . . . They can send me to prison. They can kill me. I will never give up my fight for freedom', millions of Africans applauded in their hearts and the Northern Rhodesian Government intensified its watch on ZANC as a party of extremists pledged to nullify the Benson Constitution.

When, in March 1959, the Governor banned ZANC, his action was applauded by Lawrence Katilungu. 'No statesman could have acted in a more sensible manner . . . to combat the lawless group of men whose plans of violence could be described as nothing but evil.' Less emphatically, Safeli Chileshe commented that 'all leading Africans share the demand for greater participation in politics . . . only a very small section of the people approve of gangster methods. . . . If such ruthless methods were to be used later the Government is justified in protecting the people.'[13] The unresolved question then was whether Accra and the direct influence of India on three of the ZANC leaders had turned Kaunda and his party into 'gangsters'. It was clear that the Ghana Conference had strengthened the resolve to struggle for the dissolution of the Federation. Kaunda had joined with Nkumbula, Chindele, Joshua Nkomo of Southern Rhodesia and Hastings Banda in signing a declaration affirming total opposition to the 'bogus scheme imposed on us by the British Imperialist Government' and their resolve to build a 'broad-based united front linking up the various anti-colonialist organisations in our respective countries and also to coordinate our activities with those in East Africa to win self-government and national independence for our peoples now'.[14] As 1959 began and the Nyasaland crisis suddenly sharpened, the Prime Minister of Southern Rhodesia used the 'policy of violence' there as pretext for a total ban on the S.R.A.N.C. Four hundred and ninety people, including Guy Clutton-Brock of St. Faith's inter-racial farm, were arrested. Less than two weeks later, and ten days after the Nyasaland Governor had belied his own explicit disclaimer by declaring a State of Emergency there, Governor Benson compared ZANC to the Chicago racketeers who 'established their protection rackets, corrupted the local governments, ruled by the gun, the sap, the knuckle-duster, the bicycle chain, and went on to establish the organisation of killers known as "Murder Incorporated". ' On these grounds he banned Kaunda's group which, however, he described as a party with few supporters. The vast majority of Africans in Northern Rhodesia, he claimed, were not opposed to Federation. What they opposed was 'any suggestion to remove them from the protection of the British government until they were ready for it'.[15]

What in fact was Kaunda doing between the birth of ZANC and its banning? According to the Monthly Intelligence Reports cited by Mulford, 'November was largely given over to planning among ZANC leaders.' As ANC branches in the Luapula Province and in Chinsali, Kasama, Mporokoso and Mpika swung swiftly to the new party and Isoka, Luwingu and Abercorn followed more slowly, Kaunda and Kapwepwe had made their first appearance in Ghana-type togas at ZANC rallies on the Copperbelt.[16] By early December, however, Kaunda was on his way to Accra where, though little financial assistance was forthcoming, he formed a warm relationship with Kwame Nkrumah and became known to a large number of leaders from elsewhere in the continent. He did not, however, return at the close of the conference, but remained behind because he had accepted an invitation extended to all delegates from the Extra-Mural Department of the University College of Ghana to attend a ten-day New Year School. He was also hoping, though in vain, for another meeting with Nkrumah. 'Before going to the College,' he added, 'I visited the Republic of Togoland for three days to see for myself what was happening there.' Before his return, however, the Leopoldville riots had broken the false calm in the Congo and sent a new shudder of fear through the European townships of Northern Rhodesia as news came in of the death of 'over forty Africans shot (with some estimates at least 100)', and of '208 Africans and forty-nine Europeans injured in riots'.[17]

A further heightening of tension was therefore apparent as Kaunda landed at Lusaka airport, where, according to the local press, 'a crowd of above 200 Africans . . . carried him shoulder-high along the road [and] saluted him with an enthusiastic salute, something between an ordinary military and a "Heil Hitler" salute.' A light comic note was provided meanwhile by the proposal of a recent English immigrant to Southern Rhodesia, called Blackman, that a white Congress should be formed to stem black nationalism and by the declaration of Godwin Mbikusita, now a member of the Federal Parliament, that he regarded *apartheid* as an experiment, like partnership, and as such did not dislike it.[18]

Kaunda's utterances on his return, as reported by the press, were sharp. He had signed no agreement to reunite with Nkumbula; and reaffirmed total opposition to the Benson Constitution. He also attacked the Government for openly supporting Nkumbula and 'attempting to check the influence of Zambia by threats, coercion and propaganda'. Credence was given to the belief that the Government was wooing ANC by the Governor's statement in Salisbury that Nkumbula's party was 'helping and supporting the new constitution' and also by the lifting of the ban on Congress in the Petauke area of the Eastern Province. At the same time, it was reported that ZANC planned to blow up the Secretariat Building in Lusaka, which Kaunda denied, declaring 'We do not believe in violence', and calling on the Government and ANC to 'play decent politics'. ZANC had laid its cards on the table, he said. 'If they play smear politics, they are in for a high time. . . . We are in a strong position. We have the support of the mass of African opinion. I can see the Government's dilemma. If they imprison us, we will be heroes in the eyes of the African people. If they leave us alone, we will continue our campaign for self-government. I see their threats as just the acts of frightened people.'[19]

On 23 February, however, the Government published a statement about the elections declaring that it was 'determined to maintain the public peace and . . . rigorously suppress any attempt to subvert it', at a time when many would be exercising the vote for the first time.[20] It is highly probable that the nervousness of the situation was increased by what was being said and done elsewhere. The *Northern News* saw 'a threat to western standards' if the split in the Congress were healed and if there then followed 'a dramatic swing towards unification of the movement in the three territories'. Meanwhile from Nairobi came a call for a 'White Congress' to extend European solidarity from Kenya to South Africa. Hastings Banda's proposal for separate black and white federations in East and Central Africa was at once rejected by Mukupo. Northern Rhodesia must remain whole, he said. 'We will fight for the whole of it.' More colourfully, Sipalo declared 'that every person with kinky hair, flat nose and dark skin must come into one big whole'. ZANC, he said, was 'not led by blood-thirsty and power-loving demagogues'. 'It is a genuinely determined, peace-loving and democratic movement aiming at the establishment of true democracy in which all the people in this country will feel safe.'[21]

Beyond the words of various spokesmen, however, the explosive situation developed as police became increasingly swift in acting against increasingly vocal and incalculable gatherings. Kaunda recalls one such incident. 'A little before we were arrested, Mr. Nkumbula and Mr. Katilungu went to hold a meeting in Kabwe. Mr. Nkumbula tried to be funny by saying, "All these Ks have stolen our money—Kaunda, Kapwepwe, *kabwalala*", [meaning 'thief'], Kamanga, *kabwalala*". So one of our supporters got up and said, "Mr. President, what about Mr. Katilungu, *kabwalala*?". The messengers who were obviously put there by the police arrested that man. These things happened. . . . It was becoming more and more clear that the Government was interested in supporting ANC.'[22] It was at this point that a brief disturbance took place in the shanty-township of Marrapodi, near Lusaka, involving Indians and Africans, and evoked a sharp challenge to the Government by Kaunda which, he claimed, had assembled '400 rifles,

15 machine guns, and 12,000 rounds of ammunition and put them in a basement at the Central Police Station.' 'Let them deny it', he said. 'The Government says it is well-informed about my activities. I am also well-informed about theirs. . . .' 'Zambia's policy for 1959,' he declared, 'is to warn the Government three times on an issue and then to take action, and there is no limit on what we are able to do. . . . Whatever the consequences we are prepared to pay the price of freedom. . . . Zambia may be banned but the spirit of Zambia will march on until independence is attained. . . . If the Government ban Zambia or declare a state of emergency as I hear they intend to do, Zambia will go underground and the Government will find it even more difficult to deal with it than if it was on the surface.' He then pointed to a Union Jack. 'I shall not rest,' he cried, 'until that flag is pulled down and something better put in its place. . . .' 'My supporters will send me to . . . tell the Colonial Secretary that Africans want independence. If Mr Lennox-Boyd says nothing, I shall say to you, "Come on, let's have positive action". They [the Government] will be sorry for it. . . . Zambia Congress believes in non-violence and positive action.' Inevitably there was an immediate call for action against Kaunda for 'both threatening the Government and challenging its authority with an audacity equal to Dr Banda at his worst'.[23]

In these climatic days, Kenneth Kaunda appeared as a man strained yet exhilarated. His letter to Fox-Pitt about the split with Nkumbula, on which Fox-Pitt has scribbled 'Too libellous to send out in its present form', expressed the pent-up feelings of the 'rebels' about what had been happening in Congress. 'Need I reiterate here what we have learnt from the history of freedom movements which have reached their goals, namely and mainly that no freedom movement could really free its people whose leaders are without principles, definite policies and programmes and whose leaders are self-indulgent, without personal discipline and therefore not ready to suffer and sacrifice for the cause they stand for? Because we lacked the above in the African National Congress, we have already lost so much ground in our race with settlers here. We were wooly [*sic*] and oozed about like water without a course whose inevitable end is to dry up.' He traced the decay in ANC to Nkumbula's brief imprisonment with him in 1955 and his determination thereafter not to risk being jailed again. Nkumbula's high-handed suspension or expulsion of provincial officials and demand for increased power for himself, along with his apparent submission to the influence of Harry Franklin, had at last made things 'too top heavy for him' and a split was inevitable.[24] Though Kenneth was reported as saying, in February, that he had forgotten about Nkumbula, his new role, being played in the full limelight, placed a great strain on him as Government, white settlers and African opponents mounted their attack. ANC's Propaganda Secretary lashed out at the 'political lunacy' and 'well-worded untruths of Zambia', and the Dominion Party claimed that their speeches proved that ZANC's leaders 'had criminal tendencies'.[25]

Kaunda was, however, very busy with the task of formulating his new party's policy and he has spoken emphatically of the drafting of its Constitution as fundamentally the corporate work of men 'far from being influenced by the hate bug'. It was 'an outstanding example of how our minds worked . . . the work of so many people wholly accepted by the conference that met to approve it'.[26] He personally laid great stress on a cardinal principle of the American founding fathers which was printed as the theme of the proposals submitted by ZANC to the Colonial Secretary in February 1959: 'We know of no other repository of the ultimate powers of society but the people themselves.'[27] 'No country in the world can endure', the ZANC Constitution said, 'unless there is stable social, political and economic growth of its people', and '. . . the surest way of safe-guarding the rights of any group is the protection of individual rights and uncompromisingly safe-guarding the liberty of every citizen irrespective of his colour, religion or national origin.' Therefore 'we are dedicated to the precepts and practices of democracy,' whereby 'there will be no discrimination, victimisation or any form of segregation' and 'the safeguards and protection of citizens' rights and human liberties will be buttressed by (i) uncompromising adherence to the rule of law; (ii) the maintenance of the absolute independence of the judiciary; (iii) extending the right to vote; . . . and (iv) the constant observance of the declaration of Universal Human Rights and the United Nations Charter.' On this basis, ZANC would 'work for the secession of our Motherland from the Federation of Rhodesia and Nyasaland . . . relentlessly but non-violently'. To make this aim effective, the Constitution committed the party to a radical economic programme and to cooperation with all movements aiming at the 'complete eradication of all forms of colonialism and imperialism'.[28]

ZANC's Organisation Committee, on which Kaunda, Kapwepwe and Sipalo served, devised the ZANC salute formed by 'stretching out of a right hand, unfolding all the fingers towards the audience to mean "straight to the point" and then raising of the thumb upwards to make a U sign [which] meant variously "Uhuru", "Ufulu", "Ubuntungwa" and "Ulufutuko" or "freedom" in the Swahili, Nyanja, Bemba and Tonga languages. The stretching of the arms was accompanied by a "ZA" sound for Zambia.' Sikalumbi added, somewhat vaguely, that this committee 'also devised various methods of approach to the problem of the country run by the pro-European government'. According to the Ridley Report, there were eighty-five registered branches and many more awaiting registration by the beginning of March. 'With jubilation' ZANC's National Council, meeting in Kaunda's absence on Christmas Eve, noted the forthcoming departure of Governor Benson from the territory.[30] According to Hall, ZANC 'was in a militant and somewhat desperate mood in the weeks before it was proscribed' and he quotes the 'inflammatory' call of Wilson Chakulya on Africans to "hate anything white on two legs". Yet, in Mason's judgment, 'it was not difficult to predict even at this stage that the future probably lay with the body that had broken away, not only because its more radical policies were more acceptable to the masses but because its leader was a dedicated man of simple habits and a Gandhian philosophy.'[31] The historical evidence certainly testifies that from the moment of the new party's birth Kaunda was committed with passionate sincerity to lead the country along the road of non-violent positive action to build a colour-blind society. 'To say that we are shouting "Africa is for Africans alone",' he said, 'is distorting the truth.' 'What we have said and shall continue to say—restrictions or no restrictions, prisons or no prisons— is that the MAJORITY MUST RULE. . . . the English rule England, the French rule France, Japanese rule Japan, Africans MUST RULE Africa. But this is far from saying "Africa is for Africans alone." '[32]

But the pace of events was wellnigh beyond human control.

274 Kenneth Kaunda of Zambia

The appearance of Federal troops in Nyasaland and the use of brutality as an instrument of 'pacification' there was already presaging Welensky's defeat.[33] On 26 February, as we saw above, White-head had proclaimed a State of Emergency in Southern Rhodesia, which according to Lord Malvern, was done in order that 'the Southern Rhodesia African Congress . . . be put behind wire so that they could not create a diversion and prevent us sending the necessary police and so on to Nyasaland'.[34] On 2 March a State of Emergency was proclaimed in Nyasaland and around a thousand Congress leaders there were immediately detained, including Dr. Banda, who was flown to Southern Rhodesia with some of his senior lieutenants. The next day, the Federal Government ordered the deportation of the British Labour M.P., John Stonehouse, who had visited both the Rhodesias and was on his way to meet Governor Armitage in Zomba.[35] More deaths by shooting followed the Nyasaland proclamation, the worst being what could well be called 'the Nkhata Bay massacre'.[36] In Northern Rhodesia, the elections under the Benson Constitution were due to take place on 20 March, and strong rumours were abroad that the Governor was about to take action against the Zambia African National Congress before voting took place, though, like Armitage, Benson asserted that there was no need to declare a general State of Emergency, despite Colonial Office pressure on him to do so.[37]

On 11 March, at 11 p.m., the Governor proscribed ZANC 'under the Societies Ordinance', by virtue of powers given to him in law to 'nip in the bud any plan or conspiracy which, if left to develop, might endanger the public peace'. Benson then claimed that the Accra Conference had deviated from earlier nationalist declarations about non-violence. 'They said in effect that if they found it difficult to achieve their aims, even by civil disobedience, they could use violence against any legitimate force used by the authorities against them.' Benson's assertion both ignored ZANC's repeated declaration of a policy of non-violence and put a strange interpretation upon what the Accra Conference actually stated, which was 'that the All-African Peoples' Conference . . . declares its full support to all fighters for freedom in Africa, to all those who resort to peaceful means of non-violence and civil disobedience as well as to those who are compelled to retaliate against violence to attain national independence and freedom for the people'. In

Nyasaland, Benson said, the working out of the Accra formula by Banda and his associates 'went off at half-cock'. But the Nyasaland Congress Secretary had visited the ZANC leaders and 'the object of his mission was to create such trouble in Northern Rhodesia that we would not be able to send help to Nyasaland.' However 'Zambia was not ready to put the same kind of plan into operation here.' 'My Government has information which has made it crystal clear that what was to happen in Nyasaland would form a pattern for events in Northern Rhodesia if Zambia ever became strong enough.' This statement was made only a few days after Armitage had claimed that Hastings Banda's Congress had conceived 'a murder plot' against Europeans and Asians, thereby implying that ZANC was committed to a similar plan. Benson was at pains, however to distinguish between Kaunda and Hastings Banda on the one hand, and Nkumbula on the other, giving great prominence to 'Old Harry's' respectability. Benson then stated categorically that Zambia was a subversive and seditious organisation. 'Murder Incorporated' was its model. 'This is no question of race relations,' he said, 'of black against white.' 'The main attack of Zambia is against Africans. . . .' 'For' he went on, 'Government's information about this seditious organisation is very full and detailed. We know far more about it than its leaders thought.'[38]

In view of this statement it is interesting to note that the local press give virtually no account of either violence or threats of violence by ZANC members in the period preceding the ban. Instead the following incidents were given prominence: The editor of the *African Eagle*, S. Mkandawire, claimed that ANC threatened him because they, wrongly, considered him biassed in favour of ZANC; the editor of *East Africa and Rhodesia* was shocked by Benson's 'staggering statement' that race relations in the Protectorate were better than five years previously; twelve Zambia men were arrested for entering an Indian-owned tearoom in Lusaka and shouting 'ZA' while being handcuffed; but Kaunda publicly praised the 'tact and general behaviour' of the police when delivering to Sipalo an order banning him from entering Nyasaland. However, his speech about replacing the Union Jack roused fierce reactions. The *Central African Post* warned that ZANC might be proscribed and a letter to the same paper castigated Kaunda for trying to twist the tail of the 'British Lion' by which he could be 'crushed and beaten to the ground'; and the Government distributed 60,000 copies of a circular warning Africans against 'men who are looking for power over you'. But Evelyn Hone, the Chief Secretary, affirmed on 27 February that there was 'no immediate reason' to ban either of the Congresses, and the *Central African Post*'s leader said that most Northern Rhodesians would 'agree with the Territorial Government that there are no overt signs of trouble in this country'.

Then on 6 March, two weeks before the elections, Kaunda made a strong statement warning against any form of violence as people went to the polls. 'If any man wishes to exercise the vote,' he said, 'he must be allowed to do so without criticism, interference or picketing.' 'Zambia does not accept,' he went on, 'that those who are not with them are against them.' Though the elections were 'a hollow mockery', he declared, 'no excuses shall be afforded for the use of force against innocent victims.' A few days earlier, he had cabled to the Colonial Secretary thus: 'Settlers urge Government precipitate serious situation here. Africans greatly perturbed. Anything serious, Zambia blameless. Zambia completely non-violent but unalterably opposes present constitution. Promptly send Constitution Commission.' The 'serious situation' was demonstrated especially in the Northern Province where ZANC was defying police bans on public meetings. Kaunda at once confirmed his earlier public statement, and said: 'We shall do this whenever permission is refused to us and granted to all other parties. If our speeches are inciting people to violence, then Government has every right to arrest us. We preach non-violence. We are muffled because Government has a guilty conscience.' Three days later the party was proscribed and immediately angry groups attacked shops in Lusaka, using petrol bombs and stones.[39] 'It must be common sense to any unbiassed observer,' Kaunda wrote later, 'that the moment you remove leaders from their followers, each one of those followers becomes a general unto himself.' 'There are numerous examples in the Indian struggle for independence. Whenever leaders were arrested, violence broke out almost invariably.'[40] The crux of the confrontation in Central Africa was really: who are the leaders of the people?

Undated, in the Sokoni collection, are five small papers, in Kenneth's handwriting which could be called jottings on leadership; the first of which is a quotation from Emerson: "What you are speaks so loudly that I cannot hear what you say." On the second sheet, he quoted more specifically thus: "All of us can be leaders some of the time if we learn how to be good followers most of the time." The basis of leadership was the habit of team-work, acquired through group activities. He then noted that 'high scholarship may or may not contribute to leadership' but 'the vigor-ous use of one's physical energies is a common demonstration of activities which develop leadership.' 'All of the activities mentioned above involve physical movement. . . . The leader is one who moves in advance of his followers and who must make unusual exertions on their behalf.' In dynamic, personal terms, Kwame Nkrumah of Ghana seemed to Kaunda at that time to embody such leadership, as is shown by a letter which he addressed to the 'Osagyefu' when he was at the Accra Conference. "You have set for us in Africa a goal which we must work for; you have set for me a standard of behaviour or personal discipline exemplified in your famous three 'S's: Service, Sacrifice and Suffering—with which we must equip ourselves before we can even hope to start on the great task before us. . . . You have proved to the world that black men can do everything else that a white man, brown or yellow can do. My people believe if you succeed here [in Ghana], as you are doing, we all are bound to do so in shorter periods than this world has ever dreamt of."[41]

Not long after 1 a.m. on 12 March Kaunda was arrested. His own account of that event and comments on it merit quotation at length. 'The day had been unusually hot for March and the out-of-season drought made the little ones who lay uncomfortably sprawled on their communal mats rather tired. In a two-roomed house, number 257, New Chilenje township, ten of us lived. It was everything—bedroom, living-room, dining-room—and was also used as the Zambia office. On March 10th, one of our informants came to report that all senior police officers from all Provinces had been meeting at their territorial Headquarters and he knew we were going to be arrested, either on that day or the following. We, therefore, began to prepare ourselves by combing our offices and homes clean in so far as our valued papers and books were concerned. . . . By this time we had already sent out to Tanganyika Mr. Lewis Changufu. We did not have sufficient funds but Mr. Ben Kapufi, then a business man in Broken Hill, offered to assist us. . . . On the 11th, it was clear that we were being shadowed in a very unusual way and we knew the reason for it. Late that evening about five of us got together. Perhaps our souls and bodies needed coming together. However, we were together for some good hours until someone joked that one should be arrested in the presence of his own family, and that sent us all to our respective homes. . . . I must have been asleep for an hour when I opened my eyes and noticed that a motor vehicle was approaching our home and had floodlit our bedroom.

'My watch read 1 a.m. I began to dress and told my wife to do likewise. Before we could go through there was a loud knock at our cattle-kraal-type door. In a very firm voice I said, "Just a moment, please". This was followed up by a big push and . . . in the twinkling of an eye, there was a policeman in uniform right in our bedroom. . . . He immediately ordered me to put my signature to a piece of paper which he would neither show nor read to me. . . . The younger of our two nieces sat up just as I was getting out and shouted, "Za-za-za". And just as suddenly as she had started up she fell back and slept. The whole small Landrover was full of my books and papers; so much so that I perched on my own otherwise valuable property with my left hand handcuffed to an African plain clothes man and my right to that of a white assistant inspector in uniform.' After a swift drive northwards and a change of vehicle, Kenneth found himself, together with Simon Kapwepwe, 'old John Mumbi' and others, rushed to Lusaka airport where, escorted by 'two hefty police officers', they boarded an aeroplane. At Ndola more ZANC men were picked up. 'After some two hours we landed at Balovale' and then 'at six p.m. I was handed over to the DC, Kabompo.' 'There Frank Chitambala joined me and thirty minutes later we arrived at our new "home." '[42]

Once again, the crisis found the Kaunda family in financial straits. 'On the arrest of my husband,' Betty Kaunda has recalled, 'I had only a half-penny and no food at all.' The events of the night had been dramatic and she has described them thus: 'One night in March at about 1.00 a.m. I heard the sound of heavy boots coming towards our house. There was a violent knock at the door. It happened that I had lost the lock to the door the previous day and to secure the door I had only placed a pair of scissors through the hasp. They forced the door, breaking the pair of scissors, and

flung it wide open. I said to my husband, "They've come. . . ."
I sat in the house for the rest of the night wondering what was
going to happen to my husband. In the morning we found that all
trees, poles, and walls were plastered with printed labels bearing
in Chinyanja, *ZA Aferetu*, meaning, "the Zambia African National
Congress is Banned". The Government wanted at first to send the
wives of the detained men to their home villages, but Betty refused
because this would disturb their children's schooling. The D.O.
concerned then agreed to an allowance of £10 per month. Soon
afterwards Betty heard from Kenneth that he was at Kabompo.
She went to the Boma to ask to be allowed to go and visit him,
but permission was refused. She was then expecting another child
and so Kenneth arranged for his sister to go to Lusaka from Chinsali
to look after her.[43]

While Kenneth Kaunda was removed to Kabompo, Sipalo was
sent to Feira at the confluence of the Luangwa and Zambezi rivers;
the Treasurer, Simon Kapwepwe, with Chimba and Nephas Tembo,
to Mungu, the capital of what is now called the Western Province;
Paul Kalichini, ZANC's Deputy President, to Chadiza in the east;
Wittington Sikalumbi, Deputy Secretary, to Namwala; Reuben
Kamanga, the Deputy Treasurer, to Sesheke; Makasa to Solwezi;
and Sikota Wina, who had been editor of *African Life*, to Luwingu.
Immediately, despite the strict control imposed on the detainees,
they began a network of correspondence, in which they exchanged
personal news and discussed the political situation in the country.
Arrangments were even made whereby, with the help of Josophat
Siyomunji, contributions were sent to the party Treasurer in the
Mungu detention camp. Sikalumbi meanwhile undertook the
writing of letters to friends abroad, including Bishop Jordan of
the African Methodist Episcopal Church, Fenner Brockway, Fox-
Pitt, and, later on, the Secretary for the Movement for Colonial
Freedom in London, and Guy Clutton-Brock in Rhodesia. The
letters exchanged between the various places of detention were full
of fun: Makasa addressed Sikalumbi as the 'Hon. P. I.'; Kamanga
wrote from 'Sesheke Slave Camp'; Kalichini was addressed as
'Monsieur du Paul' and Chitambala was given the nickname
Makarios; the men detained at Mungu were called 'the Guidance
Committee', and a letter was received by 'the Secretariat, Namwala'
from 'Solwezi Advisory Committee'. The usual form of address

was either 'Brother' or 'Comrade'. Stamps were sent from various
centres to Sikalumbi in order to help him to maintain his 'official'
mail. News was constantly exchanged about 'revocation orders',
family affairs, births, marriages and deaths; and the tenor of the
great majority of letters was confident, looking forward to joining
forces with 'comrades' outside the camps in the final struggle for
independence. 'You should take this detention in light heart,'
Sikalumbi wrote to 'all ex-Zambia detainees and all Freedom
Fighters' on 15 July '. . . You have nothing to lose but your chains';
and he went on to quote Kaunda's words to a news reporter shortly
before his arrest: "They would gain very little by putting Mr
Sipalo and myself in prison. We do not fancy going to prison but
we are not afraid of imprisonment or being banned. If they think
they can destroy African freedom that way, let them try it and see
what happens. In Zambia we value the cause of freedom more
than our own personal freedom."[44]

'Kabompo to us was still regarded as our HQ and K.K. was
very good at issuing instructions.' 'Every week we received circulars,'
Dingiswayo Banda recalls '. . . The general theme was that we
should never retreat, that while we were in restriction we should
still inspire those of our leaders who were not restricted to keep
on meeting people and telling them that the fight was still on.'[45]
'You know,' Kaunda wrote to his fellow-detainees, 'that the darkest
hour of night comes when it is about to dawn and now we are about
to . . . create an impact on our struggle.' 'It means that we are near
because they have started panicking.' Thus, according to Grey
Zulu, 'it was in fact a great joy to be restricted along with the
President because even in those difficult years he acted more or
less as a father to all of us.'[46]

Because restriction meant having long periods of quietness,
Kaunda, as his autobiography tells, gave much time to serious
thought and meditation. The one letter which he quotes, written
to Solomon Kalulu, revealed his fears about what he called 'moral
destruction' in the life of the nation. "The Western way of life
has been so powerful that our own social, cultural and political
set-up has been raped. . . . The economic dis-equilibrium is such
that our people . . . are now hovering around to catch up with the
outwardly superior social and cultural levels of the West. . . .
Do we sincerely work for self-government now? If so, who do

we hope to lead to our cherished land of Canaan? A nation of half-drunk, half-thinking, half-corrupted?..." "The history of the working class in Britain greatly subscribes to my fears," he added, asking Kalulu to discuss this problem with some trusted friends.[47]

At the same time, as we saw earlier, the weeks in Kabompo deepened Kenneth's sense of communion with the surrounding world of nature. It began to appear to him that 'trees and all growing things must have a language of their own but that God's creation that passes all men's understanding has kept this secret.' He believed that in the future, as was the case with other 'secrets', this one would be revealed to mankind. As he sat in meditation, 'while minutes ran into hours', Frank Chitambala would sometimes become anxious about his whereabouts and come searching for him. But for Kenneth it was easy to forget time as he sat at peace in the midst of nature's profound symphony. 'I studied the various shapes of trees and this gave me pleasure,' he has recorded. 'As the quiet breeze blew from the River Kabompo the trees and the grass around seemed to dance to a strange tune which made me feel that I was in the midst of music which would never come the way of my ears.' Yet at other times, he would be hard at work at their 'open-air office' writing letters and, in the first weeks, chatting with an increasing number of interested people from nearby villages who came to hear 'the good tidings of FREEDOM'. Once the first fear, which Kaunda blamed on deliberate propaganda by 'those in authority', was dispelled and people knew that the restricted ZANC men were anything but 'cannibals', very friendly relations developed; so much so that 'only a month after we had been there we received individual orders banning us from addressing any meeting at all.'[48]

Just as his sense of the glory of nature was deepened in those days, so Kenneth's anger at the trend of events in Northern Rhodesia was sharpened. 'Benson,' he said in a letter to Fox-Pitt written at the end of his first week in restriction, 'would do very well as a fiction writer.' Moreover it was Harry Nkumbula who, having failed to attend the meeting at Fort Jameson of representatives of the various territorial Congresses, 'was telling Benson all our arrangements.' 'He has frightened Benson into this mad action,' Kaunda claimed, 'for personal financial gains.' He followed his letter to Fox-Pitt with a note, for the Revd. Michael Scott, of the reasons given by Benson for his restriction. The core of the Governor's statement was as follows: "... I am satisfied that KENNETH KAUNDA is participating in and immediately intending and preparing to participate in the following actions, namely (a) conspiracy to use force and restraint upon and against persons in order to compel them to refrain from voting or standing for election at the General Election for the Legislative Council of the territory to be held on the 20th day of March 1959; (b) counselling the use of force against voters and candidates for the aforesaid purposes; (c) conspiring maliciously to cause damage to property and injury to person and the counselling of such malicious damage and injury; (d) conspiracy to hold unlawful meetings, the organisation of such meetings, and counselling and procuring of the holding of such meetings."[49]

The Pan-African Freedom Movement for East and Central Africa was gathering for a conference in 1959 and Kaunda prepared three lengthy memoranda for it, written at Kabompo. One of these, the second, is extant among Malama Sokoni's papers, and its ten foolscap pages of concisely written typescript suggest that the three together must have been a weighty document to come from a man, restricted to a lonely place far from home and political companions and stripped of his books and papers. The main argument of this second memorandum was directed against the so-called Benson Constitution and claimed that 'the undeveloped democracy of Ancient Greece ... enjoyed only by "freemen or warriors, barring slaves, peasants and foreigners"' was better than twentieth century democracy in Central Africa. 'Here,' he declared, 'it is Government of the SETTLERS by the SETTLERS for the SETTLERS against Africans ... according to the wicked principle of the lighter the colour of one's skin, the better the treatment.' Every African was 'treated like a potential criminal', forced to carry a range of humiliating passes, to which was added the requirement that women must be able also to produce '*michatos*', ... 'to prove they were not criminals.' Despite the official Federal policy of 'partnership', 'this business of regarding every "darkie" in his own country as a potential criminal forms the pattern in every walk of life.' Partnership had been further belied by Godfrey Huggins's definition of it as that of "rider and horse". Moreover, it was Huggins's own assertion in the House of Lords on 25 March that "Africans are all liars", that epitomised, Kaunda asserted, 'this type of prejudicial and set mind that we are dealing with in Central Africa.' In this situation it was tragic that the African political ranks had been broken despite his own anxiety, on returning from India, 'to help heal the split'. 'Brother Julius Nyerere will bear me out, for I asked him to write Mr. Nkumbula a personal letter . . . which he kindly did.' Yet, though he had been attacked, by Nkumbula and 'his henchman', 'on purely tribal lines', he still hoped that Nkumbula or his deputy would attend the PAFMECA conference.[50]

Among the few personal letters extant from Kaunda's hand while at Kabompo there was one to Colin Legum who has quoted in print this extract from it:

"I wish to state here categorically that we shall untiringly attack systems that for reasons of race alone deny about three million Africans the full enjoyment of democratic rights in this country. But I shall always pray that no bitterness shall come into the picture and that we freedom fighters shall be for ever colour-blind. We make no apologies for being in the fore-front in the struggle for national independence and self-determination. FREEDOM IS OUR BIRTH-RIGHT and we simply are determined to achieve it."

Kaunda also wrote to Colin Leys, another distinguished commentator on African affairs, in the hope that 'this might be the beginning of a long-time exchange of notes and information' and spoke warmly of Guy Clutton-Brock, whose 'efforts to effect what the Central African Governments so ceaselessly preach—PARTNERSHIP—could not have been better crowned than by his being arrested together with the leaders of the people he loves and works for.'[51]

At the same time, Kenneth wrote in a different vein to the South African High Commissioner in Salisbury, on receiving an order prohibiting his entry into South Africa. 'Die Hoe Kommissar, Sir,' he wrote, 'I acknowledge receipt of your No. S.53/7/2 in which you inform me that the Hon. the Minister for the Interior of the Union has deemed me an undesirable resident of or visitor to the Union of South Africa.' 'Let the Hon. the Minister know I accept the DECORATION OF GALLANTRY in my struggles against all that is inhuman. Let him know too that his decoration is the

4th and makes me INTERNATIONAL. The first was in 1954 when the S. Rhodesia Government declared me PI and this was followed up by the N. Rhodesia Government giving me leave to rest for a couple of months in Her Majesty's Hostels. The 3rd DECORATION has brought me here and under it the N. Rhodesia Government "has deemed me an undesirable resident" of my own home and country. We may and can deceive ourselves but history— never! My regards to Dr Verwoerd and let him know this is just the beginning.'[52]

His health had been poor for some time, and the unsatisfactory diet available at Kabompo provoked Kaunda to write an angry letter to the local District officer. 'I must say,' it began, 'that I am totally disappointed at the way I am being handled.' 'If it is the intention of Governor Benson to murder me slowly by starvation then he will go away with my blood on his conscience if he has any at all.' There were eggs, milk and fresh fruits in the neighbour-hood yet he was lacking all such foods. 'You people told me there is no fresh milk in this area and yet 50 yards from where I am caged a milkman makes his daily trip to bring up milk to you people. . . .' 'I may lack all other qualities,' he protested, 'but PATIENCE and DETERMINATION I have a surplus of.' 'I have behaved well ever since I came—you will all readily agree if you know what a prisoner without court trial is capable of doing. . . . Now tell the DC that I am giving Colonial Governor Benson notice through him that if I don't have any at all of these mentioned foodstuffs . . . I am taking the first serious step not by hanging you *but* myself and then Benson will do the rest as he likes. . . . I will go on HUNGER STRIKE INDEFINITELY.'[53]

Looking back, Kenneth recalled that letter as written in 'real anger', the same fierce resentment that broke out on another occasion—though as he said 'I remembered to keep myself to myself as much as possible'—which is described in his auto-biography. 'One day,' he wrote, 'I went to see the District Com-missioner about the insufficiency of our allowances.' 'I arrived at the offices at 8.30 a.m. At 9.30 a.m. the Hon. William Nkanza, member of the Legislative Council for North West arrived. He waited for forty-five minutes but the DC would not see him. We were just told to wait. Mr. Nkanza went back but I still continued to wait. At 12 noon I went past the messenger posted near the DC's door to stop anyone from going in. My patience was completely exhausted. I knocked at the door very angrily and entered without his asking me in. He shouted at me to get out but I refused and instead demanded to be told why he had kept me waiting for three and a half hours. He replied that he was drafting something for me to sign. I shouted back saying surely it would have been good manners to let me know and then I would not have wasted my time. . . . At this juncture, he lost his temper and called me names. Silently I went straight for him. He left his chair and we went round and round his table as he called for his head messenger. The head messenger came in and stood between us and we looked at each other like fighting cocks.'[54]

When it was announced that a special Commission was to enquire into the events leading to the proscription of ZANC, Kenneth prepared a sworn memorandum for submission to it, though his lawyers advised him not to lay it before the commissioners. In demanding self-government and majority rule, he said, ZANC had been open in its approach to Government. If its pleas were ignored, the party would warn Government three times before taking action, 'and that action . . . would be known by everybody.' This programme was the reverse of Benson's description of the clandestine plottings and terror tactics of 'racketeers'. Where facts were distorted, the local press was to blame, and, in support of this view, Kaunda quoted Sir John Moffat's recent statement that "during recent elections, . . . the local papers and the Federal Party went together like bacon and eggs."[55]

In the emotionally charged situation of Central Africa, the use of words like 'felony' by the Government was, in Kaunda's view, pernicious; for the only charge ever made against him was that of organising a meeting without police permission. 'When it was reported in the press that I was charged with conspiring to commit a felony, it appeared to the casual reader that I was planning something horrible.'[56] However, in the Lusaka Magistrate's Court, he was formally prosecuted for 'convening an unauthorised assembly contrary to Section 30 of the NR Police Ordinance, Cap. 44 . . . on or about the 8th day of March 1959 at or near Lusaka'. The occupation of the accused was stated as farmer. In view of his facility with the English anguage, it may have been a bit of fun on his part that lay behind the statement in the court record that 'Court explains both charges to the Accused in Bemba, at the Accused's request, whereupon the Accused states that he fully understands.' The trial, which began on 21 May, went on into June, his lawyer, Colin Cunningham, arguing at length with the prosecuting counsel over the validity of the restriction order. A Police Superintendent in his evidence stated that, though he did not consider Kaunda 'less of a menace' than the other people involved in the organisation of the unauthorised meeting at Matero: 'I have never attributed to the accused any statement advocating possible acts of violence. I would call the accused an intelligent man, not a thug.' The Senior Police Superintendent, however, believed that the holding of a public meeting by ZANC 'would carry with it a very great risk of disorder'. On 20 June, the magistrate, taking into account 'the arrogant and impudent way' in which Kaunda had announced his intention to defy the law, pronounced sentence of nine months' hard labour. In his concluding plea, Cunningham claimed that Kenneth was 'on the evidence of the Prosecution, . . . the non-violence advocating leader of a now banned organisation who by his sincerity has impressed those who have been called to give evidence against him. . . .' 'He is one of a growing number of men in the history of the Commonwealth . . . who have . . . graduated to positions of great respect . . . and of responsibility from the University of the Territorial Prisons.'[57]

When Kenneth was flown to Lusaka for trial, he was put into his 'old familiar cell' in Lusaka Central Prison. At once he noted some improvement from four years previously: sheets, pillows, two pairs of pyjamas. His cell was in the 'European, Asian and Euro-African quarters', which meant that he was listed as a 'special African'. Sipalo, also convicted, was in the section called 'The Confinement'. Kenneth believed this was in order to keep them apart. 'On one occasion during my trial,' he has recorded, 'the police officer who was taking me to court became annoyed with me for waving back to our people who waved when they saw me. He said to me "Why do you keep waving all the time as if you were Elizabeth the Queen Mother? If this continues, I will see to it that you come to court in the Black Maria—do you understand?" Of course I understood, but I did not say so. I continued to wave but this time very carefully. The idea of travelling by a Black Maria was not a very pleasant prospect.'[58]

His autobiography deals at length with his experience of imprisonment and with his comments on the effects of prison life especially upon young convicts. His relations with prison officers were probably affected by the work required, of him, in the category of a 'special African' among non-Africans, as cook and kitchen-hand. 'As for my fellow prisoners, I cannot remember a single prisoner who was not on good terms with me in our section. We got on very well. Some were gentle and repentant. Very apologetically they would say to me they realized I was not in for the same reasons as they were.' He was aware of the specially sad lot of what he called 'the beyond-redemption types' who 'require our sympathy more than anger'. But even for 'a special African', there was a colour bar at work in the prison. 'According to existing regulations I received four ounces less of sugar, cheese and fish than my white and brown counterparts.' In days of dull routine, which included cleaning the 'primitive bucket lavatory', he found pleasure in little distractions, and retained 'vivid memories of a little friend which had no knowledge of me.' 'This was a small aeroplane which flew over our prison almost every Sunday. At about 4 p.m. I would stand in the courtyard waiting to wave at it. . . . There were also some very friendly magpies which came to greet us when most of our friends from the African section had gone to their cells. These birds would come very close to us as if to say to us, "We bring greetings from outside". As soon as the guards came they flew out as if to say "these we cannot trust." ' The official attitude to him was demonstrated by the fact that he was not 'allowed to speak to any other African prisoner and for that matter any African warder', except those in his section.[59]

Beyond the areas of Kenneth Kaunda's confinement, the situation was not improving. While Nyasaland smouldered, conditions were developing which led the Devlin Commission to declare that 'Nyasaland is—no doubt temporarily—a police state.'[60] South of the Zambezi, despite protests by church leaders, the Bar Association and University lecturers and sharp criticism by the press abroad, the Southern Rhodesia Government was rushing through more 'security measures', while the right-wing Confederate Party, meeting freely, called on white people in Southern Rhodesia and South Africa to unite against 'the wave of Black nationalism' that was being 'aided by the Colonial Office'. The constant flow of tales of

atrocities by Government forces in South Africa continued unabated
and there was little reason to expect a long life for the newly-born
Pan-African Congress there, founded in April by Robert Sobukwe
as 'the counter-blast of Black nationalism to the forces of extreme
white nationalism'. To the north the Congo was in deep disquiet.
Not long before being banned, ZANC had protested hotly against
what it called 'the Leopoldville Massacre' and demanded the recall of
the Congo's Governor-General.[61] Meanwhile, there were widespread
reactions in various parts of the world at the news of brutalities
perpetrated against detainees in the Hola Camp in Kenya.[62] It
was this news that significantly convinced Iain Macleod of the
British Conservative Party that British colonial policy needed to
be changed 'to move much more quickly towards independence
for the African countries'.[63]

In Northern Rhodesia there was a brief proliferation of political
parties, both the African National Freedom Movement and Dixon
Konkola's United African Congress announcing a 'non-violent
campaign for self-government'.[64] In the old ANC, Nkumbula was
still at loggerheads with his subordinates and in July he seized all
the files from the secretary, Mukupo. He then suspended Mukupo,
who retorted by demanding Nkumbula's resignation. Meanwhile,
almost unnoticed, the two big mining companies withdrew financial
backing from the United Federal Party; and a beam of hope
appeared in the storm when it was announced that the new Governor
would be the present Chief Secretary, Evelyn Hone, thus following
an unusual line of promotion.[65] At the same time papers began to
pile up on Government and Congress desks as a motion by Moffat
in Leg. Co. gave birth to a Race Relations Committee, with particular
reference to places of entertainment, cafes, etc.[66] When the Committee eventually submitted proposals on how discrimination might
be progressively abolished, its report bore the signature of its
chairman, N.C.A. Ridley.[67]

Much more important to Kaunda and his colleagues was the
earlier report that came to be known by Ridley's name. Mulford's
comment on the report on ZANC's proscription is that it provides
virtually no information of merit about ZANC's actual organisation,
but that 'evidence overwhelmingly supports the view' that what
was really at work in Central Africa was a 'carefully planned
attempt to decapitate major nationalist parties in Central Africa

simultaneously in order to ensure the future survival of the Federation', and that while Benson was personally bitter against both Whitehall and what he called privately 'the sadistic and evil' utterances of Welensky, a vital part of this operation was Welensky's 'powerful Salisbury-London axis, presumably with Lord Home and the Commonwealth Relations Office'. The 'great Central African plot', as we have called it, was thus still central to the drama. Ridley, like Devlin, had no remit to comment on the deeper factors of the crisis, and so, like Devlin, he reported at length mainly on evidence of what must, nonetheless, be seen as the local people's reaction to the major action of the great plotters. His final recommendations were thus timorous and touched on little more than the 'need for urgency' in the removal of genuine grievances, citing, for example, 'the big differential in favour of European maize though the quality of the grain was the same'.

Yet Ridley provides a list of words and actions by ZANC men which, in his view, justified its proscription. He cited Sipalo's warning, in December 1958, that "if any registered voter voted, he would be watched and punished". Soon afterwards, Kalichini had promised 'trouble' to anyone going to the polls. Another ZANC man, John Mumbi, was said to have declared that "Zambia would find out and mark the houses of all voters—anyone who went to vote would be accompanied by Zambia people, and if the police fired on them they would also be firing on the voters." Kaunda was cited as stating, at Fort Jameson in February, that "they must not let any other African organisation go to the polls." Makasa, ZANC's Regional President in the Northern Province, was reported by the C.I.D. to have warned that "Government would be kept very busy in 1959" and that ZANC "would continue to derail trains". They must follow the example of Congo Africans. On a different note, Raphael Kombe of Broken Hill had said, according to Ridley, that there was no "ill-feeling against African policemen but . . . towards European policemen." "When the African policemen understand Zambia policy, they will throw their helmets away." Meanwhile ZANC had described Benson's governorship as "a tragic catalogue of terribly inhuman activities" and Justin Chimba called him ' "a murderer". And in terms of direct racial emotion, one ZANC man allegedly said that "sometimes if you see a European you can spit at him";

while Sipalo and Chakulya urged people to "hate everything
white". Speaking in Kasama, Kapwepwe had urged that "Africans should drive fear from their minds into the minds of the
white people." But while Devlin could cite Hastings Banda's
self-assertive words, "I put Salisbury on fire. . . . Everybody
knows that I got Salisbury rocking rocking", neither Ridley
nor the prosecution at Kenneth's trial could quote anything to
support the contention that his non-violence was hypocritical.[68]

'In the result,' Ridley said, 'the elections took place calmly. . . .'
'Though after the restriction of the leaders there were widespread
acts of disorder, arson and the like, the Government's action
diminished this to some degree.' The disorder included the secret
plot of the Mulongoti Branch for "special organised groups to face
the candidents [*sic*] . . . to be cleared and by means of bottles
containing petrol to destroy their hut [*sic*] by night."[69] It also
erupted on Chilubi Island in Lake Bangweulu. ANC had first
appeared on the island in 1954, but there had been a widespread
switch of loyalty to Kaunda after the split in 1958. 'We left
Nkumbula because he delayed us' in the movement for self-rule which
'Almighty God arranged', islanders told the writer eleven years
later. When the Governor banned ZANC, a Boma officer came to
effect the ban. Starting at Yombwe village, 'he so searched us,'
the people said, 'that we wondered how a white man who had
never entered an African home dare enter it now. . . .' 'In the process
of getting him out of the house he was caught on the arm and
brought into the yard. The messengers witnessed this. Then, as
he wanted to hit us, the wife of Mr. Lungoya came swiftly and
struck a blow across his face.' The officer was then escorted from
the village but arrested a man on the way to Muchinshi village.
There the local people became angry. 'Let us go and set free our
friend,' they cried. 'We are now in Zambia.' The officer agreed to
release his prisoner but sent word to his senior who came and
carried out pre-dawn arrests at Yombwe. 'We were all dragged out
from our beds naked and handcuffed.' The headman was beaten
'with long batons,' which provoked a man to spear the District
Assistant. The messengers then seized the assailant and more
beating took place. There was a burst of gunfire and four men died.
From the nature of the injuries reported, the shooting must have
been at random. Local witnesses claimed that thereafter another

officer came and set fire to a shop owned by a Zambia Congress member. By the end of the disturbance, fifty-one arrests had been made. 'When they came out of jail,' the people said, 'they never retreated. . . .' 'If the Government governed us justly, they said, we would not rise against them. But because . . . they have even started killing us, we will follow Kaunda until we are free from all this.'[70]

In many parts of the country, visits by Kenneth Kaunda were remembered as signalising a new realisation by village people of both the gravity of the issues at stake in Central Africa and their part in bringing about change. In the eyes of certain District Officers this rapport was not genuine. A Tour Report, for instance, described in 1958 how 'the hard core near Chinsali rallied to Kenneth Kaunda and chanted "one man, one vote" while the maestro wept crocodile tears.' His mother was said to be taking part in these activities, 'despite her age'.[71] Now that he was behind bars, the question for those who realised that fundamental change was now unavoidable was who would be the African leader to effect a new regime. The *Central African Examiner*, which believed that 'the tide of anti-Federation criticism in Britain was beginning to ebb', prophesied that 'as the only Congress leader from the Congo border to the Cape who is not either locked up or in voluntary exile, Harry Nkumbula, the mission boy . . . is the African nationalist most likely to make the loudest noise between now and the 1960 [Federal Review] Conference.' It also blamed 'the openly political role of the Church of Scotland missions' for fomenting nationalism and saw this as the reason for the closure of the hospitals at Lubwa and Mwenzo.[72]

In July, Paul Kalichini was released from detention in Petauke and at once announced the formation of a new party, the African Independence Party, at a time when the Government must have been not a little alarmed by the growing dissension within ANC and its increasingly apparent inability to hold the masses. Fines Bulawayo's success in late August in reconciling Nkumbula and Mukupo was to be short-lived. On the other hand, Kalichini, though flanked by the colourful Frank Chitambala clad in a Ghana-type toga, was presenting an image of statesmanship. Then, as Mukupo announced 'Harry is finished. We are busy writing his epitaph', and Bulawayo joined Nkumbula's opponents, Mainza Chona, back from London and now a barrister-at-law, appeared as

the main challenger for the presidency of ANC. At once he warned
that Nkumbula's 'leadership weaknesses and general disagreeable-
ness' were driving 'many Africans' to join the U.F.P. and Moffat's
new Central African Party. With a touch of comedy, there were
now two men called President-General of ANC and talk of a
High Court decision to settle the dispute. It was, however, the
Registrar of Societies who quietly recognised t he claims of
Nkumbula. Chona at once left ANC and joined Kalᶦchini in what
was now being called the United National Independence Party; the
name eventually chosen after Sikalumbi proposed NIP, to give
the lie, as it were, to the Governor's resolve to 'nip' the new popular
movement 'in the bud'.[73]

On 11 September, with only two Africans in court, the Chief
Justice rejected Kenneth Kaunda's appeal against conviction in
the Lusaka Magistrate's Court, but removed the element of hard
labour. Kenneth did not appear in person and his lawyer stated
that he was in Salisbury.[74] Once again we return therefore to
Kaunda's own account of his transfer to Salisbury Central Prison.
'Four of us were picked up by the superintendent and made to
dress in our own clothes. I was handcuffed to Wilson Chakulya
who had been given sixteen months for a charge of sedition. He
was Secretary of our Broken Hill district as well as General Secretary
of the Central African Road Service Union of Workers. Munukuyumbwa Sipalo was handcuffed to a man called Chirwa who had
been given twenty years for alleged derailment of a train somewhere
near Lusaka.' In Salisbury jail 'we were given a room each in a
wing that is used for the accommodation of sick people and those
in transit.' 'In the morning, we were issued with what is described
as a superior uniform; regulation wear for Indians and Euro-
Africans. We were then locked up in our respective rooms again.
This made a good number of people very curious.

'One of the most difficult prison officers to deal with happened
to be on duty on the second or third day of our stay there. As we
were parading to go in he saw us standing about five yards away
from the man at the end of the line of ordinary prisoners. Shouting
at the top of his voice he said, "KU-ANDA, get to the back and
take him with you (meaning Sipalo) or else I will cut your legs
off for you. And while doing so I shall be smiling just to show there
is no actual animosity". This man was ex-Kenya. He was in charge

of the supply of things like toothpaste. He kept me for three solid weeks without supplying me with my much-needed toothpaste. I kept on complaining to the senior superintendent until he went in to order this officer to bring a tube of toothpaste to me. He was about twenty yards away from my cell when he started calling, "KU . . . ANDA, KU . . . ANDA, KU . . . ANDA" When I did not answer, he said "Where is this native they call Kuanda?" I then said, "I am here, officer, how can I help you?" He came in and stared at me, his eyes full of anger. After he had satisfied himself he threw the paste at me. I said, "Thank you". He then replied to my thank you by saying, "Don't thank me. I don't give toothpaste to natives—go and thank the senior superintendent".

'One day I remember we received an official visit from a Federal Minister. He did not come to our workshop but when his party was about thirty yards away, the senior superintendent called out for me. The Director of Prisons introduced me to the Minister who said that we had never met before although both of us came from Northern Rhodesia. He added, "I understand you have been a model prisoner here". I thanked him and replied that I did not know about my being a model prisoner but that both the senior superintendent and the Director of Prisons might know. The senior superintendent then cracked a joke saying, "This man is here, sir, because he conspired to blow up the British Empire". The Minister replied "That should stand him in good stead for his future responsibilities." '[75]

As he looked back, after his release, to his weeks in jail, he realised that the rigours of confinement had had a refining effect on his thinking, as he said in a letter to Frank Barton. 'You are right when you speak of "a spell inside is almost a necessity for any nationalist leader". Don't ask me why, Frank, for I don't know why, but I found that I was able to ponder over problems a lot more clearly than I had ever done outside. I suppose this is due to the physically narrow confines of prisons which perhaps help one's mental faculties to be more active. In any case, whatever the reasons, I was able to see more clearly that my line of thought is the right one and I have stuck to it ever since I came out.'[76]

To help Betty Kaunda and the children while Kenneth was in jail, a fund was started and, in addition, Cunningham informed Fox-Pitt that 'the Catholic Fathers and Father Walsh are arranging

to supplement the meagre diet KK enjoys in prison with fruit and
fish.' Clutton-Brock assisted too and Kenneth wrote from his cell
to thank the friends involved. In a letter to the Fabian Colonial
Bureau, he wrote thus: 'By Time, Space and Human Activity,
we have been separated—but at Christmastide we have time and
chance to break these forces and renew that spiritual feeling that
even they cannot break. And now may we join together and sing,
"All Glory be to God on High, Goodwill and Peace to men".
Until I write again I wish all my friends and their families the
Merriest Xmas and Happiest New Year. In all this my friends,
Munukuyumbwa Sipalo and Wilson Chakulya, join me. Yours
sincerely, Kenneth— K. D. Kaunda, No. 447, HM Prison, Salisbury,
14/12/59.'[77] Before Christmas, Kenneth knew that his release was
not far off. On the fifteenth, it was announced that 'if they do not
forfeit normal remission of sentences', he and Sipalo would be
freed in January and then Harry Franklin gave the date as 10
January 1960. A government spokesman subsequently published
news of the release of the remaining ZANC detainees by 8 January.[78]

Prison experience had been inevitably grim but, Kenneth said,
'for those of us who meddle in public affairs' such experiences were
valuable for 'there we see some of God's own children who need
more care and attention than any others collected as often as courts
of law meet.' He was particularly troubled by what prison life did
to the younger inmates who 'respond very quickly to anyone offering
them protection . . . who . . . do so with terrible motives.' 'If a boy
tries to resist, his so-called protector arranges with others to thrash
him so that, by coming to the boy's protection at the right moment,
he will submit to his unnatural desires . . .' 'Is it beyond our
reach,' Kaunda asked, 'to come to grips with this problem in a
young country such as ours?' The problem was that society outside the prison walls was 'so soiled, in so far as Africans are concerned', that many of them preferred to stay inside where at least they
would not be 'harrassed by the police for passes, tax receipts and
many other things'. Such a society 'is rotten and needs burying'.[79]

Kaunda's transfer from Salisbury back to Lusaka took place
on 18 December. Had the Government been determined to keep
the principal leader of what Benson had branded 'Murder Incorporated' away from the political arena, there would have been
no apparent problem in extending his period in Salisbury indefinitely.

Moreover his release was not signalised by a 'change of tune' among his political colleagues. Mainza Chona, who, after the final break with Nkumbula, was at once seen as a rallying force in the emergent United National Independence Party, was certainly not pulling his punches. Kenneth's personal interpretation of the release of himself and the other ZANC detainees was that the Government was now more aware of a dangerous 'vacuum' and of the impossibility of going forward in any way by ignoring what was clearly the more popular group. 'It was better to release us all to be together again and guide the movement on a path of non-violence.'[80] Meanwhile in the urgent negotiations taking place between the various groups and individuals associated with the emergent United National Independence Party, it was clear that, as Chona wrote, 'everyone would like to see Mr Kaunda at the very top.'[81]

On 9 January, Kaunda was released from jail, a day earlier than originally stated on the pretext that 'no releases are made on Sundays'. Colin Cunningham was there to receive him, along with a press photographer and a reporter. He went straight to the tiny house in Chilenje where Betty and the children welcomed him and friends gathered quickly. Soon a crowd of supporters surrounded the veranda and various songs and Christian hymns were sung. It was an occasion when tears were hard to control, and which called for a message from Kenneth. He therefore issued this statement: 'Freedom! All I am asking the Africans of Northern Rhodesia is that they should remain calm and patient; and should prepare themselves for the real non-violent struggle that lies ahead. The Zambia African Congress was banned, but there is no power to ban our desire to be free, to shape our own destiny. In this struggle for freedom, we will tell the present rulers to realize that the colour of man should not count; what should count is his behaviour . . . . I repeat that the Africans of Northern Rhodesia must be patient. We will negotiate with the British government and the Governor here. I will demand constitutional changes now. I hear that the new Colonial Secretary, Iain Macleod, is a man of great understanding. I am certain he will be sympathetic. We shall soon be putting before him our constitutional proposals which will be framed at the forthcoming conference of the United National Independence Party on 31 January. It is time that power shifted from the minority group to the majority, and by this I mean universal adult suffrage which is popularly known as "one man, one vote". I am hopeful that this can be achieved through a non-violent struggle. I therefore, ask you all to be calm, patient and non-violent.'[82]

In the evening a journalist interviewed him and asked the inevitable questions as to whether he was angry at the treatment he had received. "A man who gathers honey," Kenneth answered, using a well-known proverb, "expects to be stung by the bees." I am therefore not embittered. I have come out with a clear conscience.'[83] It was a moment of renewed exhilaration.

The men who had kept up their secret correspondence with one another while in restriction were far from cowed as they re-entered society. Their leaders were obviously at concert pitch; the country was set for heightened tension and accelerated change. Indeed the continent was experiencing the strong currents of what Prime Minister Harold Macmillan aptly called 'the wind of change'.[84] For Kaunda, as for the rest, the coming months were to be severely taxing, and therefore it was perhaps a happy consequence of his period behind bars that, as Betty has recorded, he had 'looked better and been healthier in jail than he ever was out on his Party organising tours'.[85]

Thus began what Philip Mason called the 'Year of Decision'. The tension had not relaxed with Harold Macmillan's announcement, in July 1959, that a special Advisory Commission, chaired by Lord Monckton, would carry out an exhaustive survey of the situation in the three federated territories in order 'to advise the five Governments . . . on the constitutional programme and framework best suited to the achievement of the objects contained in the Constitution of 1953, including the Preamble'.[86] From his detention camp at Mungu, Simon Kapwepwe had issued a circular headed 'Talk Freedom with Detainees' and addressed to 'Sons and Daughters of the Soil', charging that the appointment of the Commission had 'sown more seeds of mistrust and hate for this pretentious Western democracy.' 'The Conservative Government', he said, 'is still treading on the sore corn of the African people. . . . We want to break this stumbling, murdering, hating Federation.'[87]

The Government's intelligence officers, sensing the depth of popular feeling, provided the Government with evidence on the strength of which a 'Preservation of Public Security Ordinance' was promulgated, giving the Governor extensive powers to rule on a virtually 'emergency' basis, arresting and detaining persons without trial as he saw fit. John Moffat, who described this document as 'outrageous', was now urging some new form of Central African association to replace the discredited Federation. 'The entire people want only one thing . . . to be quit of it.'[88] This mounting antipathy had undoubtedly been the cause of the wave of 'indiscipline' in Kenneth Kaunda's old school, Munali, on account of which the Minister of African Education, Gabriel Musumbulwa, ordered the dismissal of its four hundred and twenty pupils.[89]

For Betty Kaunda, Kenneth's return from Salisbury brought both joy and anxiety. Not being fully aware of the secret negotiations that had led to the merger of various parties that had appeared after the ban on ZANC to form UNIP, she recorded the situation thus: 'My husband . . . now started organising something else later to be known as the United National Independence Party. He went to the Municipal Office and pressed for a bigger house . . . No. 394 in Chilenje.[90] . . . My life went back to that of 1951-52 when I used to remain alone at Shambalakale farm while he was absent. . . . As it was a new Party, there were fewer contributions and so less allowances for us to live on. I had now become so used to this way of life that it worried me no more.'[91] Inevitably the family saw little of Kaunda for, from the moment of his return, he was in the public eye, and under the strain of an even more exacting role. At the first meeting he attended on leaving prison, he wept as he pointed to the poor houses of Africans in Matero and as he protested that it would be betrayal to give evidence before the Monckton Commission.

Ten days later, with the arrival of the British Prime Minister in the territory, UNIP handed to the Governor's office a 32-page memorandum for transmission to him, the preparation of which had involved Kaunda along with the Party's interim executive. The British Government 'stands like a toothless bulldog between the ever clamouring demands of the foreign settlers to whom [it] has granted more and more power, and the indigenous people whom it has betrayed . . . with an easiness of conscience which would make every protector . . . except the British . . . blush with shame.' 'Your Imperial Government,' UNIP told Macmillan, 'has retreated from promise to promise,' while in Northern Rhodesia government was now 'by gunpowder and lead'.

When Harold Macmillan appeared outside Ndola's Savoy Hotel on 22 January in steady rain, 'the biggest African nationalist demonstration' of his Federal tour greeted him with sodden banners, one of which—'To hell with Welensky'—was removed at the insistence of the police. 'Do not bring Monckton here,' one poster read, and another: 'Kaunda means Independence.'[92] It was now clear that the cordiality of the Lennox-Boyd-Welensky concordat of 1957 was withering rapidly. As it wilted, the Northern Rhodesia Government took an interesting step, in recognition of the radically changed political situation, by deciding to abolish the African Representative Council. The coming conflict was thus moving out of legislative and deliberative chambers and becoming increasingly a confrontation between Welensky and the African people. For Kaunda, the overwhelming defeat of Moffat's motion calling for some form of association other than the present Federation endorsed his conviction that 'the fight would have to be carried on by building up a strong party to force constitutional changes.' He was now even more determined on out-and-out opposition to the Central African Federation.[93]

Now, therefore, using a Landrover procured for the Party by Merfyn Temple from the United Society for Christian Literature, Kenneth and his colleagues began intensifying their contacts with the people in towns and villages, to sound public opinion and to broadcast UNIP's policies. The vehicle was soon known as 'Mother UNIP' to thousands of people all over the country. Meanwhile in South Africa the stage was being set for the massacres at Sharpeville and Langa in March and April 1960, in which 83 'non-whites' were killed and 365 injured.[94] To the north, the Congo was experiencing a wave of renewed violence, despite the Brussels Round Table Conference in February. The enmity between Kasavubu's Abaku Party and the followers of Patrice Lumumba had increased sharply. In Angola, 57 arrests had been made on charges of treason just before Christmas, 1959, and there had been a marked revival of the united 'African Revolutionary Front' against Portuguese colonialism on the one hand, and of Portuguese military activity on the other. In Kenya, there was increasing optimism about the release of Jomo Kenyatta and the effects of such a move on the timing of radical constitutional change. In Tanganyika, though

Julius Nyerere had spoken recently of independence 'within at least five years', it was beginning to look as though the pace might even be faster.

There was thus ferment at home and abroad as Kenneth Kaunda was unanimously elected President of UNIP on 31 January at a lively party conference held at Chilenje. His election was marked by a tense incident arising from the anger of a crowd, gathered for a rally at Kabwata, against white police officers who insisted on adjusting the microphone and noting each speaker's name before he spoke. 'It was with the greatest difficulty,' Kaunda recorded, 'that I managed to control the crowd but I kept on insisting that our policy was one of non-violence.' 'I remember saying "If, because of our policy, you are lifted in the air and thrown on the ground, say, kill me but I shall be free". I was determined to combine Gandhi's policy of non-violence with Nkrumah's positive action. . . . I was aware of the terrible danger of some of the young extreme elements of my party getting out of control and causing riots. In any nationalist organisation there are bound to be "roughs and toughs" who want to force the pace, and a way must be found of dealing with them.'[95]

The birth of UNIP had certainly released a new extremism into the situation, as evidenced by the November 1959 issue of *Forward to Freedom*, the newsletter started by Sykes Ndilila and others in October. While expressing anger at the closing of Munali School and demanding the resignation of Musumbulwa, the Minister of African Education, this paper carried about fifty lines of verse apostrophising 'Mr Whiteman', written by Ndilila himself. Europeans should not worry, the verses said. 'The Blackman will not chase you away.' But 'bossin' around' was finished and white people must be prepared to be 'faithful and loyal' and 'obey their African laws. . . .' 'Some of your people are gonna be taught to sing them Native songs.' Meanwhile 'jobs are plenty reserved' for white people as 'road foremen, working capitaos, barmen, cook boys and spanner boys, etc., and above all no tea at 11 a.m.' Ndilila concluded 'Why do ye panic, Mr Whiteman? . . . everything is arranged for yer MISISI and yer children.'[96] Nonetheless, the Party's more formal publications were couched in carefully chosen language, as for example, the statement of 'national political policy' issued, before Kaunda's release, over the signature of the flamboyant Chitambala, then the National Secretary. This document reaffirmed 'the absolute principle of non-violence' as fundamental to the 'fight by all Constitutional means for the attainment of full Self-Government now'. This was part of the wider intention of striving towards 'the realisation of full democratic status for all BLACK AFRICA'.[97]

In these feverish days, Kenneth Kaunda somehow found time to work with Colin Morris and Merfyn Temple in the preparation of a contribution to the wider understanding of the issues at stake in Central Africa in the form of a 116-page book published by the United Society for Christian Literature, and entitled *Black Government*. Readers are recommended to read this book in full, in view of its ability to capture the sense of commitment and urgency that impelled the new African leadership as 1960 began. *Black Government* carried a foreword by Sir Stewart Gore-Browne, now a supporter of Kaunda, in which he likened the struggle in Northern Rhodesia to 'the situation in Britain in the years just before the passing of the Great Reform Bill in 1832, when the conflict was between Privilege and the People'. Africans were demanding, Gore-Browne believed, 'what the Prime Minister of India, Mr Nehru, calls "The Fourth Freedom: Freedom from Contempt" '. Temple, in a brief profile of Kaunda, asked the question: 'Is he to be compared with a black mamba, the most deadly of snakes?', as John Gaunt had said. 'Is he a potential African Gandhi of the unborn state of Zambia? . . . Any glib answer is sure to be wrong for Kaunda is a riddle; for how can a man with as gentle a nature as Kaunda's continue to ride the tiger of "African Politics"?' In this book, Kenneth is recorded as speaking passionately yet with care and with logic on the economic plight of his people no less than on the gravity of the political crisis. Once again he made his own belief about positive action for political and social change unequivocally clear: 'I reject absolutely violence in any of its forms as a solution to our problems.'[98]

During those crucial months, Kenneth was seeking to reassure worried Europeans that under a popularly-elected government their persons and property would be protected. 'Come with us for freedom,' he called. But the N.R. Eurafrican Association, meeting at Ndola a week later, rejected appeals by what the press called 'extremist members' to support the African cause and align itself

with UNIP. Though Colin Morris, who addressed the meeting as
a visitor, along with Harry Franklin, spoke of Kaunda as 'potentially
a great statesman', he and Franklin as well as the Association's
Chairman warned against such an alignment. 'UNIP,' said the
Chairman, 'is not even recognised by better-educated and better-
class Africans.'[99] In the weeks that followed, however, a further
effort was made to draw attention to the fact that what UNIP
stood for was of concern to all. Kaunda and Nkumbula, early in
March, announced plans for a nation-wide petition, demanding
secession from the Federation and a new Constitution. Five hundred
thousand signatures were to be sought. 'We expect support from
people of other races,' said Kenneth, 'and will welcome it.' Neither
he nor Nkumbula, however, would comment on the possibility of
a rapprochement between their parties.[100]

The new Colonial Secretary, Iain Macleod, arrived in Lusaka
at the end of March, and a marked change of policy was at once
apparent. 'When Harold Macmillan . . . gave me this post, he knew
very well, and indeed it was implicit in the offer, that I was going
to operate a different form of regime to that of my predecessor.
When I took over . . . there were something like 100,000 people,
in different parts of what was then still a colonial empire, living in
detention or restriction without trial. The first minute I dictated
to my new office was in effect to say that although I fully recognised
the dangers of moving quickly, the dangers of staying where we
were or even of trying to move slowly seemed to me overwhelming,
and therefore we would move swiftly towards independence via the
traditional form of a series of independence conferences.'[101] But
when Kenneth Kaunda met Iain Macleod in Lusaka, the atmosphere
in the territory was tense. Though Kaunda was looking forward
to visiting America in less than two weeks and speaking of his
people's aspirations there in the company of Martin Luther King,
Harry Belafonte and Mrs. Eleanor Roosevelt, the home news
was disquieting. There were rumours of fresh trouble in the Northern
Province where Simon Kapwepwe was reported to have been arrested
on 'an alleged pass offence' and sixty-one other people had been
put in jail. Just previously, Kapwepwe had publicly torn the N.R.G.
bulletin on the Monckton Commission to pieces, at Fort Roseberry.[102] Macleod's public statement that he had 'no plans in contem-
plation to amend the constitution' and the U.F.P.'s jubilant reaction

to it did not augur well for the fulfilment of UNIP's dream. Macleod was inevitably embarrassed by the fact that Kaunda and his Party had operated a very effective boycott of the Monckton Commission immediately before his arrival.

The Memorandum which Kenneth gave to Macleod at this time attempted to combine the reasonableness of African demands with the urgency of swift constitutional change. "We have already submitted our case for SELF-GOVERNMENT NOW," he wrote, "but I wish to sum up the case as follows:

1. THAT we do ask for the graceful transfer of power from minority groups to the majority not only because we believe it is the God-given right of any people to rule themselves but because we believe quite sincerely that if an atmosphere of racial harmony and peace which we need in order to develop and exploit our abundant natural resources, is to be created, the majority must rule.

2. THAT [under] such government minority groups need not have any fears that their interests might be jeopardized because when we say we believe that 'all men are created equal and that they are endowed with certain inalienable rights, among them LIFE, LIBERTY and the PURSUIT OF HAPPINESS,' we mean this. . . .

3. THAT note should be taken of the fact that what is happening in both North and South Africa is influencing the situation here greatly. . . .

4. THAT the spending of *only* ten days in Northern Rhodesia and ten days in Nyasaland is a slight on the leadership of Africans of Northern Rhodesia who believe in non-violent struggle. It is being interpreted to mean that the British government will only move when there is bloodshed. To clear this unfortunate interpretation . . . I believe it is advisable for the Secretary of State to announce an earlier date than October this year for a round-table conference."[103]

Macleod was still in Lusaka when Kaunda announced that the Colonial Secretary had invited him to London for consultations. The news immediately angered Welensky, who claimed that a number of African M.P.s had protested 'on hearing that this certain Northern Rhodesian gentleman' had received such an invitation. 'Reasonable Africans were beginning to fear that it was only extremists who could hope to meet VIPs.' Kenneth, however, was hailing

Macleod's new approach to African problems. 'The Colonial Secretary has already demonstrated in Kenya and in Tanganyika what his Government will do. I have no doubt that if we carry on in the right way we shall meet with the same success in a very short space of time.' In different accents Munukuyumbwa Sipalo told a rally of around 6,000 people at Ndola that 'God brought the whiteman here and let him sit on the black people.' 'I tell God and his white brothers to clear away from Northern Rhodesia,' and Chimba went on to declare that since Europeans had declared open war on Africans, 'we are going to hit back when we get into power.' He also promised that independence would see the abolition of taxes. As this rally took place, Kaunda was completing preparations for his visit to the United States, though the remittance for his fare had not yet arrived from New York. However, he had time to cable his good wishes to Hastings Banda and sent another telegram to Macleod, praising his 'wise and firm decision' to release Banda from Gwelo. As he boarded his plane at last, on 10 April, he issued a press statement denouncing the attempt in South Africa to assassinate Dr. Verwoerd. This was 'not the way to go about political change'.[104] The realities of contemporary African politics were harsh, and fraught with peril. Kenneth's eye was still on the honey pot, but the bees were swarming angrily about his head.

---

[1]Mpashi, *op. cit.*, pp. 49-52; with quotation from p. 49.
[2]*Ibid*, pp. 51-52.
[3]TI-FM/L. Changufu, 11/7/69.
[4]Mpashi, *op. cit.*, p. 53.
[5]*NN*, 5/11/58, warning by S. G. Tembo, an ANC Provincial President; and 7/11/58, for Nkumbula declaration.
[6]TI-FM/SMK, 8/11/69, TI-FM/A.G. Zulu, 27/2/69.
[7]TI-FM/RCK, 1969.
[8]Kaunda, *Zambia*, 98-99; and *NN*, 21/11/58 and 27/11/58.
[9]TI-FM/KK, 13/7/71; Grey Zulu (TI-FM/AGZ, 27/2/69) quotes Kaunda to Nkumbula thus: 'I wanted to be very loyal to you ... but you are not really honest with me. ... However, in spite of the fact that I have resigned ... I am prepared to hand over peacefully to whoever you will appoint ... after which I want to plot out my own future.'
[10]Mason. *Year*, pp. 126-127, and Sikalumbi, *op. cit.*, p. 104.
[11]See Hall, *Zambia*, pp. 184 ff., with quotation from pp. 184-5; Mulford, *op. cit.*, pp. 79-81; Sikalumbi, *op. cit.*, p. 103 ff.
[12]See Mason, *Year*, 179; *Africa Digest*, Vol. VI, No. 5, pp. 169-170 ref. University and Dr. Bernard Chidzero; and *News Chronicle*, 28/11/58.
[13]*N.R. Press Communique*, Nos. 100, 102, 108, 12/3/59.
[14]*Africa Digest*, Vol. VI, No. 5. p. 170.
[15]*Africa Digest*, Vol. VI, No. 5, pp. 170-171; *CAP* 13/3/59. The S.R. Emergency was proclaimed on 26/2/59,

[16]Mulford, *Zambia*, p. 77 and *M.I.R.* for November 1958.

[17]TI-FM/KK, 4/9/72; *Daily Telegraph*, 9/1/59; and *Africa Digest*, Vol. VI, No. 4, p. 158.

[18]*NN*, 19/1/59 for quotation; see also 21/1/59, 26/1/59, 30/1/59.

[19]*NN*, 5/2/59 for quotation, and 19/1/59; also *Africa Digest* Vol. VI, No. 5, p. 171,

[20]*N.R. Press Communique* No. 76.

[21]*NN*, 27/1/59, 10/2/59, 12/2/59, 14/2/59.

[22]TI-FM/KK, 11/4/69.

[23]*NN*, 16-17/2/59.

[24]RH 103/2: covering letter, Fox-Pitt to 'Dear Jimmy' 16/12/58 enclosing copy of Kaunda to Fox-Pitt, 2/12/58. Fox-Pitt wrote: 'I have long thought Harry a disaster to his people and Kaunda is the sort of committed man needed to hold things together.'

[25]Federal Newsletter, 27/2/59; and *NN*, 19/2/59 and 26/2/59. ANC's Propaganda Secretary was F. N. Bulawayo, and the Dominion Party Chairman was C. I. Fleming.

[26]TI-FM/KK, 13/2/69.

[27]Kaunda, *Zambia*, pp. 100-103.

[28]RH 103/2: Constitution of Zambia African National Congress, undated.

[29]Sikalumbi, *op. cit.*, pp. 101-102.

[30]*Report of an Inquiry into all Circumstances which Gave Rise to the Making of the Safeguard of Elections and Public Safety Regulations, 1959.* (Government Printer); known as the Ridley Report; Sikalumbi, *op. cit.*, p. 105.

[31]Hall, *Zambia*, p. 187; and Mason, *Year*, p. 206.

[32]Cited in J. Stonehouse, *Prohibited Immigrant* (Bodley Head, 1960) 184.

[33]Personal observation of the writer who was in Malawi from December 1956 to July 1959 and who, with his colleagues, submitted a number of detailed protests against the brutal action of the 'security forces', particularly in the Northern Province.

[34]*Africa Digest*, Vol. VI, No. 6, p. 219, quoting Malvern's speech in the House of Lords.

[35]See Stonehouse, *op. cit.*

[36]See the *Report of the Nyasaland Commission of Inquiry* (CMD 814), July 1959, known as the Devlin Report. The writer received testimony of reliable witnesses that the death toll greatly exceeded the figure of 48 cited by Devlin (p. 119).

[37]For events mentioned in this paragraph see *Africa Digest*, Vol. VI, No. 5, pp. 165-175.

[38]*RH* 103/2: Typed extract from 'Broadcast by the Governor of Northern Rhodesia made on Thursday, March 12th, 1959', in which is inserted, under para. 8, 'The text of the resolution taken from the News Bulletin issued by the conference' in Accra.

[39]For events recorded here see *CAP* and *NN* for the period, esp. *NN*, 16/2/59 for Kaunda's 'Union Jack' remark. For Kaunda's telegram to the Colonial Secretary, see *Africa Digest*, Vol. VI, No. 5, p. 170.

[40]Kaunda, *Zambia*, p. 100.

[41]Sokoni Papers: undated jottings by Kaunda, filed among papers of this period; and Mulford, 80, quoting letter from Kaunda to Nkrumah, December 1958.

[42]Kaunda *Zambia*, pp. 104-108. His chapter 14, 'Arrest and Detention' should be read in full.

[43]Mpashi, *op. cit.*, pp. 54-58.

[44]See Sikalumbi Papers for letters between restricted ZANC men; and note Sikalumbi to (i) Bishop Frederick Jordan (African Methodist Episcopal Church), Fenner Brockway, Fox-Pitt, 20/5/59, (ii) Secretary, Movement for Colonial Freedom, 19/9/59; Clutton-Brock, 17/11/59.

[45]TI-FM/HDB, 9/5/72.

[46]TI-FM/AGZ, 27/2/69.

[47]Kaunda, *Zambia*, pp. 113-116.

⁴⁸*Ibid.*, pp. 109-111.

⁴⁹RH 103/2: Kaunda to Fox-Pitt, 20/3/59; and to Michael Scott, 3/4/59, for Governor's statement.

⁵⁰Sokoni Papers: 'Part Two of Three Memorandums of N. Rhodesia, prepared for PAFMECA Conference by K. D. Kaunda, President (until it was banned) of Zambia African National Congress' 4/4/59.

⁵¹*Zambia: Independence and Beyond* (Nelson, 1966), 36; and Centre of African Studies, Edinburgh: Leys Papers: Kaunda to Leys, 25/4/59 and 14/5/59 (by courtesy of Prof. Shepperson).

⁵²Sokoni Papers: Kaunda to S.A. High Commissioner from Detainees Camp, Kabompo, 23/4/59 (sent through his lawyer, Colin Cunningham).

⁵³NAZ: Historical MSS 35, Kaunda to McInnes, undated. The D.C. was E.C. Greenall.

⁵⁴Kaunda, *Zambia*, pp. 112-113.

⁵⁵RH 103/2: undated 'Sworn Memorandum' by Kaunda for the Commission 'to probe into the banning of the said Zambia African National Congress'. For the quotation from Moffat, see *NN*, 10/4/59.

⁵⁶Kaunda, *Zambia*, p. 100.

⁵⁷Sokoni Papers: Lusaka Criminal Case No. SP4295 of 1959, Regina v. Kenneth David Kaunda; the Police Superintendent was Jack Seed and the Sen. Superintendent was Roy Randall. The magistrate, Thomas Pickett, was appointed by President Kaunda as Chairman of Zambia's Electoral Commission soon after independence.

⁵⁸Kaunda, *Zambia*, p. 122.

⁵⁹*Ibid.* pp. 122-125.

⁶⁰Pp. 1 and 141, and *Africa Digest*, Vol. VII, No. 1, p. 1.

⁶¹*NN*, 8/1/59; and *Africa Digest*, Vol. VI, No. 6, p. 233 for reference to S.A. Pan-African Congress.

⁶²For events cited here, see *Africa Digest*, Vols. VI, No. 6, and VII, No. 1.

⁶³TI-FM/I. Macleod, London, 5/2/70.

⁶⁴*Rhodesia Herald*, 25/6/59. The two parties soon united, to form the United African Freedom Party.

⁶⁵ANC/CEO/OA/7, circular of 22/7/59; *Rhodesia Herald*, 28/7/59.

⁶⁶See Leg. Co. Order Paper, 29/7/59; and memoranda to the Race Relations Committee (in ANC files) from, e.g., Chief Musokantanda; John Gaunt, Atheneon Cafe, Chingola; Luanshya Indian Chamber of Commerce; five Greek-owned cafes; R. N. Rich, Lusaka; Mitchell's Farms, Livingstone; Race Relations Committee in Choma, Livingstone, etc.; and Gervase Clay, who said that the time had come 'to force tea-room proprietors to permit well-dressed and well-behaved Africans to enter'. If not they should (a) form a club or (b) remove themselves.

⁶⁷See footnote 30 *supra*.

⁶⁸Mulford, *op. cit.*, 103-106; and for citations here, see Ridley Report, Chapter X.

⁶⁹*Ibid.*, Chap. XVI and Chap. XI.

⁷⁰*NN*, 18/3/59 and 5/5/59 and TI-FM/Chilubi Islanders, 14/2/70. The D.C. was G. Walsh, the D.A., J. Sharp. The man who speared Sharp was Lumpa Chikoti.

⁷¹NAZ: KTQ 2/1, Chinsali Tour Reports, 4 and 12, 1958.

⁷²*Central African Examiner*, 24/4/59 and 20/6/59; see also *Manchester Guardian* 12/5/59.

⁷³For this paragraph, see *NN*, *CAP* July to October, 1959; and TI-FM/W. Sikalumbi, 7/11/71. See also ANC/CEO/OA/7 of 16/10/59—statement on 'the present state of ANC', by the new Secretary-General, J. E. Michello. Other names suggested for the new party were CHUNO (Charity, Hand, Unity Needed only) and KASIKA, the Bemba word for paddler (of the national canoe). The latter incorporated the first syllables of names like Kaunda, Kalichini, Kapwepwe, Kamanga, Sipalo, Sikalumbi. Sikalumbi rejected it, because he had once proposed Nkumbula as life president of ANC and now 'Harry is a name which stinks.' He therefore urged caution in respect of what would happen in a situation

'if some of the names incorporated in Kasika were later discredited'. (Sikalumbi Papers: letters, Kombe to Sikalumbi, 15/6/59; Sikalumbi to Kombe, 17/6/59.)
[74]*NN*, 12/9/59.
[75]Kaunda, *Zambia*, pp. 125-131.
[76]Legum, *Zambia*, p. 37, letter of Kaunda to Frank Barton.
[77]RH 103/2: Fox-Pitt to Catherine Hoskyns, 20/8/59; at which time the fund to help the Kaunda family stood at £187.8.11d.; and Fabian Colonial Bureau Papers.
[78]*NN*, 15/12/59, 25/12/59, 29/12/59.
[79]*Zambia*, 133-134.
[80]TI-FM/KK, 9/4/71; and for Chona's utterances, see ANC: 'Comment on the Answer to the Petition submitted . . . on 12 April, 1959', unreferenced, 4/10/59.
[81]RH: Fabian Papers, Chona to Lady Selwyn Clarke, 22/9/59.
[82]Kaunda, *Zambia*, 138-139.
[83]Hall, *Kaunda*, 29.
[84]From speech by Macmillan, Cape Town, January, 1960.
[85]Mpashi, *op. cit.*, p. 59.
[86]See *Report of the Advisory Commission on the Review of the Constitution of Rhodesia and Nyasaland*, (Monckton Report) October 1960—CMD. 1148, HMSO, p. 6.
[87]Sikalumbi Papers: Kapwepwe Circular from Mungu, 23/9/59.
[88]See NR *Hansard*, No. 99, 1960; and *Africa Digest*, Vol. VII, No. 5 (March 1960), p. 148.
[89]*CAP*, 18/11/59 and 4/12/59.
[90]Now a National Monument.
[91]Mpashi, *op. cit.*, p. 59.
[92]*NN*, 11/1/60; and 21/1/60 for quotation from the UNIP memorandum.
[93]*NN*, 16/1/60; and Kaunda, *Zambia*, 141.
[94]See B. Bunting, *Rise of the South African Reich* (Penguin, 1964), 205 and 174-5.
[95]Kaunda, *Zambia*, pp. 139-140; and *NN*, 1/2/60.
[96]UNIP Newsletter, Vol. II, (November 1959).
[97]RH 103/2: statement from UNIP Secretariat, (price 3d.) 1/12/59.
[98]*Black Government*, especially the Foreword, and pp. 5, 50 ff. and 99.
[99]*NN*, 1/2/60; The N.R. Eurafrican Association's Chairman was Aaron Milner, who later joined UNIP and was at one time Secretary-General to the Government.
[100]*African Mail*, 8/3/60; and see photograph in C. L. Vyas, *Flight of the Eagle* (NECZAM, 1970), after p. 34. According to Titus Mukupo (*Central African Examiner*, 19/7/60, p. 11) ANC announced the collection of 35,000 signatures while UNIP collected 305,000.
[101]TI-FM/IM, 5/2/70.
[102]*NN*, 12/3/60 and 26/3/60.
[103]Kaunda, *Zambia*, pp. 141-143.
[104]*NN*, 29/3/60, 30/3/60, 4/4/60, 5/4/60, 16/4/60.

11

Non-violence on Trial—
'A Flower in Seed'

Kenneth Kaunda's visit to America and Britain kept him away from Northern Rhodesia for over nine weeks from mid-April, 1960. Less than a fortnight before he flew out from Lusaka, Iain Macleod had publicly dampened African hopes for swift constitutional change and now events seemed to be tripping over one another in a dangerous stampede while men with loosened tongues were piling faggots for a grim conflagration. The decision to go abroad, uncertain when he would return, must have caused Kenneth much anxiety. As he boarded the plane in Lusaka and as it touched down again at Ndola on its flight to New York, via Elizabethville and Brussels, only small groups of UNIP members gathered to say farewell. 'Police told me I would be taken off the plane if there were any incidents,' he told a reporter. Pressed to outline his plans, he replied that he did not yet know what he was going to tell the Americans. Though it was even more dramatic for Dr. Hastings Banda to fly to America at the same time, so soon after his release from jail, Kaunda's country presented a graver problem. It was difficult for him to be as optimistic as Banda declared himself to be about the new regime at the Colonial Office. 'In my country,' he said, 'there are 72,000 settlers, while in Dr. Banda's country there are only 8,000.' 'I do not know whether Mr. Macleod will be bold enough to face up to the settler community in Northern Rhodesia.'[1] To such misgivings he had to add the passions of his people and the effervescent zeal of his party, which Simon Kapwepwe was to lead during his absence; and no less the passions of those white people who were increasingly responding to the utterances of John Gaunt. The ferment had meanwhile erupted in a number of schools widely separated throughout the territory.[2] Moreover, south of the Zambezi, 'security' had pounced on an economics lecturer in the University College in Salisbury and was keeping Terence Ranger and John Reed, editors of *Dissent*, under strict surveillance.[3]

The conflict in Northern Rhodesia was now the 'highly dangerous' one of 'two competing nationalisms', as UNIP had told Governor Hone on Christmas Eve, 1959;[4] a situation aggravated by the fact that, while before 1953 the military units stationed in the two Protectorates had consisted of 'mixed regiments only, such as the King's African Rifles, white-officered—by Rhodesians or Britons— but under the direct control of Whitehall, paid by the Imperial exchequer and subject to the immediate command of the British Governor', Churchill's Government had agreed, at the birth of the Federation, to the amalgamation of these units into the Federal Rhodesian Army, paid and directed by the settler Government in Salisbury.[5] The experiences of the African people in Nyasaland at the hands of units of this army, officered often by men who readily talked of 'Kaffirs', 'munts' and 'baboons', boded ill for Northern Rhodesia. Yet Kaunda was to insist unequivocally on 'non-violence' as the 'absolute principle' guiding the popular movement towards nationhood.

Kenneth's thought was early and profoundly influenced, as we have seen, by Mahatma Gandhi who illumined for him the personality and teaching of Jesus Christ. Until then, he had under- stood the Bible 'in a mission way'. Gandhi, he has said, 'helped me to understand Jesus, whom he himself almost worshipped'. Convinced that Jesus's statement that 'man cannot live by bread alone' was true, he saw 'non-violent positive action' as more than a formula for the attainment of national independence. 'I believe that man is moving towards perfection. When Jesus said, "Thy will be done on earth as it is in heaven", to me that is a statement of fundamental importance. God's kingdom is coming on earth, but He has left the whole programme to us, saying simply, "Do to others as you would have them do to you", giving us this guide, this tool, for use in man's long march to perfection, to the point in time when we begin to see God's kingdom on earth through man's behaviour to his fellow man. So this is now politics, real whole life that we are trying to improve; political, economic, social, cultural, scientific and technological life. Indeed, when we look at the millions of years behind us, I don't know at what time my seed was born; but it is a long, long march to where we begin to have some perfection. Yet we can't be despondent at this time, because we are receiving through all our commotions and conflicts a flower in seed, something better evolving. Yes, even from nuclear weapons we are receiving some good, out of our fear of each other. From the mouth of the lion some honey is coming.

'This is not to condone violence; but the fear of violence begins to show that non-violence is the only answer. Pacifists say that war is wrong, and I entirely agree. We must use all sorts of tactics to try to avoid war. But again, like Gandhi, if I had to choose between slavery and fighting for independence, I'd choose the latter. Violently, yes, I'd rather do that, though it may seem a contradiction. . . . For the way God made man was that He said, "You shall be free"—all-round freedom. So it is wrong for anyone to stand between man and the Creator who gave him all-round freedom. I'd rather die than accept to be a slave. So the question is: How non-violent is non-violence?' It is easy, Kaunda said, if you are dealing with a nation that has a conscience that can be troubled. 'But when we come to Portugal's role in Africa, I support freedom fighters with a very clear conscience. In Northern Rhodesia we had no right to train people to be anyone's cannon-fodder. In South Africa it is different. . . . My concept of non-violence is that it is the central thing; but because we've not yet attained perfection, we're bound to get lost . . . we haven't carried the weapon of non-violence far enough yet. We still tend to go the gun way. But the power of non-violence is there, perhaps like an iceberg whose top only has been seen so far, just as the atom was buried and unknown for so long. We are therefore still spending so much on destruction, so little on the investigation of the power of non-violence in human relations. Thus we rush towards the gun, to defend our independence.'

The dilemma for himself as a believer in non-violence was a conscious one, from before his election to the Presidency of UNIP. 'In Dar es Salaam,' he said, 'an Indian called Narayan told me that, as a disciple of non-violence, I must renounce leadership of my people.' 'It was a great problem for me and I thought about it, alone, for a long time. Then I decided that I wouldn't be right to judge that my fellow men were wrong to elect me as their leader, or that I should follow my own course outside party activities and Government activities. Anything that I wanted to help to do would be ineffective because people would not understand what I was trying to do. The best way for me would be to try to influence things from within the party and Government. Otherwise it would be taken as if I were deserting the people at a time when they might need my services. So I decided, in Dar es Salaam, that I'd certainly go where my people decided, and I have tried to do that ever since. ... For me, non-violence is the ultimate weapon. At the same time I realise that the situation we are dealing with is far from perfection, and the conflict demands that we refuse to sell our souls at all. This is why I find capitalism, of the west or of the east, completely unacceptable and why I consider state-capitalism in Zambia to be only a transition stage. For we must move towards a people's democracy in economic life as in political. ... In all this, non-violence is one of the good roads that lead out of the city of "Do unto others"—a good road, a hard road, with many ups and downs.'[6]

Kenneth Kaunda spoke these words to the writer twelve years after the period we are now reviewing. However, he had written, in *Black Government*, that he knew that all he could do was to 'make my policy of non-violence as widely known as possible and discipline severely any cases of unconstitutional action which came to my notice', claiming that he had recently had 'a prominent member of our party expelled for making inflammatory utterances'. On the other hand, the furore among white people over the Devlin Report's description of Nyasaland as 'a police state' proved to Kaunda that 'the European is never conscious of living in a police state.' 'There is no temptation for him to break the law while he basks in the warm sun of his superior power, his privilege and his wealth.'[7]

Just as Kaunda returned to the Protectorate from London, Welensky warned Macleod against making any concessions 'to a campaign of violence and intimidation by UNIP' and stated that 'between January and May, 84 office-bearers of this party had been convicted of 117 criminal offences, including attempted murder, riot, assaults on the police and public incitement to violence.'[8] It was, in Kaunda's view, cardinal to a mass movement that it should not be over-centralized, but this involved calculated risks should some tense local situation start a chain reaction, beyond the control of the officers in Lusaka. UNIP's opponents, however, wanted to lay full responsibility for any disturbances on the Party's national leaders, and the text on the cover of the Constitution: 'When we call the country to action, every man, woman and child shall follow our lead', seemed to imply a highly centralized control.⁹

As the situation simmered dangerously UNIP's 'top man' was far away. In the U.S.A. he met Moise Tshombe from the Congo province of Katanga, neither of them guessing how their future relations would develop; Dr. Martin King, whom he joined in a press conference; and Dr. Hastings Kamuzu Banda. 'I am sure that Dr. Banda was worried by rumours that I suffered from tuberculosis. Ronald Segal's book *Political Africa*, says I have twice been ill with TB, but I never have.' Kaunda found Banda 'very human indeed....' 'We shared a platform at the Freedom Day Rally, and were talking the same language.' The magazine *American Metal Market* spoke of Kenneth as the man 'likely to be the first African Prime Minister of Northern Rhodesia', while *Life* devoted a long illustrated article to his character and policies. Everywhere he affirmed that failure to effect major constitutional changes in his country by 1961 could lead to violence. His people were finding it 'incredibly difficult', he told a San Francisco audience, 'to maintain non-violence', He wanted 'no truck with bloodshed or with Communism', he declared. 'Our problem is practical, not ideological. We feel that we must and we will govern ourselves.'¹⁰

On 3 May, the Colonial Office announced that Macleod was willing to meet Kaunda, who had just declared that he had no bitter feelings against the British. He was still in America when Northern Rhodesia was shaken by the news of the killing of a woman, Mrs. Lilian Burton, by men who stopped her car on the road between Ndola and Mufulira, threw petrol over her in the presence of her children and set her alight. Mainza Chona declared at once that UNIP was against violence, but John Gaunt was already demanding the proscription of the Party which he described as 'the loathsome spawn of Zambia'.¹¹ On 8 May Dingiswayo Banda, UNIP's Provincial Chairman for the Copperbelt, had announced a public rally in defiance of a police ban, prior notice having been sent to the local Government officer concerned. Banda and his committee determined to defy the ban 'so that we could show that we were prepared to go to jail'. The Mobile Unit, however, swooped on this meeting at Chifubu near Ndola and a number of Party leaders were arrested. Immediately the situation became dangerous. The District Commissioner then read the Riot Act and the police charged the crowd with tear gas. It was believed that the men who killed Mrs. Burton had been among those fleeing the police. 'I was arrested with about 500 people about 10 a.m.,' Banda has recorded, 'and at 1.30 a European police officer came to me and said, "See you have killed a European woman because you cannot restrain your people", and I said, "How can you accuse me of that?" '[12]

As Kenneth was addressing a crowded press conference in London on 16 May, a journalist asked him whether he dissociated his Party from the Burton outrage. 'Only then', the journalist stated, 'did he learn from Mr Mainza Chona, his first lieutenant and deputy president of UNIP, that Mrs Burton was dead.' 'For the first and only time during a lively press conference Mr Kaunda was at a loss for words. He hesitated and then, with every sign of sincere distress, he said that he had no evidence who was responsible for the attack . . . but he very deeply regretted it. . . ."I want to go back to my own country as soon as possible to persuade as many people as possible to stick to our Party's policy of non-violence." ' Kaunda then said he believed that the ban on UNIP in the Copperbelt region might well provoke more indiscriminate violence. 'He said the restrictions placed on his district leaders would make it impossible for them to spread the gospel of non-violence.' He then announced that, when meeting the Colonial Secretary the next day, he 'would urge him to agree to the dissolution of the Federation and the formation of a new, predominantly black, government'.[13]

His opponents were not, however, moved. On hearing that Kenneth had wept while addressing the United Nations Committee on Decolonisation, John Roberts, the U.F.P. leader, referred to his 'crocodile tears'.[14] Governor Hone, in declaring UNIP an unlawful society, on the eve of a visit to the Protectorate by the Queen Mother, stated that the cause of the explosive situation was 'UNIP's defiant attitude . . . particularly in the Western [Copperbelt] Province, its deliberate flouting of the law regarding public meetings and its resistance to the police'. In America, reports had reached Kaunda that Europeans were 'buying more and more firearms', and demanding the Governor's resignation. It was not surprising therefore that his meeting with Iain Macleod was dominated by the issue of violence. The Colonial Secretary gave him what the *Northern News* called 'a blunt warning' over UNIP propaganda, and affirmed that there would be no constitutional change in 1960.[15] Macleod was very aware that one consequence of his own policy was the growth of 'a lot of feeling at the time that you virtually had to shoot your way to independence and then Britain would give in'. 'One of the reasons,' he said, 'that I pushed Tanganyika so quickly towards its independence was simply because there had been no disturbance of any sort there.' He made this point now to Kenneth in London with special force. 'Looking back,' he said: 'I may conceivably have put it in a way that made Kaunda feel I was less sympathetic than in fact he knew me to be. But I doubt it.' Kaunda shared the view that, despite the gravity of the crisis, Macleod and he understood each other.[16]

In Welensky's view, it was on Macleod's persuasion that Kenneth accepted a policy of non-violence. For he had hitherto consistently regarded UNIP's leader as a rabble-rouser. Recognising that 'real organising capacity was brought to the ANC' by Kaunda, Welensky went on to say that he had 'a strong line in mob oratory and in the vivid imagery that appeals to rural Africans'. 'Europeans were vultures hovering over the land to pounce on their African victims. Joining with the white man in Federation was like trying to share a small stool with someone with a big backside. . . . Huggins and I had our eyes on the Mwinilunga country where a mysterious mineral buried in the soil enabled aircraft to fly. . . . The fear-laden stories grew wilder as the months went by: I had ordered the African's sugar to be poisoned, so that African women might miscarry and African men become impotent; tins of meat contained human flesh, poisoned to break African opposition to Federation.' Welensky then added: 'Federation's enemies in Britain regarded this manipulation of medieval or dark age fears and hatred as enlightened democratic opinion.' Moreover, during the weeks prior to the elections in March 1959, he wrote, 'Benson, the inveterate opponent of Federation, found himself up against a different opponent, the Zambia African National Congress, whose leader, Mr. Kenneth Kaunda, made one inflammatory speech after another, in spite of the fact that he assiduously professed his belief in non-violence.'[17]

On 16 May, Kaunda issued a statement from London, reiterating what he had said as he left New York, adding these words: 'Violence, whatever its source, I condemn without reserve in that it leads to loss of LIFE, PROPERTY AND HAPPINESS, the very things we are trying to secure. I know the rude and provocative manner adopted by most white officials and police officers. Distant as I am from my country, I wish to appeal to my countrymen to refrain from any acts of violence . . . no matter how trying the circumstances.'[18] Meanwhile back at home, the Chief Secretary, Martin Wray, met a UNIP delegation, led by Kapwepwe. Wray answered the delegation's letter to the Colonial Secretary, which Kapwepwe submitted, by refuting allegations of bribery by the Special Branch and 'torturing of Africans . . . worse than the Gestapo methods', and by indicting UNIP as the promoter of lawlessness.[19]

Robert Burton and his daughters had gone to England very soon after Mrs. Burton's death. On 22 May, Kenneth Kaunda wrote a letter to him which merits quotation in full. 'Without the lead that you and the late Mrs. Burton gave us in Northern Rhodesia, and which you have continued to give us since she passed away,' he said, 'my sincerity of purpose and my strong feelings against such hooligan activities as led to the tragic death of Mrs. Burton alone could not have been sufficient to give me courage to write to you to express my personal as well as my Party's condolence to you and your children.

'Why had it to be Mrs. Burton? And why had it to be this way? Perhaps historians will give us their own interpretation of this; but whatever they write and say about this will be speculative. What is important is the lesson we all learn from your example that LOVE is by far a superior force to HATE. This is too costly a lesson to go unheeded by any of us in Northern Rhodesia. It is man's inherent weakness to learn only from tragedy.

'I do sincerely hope and pray that you will receive my message in the same spirit of wider understanding and LOVE as you have demonstrated to the entire world, and may I add that it came as a further consolation to me that you expressed yourself as confident in the future of NR. I feel encouraged to venture to say that I hope your children, after recovering from this shock, will also still regard NR as their home country.

'May God bless you and your children and may He ever be your guide as you pass through what must be your most trying period.'[20]

Three weeks later, Burton and Kaunda met in London and the *Northern News* quoted an extract from a letter Burton wrote to a friend in the Protectorate about the meeting: "I feel there is much to be learnt if you can get him to talk freely and provided you remember that all Africans are born schizophrenics." Kenneth's comment, when he arrived back in Lusaka, was that Burton 'behaved in a Christian manner which could scarcely have been expected of him in the circumstances'.[21] The other side of the agony was voiced bitterly, however, by Sikota Wina in the *Voice of UNIP*. 'After the unfortunate incident on the Copperbelt leading to the death of Mrs. Lilian Burton and the arbitrary banning of UNIP,' he wrote, 'hundreds of reports have reached National Headquarters of how Europeans hooligans there have launched a counter terror campaign. . . .' 'Africans walking or cycling on the streets in Kitwe and Chingola have been deliberately knocked down by European drivers. . . . Africans walking on the pavement are insulted by young miners and in five incidents literally spat at in the face. An African cycling home was stopped by three Europeans driving a car. The European hooligans, . . . shouting "FREEDOM", . . . assaulted him with a bicycle chain. So much fuss was made over Mrs. Burton—Funds, Monuments, Race Relations Institutes and all the rot while not a single line has been received from the Katilungus, Lewanikas and all the European Do-gooders, including Colin Morris, condemning European hooliganism. . . . It is a sad tragedy. So much has the indoctrination of the MASTER RACE gone deep that when a European is killed by Africans everyone is expected to shed tears of sorrow, but when an African is killed by Europeans it is all hush-hushed.' The *Voice* also published a telegram received from Kaunda and Chona in London, thus: "Will visit some African states as prearranged. Do not attend conference with Yamba Katilungu Chembe until they resign as M.P.s and Monckton Commissioners. Their cooperation with institutions of oppression identified them with oppressors."[22]

For Kaunda, still far from home, the question was whether
a new nation could rise from the present turmoil with non-violence
in its heart. Simon Kapwepwe's statement as Acting UNIP President
was therefore crucial. 'There are those in our ranks,' he said, 'who
will be speaking irresponsibly of bloodshed and violence. They
must be firmly told what our policy is. There are those in our ranks
who feel that, by throwing a stone at a passing car or burning a
particular building they are . . . revolutionaries engaged in revolutionary warfare. They must be told that they are working contrary
to the interests of 3,000,000 people. . . . The African people . . .
have entrusted their whole future to us and we have sworn that
we are leading them, not to death, but to a richer and more abundant
life. . . . This year we shall be taking our first major step in the
march to total FREEDOM and we are not leading corpses to this
freedom. . . . If we adopt the methods of violence against Settlers,
Government and our own African people, it is we ourselves who
will be the losers, morally and materially. . . . The power of
non-violence lies in ONENESS, TOGETHERNESS and complete
SOLIDARITY FOR ONE PURPOSE. . . . Let us be non-violent
in THOUGHT, WORD and DEED. This is the sincere appeal of
your own President KENNETH KAUNDA.' Six thousand copies
of Kapwepwe's circular were distributed throughout the country.[23]
But the wind of change was nearing gale force. Would the African
proverb be validated in respect of Kaunda's dream of a new society:
'A strong tree grows by the blowing wind.'?[24]

Another twenty-six days passed after Kenneth's meeting with
the Colonial Secretary before he arrived back in Lusaka. The plan
to visit a number of African countries was upset by his being
declared a prohibited immigrant in Kenya. He had hoped to fly
from Nairobi to both Addis Ababa and Dar es Salaam where he
would have met Julius Nyerere and attended a conference of
PAFMECA. Instead he was put on the first south-bound aeroplane,
which took him to Lusaka via Salisbury. Before he arrived home,
a police notice was published forbidding him, like other UNIP
leaders, from visiting the Copperbelt. 'I am now practically a
Prohibited Immigrant between South Africa and Kenya,' he said
at Lusaka airport. The ban on his entering the Gwembe valley was
still in operation. Two days later, addressing 1,500 people in Lusaka
under close police surveillance, he declared that Macleod 'showed

understanding—great understanding—and one thing I can announce is that the doors are still open for negotiation'. 'But,' he added 'if we have to negotiate with the British Government—and we must—we must show that we are responsible. . . . If I came out and told you everything with the Press present and informers all around . . . the Colonial Secretary would have to think twice before he asked me or anyone to go and discuss matters with him.' Responsible people in Britain were all aware that the present Constitution could not last 'for more than a year'.[25]

Harry Nkumbula's Congress, having joined UNIP in boycotting the Monckton Commission, at this time was making pronouncements on the territory's past and future very similar to those of UNIP. Nkumbula was therefore at pains to depict the break-away group as representative of a minority, led by 'power-hungry demagogues'. ANC had held its National Assembly in April, claiming an attendance of 15,000 'delegates and observers from 451 registered branches'. After declaring that he felt 'an earth tremor from Cape to Cairo and from East Coast to West Coast', Nkumbula claimed that the cry of the sons and daughters of Africa for freedom was worrying 'the forces of imperialism and capitalism'. 'European settlers all over Africa are living in fear. The missionary churches are worshipping hard,' while colonial governments were intensifying repression by 'more and more shootings' and 'more and more detention camps'. The rest of the speech was devoted to an attack on UNIP, 'an organisation which is European organised and financed in order to destroy the African National Congress and divide the Africans. . . .' 'They have no policy of their own', he said, 'only one thing they did not learn from Congress and that is the use of petrol bombs. . . .' 'We did not teach them to beat up the people who differed from them. . . . Arson is increasing in African housing areas; school buildings are also being burnt in many parts of the territory.' Nkumbula then claimed that 'in America and Northern Rhodesia Mr Kaunda . . . had several interviews with top officials of the Rhodesian Selection Trust and other financiers [who] tipped him as the most likely first African Prime Minister. . . .' 'In England they have started what they call "Kaunda Fund". . . . On April 10th, the press had reported that UNIP had 200 European members most of whom are churchmen. Before Mr. Kaunda formed a splinter group, he accused me of having European friends.' Nkumbula also blamed UNIP for the dismissal of hundreds of pupils from African schools.[26]

In view of the ferment in various schools, a special Commission of Inquiry had been set up. Its Report, published just as Kaunda returned, stated that: 'outside school bounds, office bearers and/or members of UNIP advised students, both singly and in groups to cause disturbance in their schools as a protest against the appointment of a UFP African Minister who they alleged was a "stooge" of the Europeans. . . . We have been urged to find that there is sufficient circumstantial evidence to justify . . . the conclusion that strikes were organised in the schools by a political party. On the contrary, we have insufficient evidence to support this theory . . . beyond a genuine suspicion. . . . We are nevertheless satisfied that the [UNIP] policy and the actions of certain of their members were indirectly responsible for the disturbances. . . . The very word "Freedom" which was shouted in almost every school represents opposition to authority and is one of UNIP's slogans.'[27]

On 21 July, the Bemba Paramount Chief, Chitimukulu, barred Kaunda from addressing meetings in his area and a rumour, immediately denied by the Chief Secretary, claimed that he had been arrested. Then came the news that Aaron Milner, Chairman of the Eurafrican Association, was bringing his members into UNIP. But much more publicity was being given to rumours of dissension in the Party, with Kapwepwe allegedly telling meetings in the Luapula Province, 'You can start forgetting Kaunda.' 'He is not a true Northern Rhodesian. His father was a Nyasalander.' Sikota Wina was also named by the *Northern News* as a challenger for leadership of UNIP. Kaunda, the paper said, was being blamed for retreating from his promise of independence by October; for coming back empty-handed from America and being pointedly snubbed by Macleod in London, and for rumoured secret talks with Sir Ronald Prain of the Rhodesian Selection Trust. Wina immediately issued a denial of this rumour, a denial confirmed by Kaunda the following month at a UNIP Conference.[28]

With his way blocked now into key areas of the country, Kaunda had to attempt to persuade his colleagues to accept a later date for self-government and to find ways of calling party leaders together from the provinces to strengthen contacts. Immediately the press gave prominence to UNIP's decision to accept 'a fresh "Freedom" date'. This, Kaunda had said, had been decided after extensive touring by Party leaders. Early in September there would be an Emergency Territorial Conference to test popular reaction to the leaders' willingness to make some compromise with Iain Macleod. Kenneth announced further that he and Sipalo had been ordered to leave Barotseland after making the first visit of UNIP leaders there. Indeed he claimed that Nkumbula had never visited either that region or the North-Western Province. Before being told to leave, the two men had been received by the Ngambela, 'Prime Minister' of the Lozi Kingdom, and the Kuta or royal council.[29] The late Princess Nakatindi recorded her memories of that visit and of receiving the UNIP leaders at her house. 'The Litunga, my uncle, had now agreed to the visit but people were still afraid to receive Kaunda,' she said. When Kaunda arrived, he was accompanied by a small band of UNIP musicians who carried a little generator with them and so, for the first time, there was a concert lit by electricity. After the holding of UNIP's first public meeting, word came that Kaunda's party must leave the area. Nakatindi, however, believed that 'the majority of the people favoured what Kenneth was doing', and 'many were impressed by his kindness and simplicity. . . .' 'He was fighting for people who were suffering under Federation.'[30]

UNIP's publicity team was increasingly energetic as the year went on. The *Voice* reported the appointment of Reuben Kamanga as the Party's representative in Cairo where UNIP was being 'accorded government status' already; it referred to Welensky's recent order of new weapons for the Federation valued at £3,000,000; cited a special UNIP pamphlet on the Congo; and carried a 'Presidential Message' from Kaunda. This message also referred to Federal military expansion and mentioned 'weapons which are said to be capable of cutting off a man's arm at a distance of 250 yards'. Such means of intimidation were, however, unable to overcome 'a determined and uncompromising populace.' 'We know,' Kaunda said, 'that the Welensky gang stinks with the rancid smell of a decaying Minor Dictatorship, while UNIP, the People's Own Movement, is as fresh as roses in bloom. . . .' 'We are not prepared to remain a valley of slavery while on all sides stand ridges of FREEDOM.' A few days after the issue of the August *Voice*, he announced the formation of a voluntary labour force to rebuild schools burned down in the Luapula Province by arsonists. The *Northern News* reported that 'men, women and children are turning up for work.' 'While men cut poles and make bricks, women cut grass for roofs and children carry bricks.'[31]

The Protectorate still had little to show, however, for the official Federal policy of 'partnership'. The crisis was instead rapidly worsening, though in a special UNIP pamphlet condolences were extended to all innocent victims of the Congo chaos, 'nationals of countries whose association with the Congo has been relatively recent, missionary workers and members of the Belgian community who have all along advocated a policy of sanity and freedom'.[32] Northern Rhodesia continued to practise a universal economic colour bar. On the Copperbelt, at the end of 1958, the average annual earnings of an African miner were £200, as against an average for Europeans of £1,699. The meaning of this was even more sharply illustrated by the fact that a white youth, aged 16 to 17 years, earned 23/8d per day while the minimum daily wage of an African working underground, and therefore earning more than a surface worker, was 7/6d. The maximum for long-service underground workers was 24/9d.[33] 'The African would have been gullible indeed to see partnership in a system that spends £6.2 million on the education of 1,036,000 black children and £6.1 million on 79,000 non-African ones.'[34] Could such a firmly entrenched system of privilege in the context of exploitation be changed by non-violent means?

With Welensky's military strength in a state of general alert, and supported by the territorial Police Force to maintain the position of what Lord Malvern had once called 'an island of white in a sea of black', UNIP's Emergency Territorial Conference opened in the Hindu Hall in Lusaka on 3 September. The programme offered delegates a number of 'conference slogans', in keeping with the practice inherited from ZANC. 'Our sole path to victory, is through sacrifice and consistency in sacrifice' was the first slogan, and the second took up the words of the American 'founding fathers' that Kenneth liked so much: "There is no safe repository of the ultimate powers of society but the people themselves." The third, no less of a strain on the memory, proclaimed that 'there is scarcely a single people in the world who, convinced, are unable by dint of faith, sacrifice and dynamic logic, to burst their chains in the face of their oppressors.' The key-note of the Conference was: 'Forward to Freedom Now—Long live President Kaunda—Long Live UNIP—Long live the People's Party'. As Kenneth Kaunda rose to address the Conference, he began by quoting the words of the Twenty-seventh Psalm: "The Lord is my Light and my Salvation; whom shall I fear? The Lord is the strength of my life; of whom shall I be afraid? When the wicked, even mine enemies and my foes came upon me to eat my flesh, they stumbled and fell." He then took up his main theme: the 'wind of change', as Harold Macmillan had called it, was in fact the 'WIND of FREEDOM . . . long known to the African'. It 'was born just at the same time as God made the first man'. It was now blowing strongly from the Congo, over Tanganyika and Nyasaland. 'This afternoon' it would blow over Southern Rhodesia, 'this evening over Angola and Mozambique, and next South Africa'. As Aggrey had said, Africa was a question mark, 'and only Africa is able to unearth these secrets' hidden in it.' So 'what right has a Frenchman to drop bombs on our soil?' This was a reference to the French Government's plan to stage a series of atomic tests in the Sahara.

'Independence now' was a just demand, Kaunda said, but 'we are so liberal that instead we have put forth proposals' for an interim Constitution. This would allow for a legislature of 58 elected members, apportioned thus: 44 Africans, 11 Europeans, 2 Asians, 1 Eurafrican. The Legal Ministry, Finance Minstry and Chief Secretaryship would be initially reserved for white officials, and the Governor would retain the right of veto. 'Does this mean blackmanism?' 'Does it mean barbarism?' he asked. 'We have done this because we do not wish to make the same mistake that Welensky made when he did not consider African fears.' The duplicated draft of UNIP's Constitutional Proposals incorporated a statement of 'fundamental rights' which included 'the right to freedom of peaceful assembly and association, . . . the right to form political parties and trade unions, . . . freedom of opinion, conscience and religion . . . the right to own property . . . and to receive free education.' 'No one shall be subject to arbitrary arrest, detention or exile . . . [or] be deprived of his liberty save in accordance with law.' It was now for the Conference to decide on its plan of action, said Kaunda. But, he added, 'We shall never raise an

axe, spear or any weapon against a white man.' 'I know they have
built concentration camps. What I say is let us fill these camps non-
violently and force them to build more and use up all the money
and this will force them to resign. If we must suffer, we must suffer
with dignity. . . . Lastly I wish you to join me in that big shout.
I know Welensky is on leave in Cape Town so let us shout and
make him know that something big is happening in Lusaka.
FREE . . . DOM AFRICA!'[35]

The UNIP Conference was not long over when Duncan Sandys,
Britain's Commonwealth Relations Secretary, visited Lusaka.
Kaunda and Kapwepwe met him, as did Nkumbula and the U.F.P.
leaders. Kaunda scrupulously refused to divulge the conclusions
of the meeting with Sandys despite the presence, outside the
Secretariat Building, of a large crowd of singing and dancing UNIP
supporters who greeted him lustily as he emerged at the front
door. With police permission, he spoke briefly but insisted that,
in the presence of journalists 'it would be wrong for me to reveal
the secret talks between me and the Northern Rhodesia Government.' Two weeks later he announced that he had cancelled his
plan to present a petition to the Colonial Secretary, calling for a
'democratic constitution' immediately. Macleod, whether influenced
by advance notice of Monckton's recommendation of a new
Constitution for the Protectorate or whether carrying out his own
earlier decision, had just announced that constitutional talks
would take place at the time of the Federal Review Conference,
and so there was no need for Kaunda's trip to London. Macleod's
announcement has been described by Hall as 'a landmark in Zambian
history [because] for the first time, African pressure had scored
a political victory over the settler population'. For Roberts, as the
Central African Mail said, it signalled the 'twilight of his political
career'. 'It cut the ground from beneath the middle-of-the-road
forces led by Sir John Moffat . . . [who] now lost for ever many
Africans who had been impressed by his trenchant attacks on
Federation and feared to align themselves with UNIP in case
it was banned.'[36]

Monckton's Report, which was outstripped by events before
being published, pleased no one. Kaunda flayed it as fearful of
displeasing Welensky. Welensky's anger at British machinations
was fanned by Monckton's pronouncement on secession for, he

claimed, Macmillan had 'said with emphasis that the British Government had no intention of making an extension of the Commission's terms of reference to include secession'. *East Africa and Rhodesia* echoed his reaction to Monckton's 'strong tributes to the Federation coupled with proposals for its destruction'.[37] As spokesmen of the settler community became more passionate, Kaunda spoke of the possibility of a battle of white versus white for Federal or Independent rule in Northern Rhodesia. Should British troops have to be deployed to counter Welensky's possible use of Federal forces to block a democratic constitution, 'UNIP members should give non-violent backing to the British forces.' If Welensky 'did a Boston Tea Party', Europeans in the territory should join hands with UNIP. Africans should help the British 'by not making tea'. It was, however, a time for confidence. 'Today I am a happy man. Tomorrow I hope I will be a very happy man.' 'The day after tomorrow I hope to be the happiest man,' he said, referring to the British decision to open fresh constitutional talks. 'U.F.P.' now meant the 'United Finishing Party', while UNIP had added thirty-eight Europeans, 'doctors, lawyers, professional and business men and women' to its ranks. He would not name them yet for, he said, 'We do not want them to be intimidated.' Meanwhile the tumult of the time was seen in a sudden proliferation of white political parties, each hoping to be given a voice at the forthcoming talks in London.[38]

As various people responded to the likelihood of swifter change by making new political alignments, white extremists suddenly gained a new ally in the man who had represented Kaunda at his trial in 1959 and who had acted as administrator of the relief fund for his family while he was in jail. Colin Cunningham, the Lusaka lawyer, announced at a pro-Federal meeting in Kitwe, that funds were being collected to send a delegation to Britain to speak on television and hold public meetings. This new organisation came to be known as the 'F.F.F.', the Federal Fighting Fund, sometimes referred to as the Federal Fighting Force. It pledged maximum support for Welensky and resistance 'to all opposition by any means within their power'. It was committed also to combating Communism, countering 'intimidation', supporting 'law and order' and demanding the establishment of a Federal police force. This meeting was described in the *London Dail Mail* under the headline

'Settlers run Mad'. Nearly 1,000 Europeans were present and 'pound notes were flung into buckets' for the new fund. 'Mr Cunningham called African politicians "dirty agitators". '39

Despite the pressures of his office and the various local bans upon him, Kaunda toured extensively in the dry months of 1960. His wife accompanied him to the Northern Province and had a period of rest at Lubwa while he was moving through the area. It was after her return from Lubwa that Betty learned of Kenneth's plan for her to attend a four-month course in home economics at the Mindolo Ecumenical Foundation. In order to let her take a full part in the course, he arranged for her to carry only their youngest child, Kaweche, while the other children stayed in Lusaka in the care of his nephew, Ernest Muwowo. 'Before the course ended,' Betty has recorded, 'my husband wrote saying that my child Masuzgo had been seriously ill but that he was well again.' 'He said he did not tell me this while the child was ill, as he did not want to upset my work.'40

While Betty was away, Kenneth was particularly busy not only with the preparation for the Territorial Conference but with the increasing pace of negotiations with the Government and the Colonial Secretary. He was taking great pains to persuade people everywhere of the feasibility of what he called a 'well-oiled' campaign of non-violent political action. He has described the message he gave his followers thus: 'Today, you have Special Branch men and women following wherever you go as if you were criminals; today you stand the chance of being sent to jail for shouting slogans like "FREEDOM NOW"; today you are liable to be deported from your own home for the "offence" of telling your people this was their country and it was their birthright to rule themselves. This is where we stand today. The terrible stories that have been written about struggles in India, Egypt, Ghana, and other countries that were once upon a time ruled by Britain, are taking place right here. . . . I wish to repeat what I said when in exile in Kabompo: that British imperialists never exile or imprison political fools. . . . Now in a situation like ours where the oppressor is armed to the hilt, the oppressed, before man discovered the comparatively new method of passive resistance, had either to succumb to oppression or come out in open revolt against it. . . . Succumbing to oppression is undignified and unworthy of any self-respecting man. On the other hand, open revolt often leads to the killing of countless people, those very people for whom freedom is sought. So we resort to the third method—the method of passive resistance or non-violent methods plus positive action. . . . This type of move-ment obviously calls for extensive coaching and very often results come after a long time, and this needs much more discipline that an open revolt. But the fruits of this training stand the participants in good stead when they take over the reins of government. This is the method we have chosen. We have no intention at all of making our people cannon-fodder for colonialist guns.'[41]

As the time for the Constitutional Conference in London drew near, UNIP was in good heart. ANC's membership was stagnant, while UNIP was growing at the rate of over twenty-five new branches per month. Indeed Government was concerned that the number of registered branches had risen from 28 to 482 between April and December. Three hundred and five of these were in the Luapula Pro-vince, which therefore was kept under the closest surveillance by the Government.[42] The image of UNIP at home and abroad was thus impressive as its delegates set off for the talks in London on a new Northern Rhodesia Constitution. The growth of the Party had not, however, been matched by sound financial supervision. The unhappy legacy of peculation that had bedevilled the old united ANC was now apparent in a number of provincial and district treasuries. Without a number of generous donations from sympathisers abroad[43] and a few such gifts from within the country, the position could have caused considerable anxiety.

In response to the personal plea of Iain Macleod, Kaunda had agreed to attend the Federal Review Conference which began on 5 December. Until the previous day, UNIP had been proclaiming a boycott. Kaunda 'went unwillingly, because I could see no point in reviewing a Federation which I and my party were committed to destroy'.[44] However, like Hastings Banda, he considered it import-ant to keep in touch with Macleod, who was, as it were, walking a tight-rope between fierce pressure from Welensky and massive African opposition to all that he stood for. In Macleod's own words: 'I wanted to see what in fact happened, that the two sides emerged with the Governor holding a somewhat narrow balance, while Kenneth Kaunda and his people learnt their business as politicians and then as statesmen.'[45] The new round of negotiations began against a back-cloth of continued strife in the Congo; of Welensky refusing to allow any attempt to 'bleed the Federation to death'; of Sipalo warning that the continuance of ruthless government would turn all whites into 'potential refugees'; while Sir John Moffat warned of civil war if Federation continued and Colin Morris declared just before leaving his Chingola pulpit for full-time political work, that only Moffat had the stature to win the trust of all races.[46]

'The Federal Review Conference . . . was fruitless,' as Hall has said, 'except in so far as it demonstrated to the British Government the complete lack of common ground between the nationalists and the Federationists.' It was adjourned early, *sine die*, after the 'big three of the anti-Federation cause, Banda, Nkomo and Kaunda', had walked out.

December had seen an unprecedented spate of political telegrams and despatches between Lusaka and London. Harry Nkumbula's supporters had been shocked that Kaunda and Chona had placed 'the burden of representing us in the hands of Dr Banda'. One telegram to Nkumbula read: 'YOU CARRIED ASSEGAI SHIELD COFFIN STOP SPEAR WELENSKY'S FEDERATION STOP PUT IT IN THE COFFIN AND BURY IT STOP . . . WE DENOUNCE BANDA'S PATERNALISM OVER N. RHODESIA STOP KAUNDA A SELL-OUT MUST GO TO NYASALAND WITH BANDA.' The Christmas Eve issue of ANC's *Week by Week* took the attack on Kaunda farther by claiming that, in a statement to 'Contact' the previous week, he had given assurances about the future of the copper mines which were tantamount to giving the mines away. 'We are the Government-in-Waiting,' said *Week by Week*.[47]

The Post Office was kept busy with an even greater flow of telegrams and letters from UNIP supporters to their London delegates. Moreover Solomon Kalulu had promised that 'seventy telegrams' would go to Macleod, all demanding 'African majority rule now'. One such message from the Euro-African Association denounced attempts 'by British Imperialists' to separate them from their 'blood brothers and sisters, the African people'. Another ran thus: 'WORLD TIRED WITH FRICTIONS WE HUMBLY . . . REQUEST YOU TO GRANT DEMOCRATIC GOVERNMENT'. Another declared: 'ENTIRE YOUTH OF ZAMBIA BEHIND

KAUNDA STOP REMEMBER OUR LUSAKA AIRPORT DEMONSTRATION DURING YOUR MARCH VISIT STOP VITALITY OF OUR YOUTH AND VIGOUR WILL ENABLE KAUNDA TO GAIN OUR GOAL EVEN IF YOU FAIL HIM. . . . THE BATTLEFIELD IS ON THE SACRED SOIL OF ZAMBIA.' Alex Shapi of the Luapula Province cabled Kaunda: 'EVERYBODY KNOWS LUAPULA IS KEN AND KEN IS LUAPULA', while the Barotse Anti-Secession Movement declared: 'OUR MOVEMENT SUPPORTS INDEPENDENCE FOR AN UNSPLIT ZAMBIA STOP CRASH [sic] WELENSKY WE FIX MWANAWINA.' The Revds. Jonas Sinyangwe and Kingsley Mwenda of the United Church told Macleod of the Church's 'SUPPORT FOR KAUNDA OVER SECESSION AND MAJORITY RULE'.[48]

Home from the Conference, Kaunda set off at once to tour extensively. In Kitwe, on his return from the north-west, he told a crowd of seven thousand that 'nothing, not even troops' could now stop the march to freedom. He thanked them for heeding his appeal 'to remain calm, dignified, non-violent in thought, word and deed'. In 1961, he said, 'we shall get the government majority'.

At the National Council, held soon afterwards, Kaunda declined to divulge what had happened round the conference table in London beyond confirming that when he, Banda and Nkomo had walked out of the Federal Review, 'Chiefs Chikwanda, Ikelenge, Mapanza and Undi and also the independent Bwana L. Ng'andu' had walked out with them. UNIP, he said, was 'heading for responsibility to safeguard the interests of all . . . power as an instrument to bring happiness to the common man.' Delegates should therefore bear in mind the coming new role of Parliament and the Civil Service. He then heard that the Party's paid-up membership in the land, excluding the Southern Province and Barotseland, for which no figures were produced, was 154,573, of whom 69,277 were in the Luapula Province and 39,944 in the Northern Province. He closed the Council with the words: 'We must forget our individualism and put the Nation before us. The Party is sumpreme.'[49] UNIP had meanwhile issued a policy statement on the judiciary in a self-governing state which pledged UNIP to preserve 'the law and the courts . . . inherited from England', and 'to enshrine in the permanent constitution provisions dealing with the independence and freedom of the judiciary'.[50]

Two days later Kenneth addressed a message to European civil servants which provoked an angry comment from Malcolmson of the U.F.P. It was 'impudent' of the President of UNIP, who did not even have a seat in the Legislature, to talk as though the results of the constitutional conference were a foregone conclusion. The message was written, however, on the assumption that 'Africans will shortly be in substantial control of the Northern Rhodesia Legislative Council' which would be 'a transitional stage only, leading to independence'. 'I am aware,' Kaunda wrote, 'that some, if not most, of the European civil servants of the Territory are very concerned about their future.' 'I, too, am concerned because, although it is the declared policy of the United Independence Party [*sic*] to push forward with the appointment of local officers and to put an immediate end to discrimination in recruitment and promotion in the service . . . this process can only be a slow one. . . . Both in the transitional stage and after we have attained self-government, we shall need considerable numbers of European civil servants to help us to continue and speed up the development of the country.'[51] UNIP was giving prominence now to its European membership, and Kenneth had already addressed 'five Community meetings in the European residential areas', according to the *Voice*.[52]

Faced with the U.F.P. boycott of the discussions about a new Constitution for Northern Rhodesia, Macleod began a round of private consultations with the various groups who had come to the Conference. These may indeed have influenced his thinking by suggesting to him that Moffat's Liberal Party was stronger than in fact it was. Kaunda felt that in this way, 'Macleod seemed to do a deal with the Liberals behind our backs.' His intial reaction that, despite the boycott, things were 'going quite favourably' thus gave way to anger and fear. Not only was the Federal Party's boycott supported by the Dominion Party, but both bodies were engaged in intense propaganda in Britain, with the full support of a number of well-known Conservatives and notably of Lord Salisbury, the leader of both the Rhodesia and the Katanga lobbies in Westminster. Thus a motion censuring the Colonial Secretary was signed by sixty-five M.P.s in the Commons.[53] Macleod's sympathy with the cause of Banda, Nyerere and Kaunda could not be concealed, and he described his dilemma vividly thus:

'Perhaps I should have told Kenneth a little more of what I planned for the future of Northern Rhodesia . . . that it was my belief that the facts of life would inevitably make an African majority emerge. But I didn't feel like doing this. . . . It would have been difficult to have picked one leader out and taken him more deeply into my confidence than the others. . . . I would have had to say something of the same thing to Welensky and then of course he would have set out to sabotage the exercise. In some ways I wished I had talked to Kenneth a little more at the time.'[54]

Because Macleod could not reveal his inner thinking to him, Kenneth felt that the situation was now worsening and on 9 February made a remark which evoked widespread fierce reactions. 'Should Welensky and the British Government continue to frustrate the legitimate aspirations of the African people . . . a mass rising might result . . . which would make Mau Mau seem like a child's picnic.' Mau Mau was still a fresh memory in Britain and in Africa. The Congo situation was, however, much nearer in place and time, and the past weeks had been marked by constant reports of fighting, the proliferation of armed bands, hundreds of thousands of starving refugees, while the United Nations action ran from trouble to trouble, and South African pilots were being recruited for the Katangan Air Force. The *Northern News* and certain British newspapers reported Kaunda's words as 'a threat'. In his autobiography he has expressed his own position thus: 'As far as I was concerned, Mau Mau meant not only a massacre of white people by black people, but also a massacre of blacks by whites. Over the previous months, the Europeans of Northern Rhodesia, encouraged by Welensky and his Northern Rhodesian leader, John Roberts, had been behaving in a manner likely to cause tension and crisis. Troops had openly carried arms in the streets. The gun shops on the Copperbelt were doing a roaring trade in firearms to the European population. Had my people not behaved themselves more decently than the whites, a single incident could have resulted in mass shootings of Africans by panicky white settlers. Would not then Mau Mau have looked like a child's picnic?' But it was reported that Kaunda had been 'carpeted' by Macleod who was 'said to have rebuked Mr Kaunda vigorously', and the UNIP leader, said the *Northern News*, 'apparently realised that he had made a psychological error' and 'was at pains to emphasise his wish to avoid trouble'. Kenneth, however, insisted that the arming of Europeans and the repeated raids by the Police Mobile Unit on village and urban communities were creating a highly dangerous state of affairs. But Hall quotes him as having sought at once to quieten widespread fears by saying in a message to his people, that, however much angered by Welensky, 'we must never do anything which could make posterity ashamed of us. . . .' 'I have repeatedly denounced secret societies [and] I do so now again.'[55]

Welensky's reaction, whether premeditated or not, was to call up two white battalions in the Protectorate three days later. The London Conference had clearly failed and was dissolved on 17 February. Welensky then called up four white battalions in Southern Rhodesia and 'it was known in Lusaka government circles that he had plans to arrest the Governor and the Judiciary; [and] a list of "anti-Federation Europeans" who should also be detained by the troops was drawn up by the U.F.P.' Then, on Welensky's orders, all the five U.F.P. Ministers in the Northern Rhodesia Government resigned. The evidence certainly supports the view that Welensky at this period was seriously contemplating 'a Boston Tea Party', a unilateral declaration of the independence of his Central African state. But there was news that Britain had put troops and military aircraft in Kenya in a state of alert, and, though Welensky claimed later that Harold Macmillan told him personally that 'we were collecting them there in case you needed help', this undoubtedly influenced Sir Roy's decision to go no further. Like the Canberra bombing plane that had flown, on his behalf, over Nyasaland in 1959, his sabre-rattling had only served to heighten the sense of general insecurity.[56]

A patch-work Government of Liberals and Officials took over in the Protectorate after the U.F.P. resignations. Almost immediately Macleod's famous 15-15-15 scheme was presented to the House of Commons on 20 February, just after Welensky had proclaimed his readiness to use force to maintain the Federation, and it seemed to make possible an anti-Federation majority in the Legislature. The Colonial Secretary's 'ambiguous proposals' have been summed up thus by Mulford: 'Macleod's proposals called for a Legislative Council of forty-five elected members, up to six official members and such nominated members as the Governor might appoint on instructions from the British Government. Among the elected

members, fifteen would be returned from single-member constituencies, by upper roll voters, fifteen from single-member constituencies by lower roll voters, and fifteen from National constituencies
by both rolls voting together. Candidates in National constituencies
would be required to qualify for election by obtaining the same
prescribed minimum percentage of the votes cast on each roll;
their overall support would also be expressed as a percentage
figure, calculated by averaging together their respective proportions
of votes on the upper and lower rolls. Each of the three sets of
constituencies was to extend over the entire Territory; upper roll
constituencies concentrated predominantly in urban areas, lower
roll constituencies centred mainly in the rural areas.' *The Economist*
described the 15-15-15 plan as achieving 'parity of abuse' which
would beget 'a quaint new Legco' as a constitutional 'anachronism'.[57]

At once the Federal leaders began to exploit both Macleod's
declared openness to other suggestions 'within the framework
and general spirit of the White Paper', and also Welensky's private
discussions with the British Prime Minister. ANC's leader was
meanwhile jailed for nine months on losing his appeal against
conviction of a charge of dangerous driving, and Katilungu, acting
as President, was allowed to fill Nkumbula's place in the Legislature.
As part of his drive to revivify Congress, Katilungu began a series
of negotiations with Tshombe of Katanga which helped to swell
ANC's coffers and also laid the foundation of what UNIP called
the 'unholy Alliance' of Congress, Tshombe and Welensky. UNIP
was also anxious to strengthen its external alliances and so Kaunda,
on his way back from London, had paid a personal visit to Damascus,
where he met the Egyptian President, and to Addis Ababa.[58]

In the United Arab Republic, support for UNIP from President
Gamal Nasser's regime had been developing as a result of the work
of the Party's ambassador in Cairo, Reuben Kamanga. Though
Ethiopia was far from being a modern democracy, Emperor Haile
Selassie was also showing an interest in the birth of the independent
African states and indeed his capital would later become the headquarters of the Organisation of African Unity. Though the immediate
fruits of northward and eastward links might be few for a self-
governing Northern Rhodesia, in the long run such a policy ought
to yield dividends. Indeed Hastings Banda had recently said he
hoped 'to see the day when Dar es Salaam is the capital of the

United States of Central Africa'. Ethiopia had already been associated with pan-Africanist occasions such as the Monrovia Conference of Independent African States in 1959 and had played host to a second such assembly in 1960. Kaunda's visit to the Emperor brought forth a quick response of sympathy. Haile Selassie's gift was '4,000 Ethiopian dollars or about £1,000'. When Kaunda reported in Lusaka on the audiences he had been granted in Damascus and Addis Ababa, he appeared 'grubby and dishevelled'. He had bought a vehicle in Dar es Salaam and driven it down the rough road to Lusaka. 'I wanted to drive,' he told a news reporter, 'because physical exertion helps mental relaxation.' He had been anxious to meet Nasser and Haile Selassie to ask them, as members of the United Nations, to be ready to put the African case to the world body, should the situation deteriorate.[59]

Another meeting of UNIP's National Council was held on 4 April, with fifty-five national and divisional officials attending. Colin Cunningham's 'Federal Fighting Fund' was described by Kaunda as 'Fifteen Fighting Fools'. Reports from the provinces included news of the unsuccessful attempts of Dixon Konkola and Huggins Chewe to organise a 'Republican Party' in Mporokoso and Luapula Districts. In a heated speech, Kaunda described as 'satanic' reports to the press by UNIP members about dissensions within the Party. He then took leave of the Council in order to prepare for a brief visit to the United States. But before his departure he signed a letter to the Chief Secretary listing cases of alleged victimisation and oppression of UNIP members in the Northern Province. One such allegation was that Andrew Mutemba, Northern Divisional Secretary, had been 'sent to prison for keeping Mr Kaunda in his house'. There were 'frequent mass arrests' and 'sometimes people, including pregnant women, [were] made to run as long as 10 miles, their offence being belonging to UNIP.'[60]

This second visit to America was again in connection with the celebration of Africa Freedom Day in New York. Though he was in the United States only from 8 to 12 April, he had an interview with President John Kennedy 'who pledged support to UNIP's freedom struggle'. Moreover 'his TV appearance at which he spoke of his country's future, made a very great impression, judging from the flood of congratulatory messages that poured in after the programme.' Arthur Wina's *News Survey* reported that Kenneth had 'announced that in the event of his failure to obtain majority rule . . . his alternative would be simply to resign his position and to allow other people with other methods to try whether theirs are better suited . . . in a situation where persuasion and non-violence methods appear unsuitable'. From New York, Kenneth flew to London as guest of UNIP's London Committee. Again, he had only three days to spare, but he met Iain Macleod and impressed on him why UNIP was so disappointed with the 15-15-15 scheme. Macleod 'showed signs of the strain he experienced during the deadlock of the constitutional talks', Kaunda observed. But their discussion gave grounds for guarded optimism for the outcome of renewed consultations in Lusaka. The London Committee's *Voice of Zambia*, which gave this account of his visit also reported a sympathetic resolution tabled at the sixteenth session of the United Nations General Assembly calling for the 'rapid development of Northern Rhodesia towards independence on the basis of a democratic constitution and at the rate desired by the people of the country through their true representatives'. Significantly 'even Sir Stewart Gore-Browne, pioneer settler, propertied politician and veteran of World War I and indeed one of the fathers of Federation, has deemed it wise to join UNIP.'[61]

The exhilaration of such reports was sustained by a gathering of '1,000 people of all races who crammed Ndola's Hindu Hall' to hear Kenneth Kaunda, soon after his return from London, describe a new dynamic economic programme which would be strengthened by checking the flow of money abroad through the B.S.A. Company's mineral royalties and ploughing it instead into development, including rail links from Kapiri Mposhi to Mpulungu, the country's port on Lake Tanganyika, and to Dar es Salaam. At a predominantly European gathering in Kitwe, he said that, though UNIP was not 'a party of angels', his listeners must give credit for the response of African people to appeals for calm 'in face of [sic] the great provocation from the guns of Sir Roy'. The audience cheered when he added: 'These guns . . . went back to Salisbury covered with shame.' At about the same time Kaunda issued two circulars. One of these denounced 'frustrated small men' who were 'planning not only to . . . cause disunity . . . but to cause bodily harm to UNIP members. . . .' 'We appeal to the authorities not to allow any thuggery to go unchallenged,' he concluded. His other circular asked Party organisers to avoid holding meetings on Sunday mornings and 'upsetting Church work or leaving out a considerable number of our followers who are Christian'.[62]

Despite the optimism of Kaunda's exposition to people of all races, of UNIP's design for the nation, suspicion was increasing ominously that efforts were being made to tamper with the already barely acceptable 15-15-15 scheme. Sir John Moffat warned solemnly that any such alteration could bring chaos. An announcement of the final scheme was expected in mid-June from Macleod, when, in Hall's words, 'Welensky sent Greenfield and Evans to London with instructions to influence the percentage basis for the fifteen national seats at all costs.' Suddenly the sky clouded ominously. Kaunda cabled Macmillan to insist that Africans would never accept 'the Sandys–Welensky formula' and the imposition of it would 'mean ruling at gun-point'. Perhaps the delay in resolving the constitutional tangle after Macleod's announcement in February had been due to the fact that the scheme had presented all concerned with a task of mathematical computation outside the normal capacity of politicians. It was when Kaunda and UNIP were increasingly aware of the subtle complexity of the scheme that they found an unexpected ally with a special gift for tackling such riddles.

Malcolm G. Clarke was a teacher at Munali Secondary School, an atheist innately in sympathy with the cause of the underdog. He held degrees in classics and mathematics, and had an outstanding ability both to grasp and expound the most abstruse mathematics. On examining the 15-15-15 scheme as modified under Welensky's pressure, he decided at once that it would effectively block majority rule and that the leaders of UNIP should be advised of this. The result, for him, was that Kaunda invited him to appear on the platform at a UNIP meeting. In consequence, he was warned by the Government's Chief Establishment Officer that he would face the prospect of dismissal if he repeated such an act. Some time later, Clarke was 'forced to resign his post', in Kaunda's words, 'by those in power today'. In commending him, early in 1962 to the Malawi Congress Party, Kenneth said that Clarke had 'proved himself as one of our best men among our European members'.[63]

It was before Macleod's announcement at the end of June but when the rumours of crucial alterations to his constitutional scheme were rife that Kaunda, in a black and purple toga, addressed a rally at Kitwe and announced in a 90-minute speech, a 'master plan' to end the territory's association with the Federation. He gave the British Government until 8 July, the date of UNIP's Annual Congress, to 'explain its intentions'. Though he revealed no details of the 'plan', he made certain important remarks about it. 'Remember,' he said, 'that we control the kitchens, the mines, the airways, the shops . . . everything in Northern Rhodesia. . . .' 'It is possible for us to bring everything in Northern Rhodesia to a standstill.' But, he insisted, 'we do not intend to raise a finger at any man or raise a stone or spear . . . .' 'Whatever we do, we shall do in a non-violent way. We believe in God and in the right of his people to determine their own destinies . . . we in UNIP follow the Mahatma Gandhi way. . . . But. . . . the British Government must be warned that there is a limit to what human nature will endure. . . . If our non-violence fails . . . they will have to deal with another set of leaders who have to speak the language that they, the British, may understand. . . . If U.F.P. rumours come out true, we shall be obliged to implement our FIVE POINT PLAN immediately. It is this:

(1) We will step up our anti-Federation campaign to clip Welensky's wings so that he can fly at ordinary level.
(2) Already we are consulting our constitutional experts on
    (a) What legal right has the Federal Government to stop Northern Rhodesia's constitutional development?
    (b) What are our constitutional rights and privileges as a protected people? Northern Rhodesia is a protectorate by treaties—which we believe Britain must now tell us whether she is to honour or annul them.
(3)
    (a) Prime Ministers and Presidents of some Commonwealth countries are being asked to use their good offices.
    (b) We have directed our US representative to solicit immediate support among Afro-Asian members by warning them of a possible constitutional crisis here and asking them to use their good offices at the United Nations.
(4) We are going to Accra to ask leaders of Africa to help us dismantle this federation in the same way as they are helping undo the South African Verwoerd regime.

(5) We will be obliged to press the British Government for a
    clear date for our complete internal self-government and
    independence.'[64]

Eight days later, Macleod presented to the House of Commons
what appeared at first to be a reissue of his February proposals.
There was little variation from the proposals of 21 February,
except as regards the national seats, but here the changes were
crucial. Candidates would be required to obtain $12\frac{1}{2}$ per cent or
400 votes, whichever was less, of the votes cast by both races.
In the national seats, there would never be more than 3,000 votes
cast by whites, so to qualify an African candidate would need
$12\frac{1}{2}$ per cent (about 375 votes)—which would be an insurmountable
hurdle. On the other hand, there would be a total of at least 10,000
African votes in each national constituency, so that European
candidates would only need 400 votes—which was four per cent.
'There were numerous other details which made the Constitution
the most mystifying ever imposed on a British dependency, but
they were all insignificant when set against the qualifying percentage
rule'.[65]

In retrospect, Macleod was able to claim some justification for
his action from the fact that the final result was not in fact a victory
for Welensky. 'I never dreamed that this constitution would last. . . .
We were trying to get these two contestants, Kaunda and Welensky,
into the ring, and this was an immensely difficult task. The constitution that got them there was never thought of, certainly by me,
as final. And this, I think, with respect, is where the more academic
studies of the 15-15-15 proposals fall down. Of course it was a
ludicrous conception. Indeed I've said so . . . but it was by no means
a ludicrous conception to settle the issue which it did settle. Welensky
failed to win the middle 15 which he had sworn openly that he could
win. . . . It was this that led the way to an African majority.'[66]

At the time, however, it would have been impossible for either
Kaunda or Welensky to take such a view of what Macleod had
offered them. Kenneth made a dash to London in the slim hope of
some last-minute change, but found Macleod adamant. In Salisbury
he met Nkomo briefly and declared publicly that Britain had betrayed
his people and treated them 'like pieces of dirt'. He might have to
face jail again, but UNIP was 'still prepared and even anxious
to negotiate' with Whitehall. The Annual Conference of UNIP

was due to start two days later at the Mulungushi Rock, north of Kabwe, [67] and his sincerest principles were going to be tested to the uttermost. It was as though the long grass was brittle and dry and someone was playing with matches. All the pleas for a realisation, in the places where power formally resided, of the danger of conflagration, seemed to have been ignored. The people were keyed up to concert pitch. It was as if the dancers were already in the forest clearing tensely awaiting the first beat of the drum. Cha-cha-cha was about to start.

---

[1]See *NN* for this period; also *Africa Digest*, Vol. VII, No. 6, pp. 182-184.
[2]See *Africa Digest*, Vol. VII, No. 6, p. 183: The school troubles took place at a time 'when only 60 per cent of the children [of NR could] go to school and reach Standard IV and only about 20 per cent [could] go to Standard VI, i.e. complete primary education'.
[3]The lecturer was Michael Faber—see *Africa Digest*, Vol. VII, No. 6. After being deported in January 1963, Ranger became Professor of History in Dar es Salaam. He is now Professor of History in the University of California. Reed has been Professor of English in Lusaka since 1966.
[4]RH 103/2: UNIP Memo to Governor, 24/4/59, signed: M. Chona and F. Chitambala.
[5]Keatley, *op. cit.*, p. 211.
[6]TI-FM/KK, 4/9/72.
[7]*Black Government*, 101 and 57. For an interesting comparison with Southern Rhodesia, note that Leopold Takawira, leader of the 'caretaker' New Democratic Party, said that he believed 'that an African-run party like the N.D.P. with strict principles of self-discipline, non-violence and non-intimidation, and open to all races, will hasten the day of peace'. *Dissent*, No. 16, (18/2/60).
[8]R. Welensky, *4000 Days* (Collins, 1964), 199.
[9]Sikalumbi Papers: 'UNIP Constitution', undated, issued by the National Headquarters, P.O. Box 302, Lusaka.
[10]TI-FM/KK, 9/4/71; Hall, *Kaunda*, pp. 32-33, citing the American magazines; and *NN*, 15/4/60, 30/4/60.
[11]*NN*, 4-13/5/60.
[12]TI-FM/H. D. Banda, 9/5/72.
[13]*NN*, 17/5/60; and see *Central African Examiner*, 16/7/60 pp. 10-12, article by T. Mukupo, 'Tiger or Rider in UNIP' quoting statement by Kaunda in New York, 13/5/60, after hearing of Mrs. Burton's death, in which he referred to the impact of the S.A. Sharpeville 'massacre' on N. Rhodesia.
[14]TI-FM/KK, 13/2/69; and Kaunda, *Zambia*, pp. 144-145.
[15]See *Africa Digest*, Vol. VII, No. 6, p. 182; and *NN*, 9/5/60, 21/5/60.
[16]TI-FM/I. Macleod, 5/2/70, and FM/KK, 13/8/69.
[17]Welensky, *op. cit.*, pp. 55, 134, 196; and Hall, *Zambia*, p. 197.
[18]Emanuel Papers: Kaunda's Press Statement, 16/5/60, from 22 Nevern Street, London.
[19]*Africa Digest*, VII, No. 6, p. 183; and RH 103/2: UNIP 'Emergency Letter to Macleod, signed at 11.15 p.m., 9/5/60 by Kapwepwe, Kamanga, Wina, Sipalo, Mundia and Changufu'.
[20]NAZ: HM 35, Kaunda's letter to Burton, 22/5/60, written from Papworth's address.
[21]*NN*, 15/6/60, 17/6/60.
[22]*Voice of UNIP* (ed. Sikota Wina), June 1960.

[23]FH: Press Statement, giving Kapwepwe's Circular of 3/6/60.
[24]*Voice of UNIP*, June 1960, for article by Reuben Kamanga, 'A strong tree grows by the blowing wind.'
[25]*NN*, 17-20/6/60.
[26]RH 103/2: Nkumbula's speech to ANC National Assembly, Mapoloto, Chilenje, Lusaka, 17/4/60.
[27]ICS: *Report of the Commission of Inquiry into Disturbances in Certain African Schools* (Government Printer, Lusaka) 23/6/60; and note paras, 168, 169, 172, 173. When the Hodgson Technical Training College, Lusaka, reopened in May, none of the 365 former students was readmitted. Not more than 200 new students were enrolled. (*Africa Digest*, VII, No. 1, p. 4.) The Commission was chaired by Sir W. Harragin with Chief Mapanza and Henry Makulu, (after independence Chairman, until his death, of the Public Service Commission) as members.
[28]*NN*, 22/7/60, 3/8/60.
[29]*NN*, 4/8/60.
[30]TI-FM/Nakatindi, 29/3/69. Princess Nakatindi was, before her death in late 1972, District Governor, Sesheke. Jethro Mutti later became Minister for the North-Western Province. In a letter to Kamanga, in Cairo, dated 21/11/60, Mutti said that he and two others had entered Barotseland after notifying the Barotse Native Government who 'raised no objection'. They had gone in response 'to the demand of the majority of the masses who support UNIP there'. When they protested against deportation to the Resident Commissioner he kept them waiting till the orders expired and then arrested them. 'We were taken to Lealui, prosecuted without defence and sentenced to 12 months hard labour, but granted bail pending appeal.' (FH Files).
[31]*Voice of UNIP*, No. 5, 16/8/60; and *NN*, 31/8/60.
[32]Special UNIP Bulletin entitled 'Congo', 15/7/60, published by the International and Publicity Bureau, P. O. Box 302, Lusaka.
[33]Figures from the *1958 Year Book* of the NR Chamber of Mines, published Kitwe, 1959.
[34]See Keatley, *op. cit.*, p. 316; see also his pp. 239-241.
[35]FH: File—National President: UNIP Emergency Territorial Conference, 3rd to 4th September 1960: Presidential Speech; and 'Constitutional Proposals', 4/9/60, document signed by Kaunda and Sipalo.
[36]*NN*, 15/9/60, 1/10/60; *Central Africa Mail*, 21/6/60; and Hall, *Zambia*, pp. 199-200.
[37]See Monckton Report; *NN*, 13/10/60; Welensky, *op. cit.*, 160, 207; *EAR*, 13/10/60.
[38]*NN*, 6/10/60.
[39]See *NN* for this period. The quotation from the *Daily Mail* for 26/10/60 was reproduced by the *Voice of Northern Rhodesia*, Oct-Nov. 1960, published by UNIP's office in Cairo.
[40]Mpashi, *op. cit.*, pp. 59-64, with quotation from p. 64.
[41]Kaunda, *Zambia*, 151-153.
[42]*Africa Digest*, Vol. VIII, No. 4, p. 131; and Mulford *op. cit.*, p. 174.
[43]The chief foreign donors were Ghana, Liberia, Egypt Ethiopia, TANU in Tanganyika and private groups and individuals in Britain and America.
[44]Kaunda, *Zambia*, 154.
[45]TI-FM/I. Macleod, 5/2/70.
[46]*NN* for period.
[47]ANC/2/4: Michello to Nkumbula, 6/12/60: to Governor and to Colonial Secretary, 19/12/60; 9/12/60; also telegrams of 5/12/60, 16/12/60, 19/12/60; ANC Press Statement, by Nkumbula, 12/12/60; ANC *Week by Week*, 24/12/60, pp. 5-7. Since the Accra Conference of 1958, Nkumbula had believed that Kaunda was working with Dr. Banda, 'to remove me from the international political scene'. (See RH 103/2: *Freedom*, June 1959 for Mukupo's article, 'Nkumbula on the Kaunda Split').
[48]Special Issue of *Voice of UNIP*, 12/12/60.

[49]Report of Third Session of the National Council of UNIP, held on 18 January, 1961, in Lusaka War Memorial Hall.
[50]For 'UNIP's Policy for Local Government and the Judiciary' see *Africa Digest*, Vol. VIII, No. 4, p. 130.
[51]FH: UNIP/11/NP-3: letter from Kaunda to Civil Servants, 20/1/61; also *NN*, 25/1/61 and 31/1/61.
[52]Dec. 1960.
[53]See Keatley, *op. cit.*, pp. 450-452; and *Voice of Zambia*, UNIP, London, Vol. 1, No. 1 (April 1961). Note also the role of Captain Charles Waterhouse, Chairman of Tanganyika Concessions Ltd., as founder of the two Lobbies.
[54]TI-FM/I. Macleod, 5/2/70.
[55]*NN* for the period; *Africa Digest*, Vol. VIII, No. 4, pp. 125-126, and Vol. VIII, No. 5, p. 173 for Congo situation; *Zambia*, 155-156; TI-FM/KK, 4/9/72; and Hall, *Zambia*, p. 45.
[56]See Welensky, *op. cit.*, p. 300; Hall, *Zambia*, pp. 203-204; and Franklin, *op. cit.*, pp. 199-200.
[57]Mulford, p. 184; and see *Northern Rhodesia—Proposals for Constitutional Change*, (CMD. 1295, HMSO, February 1961); also *The Economist* 25/2/61.
[58]*NN*, 22/2/61, 11/3/61; and Mulford, *Zambia*, pp. 189-190.
[59]TI-FM/KK, 13/2/69; and *NN*, 11/3/61.
[60]UNIP Minutes of the Fourth National Council, 4/4/61; and UNIP/12/298 to the Chief Secretary, 7/4/61.
[61]*NR (Africa) News Survey*. Vol. I, No. 8, (1/5/61); *Voice of Zambia* (London Committee of UNIP), Vol. II, May, 1961; and *NN*, 25/4/61, 26/4/61.
[62]*NN*, 13/5/61 and 18/5/61; UNIP/NP-13, Presidential Communique of 24/5/61; and Kaunda's letter, 29/5/61, to all Divisional Presidents on 'Public Meetings'.
[63] Hall, *Zambia*, p. 205; *NN* 17/6/61; M. G. Clarke—Personal Papers: (a) Chief Establishment Officer to Clarke, SX. 12783, 7/7/61; (b) Clarke to Chief Establishment Officer, 12/7/61 and 24/7/61; (c) Kaunda to Dr. H. K. Banda and to Kanyama Chiume, Malawi, UNIP/1/P, 27/2/62 (by courtesy of Professor Clarke). Clarke, after returning to Zambia from Ghana, was first Professor of Mathematics Education at the University of Zambia, till December, 1970, and then Secretary to the Metrication Board.
[64]UNIP 'Master Plan', Statement on Constitutional Changes by President K. D. Kaunda', 18/6/61; and *NN*, 19/6/61, 28/6/61.
[65]NR Proposals for Constitutional Change. Cmd. 1423, June, 1961; and see Mulford, *op. cit.*, pp. 194-197; and Hall, *Zambia*, p. 206.
[66]TI-FM/I. Macleod, 5/2/70.
[67]*NN*, 6/7/61; and note that Grey Zulu stated that the choice of the bare, black rock as a Party meeting place was his, as a Kabwe resident. (TI-FM/AGZ, 27/2/69).

12

Cha-Cha-Cha—Controlling a Fire

'For a long time the people had been talking of violence, of the day when they would fight the white man and win back their country—and we, the leaders . . . had prevailed on them to use peaceful methods. When some of us discussed this in June, 1961, it could not be denied that our policy to achieve a non-racial state by non-violent means had achieved nothing, and that our followers were beginning to lose confidence and were developing disturbing ideas of terrorism.'[1] These words were not spoken by Kenneth Kaunda but by Nelson Mandela in his frank, courageous defence at the end of the Rivonia trial in Pretoria in June 1964. But Kaunda could easily have spoken them as he approached the Annual Conference of UNIP in July 1961. It might have been more comfortable to have 'let sleeping dogs lie'. Despite the significant number of genuinely good people in it, the white community of South and Central Africa had in effect posted notices everywhere: 'No dogs, no natives', and Africans must be ready to have their knock answered by a sharp 'What do you want?'. Now, for Kenneth, in the tenth year of his active association with the movement of pent-up protest, there was a fresh awareness that the awakening of his people to hope for a spiritual change in the land had raised them to their feet and that it would be easy now for someone to call them to surge forward recklessly with sticks and stones to claim their heritage. If he stayed with these people of his who were 'no band of angels', he would be blamed for every incident of indiscipline. Somehow, since his friend Iain Macleod had not been able to master the powerful machinations of Welensky and his numerous allies, the five points of the 'Master Plan' would now have to be rendered in terms more practical than those he had enunciated in Kitwe, so that, hoping against hope, justice might still be done without the shedding of blood. He knew the situation might force him to hand over to more 'tough' leadership, but as long as his people would hear he would appeal to their deep humanity; for the new nation would need all the flexibility of heart, all the reasonableness, all the mercy of all its people, to grow and prosper.

As the South African ANC faced its crisis of non-violence versus violence for violence and the Congo continued to be haunted by the ghost of the murdered Patrice Lumumba and to erupt in strife and panic, the Central African conflict was aptly summarised by Southern Rhodesia's former Prime Minister, Garfield Todd, whose role as a spokesman of white sympathisers with the African cause was increasingly significant in the Colony. 'Intimidation takes many forms,' he said, 'and while it is at its crudest in the petrol bomb, it is no less undesirable in the call-up of the armed forces to "maintain law and order" when the peace is threatened simply because a racial minority refuses to abrogate its privilege.'[2] These words were spoken in the worsening security situation that had followed the promulgation of the Sandys-Whitehead Constitution for Southern Rhodesia which Joshua Nkomo had at first accepted and then rejected. It was encouraging to African political leaders that in Kenya Jomo Kenyatta was being moved step by step from ignominious imprisonment to political supremacy, and Julius Nyerere was now Prime Minister in Tanganyika. But the situation of Southern Africa was likely to wield a greater influence on Central African affairs than that of either East or West Africa. Mozambique and Angola, under severe news censorship, were increasingly experiencing tremors of protest and repression.

What seemed so ominous in the latest formula from London for Northern Rhodesia was that it was placing '*apartheid* on the Statute Book'. UNIP's London Committee, in its *Voice of Zambia*, pointed out that 'where a constituency is racially reserved for a European and an African, the candidates' names would be "arranged in two separate sections on the ballot paper" ', and that the votes of white and black voters on the Upper and Lower Rolls respectively would have to be checked according to race. 'What is to be the definition of "European" and "African"?' the paper asked. 'If the definition is to be based on some unscientific criterion of racial purity, what are the tests proposed? . . . In recent years, Dr. Verwoerd has been classifying people racially by tests such as these:

whether a pencil placed in a person's hair falls out or not on bending over; width of nose; shade of whiteness; purity of ancestry; opinion of neighbours; and many other obnoxious tests. Are these now to be applied in our country . . . [and] to persons who have escaped the South African tests by migrating to our country? . . . Racial classification is not a matter to be taken lightly—it is a sign of *Apartheid* in its advanced stage. Great personal tragedies are to be expected in the short run and irreversible racial thinking engendered in the long.'[3] The London newssheet also printed, in the same issue, a poem, by Bakali Koshikabila, entitled 'Northern Rhodesia, Awake', which cried thus:

'People of the North,
People of the North,
Let the cry go forth.
Why continue in bondage?
Where is your courage?

Before your enslaver came
You stood your own and overcame;
You proved yourselves a people
Capable of tearing the lion's jaws
Like Samson with bare hands.

Seventy years have gone by,
Enslaved, exploited, insulted, you stood by,
When will you stretch forth?
The enslaver love, charity, humility taught
But these he regarded not.

Your forefathers' honour, dignity
Do not set to naught,
How long, how long
In your own land
Shall you second class citizens be?'[4]

On his journey back to Lusaka, Kenneth Kaunda had to make the inevitable air stop at Salisbury. Though as a prohibited immigrant he was not allowed to leave the airport, he was subjected to an exhaustive search which he described as worse than any humiliation he had suffered in his life. He would now, he cried, 'declare practical war' on the Federation. The notes of his address to the Party Conference at Mulungushi, the text of his joint declaration with Joshua Nkomo and a letter from a friendly British Labour M.P. had been seized.[5] Lying on the lawn at the airport with Nkomo, he told reporters that the coming struggle in his country would be 'non-violent—something to make the working of the Federation impossible.' 'They will not have our cooperation any more. . . . I am fighting the British Government. . . . But I want a clean fight.' He did not want Whitehall to be able to claim that he had not understood the issue. He was now sure that the modified 15-15-15 scheme was 'weighted very much in favour of white candidates'. In this baleful conviction, he issued a sharp press statement during a brief stop in Ghana. Because of this crisis, he was cancelling invitations to nationalist leaders in Tanganyika, Kenya, Nyasaland, Basutoland, Southern Rhodesia and Bechuanaland to attend UNIP's Annual Conference. 'As a precaution we have already sent Party emissaries to the district warning people not to squander their month's earnings or savings on frivolous commodities.'[6]

When he rose to speak to the three thousand Party delegates on 9 July, at Mulungushi, he began with a note of ringing confidence: 'Countrymen, we meet today to decide the future of our country.' Right away he explained the absence of Chiefs, 'our natural rulers'. 'I am conscious of the danger to which we would expose them if we invited them to come here. I am glad to tell you that we have overwhelming support from them, although intimidation from those above them will often make some of them not say so. . . . I thank God for waking up this wide mass awakening among His people. . . . We are poverty stricken in the midst of plenty. Bus and other fares are fantastically high. Yet we have here three thousand delegates and official observers. . . . Congratulations, countrymen.' Then in a long, complicated speech, he attempted to explain the mathematical intricacies of Macleod's scheme and the subtle alteration of it demanded by Welensky's agents. Yet, he said: 'in my mind's eye I can still see Mr. Macleod's face. It is a trustworthy face in so far as I am able to discern faces and read other people's minds. Many fellow colonial leaders have told me the same thing.

What then has gone wrong with him over Northern Rhodesia? . . .
I know Colonial Secretary Macleod is adept at bridge. But we are
not breathless pieces of paper on a bridge table. We are human beings
who, if they will not play bridge, at least will know what is right or
wrong for themselves whether it be political, economic, social
or cultural.' The situation was rendered the more critical by the
'full military and police preparations . . . in the Union of South
Africa, in this rotten Federation . . . in Angola and Mozambique'
and by the military pacts being made 'between these three foreign
powers,' but the people must respond in courage. Here he quoted
'that great English genius', Shakespeare from *Julius Caesar*':
"You must note beside
That we here tried the utmost of our friends,
Our legions are brimful, our cause is ripe.
The enemy increaseth every day,
We, at the height, are ready to decline.
There is a tide in the affairs of men
Which, taken at the flood leads on to fortune;
Omitted, all the voyage of their life
Is bound in shallows and in miseries.
On such a full sea are we now afloat
And we must take the current when it serves,
Or lose our ventures."
'We are ready,' said Kaunda, 'not to decline but to march forward
equipped with the only weapon I know will do here—the positive
and creative force of NON-VIOLENCE.' Towards the end of his
speech, he gave special messages to European, Asian and Euro-
African 'friends and comrades in the struggle', all of whom had
to face difficulties by aligning themselves with the African cause.
Our country at this hour needs brave ones,' he declared. 'Stand
up and be brave.' He had, he concluded, demanded that the British
Government should announce the new Constitution before 8 July.
'They have done so, but it is completely unacceptable to us of your
'National Council at least. I have always asked you to be PATIENT,
NON-VIOLENT IN THOUGHT, WORD and DEED. I am
removing one of the noble words from my vocabulary and it is
PATIENCE. . . . What is important is, although I remove
PATIENCE . . . we shall remain strictly non-violent in thought,
word and deed. . . . If you refuse to recognise the new constitution,

we will have to act in a positive but non-violent way . . . [and] I shall be obliged to ask for powers to send myself as well as others to jail.'[7]

As Kenneth Kaunda was speaking, there were repeated shouts of approval and again and again the word 'Cha-cha-cha' was heard. It was the name of a popular community dance, and it could perhaps be interpreted as meaning: 'Face the music.' There were many questions about 'Cha-cha-cha' at Mulungushi. Someone asked Kaunda whether there was a book in which he had read about it, but he replied that 'it was written in his head', and added in laughter, 'If you wish to open my head you will see where it is written.' Perhaps Welensky thought that 'cha-cha-cha' was 'political agitation' only, but he was wrong. 'Cha-cha-cha means real dancing. Europeans will take part along with Africans.' 'Young children and those unborn will join in the dance,' he said. 'Hens, dogs and all our domestic beasts will join in. Yes, even the Queen will also dance Cha-cha-cha. Cha-cha-cha is for all.' It was to come to mean that the action would go on till victory was won; the whole community, as it were, dancing together in unison, refusing to be silenced. But Kaunda, again clad in his Ghana-type toga, spoke at several points under considerable emotional strain, at once point crying, 'Dear God, in the past I have appealed to my people to be patient, non-violent and dignified.' 'What shall I tell them now? And if I tell them to be patient and non-violent, will they listen to me? . . . ' 'We will witness the madness of man,' he exclaimed, near to tears, 'when he kills his fellow man because he is of a different colour.'[8]

The round timber dais was surrounded with placards, some carried by children, with texts more in tune with Sipalo's thinking than with Kaunda's: 'Quit Africa, all white men' and 'No room for white settlers'. It was at this Conference that, for the first time, there were angry shouts of 'No more non-violence' as he was speaking, and he had to plead to be allowed to explain his policy further. Civil disobedience in the form of non-cooperation had been going on for some time, which had generally meant, in the rural areas, the ignoring of District Commissioners' calls to Boma meetings and of instructions of agricultural and other officers. Now something more was expected and, according to Kaunda, the 'Master Plan' was being spoken of before it had been formulated. The

people 'had to give a demonstration of strength but we did not
know what action would be called for'. Moreover, from the outset,
he had sought to promote the initiative of local Party leadership
rather than of a centralised authority. He has recorded how,
during 1961 when he had to travel abroad extensively 'the local
chaps did most of the work, like Alex Shapi and Sylvester Chisembele in Luapula, in the north Mutemba, in the north-west Hanock
Kikombe and Mateyo Ngalande, etc.' Grey Zulu, a member of
the Central Committee where 'non-violence' had been hotly debated,
recalled that, as he bade delegates farewell, Kenneth spoke movingly
about the possibility of some dying in the coming struggle. 'Those
who believe in God believe sincerely that we will meet in heaven
as people who died for a just cause. To the few of you who die so
that others should live in peace after you, it gives a great challenge
that you should not kill anyone, for then you would be in the same
boat as those who kill us.'[9]

Convinced that it was 'the intention of the British Government
. . . to foster white oligarchy at the expense of three million African
people', the Mulungushi Conference finally resolved as follows:

'(1)   That the United National Independence Party on behalf
       of the people of Zambia totally rejects the "Macleod"
       constitutional proposals;

(2)   That the United National Independence Party regard the
       said constitutional proposals as an insult to the people
       of Zambia, both Black and White, and an insulting
       betrayal to the policy of negotiation hitherto carried
       out on behalf of the people by their leader Kenneth
       Kaunda;

(3)   That from now on United National Independence Party
       will carry on a bitter struggle to attain full independence
       for the people of Zambia and we call upon the people
       to rally to the cause of freedom in order to ensure that
       the present constitutional proposals cannot be imple-
       mented;

(4)   That time has come for United National Independence
       Party to revise the method of our struggle for freedom
       and independence and to find the means which the
       British Government will understand and obey;

(5) That to these ends this Conference, representative of all the three million African people of Zambia and thousands of members of other races, hereby grants the President of the United National Independence Party emergency powers to direct and supervise all operations for a lively and effective positive action campaign now;

(6) That these powers should include the following:
   (a) Authority to call on any individual to perform any task at any time and at a second's notice.
   (b) Authority to call, halt, prolong or suspend any campaign in any part of Northern Rhodesia;
   (c) Authority to appoint special committees.

(7) We the 4,000 delegates do hereby dedicate ourselves individually and collectively to the spirit and letter of this resolution in its entirety.'[10]

Meanwhile ANC's campaign against Kaunda as a' Nyasalander' continued unabated, with charges that he was making himself rich from his visits to America, and that the funds received by UNIP from the All-Africa Peoples' Conference in Cairo were 'Communistic'. ANC's *Week by Week* had asked why 'Kaunda (Mau Mau) (some call him Zombie because of his primitive hairdo)' should qualify to meet the President of the United States. Small but ugly inter-party clashes around Lusaka had confirmed that such enmity was on the increase.[11] Meanwhile, within UNIP itself there were fresh manifestations of dissension and a major crisis blew up at Mulungushi, over the anger of various delegates at the 'drunkness' [*sic*] of Munu Sipalo, the National Secretary. In consequence, Mainza Chona was appointed as Acting Secretary and so became Editor of the *Voice of UNIP*. The censure motion was hurriedly drafted in view of Kaunda's decision to hold unscheduled elections, thus sparing Sipalo the ignominy of dismissal.[12]

In recent months there had been, as we have seen, a great increase in the activity of UNIP's agents throughout the country and in areas like the Luapula and Northern Provinces, singing and dancing had been a feature of Party gatherings for some time. The Regional Women's Secretary for the Luapula had described how in Kazembe's area there was widespread suspicion that the Chief was working for the Boma by warning other Chiefs that the political leaders wanted to 'grab' their positions and 'declare themselves chiefs'. In reaction, UNIP's local organisation was intensified and people went about singing Party songs.

'Father Kaunda, Father Kaunda,
It's you we follow
In this journey of ours to freedom.
It is not war we want (bis)
We want the country,
There is no offence in that.'

Another song went like this:

'Never mind that the laws
Seem so harsh against us:
We shall go on meeting,
We shall not fear imprisonment,
Because all these will be testimonies
When we are free, when we are free!
Mothers and Fathers,
What are you thinking
Of this land we live in?
You say it belongs to the Incomer.
Come here and let us understand
That, like our friends in Ghana,
We're about to be free (bis)!

Yet another struck a more bellicose note

,See, we received those
Who brought us weapons
So that we could kill them all.
In our land we are the owners.
God was not stupid
To make a black man.
This is why we're calling you all—
Come, let us fight for our country.'[13]

Political songs were, of course, not new to the country. They can be traced back to the early days of forced labour and conscripted porterage. For some years now, the cry of the songs had been for democracy, about which British war-time propaganda had talked so confidently. So people had been singing:

'When talking about democracy
We must teach these Europeans,

Because they do not know.
See, here in Africa they bring their clothes,
But leave democracy in Europe.
(Chorus) Go back, go back
                And bring true democracy.
We are no longer asleep,
We are up and about democracy.
We have known for a long time
We are the majority, and we demand
A majority in the Legislative Council.'[14]

Because the colour bar begot a language barrier, such songs had often been sung with impunity when white men were near. But now, as in Nyasaland in 1959, the shout of 'Kwacha—the dawn is come' or 'Freedom' and the singing of such songs were regarded as seditious. Such shouts were now heard as incidents of violence took place, immediately after the Mulungushi Conference. A U.F.P. member of Leg. Co. had just described UNIP's leaders as 'scum of the earth', but such a remark was heard now, not simply as 'the way Europeans talk', but as bitter provocation. In various regions of the country, the party was declaring a boycott of beer halls, partly to promote sobriety as a vital part of popular organisation. There was immediately a number of 'crude attempts at sabotage by the UNIP Youth League on the Copperbelt', while the increased movement of police and military vehicles in the Luapula province was answered by the ditching of a number of bridges on the main roads.[15]

In a letter to 'Dear Freedom Fighters' in the *Voice of UNIP*, Mainza Chona wrote: 'You are all standing at attention waiting for the green light to the MASTER PLAN. Some of you are tired of waiting. . . . [At] the Mulungushi Conference . . . you were told to be "ON YOUR MARKS, GET SET". . . . But you remember you gave emergency powers to the National President. . . . who alone is responsible for directing CHACHACHA. This means that he is to blame if the campaign fails. So he has to make a careful assessment . . . before he can give the word "Go".' Chona ended with a grave word on the coming struggle. 'There will be many arrests, many trials, many imprisonments and many appeals. Try to obtain bail on your own recognizance; but if a sum of money is demanded it is no use looking to the Party for help. Just sit in custody. There will probably be thousands like you.'[16]

UNIP reports of the first wave of incidents after Mulungushi listed sixty people arrested at Kitwe in a pre-dawn raid and quoted a press notice of the death of an ANC official who had been organising opposition to the beer hall boycott there. Chisembele had at the same time cabled UNIP headquarters from the Luapula Province to report 'police provocation' and ask a national official to go north 'to calm the people'. Bridges had been destroyed and 'many people were arrested'. Southern Province officials alleged police bribery of ANC members to block the beer hall boycott, which however was 'completely effective' in the Lusaka region. Relations between Party officials and 'the authorities' in Barotseland were 'reasonably fair'. In the Eastern Province, UNIP was battling against ANC attempts to persuade people to register as voters under the new Constitution; and it was alleged that the District Commissioner of Petauke, finding that the Chiefs thought that the requirement of the Constitution for a candidate to win $12\frac{1}{2}\%$ of the votes cast was too high, had suggested that it 'could be reduced to $\frac{1}{8}$ of the votes cast'! From Solwezi in the north-west came a report of a police raid on the UNIP office. In the Northern Province where Kenneth Kaunda was touring, troubles had been reported in Chinsali and the Lungu Chief near Abercorn had, 'as an agent of imperialism', forbidden Kaunda's entry into his area. Everywhere he went on this 3,000-mile pilgrimage, Kenneth appealed insistently for 'non-violence'. But without physical violence to persons, the thousands of Party members and their allies, in the Northern and Luapula Provinces, were beginning what was in effect a sabotage campaign without awaiting a direct order from their President. When Chona was asked, on 27 July if these first outbreaks were part of the 'Master Plan', he replied, 'I really don't know,' while Kaunda himself 'called unsuccessfully for a stop to the violence, conceding that the disturbances "looked organized".'

Kaunda was convinced after his tour, that the mood of the north was bitter. When at Mpika, he had been wakened at 4 a.m. to find a number of Chiefs and other senior people dancing and singing a battle song near where he had slept which said clearly: 'War is near.' This made him insist even more strongly 'that there was to be no movement at all' until he gave the word. This instruction was communicated personally to all provincial leaders. But somehow the trigger was pulled before the order was given and it was when he was at Dar es Salaam that a correspondent of the London *Daily Mail* in Lusaka called him with the question, 'Have you heard what is happening at home?' 'I said, "No. No,"' Kaunda recalled, 'and he said, "They are burning their ICs. Is that in order?" Then I said, "Yes, this is the first part of the Master Plan."'[17]

At this point it is important now to sketch the pattern of events, mainly in the two northerly regions of the territory, as seen by people living there. Many witnesses were explicit in the view that they 'liked' Kaunda's leadership 'because there was no bloodshed in his way of fighting for our freedom', in consequence of which 'all constituency officials were going around stopping people from taking up weapons such as stones or damaging roads or bridges. . . .' 'On several occasions, we tended to force him against his non-violence policy but because of his strictness and straightforwardness, we were calmed.' In the Samfya area, where there had been early disenchantment with Nkumbula's leadership and where first ZANC and then UNIP had gained a very large following, local testimony indicates that the mass burning of *ifitupa*, as African Identification Certificates were called, was done five days before Kaunda burned his own *ichitupa* in Lusaka, probably because some delegates returning from Mulungushi had broken their pledge of secrecy. The burning at Samfya was followed the next day by similar action on the island of Chishi, and there too people testified that the burning of *ifitupa* and of *imichato* or Marriage Certificates was symbolic of a radical rejection of foreign rule.

'This time,' said Mama Chola of Mwense, 'we realised that Cha-cha-cha had started. . . .' 'Straightaway we started collecting Identification and Marriage Certificates, even from those who did not attend the meeting, and we visited the homes of all the elderly people who had not come because of the cold weather. They surrendered heaps and heaps of certificates, and when it struck 2 a.m., we set these ablaze. . . . We were then instructed to ask young children to collect the ashes of the burnt things and take them to the D.O. sent by Welensky and tell him we had burned the *ifitupa* to show that we did not like his government. If we sent adults they would be fired at. . . . From all over the place our fellow citizens, like the Watchtowers who did not join the struggle because of fear, came along with the Boma Messengers to see what we were doing

. . . . Then they muttered among themselves, "Is this the Cha-cha-cha Kaunda has been speaking of? A Cha-cha-cha of happiness?" . . . . When the youngsters reached the Boma, "These people are mad," said the D.O. . . . He looked at the children and caught them by the ears, demanding to know who had sent them to his office with the ashes. "It is President Kaunda who has sent us," they told him. Then they arrested the youngsters, shook them and then separated them to try to force them to name those responsible. But the children simply repeated: "President Kaunda sent us. . . ." He then despatched police and they began beating the people.' Mama Chola, like other witnesses, gave the names and villages of a number of people who had been arrested or beaten by the Government forces. Men and women prisoners, she said, were made to walk naked. More than two hundred arrests were made. At Samfya, the burning of *ifitupa* was concluded by the burial of a large heap of ashes and the erection of a rough wooden cross at the spot near the UNIP Constituency Office with the inscription, 'Here we have buried Welensky today.'[18]

From all the affected areas evidence was given of a variety of brutalities by the security forces, including assault and outrage upon women, which was recalled with special horror, as well as torture of men by the suspension of stones on their private parts, and by making them run and dance, naked, in this condition. In this respect, the testimony of a Scottish missionary of the United Church corroborated the indiscriminate violence which had been so marked a feature of the 'pacification' of northern Malawi during the 1959 Emergency.[19] He and his family, returning to Lubwa, Chinsali, from the north, encountered various road blocks and then found a stationary lorry loaded with people, roped hand and foot like bundles. He was shocked to see a white officer kicking some of them off the lorry. 'That kind of thing makes you boil inside,' he recorded later, 'and you don't know how to react at first.' On reaching Chinsali District, they found that, wherever there was a road block, the security forces swept into the villages nearest to it and started terrorising the people. No effort was made to ascertain people's political involvement, 'like Andrew and Susanna, for example, people I knew at Mundu.' 'Andrew was dragged from his house, thrashed, kicked, beaten about the body. His wife hung on to one of the posts of the house because she knew that if she was dragged away, they would burn the house down.' Not far from Mundu, 'there was a man who was a storekeeper.' 'His wife was dragged out and then pushed into the room again. I don't personally have any doubts about what happened then because the woman was a changed person thereafter. She had been the brightest woman in our local congregation, but now she changed completely and became depressed, ashamed to see anyone.' As he moved southwards towards the court of Chief Chibesakunda, the missionary found that 'a terrific amount of damage' had been done at Matumbo by the police and army. 'The village was practically razed and the girls were raped, without any doubt.' Many of the men in the area had gone to live in camps in the forest, which were surrounded by booby traps in case of an attack by soldiers. These men roamed at large by day, 'chanting UNIP slogans in bands of up to 1,000 strong, through the bush'. The security forces therefore terrorised the women and old people who remained in the villages. 'There was for example the old man who came into Lubwa hospital, suffering from shock. He had been in a village a few miles north of Chinsali when the Mobile Unit had come, burned the village and started picking up everything they could. . . . The Mobile Unit boys did just what they wanted, they could take food, pick up all the chickens, take away the cattle. This old man happened to be the proud possessor of one cow, but as he ran away and hid, he could see his cow being slaughtered and dumped into a lorry. He saw his house burnt down, his wife beaten . . . and it just shattered him. . . . He walked into hospital in a dazed condition and was there quite a long time. He just could not be orientated again. He had lost his bearings.'[20]

As we saw above, there had been some acts of arson against village schools in 1960. Now a considerable number of schools were burned and the testimony of village people varied substantially on this matter. Some claimed that, like the stealing and killing of cattle and the destruction of grain bins, it was done by the security forces or their agents to shatter the whole fabric of life by way of 'punishing' the populace. Others, including the Lubwa missionary, believed that the people, in the unanimity of their protest, regarded the blocking of roads and damaging of bridges as inadequate. 'Everything that was N.R.G. therefore had to be battered. Buckets, brooms, anything with the Government stamp'. The missionary recorded, however, that before a school was set ablaze, all the Bibles were removed and stacked safely away from the fire. The imposition of community fines had the effect of increasing solidarity and convincing the people that it was a 'war of the Government' against the African population. In the words of one witness, 'We did not approve of anything of the Government, not even of its institutions, like the schools.' 'We only wanted to achieve self-government. Then we would build our own schools and send our children to them. We would replace them with better ones, just as in our Bemba proverb: "*Nga twakana umuntu ifwe, twakana no twakwe*—" "If we reject a man, we reject also what is his." ' Inevitably, however, such a unanimous resolve 'to do something in their own right' evoked in turn bitter and indiscriminate anger against the people on the part of otherwise benevolent persons. The Scots missionary told of one such, the senior police officer at Chinsali, an Irishman, who had once given £100, 'the biggest donation we had ever received', for a church building, and who did numerous acts of charity to people near the Boma. The wave of popular unrest made him feel that he had somehow 'been let down', and he left Chinsali embittered. The fact that the names of white officers were often misheard and mispronounced by the local people, while almost all the people were unknown by name or face to the expatriates who operated 'law and order', further aggravated the tragedy.

If the position of well-meaning white officials was painful, that of many of the Chiefs was far more parlous. 'You Chiefs,' their people told them, 'when you see a white man you leave your chair and go and sit on the ground, you let a stranger occupy the chair of a Chief.' 'You do not realise what you are doing . . . . We shall show you real freedom when Dr. Kaunda, through God's will, gets this freedom for us.' This anger against the subservience of some Chiefs was widespread. 'On August 27th,' Headman Katambarara of Lundazi District recalled, 'I went out with Humphrey Mulemba and burned the local court . . . to show that we were taking our country back. . . . Cha-cha-cha was the end of fear. . . . We rejoiced because we were on the road to peace.'[21]

When Kenneth Kaunda made his extended tour of the north, he had made his public speeches in the presence of Government officials. At Chinsali, according to the evidence of his brother,

Robert, the D.C. and his D.O. both attended a mass rally at the Boma and heard Kaunda's explanation of the crisis and his appeal for 'non-violent positive action'. His last words were: 'If I were to order you, my people in Chinsali District, to go to the east, beyond the hills, and pull down those hills and cut down the forests, would you do just that?' This was greeted by 'a resounding YES'. 'And if I led you to the north or to the west, would you still follow me?' 'Yes,' they roared back, 'we will follow you.' 'We will do whatever you ask us to do.' 'Now, I have finished addressing you', Kaunda said, 'Stay well.' He was clearly under great tension, believing that the whole movement of political change must depend on local leadership, yet realising that so explosive a situation demanded not less than military authority, unsupported by arms, to prevent chaos. As crowds everywhere shouted 'Kaunda, Kaunda' and the exuberant scribes of the *Voice* wrote his name in every issue, with acclamations of 'Choba-e, Kaunda, Choba-e', Bemba for 'helmsman', the movement was assuming an increasingly religious fervour.

'O God', the people sang, 'Behold our sufferings.'

'What have we done against you, our Saviour?

This we know, O God,

That we are in the ditch.

But you give to each who asks

And you are our redeemer.

Come and redeem us, O God,

From everlasting bondage.

This place, brethren,

God has given us.

There is a great good fortune

Ahead for you and for us.

Let them stop mocking us,

Let them stop hating us,

Though we sing praise to our land

And comfort those who suffer,

Those who are in jail.

Fathers and sisters,

Cast away the fear inside you.

Welensky, see this land is our land!

Rejoice and be glad.'

Therefore the roads must be blocked, the bridges ditched, the telephone cables cut, the cattle pens destroyed, the Government officials, police and soldiers harassed and given no rest, until, as they said, '*Tukapoka ubuteko*'—'We shall take over the Government.'[22] For 'Cha-cha-cha didn't start in 1961, but long before', building up in peoples' heart until the pent-up protest had to burst forth, till 'the Government must look and realise that the people are really angry. "If we kill them, they won't listen. So let us now acknowledge that they must rule themselves. . . ." Moreover, we heard another report that the Governor Hone in Lusaka was well-disposed towards our freedom, really helping President Kaunda', which added impetus to the hope of early victory.[23]

Though Kaunda's flying visit to London on 13 August was to make 'a last appeal', he was determined to keep open the channels of communication with both the Governor and the Colonial Secretary; and they too were anxious to avoid a final breach. At Ndola on his way back from England via Dar es Salaam, he had said that if things were 'not very hot yet' he was coming 'to make them hotter'. These words recalled, in the minds of his opponents, Hastings Banda's words, in November 1958, about having 'the whole of Nyasaland on fire'. The next day he publicly burned his own *ichitupa* in the presence of about twenty pressmen outside UNIP's Freedom House in Lusaka. Dropping its ashes into a metal waste paper container, he cried, 'God bless Africa.' He could calm the people of the north, he declared, if he was allowed to go there 'as a free man' and not 'as a Government stooge'. Invoking the Preservation of Public Security Regulations, the Government had proscribed UNIP in the two turbulent provinces, and this meant that Kaunda could not go there as Party President. As the death toll in the north mounted, he cabled Pandit Nehru of India, begging him to initiate international action to 'stop the killing of Africans and the mass uprooting of villages', and sent a telegram to Prime Minister Macmillan demanding a commission of inquiry into the disturbances. In view of the ferocity of Government action, he said, 'I cannot go on blindly with our original plan.' 'I must now plan to meet the changing circumstances.' Within a few days, he was back in Britain, this time to take part in a Conference on World Tensions in Oxford, where he met delegates from Africa, Asia, South and North America and Europe.[24]

While Kenneth was in London, stressing his commitment to

'non-violence' despite the increasing difficulty of maintaining it, his wife Betty was busy with household chores and awaiting the birth of their seventh child. Kenneth had put up a special prayer for the coming birth, saying, before he left for London, 'Please, Providence, may I find a baby girl born of this woman.' 'She has been waiting for one for so long.' He had arranged for his mother-in-law to stay in Lusaka while he was away. 'One morning,' Betty has recalled, 'as I was sitting with my mother, a man came cycling very fast. . . .' 'He was one of the most active [UNIP] members and used to go on tours with my husband. . . . He started sobbing. . . . "The President, Mr. Kaunda, has been poisoned in the United Kingdom" he said. "Poison was put in his food and he is very ill." ' Though newspapers carried a report of Kenneth's illness, Betty was soon reassured that it was only mild food-poisoning; and a few days later, Kenneth was on his way back to Lusaka, to find their first little girl, Musata, safely born.[25]

His talks in London, though still 'inconclusive' and 'secret', had obviously kept the door open. A final breakdown would force the implementation of the third stage of the 'Master Plan'; the burning of Identification Certificates and the destruction of roads and bridges having been the first two stages. In fact, the Plan had miscarried as the first three stages had been synchronised; namely, the burning of certificates, the closure of schools and the destruction of roads and bridges. For, according to Kaunda, 'we didn't have stage four or stage five.' He had been encouraged by having access in London not only to Iain Macleod but also to his Minister of State, Lord Perth, and to the Commonwealth Relations Secretary, Duncan Sandys, though UNIP headquarters had told him not to seek any such meetings at that time. The British Ministers declared their willingness, on the cessation of violence, 'to consider representations on divergence of views about details of the proposed Constitution'. This, Kenneth said, in Nairobi, would 'spell new hope for our troubled country,' and the London *Voice of Zambia* reported that he had decided 'to *suspend* our campaign of protest and try once more to make the British Government see reason. . . .' 'In Mr. Kaunda,' said the newssheet, 'the British people as well as the people of *all races* in Northern Rhodesia . . . have not only their best friend but also their *last* friend.'[26]

The disturbances that had erupted in August dragged on into

September. Kaunda noted on many occasions that, as Hall put it, 'the "insurgents" never attacked Europeans except in clashes with the security forces.' 'At Missions for instance,' said Kaunda, 'there were no clashes at all, yet sometimes missionaries were very isolated.' 'It was a real success story.' But he was deeply perturbed by news of hunted men living in secret forest camps. 'We began to fear that something like Mau Mau might begin if we didn't handle this quickly and properly; for they might have stayed in the bush almost for ever';[27] and as he said in retrospect, 'if you drive an animal into a corner and torment it, you may expect that, in its fear and rage, it will slash back at you.'[28] The animosities within the land were sharply illustrated by Chona's article in the August *Voice of UNIP:* 'A European,' he wrote, 'spends 3/- a day feeding his dog . . . per month, £4.10.0d. . . .' 'A dog does not work. . . . Yet many of you who work for Europeans receive £3 or less per month. . . . Nothing will make this situation for you nice. . . . It is for you to decide to be free.' The burning of 64,000 *ifitupa,* as estimated by the *Voice,* signalised such a surge of liberation: 'No majority, no tax.'[29]

In October Kenneth was able to start visiting the northern districts. Over 2,600 people had been arrested, and he found nervousness everywhere. At Mwense, as Mama Chola remembered it, his visit had a dramatic effect. 'The people lined up on the road cheering and chanting political songs. But the Messengers, the police, the Mobile Unit and the Europeans ran and sought refuge' in a Government building. As he approached, women beat their breasts in lamentation. 'We asked how he had not been killed, but he said he was safe and alive. We assured him that even though we had been beaten, as long as he was safe, everything was all right. While he was still in the car, police and Messengers began to come to greet him. We wanted to stop them but the President said, "No, let me greet them." ' Kaunda paid a visit then to Mwata Kazembe, the Luunda Chief, and then came and spoke to the crowd. 'We shall get freedom sooner than expected,' he said. 'The most important thing is to do what I tell you. If I say, "Let's dance," just dance. If I say, "Let's sing," just sing. . . . You, Messengers and policemen, do not threaten your brothers and sisters. When we get our freedom, we are not going to dismiss you from your jobs. . . . We shall be leaders only because we are elected. So please do not threaten my people. As soon as I get back the country, I shall simply say to you "Right about turn" and you will turn and follow me. . . . These very people you are threatening and beating are the people who are going to save you. . . . And if you adopt cleaner methods, I shall be able to adopt mild ways of gaining independence without the shedding of blood. Then we shall lead people to peace, stability, unity and understanding.'[30]

Chinsali had been the scene of some of the worst violence. In addition to the incidents cited by the Scots missionary at Lubwa, many other testimonies exist of barbarous actions against people who did not themselves use violence against persons. The wanton destruction of granaries posed the threat of severe hunger. But one of the worst incidents was associated with the forest of Chibuba or Mwaba wa Nkulungwe, to the west of Lubwa on the road to the Chambeshi River. In a sharp encounter with soldiers, a number of people fled into this forest. 'The security forces fired into it and stopped others from going into it. So these people died and rotted there.' UNIP's document, *A Grim Peep into the North*, which we shall consider later, added that 'aeroplanes machine-gunned the villages.'

When Kaunda reached Chinsali, the ban on meetings was in force and he was anxious not to cause more suffering by letting people gather. However, he sent a private message to Lubwa asking if he might greet the church elders. The missionary agreed readily and arranged that, after Kenneth and he had had a drink of orange juice, they would meet the elders in the small domestic science room. But they found no one there and then realised that a large number of bicycles was stacked outside the large church building nearby. The church was packed, but absolutely quiet. 'Kaunda said, "This is very awkward, even in the church" ', but, said the missionary, 'I told him it would be all right. He could talk to them in a worshipful way and I would say a prayer and we could sing a hymn and have a Bible reading. He spoke very, very well. . . . I was listening very carefully to find out whether he was going to be a rabble-rouser. His line was: "We have made our point, people are beginning to understand. Now let's keep organised. Let's keep our oneness . . . and let's not destroy what we're doing by bitterness and strife. . . ." He spoke for about an hour and you could have heard a pin drop. . . . At the end he said, "Now we're going to disperse. . . . I don't want any mob outside the church, no open-air meeting or demonstration of any kind." ' The next day, however, the primary school Head Master was suspended for allegedly having allowed pupils to attend a meeting, and the missionary was forbidden to leave Lubwa.[31]

In those days, it was not only the affairs of the territory that were concerning Kenneth. On 17 September, Dag Hammarskjöld, Secretary-General of the United Nations Organisation, had been killed in a mysterious air crash over Ndola as fighting raged around Elizabethville in the Congo's secessionist province of Katanga. 'I wept publicly,' said Kenneth, 'because this man, committed to world peace, had died on our territory.' Immediately the London *Voice of Zambia* stated that 'Welensky . . . had invited Tshombe to Northern Rhodesia and hatched a conspiracy that shortly led to the ruthless murder of Dag.' Sir Roy sued the paper for libel but, on receipt of an abject public apology, six months later, dropped the action, promising to give the damages awarded to him to charity. Even more sinister than the U.N. Secretary's death, however, was the flow of mercenaries through the Protectorate into Katanga. The wooing of Lawrence Katilungu by those U.F.P. members who now realised that they could not afford to ignore Africans was increasing anxiety about the Katanga situation because of suspicions that ANC would be ready to associate inextricably with Tshombe and Welensky in a potentially anti-UNIP alliance. ANC's Berrings Lombe had announced some months earlier, that Tshombe had promised to give Congress 'a fleet of Land Rovers'.[32] In the midst of this tangle of intrigue, Kaunda found himself obliged to apologise publicly to London for the statement of UNIP's delegation to a Conference of non-aligned nations in Belgrade in September that 'a well-planned genocide operation is being conducted against three million innocent and unarmed Africans of Northern Rhodesia by the European settlers of the country with the paternal sanction of the British Government.' The security forces, Kaunda said, had been guilty of 'arson, plundering and atrocities' which Britain should investigate. But the charge of genocide was wrong. Despite his aplogy, however, some UN P leaders, according to the press, continued to publicise what they regarded as evidence of a plan to decimate the African population.[33]

The Northern Rhodesian Christian Council, meanwhile, despite the Governor's assurance that the June proposals were 'irrevocable', now issued a call for a general conference of political leaders, which Kaunda at once supported. The stirring of Christian leaders was welcome, but he was aware that many ordinary church members were still 'prevented from joining political parties', Christian teachers often fearing to be 'put on a black list by the missionary managers or their Education Officers'.[34]

It was now that Reginald Maudling succeeded Iain Macleod as Colonial Secretary. Macleod's two years had undoubtedly exposed him to extraordinary strain and his touch had been less certain in Northern Rhodesia's crisis than in the less complicated Nyasaland situation. Kenneth Kaunda, however, spoke very warmly of him. 'Mr Macleod's departure from the Colonial Office is a matter of deep regret to me because he was obviously a very progressive Colonial Secretary. But as one who counts him as friend, I am happy at his promotion and, who knows, the first African Prime Minister of Zambia might have to be welcomed into the Commonwealth by British Prime Minister Macleod. Mr. Macleod's promotion could mean he was probably consulted about his successor. We welcome Mr. Maudling to his new post. It is a difficult one. But he is obviously a modern Tory M.P. and realises only too well that "Men shall not live by bread alone." '[35]

Sir Roy Welensky was meanwhile renewing pressure for the Federal Review Conference to be reconvened, and at home his 'Build a Nation' campaign was appealing for inter-racial co-existence in goodwill. But Mainza Chona decried the 'Build a Nation' campaign as specious. People of all races, he said 'are tired of their impossible and dangerous resistance to the advent of the inevitable', and Kenneth Kaunda claimed that 'reliable sources' confirmed a secret alliance between the U.F.P. and Colin Cunningham's fanatical 'F.F.F.' Meanwhile Roberts was still refusing to join all-party consultations under the chairmanship of Hone though it was rumoured that Welensky was urging him to change his mind, now that it had been announced that Maudling would soon visit the Protectorate.[36]

A Grim Peep into the North had now been released by UNIP's International and Publicity Bureau and was eventually to be answered, in January 1962, by the Government's *Account of the Disturbances in Northern Rhodesia, July to October, 1961.* UNIP had rejected the Government report in advance on the ground that 'the accused would be their own judges.' Kaunda in his introduction to *A Grim Peep*, stated that the evidence which he had gathered in person on his trip to the two worst troubled provinces had convinced him that the 'so-called security forces' had been guilty of 'murder, arson, plunder and savage atrocities. . . .' 'The charge I make,' he wrote, 'is a serious one but it is true. . . .' 'I am positive that the Central Government does not possess full facts . . . much less His Excellency himself.' The sum of the evidence showed that 'whole villages have been razed to the ground, foodstuffs including goats, sheep and fowls have been taken away, to say nothing of clothes, pots, pans and other utensils.' 'What they could not take away they destroyed.' The Chiefs, Kenneth affirmed had received him and his colleagues on their tour 'with open hands [sic]', and he paid a special tribute to the Bemba Paramount Chief, Chitimukulu, 'my beloved natural ruler'. The campaign against *ifitupa* had been successful. In consequence, 'prisons are so full now that . . . there are as many as three prisoners to a blanket.'[37]

The immediate effect of the publication of *A Grim Peep* was that the Government set to work compiling its own account of 'Cha-cha-cha'. Of the two documents, Mulford has said that the Government's *Account of Disturbances*, although 'less flamboyant and containing fewer extreme exaggerations, was no less biased than UNIP's'. Indeed it appeared to have been consciously manipulated, accordign to a letter to the Administrative Secretary from the officer who prepared it. 'I have endeavoured to be frank enough to resist charges of white-washing and yet restrained enough to avoid making unnecessary self-inflicted wounds. I hope I have not offended the security forces by gratuitous criticism and at the same time to have disarmed those who will charge us with evasion. . . . I have been mindful of the necessity of avoiding any reference to the central leadership of UNIP, which might present new ammunition to the opposition in Legislative Council, and might embarrass us in impending constitutional negotiations.'[38]

On 1 November, Governor Hone had announced that law and order had been restored. The evidence suggests that this chance to draw breath again came, to a great extent, because Kenneth Kaunda, who had not swerved from the necessity of non-violence, had survived a crisis marked by extravagant violence upon persons and property in villages built of forest poles and roofed with grass. When Mulford writes that 'without tarnishing his image as a militant nationalist leader' Kaunda had sought to ease the party towards 'constitutional negotiations and to encourage the policy of multi-racialism', we are given the image of a delicate manoeuvrer, a politician astutely maintaining his own position. Yet the testimony of his close colleagues is that he stayed as their leader because, at one and the same time, he insisted on principles without which he foresaw chaos, while being quick to listen and open to the thoughts and concerns not only of his associates but also of people like Iain Macleod and Evelyn Hone who were nominally in the opposing camp. One might expect to find a disciple of 'non-violence' in a party of 'moderates', but what distinguished 'the struggle in Northern Rhodesia was that its most revolutionary nationalists and those most bitter against the pervasive crudities and insults of 'the colour bar' acclaimed Kenneth as their spokesman. There were undoubtedly rumblings of discontent as well as personal jealousies within UNIP, but the Party had remained loyal to the man who, in Lewis Changufu's words, kept their minds 'fixed on the struggle for freedom' and whose 'determination and clear thinking' gave so much encouragement to them. The man who 'kept them on their toes' was the same man who pointed constantly to a new society to be attained without hatred or bloodshed.[39]

The memorandum which Kenneth Kaunda submitted to the new Colonial Secretary called for a clear African majority in the Legislature, affirmed the failure of the Lancaster House Conference, declared that the African people would not 'swallow' an imposed settlement, and pressed for a legislative majority representing the electoral majority. A few days later, on 12 December, Kaunda said that UNIP was declaring 'political war' on the draining from the country of vast sums of money in the form of B.S.A. Company royalties. There was information in his possession which would not be released yet to the effect that the Company was politically linked with what was going on in Katanga as well as in Angola, Mozambique and South Africa.[40] This fresh attack on the British South Africa Company was being joined by well-informed critics of white supremacy abroad. Fenner Brockway called the Company 'the evil genius of Rhodesia' and quoted Welensky's strictures, made thirteen years earlier in Leg. Co., upon "agreements, if

you can call them that . . . negotiated in the early part of the
nineties . . . ." "The Company knew what it was after" Welensky
had said, "but I certainly question whether any African chief
. . . knew that he was disposing of . . . mineral rights." ' The
Company, Brockway pointed out, was so wealthy that 'even in a
lean year it is able to pay a dividend of 30%. . . .' 'Until 1964
it is to have half the proceeds of land disposed of by the Government
of NW Rhodesia.' Moreover 'it owns 99% of the shares of the
Rhodesia Railway Trust.' Obviously 'the African people of Northern
Rhodesia, existing in poverty, are not likely to allow one alien
company to net millions of pounds a year from royalties on their
natural resources.' Brockway then showed what in fact this 'net-
ting' represented. 'If one takes an average year, between boom and
slump, the mineral royalties . . . amounted to £8,857,691, while
the 39,000 African miners were paid £7,341,374 in wages.' That
figure gave an average annual wage for these miners of about £190.
Not surprisingly, as the *Northern News* had stated 'right from
the beginning of Federation, the BSA Company and the big mining
companies have been paying a considerable subsidy to the United
Federal Party.' Welensky, who as a settlers' leader in the nineteen-
forties had wanted the wealth of the Company for his compatriots,
had come to realise a common interest between his U.F.P. and the
B.S.A. in face of 'the wind of change' in Central Africa.[41]

As the spotlight turned upon the B.S.A. Company's role and
UNIP drew closer to the African Trade Union movement, it was
proving very difficult to avoid racial polarisation. Kenneth Kaunda
had expressed his deep concern to Harold Macmillan, in the critical
period in July, over the fact that the Federal call-up could apply
to provincial officers. 'The arming of our white people . . . against
the British Protected black people' posed a grave enough danger
of breeding race hatred, but the conscription of men sent from
Britain as colonial officers meant that they were 'compelled to
owe their first allegiance to the Federal Government . . . and not
to the Imperial Government. . . .' 'Therefore' he said 'your
Government can no longer protect my black people nor the
thousands of white people and Asians who object to being ruled
from Salisbury.'[42]

There was, moreover, a regular flow to UNIP headquarters
of reports of 'brutalities' done by police and other officials, listing

the names of persons tortured and specifying the form of torture inflicted, which allegedly included locking in an ice-chamber, use of hot irons, assault of private parts, and forcing people to spend a night on a wet floor. The prospect of a further extension of military action throughout the territory was seen as a grave threat to any attempts to restore confidence and peace. Mainza Chona ended one statement on 'Police Brutalities' by saying: 'If this is what Christianity and civilisation are, I tell every European civiliser to pack up and go without leaving a single Bible behind. Colonialism stinks and is a sinful evil.'[43]

In retrospect, Kaunda has spoken of police excesses as 'a scar that has been very difficult to clear'. Among his personal experiences, he has told of an occasion, in the 'Cha-cha-cha' period, when after he had been working late in his Lusaka office, he was about to set off for the Copperbelt with Sikalumbi. As they sent out for fish and chips to eat on the way, Sikalumbi was called by the police. 'Where is Kaunda going?' they asked. Kenneth himself answered that they had 'no business' to ask this question. 'You'll soon learn,' Kenneth replied, 'that what I'm doing isn't mischievous.' At this, the officer began to search him roughly, and Kaunda said, 'Be careful. You might have to pay for this one day.' They had not gone far when they were stopped by another group of police who 'manhandled' the driver. 'Who are you?' an officer shouted at Kaunda, 'You're a trouble-maker.' 'I may be today,' Kenneth retorted, 'but I won't be tomorrow.' He was certain that his Party was 'on the winning side' at that time, but keenly aware that 'the image of the police was so bad that it would be very hard to reconcile the people to them'. Again, in his northern tour in November, he found the police and District Messengers constantly on his trail. This was the time when, as he recalled, he 'received so many blessings from the Chiefs, a total of 12 deportation orders'.[44]

We have cited sufficient extracts from UNIP's documents to confirm the forceful utterance used by many of its publicists. Among the many communications emanating from UNIP headquarters in the latter part of 1961, the following specially reveal both the range of international concerns pressing upon the Party and the pungency of its message. For instance, Kapwepwe rebuked the leaders of 'the Pan-Africanist Congress outside South Africa' for selling the principles of the movements' martyrs. 'I think if

Mangaliso [Sobukwe] could be allowed by these cruel Boers to peep outside his jail . . . he would, I am sure, die of shock.' Nearer home, the activities of Colin Cunningham roused the fury of Mukuka Nkoloso who wrote to the press accusing him of 'growing bigger than his political boots' by propagating the 'venomous and acrid poison of racialism' through his Rhodesian Republican Party, 'a gang of ferocious mercenaries'. In December, Sikota Wina issued a statement welcoming the retirement of Martin Wray, the Chief Secretary, whom he accused of 'intemperate and unwarranted hysterics' at the time of the revelation, through UNIP, of the mathematical 'hidden meaning of the Macleod June Plan'. Wina then stated that Sir Evelyn Hone was 'not a good Governor but . . . probably the best Northern Rhodesia has had for a long time . . . [and] would have been much better' but for 'the ill-intended advices [*sic*] of his Chief Secretary'. At the same time, just before the New Year, Chona wrote to the United Nations in New York condemning Welensky's demand for an investigation of U.N. conduct in Katanga as 'an endeavour to focus world attention away' from the Federation's plan to use secessionist Katanga as 'a buffer against the Independent African states'. Welensky had expressed his hope, in 1960, that 'this vast and rich part of the Belgian Congo . . . could throw off its old ties and join the Federation'. Since then, Chona alleged, there had been an 'office to recruit mercenaries' for Katanga opened in Lusaka. Katangan planes had been given use of Northern Rhodesian aerodromes 'without hindrance'. This was creating a grave threat to peace in Africa and beyond and so Kaunda, on behalf of 'the major political movement in Rhodesia' was 'prepared to appear before the UNO in person'.[45]

Kenneth Kaunda was meanwhile making prolific use of his pen, despite his ceaseless travel in the country and abroad. Party organisation was worrying him in the wake of the northern disturbances and, in a circular calling for vigorous discipline and systematic communication within UNIP, he warned that he was 'going to check on every branch' week by week. By press statements in late September and October, he warned strongly against the military activities of the U.F.P. 'They must be told,' he said, 'that we would lack neither courage nor resources of dangerous weapons.' 'We could get anything here tomorrow,' if the building of 'U.F.P. resistance armies' went 'too far'. A lengthy statement was devoted to the alteration of Macleod's orginal 15-15-15 'parity' proposals, which, he said, must have been made on the recommendation of 'senior advisers in Northern Rhodesia'. Though it had 'been said in Sir Evelyn Hone's favour that he did not understand his own proposals', he had taken responsibility for them by signing them. This statement ended with reference to the trial in Lusaka recently of a white man who had assaulted the American Assistant Secretary of State for African Affairs, G. Mennon Williams. In this case, the magistrate, ruling out a political motive, had handed down a fine of £50. 'Do you think,' asked Kaunda, 'that the magistrate would have fined a UNIP man £50 for an offence of this type?' 'No . . . he would have handed out 2 years hard labour and 12 strokes of the cane' for a "criminal political assault".' 'Is this what is meant by British Justice? Are these the laws our students are being taught in universities overseas?'[46]

Above all, however, it was the need for a forward look to galvanize creative energies and build unity on a basis sounder than the sharing of a common enemy that was uppermost in Kenneth Kaunda's mind at this time. Therefore, a week before Christmas, he issued a confidential circular to the Party's Central Committee. 'Very often,' he began, 'we have stressed to the British Government that they could not decide on anything pertaining to our country in isolation from what is taking place elsewhere on the Continent.' It was no less essential for his people to be aware of what he called 'the international financiers'. The Congo tragedy brought out in sharp relief the mercilessness of their power. Patrice Lumumba, 'never a communist', had appealed to Russia before he had 'consolidated his forces'. Thus 'Tshombe', he wrote, 'was used only as a tool in this sad tragic event' of Lumumba's death. This international power block had also effected President Kennedy's very recent swift *volte face* from his declared support for United Nations action in the Congo. South Africa, Portugal and Welensky were in alliance with this bloc. But, he went on, 'this paper is not designed to scare us into submission to the forces of oppression. . . .' '[They] are powerful and it would be tragic to ignore them. . . . [But] it cannot be overemphasised that the answer lies in effective organisation. This means a careful study of our cultural, social, economic and political problems at all levels. . . . There is a real need to come down to the people. . . . One other factor . . . is that the purchasing of landrovers for divisional leaders has made a good number of them reluctant to walk, run or cycle.' He proposed therefore a dividing of the present divisions into regions which, he believed, would 'help to build a new spirit among our people and . . . keep the government of an independent Zambia intact.'[47]

New Year 1962 began with a cautionary note from Maudling about demands for independence, and a bitter broadside from Welensky against the past year's pattern of 'liberation for colonial peoples' whereby, he claimed, 'in Africa, fresh areas of chaos and depression were opened up.' Harry Nkumbula then came out of jail to a Congress cocktail party, and at once resumed the Congress Presidency, which had been held by Mungoni Liso since the death of Katilungu in a road accident in November. Just as UNIP threatened to resume its 'Master Plan' there was a 'leak' from London to the effect that Maudling's revision of Macleod's June 1961 plan would favour African candidates. The Colonial Secretary, it was said, was 'eager to dispose of the Northern Rhodesia question'. Kaunda's concern over Maudling's delay led him to warn that he might have to move a 'mass mine strike' from the fifth to the third stage of his 'Plan'. He was at once countered by John Chisata's declaration that the A.M.W.U. 'could not stand a strike'. Sikota Wina however took the threat further by talking of 'country-wide strikes to bring to a complete standstill every activity'. The welter of prejudice and passion was further agitated by more news of mercenaries, this time a group of 35, passing through Ndola on their way to help Tshombe and by U Thant's specific reference, which Welensky did not deny, to 'the activities of a Dornier aircraft based at Ndola and piloted by one Mr Wickstead'. As January drew to a close, Kaunda said he had an authoritative report of a meeting between Tshombe and Welensky in the Queen's House, Kitwe. Meanwhile in Southern Rhodesia the National Democratic Party had been banned in December, and the former Chief Justice, Sir Robert Tredgold, had warned that, by extinguishing 'the only political organisation that could claim a wide measure of African support,' Whitehead had moved 'towards the one-party system of government, which is totalitarian'.

The press now reported the possibility of a split in the British cabinet with Maudling and Macleod lined up against a group led by Lord Home who held that it was 'vital not to antagonise

Sir Roy'. But telegrams were piling up on Kenneth's desk demanding action on the 'Master Plan' and Justin Chimba feared that they indicated tension so high that 'an eruption of some sort' might happen without instructions from the Party President. Kaunda's reaction was to reiterate that it might be necessary to paralyse the mines and that, in preparation for such a possibility, people should not spend money on drink and on clothing, for 'who knows how long a strike will last?' Then, as at previous moments of high tension, he went abroad, this time to Ethiopia. 'While I am out of the country, nothing must happen,' he ordered. 'But if I don't take the strike action if the Constitution does not come out right, I must be prepared to be overthrown and let other leaders take my place.' Meanwhile, he urged, people should await word of changes in the Constitution and 'drink milk instead of beer'.[48]

The correspondence columns of the press were increasingly filled with letters for and against UNIP. One African correspondent blamed Kaunda because 'unlike the Moffats, he has taught us disrespect for chiefs and how to hate one another [and] also frightened away capital'. Meanwhile, some members of UNIP were talking of the men hanged 'for the alleged murder of a European woman' as 'freedom fighters'. Once again, therefore, Kenneth made a public apology, on UNIP's behalf, for this statement, repeating his 'shock' at the murder and his condemnation of it. 'On the other hand,' he said, 'the act of the four men who had to find an outlet for their pent-up nationalism can be understood.' He was continuing his programme of meetings with 'non-Africans', at which the death of Mrs. Burton was constantly raised. Robert Burton was again involved in the controversy and asked for further reassurance from Kaunda. 'I had always held the view,' he wrote, 'that the incident of 8th May, 1960, was one of vandalism, not one of political violence laid at the door of any party.' 'It seems I was wrong.'[49] A considerable number of Europeans still echoed the sentiments of one letter to the *Northern News* which said that 'the African has subscribed literally nothing to the development of his country except to shout "Kwacha". '

Roy Welensky meanwhile rejected any 'compromise with Pan-Africanism' whereby 'a man's race is to count, not his ability', as news was recived that the Pan-African Movement of East and Central Africa was to discuss positive aid to the recently formed

Zimbabwe African People's Union and to UNIP. At PAFMECA's meeting at Addis Ababa in February 1962, Kenneth Kaunda was elected President, and word came from Addis that he had demonstrated to other leaders that 'the spearhead of African liberation had now reached' his own country. The U.F.P. line was therefore more and more to build up the reputation of 'moderate Africans'. Godwin Mbikusita's remark that, in the eyes of the Chiefs, UNIP and 'other racialist parties were "youth clubs" ' to which it was unbelievable that Britain should pay attention, made him an ideal model of such 'moderation'.

Cha-cha-cha, as a popular 'dance' towards independence, had not ended with the Governor's statement that the situation in the north had been brought under control. The drums were still throbbing though the ecstasy had slackened, and for months to come the land was to be filled with agitation. Just after 16,301 out of 16,601 A.M.W.U men had voted in favour of a strike, fear mounted that Britain was planning to encourage the secession of Barotseland. Meanwhile Cunningham's Rhodesian Republican Party and the Dominion Party were considering a merger to force Welensky's resignation, for being too 'moderate', which may have pushed Welensky into making his famous utterance about being 'prepared to fight . . . to go the whole hog if necessary'. Immediately UNIP's Chona and Wina retorted that, if Welensky were to use force, it would be 'a signal for red war'. On the same day, news came that the Revd. Michael Scott's World Peace Brigade was planning to march into Northern Rhodesia from the north, and the question arose, what would happen if they reached the line of rail. But, said Kaunda, now back from Ethiopia, they would 'not be equipped with guns but with Bibles'. The silence of the Colonial Secretary was forcing a rapid deterioration in the situation, and Kenneth warned again that the country might have to face 'a six-month strike'. This renewed call to 'the people of Zambia' to use only 'non-violence' but in a most positive way, came just after Welensky had exclaimed: 'I would never have been prepared to face events without a properly equipped and properly manned Army and Air Force.' Welensky's friends abroad were likely to rally to support such a posture. The London *Daily Express* presented him the more favourably by listing among the 57 nations that had condemned the Federation at the United Nations, '27 dictatorships,

27 [that] have defaulted in the United Nations subscriptions, and 16 [which] suppress minorities'.[50]

Once again, however, Kenneth saw signs of hope. Chief Secretary Martin Wray had just been replaced by Richard Luyt, a South African by birth, who had once been a Labour Officer in the Copperbelt, and who later became Principal of the University of Cape Town. Kaunda regarded Luyt, like Hone, as 'a very good friend'. He did not fail either to appreciate the news that Britain's 'Young Tories' had affirmed their belief in the goal of 'one man, one vote' for Africa. More negatively, he welcomed the news, on the last day of the month, that Welensky had made a sudden flight to London, as a sign that Maudling's new plan for the country was not in Sir Roy's favour; which was confirmed the next day by the publication of the new constitutional plan. It 'could open the way to black control of the Legislative Council', said the *Northern News*. Though Maudling had 'dodged the issue', Kaunda was ready to give 'serious thought' to the plan. Maudling proposed elections in October and, though UNIP regarded this as far too late, it was soon to be clear that the 1962 General Election 'marked a change of revolutionary proportions in Northern Rhodesia politics' whereby 'Africans and Europeans joined for the first time in an electoral battle which not only brought Black Government . . . but also dealt the *coup de grace* to Federation in Central Africa.'[51]

The immediate reactions to the plan were varied, however. Nkumbula rejected it. John Gaunt saw it starkly as 'the end of Northern Rhodesia as we have known it'. An Indian M.L.C., Mistry, was simply very disappointed, while Moffat was impressed by the note of anticlimax. 'One wonders,' he said, 'what all the terrific thunder and lightning was about to produce this cupful of rain.' While Colin Morris remarked that Maudling's scheme was 'a decided improvement', Welensky rejected it angrily. 'People in Britain seem anxious,' he exclaimed, 'to pave the way for control . . . by a party whose mouthpiece, the "Voice of UNIP", has idolised the murderers of Mrs. Burton and 2,000 of whose members were imprisoned last year for serious crimes of violence.' Kaunda described the plan as 'the most racial yet devised' and declared his rejection of its ultimate objective. But he was ready to lead his Party to participate in a General Election if five important conditions were met: there must be an independent commission to delineate constituencies; 'national' seats not filled by election must not be filled by nominees of the Governor; an amnesty for banned political parties and leaders must be proclaimed; there must be no Federal Review until the attainment of representative government in the Protectorate; and the date of the elections must be brought forward. Superficially, the only difference between Maudling's plan and Macleod's June proposals was the lowering of the percentage requirement of votes cast by each race for the 'national' seats from $12\frac{1}{2}$ per cent to 10 per cent. In effect, however, it would increase the roll of eligible voters from 30,000 to 100,000.[52]

On the day after Maudling's announcement, the press reported that Kaunda had informed the Governor of an alleged plot by Welensky to arrest Hone and other senior Government officials and 'high ranking police'. The source of his information was the one that had uncovered Welensky's secret meeting with Tshombe. There would be 'terrible bloodshed', Kenneth said, if Welensky was allowed to take such action. After meeting the Governor, he expressed his full satisfaction with the reception he had received from Hone. No official comment came from the Government but the *Manchester Guardian* advised that Kaunda's report should not be dismissed 'as entire fantasy'. 'Men with long memories' would recall a similar rumour a year earlier, never refuted by Welensky, despite the serious publicity given to it by the *Economist*. Though Welensky called the report 'drivel', Kaunda maintained that he had reason to believe it. 'I wasn't good at playing up things like that,' he said. Then, on 6 March, the *Guardian* published a report on Federal plans for 'hard action' made at an emergency U.F.P. conference at Broken Hill, in which Julian Greenfield hda figured prominently and given an assurance that Welensky and he 'would back unconstitutional means' of opposing Britain's 'retreat'.[53]

As we review Kenneth's words and actions at this period, it is clear that he was striving hard to persuade people to look positively and creatively at the situation. This was shown at yet another Hindu Hall meeting in Ndola attended by 400 Asian and Eurafrican and 80 white people. With baleful inevitability, the killing of Mrs. Burton was raised by a questioner and again Kaunda deplored it as 'a shameful act'. . . . 'I will regret it as long as I live,' he said. 'But the guilty people have been punished and it serves no useful purpose to bring the tragedy back. You cannot condemn a whole community for such an action.' A couple of days later he was challenged over news of an attack on a white South African after a UNIP meeting in Luanshya. Would he support those 'who slashed a white man', he was asked. 'If the questioner could give me details of this attack,' he answered, 'I shall certainly see that the culprits are found.' 'It is not my Party's policy to go about attacking people.' Shortly afterwards he suspended the strike plan 'and called off Michael Scott's "Peace March" ' as he 'didn't want to let sympathisers suffer'. He therefore 'soft-pedalled it' despite the sharp anger of UNIP against the Government's ban on meetings of more than three people in the Abercorn and Isoka Districts, through which the 'Peace Brigade' would have had to pass. In retrospect he remarked that he 'hadn't then developed sufficient internationalism. . . .' 'Today', he added, 'I might have said "Go ahead." '[54]

As the British press played its spotlights almost daily now upon Central Africa, the failure of the Federation was described as 'one of this century's great tragedies', and the left-wing *Reynolds News* called Welensky 'an honest man with a false vision'. The *Daily Express* reported an interview with Sir Roy in which he spoke of discussions with Tshombe about 'the possibility of a union' of Katanga, with its mineral wealth, and the Rhodesias. Such an idea, Welensky claimed, 'scares the daylights out of the United Nations'. However, Kenneth Kaunda's reluctant agreement to contest elections on Maudling's formula evoked sympathy in Britain, where some members of all three main parties launched an appeal for funds to support UNIP's electoral campaign. Commenting on this appeal, *East Africa and Rhodesia* quoted Fenner Brockway's description of Kaunda as 'the Gandhi of Africa' and his remark that, unless he received 'the greatest possible assistance . . . Britain would face a situation as serious as the Boston Tea Party or the Gandhi Salt Party'. The opposing view was that of Lord Malvern whose words won a wave of applause in the House of Lords; one English peer describing Kaunda as 'a ruthless man, using the weapons of murder, violence, sabotage and intimidation to achieve his own ends'. However, the Colonial Under-Secretary had recently spoken of his 'warm personal regard for Mr. Kaunda'.[55]

UNIP's fortunes were meanwhile moving from crisis to crisis.

Sudden police raids on its offices in places as widely separated as
Monze, Lusaka and Fort Jameson had caused alarm, and in February
and March Justin Chimba and Mainza Chona were charged with
spreading rumours and issuing a seditious circular respectively.
In Lusaka ANC was accusing UNIP officials of telephone 'sabotage'
and inter-party 'gang' battles were increasing dangerously in the
Copperbelt towns as well as in Lusaka. Then came a report, soon
afterwards, of 'a threat to kill' Kaunda on his return to Lusaka from
Kapiri Mposhi in early April. A heavy police escort had to be
provided, which led UNIP supporters to think that he had been
arrested. In Lusaka, 19 UNIP members were charged with the
illegal wearing of Party 'uniforms' and a press report spoke of
UNIP's plan to have 'political commissars', for its election drive,
even though Kaunda was 'a pure nationalist with no communist
leanings'. The 'red bogey' nonetheless touched the frayed nerves
of many white people at the news of a police haul of 'piles of
communist books' from a 'red cell' uncovered on the Copperbelt,
even though it was stated explicitly that none of the country's
political parties was in league with the 'cell'.[56]

It was now that Harold Macmillan made a new move to resolve
the Central African crisis by appointing his Home Secretary,
Robert Butler, as Minister with special responsibility for the Federal
area. At once however, both ANC and UNIP voiced their 'suspicion'.
Britain appeared to be anxious to reassure the wrong people, they
felt; though Welensky himself was declaring that he had 'no loyalty
to the British Government, only a profound loyalty to the Queen
in person', and that the Federation's £8,000,000 Defence Bill was
a matter of 'sheer necessity'. Colin Morris, however, was calling
on Europeans to realise that they must 'deal with the *de facto*
leaders of the African people just as they are . . . if multi-racialism
can provide no solution', and make 'a hard-headed deal'. The
fact that Europeans had 'fought a last battle for the control of
the Legislature had resulted in all the dynamism of the African
nationalists being concentrated upon dislodging them to the complete
disregard of economic reality . . . for every proletarian African
is a nationalist'. The bitterness was still in spate when Kenneth
Kaunda set off on 9 April, with Sir Stewart Gore-Browne and
T. L. Desai to present the cause of Zambia before the United Nations
Committee on Colonialism.[57]

When the inner communications of UNIP are known, it will become even clearer that Kaunda, though only thirty-eight years of age in 1962, was constantly facing the challenges of a type of leadership that was a macrocosm of the role of a headmaster. Now, just as he was set to carry UNIP's cause to New York, Sikota Wina made a statement in Salisbury which created a furore and involved Kenneth at once in the double task of explaining away his colleague's words and yet retaining Wina's enthusiasm for constructive work. Speaking at a meeting with the recently formed Zimbabwe African People's Union, Wina declared that one of UNIP's first acts on attaining control in Northern Rhodesia would be to declare Welensky a 'prohibited immigrant' as part of the Party's programme of 'demoralisation of the white man'. Kenneth's immediate comment was that 'what Wina did say was that the first thing we would do was to demoralise those white men who believe in Federation, like Welensky . . . not a declaration of colour but against Federation.' But he followed this protective comment by a strong reiteration against violence. 'UNIP stands a good chance of winning the coming elections,' he said, 'and therefore stands to lose if a wave of violence should sweep the country. . . .' 'Violence is wrong and I continue to condemn it.' A week later, however, Wina resigned his important post as UNIP's Director of Elections, and was replaced by Solomon Kalulu. Kaunda then stated that the alleged remark about 'P.I.ing Welensky had been wrong as the Central Committee has reached no such decision'. Two journalists meanwhile confirmed that Wina had definitely spoken of 'a programme for the demoralisation of the white man in Central Africa'. Nine years later, in an interview with the *Sunday Times of Zambia*, Wina gave his version of the incident thus: 'Once before Independence I told a large crowd that, in order to solve our problems, we must first demoralise the white man. The President was furious when he heard . . . [and] said "I want you to understand that I am not interested in the colour of a man's skin", and he asked me to resign from my job as publicity director. I was sacked for two months because of this remark.' But it would have been easy to expose him then to public disgrace and indeed to cause others of the more extreme Party men to rally round him and so promote dissension. Instead, as a man who became a Cabinet Minister said, 'He does not punish people when they ought to be punished. . . .' 'We

Kenneth Kaunda of Zambia

may take this as a weakness . . . but it has solved more problems than the problems that have been created by not taking firm action immediately.'[58]

Though Wina had to accept disciplinary demotion, he was engaged in early April in organising what was called the 'Committee of Thirty', a special body established to formulate UNIP's policies, for presentation to the electorate, on agriculture, education, health, economics, foreign trade and commerce, local government, the judiciary, prisons, etc. This 'high-powered top-level' group was 'drawn from the intellectual cream of Northern Rhodesia Africans'. As Chairman of this 'Easter School of Political Policies', Wina laid down that it would be held in private houses as hotels were 'undesirable for security reasons'. One member wrote to say that it would be difficult to participate. He was a doctor in Kitwe. 'The sad thing,' he wrote 'is none of my colleagues can swap duties ever with me because I am not allowed to touch European patients.' From this Easter conference came eventually the 60-page election brochure called *UNIP Policy* which we shall note later, and also the ten 'Parliamentary Committees' which would be listed in a Press Statement in early October, when Kaunda announced the names of UNIP's election candidates.[59] A few days later, the local press reported that Angolan refugees were streaming into the Congo at the rate of over 200 daily, the total now exceeding 150,000. They were in flight from Portuguese napalm bombs dropped to 'punish' villagers as the great revolt dragged on behind a heavy wall of censorship.[60]

As Kaunda sped on his travels to America and then Britain, the death toll in the Copperbelt inter-party clashes rose sharply and Kapwepwe had emergency talks, described as 'cordial', with the Provincial Commissioner. Aaron Milner, he heard, had had to flee from Fort Jameson because of an ANC threat against him, and as the Police intensified anti-riot measures, the *Northern News* declared again that the disturbances showed that UNIP was 'its own worst enemy'. As May began, John Chisata further heightened the tension by announcing a massive strike of African miners. '5,000 European miners,' he claimed, 'grossed a total of £14 million per annum, while 37,000 Africans earned only £6 million.' The strike was non-political '—not part of Kaunda's "Master Plan" ' and the European Union, this time, offered 'moral support', though not by either a 'go-slow' or by refusing to work. Solomon Kalulu then commented that, because their grievances were so great, Africans might be driven to boycott the October elections. 'The Argus Press, the Government and the Police' were all working against the African people. The conviction of Chona on a charge of sedition for his statement attacking the work of District Commissioners as magistrates in cases involving political unrest was yet another sign of the gulf of misunderstanding in the land; and a pronouncement by the Litunga that a victory of the African nationalists in October would be a signal for the secession of Barotseland confirmed that UNIP's overtures to Mwanawina had still not succeeded.[61]

Moreover, prominence was being given to Kaunda's reported statement in America that he was 'not unsympathetic' to the idea of a one-party state. The 'one-party' issue, which provoked a sharp retort from Nkumbula, became increasingly contentious as weeks went by, and so, in September, Arthur Wina, who had been with Kaunda in New York, quoted verbatim from the official record of the United Nations. In answer to the question of an Indian delegate, Kenneth had said: "I do not remember saying at any time that I favour a one-party system. . . . If the people decide that there should be one party by electing members of one party to fill, for instance, all the seats in any Constituent Assembly, I see no reason why we should try to encourage an opposition just for the sake of opposition. . . . But if my policies and those of my party are sufficiently good, sufficiently appealing to the people, I see no reason at all for fearing opposition . . . we would allow any number of political parties to function in the country, provided they did not play a devastating game that would destroy the Government, provided they did not play in [*sic*] the hands of foreign elements, provided they did not plan to overthrow the Government through use of force."[62]

Kenneth stopped in London, after leaving New York and addressed a large gathering, chaired by the Bishop of Woolwich, at which he prophesied the death of the Federation in the face of African determination 'to build societies responsive to their own traditions'. He also asserted that UNIP had known what 'the rest of the world did not know', namely that Welensky was in close touch with Tshombe. As he spoke, a woman heckler, shouting

'Murder, murder' was hustled from the hall. From London he went to Sweden to lay a wreath on the grave of Dag Hammarskjöld. This visit was followed by a gift of £20,000 to assist UNIP from the Swedish Liberal Party and some Social Democrats who described Kenneth as 'the central figure in the movement for independence'. When, therefore, he stopped at Mbeya in Tanganyika for a meeting of PAFMECA, he was hailed as 'guest of honour', for, as the *London Times* had remarked, he had succeeded at the United Nations Committee in making 'a damaging attack' on the Federation 'in a widely publicised forum that listened to him with the greatest sympathy'. Not surprisingly, the British delegate had responded 'with reluctance and evident embarrassment, for Northern Rhodesia is not a United Nations trust territory and, strictly speaking, is not subject to United Nations investigation'. Kenneth had 'shown little concern about such niceties' and been 'unsparing in his criticism of the failure of the Government to take into account the opinions of Africans'. Zambia was on the way to 'a place in the sun'.[63]

Kenneth had told the U.N. 'Committee of 17' that his country consisted of 'four watertight compartments—the area of the white settlers, the "second-class" area of the Asians, the area of the Eurafricans, and finally the compounds of the Africans', and that this must be changed. The *Voice of UNIP* was still talking of the 'four heroes' who had been hanged for killing Mrs. Burton, and attributed to Cresta Ngebe, before his execution, a farewell message bidding people to "bear in their minds that we shall not die at all in spirit [but] be with them wherever they are carrying on the national work". The *Voice* had carried other messages likely to rouse bitterness. A. J. Soko gave a personal account of his experiences in Bwana Mkubwa maximum security prison, where, he alleged, boys and old men were stripped, forced to run naked, beaten and cursed. Throughout the towns, racist 'pinpricks' continued as before, but were now receiving more publicity, as when a team from Katanga was evicted from 'Europeans Only' seats in the Nchanga football stadium and a 'race row' blew up in consequence.[64] The *Zambia Times*, Ndola Branch's periodical, portrayed a future free of all the restrictive and oppressive practices that still distinguished colonial rule. 'If we follow Kaunda . . . the mass arrests in our stinking locations . . . will come to an end, for he will form a government that will express the will of the people and not only that of Europeans. . . . Poll tax shall be abolished because it is unfair . . . in that people who have no work are forced to pay while a European who has no job does not pay income tax. . . . If we follow Kaunda, this slave-tax and the company that introduced it will come to an end. The £10,000,000 paid to the B.S.A. Co. annually as royalty shall be spent on education, hospitals, wages for the miners and family allowances. . . . Poll-tax forces our people to leave villages to become cheap labourers in the mines, on the farms and railways. . . . When Kaunda comes to power, there will be promotions . . . based on merit, in all directions.'[65]

This was the mood that prevailed as the turgid year rushed on towards October, and it gave thrust to the campaign to encourage voters to register. Thus Solomon Kalulu protested at the slowness of registration and declared that only a third of the 100,000 eligible would be registered by the end of June.[66] As the only party that was organised on a territorial basis, UNIP had 1,799 branches in May 1962, having added 200 in the previous six months.[67] The non-African membership of the Party was growing significantly and Kaunda was insisting on 'non-racialism' as a cardinal pre-requisite of peace. 'Do you hate white men because they are white?' he asked a huge rally in Lusaka in May. 'No,' the crowd roared back. Then turning to Joshua Nkomo who was with him on the platform he said: 'We don't support you because you are black, but because your cause is just and right. If you came into power and started kicking about the whites we would oppose you.' A month afterwards, Sir John Moffat declared that the African nationalists' political objectives were going to be attained, and represented 'a vital dynamic force'. Then as another huge crowd of well over 20,000 gathered in Kitwe for a much publicised pre-election rally, James Skinner exclaimed that 'the golden bell of liberty' was ringing, and Kaunda began his speech by declaiming: 'We are better organised than two years ago. . . . This is my final warning.' But he affirmed, 'we want only peaceful advancement.' 'Even if they kill me, I want you to promise you will not hit back. There are others to take my place.' A roar of disapproval came from the crowd. 'We want power,' he went on, 'agreed.' 'But only so that we can use it for the good of all. . . . We can promise this because we fear God. . . . The rule of law will prevail.'

It was now being recognised both in Central Africa and abroad that Northern Rhodesia was witnessing a popular resurgence of powerful proportions. In the words of a missionary priest, UNIP was not just a political party, but 'a folk movement, the soul awakening of a people.' 'We should welcome this movement in trembling and joy', wrote the missionary to the *Northern News*, and 'anyone who looks back nostalgically to the peaceful days before the politicians interfered can only expect the fate of Lot's wife.'[68]

---

[1]Speech by Nelson Mandela at the end of the Rivonia Trial, June 1964, reproduced in J. Kantor, *A Healthy Grave*, (Hamish Hamilton, 1967), 221-227.

[2]*Africa Digest*, Vol. VIII, No. 6, p. 225.

[3]Vol. I, No. 4, (July 1961), pp. 5-6.

[4]*Ibid.*, p. 1.

[5]UNIP/2/PUB/GEN, 28/6/61: Joint Statement issued by President Kaunda and President Nkomo, National Democratic Party, Salisbury Airport.

[6]*NN*, 6/7/61; and FH: Kaunda's Press Communique, Accra, 27/6/61.

[7]'UNIP Conference, July 8th, D-Day—"We have Power"—National President's Address to the Territorial Annual Conference', 9/7/61. The quotation from *Julius Caesar* is to be found in Act IV, Scene 3, lines 212 ff.

[8]FH: Notes (undated) on the Mulungushi Conference.

[9]*NN*, 10/7/61; TI-FM/People of Mwense, Luapula (in Bemba) incl. Mama Chola, UNIP Regional Women's Secretary, 15/2/70; TI-FM/KK, 11/4/69 and 9/4/71, and FM/AG Zulu, 27/2/69.

[10]FH: 'Resolution passed at the Second Annual Conference', UNIP, Mulungushi, 10/7/61.

[11]ANC/CEO/OA/7 *Week by Week*, 28/4/61; and Typed Report of Rioting in Chibolya, Kalingalinga, Howard and Mandevu compounds, 14-17/51.

[12]E.g. FH: Report by J. M. Chapoloko, W. Province President to 5th National Council, 30/6/61, blaming Hyden Banda (currently in jail) for encouraging arrogance of UNIP Youth Brigade leaders; and Sikalumbi Papers: Mulungushi 'Resolution on the General Secretary', with 32 signatures. moving 'a Vote of No Confidence in the National Secretary through the drunkness [*sic*].' On the election of Chona as Sipalo's successor, the former Chairman of the N.R. Eurafrican Association, Aaron Milner, became Deputy Secretary.

[13]TI-FM/Mwense, testimony of Mama Chola. 'The Incomer' is a translation of the Bemba '*Mwisa*' meaning colloquially 'European'.

[14]Quoted in Ruth Finnegan, *Oral Literature in Africa*, (O.U.P., 1970), pp. 294-295. The political songs quoted here are translated from original songs in local languages.

[15]See Hall, *Zambia*, pp. 208-210; Mulford, *op. cit.*, pp. 199-200; and African Archives Folio 2 'Cha-cha-cha' by B. S. Krishnamurthy (Lusaka: O.U.P. and Neczam, 1972).

[16]*Voice of UNIP*, undated, but around 25/7/61, ed. M. M. Chona.

[17]TI-FM/KK, 11/4/69; and see *NN* for the period; the *Daily Maily* correspondent was John Dickie.

[18]Extracted from TI-FM/Samfya, 12/2/70; Mbabala Island, 13/2/70; Chishi and Chilubi Islands, 14/2/70; Mwense, 15/2/70; the fullest evidence being that

of David Lukwesa, Gordon Mulongwe, William Mwape and Mama Chola, with evidence of the events in Chinsali from Mr. Chanda, at Chilubi (all interviews in Bemba); and see *African Eagle*, 22/8/61 for note on timing of start of 'Cha-cha-cha'.

[19]E.g. as recorded in testimonies of Chief Chikuramayembe, Sub-chief Mwalweni, Revd. S. K. Msiska, various student teachers; and an account of 26 brutal assaults at Chitimba Village, 20/3/59 by 'security forces', by the Principal (the writer) and staff of Overtoun Institution, Livingstonia.

[20]TI-FM/Revd. W. Mackenzie, 19/2/70.

[21]*Ibid.*; TI-FM/People of Mwense, 15/2/70; and testimony of Headmen Katambarara and Nguwe, M. S. Mwale, recorded at Lundazi Local History Seminar, 24-25 June, 1972.

[22]TI-FM/RMK, 15/6/71, and FM/People of Chishi Island, 14/2/70.

[23]Oral History Seminar, Mungwi, Kasama, 3-4 June, 1972; testimony of M. Chibolya (Bemba).

[24]*NN*, 18/8/61, 19/8/61, 24/8/61; and *Sunday Times of Zambia*, 28/1/73 for K. das Gupta's article, 'The Peace Prize for Dr. Kaunda'.

[25]Mpashi, *op. cit.*, pp. 65-66.

[26]*NN* for the period. *Africa Digest*, Vol. IX, No. 2, pp. 39-40; TI-FM/KK, 11/4/69; and *Voice of Zambia*, September 1961. The opposition of UNIP leaders to Kaunda's visit to Macleod, etc. was modified by receipt of a letter of 3/9/61 from the Labour M.P., Hilary Marquand, explaining how and why these unofficial meetings had taken place, and counselling 'patience'. Marquand praised Kaunda's public relations work very highly. (ANC/ATT).

[27]Hall, *Zambia*, 209: TI-FM/KK, 11/4/69, 13/8/69 and FM/KMK, 15/6/71.

[28]Kaunda, *Zambia*, 160.

[29]*Voice of UNIP*, August, 1961.

[30]*Africa Digest*, Vol. IX, No. 3, p. 72; TI-FM/Mwense, esp. testimony of Mama Chola, 15/2/70.

[31]TI-FM/J. M. Sokoni, 6/10/69; *A Grim Peep into the North*, ed. N. Mundia (October 1961), 13; TI-FM/W. Mackenzie, 19/2/70.

[32]*Voice of Zambia*, September, 1961; *Guardian*, 15/3/62; *CAP*, 24/2/62; and *NN* 13/10/61, 19/10/61, 23/10/61.

[33]RH 106/1: 'UNIP Memorandum to the Belgrade Conference' 19/9/61. The delegates, R. C. Kamanga, C. Kamalondo and M. Sipalo, also submitted to the Conference a document purporting to be a copy of a 'confidential document of one top Cabinet Minister' in Britain, (to 'My dear J', from 'Sandy') explaining a plan to secure Welensky's objectives by seeming to support 'Kaunda and Company'. *Ibid.*: 103/2. Kaunda described the letter as 'probably faked'. Kamanga and Sipalo wrote an article on his alleged 'British Secret Plan' in the UNIP 'official organ' of the Broken Hill Division, entitled *Dawn*, Vol. IV, No. 1, (30/11/61) pp. 4-5; see also *NN*, 25/11/61; quoting Chona's proposal for distribution of 2,000 copies of the Belgrade Memorandum.

[34]Kaunda, *Zambia*, 149-150; and *NN* for period.

[35]Extract from Kaunda's Introduction to *A Grim Peep*.

[36]*NN* for period.

[37]*A Grim Peep*, p. 1.

[38]Mulford, *op. cit.*, 206; and see *Account of the Disturbances in N. Rhodesia, July-October, 1961* (Govt. Printer, Lusaka).

[39]See Mulford, *op. cit.*, 191-193; and TI-FM/L. Changufu, 11/7/69.

[40]*NN*, 2/12/61, 13/12/61.

[41]Brockway, 'Evil Genius in Rhodesia,' *Tribune*, citing *NN* in 1959.

[42]UNIP I/P—Kaunda to British Prime Minister, 22/7/61.

[43]See (e.g.) in ANC/ATT circulars from UNIP on Police Brutalities; 'Police Suppression' and 'Intimidation', 3, 14, 28 August and end of August, 1961. One person named as a victim was W. K. Sikalumbi, then UNIP's Accountant-General. Note that correspondence from the Secretariat (e.g. S/S.108/06 of 23/8/61 and S/S. 116.05 of 9/10/61) revealed vast divergence of reporting, as when UNIP claimed that a crowd of 8,000 had gathered and the Administrative Secretary gave the number as 100. The end of August circular contains the quotation from Chona; the 14/8/61 circular refers to Sikalumbi.

[44]TI-FM/KK, 13/2/69 and 11/4/69.

[45]FH: UNIP/TO/67: Kapwepwe to Peter Molotsi, 18/10/61 and 1/11/61; (Mangaliso was Robert M. Sobukwe, jailed after the Sharpeville 'massacre'); also Press Statements, Nkoloso to *CAP* and *NN* 5/11/61; Wina on Wray's retirement, 14/12/61; Chona to Acting Secretary-General, U.N., 28/12/61. See also UNIP 2/00/30/413, Chona to Tshombe, 22/12/61.

[46]UNIP/1/P, Instructions to all Branches (sgd. K. D. Kaunda) 25/9/61; Press Statements (K. D. Kaunda), 28/9/61, 12/10/61, 15/10/61. G. Mennen Williams arrived in Lusaka on 27/8/61. He was assaulted at the Airport by S. Finlay Bissett, formerly a fish trader at Mpulungu, who was defended by Colin Cunningham before Resident Magistrate Ivor Evans.

[47]FH: (President): Kaunda's Confidential Memorandum, 18/12/61.

[48]*NN* for January 1962.

[49]*NN* for the period 2/2/62 for Burton letter; and *Voice of UNIP*, Jan. 1962, pp. 13-14, for ref. to Burton murder.

[50]*NN* for period, 27/2/62 for quotation from *Daily Express*.

[51]TI-FM/KK, 9/4/71; *NN*, 15/2/62, 27/2/62, 1/3/62; and cover of Mulford, *Northern Rhodesia General Election*, 1962 (O.U.P., 1964).

[52]*NN* for period; Hall, *Kaunda*, p. 54; and *EAR*, 15/3/62.

[53]*NN*, 2/3/62; *Africa Digest*, Vol. IX, No. 5, p. 139; and Hall, *Zambia*, pp. 203-204 for an analysis of Welensky's activities in February 1961, and the 'Tea Party'; TI-FM/KK 13/7/71; and *Guardian* 6/3/62; article by Clyde Sanger, quoting Appendices B and C of Minutes of U.F.P. Emergency Conference called (September 1961) after Britain had agreed to reconsider Macleod's June Proposals.

[54]TI-FM/KK, 13/7/71; and *NN* for period.

[55]In order of reference, see *Guardian*, 26/2/62, *Reynolds News*, 3/3/62, *NN*, 6/3/62 for quotation from *Daily Express*, *Scotsman*, 23/2/62, *Guardian*, 13/3/62 (The chief sponsors of the appeal were the Tory Lord Hemmingford, the Labour Lord Listowel and Mrs. Grimond, wife of the Liberal Leader.) *EAR* 15/3/62, *Guardian*, 28/3/62, and *EAR*, 3/5/62, citing attack on Kaunda by Lord Colyton; also *EAR*, 14/12/61.

[56]*NN* for the period. Chimba was acquitted, 7/3/62, on the charge of spreading a rumour that the Governor 'was going to shoot Africans who did not accept the new Constitution'.

[57]*NN* for period.

[58]*NN* 10/4/62, 11/4/62, 17/4/62; *Sunday Times of Zambia*, interview with S. Wina 6/6/71; and TI-FM/A. G. Zulu, 27/2/69.

[59]FH: Elections (C): S. Wina, Confidential Circular on the Committee of Thirty, 17/3/62; Election (M), Dr. M. Nalumango to S. Wina, 5/4/62; Press Statements, Circular on 'Parliamentary Committee', early October 1962.

[60]*NN*, 18/4/62.

[61]*NN* for the period. 'Arson and beatings' were reported and seven deaths after mob violence in Ndola. The strike lasted a month but no violence of any kind occurred.

[62]UNIP 7/BP/GEN/10-5746 of 19/9/62, A. Wina to Editor, *Northern News*, citing UNO Official Record A/AC. 109/PV. 30, 18/4/62.

[63]*NN* for the period; and *London Times* 18/4/62.

[64]*Voice of UNIP*, January 1962, pp. 13-14 and 11-12. *London Times*, 18/4/62.

[65](Edited by Nephas Tembo), 24/6/62. There were 401 arrests in the Ndola 'townships' in May.

[66]FH: Press Statements: Kalulu, on registration of voters, 17/5/62.

[67]For an analysis of the state of the parties in N. Rhodesia before the October election, see Mulford, *The Northern Rhodesia General Election 1962* (O.U.P., 1962), pp. 31-49.

UNIP's branches by provinces numbered as follows (*Ibid.*, p. 48):

Northern Province	467
Luapula Province	358
Western Province	250
Central Province	230
Eastern Province	210
North-Western Province	199
Southern Province	55
Barotseland (unofficial)	30
	1799

[68]*NN*, 21/5/62; 23/6/62; and 1/6/62 for the letter of Canon John Kingsnorth of the Universities' Mission to Central Africa (Anglican).

13
'Man Must Come First'

'For a long time I have led my people in their shouts of KWACHA, the dawn. We have been shouting it in the darkness; now there is the grey light of dawn on the horizon and I know that Zambia will be free.' With these words Kenneth Kaunda concluded his autobiography, published in 1962.[1] Three years earlier the use of the name 'Zambia' had been a criminal offence. The assurance which he had sent to his 'comrades' from Kabompo was now the supreme reality: 'The greater name of *freedom now* is spiritual. It is beyond their reach and so they cannot ban it. We shall organize our people . . . in the name of *freedom now*. Africa, our mother Africa must be free and it has fallen to our lot to free this part. Be of good cheer, we are just beginning.'[2] Now, even the most implacable enemies of the African cause knew that it was on the way to victory, and history was to confirm in a host of tragedies and of triumphs that the 'continental African' who was leading Zambia was right to link his country's resurgence with the rest of 'Mother Africa'.

Enemies and friends alike would often wonder and sometimes mock at what was of supreme import in Kenneth Kaunda's life, namely that he saw the struggle not just as a horizontal grappling of men against men, where, in common parlance, might is right. It was somehow, constantly and practically, a three-dimensional encounter, with God actively participant and the spirit of man therefore made stronger than guns and chains. Kenneth could thus say, without pretension, that 'his dearest prayer' was that God should help him to contribute to his country 'the type of government that should be the envy of other countries'. Even more personally, he could claim that, though he was 'in many ways a rebel against organised church religion', yet his sense of the presence of

God was 'completely indescribable.' 'Very often,' he said, I'm in very tight situations and I've felt completely lost.' 'All of a sudden I've remembered "Good heavens, I haven't said my prayers!" Then I've stopped to retrace my steps, go back to where I started thinking about this problem and say a word of thanks and ask for guidance.' From this uncomplicated standpoint has come Kenneth's sharp impatience with the divisions within the Christian Church and, no less, his deep conviction about the positive imperative of 'non-racialism' in the context of Africa's crisis. 'How can God be so kind to me as to guide me in my work and at the same time be a God who entertains divisions? It can't be!'[3]

Nineteen sixty-two, as we have seen, was a year of brutal, irrational realities in the life of Northern Rhodesia and there seemed no end to strife. As the registration of voters went on, Roberts of the U.F.P. accused UNIP of 'a tremendous vote fiddle' and Nkumbula claimed that the Government was now favouring UNIP. Welensky joined the anti-Kaunda chorus with a statement that Kenneth was not 'a peace-loving man overflowing with Christian virtues' and warned of the ruthless suppression of 'any Mau Mau attempts'. Kaunda retorted that Welensky was trying 'to assassinate' his character. But at that same moment, Kaunda and his wife undertook what the press called 'a social gamble that paid off', by holding a reception in Kitwe's Hotel Edinburgh at which a third of the 300 guests were Europeans. Dixon Konkola, meanwhile, belatedly urged the imprisonment of Kaunda for burning his *ichitupa*. Kenneth, ignoring this, offered to meet Welensky to discuss 'the ending of the Federation. . . .' 'How do we cooperate to bring it to a peaceful end?' Such a meeting would have to be in Lusaka, 'since I am a PI in Southern Rhodesia'. But Welensky was, at this moment, having a further secret meeting, in Salisbury, with Moise Tshombe, ostensibly about 'trade and commercial matters', as another large exodus of Africans from Elizabethville began in fear of an attack by United Nations forces.[4]

At the end of July, Chief Secretary Luyt made a strong appeal against 'intimidation'. 'This evil can destroy us,' he said. But there were huge Federal troop movements, described as 'routine' going on in the Zambezi Valley, and in the north many UNIP members were being arrested in an intensified campaign of tax collection. Such raids and arrests had been going on since the latter part of

1961 and had been the subject of a hot protest to the Chief Secretary in December by Chona, who feared that UNIP might be forced to withdraw from the elections. Thus the sequence of threat for threat went on. Kaunda paid a call on Luyt to underline the danger of attempting to handle 'administratively' the recovery of tax from people who had a year before declared the invalidity of their identification and tax certificates.

Butler meanwhile had so far failed to win anything like the degree of confidence that Africans had given to Macleod or even to Maudling. In a memorandum about the five conditions for UNIP's participation in the elections, dated 21 May, Kaunda and his 'cabinet' had said that his visit to the Protectorate called for more seriousness than a round of cocktail parties. 'Something needs to be done,' they said bluntly, 'if Britain's name is to be salvaged from wreckage, a wreckage which has been echoed in the august chambers of the United Nations'. However, a letter from an African reader to the *Northern News* displayed more prescience by suggesting that Butler's real role could be described by paraphrasing Shakespeare's famous speech of Mark Anthony at Julius Caesar's grave: 'I came to bury Federation though I praise it'.[5]

Also at the end of July, UNIP announced that Kenneth would be a candidate in the territorial elections. ANC said that many Africans were registering as voters twice, and Roberts accused the Government of 'stooping . . . before UNIP's war of nerves'. But Luyt replied that the greatest possible care was being exercised in ensuring the accuracy of the voters' rolls, while Skinner, as UNIP's Deputy Director of Elections, prepared a clearly-worded manual for general circulation, *How to Vote*. Kaunda, who had just had a hairbreadth escape, with Milner, when their car scraped a tanker near Broken Hill, was meanwhile preparing for the Party's Conference, to be held at Magoye in the Southern Province. He went there cheered by news of 'full agreement' between the A.M.W.U. and the mining companies, whereby an extra £1.25 million was to be paid in wages to African miners. Another matter of gratification was his recent welcome in Barotseland. In Sikota Wina's view, the reception at Mungu by 6,000 people had shown that 'UNIP has the nearly unanimous support of the Lozis . . . and the goodwill of many Europeans' in the province.[6]

At the Magoye River Conference, it was clear that the Cha-cha-cha spirit was still strong and it would take little to set UNIP dancing again. The wave of arrests in the villages of the north and a report by secret Party envoys to Katanga that members of ANC were receiving military training there kept the tension high; and Sikota Wina added dramatically that 'if ever Mr. Kaunda thought', after the elections, 'that not enough progress was being made in Leg. Co., all he had to do was lift up a telephone, put a call through to Freedom House and say, "Boys, do it the UNIP way." ' Kaunda, however, appealed to delegates in the words of Jesus Christ: ' "Love your neighbour." ' The accession of 'black government' would require 'respect for the European point of view'. As applause punctuated his speech, he challenged the conference: 'Don't keep on cheering if you don't agree with me!'[7]

He was at this time writing to a number of Chiefs, assuring them that UNIP wanted to restore the dignity and authority of the 'natural rulers', degraded under European rule, in order 'to build a refined and strong nation which is God-fearing and loving all people as children of the Creator'. Chief Puta of the Luunda then invited him to visit the Kawambwa area and revealed that 'Chiti-mukulu of the Bemba Empire' and 'almost all chiefs' had been genuinely concerned about being 'no longer represented' under 'a total black government'. Similarly Kankomba of the Lala urged Kenneth to remember that, because Nkumbula had failed as a leader, the country 'elected you to liberate the nation'. At this time, too, Kaunda made a statement on UNIP's attitude to the Liberal Party, with which there had been discussion as to possible cooper-ation. 'Sir John Moffat needs to be congratulated for his sincere efforts to achieve unity,' he said. 'Unfortunately he is surrounded by people we can never trust.' Kenneth was at this time, however, continuing his programme of meetings with Europeans and Asians, characterised by his readiness to answer questions and criticisms. His condemnation of Welensky's vast expenditure on 'defence' provoked one questioner to justify it as a means 'to fight com-munism'. To this, Kenneth replied: 'Communism isn't shootable. It can only be fought by building a happy and contented society.' One fruit of his meetings with Europeans had been a suggestion from a white woman that UNIP members should visit white schools 'to dispel the fog of ignorance and prejudice about Africans'.[8]

Yet the charge of Communist leanings was still being hurled at

Kaunda. Welensky declared that Communism was the inspiration of the African nationalists, and in his *4,000 Days* he has recorded that when Kaunda spoke of nation-wide strikes he 'related this utterance by a man who in London and New York habitually passed as an apostle of peace and non-violence and all the Christian virtues to the wider pattern of western appeasement, folly, prejudice and ignorance in African affairs, and then to the grand Communist design for the whole continent'. Nkumbula now described Kaunda and Hastings Banda to a rally of 5,000 ANC supporters as 'the chief agents of Communism in Central Africa'. U.F.P.'s Simukondah added that 'Zambia Police' were being paid to perpetrate intimidation, and Dixon Konkola reported that UNIP followers had attacked him in his bed. However, once again the 6,000 who gathered at Magoye confirmed Kenneth in unchallenged leadership, and the Annual Report which Wina, as Publicity Director, submitted to the Conference reflected the growing sense of hope that the way was opening for a swift dismantling of the Federation. As a result of the British reaction to Kaunda's insistent demands, the U.F.P. had been 'deprived of political power'. It had not therefore been necessary to implement the third stage of the Master Plan, secretly fixed for 12 March. Everywhere the slogan had been: 'Choba-e, yes, Kenneth Kaunda, Master Plan No. 3, Cha-cha-cha, Bulala Zonke'. But Maudling's scheme, long delayed, had come in the nick of time.[9]

At the end of August an Order in Council ruled that people with prison records would not be debarred from standing as candidates for Leg. Co., thus making it legal for both Nkumbula and Kaunda to stand. In mid-September, Kaunda read to a rally of 15,000 people in Lusaka the names of UNIP's candidates which included veteran trade unionists, like Chisata and Mwendapole, and intellectuals like Mwanakatwe, along with the Lozi Princess Nakatindi, Gore-Browne, Merfyn Temple and James Skinner. But the jubilation at this announcement was severely dampened by news of violence in Southern Rhodesia, with the Air Force aiding the hunt for 'terrorists', and of Tshombe's further 'meddling' in Central African affairs, with a report that Katanga had given £90,000 to three political groups to fight 'Lumumbist Communist parties'. Clearly the beneficiaries were ANC, Konkola's Central African Peoples' Union and the Zimbabwe National Party, led by Patrick Matimba.

The ANC-Katanga-U.F.P. association was to be corroborated soon afterwards by a circular, issued under UNIP's auspices in early November by Huggins Chewe who had been in ANC and then in Konkola's CAPU before they merged. Chewe claimed that talks had started in 1961 and that 'fantastic aid' had been made available to ANC, for which 'UFP or the Federal Government' had negotiated with Tshombe. The *London Observer* cited one amount received by Nkumbula in April from Katanga as £24,000 and then, presumably from the B.S.A. Company, £30,000 as a gift and £30,000 as an interest-free loan, which 'some of his lieutenants have admitted'. In a message to PAFMECSA in May, UNIP had claimed that 'the ANC . . . which was bankrupt, has suddenly become very wealthy . . . purchasing 20 motor vehicles . . . .' 'The leader himself has bought a house worth more than £3,000 . . . . ANC is importing people from Katanga to come and kill UNIP people . . . our own security forces have it that a strong white group is behind the mysterious troubles. In Lusaka alone there are over 80 Katangese thugs. The ANC has donated a piano worth £350 and £100 in cash to the African Methodist Church.' Moreover 'to get UFP African supporters by corrupt means . . . the ["Build a Nation"] campaign was launched with an initial capital of £250,000 from the BSA Company.' The UNIP statement to PAFMECSA was signed by Chona, Jonathan Chivunga, Sikalumbi, J. K. Mulenga and Makasa.

Kaunda took so grave a view of the situation that he made a secret trip to Elizabethville to meet Tshombe. There had been a number of approaches made by Tshombe to him through an Italian journalist which he had rejected. But news of a plan to supply Nkumbula with firearms made him undertake a mission which, as Wina said, would have been unanimously opposed by UNIP's Central Committee if Kaunda had consulted them. Kaunda 'admitted that he regarded his going to Elizabethville as a "plunge" into death' and was 'glad to return alive'. He was 'not entirely satisfied with his talks with Tshombe' but felt it had been important to warn him against his association with the two 'dying horses', Welensky and Nkumbula, and against supplying 'pistols' for use by ANC. For he saw the situation as a plot on Welensky's part to boost Nkumbula, through Tshombe, against the cause of Zambian independence.[10] A British journalist had meanwhile described his visit to a camp near Elizabethville in which 'there were about 200 Northern Rhodesians'. 'Mukuba House', as Congress was naming its headquarters, retorted that the stories about military training in Katanga, like the report of Welensky's plan to arrest the Governor, and of a plot to kill Kaunda 'and 33 others', was a fabrication of Kaunda's guilty conscience. ANC had information, Nkumbula claimed, that 200 UNIP men had been to Moscow, via Tanganyika, 'to be trained in subversive activities'.[11]

Pictures, advertisements and social notices in the local press still portrayed Europeans to the almost complete exclusion of the African population. Mainza Chona was therefore infuriated by a report that 'the three year old son of anti-everything-Federal, UNIP leader Kenneth Kaunda had his tonsils removed . . . in Kitwe's Federal Llewellin Hospital.' This Chona regarded as 'cheap' and went on to allege that the *Northern News* had a heavy bias towards the U.F.P. 'and their African wing', ANC. 'Today most of us believe,' he said, 'that your editorials are drafted by top-ranking UFP office-bearers.' A week later, Chona wrote again to the *Northern News* declaring that the 'pro-Welensky press' was campaigning, by distortion of facts, to discredit UNIP 'with the approach of October 30', and denying that the Party was 'scorning a helping hand' by breaking off negotiations with Moffat's Liberal Party. Kaunda had made it plain that he would welcome people like Sir John to 'play their role in UNIP'. As one African letter-writer to the press said aptly, 'The fight is between UNIP and UFP.'[12]

Welensky continued to evoke deep passions in many African leaders. Nalumino Mundia, for example, had recently come from his 'Iron Curtain prison' and wrote at once to all regional secretaries a letter in which he described Sir Roy as a 'classical hypnotist . . . transforming his audience into somnambulists cheering at every unethical poppycock he utters [and] rattling the phantasmal ghosts' threats of Communism and intimidation . . . the usual tricks of a discredited jingo. . . .' 'In the meantime an irrefragable African leader' had emerged, 'to create a true non-racial society'. Despite the fact that 'treatment in Federal Prisons to political prisoners' was 'barbaric inhumanity, revenge would be savagery', Mundia said, and would 'only help to create strife and chaos in the country to the suffering of us all'.[13] Nevertheless, the unabating winds of passion were sharpened by mass boycotts, which Wina decried on behalf of UNIP, involving the refusal of thousands on the Copperbelt to participate in an inoculation campaign against poliomyelitis. The Medical Officer in Kitwe praised UNIP's co-operation, but vaccine teams were stoned in some places and the Party was widely blamed for fomenting this wave of irrational protest. Unemployment was meanwhile growing ominously on the Copperbelt, and police patrols were intensified.[14]

Kenneth Kaunda gave little attention, in the weeks before polling-day, to the spate of personal attacks upon him. Instead he appealed to people to save money 'before the master plan to end Federation is launched', the election campaign being seen now as the new 'Master Plan'. The consistency of his thought and utterance received a back-handed tribute when a leading article said that, unless UNIP could prove that 'it means what Mr. Kaunda says and not what some other people in his Party have said, the great majority of Europeans will, like ourselves, be sceptical'. Kenneth had good news to offer, however. The World Bank would assist in the country's industrial expansion if UNIP won the election, he reported. He ignored a press report of a rumour that, as people went to the polls, he would be flying round in the air, invisibly checking on how they voted! Instead, he offered another Hindu Hall meeting, this time in Broken Hill, the assurance that, because 'such organisations as the Rhodesia Railways and mines are running efficiently . . . yielding substantial revenue' there would be no point in 'interfering' with them. At a similar meeting in Ndola, he promised peace if UNIP won at the polls. 'I have a good grip on the Party.' In a letter to the press, Merfyn Temple described UNIP as 'doing its utmost to control a mass movement in which there are thugs, delinquents and intimidators'. Meanwhile, the *Northern News* began a series of articles called 'Political Profiles', with a portrait of Kenneth, and forecast a landslide victory for UNIP. 'Two years ago, a year ago, the role of national leader seemed too big for Kaunda . . . . I saw him at a great gathering of African nationalists in Tanganyika and his personality was overshadowed. But in the past six months, he has grown steadily in maturity, in self-confidence, in suavity. Nothing will shake that confidence.'[15]

Federal Customs officials at Ndola had, however, just seized the first consignment of Kaunda's *Zambia Shall be Free*. Justin Simu-kondah's 'anti-UNIP drive' was receiving generous publicity.

Kenneth Kaunda of Zambia

'UNIP burns schools,' it said. Konkola produced a leaflet, for extensive distribution, entitled 'You have been warned', which Mulford, who was in the country at the time, has described as 'the most decisive brochure of the campaign'. The leaflet, which reached many white voters, was 'cleverly designed to summarize the European's worst fears' by providing documentation to establish that UNIP had been responsible for the murder of Mrs. Burton; citing the threat, by Kaunda, of something far worse than Mau Mau; Sipalo's call to 'hate everything white that has two legs'; and the destruction of '64 schools, 28 churches, 86 houses, 2 hospitals, 64 bridges, 13 railway lines, 69 motor vehicles' in 1961. 'Actions speak louder than words' was the theme of the leaflet. But, as a horrific crisis suddenly developed between America and Russia over Cuba, UNIP was engaged in a maximal effort to mobilize Copperbelt support, dancing now in a more lightsome mood.[16]

The colourful trappings of UNIP rallies were now a regular feature of life; the black, red, green and orange colours of the Party festooned around the place of assembly; the dais constructed of bush poles and roofed with grass; the strident music of the band caught and broadcast by a battery of microphones; Youth Brigade lads, known as 'Zambia Police', wearing lion skin bonnets, and marshalling the people with quips and prods until the platform party arrived. Then praise songs would be sung, such as this:

'Kaunda will politically get Africans freed from the English
who treat us unfairly and beat us daily.
UNIP as an organization does not stay in one place.
It moves to various kinds of places and peoples,
Letting them know the difficulties with which we are faced.
These whites are only paving the way for us.
So that we come and rule ourselves smoothly.'

Increasingly, songs at political rallies struck a polemic note against other political parties, like these;

'The walking stick of Mr. Kaunda appears crooked;
The walking stick of Mr. Kaunda appears crooked.
If Welensky sees it, his heart drops to the ground—
His heart fears and drops to the ground.'

or

'Do you know what Tshombe did?
He killed his Premier, Lumumba—

As if he was clever, but in the end he was known
to have done the murder.
CHORUS:
It is horrible.
When we remember what Tshombe did.'
As a close observer of the campaigning patterns of the parties,
Mulford has described how 'often during speeches there were
exchanges between the speaker and the crowd.' 'The most common
exchange was started by the speaker shouting "UNIP", and the
crowd roaring in response "MEANS WORK" or "KWACHA"
(the dawn) .... Though men like S. Wina and Kapwepwe were
especially popular with the crowds, no one moved the people like
Kaunda. The crowd responded to each of his motions, interrupted
his speech and chanted his name over and over again. When he
finished speaking and left the rally, people pressed forward to greet
him and rushed to touch him or his car, all the while chanting
KAUNDA—KAUNDA—KAUNDA!' Mulford also tells how
UNIP's extensive splashing of notices in white paint on roads
and buildings, 'UNIP is power', 'Vote UNIP', was countered by
the militant 'United Anti-UNIP Movement', and how U.F.P's
Cecil Burney supplied a 'team of 16 toughs' each receiving £2 a
week 'to protect ANC canvassing teams'.[17]

On the eve of polling-day, Kenneth Kaunda's message contained
these words: 'I decry those who accuse me of putting on a cloak
of sweet reasonableness for the sake of 10% European support.
My personal campaign among non-Africans started immediately
before the June troubles of 1961.' There was no ulterior motive,
he said, only a genuine desire to eradicate racial bitterness. Governments controlled by Europeans did not present an assuring picture,
he added, citing 'assassination attempts on de Gaulle, endless
revolution in South America, refugee trails from East Germany,
mass arrests in South Africa, looting and burning in Southern
Rhodesia'. In another statement, he said: 'Not unnaturally, all
of us have made mistakes in the past ... but men do not live in
the past; they live in the present and plan for the future. ... Of
late people of all races have begun to meet and discuss their
problems more and more. This is a healthy sign. ... The sures
way of safeguarding any society is to safeguard the individual.
Then, 'the problem of entrenching in your constitution melts away;

but if it is the wish of the majority of the minority that we entrench their rights in the constitution we shall be happy to do that . . . .'
'We know that we are winning these elections and we promise to make our victory at the polls a victory of all the people of Mother Zambia and a shock to none. We love our God, and that is meaningless if we do not love His people. We want power not to destroy people's lives but to serve them.'[18]

The press hailed 30 October with the headline: 'The Oh-so-peaceful NR Election', but three days earlier an ANC man had died in Kitwe, and Kaunda had therefore asked people to impose a voluntary daily curfew on themselves. Though Kenneth was sure that the ANC-U.F.P. pact would be 'the ruination of ANC', Congress was effectively in league with its traditional foe as the country flocked to the polls, and the chant went on:

'Upper roll voting papers will be green;
Lower roll voting papers will be pink.
CHORUS:
Green paper goes in the green box;
Pink paper goes in the pink box.'

By nightfall, it was known that there had been a 90 per cent poll, but that on the upper roll, U.F.P. had scored massive support. Of 76,315 votes cast on the lower roll, UNIP won 59,648 against ANC's 16,268. The high level of polling and the orderly conduct of the elections demonstrated the thoroughness of the instruction that had been given to an electorate for many of whom this was their first encounter with the ballot box. Some rural voters had had to walk up to sixty miles to the nearest polling booth. But the results did no more than to confirm Kaunda's first reaction to Maudling's constitutional scheme. When the votes were all counted, the new Legislative Council was found to be composed of the following racial and party elements:

	UNIP	U.F.P.	ANC	TOTAL
Europeans		13	1	14
Africans	12	2	4	18
Asians	1			1
Eurafricans	1			1
State of Parties	14	15	5	34

At once the dilemma of the African parties was apparent and the news went out that Kenneth Kaunda was seeking ways of persuading Nkumbula to form a coalition government with him. Nkumbula declared openly that he would 'be politically killed' if he supported U.F.P. now and put the onus of decision on ANC's National Assembly.[19]

In sum, the Liberal Party was extinguished, only less dramatically, on the upper roll, than the 'white extremist' Rhodesian Republican Party. But the news that U.F.P. won 90 per cent support among Europeans demonstrated the tragic fact that what Kaunda had called 'the most racial constitution ever devised' had thrown the racial alignments in the territory into the sharpest possible relief; and precipitated 'a full-scale national crisis'. Yet it had its comic features. The *Northern News*, for instance, made the amazing assertion, on the evening of 1 November, that 'the most important single politico . . . tonight is Mr. C. E. Cousins', because he had won 76.5 per cent of the European votes in the Luangwa rural constituency on an ANC ticket.' The more bizarre fact was that both Kaunda and Roberts were now obliged to seek Nkumbula's agreement to a coalition government in order to break the deadlock. Nkumbula began at once exploiting his bargaining power, demanding that Kaunda denounce intimidation and Communism and that Roberts abandon 'political Federation' and agree to replace it with 'only an economic association'. While 'Old Harry' temporised, Kenneth declared that, if need be, UNIP would 'go it alone' and 'go the whole hog', which inevitably brought a storm of questions on his head. 'I am merely following in the footsteps of Sir Roy,' he replied. 'I mean exactly what he meant. If he means peace, I mean peace. If he means trouble, I mean trouble.' But the wooing of Congress had to go on. Chona called on all UNIP members 'to show cordiality and brotherhood towards members of ANC', while Kenneth himself asked the Chiefs to press Nkumbula to form a coalition with UNIP, to which the 'natural rulers' responded immediately and positively, despite Nkumbula's rebuttal of their overture.[20]

Kenneth Kaunda was physically exhausted in the wake of the election climax. As one British reporter said, 'UNIP's lead had been gained by the superhuman efforts of its President . . . sleeping nearly every night in the back of a speeding car, he has criss-crossed the country for six weeks to reassure European and Asian audiences of the Party's constructive intentions. Speaking without notes on television he impressed many with his sincerity.' Yet many Europeans had been 'driven back into the white man's laager' during the previous two weeks by U.F.P.'s 'campaign of vilification' against UNIP, and there were sneers in plenty about this man whose deep feelings often overwhelmed him as he pleaded for a new pattern of society. One letter to the press chided his 'childish tantrums' and proposed a special fund to provide him with handkerchiefs 'as he is sure to be weeping copiously at the Colonial Office'. As Moffat said, when disbanding the Liberals, Welensky's party had 'fought on three points—that UNIP was lying; a "hate UNIP campaign"; and an attempt to split the African nationalist movement'.[21]

In a circular to UNIP on 'unity talks' with Nkumbula, Kenneth commented in detail on the election results: 'The total anti-Federation vote, taking the two rolls combined, was 85,071 as against 21,803. . . . Can anyone say in fact or in conscience that we are not entitled to the Government of the country? My party if therefore being alerted to face the struggle once again. At this time we are aware of all the implications . . . a ruthless and heavily financed professional machinery which is backing the UFP in face of [*sic*] all logic; a weakened but once mighty overseas colonial power which dithers between hypocrisy and constitutional deceit. Whatever the cost, we must win.'[22] In a short letter to Nkumbula about the 'national crisis', Kaunda then wrote: 'We cannot continue to live in the past—even when the whole nation is on the brink of disaster. I am not for the moment suggesting that we bring our parties together, but I am thinking of our parliamentary groups coming together in order to break the United Federal Party stranglehold on our country.'

Meanwhile over 100 telegrams streamed into Freedom House in support of a coalition, and Nkumbula also received strong pressure to 'bury the hatchet'. A summary of messages received at his office showed 21 in favour and 14 against. One of them read: 'The future of our children depends upon what two great and strong men, Mr. Kaunda and Mr. Nkumbula, will decide today.' From south of the Zambezi came the cry: 'Africans in Zimbabwe implore you accept Brother Kaunda appeal.'

The *Central African Mail* made a scathing comment on the aftermath of the election: 'Northern Rhodesia's 70,000 Europeans, led by Sir Roy Welensky, last week marched triumphantly into a dead end. . . . His United Federal Party collected less than 22,000 scared White votes. UNIP won over 60,000 votes. Africans put their crosses in 99.5 per cent strength for anti-Federation parties. . . . UNIP, which scored 60 per cent of the total votes cast, ends up with only fourteen of the declared thirty-four seats; a candidate like Sir Stewart Gore-Browne who got 12,000 African votes could not secure a seat because 10 per cent of the few Europeans did not vote for him; and the UFP, which got only 180 African votes and nearly a fifth of the total votes cast, emerges as the strongest single party.' While indecision continued, the Governor accepted the resignation of all the Liberal members of the Executive Council, and announced that a 'caretaker' Cabinet of civil servants, along with one nominated African M.L.C., would advise him until a solution was found to the 'deadlock'.[23]

Nkumbula's decision to accept a 'deal with UNIP' came sooner than seemed possible, and just after a newspaper report that Welensky had met Tshombe again for 'hush-hush talks'. He explained his decison by saying that he had been 'used' by the U.F.P., and attributed this change of mind, in twenty-four hours, to 'public opinion here and overseas that there should be a stable government. . . .' 'It must be an African government. . . . I don't care who leads as long as it is stable.' Though some of his lieutenants demanded his resignation, he replied that Kaunda had assured him that he was 'not inclined to Communism' and was now 'favourable to Tshombe'. Then, on 16 November, he and Kaunda issued a joint statement, calling all their followers 'to cease all hostilities . . . both collectively and individually' and to realise that they had shared over twelve years in the struggle 'for the advent of an African Majority Government' with 'the support of the entire African population'. Now, they said, 'we are nearing the end of our hard-trodden road.' Jointly they denounced 'in no uncertain terms, intimidation, violence, Communism and racial bitterness', and promised to enshrine a Bill of Rights in the new nation's Constitution and live in 'friendly neighbourliness' with 'all the independent states of Africa, including Katanga'.

Kenneth, who was both leader of UNIP and Chairman of

PAFMECA, went almost immediately to meet Tshombe again in secret, this time taking Andrew Mutemba with him. Meanwhile, as most delicate negotiations were thus in progress, a large-scale boycott of European and Asian shops began and Kaunda had to dash to the Copperbelt to 'assess' it. The press blamed it on UNIP, but he told the British High Commissioner, Lord Alport, that it should be seen rather as 'an expression of the discontent of the African people against a stupid racialist constitution', and blamed the *Northern News* for 'fanning up' the boycotts. As the wooing of Nkumbula proved Kaunda the more persuasive suitor, the two men met in Nkumbula's house, Nkumbula dramatically announcing that he had 'turned Roberts from the door' because U.F.P. had cheated ANC.[24]

The new relationship between Kaunda and the Congress leader was demonstrated further by PAFMECA's sponsoring of a journey to London by Nkumbula which was soon followed, presumably as pre-arranged, by Kaunda's departure to join him in discussions with the Colonial Office. Simoloka of ANC then renewed the dormant rumour that Kapwepwe and Sikota Wina were about to 'split' UNIP. But Welensky admitted that it would be 'extremely difficult' for his party if the two nationalist parties in Northern Rhodesia began to cooperate. The atmosphere of reconciliation was extended when, at his second meeting with Tshombe, Kaunda and the Katangese leader spoke of hope for 'a vast United States of Africa' and a UNIP Press Release on the meeting announced that they had discussed 'the possibility of a new Federation of Central African countries including a link between Northern Rhodesia and Katanga. . . .' 'The talks, which Mr. Kaunda held in his capacity of PAFMECA Chairman were . . . intended to create more understanding among Africans and eventually bring Mr. Tshombe into line with the Leopoldville Government.' In more practical terms, the Union Miniére was ready to arrange to divide the portion of profits, assignable within the former Belgian Congo, between Elizabethville and Leopoldville. The main cloud in the Protectorate seemed to be, therefore, the wave of arrests of tax-defaulters, which Kaunda discussed urgently in person with the Chief Secretary. He then appealed to the Northern Province to keep calm. When Kenneth arrived in London at the end of November, he could honestly declare that 'minority rule was over'. The

UNIP-ANC coalition was formally announced in London on 28 November, subject to ratification by ANC's National Council, with a demand for 'home-rule' for the Protectorate.[25]

The new association with Nkumbula was far from reliable, however. Though the 'Old Man' and he had 'come closer together than ever before' when in London and Nkumbula had said that 'it was inconceivable' that he should 'stand in the way of African government . . . after a 20 year struggle', Kaunda knew that the chains that bound ANC to Welensky and to Tshombe had been forged skilfully. One of Nkumbula's most determined 'advisers' was Roy Horrell, who had been a U.F.P. organiser in Southern Rhodesia and who, after the elections, was known to be heading the opposition within ANC to a deal with UNIP. On 12 December, Congress held its National Assembly and, though Nkumbula met with fierce opposition especially from his Copperbelt members, backed by Horrell, he demonstrated a new decisiveness as he swept into the Assembly with Kaunda at his side, and asked sharply: 'How many favour African Government now? How many are behind me?' As the majority of hands rose in affirmation, he left the meeting to go straight, with Kenneth, to Government House. Thus the coalition was born, despite a last-minute battle over the number of seats each party demanded in the 'Cabinet'. Another quirk of fortune put Nkumbula into a strong bargaining position and enabled him to attain parity with UNIP in the Executive Council, though Congress had only seven seats as against UNIP's fourteen. This was due to the fact that the Constitution laid down that at least two of the elected members of the Council must be Europeans. Nkumbula, who could provide these in the persons of Stubbs and Cousins secured three Ministries, with himself as the only African representative of the African National Congress. Kaunda meanwhile took Kapwepwe and Kamanga into the 'Cabinet'. UNIP's reaction to the conclusion of the Maudling elections was to declare jubilantly: 'Zambia is born—December 14th, 1962'. 'The battle has been long and bitter,' wrote John Malama Sokoni, in a special message to the country's Chiefs, '. . . Bless heavens the white man's rule has ended today. . . . I hope your Royal Highnesses will trust those children of yours to whom, by virtue of their ability, this country has entrusted its affairs.'[26]

Nineteen sixty-two ended thus with the certainty that it would

not be white minorities, drawing strength from superior wealth,
military power and a technological system buttressed by an industrial
colour bar, who would shape the future of the lands north of the
Zambezi. In Southern Rhodesia, a third but different blow had
been struck against Welensky at the elections in mid-December.
There, however, despite the fact that both Banda and Kaunda
praised the 'frankness' of Winston Field, the new Prime Minister
of the triumphant Rhodesia Front Party, history records an immediate and steady hardening of 'white supremacist' policies until
at last, in November 1965, Ian Smith would declare uniliterally
the 'independence' of Rhodesia. By giving Ministerial rank to
Smith as well as to John Gaunt, Field offered immediate augury
of the direction of events in the 'Crown Colony'. As the cold war
of the super powers of the West and East continued, negotiations
broke down in the Congo and Tshombe fled to Salisbury in a Royal
Rhodesia Air Force plane, while reports came from Katanga of the
'mortar-bombing' by U.N. planes of Lubumbashi Hospital, and
floods of refugees were again expected.[27]

   At this moment in Northern Rhodesia, it was most important
to be aware of what was being said in languages other than English
about the country's history and present turmoil. Indeed, there is
place for a study of such utterances in what were called by the
strange, tendentious name of 'the vernaculars'. The *Voice* carried
an article in Bemba entitled '*Mwisa, wailetelela*'—'Intruder, you have
brought calamity on yourself', which spoke of the behaviour of
white men as characterised by self-aggrandisement and by the
cursing and oppressing of the African people. 'Go to Bembaland,'
it said, 'and see the evil of the white man', citing the burning of
villages, including foodstores, and the destruction of livestock
by the Security Forces in 1961. Moreover, while white children had
had ample educational opportunities, African education was
stultified. That regime was now finished, said the article. 'The white
man who wants to stay in this country must now obey the laws
of our government. If not, let him start packing his luggage. LET
HIM WHO CAME GO. We did not call him. If the black man
cannot find prosperity in his own land, where else will he find it?
. . . If there are those who want to disrupt and confuse the leadership of CHITWE MAMBO NKAMYA MILONGA KENNETH
KAUNDA, let them know that we have vowed a mighty vow that

this shall not be so.'[28]

Kenneth Kaunda was in Leopoldville, as the year ended, for a meeting of PAFMECA. He had left Lusaka soon after the Governor had announced what Mulford calls the 'first African Government', though the number of Officials in the Executive Council still gave it more white faces than black. Kaunda had secured the portfolio of Local Government and Social Welfare; Kapwepwe became Minister of African Agriculture; and Kamanga of Labour and Mines. Nkumbula, who had hotly rejected the portfolio of Transport and Works, saying that he would not 'talk to roads and bridges', took over African Education, while Stubbs and Cousins were given Transport and Works and Lands and Natural Resources respectively. UNIP, however, held both the post of Chief Whip, in the person of Sikota Wina, and four, as against ANC's three, Parliamentary Secretaryships. In this respect, Kenneth had a notably stronger team, for three of his four Parliamentary Secretaries were graduates, two of whom had university qualifications closely related to their portfolios. Arthur Wina, an economist, was attached to Finance and Elijah Mudenda, a B.Sc. in Agriculture, was to support Kapwepwe in the Ministry of African Agriculture. The third graduate was John Mwanakatwe.

Party organisation was meanwhile as important as ever and Sokoni instructed regional officers to ensure that Chiefs were informed of 'all the current events and progress we make politically', signing his circular 'Yours in it . . . !' Nineteen sixty-three began for UNIP with a list of 'New Year Resolutions' for each month of the year which showed that 'the fighting spirit' of the Party was high. Members were called to trust in their 'black government'; to realise that 'non-violence does not provide a satisfactory answer to . . . what should be done if peaceful means do not bring the desired results'; to 'pray for the souls of those who died on the political battlefield'; to practise self-control; to share generously; to visit political prisoners; to stop calling Europeans 'bwanas'; to be active in the Party; to keep secrets; to campaign for African unity; to ignore imperialist Christmas messages; and, in sum, to 'remember: UNIP to UNIP—BUY UNIP—WALK UNIP—FEEL UNIP—KWACHA.' The optimism of the moment was, however, summed up by a caption in the *Voice*: 'No peace so deep as that by struggle won'.[29]

402 Kenneth Kaunda of Zambia

The *Manchester Guardian* had described the negotiations of the two African leaders in London under the headline: 'No more thunderbolts from Mr. Kaunda: a model of mature confidence'. The question now was whether the results of the ballot-box would be allowed to guide the future or whether there was substance in Sir Roy's continued sabre-rattling. For he had just told a Johannesburg audience that 'Pan-Africanism has neither budget nor army' and elsewhere had called on an entirely white gathering to provide him with 'the sinews of war'. Thus, though our main concern is with what Mulford calls the 'phenomenal political metamorphosis' of late 1962 in Northern Rhodesia, the affairs of the territory cannot be viewed in isolation. For example, what the *Guardian* described as 'the fitful, often reluctant, but still measurable advance towards a non-racial state' in Southern Rhodesia under Whitehead, had ended within days of the announcement of Northern Rhodesia's African coalition, with the victory of the Rhodesian Front.[30]

In the preceding chapters we have been watching, as it were, the rise of the waters behind the dam. The essence of rising waters is the breathless expectancy which they generate and the history of Northern Rhodesia, and the record of Kaunda's role in it prior to the vital election, have thus fixed the pace of our narrative hitherto. But now we have witnessed the watershed and what follows is the swift surge to full independence. The odds against the realisation of Kaunda's vision were still, as we shall see, grim. But the pace changed and the narrative must now seek to catch the rhythm of the river in spate. Yet rocks were to abound, breaking the flow angrily, right up to the moment of replacing the Union Jack by the flag of Zambia. Because Nkumbula was so heavily in debt to Katanga, he could not be expected to cut his chains at once, if at all. The coalition could not therefore fail to have an air of unreality about it, even though the split in the African nationalist movement continued to be, as it had been in 1958, fundamentally a clash of personalities and indeed the basic common purpose had been recently underlined by a slogan used before the by-elections:

'UNIP and ANC
Stop and look
Our common enemy
The lion, the snake, UFP must die.'

Yet the exaltation of the moment was irrepressible, and, though Nkumbula maintained that his interest in the coalition was 'solely to be a moderating influence' on UNIP's inherent violence, the *Voice* praised his far-sighted patriotism in resisting Roberts's efforts to 'buy him out' and realising that 'these glorious offers [of four portfolios and for himself the post of Chief Minister of a U.F.P.-ANC government] . . . were in direct conflict with the African people's desire. . . .' 'Nkumbula's final decision has been an answer to our baffling problem. Here is the positive and progressive essence of what is time and again referred to as "THE AFRICAN PERSON-ALITY." ' The gaiety still remained, though the mood was changing as the next issue of the *Voice* published this doggerel 'Ode to a Politician':

'Our dear Harry Nkumbula;
Has made an awful Nkbloomer!
By switching with impunity;
From UFP to UNIP!

Now finding his balance of power;
A strange, rare exotic flower!
The bloom fast wilting and lank;
Now ANC claim it stank!

Wise men counsel our dear Harry
On political paths not to tarry!
But give way to K. Kaunda;
Whose path to freedom does not wander!

Any credit for his stand must be;
From here until Eternity!
Disappointed UFP and Roberts;
Harry Nkumbula and his ANC!

Africa needs a new type of man;
A dedicated, modest, honest and devoted man!
A man who submerges self in service to his nation and mankind;
A man who abhors greed and detests vanity!

A new type of man whose meekness
Is his strength and whose integrity
Is his greatness!
Africa's new MAN must be a MAN indeed.'[31]

One of Kenneth Kaunda's first tasks as effective 'leader of the Unofficials' in the Legislative Council was to try to halt the eruption of strikes on the Copperbelt, where there was grave deterioration in the relations of the United T.U.C. and the break-away Zambia T.U.C., dominated by the huge A.M.W.U. Jonathan Chivunga was leader of the U.T.U.C. while John Chisata and Mathew Deluex Nkoloma were the chief rival spokesmen. There was considerable defiance of their leadership within the A.M.W.U., and it appeared that the primary cause of the strikes was a grave clash of personalities. Ten days after Kaunda's meetings with the rival groups, the strikes ended; the *Central African Examiner* declaring that they had reached 'a climax of absurdity' before they abruptly stopped. The urgency of constructive unanimity in the life of the nation was then further emphasised by Kaunda and Nkumbula in January. Their victory at the elections gave them, they said, 'a clear mandate from the people . . . that they wish to have nothing to do with Sir Roy's Federation'. Its continuance would make it impossible to 'guarantee peace and order'. They then offered an apparently agreed upon and detailed proposal for a 65-member House of Assembly, universal adult franchise which would include both British Protected Persons and United Kingdom Citizens, a 15-man Cabinet led by a Prime Minister, a House of Chiefs, and a Bill of Rights. They specifically required that 'the House of Assembly will be unfettered in its legislative power save that it will be precluded from enacting laws which are *ultra-vires* the constitution. . . .' 'The powers of legislation reserved to the Governor shall not be continued.' A delegation representing the two parties spoke to these points in a meeting with Butler, adding that under their proposals, 'members of the Federal Civil Service . . . will be given conditions of service comparable to those operating in Northern Rhodesia when their present services revert to Northern Rhodesia.' They would not 'stand to lose'.[32]

Under the superficial solidarity there were, however, serious tremors. Kaunda was embarrassed by manifestations of bitterness that showed that the 'dancing' of Cha-cha-cha was still going on here and there. When Chief Mwase of Lundazi, who had shown uncommon cooperation with the Government by the manner of his banning of UNIP, was elected to the House of Chiefs, an angry demonstration took place outside the chamber in the Secretariat. Immediately, as Minister of Local Government, Kenneth wrote to

the President of the House to express 'sincere regrets that this shameful incident ever took place at a critical time when all those striving
to set the Government . . . on its proper footing should be seeking
cooperation with our natural rulers . . . [as] we regard your institution [of chieftainship] to be above the normal rough-and-tumble
of party politics'. It is noteworthy, however, that the new policy
was in direct contradiction to the colonial approach whereby Chiefs
were dealt with in their own areas only. The old ANC, as we saw,
had started a national approach to Chiefs which was to be the policy
of the new Government. But, as letters to Kaunda showed, new
problems and rivalries appeared as Chiefs were drawn closer to one
another. Meanwhile what Mulford calls 'the UFP rebel group'
wanted to recognise the *de facto* end of Federation by forming a
new party to renew the wooing of ANC, while at the same time,
Welensky was trying to persuade some of Nkumbula's dissident
members to form a new African party to accelerate cooperation with
the U.F.P. This dissident 'Mukuba Group' was to disturb the
fortunes of ANC for some time.[33]

In the certainty of the death of Federation, Kaunda was trying
also to encourage the hope of a new era of cooperation in Central
Africa. On his way home from the Leopoldville Conference of
PAFMECA he had said that, if Joshua Nkomo and other Southern
Rhodesia nationalists were allowed 'to organise peacefully', he saw
no reason why the Central African territories should not be able to
work together 'to their economic advantage'. The new government
south of the Zambezi seemed to him to be 'an improvement on the
old one inasmuch as it will help to dismantle the Federation quickly'.
But when Liso of ANC expressed himself in favour of accepting
Field's invitation to inter-governmental talks, Kenneth said he
found it 'very embarrassing' to cooperate with such an undemocratic
regime.

'UNIP is WORK' had been one of the popular slogans of the
election campaigns and it was now a matter of the highest priority to
channel the energies of the people, which Moffat called 'enormous',
into the establishment of a 'truly non-racial society'. Kaunda stressed
this in his maiden speech as a member of the Cabinet and declared
that the parlous economic situation of the territory was the result
'not of irresponsible behaviour in the big political parties', as
U.F.P. had claimed, but of the inability of the former regime to

function as a government. 'A completely new non-discriminatory constitution' would take the country 'a long way to solving' its problems. Kaunda then said that there would be no nationalisation of the press 'as long as I am leader here', and he and Nkumbula, at a joint press conference, 'confirmed that they did not believe in a one-party system'; that both parties would retain their identities and would oppose each other at the next election; but that they were both issuing orders down to branch level in their organisations to the effect that there must be an end to inter-party clashes.[34]

On 1 February, Dr. Hastings Kamuzu Banda was sworn in as first Prime Minister of Nyasaland, and Kaunda went with Kapwepwe, Kamanga, Michello and John Banda, to the celebrations. On arrival, after a brief visit to the Governor, Sir Glyn Jones, they went to Banda's house but had to wait for over three hours before they were led to the front of the building to join a large crowd of visitors. There Kaunda was amazed to hear the Prime Minister singing a song, in the Chewa language, in his own honour: '*Zonsi zimene za Kamuzu* . . .' '—Everything belongs to Kamuzu—Nyerere, Kaunda, Kapwepwe, Kamanga, Nkomo—all belong to Kamuzu.' Banda's lieutenants were saying, during this period that there were 'only two important people. God in Heaven and Kamuzu on earth'. In recalling this, Kaunda said that he was troubled when, at UNIP rallies, slogans such as 'One Zambia, one Nation; one Leader, Kaunda' were shouted; for the slogan should simply be: 'One Zambia, one Nation.' 'You've got to stop there,' he told his followers. The image of leadership in Nyasaland was in sharp contrast to what he knew in his friend, Nyerere, underlining the grave pressures of such a role upon a man's personality.[35]

As he and his colleagues returned to Lusaka, their uncomfortable experiences were crowned by being detained for seven hours at the airport in Salisbury, where they had to sleep on benches. However, what was concerning the new Government of Northern Rhodesia was the need to press home the victory over Welensky before he built up his strength for a counterattack. Therefore Kenneth was gratified that, after a stormy six days of debate, a motion, moved by Nkumbula and seconded by himself, calling for secession from the Federation, was passed by Leg. Co. The next day, he introduced a motion in the Council, calling for a new

Constitution forthwith, which was adopted by 21 votes to 14, as Nkumbula's motion had been. Now, said Kenneth, 'we can quench Sir Roy's fire-power.' 'If he uses fire-power, we have sufficient water to extinguish it.'[36]

The two debates had given prominence to the need for a Bill of Rights to guarantee the civil liberties of individuals, and Kaunda insisted that such a safeguard was desirable, and also that there would be no victimisation of members of the civil service. 'We have no intention of establishing a dictatorship and whether we have two, three, four or twenty parties depends on the people.' These words were spoken as evidence accumulated of growing repression in Southern Rhodesia, as shown not only by the re-arrest of Nkomo, but also by the re-introduction of social segregation in public swimming baths and the deportation of Dr. Terence Ranger. As police action increased in the south against African people, Sikota Wina, now a Parliamentary Secretary, made a sharp attack on the 'mobile unit' of the police for their 'brutal' actions against ordinary people. The 'riot squads' were made up of largely illiterate Africans led, in the main, by white officers of South African origin. Kaunda had just used his authority as a Minister to prevent the 'mobile unit' from moving in to Lundazi District in the east to quell a demonstration against the banning of a UNIP meeting. Wina proposed that, to give them a sense of social responsibility, the men of this unit should be put onto community projects when not on duty. There was, however, growing evidence that a number of industrialists and businessmen were planning to move in swiftly as the new state was being born. The promise of the reality of a harmonious multi-racial state, already being tested, could, Kaunda believed, proclaim convincingly that southern Africa's *apartheid* was indefensible. Yet non-Africans must be ready to face change and, as Minister of Local Government, Kenneth was anxious to apply the principle of adult suffrage swiftly to local government elections. He therefore moved to postpone until April 1964, elections due to take place in the near future, and went to meet the Municipal Association to allay its anger and fear at this move and to assure its members that there must be no lowering of standards in the administration of municipal government.[37]

In much hotter accents, at this time, the *Voice of UNIP* was speaking of 'panic-stricken whites fleeing southwards', like John

Gaunt, and denouncing 'white settlers in and outside the government service, posing as friends of the people.' 'A stream of lies',
the *Voice* declared, 'is continuously disseminated through churches,
schools, multi-racial organisations, capitalist-owned newspapers
and radio. . . .' 'Which fool can believe this cheap propaganda of
self-proclaimed friends of the Africans? Why promise the people
a bright future and freedom which yesterday was denied to them
with long prison sentences, machine guns and massacres?' The
Voice admitted, however, that 'forward-looking whites' were glad
to stay under a black government, but the reported exodus of
Europeans proved that they had 'been contributing to the oppression
of the African . . . the deprivation of his political rights and . . .
economic opportunities'. 'You shall run from here to Southern
Rhodesia where we shall follow you with a hot poker,' said the
Voice ' . . . to South Africa, even there we shall follow you and throw
you in the ocean. . . . When Zambians are free, they shall march
southwards to liberate the millions of their brothers and sisters . . .
even at the point of a gun.'[38]

In mid-March, the mobile unit broke up an ANC meeting at
Ndola after clashes of Congress and UNIP gangs, just when Kaunda
had called on Nkumbula to renounce violence. But the wave of
violence was not confined to the Copperbelt. Kaunda then issued
an order that any UNIP member who committed violence or
intimidation must be suspended from the Party. In the Southern
Province, Lusaka and Mufulira, and later in Lundazi, the disturbances were most severe, undoubtedly worsened by rumours of a
revival of ANC-U.F.P. relations, which provoked Kaunda to
threaten that he might call for an immediate election to 'let the
people decide who goes into power'. The fear of ANC acting
treacherously towards the new nation was inevitably increasing
pressure in UNIP for the banning of the opposition. As 'Freedom
House' and various regional offices issued stern statements on the
unrest, it became necessary for UNIP to deny as 'absolutely untrue'
the accusation of a U.F.P. M.L.C. that the Party in general and
Kaunda and Kapwepwe in particular 'believed in one party system'
[*sic*].[39] However, March had seen yet another crisis following a
statement in the *Voice* against Christianity, the observing of
Christian holidays, and the 'imperialist introduced' Bible. A protest
by the Christian Council expressed both 'great shock' and the belief

that Kaunda, 'son of an African Church of Scotland missionary', would not condone such pronouncements. The *Voice* had added that 'violence pays'. Sikota Wina then stated that some such recent articles were 'clearly contrary to party policy', that there was no intention whatsoever to abolish Christian holidays, and that Party publications would be brought into line with 'the responsibilities which our leader and his lieutenants have assumed' in national government.[40]

Kenneth left Lusaka a few days after a weekend meeting of UNIP's National Council, where, under the chairmanship of Grey Zulu, and with over 100 delegates, there had been signs of disquiet about the London Conference. The minutes recorded that at one point 'the National President asked if there way any doubt in the leadership.' 'He thought everyone knew what our stand was on secession.' The emotional atmosphere was, however, expressed by one delegate's announcement that 'their new slogan in his region was that if there was no new constitution, TWIST,' while another delegate 'regretted the words of the National President which made people refrain from speaking their minds'. Mainza Chona 'wondered why the delegates were going to London at all'. After many delegates had spoken, the minutes recorded that: 'Bwana Kaunda urged that we should not make a public stand on the question of whether the British Government should make it clear that Northern Rhodesia will secede. . . . He was not a coward and everyone knew it but he warned against any situation that would give rise to the use of Federal troops.' The Council had opened with a speech by Kenneth in which he said that in the present wave of violence, '60% of the incidents were started by the ANC and only 40% by the UNIP.' He proposed that UNIP members should join the Police Reserve. Wina however argued that 'the Police must be independent of politics', and Kaunda agreed that his proposal should not be made public.[41]

An undated typescript in the Sokoni Papers, which gives an extract from a speech by Kaunda that appears to belong to the period under review, merits citation here: 'We have got to think not like fish in water but like human beings. . . . Let us make our mind's body fly up very high then look down as the stream of history flows on. . . . The question is, "What kind of society do we want to see?" What we decide in here is what is going to be if we can put it successfully to those concerned and if together we can give shape or form to our decisions. . . . We realise that Federation is dead. . . . We realise too that the cost of the burial will be terrific. But we are prepared. We have an international commission looking into this. As soon as they have allowed us we will let the public know. We are prepared to shoulder part of it if only to save Britain from the overwhelming economic difficulties. We are prepared to negotiate. . . . We are sure we are winning. But the country can rest assured that this will not be a Party victory, but right and reasonableness triumphing. There will be no Nuremburg trials and no Eichmans to hang.'[42]

As we have seen, the majority Party had no reason to be happy about security in the land. There were now increasing signs of a sinister situation in Kenneth Kaunda's home district of Chinsali and neighbouring areas as a result of the way in which what had come to be called the Lumpa Church was developing. We noted the beginnings of this movement earlier. However, between early 1961 and mid-1962, Lenshina was away from home on an extended and unchronicled tour on the Copperbelt and southwards beyond the Zambezi. She had thus missed the tumults of Cha-cha-cha. On returning home, she issued an injunction to her followers to forswear political affiliation, raising at once the question why she should take such a line. Though Andrew Roberts, in his authoritative account of the Lumpa Church, finds no proof of the widespread rumours that she 'had made some sort of alliance with the white settler United Federal Party', Robert Kaunda, who was a Lumpa 'deacon', has stated that an offer of £8,000 was made to her, when in Southern Rhodesia, by agents of Welensky's Party. 'At first she refused and told them she had not gone there to negotiate for money but to convert people. . . . After a while, word reached her brother in Kabwe, Mr. Lubusha. . . . He told her she had done an unwise thing to reject the offer, and . . . they finally agreed to get the money. . . . Now then, when Lenshina finally gave way and accepted this money, she returned to her headquarters in Chinsali, a village she named Sioni [Zion] previously known as Kasomo . . . [and] started to summon her elders and deacons . . . to tell them that there was no understanding now between them and those of UNIP . . . . "When I tell them to do something, they don't respond . . . so I am now ordering everyone in this village to destroy their UNIP cards. For I have now discovered there is a devil." UNIP cards, she said, were an evil, satanic thing. "We who believe in our Church, cannot afford to serve two masters." '43

Roberts notes that at that time 'the local administration was widely assumed to be in league' with the U.F.P. and 'some victims of Lumpa violence despaired of redress through official channels.' Then, 'in July 1962 five small Lumpa churches in Chinsali District were burned down.' Despite the improvement in the relations of 'native authorities' and UNIP after the 1962 elections, Lumpa remained suspect and hostile and 'those who withheld support from the United National Independence Party were implicitly regarded not just as political opponents but as enemies of the nation.' In the words of the 1965 *Report of the Commission of Inquiry into the former Lumpa Church:* 'The first few months of 1963 saw the fears and tension of 1962 between the Lumpa Church and non-Lumpa followers increase considerably. . . . During April and May, 1963, numerous incidents of arson, mainly of village Lumpa churches, were reported from both the Chinsali and Lundazi districts.' In May, ANC addressed a message to 'all leaders of Christians' in the Northern Province, accusing UNIP of turning 'against Mama Lenshina' as part of its plan 'to stop people not to keep the instructions of their own churches' and 'to ban Holy Days'. It is nonetheless difficult to avoid the conclusion that this major and well-nigh lethal scourge in the period of the birth of Zambia can be traced, in part at least, to a desperate attempt by the arch-enemies of Kenneth Kaunda's people to add, to the alliance with Tshombe, another weapon forged to strike at UNIP in the months before the crucial election; a weapon which effected, as it were, a haemorrhage in the body of rural society that was to continue bleeding right to the eve of independence.[44]

Despite the still rampant bitterness of the forces against his cause, Kaunda arrived in London 'confident of achieving his aims.' He had just issued jointly with Nkumbula another appeal to the country for an end to incidents of 'stonings, assaults, unlawful assembly, riot, arson, murder, unlawful wounding and obstruction of the police'. During their absence in London the country must experience 'the beginning of a period . . . when people of all races shall live in the knowledge that both their person and their property are safe'. By walking out on the first day of the Conference, Kaunda and Nkumbula had shown that their demand of secession before discussion on the Federation was made in earnest, and they threatened also that they must be assured of a new Constitution before they would join the Central African negotiations. Along with Nkomo, Nkumbula and Kaunda refused to talk with Welensky, who, by the testimony of the polls of all three Federal territories, was now in their eyes, as Kaunda said, 'Lord Broken Reed'. Thus, unceremoniously, it happened that the Federation's death occurred as Butler was forced to acknowledge 'in 16 crisp words' the historic fact: 'We accept that none of the territories can be kept in the Federation against its will.'[45]

This trip abroad was the first in which Kenneth was accompanied by his wife and he was anxious that she should see as much as possible of interest. A visit to Scotland was planned but cancelled at the last moment because Betty was invited to Ireland and to New York. Kenneth had left her in Britain while he went back to Lusaka, during which time she was in London, Oxford, Brighton and the Lake District. When he returned, six weeks later, he took her to New York and to Sweden and Italy before going home. 'By the time I came to Zambia,' Betty recorded, 'I had a very much wider outlook.'[46]

The real danger in Central Africa now was that the affairs of Southern Rhodesia were in the hands of men more reactionary than Welensky's entourage. Moreover Field commanded financial and military power as well as the loyalty of a now more fiercely racialist electorate, whose attitude to Britain, according to the *Guardian*, was expressed by this 'sour joke': 'Why is the British Government like a banana? Because it is yellow and soft, is never straight and ultimately goes black.' *East Africa and Rhodesia* then gave prominence to that 'slogan printed in bold type' in the March issue of the *Voice of UNIP*, which had been disclaimed by Sikota Wina: 'Violence pays: peace does not pay.' Macmillan's Government had, said this journal, destroyed the Federation by its 'supine surrender to threats'. It was also noted by the British press that in the nothern territory 'the winds of change' were 'not on the side of the BSA Company' any longer, though its income from royalties in the Protectorate in 1962 had been £11,000,000. On his return to Lusaka, Kaunda had, however, to try to explain that, despite the unacceptable character of Field's Government, there would have to be discussions with him about common services such as railways, airways and Kariba power, which would make 'some sort of economic association' inevitable. For, he said, 'you cannot build a wall across the Kariba dam.'[47]

Recognising that the day of an 'independence' ceremony is never the actual birth of a new nation, various dates have been suggested, like Sokoni's 14 December 1962, as Zambia's natal day. The March/April issue of the London *Voice of Zambia* underlined the importance of 29 March at 17.00 G.M.T. as marking the end of Federation, when Britain 'acted just in time, and wisely in that their action is to the greatest advantage of all, including the 70,000 white settlers . . . who, for the past 60 years of foreign rule, have lived in a fool's paradise'. The paper also quoted Kaunda's answer at a London press conference to a question about what job he would offer Sir Roy after the burial of Federation, to the effect that 'there was a prosperous opening for an experienced railway worker to rise to the post of District Manager of Zambia Railways.' However, he added, "There is no question of any person, simply because he is white, being denied the right to remain in Northern Rhodesia, but . . . they will have to accept black leadership." "Sir Roy and his followers can, therefore, stay if they wish to."[48]

A considerable body of opinion, however, would have welcomed the departure of white people, especially the Afrikaans community, known as *Bambunu*. Therefore when Kaunda was misquoted as saying that South African passports would not be valid in the new nation of Zambia, the *Voice* carried these verses, entitled 'Boer Swan Song (to be sung, more or less, to the tune of Saries Marais):

> 'We're on our way to the old Transvaal
> Cornelious, Jannie and me,
> Zambia's no longer a place for us
> Now that the "Kaffirs" are free.

CHORUS: Pack your clothes in the old sports bus,
> Rugby kit, the old TV
> Do not forget the Copper bon-us
> Earned by the "Kaffirs" and me.

> Pietersburg, Nelspruit, Potgeitersrust,
> Cornelious, Jannie and me,

Apartheid's the proper job for us.
Why should the "Kaffir" be free?

Follow Mr. Swarts and old voevarts [*sic*]
Not forgetting Mr. Fouchie,
They say Zambia's not so smart
For Cornelious, Jannie and me.

Suppose the "Kaffirs" catch up with us
In Jo'burg and Kimberley,
Take over "our" Zuid Africa
From Cornelious, Jannie and me.

CHORUS: Leave clothes and the old sports bus,
                 Rugby kit, the old TV
                 Zambia's the proper place for us
                 Even if the African is FREE!
                              Ach—man what a puzzle.'[49]

It was increasingly clear that a large number of African people
believed that, with their leaders now in the Government, poll-tax
had ended; and so Kaunda and his colleagues had to explain clearly
that the burning of Identification Certificates had not meant the
end of the unjust tax, which could only be abolished when a new
tax structure was established. People had been 'so drilled for a very
long time in the nursing of *situpa* (*ifitupa*) along with poll-tax
receipts', that they thought both had ended with Cha-cha-cha.
Meanwhile, since health was still a Federal matter, 'Welensky's
rotting government', in Chona's phrase, was bringing fresh oppro-
brium upon itself by the introduction of a maternity levy of 30/-
and a theatre fee of £5 for any surgery required at confinements.
Chona further rejected the Federal reply that a 'destitute' or
'indigent' woman would receive exemption if she produced a
certificate to that effect, since she would have to be formally listed
as 'destitute' and also since the differential between European and
African incomes was so great.[50]

In May, there was a revival of press rumours about dissatisfaction
in UNIP with Kaunda's leadership, which mentioned Simon
Kapwepwe again as a rival. But Kapwepwe made a fresh pledge
of 'full support' for Kenneth, which was endorsed by a vote of
confidence in his 'unquestioned leadership' at the Youth Brigade's

Annual Conference. Alexander Chikwanda, Youth Secretary in Kitwe, then denied that Kaunda was 'losing his grip' on the Party's youth organisation.[51] However, for all its tremors, May ended with a brief journey to America, via Britain, Sweden and Italy where Kenneth discussed the possibility of economic assistance for the new nation, and also had informal talks with Butler, during which he mentioned the need for a railway between Lusaka and Dar es Salaam, to reduce dependence on hostile territories to the south.

The journey had been arranged primarily, however, so that he could receive an Honorary Doctorate of Laws of Fordham University, a Jesuit foundation in New York State. Since he had rejoined Betty in London, she was with him at the academic ceremony, and in his speech he spoke of her thus: 'Fortunately for me, my wife has stood by my side. I know it hasn't been easy for her, it has meant great sacrifices on her part, from the comforts of a headmaster's home to one in which even finding food became a problem; long absences from home on my part have been common features of our life. I was either agitating within the borders of our own country or among friendly nations, or away as a guest in one of Her Majesty's hostels. It was a trying period for her, especially when you think of our private army of six boys and one girl that she has to look after. I cannot repay her for all this.' In the citation conferring the degree, the University spoke of him as one who "through varying chances and so many hazards . . . now stands forth a leader of his nation, whose reputation has reached all parts of Africa and the whole world".[52]

In his speech at Fordham, Kenneth began with words couched in light, colloquial English: 'Whilst acknowledging that imperialism and colonialism are the same the whole world over, I am nevertheless inclined to agree with the Mahatma Gandhi when he expressed the view that there was a difference between British colonialism and that of other colonial and imperial powers represented at the Berlin Conference. Although the British will harass and embarrass you, beat you up, send you to prison, shoot and kill some of you, if you still have guts, when you come out of these detention camps and prisons, to continue to do what you believe in—and this process may be repeated several times—in the end they say, "These fellows are determined, give them some little power and let's see how they behave", they will eventually give you what you want.' He concluded in a lengthy discussion of non-violence, by declaring that it was not a primarily religious question. 'It is political, economic, social and spiritual. It brings man, as an individual living in society, back into the centre of things. Nothing is more necessary, for we are now in danger of getting so wrapped up in machines, organizations and plans that man who is the purpose of it all is treated like an instrument. Man must realize his own importance, both as an individual and as a member of society.'[53]

The Northern Rhodesian Coalition Government certainly had not drawn the two African parties closer. On issues like the plan for a rail link with East Africa, while Kaunda told a vast 'welcome home' rally that there was a company ready to build a line to Dar es Salaam in two years, Nkumbula wanted any railway expansion to be in the form of internal lines and his colleague, Stubbs, called the UNIP idea 'a white elephant'. But Nkumbula, whom one British newspaper described as 'the white sheep among black nationalists', was facing threats of revolt within ANC. His statement that he had been talking with UNIP, while Kaunda was abroad, about a possible 'merger', angered the 'Mukuba Group' within Congress, and Michello appeared as Nkumbula's chief rival. Pleas poured in to Nkumbula's office, calling him to action. 'You are just as a small boy of Kaunda all the time, why?' said one sad supporter. 'Is this your wishes to be not popular like what they do to Kaunda and his collidges [sic]?. . . . You better shake these things.' Another letter said: 'Mr. Kaunda immediately he returned from London . . . addressed six meetings, covering the whole of the Copperbelt main centre . . . we hardly see one from ANC.' Meanwhile it appeared that the violence sweeping the towns was more than political in origin, as was stated by a special Commission of Inquiry into Unrest on the Copperbelt. Political frustration merely added to the cumulative dynamite of unemployment, illiteracy, homelessness, and hunger. There were 50,000 unemployed persons in the mining towns in the middle of the year, and the situation was deteriorating fast.[54]

Seething impatience thus characterised the dry season of 1963. UNIP was showing that it could barely tolerate this harvest of 'mathematical constitutions' which, as the London *Voice of Zambia* said, had merely encouraged 'corruption, bribery and sinister pacts between parties of opposing principles'. There could be no progress when no one knew who was friend or foe. The expressions of good will to both African parties by the heir of the U.F.P., which Roberts and van Eeden were now leading under the name of the 'National Progress Party', evoked little response, for there was still deep suspicion of U.F.P. even in a new guise, and as Mulford shows, at that very time, ANC received an offer of £100,000 from Tshombe, on condition that there was vigorous reorganisation of the party and a drastic reduction of Nkumbula's presidential powers. The N.P.P. proposed, surprisingly, the development of trade with the north, where 'future principal markets must lie', pledged itself not to 'undermine any African political party' that could give the country stability and economic growth, and hoped 'at a later stage . . . to participate in a non-racial government'. UNIP's energies were being concentrated rather on preparing for new elections and on laying 'more emphasis than in the past on organising Europeans' though 'their votes are few and negligible', as Chona said.

Kenneth Kaunda was busily buttressing confidence in the coming independent nation and declared that Sir Evelyn Hone or Chief Secretary Luyt would be welcome as the new state's 'first Governor-General'. There was no attempt to conceal the warm personal relations between Hone and Kaunda, as had been illustrated by what happened as the two men arrived back from London on 6 April. A huge crowd was cheering and as the aeroplane door opened, Kaunda urged Hone to go first. 'For several seconds both hesitated. . . . An air hostess broke the deadlock by suggestion: "Why don't you both go out together? Then you can give each other moral support". The hint was taken, and fittingly both men were garlanded with flowers by the Asian community.' Meanwhile confidence in Northern Rhodesia's economic strength, real and potential, had recently been affirmed vigorously by Sir Ronald Prain of the Rhodesian Selection Trust, who believed that Europeans and Africans in responsible positions would 'have to balance up the conflicting claims of the mineral heritage of an African people, the fact that political power will rest with Africans while the technical skills will rest for many years with Europeans, that jointly Black and White have to work out a new accommodation which does justice to all these considerations'. Despite all the babel of contentious accents, no one was disposed to ignore the voice of big business at this juncture.[55]

The Victoria Falls Conference of 28 June could not have contrasted more sharply with the gatherings at the same venue in February 1949, at which, with no Africans present, the plan for Federation had been discussed, and again in September 1951 when African opinion had been overwhelmed and the principle of Federation confirmed. Now, in 1963, the assembly of political luminaries was, as it were, a funeral party, in advance of the actual demise, concerned with the swift distribution of the estate. Yet the essential fraudulence of the moribund Federation was seen even now when Liso and Banda of ANC were ordered out of the dining-room of a Wankie hotel and told to get food from the kitchen at the back. But Kaunda was able to pay tribute to Sir Roy, 'though misguided' for his attitude at the Conference, and to couple this with appreciation of Butler's approach. In a brief meeting with Winston Field and Ian Smith, Kaunda said, 'I am offering Northern Rhodesia's good offices, if you'd like us to mediate between you and the African nationalists.' Field looked at him intently and then said, 'If I didn't know you were sincere in saying that, I'd tell you to mind your own business', to which Kaunda replied, 'Thank you. Goodbye.'

In reviewing the Conference, Kaunda said that he 'would not be saying too much' if he suggested 'that Sir Roy Welensky might still use his great energies for the good of the country he chooses to settle in. . . .' 'We don't consider that any one man was the victor or the vanquished, but just that common sense prevailed.' The Conference achieved the supreme purpose of setting 31 December as the date for the dissolution of the Federation, but nevertheless it had some bitter results. Federal civil servants expressed fury at a report that Kaunda had proposed the 'drafting' of such officers if they were loath to serve under a new regime. 'Who does Kaunda think he's dealing with?' they cried. 'An army platoon, a pack of sheep, or what?. . . . We're not vegetables.' Much more sinister, however, was the decision swiftly made, to let the Air Force of seven squadrons, including eighteen Canberra bombers and twelve Hunter fighters, revert to Southern Rhodesia, though the north might be given some transport aircraft.[56]

The ominous situation in southern Africa added to the urgency of a Constitution based on universal adult suffrage for Northern Rhodesia. There were rumours that, as a result of a series of meetings with the Governor, a scheme might emerge whereby Nkumbula

would be President and Kaunda Prime Minister of a new Republic,
but police officers maintained that in fact UNIP was campaigning
on the Copperbelt to 'liquidate' opposition and they quoted a
figure of over 1,300 convictions for political crimes in six months,
five times as many as for the same period in 1962. The coalition had
not brought stability, and this affected economic as well as social
life severely. In an address to the Medical Congress, Kaunda showed
that he was aware of the reluctance of professional people to serve
in the new nations of Africa and the need to devise schemes whereby
qualified and experienced people would come on short-term contracts
without upsetting their own careers in their home countries. The
Northern News reported his remarks with the headline: 'We need
someone to hold our hand.' 'We need from outside,' he said, 'not
people who will exploit our weakness and inexperience but . . . who
would be willing to bear with us over the difficult years of our early
development.' As the exodus of Europeans continued to reveal
their fears of conditions in an independent nation, he was sad that
more could not be done to 'make public UNIP's approach to a non-
racial state'. Surely, he said, 'our kith and kin are those who agree
with us that we can make Northern Rhodesia, the continent of
Africa and indeed the entire world, a happy place for everyone.'
Small-pox then suddenly appeared in the Eastern Province and
Kenneth called on people everywhere to cooperate with a nation-
wide vaccination campaign. 'Medical people, black and white, are
not in any way involved in Federal politics. In any case I am taking
over this Ministry fairly soon.'[57]

Also in September, UNIP welcomed as a member Richard
Sampson who had been Mayor of Lusaka and who, said Chona, had
'refused to be intimidated by racialist critics'. Sampson's accession
would bring other associates with him, just as the resignation of
Shadreck Soko from ANC in July to join UNIP had boosted the
Party's standing in the Eastern Province. As UNIP postponed its
Annual Conference to devote itself to preparing for an election now
expected early in the New Year, Kaunda issued a pre-election
advertisement, reiterating the paramountcy of respect for individual
rights. The killing of an Assistant Police Inspector in yet another
outbreak of violence at the end of September evoked from him a
'very strong condemnation of one of the most outrageous crimes
against our society . . . [for] without law and order our country is

finished'. Very soon after this, word reached him that 'hundreds of
well-armed mercenaries from France, Portugal, Spain and South
Africa were massing in Angola' in support of a plot to create
a new country linking Katanga to the Copperbelt. It was clear,
Kaunda said later, that 'Nkumbula was still flirting with Tshombe
and Welensky had said that if they got Katanga and part of Northern
Rhodesia, the rest could go to Malawi. So I wanted to bring this to
light and frighten them by the fact that we knew all about it. My
sources were very reliable.'[58]

It was now five years since someone had painted a simple sign over
the door of the office of the newly formed Zambia African National
Congress thus: 'Culture, Simplicity, Freedom, Sacrifice, Immediate
Self-Government. Please Join.' The split from ANC then had been
made because some of these vital elements of the quest for nationhood had been eroded beyond repair. Now there was renewed
pressure for a UNIP merger with ANC. Chona, however, replied that
at the next election there would 'not be a single ANC follower'.
'... So with whom is UNIP going to merge?.... UNIP has opened
its door to all who believe in freedom and independence.' But in
fact the issue was not simple, for as Sokoni explained to the Chiefs
and Chona to Party officials, ANC was still inextricably involved in
intrigues. Yet, Chona had said, 'Old Harry was prepared to be a
stooge but within certain limits. . . . Hence his refusal to form a
coalition government with the UFP.' Moreover, UNIP's Caucus
Secretary had produced a research bulletin 'UNIP inside the Leg.
Co.', which furnished figures and graphs of five years' growth,
with comparative statistics for ANC. While ANC had formed 265
branches in the period, UNIP had formed 2,393 and, though the
Litunga still had refused to allow registration of parties, the 90 per
cent vote for UNIP in Barotseland helped to give grounds for
confidence that the next election would give Kaunda a resounding
victory. When, therefore, someone fired a gun in Kaunda's direction
at a rally in Lusaka in mid-November, piercing the straw hat of one
of his followers, he knew that his own reaction could have important
consequences on the behaviour of others. 'Put this down, as I do'
he said, 'to the work of an individual, a crank. . . .' 'It is difficult to
say whether the shot was fired at me. . . . I don't want my supporters
to think that . . . it was the work of any particular party.' Looking
back on the incident nine years later, he acknowledged that the

man who fired the muzzle loader was a known member of ANC. Yet at the time his words undoubtedly quietened the situation. Moreover, Princess Nakatindi, who was on the platform, confirmed, in conversation with the writer, that his reaction to the gun-shot amazed all who saw it. As the shot rang out, there was inevitable confusion and then a group of men dashed from the crowd in pursuit of the fleeing gunman. Kaunda at once left the platform and set off after them. He found them with the man some distance away, beating him. At once he ordered them to stop, called for people to carry the man to hospital and commanded that no violence must be done to him.[59]

A few days after this, Kenneth told 'an enthusiastic and orderly crowd of about 6,000' that when UNIP won the elections, it would not tolerate anyone who tried to terrorise the country by any means. Some people were preparing arrows and other weapons to destroy public peace, and he warned that 'those who rise by the sword will perish by the sword.' But, he added, 'I don't want you to touch any ANC supporter physically, only mentally.' Clearly, as Richard Hall wrote in the Edinburgh *Scotsman*, Kaunda was going to 'need a strong hand on the levers.' 'He will be assisted by the virtual one-party state which UNIP's dominance will secure. . . . The guitar-playing Bible-reading clergyman's son has a mystical faith in kindness as a conquering force. Zambia 1964 will put this novel idea to the test.' Kenneth had already revealed that he would like the country to attain its independence on United Nations Day in 1964, 24 October. It was not the time-table that was complicated but the jig-saw of people, pressures and potential explosions that made the birth of this potentially 'most powerful black state south of the Equator' so critical. As the year ended, Kenneth had to dash north to Chinsali to try to halt a virtual vendetta between his followers there and members of Lumpa, some of whom had hacked two UNIP men to death in an outburst of bitter violence.[60]

On 3 January, 1964, an Order In Council formally conferred self-rule upon Northern Rhodesia, whereby only defence, foreign affairs, public order and the police would remain in the Governor's control. The new Constitutional instrument confirmed that every person was 'entitled to the fundamental rights and freedoms of the individual, of whatever race, place of origin, political opinions, colour, creed or sex, but subject to respect for the rights and freedoms

of others and for the public interest.' UNIP's election manifesto and
supporting documents revealed careful, corporate thinking, with an
insistence upon the need for compulsory education as soon as
possible, the brochure aptly quoting a dictum of H. G. Wells:
"Human history becomes more and more a race between education
and catastrophe."[61] Roberts of the N.P.P. declared that his party
was 'in every way dedicated to the national effort . . . [but] you don't
have everybody belonging to one party to be a united effort'.
Nkumbula, whose Director of Elections had defected and fled to
Tanganyika just before the close of nominations, was so angry when
his request for postponement of the elections was rejected that he
called for the removal of the Governor. He further threatened a
'Master Plan' to force the deferring of the elections and there was a
nasty rumour that ex-gendarmes from Katanga might be brought
in to effect his 'plan'. In advance of the elections, Kenneth Kaunda
had been stressing that the country must now be, not two nations
but one, and that therefore the reserved seats for Europeans should
be abolished before Independence Day. 'All tribal and racial
opposition,' he said, 'we intend to make completely ineffective in
and outside Parliament' ' . . . . Europeans, Asians, Eurafricans and
Africans will be fully represented, but certainly not on racial lines.'
The indecision of white voters was noticeable in the weeks before
the election day, though UNIP's meetings with them compared very
favourably with N.P.P. meetings. It was widely believed that the
news of army mutinies in Tanganyika and a threat to the rule of
Nyerere, whom many regarded as Kaunda's 'model', deprived UNIP
of any chance of capturing 'reserved seats' from the N.P.P.

On the morning of 20 January huge queues had gathered hours
before the polling stations opened. Once again many rural people
had made long walks from their homes to vote, and once again the
average percentage poll was very high, this time 94.3 per cent. When
the ballot-boxes were checked, it was also clear that UNIP had
made virtually no impact on the ANCs strongholds in the Southern
Province. The overall results, however, were a resounding victory
for UNIP, which won 55 seats against 10 for ANC and 10 for
N.P.P. The *Northern News* hailed this with a banner headline:
'Kaunda's Greatest Triumph'.[62]

[1]*Zambia*, p. 160.
[2]Kaunda to 'Dear Comrades', Kabompo, 28/4/59, quoted in Rotberg *Rise*, p. 303.
[3]TI.-FM/KK, 22/9/69 and 13/2/69; and for perceptive comments on the 'spiritual' quality of Kaunda's character, see especially Hall, *The High Price of Principles—Kaunda and the White South* 36-51; Legum, *Zambia—Independence and Beyond*, vii-xiii.
[4]*NN*, 7/6/62-9/7/62.
[5]UNIP: Chona to Chief Secretary, 1/0G/410 of 22/12/61, in which Chona asked: 'Why don't you arrest Mr. Kaunda who burned his I/C publicly?'; UNIP's Memo to Butler of 21/5/62 was signed by Kaunda, Chona, Kapwepwe, Milner, Wina and Kalulu; FH Statement to PAFMECSA, 13-14/5/62; and *NN*, 26/7/62 with letter by Kasakula, parodying Shakespeare, *Julius Caesar*, Act III, Sc. 2, line 80.
[6]*NN* for the period; *EAR* 17/5/62 for a report of the Barotse National Council's Resolution of 7/5/62; and *Guardian*, 25/7/62. See also UNIP 2/PUB/18-5097, J. Skinner, *How to Vote*, 10/7/62.
[7]*NN*, 6/8/62-9/8/62.
[8]UNIP: 9CG/WP/5, Kaunda to 'Royal Highness', Western Province, 2/8/62; 9/CH/EP—5294 and 5318, Kaunda to Chiefs Kambombo and Chikuwe, 16/8/62 and 17/8/62; 9/CH/WP/5/5455, to Chief Nkana, 28/8/62; 9/CH/NW-5498 to all NW Province Chiefs, 29/8/62; FH; Lunda NA, Chief Puta to Kaunda; 239/Legis/2 of 4/9/62, Kankomba we Lala to Kaunda, 29/9/62 and Kaunda to Kankomba 6/10/62; UNIP Press statement (undated) on 'policy towards the Liberal Party'; *NN*, 22/8/62; and letter, A. Rawlins, to *NN*, 30/6/62.
[9]*NN*, 13/8/62, 20/8/62, 15/8/62, 14/8/62; *UNIP Annual Report, August, 1961-July, 1962*, esp. pp. 6-7; and see Welensky, *op. cit.*, pp. 342-343.
[10]*NN*, 31/8/62, 17/9/62, 13/9/62; FH: Press Statement, S. Wina, 10/9/62, on Kaunda's Katanga trip; TI-FM/KK, 13/8/69; also FH: Press Statement:—Huggins Chewe, ex. ANC, on ANC-Katanga 'link', 7/11/62; UNIP Statement to PAFMECSA, 13-14/5/62; and *London Observer*, 29/7/62. Note that a letter from Chief Sakavungu to Kaunda, 9/1/63, mentioned a strong rumour that Tshombe had given guns to Lunda Chiefs to fight the Luvale in 1962. (FH: Presidential).
[11]UNIP/2/00/GEN-5316: circular by M. Chona on Katanga 'soldiers', 17/8/62; *Scotsman*, Edinburgh, 1/8/62, article by Andrew Wilson, and *London Times*, 16/8/62, for report of Kaunda's allegation of a plot to kill him and 33 others, as proof of which Kaunda had 'held up a blue notebook' at a Lusaka press conference; ANC: Press Statement on 'Mr. Kaunda's Allegation of the 200 soldiers in Katanga and the Assassination Story', signed: H. M. Nkumbula, 17/8/62. 'Mukuba'=copper; the local name for Broken Hill being *Kabwe ka mukuba*—'Little Copper Rock'. Broken Hill was renamed Kabwe after independence.
[12]FH Press Statement: Chona 'Open Letter to Welensky', 20/9/62; Chona to *Northern News*, 27/9/62; and *NN*, 3/10/62, letter by K. W. Chituta.
[13]FH: Election: Mundia, circular letter, 1/9/62.
[14]*NN*, 11-12/9/62.
[15]*NN*, 28/9/62-12/10/62, 18/10/62; and Temple Papers: letter to *Northern News*, 8/10/62.
[16]*NN* for October, 1962; FH; Press Statements 13/10/62; Mulford, *NR General Election*, 116, which refers specifically to the leaflet.
[17]Mulford, *NR General Election*, 134-136.
[18]*NN*, 27/10/62; and Sokoni Papers: Note entitled 'President Says—'.
[19]Mulford, *NR General Election 1962*, 145 ff. The table of 'Racial and Party Composition of Elected Members' appears on p. 147. Note: Mulford was in the territory from August 1962 to January 1963, and has enriched an excellent analysis of the elections with first-hand knowledge of the situation at the time. Note the surprise defeat of UNIP's Solomon Kalulu and ANC's Job Michello.

[20]*Ibid.* and *NN*, 1-9/11/62; *Africa Digest*, Vol. X, No. 3, pp. 80-81.
[21]*Guardian*, 30/10/62; *NN*, 6/11/62 and 19/11/62, letter by S. N. Oldfield about Kaunda's 'tantrums'.
[22]FH: Presidential Circular, 6/11/62, and note Kaunda's error in totalling anti-Federation Upper Roll votes, which was actually 29.3 per cent.
[23]*NN*, 10/11/62; ANC: 'Telegrams Received in Favour and Against Coalition Government with UNIP' (undated), with Kaunda's letter to Nkumbula attached; and *Central African Mail*, 6/11/62.
[24]*NN*, 14-19/11/62; and FH: ANC-UNIP Joint Press Statement, 16/11/62, signed, H. M. Nkumbula and K. D. Kaunda.
[25]*NN*, 19-29/11/62; and UNIP Press Release 20/11/62, on Kaunda's meeting with Tshombe in Kitwe; also *Scotsman*, 1/12/62; and *Guardian*, 3/12/62.
[26]Mulford, *NR General Election*, 173, 105, 174-182; *NN*, 15/12/62; *Voice of UNIP*, Jan. 1963, J. M. Sokoni, pp. 25-26; Sokoni was entitled 'Under Secretary to the National President'.
[27]*NN*, 15-31/12/62.
[28]January 1963 (ed. Moses Makwaya), pp. 29-31, article in Bemba by Aaron Milner, UNIP's Deputy National Secretary. *Chitwe Mambo* is an honorific title to describe one who, at the centre or control, is there by rightful inheritance. *Nkamya Milonga* is also honorific, meaning literally 'Drier of the rivers'.
[29]Note: The Pan-African Freedom Movement of Central Africa, PAFMECA, was still often called PAFMECSA, to include Southern Africa. For an analysis of the 'first African Government', see *NR General Election*, 180-182; and *Voice of UNIP*, January 1963 for brief biographies of 'African Cabinet Ministers and their Parliamentary Secretaries', pp. 21-22; also FH: Election (A): UNIP, M. Sokoni to Regional Secretaries, 18/12/62; Sikasula to Regional Secretaries, 5/12/62; and *Voice of UNIP*, January 1963, pp. 7-8 and 20.
[30]*Guardian*, 6/12/62 and 17/12/62; Keatley, *op. cit.*, pp. 491-492 and 477; and indeed the whole of his 'Postscript'; *Scotsman*, 6/12/62; *NR General Election*, p. 183; and note Welensky's claim that Butler had promised that British troops would not be used against the Federation (*Glasgow Herald*, 21/12/62).
[31]January 1963, pp. 23-24; and February, 1963, pp. 10-11; and *Central African Mail*, 10/11/62, slogan written by Unia Mwila.
[32]*Guardian*, 7/1/63 and *Africa Digest*, Vol. X, No. 5, pp. 152-153, citing *Central African Examiner*; FH: Press Statements, Joint ANC-UNIP, 15/1/63 and 25/1/63; and 'Joint ANC-UNIP Memorandum to the Rt. Hon. R. A. Butler', 24/1/63.
[33]*NN*, 9/1/63; FH: UNIP 9/CH/WP/5-131 of 19/1/63, Kaunda to Chief Shimukani, Luanshya; the Luvale Chief Sakavungu to Kaunda, 9/1/63; Mwata Kazembe to Kaunda, 8/3/63; and UNIP/1/A/NP/1 of 22/4/62, Sylvester Chisembele to Kaunda ref. chiefly rivalries in the Luapula Province; also Mulford, *Zambia*, pp. 304-305; *NN*, 25/1/63 and 13/3/63.
[34]*NN*, 3/1/63, 19/1/63, 16/2/63, 25/1/63, 1/2/63.
[35]TI-FM/KK, 12/3/70.
[36]*NN*, 4/2/63 and 15/2/63; and *London Times*, 14-15/2/63.
[37]*NN*, 15/2/63; *Guardian* 26/2/63 and *Scotsman* 26/2/63, 7/3/63; *NN*, 8/3/63.
[38]Feb. 1963, p. 12.
[39]*Glasgow Herald*, 11/3/63; *NN*, 11/3/63, 20/3/63; FH: Central Province Regional Secretary (S.C. Mukando) on Monze disturbances at rally addressed by Kapwepwe, 3/5/63; Press Statements, 24-25/4/63, 3/5/63, 7/5/63, 18/5/63, (by W. P. Nyirenda), 20/5/63, (by A. Milner). The denial of a one-party system is from the press statement of 3/5/63.
[40]*Guardian*, 15/3/63 ref. to protest by N.R. Christian Council Secretary, Revd. E. G. Nightingale.
[41]UNIP: Minutes of National Council, 15-17/3/63.
[42]Sokoni Papers: 'President Speaks to National Council', undated.
[43]TI-FM/RMK and others, 15/6/71.
[44]*Op. cit.*, esp. pp. 34-36; *Report of Lumpa Commission, 1965* (Govt. Printer,

Lusaka) esp. pp. 10-11; ANC/PHQ/5/6 (Kasama), 7/5/63; and TI-FM/J.M. Sokoni, 6/10/69, and FM/SMK, 8/11/69.

[45]*Glasgow Herald*, 25/3/63; FH: Joint Press Statement, Kaunda and Nkumbula, 22/3/63; *Times*, 30/3/63; *Guardian*, 26/3/63, 30/3/63. For Kaunda's description of Welensky as 'Lord Broken Reed', see *Voice of Zambia* (London), Vol. I, No. 18, March-April, 1963, p. 2.

[46]Mpashi, *op. cit.*, pp. 67-68.

[47]*Daily Telegraph* and *Scotsman*, 30/3/63; *Observer*, 31/3/63; *Guardian* 28/3/63 and 1/4/63; *EAR* 4/4/63 pp. 660-661; *Scotsman*, 17/4/63; *NN*, 11/4/63.

[48]*Voice of UNIP*, January 1963, p. 25; and *Voice of Zambia*, London, March/April, 1963.

[49]*Voice of UNIP*, July 1963, p. 26.

[50]*NN*, 20/4/63, 29/4/63; FH: Sundry: UNIP 9/CH/EP/12-822, Kaunda to Undi, Paramount Chief of Chewa, 8/5/63; and UNIP 9/CH/CP/1-2344 to Mkushi Native Authority; UNIP 7/HQ/9-855, Chona to all Regional Secretaries 16/5/63; Press Statements on Maternity Levies, 16/5/63 and 22/5/63.

[51]*NN*, 1/5/63, 8/5/63, 13/5/63; and *Scotsman*, 25/5/63.

[52]Melady, *op. cit.*, p. 211 and Legum, *Zambia*, p. 247.

[53]Legum, *Zambia*, pp. 248-9, 252-3.

[54]*Guardian*, 3/6/63; Hall, *Zambia*, pp. 222-223; ANC: Unsigned letter to President, 16/4/63; H. P. Ngoma, Livingstone, to Nkumbula, 19/4/63; D. Simoloka, ANC, Ndola, to Administrative Secretary, 29/4/63; 'Monthly Circular' (Old Man), 7/5/63. See also Report of *Commission of Inquiry into Unrest on the Copperbelt*, August, 1963 (Government Printer, Lusaka).

[55]*Voice of Zambia*, April 1963; Mulford, *Zambia*, p. 309; ANC: Policy Statement of NPP, issued by G. van Eeden, 10/5/63; *Voice of UNIP*, July, 1963, p. 14; *NN*, 22/6/63; Hall, *Kaunda*, pp. 63-64; *Africa Digest*, Vol. X, No. 6, p. 180.

[56]*Times*, 1/7/63; *Report of Central African Conference, 1963* (Govt. Printer, Lusaka); *Africa Digest*, Vol. XI, No. 1, pp. 8, 10, and 5; TI-FM/KK, 9/4/71; *NN*, 24/7/63, 4/7/63.

[57]*Scotsman*, 30/7/63; *NN*, 31/8/63; 11/10/63, 24/10/63; and FH: Press Statements by Kaunda, 14/9/63, 17/9/63.

[58]FH: Press Statements, Chona, 17/7/63, 13/9/63; Kaunda 21/9/63 and 28/9/63. The murdered policeman was Assistant Inspector Chito; UNIP 7/HQ/CIRC/9-269 of 14/9/63; Election Advertisement, signed: K. D. Kaunda, undated; also *NN*, 9/10/63; and TI-FM/KK, 9/4/71, quoting one source of the 'mercenaries' report as Timothy Kankasa who was assigned to check on developments to the north-west.

[59]FH: Press Statement, Chona, 12/9/63; No. 7/HQ/CIRC/9 (Chona) 29/7/63; UNIP Research Bulletin, *UNIP in the Leg. Co.*, July 1963; *NN*, 14/11/63; and TI-FM/Nakatindi, 29/3/69.

[60]*NN*, 23/11/63, 5/12/63, 9/12/63; *Scotsman* 21/11/63, 6/12/63; and *Guardian*, 30/12/63.

[61]*Africa Digest*, Vol. XI, No. 4, pp. 94-95; UNIP, election brochure, *Path to National Salvation*, 5.

[62]*CAP* 20/12/63; Hall, *Zambia*, p. 227; *NN*, 23/1/64. Note: ANC's defecting Director of Elections was John Banda.

14
Kwacha Ngwee—Into the Zambian Morning

Nineteen sixty-three had been a year of conflict and confusion, yet it had been certain that the goal of all the striving would be reached. As some of the nationalists had prophesied on several occasions, it had been the darkest hour before the dawn, a time when agitated people were rushing up and down, as it were, stumbling blindly, shouting, knocking into one another roughly and unreasoningly in the darkness. Then, like a tiny strip of light, at first no bigger than a man's finger, the dawn had begun to reach from the east into the area of jaded, sleepless strife, coming from where national sovereignty was virtually an accomplised fact, in East Africa and in the land soon to be called Malawi. For Northern Rhodesia, 1964 was to be the time of the lightening of the sky, in which the country was to move swiftly through what one commentator would call 'the most amicable pre-independence talks' with Britain 'for the past five years', to the status of a republic within the British Commonwealth, welcomed into the United Nations Organisation, and widely acclaimed as a star of hope in Africa.

This realisation of a new dispensation was what was meant, in essence, by the slogan 'KWACHA NGWEE'. Indeed the word '*Kwacha*' had, as we have noted, been the watchword of the nationalist movements of both Central African Protectorates, a word meaning either 'The dawn is about to break' or 'The dawn has come', according to the inflection of the voice. '*Ngwee*' is one of a group of expletives of intensification in which African languages are so rich. It is the root of a verb, *kungweruka* in the dialects of eastern Zambia and Malawi, which means 'to be light', as, for example, the lightening after clouds have gone or the white light of a new day. Shouting '*Kwacha*' had been a criminal offence in both territories in the various 'emergencies' which preceded the dismantling of the Federation. After formally attaining independence, both new nations would use the word *kwacha* for their main denomination of currency and Zambia would use *ngwee* for one hundredth of a *kwacha*. In this dawn there would still be confusion and strife, but what Welensky, Greenfield, van Eeden, Field, Smith, Verwoerd and Vorster stood for would not now oppress people's personalities and aspirations or treat of two levels of humanity, one superior and one inferior, which is the essence of *apartheid* and *herrenvolk* and the ultimate negation of Kenneth Kaunda's cardinal conviction that, however human societies may be structured, 'MAN must come first'.[1]

In these pages, it has not been possible to give an adequate picture of the social forces at work over the seventy crucial decades of what Gann called a 'plural society'. It has been necessary to give place to the endless chain of stresses and clashes that brought to the situation an element of real peril, and to attempt to present these as they impinged upon the majority of the country's people and upon Kaunda in particular. The deficiencies of such a survey are patent. Little notice has been given to the ordinary doings of quiet people, or, for instance, to the significant increase of Europeans with an understanding of the need for change and a readiness to participate in making the situation better. There is need also to study more closely than has been possible here, the awakening of the churches, however belated, to the 'signs of the times'. The amelioration that was discernible, alongside increasingly articulate 'reactionary' utterances and actions, was the work of more than a handful and, as we have noticed, UNIP's leaders paid numerous tributes to the contributions of good men to a better society. It is nonetheless a historical fact of considerable importance that Zambia's attainment of independence and her international standing and influence thereafter have been realised, to a great extent, because people who have exercised power have been magnetized by the quality of sincerity and honesty of mind, manifested without arrogance or self-praise, in the nation's young leader.

We have already noted how quickly and positively Iain Macleod had reacted to Kaunda's character. Hard-headed men, no less than others, have commented on the effectiveness of the combination, in his character, of spiritual integrity and clear-headed realism.

John Stonehouse of the British Labour Party, who was deported from the Federation in 1959, and who 'judged people by their ability to achieve their objectives and above all to survive', has traced Kaunda's ability 'to ride the tiger' to the fact that 'what appeared to be weaknesses years ago are in fact his strength because he needs deep emotion in order to be able to communicate with the masses of Zambia.' 'They've got to feel that they have a chap at the top who has this basic sympathy.'[2] In the opinion of another Labour Party man, Frank Judd, who has associated himself closely with the 'Zambia lobby' in Westminster, the most impressive quality in Kaunda was 'his willingness to talk about the values which he believes should be relevant in political action', a quality which we have seen extensively in his circulars and speeches to his followers since 1953. Kaunda, Judd noted, did 'not hesitate to admit that he himself and his government may fall far short of the standards which they set themselves', while evincing a response to 'the real challenge to see how one must present one's arguments for the things in which one believes, in order to change the state of public opinion'.[3] Thus, what caught the attention of many who met him and watched his leadership in action was that it was 'the man more than his politics' which they were encountering. A Conservative M.P., Noel Fisher, who had rallied support for Macleod in early 1961, had met Kenneth when on an unofficial tour of the Federation in mid-1960, and at once understood the aspirations which he expressed, though 'technically at that time he could have been regarded by some people as an extremist.' Fisher saw Kaunda as a man who passionately wanted a profound change in race relations, a man 'whose record, from my point of view, was terribly good'.

Harold Macmillan, Fisher has recorded, shared his own shock at the patent fact that Welensky did not seek to know African leaders personally though he claimed to be the spokesman of the Federation. Kenneth, on the other hand, had no such 'colour bar' in his thinking and readily gave and expected trust.[4] It always shocked Kenneth that, as he said when he heard on the radio that Macleod had agreed to a crucial modification of the 15-15-15 scheme in Welensky's favour, 'a man would say one thing and do another'. This *cri de coeur* has been vividly recalled by Father Patrick Walsh who was with him and his colleagues in Freedom House when the report of the constitutional adjustment was broadcast. 'I'm giving it as an instance of the integrity and honesty which I've always found to be a very characteristic trait in Dr. Kaunda,' said Walsh. 'He couldn't deceive a person. It wouldn't matter whether the decision he had to make was popular or unpopular. If he thought it was the right thing to do, he would do it, and he would not deceive people about what he was thinking and what he was going to do.' Incidentally, Walsh had also been especially able to witness at close range what he called 'the silent, womanly suffering' of Betty Kaunda, 'during the hard times of the fight for freedom....' 'She never complained, there was never any sign of bitterness. She always seemed to be the image of the "valiant woman", who knew her husband had to work and suffer for his people, while she bore the loneliness and hardship with stoic silence.'[5]

A few days before the elections in January 1964, Harry Nkumbula made an amazing broadcast in which he responded to a question about his future, by saying 'I shall be Harry' and then adding, 'My men can leave me one by one.' 'They are spineless, uneducated primitives. But I choose not to be bought . . . not to be kicked out the back door. . . . I come from a line of chiefs. My ancestors bought slaves—not that I agree with that, it was all wrong. I am a Marxist, and that doesn't mean I'm a Communist.'[6] Perhaps the split of 1958 had been both inevitable and irreconcilleable because Nkumbula had been relying on egotism and on slogans and had therefore failed to chart a way forward; whereas, as a one-time associate said of Kaunda, 'he gave a tremendous amount of thought to what he was saying . . . was really conscious of where he might be going, where he might not be going, what all this could mean.' Other chroniclers will trace the development of Zambia's international relations in the years after independence and attempt to reconstruct the multifarious network of information and counsel on which the President and Government had to rely in shaping foreign policy. In the years before 1964 it was clear that Kenneth Kaunda was trying to place reliable, perceptive men of initiative in key foreign capitals but that there was no cadre of trained diplomats to draw upon and so he supplemented their work by an informal system of consultation whereby he sought corroborative evidence and comment from people in the countries concerned whom he believed he could trust. At first, naturally, there could be only a handful of such confidants but the awareness that his country was moving swiftly, not only to the coveted status of national sovereignty but to an increasingly crucial role in continental African affairs, necessitated a concerted programme of personal contacts.[7]

The Pan-Africanist role that, as we have seen, Kaunda played almost constantly during the years immediately before independence, was the fulfilling of a vision that he shared with other leaders but which he had largely pioneered in the Protectorate. Within a few days of his appointment as Nkumbula's Secretary-General in 1953, he had written to Nairobi and Johannesburg, responding to a suggestion of the Kenya Africa Union and the South African ANC that Lusaka should be the rendezvous of nationalists from countries south of the Sahara. As we saw, this led to his planning an abortive Pan-African Regional Conference. What was significant was that the Kenyan and South African letters, which had been lying in the Congress office for some weeks, were now answered by Kenneth with enthusiasm. 'One cannot help dropping a tear of joy,' he had written then, 'when one notices the fact that our long-dreamt of Pan-Africanism is now afoot and one can foresee the fruits of this on-coming cooperation.' He had thus seen the growth of both PAFMECA and, from meetings of the All-Africa Conference, the Organisation for African Unity, and, as the *London Financial Times* observed, he had been a leading figure in all the inter-African conferences since the big gathering at Addis Ababa in 1960 of Independent African States.[8] The exploitation of every opportunity to send young colleagues abroad had been necessary not only to the welding of fraternal relations but to the injection into his Party of a sense of belonging to a wider community.

The writings and speeches of Kenneth Kaunda reveal that, during the 'long, hard march' to independence, he rarely talked about himself or his reactions and actions. Though Hall entitles a chapter of his little book on Kaunda, 'In the Ring with Roy', Kenneth's own speeches did not spotlight himself in a hero's role. They lacked the egotism that Hastings Banda revealed so often, as when, in June 1964, he heard that Welensky was planning to enter Southern Rhodesian politics. If so, said Banda, 'I will throw to the wind my policy of non-interference in the affairs of other countries . . . .' 'Welensky is my enemy, no matter where he is, even in hell.' It was not by self-projection that Kenneth earned the tribute of the *Northern News* that the country's swift and smooth progress to independence was largely due to 'the unusually sweet reasonableness of its leader' who had 'won the hearts of the British Prime Minister, the leader of the Opposition, the former Dominions and the United States, to say nothing of the United Nations'.[9] Moreover, UNIP had not produced any glossy pictorial brochures of its leader even when he was about to become Prime Minister. There had been only a 28-page booklet produced in Bemba by Andrew Mutemba in 1962, which, despite its crudity of production and format, was meant to inform the Party's Bemba-speaking membership about Kaunda's life. Entitled '*Umweo no kufyalwa kwa Ba Kaunda mu bwipi*'— 'The Life and Birth of Mr. Kaunda in brief', the booklet told of his parents and their life in Chinsali District; his birth, childhood and youth; his education, teaching work and wanderings; his return to Lubwa and the growth of misunderstanding with the Mission there; his full-time work for Congress and travel abroad; the split with Nkumbula; ZANC and its leaders' detention, and Kenneth's imprisonment. Mutemba told how, when Kaunda went home to Shambalakale, he had no opportunity to see his family there in peace because of endless streams of visitors. The rearing of a big family had meant, as we have seen, privation for them all and loneliness for Betty Kaunda, and Mutemba said that the names of their children showed that the Kaundas had often faced troubles: one was 'Perhaps', one was 'What shall we eat?', another was 'Troubles'. The second son, Wazamazama, once said to his father, "Europeans aren't pleased that you have grown a beard on your chin." "When I grow up, I'll grow a beard all over my face." This seemed fitting in the son of a man who, as Mutemba saw him, 'always refused to be frightened by anyone'.

Like his second son, Kenneth had loved to model in clay as a child. In youthful maturity, he had become convinced that the future of his impoverished land lay in using its natural resources. When later, he gave the slogan 'UNIP IS WORK' and the movement adopted the hoe as its symbol, the same idea was developing. In a speech to the Staff Training College in December 1963, he sought to press home this concept of self-reliance in a situation in which massive dependence on imported goods and food-stuffs since the early decades of the century had fostered a notion of local inadequacy to provide the necessities of life. The development of the nation from within was paramount. This was why he had given an assurance in his maiden speech in Leg. Co. that, despite his dedication to continental unity, he would not 'place the interests of Northern Rhodesia second to Pan-Africanism'; and why also he insistently stressed that national development must be non-racial. When, three weeks before independence, the negotiations for the end of the B.S.A. royalties were still inconclusive and Kenneth threatened to put the issue to a national referendum, a notably sympathetic commentator found 'an incidental paradox . . . in that, of all the Prime Ministers in all the territories in British Africa, going forward to independence, none has been more committed to a policy of good relations with the European than Dr. Kaunda, the missionary's son'. Yet, surely the comment confused the issue, and moreover wrongly implied that Kaunda's 'policy of good relations' was to 'the European' qua European. For Kenneth the issue was clear. The B.S.A. royalties symbolised gross exploitation of the potential wealth of the many for the vast enrichment of a few whose interests lay outside the country. It was not a question of the colour of either exploiter or exploited.[10]

As news came in that a total of 800 white families had left in December 1963, Kenneth had the experience of being 'lost' for nearly an hour while his plane tried to find the rough airstrip at Mwinilunga, in the remote north-west, in very bad weather. He was on an electioneering tour there, appealing as everywhere for peace. The printing by a paper called the *Voice of Zambia Front* of a suggestion that Kapwepwe should be UNIP's leader and first Prime Minister evoked Kaunda's anger. 'It is the work of lunatics,' he said. The police, the press announced, were ready to cope with election violence and the rumour of ANC's plan to disrupt the elections by use of ex-gendarmens from Katanga was still abroad, despite Nkumbula's denial. Sikota Wina pleaded, therefore, that people should realise that Kaunda was first and foremost a humanitarian. 'It was he who personally proposed at the Lancaster House Conference in 1961 that a Bill of Rights, not to protect ethnic or racial groups but to protect the individual, be enshrined in the Constitution.' The bitterness of the past had to be forgotten, and this prompted Kenneth's remark, which was open to misunderstanding, that 'just as water takes its colour from its container, so a well-trained police force reflects the calibre of the government in power.' This, he had to explain, was meant to help the police and not to

adumbrate their subordination to 'UNIP's thumb'. Moffat, meanwhile pleaded with white voters to realise that, though Kaunda had
'all the power he needs, . . . rejecting him would be like a kick in the
teeth to a boxer, and would show that the Europeans, by electing
10 old stalwarts of the UFP, were persisting in the undeviating
hostility to African government which was their trade mark'. But
there were also reports by foreign journalists that an anti-European
'ginger group' was active within UNIP and Kenneth issued an
angry, categorical denial of this. What mattered was that the
country would be independent by October 'with or without European
support'.[11]
  We have already noted the results of the January elections.
Though UNIP's victory was clear, there were causes for concern.
'A tiny cloud in Kaunda's happy hoe-down', as the *Northern News*
said, was the solid vote against UNIP amongst the 'Bantu Botatwe'
as the Ila, Tonga and Lenje peoples were called. He would need
'all his tact and finesse . . . to achieve a national omelette from the
eggs in his basket'. The arrest of 80 Mufulira rioters showed that
there was unrest on the Copperbelt as well and Kaunda was sure
that ANC needed a fresh warning against 'misbehaviour'. The
Voice of UNIP editorial in its January 1964 edition, however,
added to the embarrassment of the situation, this time by a statement,
which Kapwepwe denied, that there were plans for violent attacks
on the racist regimes to the south. Instead, said the Minister of
Home Affairs, 'we shall be standing to teach South Africa the
human principles cherished by the people of the world.' Welensky
was, however, proclaiming that the Russians had already won
more than half the battle for Africa as violence flowed in Salisbury
and as, by contrast and for the first time, classes of black and white
children together were pictured in the *Northern News*. The South
African government, no doubt well-informed of the trends in the
new nation, was reportedly split on its reaction to Kaunda's proposal
to Britain for an exchange of diplomats between Lusaka and
Pretoria. Soon afterwards, however, the offer was rejected as
'lacking in sincerity' and Kenneth said: 'If South Africa doesn't
want to have friends on this continent, it's just too bad.' As Northern
Rhodesia lifted the ban, imposed by the Federal Government, on
John Stonehouse, John Papworth, Terence Ranger, Thomas Fox-
Pitt, Michael Scott, Michael Faber, George Houser and Simon

Zukas, Kaunda offered the country as a base for British troops in the event of an illegal independence declaration by Southern Rhodesia, but hoped that Field would be able to control his supporters.[12]

It was at this time that twins were born to the Kaundas, Kambarage, the second name of Julius Nyerere, and Cheswa, a Bemba word meaning 'broom', and by extension, 'service'. In previous ages among various African peoples, twin birth had been at best a cause of deep awe and trembling and at worst a sign of a threat to the community, which could only be removed by killing the twins. Among Kenneth's mother's people, parents of twins had been ostracised and then readmitted by a special rite into the community, for this irregular birth presaged calamity. It had therefore been necessary for the parents to leave their village in haste. When they were allowed to return from their *chisakasa* or grass shack, the whole village had to partake together with them of porridge medicated with special herbs in order to ascertain that no disaster would come.[13] In 1964, however, the birth of the twin grandchildren of David and Helen Kaunda was hailed with delight and the titles, *ShiMpundu* and *NaMpundu*, father and mother of twins, were now titles of honour. On the day after their birth, Kenneth welcomed the first flight of Zambia Airways, the national airline that would replace the Federal Central African Airways. Another birth announcement, as it were, was the statement by the Minister of Education that Zambia's University would, from the outset, award its own degrees. Its primary principles would be that it would be 'responsive to the real needs of the country' and that 'it must . . . on merit win the respect and proper recognition of the university world.' As there was drafted for Parliament a bill abolishing the Rhodes' and Founders' holidays as now unacceptable and as the copper 'boom' raised the value per ton by a bigger leap than since 1956, Kaunda announced a special £5 million vote for development as 'only a start' and an agricultural revolution was promised. When Parliament opened, it was hailed for the first time by traditional African dancing as the Prime Minister embraced his guest, Cyrille Adoula, Prime Minister of the Republic of Congo, and news was received of the recommendation of a United Nations economic team that the nation should launch a £450 million development programme.[14]

As people crowded round the honey-pot, the bees were still stinging, however. A UNIP demonstration was staged in Livingstone in late February against the appointment of a Provincial Commissioner who, they alleged, 'was partly responsible for the massacre at Gwembe' six years earlier.[15] The February issue of the *Voice of UNIP*, in an article, immediately repudiated by Kapwepwe, made statements of racial bitterness thus: 'There are no more than 20 settlers who are not devils. . . . People who have been your oppressors in the past cannot be your friends in 1964. . . . From now on we shall regard every white person as an enemy of the people of Zambia. . . . Help your Government plan the liberation of millions in the cruel hands of oppressors.' Meanwhile the Union of African Railwaymen threatened a strike over 'insults and beatings' by white railway staff and named one particular 'European troublemaker'. Just across the Zambesi, police were firing on African strikers in the coal mining town of Wankie. Wage discrimination was focused again by a threat of strike action by African teachers. Meanwhile, the exodus of white residents went on, and Kaunda announced to Parliament that more than one-third of the European police officers had resigned during the year preceding September. Moreover, there were 1,100 empty places in the formerly all-white fee-paying schools, despite vigorous efforts to find black pupils to fill them. Across the western borders, Angolan 'rebels' were warned by Adoula to 'keep the cold war out of Africa' and, with the news that Tshombe was planning to return home, Adoula reacted to ANC's demonstration against him in Lusaka by calling Nkumbula 'that devious valet of Tshombe'. 'Old Harry', however, was now favouring a merger with UNIP. 'More of my friends are in UNIP than in ANC,' he said. He would therefore like an 'honorary post' in the Government, for, he claimed: 'I have achieved my purpose. I destroyed Federation. I got self-government. I smashed racial discrimination.' It would be adequate reward if 'they pay me by doing a decent job in governing this country'.[16]

Shops were now advertising 'kwacha cloth' in preparation for independence, bearing a print of Kenneth Kaunda's head and the words 'Freedom and Labour'; and there was a public competition for the composing of words for a Zambian National Anthem which would be sung to the tune of Professor Jabavu's *'Nkosi, Sekelel' iAfrika—'* 'Lord, bless Africa', that had come to be known as the

Bantu National Anthem. Lusaka had appointed its first non-European mayor, Safeli Chileshe, a founding member of the African National Congress. Simon Zukas was back, responding to a 'hero's welcome' by saying simply 'I was right and they were wrong.' 'Federation is dead and we have universal suffrage.' Kaunda was now initiating inter-party talks on the Constitution of the new Republic, though ANC was suspicious of a UNIP coalition with the N.P.P., whose policy appeared now to be one of cooperation. Even on the issue of the B.S.A. Company mineral rights, Roberts was supporting Kaunda. But as both opposition parties constantly reiterated their complete opposition to a one-party system, Mundia announced that ANC would be debarred from the forthcoming Independence Conference in London, and Nkumbula said that he was receiving assassination threats by letter, designed to keep him away from the London talks. Kaunda had to refute Mundia's assertion at once. 'It was purely a personal statement' of his own opinions, he said, though he blamed himself for failing to brief his colleagues adequately. These was no intention to remove parliamentary opposition by governmental action, he reaffirmed. 'A one-party system might be set up if the people elected only one party. . . . It would then be only according to the wishes of the people as expressed at the polls in any future elections.'[17]

Furthermore, he declared, 'If Kaunda himself misbehaves, the law must not falter.' Northern Rhodesia must become a 'republic' with 'only free citizens of Zambia', all under the law. This concept of freedom, as he constantly insisted, had to mean real liberty to think, speak and act, real personal safety from persecution. 'We intend to establish a society,' he had stated publicly, 'in which I myself as President of UNIP will not be afraid of my own safety should another man take over from me. . . .' 'In this our coming society, we undertake to see that . . . elections are going to take place periodically. This will safeguard the nation against any selfish interests driving any group of men and women to a position where they might be power-hungry and try to destroy all those who don't see eye to eye with them.'[18]

On 24 April, four days before his fortieth birthday, Kenneth Kaunda, as Prime Minister, formally received, from the British Government through the Governor, responsibility for the maintenance of law and order in Northern Rhodesia. Announcing this, the *Northern News* had said that Kaunda appeared 'to have beaten the gangs that were threatening to reduce Northern Rhodesia's chances of securing early independence'.[19] The new Government had already earned a reputation for hard and expeditious work in various fields. According to a British journalist, Kaunda and his Ministers worked 'hard, fast and unstuffily, and this is reflected in their sartorial habits.' 'Working clothes for Dr. Kaunda are khaki bush-shirt topped with a bright, royal blue, silk scarf; Mr. Simon Kapwepwe . . . wears a black, Chinese style, short-sleeved, collarless shirt (which he insists comes from Japan); and Mr. Elijah Mudenda . . . sports a black leather jacket and a check [sic] cowboy-style shirt.' As the Industrial Development Corporation tackled its work, it was clear that the death of Federation had given Lusaka an amazing 'shot in the arm' and its hotels were 'bursting with business-men sniffing prospects'.[20] Yet not only were the country's social clubs still almost entirely for 'Europeans only', but Dr. Konoso, M.P., was arrested in Livingstone following a row with the manager of a hotel which refused to admit him. The manager's excuse that he did not know who Konoso was was obviously unacceptable to the new regime.[21]

The London Conference on Zambia's Independence began on 2 May. Kaunda had taken a delegation of six Party leaders, selected with the approval of the National Council: Kapwepwe, Arthur Wina, Mudenda, Milner, Chivunga the trade unionist, and Hanock Kikombe from the North-Western Province. Shortly before leaving Lusaka, they had heard of a violent riot in Mufulira following an ANC rally addressed by Nkumbula, just as Kaunda was paying a quick visit to the Lozi Litunga to assure him of the Government's sincerity. Kaunda had also just secured London's consent for an announcement of free pardon for hundreds of people jailed for political offences, 'prison graduates' who would naturally look for some reward from the nation for which they had suffered. Apart from the main Conference agenda, there was much to be done now in London. Pressure had to be put upon Whitehall not to admit the 'Canute of Africa', Ian Smith, to the Commonwealth Prime Ministers' Conference in July in the knowledge that the Rhodesian Front had many sympathisers in Britain. The *Daily Telegraph* had recently spoken of 'a group of British people like ourselves . . . [who] face the fanatical power of black nationalism', and far more

British people read that paper than the number who read the bulletin of the International Commission of Jurists which had protested when a young African was sentenced to death in Rhodesia 'for participation in an offence causing only £17.10s of damage'.[22] The recognition of Ian Smith's regime would do great damage to Britain's standing in Africa and elsewhere, where he was seen as a 'fascist'. Progress had to be made also in the negotiations to end the B.S.A. royalties and the Barotseland issue had to be settled once and for all. Three weeks earlier, Kenneth had scotched a rumour that Zambia would buy out the B.S.A. Company for £30 to £50 million, but he had argued that 'willingness to negotiate was not a sign of weakness'. His Government regarded 'the circumstances under which the British South Africa Company acquired these royalties' as placing the issue 'outside the normal commercial or industrial activity existing anywhere in the world today'. What was important now was to make contact with persons of influence in London whose understanding of the case against the Company could help in bringing a satisfactory settlement.[23]

The work of the London Conference was, in effect, to formalise a *fait accompli*, as Governor Hone predicted that Zambia would be 'a nation of lasting significance in the world'. Roberts supported UNIP's plan for an executive President, 'one man for the dual role of President and Prime Minister' with '. . . the necessary powers to maintain command'. Nkumbula objected to the continuation of provision for 'reserved seats' on which Kaunda had recently apparently changed his mind, when he had stated that those seats would be retained after independence. In the arguments over this issue in London, however, Kaunda said that the Government was 'in the middle' between the two opposing delegations. By making his 'disgruntled and not very coherent speech', Nkumbula provided 'the sole fly in the honey pot', in the words of the *Guardian* correspondent. Undoubtedly, the smooth conclusion of the Conference's constitutional discussions reflected the British Government's manifest trust in Kaunda as a man. 'His universal appeal,' the *Northern News* observed on 8 May, 'is as a man without a tribe,' and added soon afterwards that 'any anxiety Europeans may have about placing great power in the hands of one man is allayed principally by the person of that one man. Dr. Kaunda is as acceptable to them as he is to Africans.'

As Kenneth spoke of his Government's intention to apply formally for membership as a republic within the Commonwealth, he declared: 'There is no bitterness in our hearts.' It was, as the *Guardian* said, 'a recurrence of the phenomenon of all these colonial independence conferences, the testimony of the man who has done time in British prisons for political offences and yet, paradoxically, bears no ill will.' 'Dr. Kaunda, the Church of Scotland missionary's son, who four years ago . . . was contracting, in detention camps, the chest troubles which have plagued him ever since, spoke with the quiet authority of one who expects to lead his country into nationhood' when he said, "We offer the hand of friendship to all men, whether they have been our friends or opponents," adding that "when we embarked upon this struggle . . . our origins were humble but our heads were high. . . ." "When we look back along the path which led to this conference room today, we cannot entirely forget—but we can forgive—the days of our imprisonment." The *Guardian* more accurately summarised the three stages of Northern Rhodesia's development, from the British standpoint, as 'dependency, infernal nuisance, republic'.[24]

Kenneth Kaunda was absent from home for four weeks in May. After the Marlborough House Conference in London, he went to Paris on 20 May while Kapwepwe visited Sweden. There were now about twenty men and women undergoing 'crash courses' of training for foreign diplomacy. Zambia was to move to full republican sovereignty faster than any other British dependency, with a Constitution which, as Duncan Sandys said, 'combined important features of the British and American systems . . . in a novel manner' to provide executive strength along with safeguards of individual and minority rights. Kaunda, as 'chief executive', had to give high priority to the development of international relations, especially since much of Zambia's diplomatic activity would be bound to centre upon the explosive situations in southern Africa. The white regimes there had strong ties of blood and of financial interest with the leading Western nations, and so Zambia's diplomacy would need sophistication, flexibility and persuasiveness from the very start. It was highly likely, as Hall had said in an interview with Kenneth in January, that Lusaka would become 'the headquarters of the anti-white-rule forces in Africa'. The Pan-Africanist policies, of which Kaunda was widely regarded as a leading spokesman, would have to be harmonised with his initiative in seeking some diplomatic association with Pretoria. But Europe was far from leaving Africa alone, despite the series of independence settlements. 'Neo-colonialism' was undoubtedly growing. Zambia had to belong right away to the community of 'non-aligned' nations, yet to keep constantly in touch with nations within the major opposing 'camps' of Moscow and Washington. Nationalism could never be, in ideal or in real terms, either an exclusive condition of living or an end in itself. 'Let us think *now* as world citizens,' Kaunda said to the country's 'trainee ambassadors' at the first Foreign Service Seminar.[25]

The United Nations Economic Commission's 'blueprint' was, of course, a source of encouragement, but the entail of the Federation had to be removed by requiring from Britain, 'not as aid but as justice', immediate relief from Northern Rhodesia's share of the Federal debt, which was estimated at about £88 million. In this the UNIP leaders were supported at Marlborough House by John Roberts. Moreover, the issue of future economic development required a strong drive, again backed by the N.P.P., to end the B.S.A.'s milking of the country's wealth. To embark on an educational programme which Mwanakatwe was to describe, a few months after independence as 'virtually unparalleled in Africa', Zambia would need good relations with a wide range of countries from whom personnel and technical aid might be drawn, without the taint of racism or of 'neo-colonialism'. All this planning demanded that the tentacles of the B.S.A. Company must now be cut, and it was one of the outstanding achievements of the new Government that, on 23 October, it could be announced that, at the cost of £2,000,000 each to Lusaka and London, one saga of exploitation was ended. Furthermore, Zambia's bargaining strength had been demonstrated by Kaunda's personal refusal, at a London luncheon with representatives of both the B.S.A. and the copper companies, to make a deal on terms that would imply his recognition of a moral obligation to compensate 'Chartered'.[26]

As he arrived back at Lusaka Airport to a tumultuous welcome and Sikota Wina and his wife danced for him, wearing 'kwacha cloth', Kaunda said triumphantly: 'I told you before we left that we were going to collect a republic in a big envelope. We've brought it back to you.' Just then, however, beyond the country's borders, a furore had arisen on the publication of Sir Roy Welensky's *4,000 Days*, which swiftly involved John Roberts. The book was reviewed in the *Spectator* by Iain Macleod, under the headline 'Welensky's World—or the Cops and Robbers Theory of History'. The *Northern News* summed up Macleod's review with the words: 'Sir Roy lied—and Roberts was weak', and Welensky likened the effect of Macleod's article to 'being bitten by a sheep'. The *4,000 Days* caused little stir, however, in either Zambia or Malawi, for as another British reviewer said, the book was the record of 'Sir Roy's Decline and Fall'. Federation was dead. The long-term question was nevertheless whether, as yet another reviewer asked, Sir Roy had offered his script of an 'unfinished tragedy'.[27]

Yet Kaunda's daily balance sheet showed a growing column of credits. The Central Statistical Office gave figures revealing a 'dramatic upward trend' in the economy and reason for hope of 'golden days ahead'. Social growth was also discernible and, as Kenneth told an inter-church conference at Mindolo, 'those who said that the end of Federation would end the chances of a multi-racial society' were being confounded. The acceptance by the mining companies of a new wage scale whose lowest rate would be 11/10d per shift, was another earnest of a desire to lessen tension and to see justice as in the interests of employers no less than of employees. The strengthening of governmental administration also continued with the appointment of thirty-eight 'shadow' Permanent and Assistant Secretaries, ten of whom were university graduates. The phased release of political prisoners of both UNIP and ANC betokened another act of healing, as 'rail saboteurs' and 'mission burners', to quote the *Northern News*, re-entered society, each receiving through Nephas Tembo, the Parliamentary Secretary involved, a personal message from the Prime Minister. A group of ANC men who had been charged with inciting others to 'cook Kaunda' were acquitted, thereby removing a potentially inflammable issue. The flag of Zambia was then revealed to the nation, its colours being, as Kaunda said, green for the natural resources of the land, black for the majority of the people, red for the blood of the nation's martyrs, and orange for its mineral wealth. It had also just been announced that the memory of the martyrs and the hope of future prosperity would be celebrated together annually in the new 'Heroes and Unity' holidays. A lighter note was meanwhile struck by the admission of Dixon Konkola to UNIP.[28]

Then it was that the Lumpa struck and for the next three months the country was to witness an upsurge of fanatical brutality which would take a death toll of well over 500, scatter terrified people into the forests, stir deep passions of revenge and necessitate the banning of Lenshina's movement as a threat to national security. In stockaded Lumpa villages exempt, for no known reason, from visitation by provincial officers, fearsome weapons had been fashioned secretly over the preceding months. Rumour had it that some of the gun-smiths had come from south of the Zambezi. Other people believed the weapons were made by fugitives from Tanganyika. Kenneth Kaunda himself visited Chinsali two weeks after the first 'pitched battle', involving 200 Lumpa followers, and believed that it had been possible to go 'a long way towards reaching a settlement'. But, as Andrew Roberts says, 'by this time the battle lines had been drawn.' On 24 July a European Police Inspector and an African Constable were brutally done to death in a settlement. called Chapaula and five days later the administrative township of Lundazi, in the Eastern Province, was overrun by Lumpa warriors. On 30 July Lenshina's brother, Abel Lubusha, called on her to surrender. One of the most horrifying incidents of the 'war' was an act of vengeance struck at a Lumpa settlement in the east by outraged villagers who killed 40 people there just before the settle- ment was due to be encircled by police and soldiers. There was widespread suspicion that the manner and thoroughness of Lumpa fighting confirmed that the uprising was not a simple spontaneous eruption. There had been 'outside influences', said Kaunda, and the disturbances had been 'definitely exploited by some well-informed minds in the military sense'. According to the Scots missionaries at Lubwa it was '*rumoured* that for over a year the Lumpa prepared spears and arrows, aided by tribesmen from Tanganyika and the Congo' and 'that some outside agency, said to be European, bribed Alice to interfere in the internal politics of the district by sponsoring ANC in a dominantly UNIP area'.[29]

The last major incident of the 'war', in which 60 Lumpa warriors died, took place less than two weeks before Independence Day. Right to the end, soldiers were reportedly impressed by the 'incredible ferocity' with which Alice's people fought, and the press described them as 'the suicide sect'. Lenshina had meanwhile been captured on 12 August, just over a week after the *Northern News* had carried a picture of her with the text: 'Dr. Kaunda, Northern Rhodesia's Premier, said in Lusaka yesterday: "We are going to arrest Alice Lenshina. She has got to answer for her crimes. Dead or alive she has got to be brought here." ' The proscription of the sect was announced by Kaunda on 3 August. The writer visited Chinsali in late August, 1964, and heard of joint UNIP and Church action to feed starving Lumpa followers hiding in the forests. UNIP branches in the Copperbelt sent food for refugees from the fighting and an inter-denominational 'mission of reconciliation', led by the Revd. Colin Morris, was mounted by various churches. As the war moved into a macabre diminuendo, the Government set up rehabilitation camps to shelter terrified 'ex-Lumpas'. The writer was told by many people in different parts of the Chinsali District that the situation had altered markedly after Kenneth Kaunda's instruction to the army not to shoot unless absolutely necessary and his plea to the people to avoid acts of personal vengeance at all costs, 'lest the country be drenched in blood'.

In a radio broadcast and a statement to the National Assembly, Kaunda affirmed the Government's attitude to religion. 'Freedom of worship is something that I and my Government hold very dear.' In refutation of the simplistic view that action against Lumpa was proof of an anti-religious bias, he said: 'We are dealing with a completely fanatical sect whose members are not only prepared to die for their faith and consider it a passport to Heaven to do so, but who are also prepared to kill as many other people as they can before they die themselves.' The baleful irony of the situation was that Governor Hone had to invoke, against the Lumpa sect, Emergency powers first enacted in the Preservation of Public Security Ordinance by a virtually white Legislature to counter Kaunda's movement for national sovereignty. The more personal irony was that Kaunda and Lenshina belonged to the same part of the country and his brother was one of her well-known lieutenants right up until the sect was banned.[30]

As Malawi celebrated her independence, six years to the day after Hastings Banda's return, on 6 July, 1958, to his native land, the *Northern News* commented that Northern Rhodesia was fortunate 'that, unlike Dr. Banda, Dr. Kaunda not only says he believes in a two-party system, but is ready to practice it'. Kaunda sent two

Ministers to the Malawi celebrations but did not go himself.
Tshombe, meanwhile, had returned to the Congo, apparently on his
own terms, and President Kasavubu had accepted his Cabinet list
and made him Prime Minister, whereupon he released 600 political
prisoners. In consequence of Tshombe's return, the Organisation
for African Unity, meeting in Cairo in July, resolved to exclude
him. Kaunda opposed this decision, however, asserting that the
selection of its leaders was 'a sacred trust of any people' and calling
for 'a spirit of forgiveness'. As splitting and polarization threatened
on the continent, Kenneth told the O.A.U. that he would like to
see in his lifetime 'the dream of Cecil Rhodes come into effect—
a Cape-to-Cairo road'. Somehow, he said, the man in the street
must share in the movement for African unity. But the tangled
nature of inter-African affairs was further illustrated when Tshombe
laid a wreath on the grave of Patrice Lumumba a few weeks
before a new Congo revolt, this time in the Bukavu area, killed
hundreds in an orgy of brutality and news came of a stream of white
Southern Rhodesian mercenaries joining the Congo National Army.
At the end of August, Kaunda declared that he had in his possession
a copy of a 'plot' for the blockade and economic strangling of
Zambia by Southern Rhodesia by the withdrawal of exports, the
stoppage of coal supplies from Wankie and the switching off of
electric power from Kariba. The hard fact was that his country still
drew two-thirds of its imports from southern Africa, and it was
obvious that these hostile sources of vital supplies had allies within
Zambia. This posed a far graver threat than the 'Zambia Freedom
Army' of '4686 trained soldiers' who were allegedly plotting to
stage an armed Communist coup on 24 October.[31]

The kidnapping of an English teacher from his house at Munali
School in Lusaka at the end of August was yet another proof of
external hostilities. Dennis Higgs had been dragged from his house,
bound, and thrown into a vehicle which raced across the border on
its way to Johannesburg. His kidnappers released a statement that
they were 'not finished with Higgs'. Arrangements for his return
were quickly made by Pretoria, however, and Kaunda praised
both the British Ambassador there and the 'good international
relations' of the South African Government. The kidnapping had
taken place within a few days of the end of a trial of strength so
dangerous that Kenneth had called it 'a national disaster'. Early

in August the majority of European railwaymen had gone on strike, offering no specific complaint to justify their action. For over two weeks, approaches to the strikers were made by various administrative officials and latterly by the Minister of Transport and Communications and the Minister of Labour and Mines. The European Union's President broke his silence to announce that one special train would be run to allow white school-children from the south to come and visit their parents. Otherwise, nothing would be done to move the coal to the mines or to carry away the vast stocks of copper accumulating there, let alone to move passenger traffic.

The writer recalls Kaunda's words about the strike to a huge rally on the Copperbelt. It was, he said, 'a stab in the heart of the nation'. The Government's apparent inaction, said Kaunda, might have worried many people, but in fact there had been feverish activity. Thus, though the Union responded, on 17 August, to his 48-hour ultimatum by the retort, 'We are not calling off the strike', all the men were back to work within a day. 'The Government,' Kaunda declared, 'does not normally interfere with the process of collective bargaining and . . . has not interfered in the present dispute.' When, however, the Union's president, Lennon, announced the end of the strike, it was, he said, 'because I think the Government intends to invoke emergency powers'. The strike had clearly been yet another last-minute attempt to embarrass the new nation with a threat of economic strangulation inseparable from the political hostility of the south to Zambia's independence. Whatever the outcome, this issue stirred Zambian patriotism as witnessed at the Copperbelt rally, when thousands of hands were raised in response to Kaunda's call for volunteers, if need should arise, to carry copper to Dar es Salaam on their shoulders. Mundia repeated the call a few days later. 'If Dr. Kaunda calls upon you to carry copper on your shoulders . . . if he wakes you up at night to prepare roads to Mpulungu . . . be ready to do so intantaneously', for 'the way in which Dr. Kaunda handled both tragedies', the Lumpa rising and the railway strike, 'had made our Prime Minister even greater in the eyes of the world than before'.[32]

During those grim weeks, Kenneth Kaunda conducted a series of huge rallies in different parts of the country and specially in the populous Copperbelt towns. It was most important, at this stage, he believed, to keep the people informed of what was happening.

His monthly press conference plan was part of the same policy. In the preceding decades no such relationship had existed between the rulers and those whom they ruled. Under elected government, it was vital to maintain and enlarge this awareness, for universal suffrage required 'political literacy' in both urban and rural areas. But the nature of the swift movement of revolution in the land was such that people wanted a hero, and so, with models from other countries, there was a growing demand, even before Kenneth's formal election as President, that he should be proclaimed Life President of UNIP. On 7 September he repeated his unequivocal rejection of the principle of life presidency thus: 'If I accept the Life Presidency of the governing Party all that which is my spiritual strength would be cut across and I believe I would find myself very ineffective. Much more time would be spent on safeguarding my position as Life President of the Party than on service to my country and the people I love.' For, he said, 'all my life I have not found any comfort in rank and position.'

At another rally at this time, the writer heard him speak on this issue as well as on the Lumpa tragedy and the European rail strike, and vividly recalls the atmosphere of that vast assembly, where people were packed together, shoulder to shoulder, head to head, their legs somehow tucked beneath them. The rally began with the usual choirs of young men and women, praising the new nation and its leader, their songs interspersed with drumming and dancing. One song in Kaunda's honour had a verse ridiculing Harry Nkumbula. As he stepped forward and after he had given the watchword 'One Zambia' and the crowd had thundered their response 'One Nation', Kaunda began to speak. He thanked the singers and dancers, but said that he was sad that they had used the occasion to mock Nkumbula. There would be no place for derision in the new nation. The speech that followed was long and he spoke generally with an unstrained voice. At last he came to the matter of the life presidency and it seemed as though written messages were being passed to him, as he spoke, from branches around the country, calling on the Party to accord him life tenure. The gist of what he said in response was this: 'I suppose I should thank you. But first I must say that you must not do this to me. For if I were Life President, I would be concerned more and more with my own image, and less and less with the work of being your President. Indeed I

could no longer really be your President, serving you as I should . . ..
And this would come between me and my God, so that I could not
talk with him in the morning. So please do not do this to me.'
The people were listening intently and as he concluded, the writer
heard all around him spontaneous spoken assent, '*Ni fyo fine*'—'So
it is. He is right.' For, as he said soon afterwards, if UNIP persisted
in the demand for life presidency it 'would be robbing itself of one
of the best freedoms men ever discovered, the freedom to choose
their leaders from time to time'.[33]

On 25 August, the Chief Justice formally declared Kenneth
Kaunda to be President-elect of the soon-to-be-born Republic of
Zambia. Though Nkumbula had said that he and his party would
never accept the mode of election employed on this occasion,
namely, by Members of Parliament, and so both refused to endorse
Kenneth's nomination and boycotted the ceremony, there were no
other candidates. The election was announced at a time of grave
crises, as we have seen. In an editorial comment on Kaunda's
election, the *Northern News* commented that he had 'come a long
way, along a hard road, since those days when, dressed in a leather
jacket, riding a bicycle, and carrying a guitar, he toured the country,
whipping up support for African nationalism'.[34] Eleven years earlier,
almost to the day, Kenneth had written in a letter to the *Central
African Post*, that 'it would take at least ten years for the Africans to
reach the point where they could meet the Europeans with a voice
which would have to be heard' and that a programme of action was
therefore needed. 'First we must do three things,' he had said then.
'We must educate our people; we must abolish the fear they have;
and we must instil into them the realisation that they are masters
of their own fate.' Thereafter, 'time alone will tell.'[35] Now, in
response to the cheers of his fellow legislators and the large crowd
gathered outside the High Court, Kaunda said: 'We can make
Zambia an exemplary country where people of all races, beliefs
and opinions will be able to live happily in harmony. . . . I will be
President, not only of UNIP or NPP followers, who have supported
my candidature, but also of the ANC members. I ask for their
cooperation. I shall not discriminate.'

This occasion was marked by an access of benevolence among
men habituated to strife. 'If he has any doubts about ANC loyalty
now,' said Nkumbula, 'let him dispel them. . . .' 'I assure him that

he will have our fullest support.' John Roberts, who had signed Kenneth's nomination, playfully suggested that since the name 'United National Independence Party' would soon be anachronistic, 'if the Government comes to join us, we can change the name to United National Progress Party.' The Speaker, recently knighted as Sir Thomas Williams, added his tribute. 'I am quite satisfied that when there is a great need in a nation, God raises up a man to satisfy that need.'[36] It was true that Kaunda had 'come a long way' through innumerable adversities and at least as true that his wife had had to push doggedly against the weight of loneliness, lack of money, lack of space for her big family, and lack of peace. On his appointment as Minister, however, they had moved from the cramped house in Chilenje to a spacious mansion, formerly the property of the B.S.A. Company, in Prospect Hill in the vicinity of Government House. It was a far cry now from the days in Mufulira when she had cooked on a grate made of the little grey anthills called *mafwasa* and from all the years of drawing water in buckets and carrying loads of firewood on her head.[37]

Rehearsals of the national symphony of independence thus went on against an obligato of persistent discord. Across the Zambezi, Ian Smith banned both Sithole's ZANU and the People's Caretaker Council, which had been created for Joshua Nkomo's followers when ZAPU was proscribed earlier. On the day of the banning order, all Africans leaving the Salisbury suburb at Highfield were 'screened'. The *Daily News*, a Southern Rhodesian newspaper of the Thomson organisation, was also banned, as subversive. It had recently printed a story of a man who had taken his dog to advertised obedience classes. 'They were turned away. Not because the dog wasn't acceptable—it has a pedigree—but because the man isn't white.' Meanwhile, Nkumbula's party was facing more internal turbulence. Simukondah and Mumbuna resigned, soon after Nkumbula had accused 'sweet life addicts' in Congress of trying to 'smear' him. Though he hotly denied that he was considering throwing in his lot with UNIP, he said a fortnight later that Kaunda wanted him to join the Government as 'he needs my services.' Suddenly at the beginning of September, news broke from Malawi of the dismissal by Banda of three of his leading Ministers, followed at once by the resignation of four other Ministers, including the Scots lawyer who had held the portfolio for Transport and Communications. Events moved swiftly and by the beginning of October, Henry Chipembere was first restricted and soon afterwards hunted by soldiers in the forests around Fort Johnson, while other 'rebel' Ministers went into exile. However, both the Malawi Congress Party and Parliament, on 9 September, declared their confidence in Banda as he cried 'I am a Prime Minister with a spine, not a jelly-fish type. . . .' Therefore I run this state as if it were my own property.'[38]

Arthur Wina meanwhile declared that 1964 was 'Northern Rhodesia's boom year' with a favourable trade balance of over £12 million. Yet it was impossible to overlook the tenuousness of Zambia's trade routes and the fact that their maintenance was inextricably tied up with the incalculable political situation in the south. Kaunda had recently committed himself to the statement that the rail link with Dar es Salaam would not be able to be started before the liberation of southern Africans was accomplished. The Government had therefore begun to move quickly with the establishment of its first seven diplomatic missions in New York, Washington, Moscow, Cairo, Dar es Salaam, Leopoldville and Accra, with of course a High Commissioner in London. The nation must have strong external links as much as internal security. With this is mind, Kenneth warned, a few days before independence, that the people must beware of infiltrators and that treason carried the death penalty.[39]

In the days when the colour bar shaped Northern Rhodesian life, the future of those young Africans who did not stay in their village, lay in labouring or, for the few with some schooling, in clerical work teaching or in hospital work as orderlies. Now, in addition to a huge expansion programme for schools, there was at last an opportunity for promotion in mines, railways and the like. The opening of the Northern Technical College at Ndola in late September 1964, was therefore another milestone on the road to a new social and economic order. Kaunda inaugurated the College, which incorporated in a larger concept the Copperbelt Technical Foundation, set up jointly by the two mining companies in early 1958 but used almost entirely for European mine trainees. NORTEC, as it came to be called, had 'satellite centres' in the various mining towns.[40] The new Government was also, however, gravely concerned about young people with nothing to do, drifting around in the towns. The

Zambia Youth Service, of which Mervyn Temple was the first director, was an attempt to tackle this problem. The challenge for the future involved much more than a change in thinking and in in social manners. As a second United Nations Commission in December 1964 was to state starkly: 'The great majority of the people in Zambia are poor, under-educated (if not illiterate) and unhealthy.' UNIP's Mulungushi Conference, held on 12 and 13 September, thus had a very different agenda from previous gatherings at 'the Rock'. As Legum says, 'with Independence only a stone's throw away, the hardened old nationalists, the enthusiastic agitators, the young rebels, and the ordinary rank-and-filers came together for the last time in an unfree country to take counsel with their leaders about their future . . . .' 'It was all right to sing hosannas for freedom; but it was not all right to suppose that these hosannas would bring forth manna from heaven.'

Repeatedly, therefore, Kaunda insisted that there must be radical practical planning. There was little place for slogans on an occasion like this. Quoting what he had said in 1960, he now declared: "We are not concerned solely with the rights of Africans, we are struggling for *human* rights . . . . Our moral and Christian right to fight against the Government of our country rests on a determination to replace it with a system that is grounded in the Christian belief that all men are equal in the sight of God." 'Exactly three years ago at this same place, . . .' he said, 'the spirit of the last stage of our *revolution* was reborn.' 'We arrested the tide at its height and gave it a direction . . . . We can be proud that our plans worked well in that we took no life and, indeed, our people fell at the hands of the forces of oppression without those of us remaining hitting back . . . . We stand here today with our heads up, ready to take on NEW THOUGHT AND NEW ACTION.'[41]

Part of this programme of new thinking was the need to understand and interpret 'Pan-Africanism' in positive, creative terms. From the days of the birth of the movement in exile, among people who had slavery in their ancestry, the movement had been suspect in the eyes of 'white civilisation', for it seemed in essence to imply a judgment and adumbrate a vengeance. In the 1960s, Kaunda had said, 'to the West it is on a par with Communism and therefore must be resisted.' 'To the East it is a barrier in their struggle with the West.' But Pan-Africanism had to be constructive, working for continental unity beyond the current struggle for political emancipation. At the end of September, he spoke to Zambia's newly designated ambassadors on Pan-Africanism in relation to nationalism and non-alignment, quoting Patrice Lumumba's saying that "a man without nationalism is a man without a soul." 'Nationalism then was the forerunner and mainspring of Pan-Africanism; . . . but these forces are means to an end, and not an end in themselves. In these years of suffering and struggle and humiliation we did not forget that our aim was, in our lifetime, to allow no-one any more to make Africans fourth-class citizens in the land of their birth . . . . I said then also that we are not concerned solely with the rights of Africans', but with 'the inalienable rights *of all men*.' 'We have been African nationalists, we have been Pan-Africanists, and now we must be international and think of man everywhere. If we do this then men elsewhere will understand that the world is not divided into compartments like a train, with first-class, second-class and so on. We are travelling together as equal passengers on the dangerous journey of life.'[42]

These words were spoken in Kenneth's last few days as an M.P. and it was then that Mungoni Liso of ANC blamed Ministers, during the discussion of the Public Seal of Zambia, for paying special attention to the opinions of European Members of the House. Kaunda reacted in fury to this. 'We listen to sense,' he shouted, 'we do not worry about a person's colour . . . .' 'We are tough in every way. It is utter nonsense, utter rubbish, stupid nonsense to suggest that we suffer from inferiority complexes. We intend to cooperate with anyone willing to cooperate with us. So long as we have the mandate from the people to rule, we are going to rule, and we will meet any nonsense, force with force. Any law-abiding Member of the Opposition will have our fullest cooperation. But anyone who goes to the darkest corners of this country to preach subversion will be put right.' Liso protested at the tone of the Prime Minister's anger. 'If members cannot have free expression in the House, then where can they have it?' he asked. ANC then briefly boycotted Parliament. 'The Government has nothing whatsoever to lose by an ANC boycott,' said Kaunda. The next day he was still bitter about the inference of Liso's remark. The ANC, he said, was just 'not following Nkumbula's peace policy'.[43]

The team of Ministers whom Kaunda chose to be the first

Cabinet of Zambia numbered fourteen. At the reshuffle announced on 24 September, Reuben Kamanga became Deputy President, Kapwepwe took the portfolio of Foreign Affairs, while Home Affairs were transferred to Chona. The other new appointments were: Sikota Wina to Local Government, Sipalo to Health, Skinner to Justice, Zulu to Transport and Works, Kalulu to Natural Resources, Mundia to Commerce and Industry. Mudenda, Mwanakatwe, Chimba, Arthur Wina and Dingiswayo Banda retained the portfolios of Agriculture, Education, Labour and Mines, Finance, and Housing and Social Development respectively. It had not been easy to decide on the final allocation of responsibilities. According to Mulford, Kaunda had been threatened with assault when selecting his earlier team in January. His own earlier experience of frustration in the face of Nkumbula's patent lack of organisational acumen when they had been together in the old ANC had sharpened his sense of the paramount importance of the right use of human resources in effecting political revolution. In Mulford's words, Kaunda 'devoted almost fanatical attention' to organisational detail and thus finally 'formed a well-balanced and extremely capable Government'.[44]

The choice of ambassadors to key capitals of the world required scarcely less care. In early October it was announced that Fwanyanga Mulikita, a University graduate and a Lozi, would be Zambia's first Permanent Representative at the United Nations. Two shrewd men, Simon Katilungu and Hosea Soko, would go to London and Washington respectively, while Vincent Nsomi would tackle the task, complicated by language and cultural barriers, as first envoy to Moscow. Together these pioneer spokesmen of Zambia were now preparing for an occasion of extravagant pomp and panoply on 24 October, when the nation was to draw heavily on ancient British ceremonial modes. This was seen when Kaunda was made a Freeman of Broken Hill and when he took delivery of a £3,800 'copper car', on loan from the Chrysler Company for the occasion. When the Mayor, Ibraim Nkonde, invested the town's second Freeman, a message was received from its first, Sir Roy Welensky, thus: 'Please convey to Dr. Kaunda my congratulations on being made the other Freeman of Broken Hill.'[45]

There was a sense of elation in the air as, all over the country, bunting was collected, dances and songs were rehearsed and schoolchildren everywhere were drilled in the rendering of the Zambia National Anthem. Kapwepwe was reported, on several occasions at this time, as calling his fellow countrymen to a festival of rejoicing. Let there be 'unreserved hospitality,' he said. 'Let there be peace over the days of joy.' For Kaunda, a brief trip to Cairo for a conference of forty-seven non-aligned nations meant another grim look at what was happening in the south. Unless there was radical change now, he said, 'South Africa will reap a whirlwind of disaster which will herald one of the world's greatest tragedies.' At the same time, however, he welcomed the British Labour Party's victory, however narrow, at the polls. It was time for a change, he felt. Meanwhile, just as Douglas Home handed over No. 10 Downing Street to Harold Wilson, Nikita Kruschev was replaced in the Kremlin by Alexander Kosygin. At the same time, Kaunda announced that the East African 'troika' had approved plans for the rail link between Zambia and what was soon to be called Tanzania, the United Republic formed by the merger of Tanganyika and the turbulent island state of Zanzibar.[46]

'We are a people united by the grant of independence,' said Kaunda on 18 October. It must now be 'one for all and all for one. . . .' 'Let us go forward as one Zambian family to find our destiny.' The price of copper stood healthily at £494 per ton as greetings poured in from many nations. Obote of Uganda, Nkrumah of Ghana, Shastri of India, Margai of Sierra Leone, Banda of Malawi and Nyerere of Tanzania sent warm messages to Kaunda. The Princess Royal arrived from Britain to represent her niece, Queen Elizabeth, at the celebrations, and she and Kenneth Kaunda were both made Freemen of the City of Lusaka. There was indeed the full gamut of ceremonial splendour, banquet and dance, with the Princess, escorted by the new President as her partner in the ballroom. Kaunda was then proclaimed Commander-in-Chief of the Armed Forces of Zambia, just as Ian Smith dismissed the officer commanding the Rhodesian army. The Rhodesian Front had been under censure from Prime Minister Home in London for departing from the idea of a national referendum on the country's future in favour of checking the opinions of the Chiefs, and General Alexander's loyalty to Smith, in case of a unilateral declaration of independence, could not be relied on. But in Lusaka, the banners and buntings were up and on the great night, as the Union Jack came down and the new flag rose, fireworks soared in the shape of Kenneth's head and of the flag, and a copper chariot, drawn by two huge eagles and controlled by a charioteer with a spear, cavorted in the stadium. There was an atmosphere of gay abandon and at one moment Simon Kapwepwe nearly swept Kenneth off his feet as he embraced him exultantly. The switching off of the lights in the stadium as the British flag was lowered and then the switching on again as the Zambian flag was unfurled, to a thunderous roar from the 30,000 people thronging together, was meant to symbolise the light of a new day. Thus, amidst all the din of festivity, there was solemnity, especially for those who were now 'masters of their own destiny'. For Zambia's first President, the commitment had to be public and yet personal as he took his vow of office: 'I, Kenneth David Kaunda, swear that I will faithfully and diligently discharge my duties and perform my functions in the high office of President of the Republic of Zambia; that I will maintain the Constitution of Zambia and uphold the laws and welfare of the people of Zambia without fear or favour, affection or ill-will. So help me God.'[47]

In honour of Kaunda's elevation, UNIP issued a special bulletin entitled *Dr. Kaunda is the President of the Republic of Zambia*, compiled by the Secretary of the Party's Parliamentary Caucus and Research Bureau, K. A. T. Kangwa. In his foreword, Kangwa wrote that Kaunda's name 'which once created fear and despondency in the hearts of white imperialists and black reactionaries, today is at [sic] the lips of every man, woman and child—Dr. Kaunda has undoubtedly . . . emerged not only as a dynamic and formidable politician but also as the father of the fatherless.' 'His ideals and dreams have never belonged to the realm of fiction, but he has truly and ably interpreted them into reality. Through him, the dreams of our forefathers, to see this land of ours free, have come true.' The bulletin provided an anthology of tributes which included one from prisoners in the Maximum Security Prison at Broken Hill. "We remember very well," they said, "how you used to work day and night without any proper resting for the sole purposes of liberating the sons and daughters of this beloved Zambia." They then paid tribute "to the noble sons and daughters, dead and alive" who helped to bring "the historical day when our Redeemer, the Saviour has been elected the first President Designate".

In a summary of the speeches made on the day of the declaration of Kenneth's election to the Presidency, the bulletin quoted Mainza Chona: "With some leaders, I have not been very impressed by the way they have spoken because all they have said is 'I did this and I did that', as if there were no other people...." "But with our hon. leader ... you will find far too many 'we's' and in fact some people have ... wished that he would say 'I' in certain cases.... Another thing I am impressed of Dr. Kaunda is that I remember during the 'Master Plan' when I must admit I could not help being anti-European at some time or another.... The Prime Minister could stand up at such a time and say, 'Look, I condemn those people who hate Europeans collectively because some Europeans are good.' " Kapwepwe was also quoted: "One thing very clear is that even those people who say 'I hate Kenneth', when Kenneth comes they do not hate him. His smile is peaceful and his thinking.... Some people question, 'Why is he so friendly with Kapwepwe who is so violent?' But he is a man who accommodates poor, rich, violent and anybody." Kaunda, said Princess Nakatindi, was "the Moses of Zambia, who has led the people ... out of poverty into the land flowing with honey and milk". Kangwa included also some excerpts from Kaunda's speech at Fordham University in May 1963; "We believe that if you harbour bitterness and think of vengeance, you cloud your thinking so much with these destructive thought-forces that you have no time for constructive thinking." Under the headline: 'Kent women admire Ken', the bulletin reproduced a message to Kaunda in June, 1960, by 'the secretary of the European white women of Kent' thus: "We respect and admire you in your fight for freedom and decent living. Skin colour does not make the slightest difference to a person's intellect or soul— we are all human beings."

The 'messianic' note appeared in various tributes and was notable in the placards carried to the High Court on 25 August. 'Dr. KAUNDA the Son of David is our Saviour here in Zambia'— 'Dr. Kaunda the Son of God who was sent to liberate the Black Zambia'; and Kangwa hailed the day when 'our Messiah, Chitwe Mwine Mambo Dr. Kenneth Buchizia Mutepa Kaunda' became first President. A praise-song from the 'Prison Graduates' of Broken Hill was also reproduced, the refrain of which went thus:

> 'Bowing low at his throne
> Which the masses so adore,

Struggling through to kiss him,
For he's our Redeemer,
And he will reign for ever,
For ever and ever,
Rejoice, rejoice, Kaunda is King'.

The bulletin also printed the authorised text of the National Anthem:
'Stand and sing of Zambia, proud and free,
Land of work and joy in unity,
Victors in the struggle for the right,
We've won freedom's fight.
All one, strong and free.

Africa is our own motherland,
Fashion'd with and blessed by God's good hand,
Let us all her people join as one,
Brothers under the sun.
All one, strong and free.

One land and one nation is our cry,
Dignity and peace 'neath Zambia's sky,
Like our noble eagle in its flight,
Zambia—praise to thee.
All one, strong and free.

CHORUS: Praise be to God,
Praise be, Praise be, Praise be.
Bless our great nation,
Zambia, Zambia, Zambia.
Free men we stand
Under the flag of our land.
Zambia—praise to thee.
All one, strong and free.'48

Colin Legum's book, *Zambia—Independence and Beyond: The Speeches of Kenneth Kaunda* has provided extracts from Kaunda's utterances between 1962 and 1965, which show the flowering of his thought as the nation moved from 'the old order' to 'the morrow of Independence.' *A Humanist in Africa*, compiled by Colin Morris from correspondence between Kenneth and himself, developed from intensive discussions between them, during the Lumpa crisis, is also essential reading. Richard Hall's analysis of Zambia's position vis-a-vis Southern Africa contains a perceptive chapter on 'the character of Kaunda' and develops the theme that, in the post-independence years, Kaunda and Zambia were to pay 'the high price of principles' in their stand for non-racialism on the continent.[49]

An entirely different interpretation of our subject has been written by a South African journalist to describe the alleged involvement of Kaunda with a 'double agent' called Brumer whom 'Kaunda commissioned to create and control the entire Intelligence and Security services of Zambia' and who, until the British 'unmasked' him was working in fact on behalf of Ian Smith 'to counter Communism'. The book claims that the 'agent extraordinary' made his first contact with Kaunda in September 1963; found him 'a hard-working and conscientious man who does not tolerate fools or favour-seekers gladly' yet by whom he was 'ceremonially clasped to the bosom of Zambia', and that Brumer then proceeded to pass all that he could glean to his colleagues in Salisbury.[50]

Our readers will have realised the special value of Mulford's two books, *Zambia: the Politics of Independence* and *The Northern Rhodesia General Election 1962* in reviewing crucial periods of history through the microscope of political science and enriching the value of their conclusions by the fact that Mulford was in the country at the time of the climactic election. His concluding sentence merits quotation here: 'Kaunda matured, sharpened his political sensitivities and devoted all his energies to building a modern and efficient party of the people. He pulled together Northern Rhodesia's diverse tribal and linguistic groups, merged them in his party and in the highest council of the land. Kaunda offered leadership to Northern Rhodesia's whites as well; for over two years before independence he devoted much of his energies to securing lasting support from Northern Rhodesia's Europeans. When Zambia achieved independence in October 1964, Kaunda became President of all the people, white and black alike, leader of one of Africa's great political parties and the hope of the new nation of Zambia.'[51]

In this survey of Kenneth Kaunda's life, thought and action, in the context of traumatic developments in continental Africa, we have tried, as far as possible, to let him speak for himself. From the first circulars that he typed in the old ANC office in Chilenje to the day of independence, he has been seen to be working for something in which he believed, with a clear and uncomplicated belief, something which prompted Kangwa to describe him as a man 'whose noble simplicity, energy, honesty, integrity and indomitable dynamism are a model for the youths . . . the man who is always so near to the heart of the masses and listens to its beat and listens to its aspiration and interest. . . .' 'The whole life of Dr. K. D. Kaunda,' Kangwa went on, 'brings to my memory words of Long-fellow:—

> "The heights by great men reached and kept
> Were not attained by sudden flight,
> But they, whilst their companions slept,
> Were toiling upwards in the night.
>
> Lives of the great men all remind us,
> We can make our lives sublime;
> And, departing, leave behind us,
> Footprints in the sands of time.
>
> Let us, then, be up and doing,
> With the heart for any fate;
> Still achieving, still pursuing:
> Learn to labour and to wait."[52]

In the years before and after independence, Kaunda's mode of address to his hearers was that of a philosopher and teacher, indeed often prompting comment that he preached sermons at the huge rallies that were so marked a feature of the period. But the philosophy and the sermons were not formulated on the sidelines of life, distilled in seclusion or even penned, as it were, in the theatre stalls as a critic might do who sits aside from the drama and can take from it, at leisure, dispassionate extracts of meaning and motive. Kenneth's thinking flowered instead on the path that he was tread-ing, not alone but in the midst of the throng which, like all throngs, mingled zeal and fickleness, passion and irresponsibility, error and truth. His, then, had to be an empirical, pragmatic and fundamental-ly spiritual philosophy in so far as he was always conscious of the essential futility of any endeavour done independently of the divine spirit moving in the world. 'Intellectuals' might thus be loath to count him in their number. What mattered to him was that a people on the move should see where they were going. And since this was an adventure of people with people, surging from a situation in which criteria of race and colour had so poisoned the past, into a wholly new matrix of relationships, it was not surprising that his thinking had within it the seeds of what was to be known later as 'humanism'. It had been so often, as it would certainly be in the future, easy and indeed natural for people to demand that nothing should challenge the totalitarian demand of national unity, that revolution and redress, solidarity and the attainment of power must subordinate all other considerations. It would have been easy to accept fatalistically that as repression demanded revolution, so revolution must release retaliation, and the old racism must give way to a new racism, enlarging the baleful entail of hate for hate, hurt for hurt in a seemingly inevitable vicious circle of unending wrong. This, Kaunda believed, was not the only way. 'Go back and tell our people,' he ordered the members of UNIP's National Council in August 1963, 'that this word revenge is out of UNIP's vocabulary.'[53] For Kenneth, as he rubbed shoulders with his 'comrades', and shared so deeply their sense of how much their new patriotism meant, his heart and mind made it imperative for him to assert insistently that man mattered most.

This paramountcy of what we might call 'humanity incorporate', people realising their personalities only in community, had led Kenneth early to the belief that, as we saw above, he must go 'where the people decided'. This was not, however, blind following of popular whim, for he was always seeking to lead his countrymen's thoughts into paths of reason and peace. But his face was set against making decisions on his own, and this has been borne out by the testimony of scores of people interviewed by the writer. Decision-making in 'the struggle', as after independence, would always be important and could have grave consequences, but, as a Zambian proverb puts it, 'One finger cannot pick up a louse.' Delicate decisions, great or small, had to do with the health of the body of society, like removing a louse; often the decision could not be postponed, lest irritation or disease set in and spread like a rash; therefore joint action had to be the rule of life, and this in turn required constant moments of relaxed listening and discussion so that quick, yet unhurried, decisions could be made. There had to be a circle of peace, at all times, at the heart of the cyclone of political and social revolution, so that there would always be a team sharing in the forward look without which any movement of change can so readily become a vicious circle. The leader had to have friends whose friendship had the essential quality of reciprocity, lest, by default, he might be isolated at the apex. For power is like a pyramid. It may be the apex that catches the eye, but what matters for future stability is the strength of the base. Kenneth's notion of what he would later call 'participatory democracy' was that, for Lincoln's dictum to be fulfilled, people must be able to speak and their leaders to hear. Certainly therefore Kenneth Kaunda's philosophy could be summed up in the biblical words: 'Where there is no vision the people perish.'[54]

Perhaps then the last word here should be left to Kaunda himself; and so we first listen to a passage which expresses what is clearly central to his personal experience: 'The secret of the love of Jesus rests with the fact that He does not judge people in terms of their accidental group-membership. To Him each man, woman and child, irrespective of colour, is unique, endowed with ultimate worth and dignity, because to Him each of them is first and foremost the object of God's infinite love. Thus Christ cuts right through the artificial cloaks with which we surround ourselves and by which we endeavour to give meaning and status to our lives. He uncovers the ultimate truth behind it all and, though often costly and painfully, liberates man from his self-made prison and makes him available to God and thus free from others. In this sense, I take it, a true Christian is a *servant of man*. Servant not in any particular way, but rather as an instrument of the love of Christ which challenges men to become their true selves. The basic answer to the question of Christian practice and desirable action, not only with regard to social action and race relations but with regard to any situation in history is, therefore, simple in principle though difficult in actual demonstration. It would seem to be the Christian's duty in whatever circumstances, to press for ultimate truth and fearlessly seek and promote such decisions as are dictated by truth alone, not mitigated by selfish motives. In this sense Christian practice is not a particular brand of action appearing alongside other endeavours. Rather, it blends with the efforts of men and becomes effective in establishing the promises and opportunities contained in given situations and in warding off fateful developments. It is in this sense that I understand Jesus' description of His disciples' ministry in terms of being "salt of the earth".'[55]

Since the theme here has been the birth of the nation and Kenneth Kaunda's role, as it were, as midwife, it is fitting to finish our record with words of his which perhaps capture best the core of his whole life and action; reminding us, as they do, that the attainment of independence was not in any sense the end of the people's endeavour but instead a rebirth of hope. 'If we want independence to have meaning in whatever we do, MAN must come first. In other words what we loosely call "independence", "freedom", "uhuru", etc., will be meaningless unless, as I say, MAN is put first, so that in fact he does not just become a meaningless cog in the wheel, but an important key-stone on which development hinges. After all, you want independence to plan for a better future for your people. The word "people" is rather abstract unless you come to the single unit in that people, and this is MAN. If I over-emphasize the importance of MAN it is because I fear young countries are in danger of repeating the mistakes of older countries both of the East and the West, where material development has been so large that plans to advance more and more have become more important than MAN for whom these plans, after all, are made, or are supposedly made. . . . The people are expectant. Let us respond by meeting their needs through their active participation as individuals in the heavy programme of national development. . . . Self-help has a double meaning to any individual if properly taught him. His inner self grows tremendously in self-confidence and we all know a man who understands himself has more chance of actively contributing to his own family's good as well as to the national good. His spiritual and moral strength stands him in good stead against any outward forces of destruction and disruption like bribery, corruption, drunkenness and all forms of hooliganism. Secondly a man with this type of self-confidence will definitely find the physical burden of life less trying. Once we succeed in doing this, then the sky is the limit to what can be achieved by individuals as well as by the nation. We shall then start building, through their efforts and energies, as indeed we destroyed through their efforts and energies. Where once we had doubts, fears and hatred, we shall have confidence, courage and love. In short, independence could act as some sort of magic wand. What is required is to heighten the people's imagination, to inspire enthusiasm and capture both forces and direct them into constructive channels. . . . The forces and tools of progress are here—let us use them.'⁵⁶

---

[1]Words used by Kaunda in address to Staff Training College, Lusaka, Dec. 1963 as quoted in Legum, *Zambia*, p. 29; and *NN*, 8/5/64 for comment on Independence Conference in May, 1964.
[2]Gann, *Birth*; TI-FM/J. Stonehouse, London, 20/1/70.
[3]TI-FM/F. Judd, Lusaka, Feb. 1970.
[4]TI-FM/N. Fisher, London, 21/1/70.
[5]TI-FM/Father Walsh, 13/3/70.
[6]*NN*, 17/1/64.
[7]TI-FM/Archie Levin, London, 6/2/70.
[8]ANC: Kaunda to Walter Sisulu, D/6-10, 24/8/53; *London Financial Times*, 23/1/64; and for a study of Kaunda's role in Pan-African affairs, see R. Cox, *Pan-Africanism in Practice* (O.U.P., 1964).
[9]*NN*, 30/6/64 for quotation, and see also 8/5/64.
[10]Legum, *Zambia*, pp. 33 and 5; *NN*, 1/10/64, quoting P. Keatley in *Financial Times*.
[11]*NN*, 11-24/1/64.
[12]*NN*, 25/1/64-17/2/64; and *Guardian*, 31/3/64.
[13]For an account of Tumbuka birth customs, see Cullen Young, *op. cit.*, pp. 37-38.
[14]*NN*, 17/2-20/3/64; and *Report on the Development of a University in Northern Rhodesia* (Government Printer, Lusaka, Nov. 1963. The UN Economic Mission forecast increased employment at the rate of 25,000 p.a.
[15]*NN*, 20/2/64; and Voice of UNIP, February 1964.
[16]*NN*, 20/2/64-20/3/64.
[17]*NN*, 19/3/64-20/4/64; and FH: Press Statement (Mundia) on 'ANC Discredited', 17/3/64.
[18]Melady, *op. cit.*, p. 238.
[19]*NN*, 23/4/64.
[20]*Scotsman*, 4/3/64; and Hall, *Zambia*, p. 228.
[21]*NN*, 8/5/64.
[22]*NN*, 27/4/64; *Guardian*, 21/4/64, 23/4/64; *EAR*, 30/4/64 (quoting *Daily Telegraph*); and *Africa Digest*, Vol. XI, No. 5, p. 132, quoting *Bulletin of the International Commission of Jurists*, No. 18.
[23]*NN*, 2/4/64; and *Central African Mail*, 3/4/64.
[24]*NN*, 6/5/64; *Guardian*, 6/5/64; *NN*, 8/5/64; FH: Press Statement (Kaunda) 14/1/64; *NN*, 18/4/64; *EAR*, 7/5/64 for text of main Conference speeches; *Guardian*, 20/5/64.
[25]*NN*, 19/3/64; *EAR*, 21/5/64; Legum, *Zambia*, p. 67, quoting interview with Dick Hall, the Editor of the *Central African Mail* two days after he became Prime Minister, and p. x, quoting Kaunda on 'world citizens'. See also Legum, *Zambia*, pp. 66-69, 160-65, and Introduction.
[26]*Guardian*, 6/5/64; Hall, *Zambia*, pp. 242-244; N.R.G. White Paper, *British South Africa Company's Claim to Mineral Rights in Northern Rhodesia* (Govt. Printer, 1964); and see Hall, *High Price*, pp. 71-85.
[27]*EAR*, 4/6/64; *NN*, 27/5/64-2/6/64; *Spectator*, 29/5/64 for Macleod's review; *Observer*, 24/5/64 for Legum article, 'Sir Roy's Decline and Fall'; *Glasgow Herald*, 25/5/64 for Kernohan's article, 'Welensky—Unfinished Tragedy', and *NN*, 16/6/64.
[28]*NN* for June, 1964; and *Africa Digest*, Vol. XII, No. 1, p. 4.
[29]Roberts, *op. cit.*, pp. 41-50; TI-FM/RMK, 15/6/71; *NN*, 30/6/64, 14/7, 27/7, 29/7, 31/7, 3/8-15/8, 4/9, and 13/10/64; *EAR*, 13/8/64; Kenneth MacKenzie Papers: Circular letter of Scots missionaries, August, 1964, sgd. Mae McKenzie, Margaret and Bill McKenzie, Alex Slorach.

[30]*NN*, 4/8/64. See 'Makulu Commission' on 'Former Lumpa Church' and Legum, *Zambia*, pp. 106-107; and note while official figures gave 491 killed and 344 wounded during the 'Lumpa War', Legum (p. 104) gives a figure of 650 'Lumpas and their victims' killed.

[31]*NN*, July-August and 4/9/64.

[32]*Ibid.*: 1-19/8/64, 4/9/64.

[33]UNIP: Statement on the Life Presidency, 7/9/64; and *NN*, 1/8/64 and 14/9/64.

[34]*NN*, 22-26/8/64. The Chief Justice was Sir Diarmaid Conroy.

[35]*CAP*, 28/8/53.

[36]*NN*, 28/8/64; and *Africa Digest*, Vol. XII, No. 2, p. 39.

[37]Mpashi, *op. cit.*, pp. 66-67.

[38]*NN*, 27/8/64; *Africa Digest*, Vol. XII, No. 2, p. 43; Salisbury *Daily News*, 18/5/64; *Africa Digest*, Vol. XII, No. 2, p. 39. The dismissed Malawi Ministers were K. Chiume, O. Chirwa, A. Bwanausi; those who resigned were Y. Chisiza, W. Chokani, H. Chipembere, C. Cameron; *Africa Digest*, Vol. XII, No. 3, pp. 66-68.

[39]*NN*, 29/8/64, 3/7/64, 10/10/64; and *EAR*, 1/10/64.

[40]*NN*, 21/9/64; and Legum, *Zambia*, p. 129.

[41]UN/ECA/FAO report cited in Hall, *Zambia*, 237; Legum, *Zambia*, pp. 151-153.

[42]See Legum, *Zambia*, pp. 43, 144-145.

[43]*NN*, 24/9/64.

[44]See Mulford, *Zambia*, pp. 330-331 and 342-343; and *NN*, 25/9/64.

[45]*NN*, 2/10/64, 12/10/64.

[46]*Ibid.*: 9/10/64, 15/10/64, 16/10/64, 17/10/64, 19/10/64, 22/10/64.

[47]*Ibid.*: 28/10/64.

[48]UNIP Bulletin, *Keeping up to Date—Dr. Kaunda is President of the Republic of Zambia*, 1/9/64.

[49]Legum, *Zambia*; Kaunda and Morris, *op. cit.*; Hall, *High Price*, esp. pp. 36-51.

[50]R. Christie, *For the President's Eyes Only*, (Keartland, 1971), with quotations from the jacket and from p. 32.

[51]Mulford, *Zambia*, esp. p. 343.

[52]UNIP Bulletin (Kangwa) 1/9/65, quoting verses from Henry Wadsworth Longfellow's poems 'The Ladder of St. Augustine' and 'A Psalm of Life'.

[53]See Melady, *op. cit.*, pp. 213-220 for Kaunda's address to UNIP National Council, 3/8/63.

[54]Proverbs 29:18.

[55]See Legum, *Zambia*, pp. 111-112.

[56]*Ibid.*: pp. 31-33.

List of Abbreviations

A.M.W.U.   African Mine Workers' Union
ANC   (pronounced *ank*) African National Congress
A.R.C.   African Representative Council
A.T.U.C.   See T.U.C.
B.S.A.C.   British South Africa (Company)
CAP   Central African Post
C.C.W.M.   Congregational Council for World Mission, London, which holds London Missionary Society archives
C.S.   Chief Secretary
D.C.   District Commissioner
EAR   East African and Rhodesia
F.A.S.   Federation of African Societies
F.H.   Freedom House (UNIP Headquarters in Lusaka)
F.O.   Foreign Office
H.M.G.   Her Majesty's Government
LEG. CO. Legislative Council
L.M.S.   London Missionary Society
M.I.R.   Monthly Intelligence Report
M.L.C.   Member of the Legislative Council
M.P.   Member of Parliament
N.A.   Native Authority
NAZ   National Archives of Zambia
N.E.C.   National Executive Committee (of ANC)
NN   Northern News
N.R.(G) Northern Rhodesia (Government)
N.R.T.U.C.   See T.U.C.
PAFMEC(S)A   (so pronounced) Pan-African Freedom Movement for East, Central (and Southern) Africa
P.C.   Provincial Commissioner
Q.C.   Queen's Counsel
RH   Rhodes House, Oxford
R.S.T.   Rhodesian Selection Trust
SA   South Africa(n)
S.C.M.   Student Christian Movement
S.N.A.   Secretary for Native Affairs
SOAS   School for Oriental and African Studies, University of London
SR   Southern Rhodesia(n)
TI-FM/   Tape-recorded interview between the author and the person(s) whose name(s) or initials(s) follow the oblique stroke
T.U.C.   Trade Union Congress
U.C.A.A.   United Central Africa Association

U.F.P.   United Federal Party
U.K.   United Kingdom
U.M.C.A.   United Missions in Central Africa
U.M.C.B.   United Missions in the Copperbelt
UNIP   (pronounced *yew-nip*) United National Independence Party
U.N.O.   United Nations Organisation
U.S.A.   United States of America
U.S.C.L.   United Society for Christian Literature
ZANC   (pronounced *zank*) Zambia African National Congress

Select Bibliography

Ballantyne, M. M. S. and Shepherd, R. H. W. (eds.) *Forerunners of Modern Malawi* (Lovedale, 1968).

Barnes, J. *Marriage in a Changing Society* (Rhodes-Livingstone Papers, No. 22; O.U.P., 1951).

————, *Politics in a Changing Society* (Manchester, 1954).

Bates, H. M. *Report on the Rhodesias* (Melrose, 1953).

Benson, M. *The Struggle for a Birthright* (Penguin, 1963).

Blaikie, W. G. *Personal Life of David Livingstone* (Murray, 1913).

Brelsford, W. V. *A Generation of Men* (Stuart Manning, 1965).

Brookes, E. H. and Macaulay, J. B. *Civil Liberty in South Africa* (O.U.P., 1958).

Broomfield, G. *1960-Last Chance in the Federation* (U.M.C.A., 1960).

Bunting, B. *Rise of the South African Reich* (Penguin, 1964).

Cairnes, H. A. C. *Prelude to Imperialism* (Routledge and Kegan Paul, 1965).

Christie, R. *For the President's Eye Only* (Keartland, 1971).

Churchill, W. S. *My African Journey* (Holland Press, 1908).

Clutton-Brock, G. *Dawn in Nyasaland* (Hodder, 1959).

Coillard, E. *On the Threshold of Central Africa* (Hodder and Stoughton, 1902).

Colson, E. *Social Consequences of Resettlement* (Kariba Studies, IV; Manchester, 1971).

Coombe, T. *Origins of Secondary Education in Zambia* (Harvard, 1968).

Cox, R. *Pan-Africanism in Practice* (O.U.P., 1964).

Davidson, B. *African Awakening* (Jonathan Cape, 1955).

————. *Report on Southern Africa* (Jonathan Cape, 1952).

Decle, L. *Three Years in Savage Africa* (Methuen, 1898).

Duffy, J. *Portuguese Africa* (Cambridge, Mass., 1959).

Elmslie, W. A. *Among the Wild Ngoni* (Oliphant, Anderson and Ferrier, 1899).

Epstein, A. L. *Politics in an Urban African Community* (Manchester, 1958).

Fagan, B. (ed.) *A Short History of Zambia* (O.U.P., 1972).

————. *Southern Africa* (Thames and Hudson, 1965).

Finnegan, R. *Oral Literature in Africa* (O.U.P., 1970).

Fraenkel, P. *Wayaleshi* (Weidenfeld and Nicholson, 1959).

Fraenkel, S. H. *Capital Investment in South Africa* (Macmillan, 1938).

Franklin, H. *Unholy Wedlock* (Allen and Unwin, 1963).

Gann, L. H. *The Birth of a Plural Society* (Manchester, 1958).

————. *A History of Northern Rhodesia* (Chatto and Windus,

1964).
Gelfand, M. *Northern Rhodesia in the Days of the Charter* (O.U.P., 1961).
Gray, R. and Birmingham, D. (eds.) *Pre-Colonial African Trade* (O.U.P., 1970).
Hailey, W. M. (Lord) *African Survey* (O.U.P., 1956).
Hall, R. *Kaunda—Founder of Zambia* (Longmans, 1964).
————. *The High Price of Principles* (Hodder and Stoughton, 1969)
————. *Zambia* (Pall Mall Press, 1965).
Hanna, A. J. *The Beginnings of Nyasaland and North-Eastern Rhodesia* (O.U.P., 1956).
Horrell, M. (ed.) *Bantu Education to 1968* (S.A. Institute of Race Relations, 1968).
Huddleston, T. *Naught for Your Comfort* (Collins, 1956).
Jack, J. W. *Daybreak in Livingstonia* (Oliphant, Anderson and Ferrier, 1901).
Johnson, H. *Night and Morning in Dark Africa* (L.M.S., 1902).
Kantor, J. *A Healthy Grave* (Hamish Hamilton, 1967).
Kaunda, K. D. *A Humanist in Africa: Letters to Colin Morris* (Longmans, 1966).
————. *Zambia Shall Be Free* (Heinemann, 1962).
———— and Morris, C. *Black Government* (U.S.C.L., 1960).
Keatley, P. *The Politics of Partnership* (Penguin, 1963).
Laws, R. *Reminiscences of Livingstonia* (Oliver and Boyd, 1934).
Leakey, L. S. B. *Defeating Mau Mau* (Methuen, 1954).
Legum, C. *Congo Disaster* (Harmondsworth, 1961).
————. *Zambia: Independence and Beyond* (Nelson, 1966).
Leys, C. *European Politics in Southern Rhodesia* (O.U.P., 1959).
Livingstone, W. P. *Laws of Livingstonia* (Hodder and Stoughton, 1921).
Lucas-Phillips, C. E. *The Vision Splendid: The Future of the Central African Federation* (Heinemann, 1960).
Luthuli, A. *Let My People Go* (Fontana, 1962).
———— et al. *Africa's Freedom* (George Allen and Unwin, 1964).
Macnair, J. *Livingstone the Liberator* (Collins, 1940).
Makulu, H. F. *Educational Development and Nation Building in Independent Africa* (S.C.M. Press, 1971).
Martelli, G. *Leopold to Lumumba* (Chapman and Hall, 1962).
Mason, P. *Birth of a Dilemma* (O.U.P., 1968).
————. *Year of Decision—Rhodesia and Nyasaland, 1960* (O.U.P., 1960).
Mbiti, J. *African Religion and Philosophy* (Heinemann, 1969).
Meebelo, H. S. *Reaction to Colonialism* (Manchester, 1971).
Melady, T. *Kenneth Kaunda of Zambia: Selections from his Writings* (Praeger, 1964).
Mpashi, S. *Betty Kaunda* (Longmans, 1969)

Mulford, D. C. *The Northern Rhodesia General Election 1962* (O.U.P., 1964).

————. *Zambia: The Politics of Independence* (O.U.P., 1967).

Mwanakatwe, J. *The Growth of Education in Zambia Since Independence* (O.U.P., 1968).

Nyerere, J. *Freedom and Unity* (O.U.P., 1967).

Ogot, B. A. and Kieran, J. A. (eds.) *Zamani* (Longmans and E.A.P.H., 1968).

Omer-Cooper, J. *The Zulu Aftermath* (Longmans, 1966).

Polak, H. S. *et al. Mahatma Gandhi* (Odhams, 1948).

Powdermaker, H. *Copper Town* (Harper and Row, 1962).

Ranger, T. O. *The Agricultural History of Zambia* (NECZAM, 1971).

————. *Revolt in Southern Rhodesia, 1896-7* (Heinemann, 1967).

Rayner, R. M. *Nineteenth Century England* (Longmans, 1938).

Rayner, W. *The Tribe and its Successor* (Faber and Faber, 1972).

Roberts, A. D. *The Lumpa Church of Alice Lenshina* (O.U.P., 1972).

Rodney, W. *How Europe Underdeveloped Africa* (Bogle-L'Ouverture, 1972).

Rotberg, R. I. *Christian Missions and the Creation of Northern Rhodesia* (Princeton, 1965).

————. *The Rise of Nationalism in Central Africa* (Harvard, 1965).

Rubin, L. and N. *This is Apartheid* (Christian Action, 1965).

Shaw, B. 'Man of Destiny', in *Plays Pleasant and Unpleasant* (Constable, 1908).

Shepperson, G. and Price, T. *Independent African* (Edinburgh University Press, 1958).

Sithole, N. *African Nationalism* (O.U.P., 1959).

Smith, E. W. *The Secret of the African* (U.S.C.L., 1938).

Sokoni, J. and Temple, M. *Kaunda of Zambia* (Nelson, 1964).

Stephenson, J. E. *Chirupula's Tale* (Geoffrey Bles, 1937).

Stewart, J. *Dawn in the Dark Continent* (Oliphant, Anderson and Ferrier, 1903).

Stokes, E. and Brown, R. (eds.) *Zambesian Past* (Manchester, 1966).

Stone, W. V. 'The Livingstonia Mission and the Bemba', *African Church History Bulletin*, Vol. II, No. 4.

Stonehouse, J. *Prohibited Immigrant* (Bodley Head, 1960).

Taylor, J. V. and Lehmann, D. A. *Christians of the Copperbelt* (S.C.M. Press, 1961).

Tempels, P. *Bantu Philosophy* (Presence Africaine, 1952).

Trine, R. W. *In Tune with the Infinite* (Bell, 1897).

van Eeden, G. *The Crime of Being White* (Nasionale Boekhandel Beperk, 1965).

van Velsen, J. *Politics of Kinship* (Manchester, 1964).

Vansina, J. *Kingdoms of the Savanna* (Wisconsin, 1966).

Vyas, C. L. *Flight of the Eagle* (NECZAM, 1970).

Watson, W. *Tribal Cohesion in a Money Economy* (Manchester, 1958).

Welensky, R. *4,000 Days* (Collins, 1964).

Wills, A. J. *Introduction to the History of Central Africa* (O.U.P., 1963).

Wills, R. G. *The Fipa and Related Peoples* (International African Institute, 1966).

Young, T. C. *Customs and Folklore of the Tumbuka-Kamanga Peoples* (Livingstonia, 1931).

Acknowledgements

The completion of this work would not have been possible without the kind assistance of many persons and institutions. For access to written documents, I am most grateful to the following:

The Africa Secretary, Church of Scotland Overseas Council, Edinburgh.

The Archivist, White Fathers, Rome.

The British Museum Newspaper Library, Hendon, London.

Mr. M. G. Clarke, Lusaka, for access to his personal collection.

The Director, National Archives of Zambia.

Mr. Phillip Emmanuel, Afrika-Studiecentrum, Leiden, Holland, for access to his collection.

The Librarian and the Archivist, Rhodes House, Oxford.

The Librarian, Congregational Council for World Mission, London.

The Librarian, Institute of Commonwealth Studies, and the Librarian, School of Oriental and African Studies, both of the University of London.

Mrs. M. MacKenzie, Edinburgh, for access to numerous files of papers on Central Africa collected by the late Reverend Kenneth MacKenzie.

Mr. Robert Makasa, for access to his personal collection.

The Minister of State in Charge of Publicity, Freedom House (UNIP Headquarters), Lusaka.

Mr. Patrick M. Mumba, for access to papers of his late father, the Reverend P. B. Mushindo.

Mr. Harry Nkumbula, for access to files of the former ANC.

The Public Records Office, London.

The Secretary, Kenneth Kaunda Foundation, Lusaka, for access to papers of its first research historian, the late Dr. W. A. Hunton.

The Secretary, National Library of Scotland, Edinburgh.

Professor George Shepperson, Edinburgh University, for access to his personal collection of 'Life and Work in British Central Africa' and to papers held by the African Studies Centre, Edinburgh.

Mr. Wittington Sikalumbi, for access to the manuscript of his *Before UNIP* (to be published soon by NECZAM, Lusaka) and to his personal collection of documents, including copies of the *Voice of UNIP* and other UNIP papers.

Mr. Malama Sokoni, for extended loan of his personal collection.

Reverend Merfyn Temple, for access to his personal collection.

For personal testimony, given in tape-recorded interviews and by letter, I am grateful to all those cited in the text and especially to President Kaunda himself.

In the preparation of the photographic section, I have been greatly indebted to the persons and institutions named in the list of illustrations. In addition, Zambia Information Services and Mr. R. S. Patel of Fine Art Studios, Lusaka, generously assisted in the preparation of negatives and prints.

I would like to thank also Dr. Ellen Kitonga for meticulous editorial work, Mrs. Njeri Muriuki for preparing the index and my wife for typing the manuscript through its various stages.

I also gratefully acknowledge receipt of financial assistance towards travel abroad for research in libraries, archives and other collections in England, Scotland, Italy and Holland. An initial grant was made for this purpose by the Roan Selection Trust Ltd., Mpelembe House, Ndola; and through the kindness of Mr. John Mwanakatwe, then Minister of Finance, donations were received towards the cost of a second journey abroad from the Commercial Bank of Zambia, Ltd., the National Commercial Bank, the Zambia National Building Society, the Zambia State Insurance Corporation and J. H. Minet, Zambia, Ltd.

The publishers are grateful to the following for permission to quote from the books listed:

Bell: *In Tune with the Infinite* (R. W. Trine, 1897); Fontana: *Let My People Go* (A. Luthuli, 1962); Harper and Row: *Copper Town* (H. Powdermaker, 1962); Heinemann: *Zambia Shall Be Free* (K. D. Kaunda, 1962); Longmans: *Betty Kaunda* (S. Mpashi, 1969); Lovedale: *Forerunners of Modern Malawi* (M. M. S. Ballantyne and R. H. W. Shepherd, eds. 1968); Nelson: *Zambia: Independence and Beyond* (C. Legum, 1966), *Kaunda of Zambia* (J. Sokoni and

M. Temple, 1964); OUP: *Northern Rhodesia General Election 1962*
(D.C. Mulford, 1964); Praeger: *Kenneth Kaunda of Zambia:
Selections from his Writings* (T. Melady, 1964); U.S.C.L.: *Black
Government* (K. D. Kaunda and C. Morris, 1960).

Index

Abrahams, Peter, 92
Africa and the Colonial World, 170
Africa Digest, 199
Africa Freedom Day, 332
African Congress, 81, 83, 86, 87, 88–89, 91, 92, 116, 138, 189
    Chinsali Branch, 81, 82, 92
    Youth League, 254
African Liberation Committee, 209
African Methodist Episcopal Church, 145, 153, 279
African Mine Workers' Union, 109, 121, 141, 169, 189, 197, 368, 370, 386, 404
African National Congress (ANC), 16, 123, 130, 136, 138, 150, 151, 153, 154, 167, 169, 177, 178, 182, 186, 187, 189, 197, 202, 207, 215, 223, 238, 240–41, 249, 251, 259, 270, 271, 290, 317, 386, 389, 394, 405, 408, 420, 422, 435, 451
    Action Council, 109, 124
    Action Group, 147, 172, 187
    Coalition with United Federal Party, 389, 394, 408; United National Independent Party (UNIP), 397–99
    Executive Council/Committee, 147, 151, 159, 172, 177, 181, 184, 188, 202, 211
    Official Gazette, 172, 173, 177
    Women's League, 157, 176
African National Freedom Movement, 288
African Railway Workers' Union, 109
African Representative Council, 138, 143, 177, 185, 214
African Shop Assistants' and Tailors' Committee, 143
African Urban Advisory Council, 124
agrarian development, 149
Anglo-American Corporation, 169, 188
Angola, 2, 103–104, 298, 321, 341, 344, 363
Angoni the, 4, 7
Anti-Federation Action Committee, 96
apartheid, 100, 101, 122, 162, 218, 341, 342
Arabs the, 12, 23, 92

Attlee, Clement, 112, 113, 136

Banda, Miss Betty 69; *see also* Mrs. Kaunda
Banda, Dr. Hastings Kamuzu, 17, 92, 93, 149, 158, 229, 258, 266, 267, 270, 271, 274, 275, 290, 303, 307, 311, 325, 326, 328, 331, 406, 443, 448
Banda, Hyden Dingiswayo, 195, 248, 258, 311, 452
Barotseland, 14, 319, 327, 350, 370, 377, 438
Bemba the, 4, 64
Bledisloe Commission, 17
boycotts, *see* political weapons
British South Africa Co., 2, 5, 9, 10, 13, 34, 53, 64, 90, 180, 257, 333, 363 379, 389, 412, 436, 438;
    rule of, 11, 15, 64
Broken Hill, 100, 123, 124
Brown, David, 67
Burton, Robert and Lilian, 312, 314, 315, 369, 371, 372, 378, 392

Capricorn African Society, 115, 116, 207, 259
Caprivi Strip, 2
Cato, George, 65, 67
Central African Council of Congresses, 153;
    Federation, 17, 19, 61, 76, 85, 86, 88, 89, 90, 92, 95, 112, 121, 122, 124, 130, 135, 136, 140, 146, 158–9 168, 181, 183, 217, 229, 230, 244, 272, 291, 313, 335, 371, 386
Cha-cha-cha, 337, 340, 345, 349, 352, 354, 356, 362, 370, 386, 388, 404, 414
Chiefs, the role of, 15, 61, 87, 93, 108, 113, 117, 122, 180–81, 240, 354, 387, 401
Chileshe, Safeli, 108, 124, 135, 138, 253, 267, 436
Chimba, Justin, 208, 209, 238
Chinsali District, 33, 34, 35, 36, 39, 40, 41, 44, 45, 50, 64, 66, 68, 69, 72, 80, 93, 94, 123, 178, 179, 352, 359, 410, 442;

Youngmen's Farming Association,81
Chirwa, Jonathan, 30
Chitambala, Frank, 1, 213, 256, 291
Chona, Mainza, 219, 231, 291, 292, 295, 311, 315, 347, 349, 361, 370, 386, 390, 409, 452
Church of, Central Africa, 75; Scotland mission, 68, 71, 107, 291
Chuula, Fitzpatrick, 231
civilising mission 4, 7, 58
Clutton–Brock, Guy, 163, 164, 268, 279, 294
Coillard, Francois, 4
Colonial Office, 12, 17, 19, 53, 87, 88, 119, 201, 216, 229, 239, 265, 287, 361, 398
colonial rule, African submission to, 13–14, 19, 23, 93, 152
colour bar, 16, 17–18, 75, 104, 140, 147, 177, 188, 200, 212, 214, 254, 363; reaction to, 147, 148–49, 150, 151
Confederate Party, 136, 141, 287
Congo, 15, 56, 102, 229, 269, 288, 319, 320, 321, 326, 367, 444
Congress Circular, 182, 184, 202, 204, 205, 209, 211, 220, 221, 222, 249, 252, 254
Congress News, 19, 139, 144, 172
Congress of Peoples against Imperialism, 155, 208
Congress Political Party, 234
Congress Women's League, *see* African National Congress Women's League
Copperbelt the, 5, 6, 16, 17, 55, 68, 109, 118, 143, 248, 311, 320, 370, 374, 408, 419

Dalgleish Report, 131, 141
Devlin Commission, 287

East Africa and Rhodesia, 123, 275, 323, 373, 412
Easter School of Political Policies, 376
Ethiopia, 332, 369
Eurafrican Association, *see* Northern Rhodesia Eurafrican Association
European, Mine Workers' Union, 188; Unofficials, 136, 208

Fabian, Colonial Bureau, 19, 243, 294; Society, 93
Federal, Constitution, 96, 187, 217; Fighting Fund or Force, 323, 332, 361; Parliament, 126, 155, 175, 184, 234, 269;

Review Conference, 230, 322, 325, 326, 361
Federation of Welfare Societies, 81, 86, 92 (*see also* Northern Rhodesia African Congress
Foreign Jurisdiction Act of 1894, 119
Fox-Pitt, Thomas, 116, 119, 207, 230, 231, 271, 279, 293, 433
Franklin, Harry, 165, 202–3, 272, 301
The Freedom Newsletter, 96, 198

Gandhi, Mahatma, influence on Kaunda, 70, 105, 140, 308, 335, 415
Gaunt, John, 136, 206, 216, 247, 300, 311, 371, 400
General Missionary Conference, 12, 18, 143
Gore-Brown, Sir Stewart, 66, 70, 82, 83, 86, 91, 96, 106, 167, 183, 235, 300, 333, 374, 397
Griffiths, James, 96, 99

Hopkinson, Harry, 119
Huggins, Sir Godfrey, 19, 89, 94, 96, 99, 100, 108, 112, 118, 130, 152, 153, 157, 158, 162, 173, 176, 186, 190, 215

Jones, Creech, 96, 143, 231
Johnson, James, 239, 240
Johnston, Harry, 4, 5, 6, 11, 234

Kabompo, 1
Kabulonga Club, 165–66
Kalulu, Solomon, 379
Kamanga, Reuben, 211, 255, 265, 279, 319, 331, 399, 401, 406, 452
Kapwepwe, Simon, 36, 46, 64, 65, 67, 71, 72, 73, 106, 165, 171, 172, 194, 210, 223, 235, 243, 259, 265, 279, 290, 296, 301, 307, 315, 318, 322, 365, 398, 399, 401, 406, 414, 435, 437, 439, 452, 453, 455
Kariba Project, 214, 444
Kasama Africans' Institute, 67
Katanga, 2, 102
Katilungu, Lawrence, 109, 121, 135, 138, 146, 169, 213, 240, 247, 267, 270, 315, 331, 360, 368
katundu (loads), 8
Kaunda, Mrs. Betty, 69, 80, 111, 125, 132, 157, 170, 171, 196–7, 264, 278–9, 297, 324, 429; visit to-Britain, 412, Italy, New York, Sweden, 412
Kaunda, David Julizya, 28–41
Kaunda, Kenneth, 1, 3, 16, 18, 19, 23,

36, 43, 45, 46, 50, 51, 61, 73, 74, 80, 91, 99, 102, 117, 131, 195, 200, 371, 372;
education, 43, 45, 52-53, 54, 55 56, 63; farming activities, 80-81; imprisonment of, 169, 170-71, 172, 277-87, 292-95; Minister of Local Government and Social Welfare, 401-17; parents of, 26-41; personality, 1-2, 42, 47, 54, 55, 64, 70, 78, 118, 163-64, 166, 194, 196 228-29, 232, 239-40, 265, 428-30, 438-39, 458, 460-62;
Political career, 6, 76, 77, 82, 83, 88, 89, 94, 95, 96, 104, 106-7, 109, 110, 113, 116, 126, 130, 133, 135, 137, 148, 153, 154-5, 175-6, 180, 201, 202, 206, 211, 216, 219, 224-5, 249-51, 255, 269-70, 318-19, 322, 336, 350-54, 359-69, 385-96;
President of UNIP, 299-325, 328, 332, 374, 436; President of ZANC 265-68, 272; President-elect, 447-53; President, 454-62; Prime Minister, 436-46; Secretary-General of ANC, 148, 153, 154-55, 156, 158-59; social life and family, 46, 55, 56, 64, 67, 68, 132, 172, 196, 264, 357, 448;
Teaching, 63, 65, 66, 68, 70, 72, 74, 77; early life, 40, 41, 42, 44, 62; Travels in—America, 307, 311, 332, 376, 377, 415; Britain, 376, 377, 402; Cairo, 453, Ethiopia, 369, 370—India, 256-57, 259,—Leopoldville, 401,—London, 229-48, 307, 312, 314, 315, 316, 325-27, 329, 333, 356-57, 411,437-39; Nyasaland, 406; Paris, 439; Sweden, 378
Kaunda, Robert, 47, 54, 63
Kazembe, King, 5
Kenya, 56, 83, 103, 114, 118, 122, 158, 198, 212, 216, 240, 247, 270, 288, 298, 303, 316, 330
Kenyatta, Jomo, 92, 124, 298, 341
King, Martin Luther, 311
kingdoms, the rise of, 23, 27
Kitwe, 73, 74, 109, 121
Konkola, Dixon, 92, 124, 126, 169, 173, 211, 214, 216, 217, 233, 265, 388, 392, 442
Koyi, William, 29, 30

Lala the, 6
land, alienation of, 13; Apportionment Act, 200
Lennox-Boyd, Alan, 215, 216, 217, 230, 232, 239, 244, 258, 271

Lenshina, Alice, 178, 179, 238, 410, 411, 442-43; Movement, *see* Lumpa Church; sect, 214
Leopold, King of Belgium, 2
Lisali, 28
Liso, Edward Mungoni, 211, 213
Livingstone, David, 3, 4, 6, 7, 23, 38, 53, 57
The Livingstone Mail, 83
Livingstonia Mission, 29, 32, 33, 58
Lochner concession, 5
London Missionary Society, 4, 11, 58, 59, 69
London Observer, 119
Lozi, Kingdom, 5, 58, 59
Lumbwa, 61-70, 72, 94, 105, 107, 111, 166, 178, 179, 324, 352; Mission, 107, 178
Lugard, Frederick, Lord, 14, 19
Lumpa, Church, 179-80, 410-411, 442, 443; cult, 178; *see also* Lenshina
Lusaka, 112, 113, 117, 120, 132, 187, 317
Luunda/Lunda, 5, 14
Lyttelton, Oliver, 99, 101, 146, 148, 158, 198

Macdonald, 9
Macleod, Ian, 301, 303, 307, 311, 313, 319, 322, 325, 328, 329, 330, 333, 334, 336, 344, 357, 363, 441
McMinn, Robert, 33, 35, 37, 39, 40, 66
Makasa, Robert Speedwell, 81, 92, 94, 96, 106, 117, 124, 178
Makerere, 91
Malawi, 27, 30, 35, 89, 164, 426
Matabele Rebellion, 5
Mau Mau, 103, 118, 122, 136, 170, 216, 229, 234, 235, 247, 329, 385, 392
Maudling, Reginald, 361, 368, 371, 372, 388
Maxwell-Robertson, Revd. David, 47, 55, 70
Mboya, Tom, 198, 229
missionaries, 6, 8, 11
missionary impact, 57, 61, 62, 63
Mitchell, Sir Phillip, 103
Mkochi, 30
Moffat, John, 297, 298, 322, 326, 334, 371, 379, 387, 405; Resolutions, 154, 167, 184
Monckton Commission, 297, 301, 315, 317, 322
Mozambique, 2, 103-104, 321, 341, 344

Mpezeni, Chief, 5, 6, 36, 119, 149
Mporokoso, Chief, 5
Mtepa, 28
Mufulira, 23, 62, 68, 74, 77, 83, 84, 91, 106, 149, 203, 204, 437
Mukupo, Titus, 139, 211, 219, 224, 233, 239, 240, 243, 244, 245, 247, 248, 249, 266, 270, 288, 291
Mulenga, Alice Lenshina *see* Lenshina
multi-racialism, 163, 199, 204, 236
Munali, 52, 53-54, 55, 56, 63, 68, 195, 228, 297, 299, 444
Municipal African Affairs Committee, 255
Mushindo, Revd. P. B., 94
Mwanakatwe, John, 195, 196, 388, 401, 440, 452
Mwezo, 34, 37, 38;
 Welfare Association, *see* Welfare Associations

Nabulyato, Robinson, 81, 93, 96, 135, 138, 158
Nalumango, Nelson, 17
Nasser, General Gamal, 124, 331, 332
National Progress Party, 417, 422, 440
Nehru, Jawaharlal, 140, 256
'New Look Policy', 208–09, 211, 213, 215, 236
The New Statesman, 131
Ngoni the, 5, 6, 27, 28, 29, 30, 31, 35, 38; the Church among the, 29–30
Ngungu, *see* McMinn, Robert
Mkolomo, Mathew, 213
Nkomo, Joshua, 267, 326, 341, 343, 379, 412
Nkrumah, Kwame, 92, 124, 140, 217, 237, 268, 277, 299, 453
Nkumbula, Harry Mwaanga, 1, 3, 17, 91–93, 96, 103, 106, 108, 109, 112, 115, 119, 121, 123, 126, 132, 133, 136, 153, 156, 158, 166, 172, 173, 174, 175, 180, 188, 200, 201, 202, 203, 208–9, 216, 217, 244, 247, 288, 295, 317, 322, 326, 331, 368 371, 388, 389, 395, 396, 401, 403, 412, 416, 429, 438;
 conflict with ANC, 258, 271;
 decline of, 228, 232, 236, 257-9, 291, 387, 446;
 Harry Franklin's influence on, 202, 203, 272; imprisonment of, 169, 171; in London, 229, 230, 232
Non-cooperation without violence, 135, 137, 147, 148, 150, 157, 168
Non-violent positive action, 70, 104, 105, 124, 146, 201, 204, 205, 220, 225, 234, 247, 257, 264, 273, 296,

299, 308, 309–10, 312, 316, 325, 335, 344, 355, 363
Northern News 90, 103, 109, 113, 121, 126, 156, 170, 233, 248, 253, 270, 313, 315, 318, 329, 364, 369, 371, 380, 386, 390, 395, 421, 422, 441, 443, 447
Northern Rhodesia, 1, 4, 90, 92, 99, 101, 104, 112, 113, 120, 130, 150, 164, 228, 270, 274, 295, 331, 344, 371, 385, 400, 409, 426, 437;
 African Congress (NRAC), 3, 76, 85, 87, 91, 95, 96, 101, 103, 108, 114, 116, 119, 120, 124, 125; Chinsali Branch, 94, 111, 125; Supreme Action Council 109, 110, 124;
 African Education Organisation, 135;
 Congress, 92;
 Eurafrican Association, 300, 318; Trade Union Congress, 215
Northern Rhodesian Christian Council, 360
Northern Technical College, 449
Nsama of the Tabwa, 6
Nyasaland, 4, 17 ,56, 126, 216, 267, 268, 274, 275, 287, 308, 321, 330, 361; Congress, 139
Nyerere, Julius, 124, 151, 164, 256, 283, 299, 328, 341, 422, 453

Obote, Milton, 124, 453
Odinga, Oginga, 198
Organization of African Unity, 331, 444
Overtoun Institution, 31, 32, 34, 39, 41

Padmore, George, 92, 222, 244
Pan-African, Council, 145;
 Freedom Movement for East and Central Africa, 282, 369–70, 378, 389, 398, 401, 405;
 Regional Conference, 134, 144, 153, 430
Papworth, John, 239, 244
Paris Evangelical Mission, 59
Plewman Commission Report, 200
politicalweapons, strikes and boycotts, 122, 142, 201, 202, 203, 212, 214, 223, 235, 240–41, 247, 350, 390
Ponde, Chief, 5
Portuguese the, 2
Preservation of Public Security Ordinance, 296
Public Order Ordinance of 1955, 200, 214
Puta, Robinson, 126, 211

Race Relations Committee, 288
racial discrimination, 147; *see also* colour bar
religious protest movements, 131
Rennie, Gilbert, 137
Rhodes, Cecil, 2, 4, 5, 6, 9, 231
Rhodes' Company, 18, 40
Rhodesian Selection Trust, 144, 169, 188, 199, 318
Riot Damages, Bill, 200; Ordinance of 1955, 212
Royal Charter, 9

Scots Mission, 4, 11, 61
Scott, Dr. Alexander, 122, 183, 190, 203
Scott, Revd. Michael, 230, 252, 370, 433
Selassie, Emperor Haile, 331, 332
Sharpe, Alfred, 6
Sharpeville massacre, 298
Sikalumbi, 109, 125, 138, 145, 171, 178, 184, 187, 202, 208, 209, 255, 258, 266, 279, 292
Sipalo, Munukuyumbwa, 195, 210, 217, 265, 275, 303, 319, 326, 452; imprisonment of, 279, 286, 292
Sithole, Ndabaningi, 115
Slave-trade, by Arabs, 4, 7, 11
Sokoni, John Malama, 36, 42, 44, 64, 71, 73, 77, 78, 91, 106, 117, 129, 228, 237, 399, 401
Sokota, Paskale, 126, 138, 176, 211
Somalia, 56
Sonquishe, Daniel, influence of, 55, 56, 78, 100; 104, 228
South Africa, 13, 17, 43, 56, 61, 91, 99, 100, 104, 105, 164, 174, 186, 270, 321, 367
Southern Rhodesia, 92, 96, 99, 100, 101, 114, 126, 137, 138, 156, 321, 368, 400; African Congress, 274
Stephenson, 'Chirupula' 6
strikes, *see* political weapons
Sudan, 216
Swann, A. J., 11

Tanganyika, 3, 56, 71, 102, 198, 298, 303, 313, 321, 341, 378, 442; Lake, 4, 178.
Tanzania, 130; *see also* Tanganyika
tax, 8, 10, 11, 12, 14, 15, 39, 40, 379, 386, 414
Thomson, Moffat, 15
Tonga the, 27, 28, 29
treaties, 3, 4, 6, 108

Tshombe, Moise, 311, 331, 360, 367, 377, 385, 388, 389, 397, 398, 411, 435, 444
Tweya, Hezekiah, 30

Union Defence Force, 146
United African Congress, 288
United Central Africa Association, 112
United Federal Party, 122, 146, 156, 248, 288, 292, 301, 312, 318, 323, 328, 330, 335, 361, 364, 366, 385, 390, 394, 395-6, 397, 408; Coalition with ANC, *see* African National Congress
United Missions, 70, 74
United National Independence Party (UNIP), 1, 292, 295, 301, 302, 308, 311, 317, 318, 319, 332, 335, 346, 350, 361, 362, 363, 369, 370, 371, 380, 385, 386, 390, 391, 392, 394-5, 397, 408, 414, 420-21, 435, 447, 450; banning of, 315, 422, 440; coalition with ANC, 397-99; Youth League, 349
United Northern Rhodesia Association, 166, 197, 203

Verwoerd, 122, 205, 284, 303, 341
Victoria, Falls, 15; Conference, 418; Queen, 3
Voice of UNIP, 315, 347, 349, 358, 378, 407, 412, 435
Voice of Zambia, 315, 319, 328, 341, 355, 357, 360, 413, 416

Welensky, Roy, 19, 53, 61, 76, 81, 82, 89, 90, 99, 103, 110, 112, 114, 115, 116, 118, 122, 129, 130, 136, 157, 163, 166, 183, 190, 201, 204, 206, 216, 217, 222, 241, 274, 298, 313, 319, 322, 330, 336, 367, 369, 370, 371, 372, 385, 389, 441
Welfare Associations, 84, 85, 143; Chinsali, 66, 67, 81; Kitwe, 91; Livingstone Native, 91; Mwezo, 38-39, 65, 84; Ndola, 84
White Fathers, 59; mission, 10
Wills, A. J., 12, 13
Wina, Sikota, 315, 366, 368, 375, 398, 401, 407, 412, 437, 452

Yamba, Dauti, 85, 93, 131, 135, 138, 184
Young, Robert ('Bobo'), 5, 33, 34, 38

Zaïre, 2, 23
Zambesi, 1, 2, 4, 5

Zambia, 1, 2, 5, 7, 16, 23, 25, 59, 89, 253, 260, 271, 453, 454; people of, 25–6;
African National Congress, 1, 260, 264, 265–7, 272, 275, 289, 290; banning of, 268; inquiry into banning of, 3; Organisation Committee 273;
United Church of, 62;
Youth Service, 450

Zimbabwe Africa National Union (ZANU), 61

Zimbabwe, African People's Union, 370, 375

Zulus the, 4
Zwangendaba, 27, 29

Printed by Kenya Litho Ltd., P.O. Box 40775, Changamwe Road, Nairobi, and published by Oxford University Press, Eastern Africa Branch, P.O. Box 72532, Electricity House, Harambee Avenue, Nairobi, Kenya.